media editic

Special Education in Contemporary Society 4

Dear Professor:

Special Education in Contemporary Society is first and foremost a textbook about people – individuals, who in many ways are very similar to their peers without a disability. Second, this book serves as a comprehensive introduction to the dynamic field of special education and the children and young adults who benefit from receiving a special education.

My intention in writing this book was to provide you and your students with a readable, research-based book that also stresses learning in inclusive settings and classroom application. By blending theory with practice, my aim was to provide preservice educators and practicing professionals with the knowledge, skills, attitudes, and beliefs that are so crucial to constructing learning environments that will allow *all* students to reach their full potential.

I also wanted to portray the "human" side of special education. The field of special education is about children and their families – their frustrations and fears – but perhaps more importantly; it is also about their accomplishments, successes, and triumphs. To me, special education is real. I personally live with it on a daily basis – it is my passion.

The Media Edition offers you and your students the opportunity to go beyond the pages of the text and explore the world of special education through media in the form of in-text links to the Interactive eBook, video clips on additional key topics, and expanded student study site resources.

With my best regards,

Richard

Richard M. Gargiulo

How does the Media Edition benefit students?

In-text links to the Interactive eBook allow students to listen to audio and watch video that relates to the content.

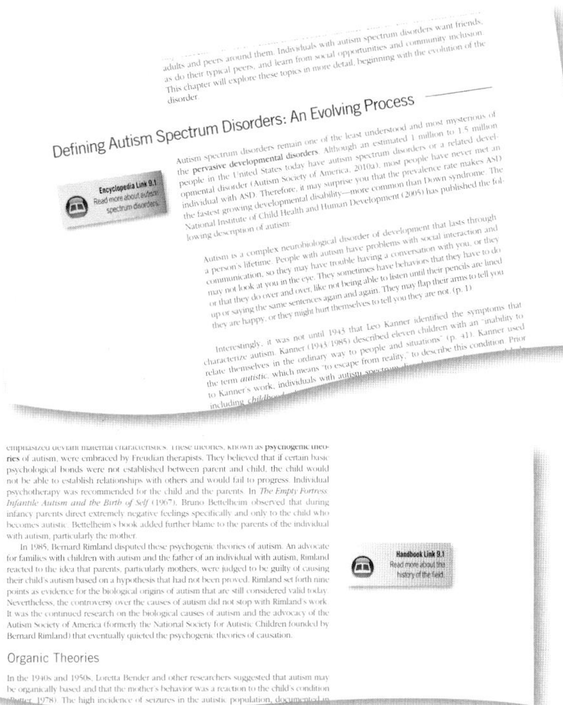

Defining Autism Spectrum Disorders: An Evolving Process

Encyclopedia Link 9.1 Read more about autism spectrum disorders.

Handbook Link 9.1 Read more about the history of the field.

Organic Theories

Audio Link 9.1 Listen to more about etiology.

Cerebral cortex - a thin layer of gray matter on the surface of the cerebral hemispheres. Two-thirds of its area is deep in the fissures or folds. Responsible for the higher mental functions, general movement, perception, and behavioral reactions.

Basal ganglia - gray masses deep in the cerebral hemisphere that serve as a connection between the cerebrum and cerebellum. Helps to regulate automatic movement.

Amygdala - responsible for emotional responses, including aggressive behavior

Hippocampus - makes it possible to remember new information and recent events

Screening and Diagnosis

Journal Link 9.1 Read more about assessment.

AUTISM FROM A PERSONAL PERSPECTIVE: A TRUE STORY OF BEATING THE ODDS AND WINNING

I would like to begin by dedicating my story to my parents, who never gave up, and to the loving memory of my grandmother, who would become a very instrumental person in my life. May her legacy live on through my words and testimony.

When I was 18 months old, a military psychiatrist diagnosed me with early childhood autism. My parents and I were living in Germany while my dad was serving in the army. My parents were told that the military could not provide any treatment or intervention, but if it found a program that I could benefit from that was located near a military base, the army would take care of relocating us. We came back to Anniston (Alabama), which is my hometown, and we lived with my grandmother for a few months until we knew what to do and where we were going. My first symptoms started with being nonverbal, rocking, sound sensitivity, and resistance to change.

However, I had some special abilities such as drawing, and I loved music. I'm also visually impaired, which has bothered me since birth but never had anything to do with autism. This was a disability I already had. I got my first pair of glasses after I turned a year old. I no longer drive because of my extremely low vision. I currently use transportation services to get around town. After coming home...

Video Link 9.1 Watch more about autism.

Video clips on additional key topics such as response to intervention, co-teaching, and differentiated instruction further engage students and put concepts into action – bringing the content alive!

Expanded student study site resources provide students with opportunities to apply knowledge and practice skills learned in the classroom. These open-access resources include Video links, Self-quizzes and e-flashcards, recent and relevant articles from SAGE's leading research journals, and Web exercises.

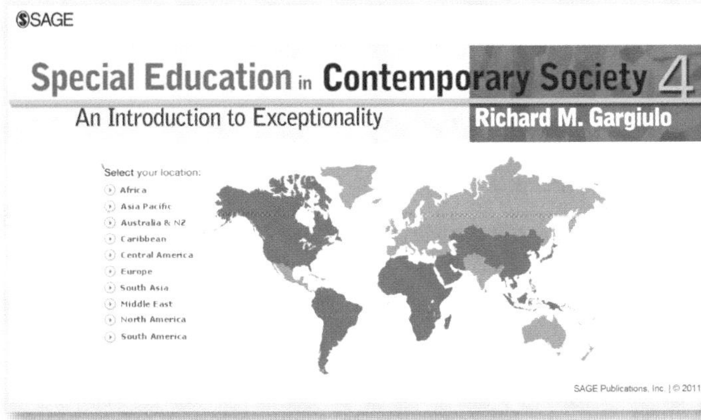

How does the Media Edition benefit students?

Richard Gargiulo's goal in writing *Special Education in Contemporary Society* is to help preservice teachers and practicing professionals develop an appreciation for and an understanding of the children whose lives they will touch. To this aim, and to make the textbook meaningful, practical, and also enjoyable to read, we have incorporated several distinct features.

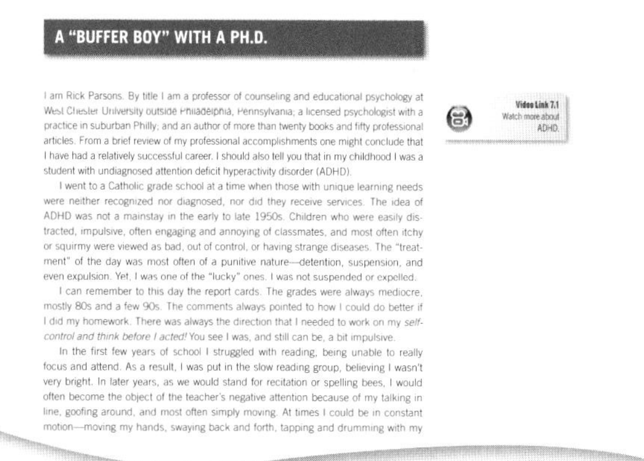

A "BUFFER BOY" WITH A PH.D.

I am Rick Parsons. By title I am a professor of counseling and educational psychology at West Chester University outside Philadelphia, Pennsylvania; a licensed psychologist with a practice in suburban Philly; and an author of more than twenty books and fifty professional articles. From a brief review of my professional accomplishments one might conclude that I have had a relatively successful career. I should also tell you that in my childhood I was a student with undiagnosed attention deficit hyperactivity disorder (ADHD).

I went to a Catholic grade school at a time when those with unique learning needs were neither recognized nor diagnosed, nor did they receive services. The idea of ADHD was not a mainstay in the early to late 1950s. Children who were easily distracted, impulsive, often engaging and annoying of classmates, and most often itchy or squirmy were viewed as bad, out of control, or having strange diseases. The "treatment" of the day was most often of a punitive nature—detention, suspension, and even expulsion. Yet, I was one of the "lucky" ones. I was not suspended or expelled.

I can remember to this day the report cards. The grades were always mediocre, mostly 80s and a few 90s. The comments always pointed to how I could do better if I did my homework. There was always the direction that I needed to work on my *self-control and think before I acted!* You see I was, and still can be, a bit impulsive.

In the first few years of school I struggled with reading, being unable to really focus and attend. As a result, I was put in the slow reading group, believing I wasn't very bright. In later years, as we would stand for recitation or spelling bees, I would often become the object of the teacher's negative attention because of my talking in line, goofing around, and most often simply moving. At times I could be in constant motion—moving my hands, swaying back and forth, tapping and drumming with my

Chapter-opening vignettes in the categorical chapters offer personal stories on the exceptionality studied in a specific chapter. Through these vignettes, students gain a firsthand, vivid account of these parents, their fears and frustrations, their accomplishments and triumphs and the issues they face on a daily basis.

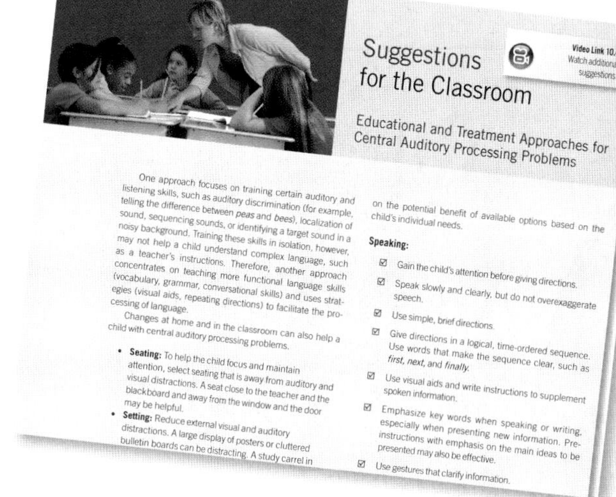

Suggestions for the Classroom

Educational and Treatment Approaches for Central Auditory Processing Problems

One approach focuses on training certain auditory and listening skills, such as auditory discrimination (for example, telling the difference between *peas* and *bees*), localization of sound, sequencing sounds, or identifying a target sound in a noisy background. Training these skills in isolation, however, may not help a child understand complex language, such as a teacher's instructions. Therefore, another approach concentrates on teaching more functional language skills (vocabulary, grammar, conversational skills) and uses strategies (visual aids, repeating directions) to facilitate the processing of language.

Changes at home and in the classroom can also help a child with central auditory processing problems.

- **Seating:** To help the child focus and maintain attention, select seating that is away from auditory and visual distractions. A seat close to the teacher and the blackboard and away from the window and the door may be helpful.
- **Setting:** Reduce external visual and auditory distractions. A large display of posters or cluttered bulletin boards can be distracting. A study carrel in

on the potential benefit of available options based on the child's individual needs.

Speaking:

- ☑ Gain the child's attention before giving directions.
- ☑ Speak slowly and clearly, but do not overexaggerate speech.
- ☑ Use simple, brief directions.
- ☑ Give directions in a logical, time-ordered sequence. Use words that make the sequence clear, such as *first*, *next*, and *finally*.
- ☑ Use visual aids and write instructions to supplement spoken information.
- ☑ Emphasize key words when speaking or writing, especially when presenting new information. Pre-instructions with emphasis on the main ideas to be presented may also be effective.
- ☑ Use gestures that clarify information.

"**Suggestions for the Classroom**" boxes provide instructional strategies, tips, techniques and other ideas.

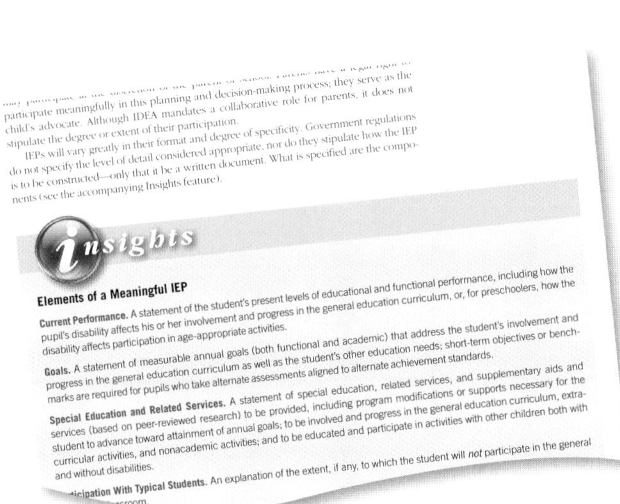

participate meaningfully in this planning and decision-making process; they serve as the child's advocate. Although IDEA mandates a collaborative role for parents, it does not stipulate the degree or extent of their participation.

IEPs will vary greatly in their format and degree of specificity. Government regulations do not specify the level of detail considered appropriate, nor do they stipulate how the IEP is to be constructed—only that it be a written document. What is specified are the components (see the accompanying Insights feature).

insights

Elements of a Meaningful IEP

Current Performance. A statement of the student's present levels of educational and functional performance, including how the pupil's disability affects his or her involvement and progress in the general education curriculum, or, for preschoolers, how the disability affects participation in age-appropriate activities.

Goals. A statement of measurable annual goals (both functional and academic) that address the student's involvement and progress in the general education curriculum as well as the student's other education needs; short-term objectives or benchmarks are required for pupils who take alternate assessments aligned to alternate achievement standards.

Special Education and Related Services. A statement of special education, related services, and supplementary aids and services (based on peer-reviewed research) to be provided, including program modifications or supports necessary for the student to advance toward attainment of annual goals; to be involved and progress in the general education curriculum, extracurricular activities, and nonacademic activities; and to be educated and participate in activities with other children both with and without disabilities.

Participation With Typical Students. An explanation of the extent, if any, to which the student will *not* participate in the general ...room.

The **Insights** feature contains relevant information that adds depth and insight to particular discussion topics.

First Person: Christopher In His Own Words

What can you tell us about yourself and your family?

My name is Christopher. I am a freshman at Oak Mountain High School. I am dyslexic and have a hard time reading and spelling. I have to get audio books or friends and family to help me with reading. I enjoy hands-on activities like building and drawing. I play football, lacrosse, and I also wrestle.

I have a brother and a sister who are also into sports and, like me, enjoy playing video games. My brother is visually impaired (around 20/600) from cone and rod dystrophy. I have to help him a lot with simple tasks at home and wherever we go. He helps me with spelling and math because he is really smart. He would help me more with reading if he could see better. My sister loves animals and rides English style in horse shows.

We go up to Pennsylvania once a year during Thanksgiving or Christmas to visit my relatives on my mom's side. All of my relatives on my dad's side live in Alabama so I get to see them a lot.

What do you like to do in your free time?

I spend most of my free time playing sports and video games. For football, I play on the defensive line (noseguard) ... started last fall for the Oak Mountain freshman team. ... for Oak Mountain High School. Although ... the bottom of the 215 ...

all of my friends and talking with them. My least favorite thing about school is homework because it takes me two times longer to do it than regular kids. I also count studying as homework. Unlike all of my friends (my friends don't consider studying homework and don't study!), I will study for several hours, sometimes staying up late at night and waking up very early in the morning before school.

One of my favorite memories of school is yelling my lungs out with my football friends at the pep rallies. My favorite subjects in school are science and history. I have all As in school.

What can you tell us about your work background?

The only work experience I really have is refereeing soccer games. I started refereeing when I was 12 years old. Unlike other jobs, I get to pick my own schedule, and the pay is good. I enjoy working with other referees I have gotten to know. I usually referee four or five games a week when I don't have a conflict.

What do you see yourself doing in the future?

I am not exactly sure what kind of job I want, but I know I want to do something hands-on. I plan on going to college, but I am not sure what my major would be at this time. As a part of my IEP ... opportu-

The "**First-Person**" feature adds a human touch to the information students are learning. These stories, written by or about individuals with exceptionalities, provide an up-close and personal encounter with children, adults, and families.

How does the Media Edition benefit students?

Making Inclusion Work

As an eighth-grade English language arts teacher with over a decade of teaching experience, I find teaching to be a new adventure every day.

I strive to enhance the learning opportunities for all of my students. Many of my current students are struggling writers, as identified by teachers from previous years. Keeping these students involved, interested, and yearning to learn, but at the same time making sure that every child is challenged and thriving, can sometimes be a difficult task. But I have asked for this setting because I want to rise to the occasion and see my students succeed.

Inclusive Education Experience

Working in an inclusive classroom takes careful planning. First, I make sure that I know my students' abilities and weaknesses. I make the classroom inclusive of all learners, which builds a positive community. I have had students in my regular English classes who are visually impaired, students who are in wheelchairs, and students who are self-contained in another teacher's room except for reading class. I have come to understand the importance of community and peer support. The teacher in any classroom, but especially the inclusive classroom, becomes the coach or facilitator of learning. Since the children come to school at multiple levels of learning, the teacher must … student where he or she is in the learning process … point.

I am constantly working on resolutions for my dilemmas, however, and I come closer to my answers every day. I rely on my colleagues for ideas that work in their classes. We have an idea exchange at team meetings as we discuss pedagogy and students. I learn from reading professional articles and books. I have always individualized my instruction, but I have learned to do it more effectively.

Strategies for Inclusive Classrooms

Collaboration with special education teachers is a must. They have teaching tips that work well with all students.

- Accommodate instruction and assignments as needed to ensure success for all students, not just those with IEPs; however, only modify assignments for those students who have IEPs. Simple accommodations include providing a word bank for vocabulary quizzes, a study guide before a test, rubrics before a project, a copy of class notes, a book on audiotape, and the use of a computer. Testing or quizzing accommodations include reading a quiz or test aloud to a student, allowing the student to read the quiz or test aloud, explaining directions or language, reducing the number of choices but covering the same objectives, extending the time permitted, allowing the student to dictate his or her answers, allowing mistakes to be corrected for extra points, or allowing a test to be retaken for an average of both scores.
- Understand the importance of presentation. Type assignment directions, activity sheets, quizzes, and tests in a larger …

The "**Making Inclusion Work**" feature highlights special and general educators offering candid perspectives and practical advice about providing services to students with special needs in inclusive settings.

STUDY QUESTIONS

1. What do the terms *culture* and *cultural diversity* mean to you?
2. At one time, the United States was described as a melting pot. Why? Metaphorically speaking, American society is now characterized as a floral bouquet or patchwork quilt. What factors contributed to this change in thinking?
3. Define the following terms: *cultural pluralism, multicultural education*, and *bilingual education*.
4. Why is bilingual education a controversial topic?
5. Compare and contrast the various instructional models used with students who are bilingual.
6. Explain why pupils from minority groups experience disproportional representation in some special education programs.
7. What are the consequences of disproportional representation?
8. Why is the assessment of culturally and linguistically diverse students perceived to be problematic? How might these difficulties be corrected?
9. Define portfolio assessment. Identify the advantages of this strategy for evaluating the performance of children who are culturally and linguistically diverse.

KEY TERMS

melting pot 88
cultural pluralism 88
culture 88
multiculturalism 89
multicultural education 89
bilingual education 89
ethnocentrism 90
macroculture 91
microcultures 91
limited English proficient (LEP) 92
bilingual special education 96
overrepresentation 97
underrepresentation 97
field dependent/sensitive 101
field independent 101
nondiscriminatory testing 104
multiple intelligences 105
portfolio assessment 106

LEARNING ACTIVITIES

1. Talk to a school psychologist, an educational diagnostician, or another assessment specialist about strategies and procedures used when evaluating students from a culturally or linguistically diverse background. What types of modifications, if any, does he or she use? Does he or she have any concerns about the validity of the assessment process? What is his or her opinion about alternative assessments such as portfolios?
2. Visit several different schools in your area. Interview administrators or teachers about services available for pupils from culturally and linguistically diverse groups. Is there a problem of over- and underrepresentation in special education classes? What types of modifications are available to meet the needs of these pupils? How are parents and other family members involved in the school? Is multicultural education reflected in the school environment?
3. Attend various functions sponsored by ethnic groups in your community. Activities may include musical programs, art exhibitions, festivals, religious celebrations, school functions, and other ceremonies. How did you feel about participating in these activities? What did you learn as a result of your involvement? Were your personal viewpoints and stereotypes challenged as a result of this experience?

Study questions at the conclusion of each chapter are designed to help students focus on key chapter content and gauge understanding of the material.

resonance 369
hypernasality 369
functional 373
organic 373
augmentative or alternative communication (AAC) 388

LEARNING ACTIVITIES

1. Visit an educational setting serving students with speech and language impairments. How was the students' classroom performance affected by their communication difficulty? How were their social interactions with other students and teachers affected? Were any special teaching techniques used or classroom modifications made to enhance their performance? Was therapy given outside of the general education classroom? Was this arrangement positive or negative? How did intervention differ for older children? What was your overall impression of the services provided?
2. Visit a clinic or hospital in your community providing services to persons with speech and/or language impairments. Interview the speech–language pathologist. What types of disorders are served? Are there special challenges in assessment techniques? What types of intervention strategies are used? What interaction does this professional have with the community at large? With area schools? Is there a team approach in use? Is there a family-centered remediation model for implementing therapy?
3. Prepare a resource book for your class that describes common types of speech and language impairments and their characteristics. Include appropriate assessment, referral, and remediation strategies. Provide information on causes and prevention, assistive technology, need for early intervention, and classroom strategies. Provide some websites of interest for each disorder.
4. Compile a list of local agencies (public and private), medical facilities, civic groups, and educational settings that provide services to persons with speech and language impairments. Be sure to include contact information as well as a brief description of services provided.
5. Visit a local preschool program for children at risk for language delay. Interview a staff member. Find out how young children are screened for speech and language problems, and describe the process. Volunteer to help with screenings if possible. What types of language stimulation activities are used? How are families included in this process? What is your opinion regarding the effectiveness of the program?

A series of **learning activities** brings the content to life. Many of these suggested activities ask you to engage in a wide variety of meaningful and worthwhile tasks.

ORGANIZATIONS CONCERNED WITH SPEECH AND LANGUAGE IMPAIRMENTS

Alliance for Technology Access
1119 Old Humboldt Road
Jackson, TN 38305
(800) 914-3017
(731) 554-5284 (TTY)
(731) 554-5283 (Fax)
http://www.ataccess.org

American Speech-Language-Hearing Association (ASHA)
2200 Research Boulevard
Rockville, MD 20850
(800) 638-8255
(301) 296-5650 (TTY)
(301) 296-8589 (Fax)
http://www.asha.org

ORGANIZATIONS CONCERNED WITH HEARING IMPAIRMENTS

American Speech-Language-Hearing Association
2200 Research Boulevard
Rockville, MD 20850
(800) 638-8255
(301) 296-5650 (TTY)
(301) 296-8580 (Fax)
http://www.asha.org

Alexander Graham Bell Association for the Deaf and Hard of Hearing
3417 Volta Place N.W.
Washington, DC 20007–2778
(202) 337-5220
(202) 337-5221 (TTY)
(202) 337-8314 (Fax)
http://www.agbell.org

Council of American Instructors of the Deaf
P.O. Box 377
Bedford, TX 76095–0377
(817) 354-8414 (Voice/TTY)
http://www.caid.org

National Association of the Deaf
8630 Fenton Street
Suite 820
Silver Spring, MD 20910–3819
(301) 587-1788
(301) 587-1789 (TTY)
(301) 587-1791 (Fax)
http://www.nad.org

Self-Help for Hard of Hearing People
7910 Woodmont Avenue
Suite 1200
Bethesda, MD 20814
(301) 657-2248
(301) 657-2249 (TTY)
(301) 913-9413 (Fax)
http://www.icdri.org/dhhi/shhh.htm

At the conclusion of each chapter there is a **list of professional organizations and associations** that you may wish to contact for further information about a particular topic of interest.

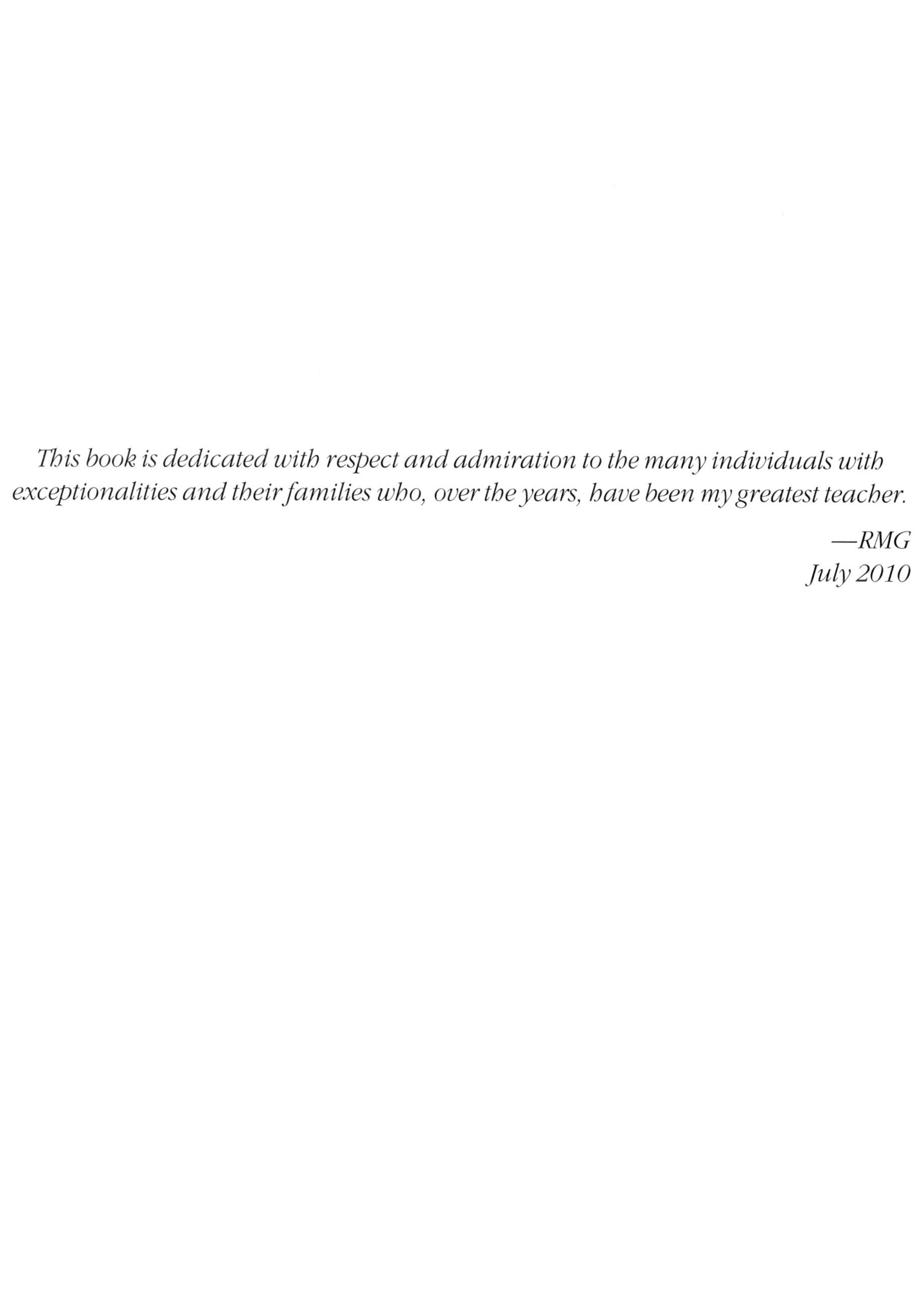

This book is dedicated with respect and admiration to the many individuals with exceptionalities and their families who, over the years, have been my greatest teacher.

—RMG
July 2010

media edition

Special Education in Contemporary Society 4

An Introduction to Exceptionality

Richard M. Gargiulo
University of Alabama at Birmingham

Los Angeles | London | New Delhi
Singapore | Washington DC

For information:

SAGE Publications, Inc.
2455 Teller Road
Thousand Oaks, California 91320
E-mail: order@sagepub.com

SAGE Publications Ltd.
1 Oliver's Yard
55 City Road, London, EC1Y 1SP
United Kingdom

SAGE Publications India Pvt. Ltd.
B 1/I 1 Mohan Cooperative Industrial Area
Mathura Road, New Delhi 110 044
India

SAGE Publications Asia-Pacific Pte. Ltd.
33 Pekin Street #02-01
Far East Square
Singapore 048763

Printed in Canada

A catalog record of this book is available from the Library of Congress.

978-1-4129-9695-2

This book is printed on acid-free paper.

11 12 13 14 15 10 9 8 7 6 5 4 3 2 1

Executive Editor:	Diane McDaniel
Associate Editor:	Megan Krattli
Assistant Editor:	Rachael Leblond
Editorial Assistant:	Terri Accomazzo
Digital Content Project Editor:	Sarah Quesenberry
Production Editor:	Brittany Bauhaus
Permissions Editor:	Adele Hutchinson
Copy Editor:	Melinda Masson
Typesetter:	C&M Digitals (P) Ltd.
Proofreader:	Jenifer Kooiman
Indexer:	Michael Ferreira
Cover Designer:	Gail Buschman
Marketing Manager:	Katharine Winter

About the Author

I have always wanted to be a teacher. I guess I am a rarity in that I never changed my undergraduate major or left the field of education. Teaching must be in my blood. I grew up in Staten Island, New York, in the shadows of Willowbrook State School, a very large residential facility serving individuals with developmental disabilities. As I recall, my initial exposure to people with disabilities probably occurred when I was about 10 or 12 years of age and encountered some of the residents from Willowbrook enjoying the park that was adjacent to their campus. This experience made a huge impression on me and, in some unknown way, most likely instilled within me a desire to work with people with disabilities.

I left New York City in 1965 and headed west—all the way to western Nebraska where I began my undergraduate education at Hiram Scott College in Scottsbluff. Three years later I was teaching fourth graders in the Milwaukee public schools while working toward my master's degree in mental retardation at the University of Wisconsin–Milwaukee. At the conclusion of my first year of teaching I was asked to teach a class of young children with intellectual disabilities. I jumped at the opportunity and for the next three years essentially became an early childhood special educator. It was at this point in my career that I decided to earn my doctorate. I resigned my teaching position and moved to Madison, where I pursued a Ph.D. in the areas of human learning, child development, and behavioral disabilities. Upon receiving my degree I accepted a faculty position in the department of special education at Bowling Green State University (Ohio), where for the next eight years I was a teacher educator. In 1982 I moved to Birmingham, Alabama, and joined the faculty of the University of Alabama at Birmingham, where I currently serve as a professor in the Department of Leadership, Special Education, and Foundations.

I have enjoyed a rich and rewarding professional career spanning more than four decades. During the course of this journey I have had the privilege of twice serving as president of the Alabama Federation, Council for Exceptional Children, and also as president of the Division of International Special Education and Services (DISES), Council for Exceptional Children. Currently, I am the president-elect of the Division on Autism and Developmental Disabilities (DADD), Council for Exceptional Children. I have lectured abroad extensively and was a Fulbright Scholar to the Czech Republic in 1991. In 2007 I was invited to serve as a Distinguished Visiting Professor, Charles University, Prague, Czech Republic.

I mentioned earlier that teaching has always been my passion. In 1999 I was fortunate to receive UAB's President's Award for Excellence in Teaching. In 2007 I received the Jasper Harvey award from the Alabama Council for Exceptional Children in recognition of being named the outstanding teacher educator in the state.

With a background in both educational psychology and special education, my research has appeared in a wide variety of professional journals including *Child Development, Journal of Educational Research, Journal of Learning Disabilities, American Journal of Mental Deficiency, Childhood Education, Journal of Visual Impairment and Blindness, British Journal of Developmental Psychology, Journal of Special Education, Early Childhood Education Journal, International Journal of Clinical Neuropsychology,* and *International Journal of Special Education,* among others.

In addition to the present text, I have authored or coauthored nine other books, ranging in topics from counseling parents of children with disabilities to child abuse, early childhood education, early childhood special education, and my most recent one, teaching in inclusive classrooms.

Brief Contents

Detailed Contents

PART II. A Study of Individuals With Special Needs

Tongue Coolers

Preface

Special Education in Contemporary Society is first and foremost a textbook about people—individuals who, in many ways, are very much just like you. Yet these individuals happen to be recognized as exceptional—either as someone with a disability or as someone with unique gifts and talents. Second, this book serves as a comprehensive introduction to the dynamic field of special education and the children and young adults who benefit from receiving a special education. My intention in writing *Special Education in Contemporary Society* was to provide you with a readable, research-based book that also stresses classroom application. By blending theory with practice, my aim was to provide teachers-in-training and practicing professionals with the knowledge, skills, attitudes, and beliefs that are so crucial to constructing learning environments that allow all students to reach their potential. I also wanted to portray the "human" side of special education. The field of special education is much more than meetings, forms, legal issues, or specific instructional strategies; it is about children and their families—their frustrations and fears—but perhaps more important, it is also about their accomplishments and triumphs. As a father of four daughters, I have traveled this rocky road. Each of my girls is recognized as exceptional: Three are gifted, and one has a disability. To me, special education is real. I confront it on a daily basis—it is my passion. I hope that by studying this book you too will develop an appreciation for and an understanding of the children whose lives you will touch.

Audience

Special Education in Contemporary Society was written for two primary audiences. First are those individuals preparing to become teachers, either general educators or special educators. Because meeting the needs of students with exceptionalities is often a shared responsibility, this book is also appropriate for professionals who work with individuals with special needs. Physical therapists, school psychologists, orientation and mobility specialists, and speech–language pathologists are only a few of the individuals who share in the responsibility of providing an appropriate education.

Organization of the Text

The first four chapters constitute Part I and focus on broad topics affecting all individuals with an exceptionality; these chapters are foundational for the remainder of the book. Chapter 1 introduces the field of special education, providing an overview of important terms, the prevalence of children and young adults with disabilities, and a framework for understanding exceptionality. An overview of important litigation and legislation, the identification and assessment of individual differences, the development of meaningful individualized instructional programs, and the issue of where students with exceptionalities are to be served are addressed in Chapter 2. In Chapter 3 we examine cultural and linguistic diversity and its relationship to exceptionality. The final chapter of Part I looks at issues confronting the parents and families of individuals with special needs.

Part II consists of ten chapters that thoroughly examine particular categories of exceptionality using a life span approach. We will talk about intellectual disabilities; learning disabilities; attention deficit hyperactivity disorder; emotional and behavioral disorders; autism spectrum disorders; speech and language impairments; hearing impairments; visual impairments; and physical disabilities, health disabilities, and related low-incidence disabilities; we conclude by looking at individuals who are gifted and talented. Despite the diversity of these topics, each chapter follows a fairly consistent format. You will learn definitions, historical information, prevalence, causes, characteristics, assessment techniques, educational considerations, services for young children as well as adults, family issues, diversity, the role of technology, and current trends and controversies. Each chapter in Part II begins with a vignette offering a personal perspective on the exceptionality you will be studying. These stories should remind you that you are learning about real people who confront a myriad of issues that most individuals will never have to deal with.

Key Features of the Text

In order to make this textbook meaningful, practical, and also enjoyable to read, we have incorporated several distinct features. These learning tools include the following:

Chapter-opening vignettes in the categorical chapters, primarily written by parents of children with disabilities, offer personal stories on the exceptionality studied in a specific chapter. Through these vignettes, students gain a firsthand, vivid account of these parents, their fears and frustrations, their accomplishments and triumphs, and the issues they face on a daily basis.

"Suggestions for the Classroom" boxes provide instructional strategies, tips, techniques, and other ideas.

The **Insights** feature contains relevant information that adds depth and insight to particular discussion topics.

The **"First Person"** feature adds a human touch to the information students are learning. These stories, written by or about individuals with exceptionalities, provide an up-close and personal encounter with children, adults, and families.

The **"Making Inclusion Work"** feature highlights special and general educators offering candid perspectives and practical advice about providing services to students with special needs in inclusive settings.

Each chapter concludes with **study questions** designed to help you focus on key chapter content and gauge your understanding of the material.

A series of **learning activities** brings the content to life. Many of these suggested activities ask you to engage in a wide variety of meaningful and worthwhile tasks.

Additionally, you will find a **list of professional organizations and associations** that you may wish to contact for additional information about a topic of particular interest.

Margin Icons

Icons appearing in the margin of the text will direct you to the additional media such as video, audio, and journal articles that correspond with the discussion to elaborate on key concepts.

Video clips of interviews with educators, parents, and individuals with disabilities are now available on the student study site. The videos provide insight to real experiences, challenges, and successes in the lives of exceptional children. Ideas from parents and educators detailing the best strategies and approaches to inclusion learning and a person-first approach to teaching are also included. Teachers and parents discuss the powerful impact that children with special needs have made on their lives.

Video clips on key topics such as Response to Intervention, Co-Teaching, and Differentiated Instruction are also available on the site.

New to This Edition

In addition to its key hallmarks, the fourth edition incorporates the following new or updated features and content:

Additions Found Throughout the Book

- Chapter topics, illustrative material, and references have been revised and updated throughout to reflect the most current legislation, terminology, and research in the field.
- New chapter-opening Learning Objectives guide the reader to the most important points to be gleaned from the chapter.
- End-of-chapter key terms include the page number where the term first appears.
- Five new First Person profiles of individuals with special needs have been added to the text. This feature now appears in every chapter.
- Two new Making Inclusion Work profiles of teachers who work with students with special needs have been added to the text. This feature now appears in every chapter in Part II.
- Photos of contributors have been added to the Making Inclusion Work feature to personalize special and general educators' experiences in the classroom.
- Links to web pages have been added to each chapter-specific organization found in Part II, facilitating the search for additional information and inquiry.
- New video clips of educators, parents, and individuals with special needs talking about their experiences are available on the open-access student study site. The video clips provide insight to real experiences, challenges, and successes in the lives of exceptional children. Icons for these video clips have been placed in the margins of the text at the point where they are most relevant to the content presented.
- Video clips on key topics such as Response to Intervention, Co-Teaching, and Differentiated Instruction are available on the open-access student study site. Icons for these video clips have been placed in the margins of the text at the point where they are most relevant to the content presented.

Chapter-Specific Additions

- Chapter 2 on policies, practices, and programs has been reorganized so as to present the content in a more coherent and logical fashion. A First Person profile has been added to this chapter.
- Chapter 3 now includes a First Person profile.
- Chapter 5 includes the 2010 definition of intellectual disabilities offered by the American Association on Intellectual and Developmental Disabilities as well as information on the Supports Intensity Scale
- Chapter 6 now includes a First Person profile.
- Chapter 7 incorporates additional information on the prevalence of ADHD. A Making Inclusion Work profile has been added to this chapter.
- Chapter 8 includes more on the topic of emotional or behavioral disorders (risk factors, learning, language/communication characteristics). A First Person profile has been added to this chapter.
- Chapter 9 has additional information on Asperger syndrome (characteristics) as well as coverage of effective programs for preschoolers with autism spectrum disorders and the transition into adulthood

- Chapter 10 includes additional information on children born with a cleft lip/palate. First Person and Making Inclusion Work profiles have been added to this chapter.
- Chapter 11 now includes a First Person profile.
- Chapter 12 has added material on academic performance and visual impairments

Ancillaries

Additional ancillary materials further support and enhance the learning goals of the fourth edition of *Special Education in Contemporary Society: An Introduction to Exceptionality*. These ancillary materials include the following:

Student Study Site: www.sagepub.com/gargiulo4emedia

This open-access student study site provides a variety of additional resources to build on students' understanding of the book content and extend their learning beyond the classroom. Students will have access to a sample individualized education program and an individualized family service plan, in addition to the following features for each chapter:

- **Self-quizzes** with twenty-five to thirty multiple-choice and true/false questions for every chapter allow students to independently assess their progress in learning course material.
- **E-flashcards** reinforce student understanding and learning of key terms and concepts that are outlined in the book.
- **Web resources** and **media links** to various sites on the web for further research and for real-life stories and situations related to the chapter topic.
- A "**Learning From SAGE Journal Articles**" feature provides access to recent, relevant full-text articles from SAGE's leading research journals. Each article supports and expands on the concepts presented in the chapter. Discussion questions are also provided to focus and guide student interpretation.
- Carefully selected, web-based **video link** resources feature relevant content for use in independent and classroom-based exploration of key topics.
- **Web exercises** direct students to various sites on the web and ask them to apply their knowledge to a particular topic.

Instructor Teaching Site: www.sagepub.com/gargiulo4emedia

The new instructor teaching site provides one integrated source for all instructor materials, including the following key components for each chapter:

- An updated **electronic test bank**, available to PCs and Macs through Diploma software, offers a diverse set of test questions and answers to aid instructors in assessing students' progress and understanding. The software allows for test creation and customization, and each chapter includes multiple-choice, true/false, short-answer, and essay questions. The test bank is also available in Microsoft Word.
- **PowerPoint presentations** designed to assist with lecture and review highlight essential content, features, and artwork from the book.
- **Lecture notes** have been provided for each chapter that can be used to structure daily lesson plans.
- **Classroom activities** and **discussion questions** are provided to reinforce active learning.
- **Informative websites** and **media links** provide your students with another source of enrichment material related to each chapter's content.
- Carefully selected, web-based **video link** resources feature relevant content for use in independent and classroom-based exploration of key topics.
- Suggested answers to end-of-chapter study questions are provided.
- Links to state-specific **special education standards** are provided for easy access.

Key Features of the Text

Effective Instructional Practices

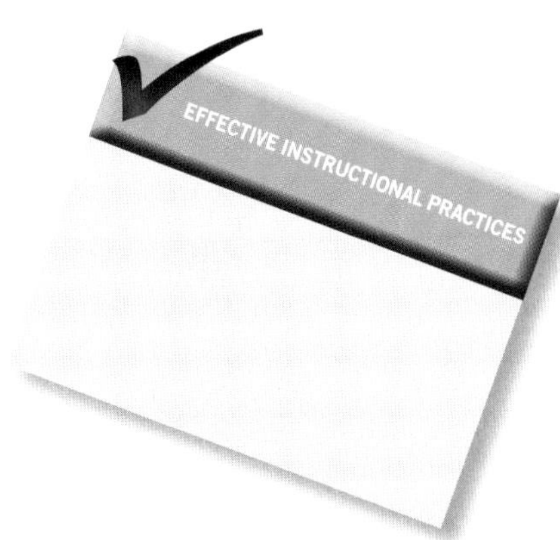

First Person

Insights

Making Inclusion Work

Making Inclusion Work

Suggestions for the Classroom

Key Features of the Text

Effective Instructional Practices

First Person

Insights

Making Inclusion Work

Suggestions for the Classroom

Acknowledgments

Writing a textbook is a team effort, and this one is no exception. I owe a huge debt of gratitude to several friends and colleagues who shared my vision for this book and were also gracious enough to contribute their talents and expertise by writing chapters. I wish to publicly thank them for their hard work, dedicated effort, and patience with my compulsive behavior and attention to detail.

- Lou Anne Worthington, University of Alabama at Birmingham, "Individuals With Emotional or Behavioral Disorders" (Chapter 8)
- Karen B. Dahle, University of Alabama at Birmingham, "Individuals With Autism Spectrum Disorders" (Chapter 9)
- Betty Nelson, University of Alabama at Birmingham, "Individuals With Hearing Impairments" (Chapter 11)
- Carol Allison and Mary Jean Sanspree, University of Alabama at Birmingham, "Individuals With Visual Impairments" (Chapter 12)
- Kathy W. Heller, Georgia State University, "Individuals With Physical Disabilities, Health Disabilities, and Related Low-Incidence Disabilities" (Chapter 13)
- Julia L. Roberts, Western Kentucky University, "Individuals Who Are Gifted and Talented" (Chapter 14)

I am especially grateful to the following individuals who reviewed the fourth edition of this book. Their guidance and professional expertise, eye for accuracy, and thoughtful suggestions contributed immensely to making this edition of *Special Education in Contemporary Society* a market leader. I applaud and deeply appreciate the generous assistance of the following individuals: Julie R. Alexandrin, University of South Maine; Rahul Ganguly, Kent Sate University; Teresa Gardner, Jacksonville Sate University; Jennifer Lancaster, St. Francis College; and Karen A. Vuurens, South Texas College.

I would also like to thank those professionals who reviewed previous editions, including

J'Anne Affeld, Northern Arizona University

Mark Alter, New York University

Michele Augustin, Washington University in St. Louis

Emiliano C. Ayala, Sonoma State University

Pam Baker, George Mason University

Andrew Beigel, Keuka College

Kristin Bewick, Wilkes University

Cheryl Camenzuli, Molloy College

Domenico Cavaiuolo, East Stroudsburg University

Walter Cegellka, St. Thomas University

Patricia Morris Clark, University of Maine at Augusta

Jo Beth DeSoto, Wayland Baptist University

Beverly Doyle, Creighton University

Teresa Gardner, Jacksonville State University

Heather Garrison, East Stroudsburg University

Annette Gorton, Miles Community College

Janice Grskovic, Indiana University Northwest

Robert Harrington, University of Kansas

Thienhuong Hoang, California State Polytechnic University

Pomona; Jack Hourcade, Boise State University

Sheila Dove Jones, Bloomsburg University of Pennsylvania

Juanita Kasper, Edinboro University of Pennsylvania

Donna Kearns, University of Central Oklahoma

Craig Kennedy, Vanderbilt University

Ava Kleinmann, Western New England College

Michelle LaRocque, Florida Atlantic University

Marcel Lebrun, Plymouth State University

DeAnn Lechtenbrger, Texas Tech University

Diane K. Mann, Edinboro University of Pennsylvania

Maria L. Manning, James Madison University

Nancy Marchand-Martella, Eastern Washington University

Teresa Oettinger Montani, Fairleigh Dickinson University

Rita Mulholland, The Richard Stockton College of New Jersey

Charolette Myles-Nixon, University of Central Oklahoma

Kimberely Fletcher Nettleton, Morehead State University

Ashley A. Northam, Chemeketa Community College

Holly Pae, University of South Carolina Upstate

Lee R. Pearce, Black Hills State University

Nicole Phillips, Daemen College and Frontier Central School District

Shaila Rao, Western Michigan University

Saleem 'A Rasheed, Indiana University Northwest

Bruce A. Shields, Daemen College

Dale Smith, Alvernia College

Angela Snyder, Virginia Commonwealth University

Terry Spigner, University of Central Oklahoma

David W. Steitz, Nazareth College of Rochester

Suzanne Swift, Eastern New Mexico University

Ron Tinsley, Richard Stockton College of New Jersey

Sheila Marie Trzcinka, Indiana University Northwest

Tandra Tyler-Wood, University of North Texas

Linda B. Walker, Kent State University

Ronald P. Weitzner, Cleveland State University

Julia Wilkins, St. Cloud State University

Denise Winsor, University of Nevada

Las Vegas; Penelope Wong, Centre College

Ann K. Yehle, University of Wisconsin–Madison and;

Cheryl Zaccagnini, Shippensburg University

I would like to thank all the people who participated in the advisory board and focus groups. Their insights helped to make a more integrated digital edition:

Sloane Burgess, Kent State University

Pamela Campbell, University of Nevada-Las Vegas

Morgan Chitiyo, Southern Illinois University

Laura Geraci-Crandall, SUNY College at Fredonia

Joanne Healy, University Of Alaska, Fairbanks

Candice Hollingsead, Northern State University

Jack Hourcade, Boise State University

Mary Beth Kelley, University Of Minnesota, Twin Cities

Arlene King-Berry , University of District of Columbia

Pamela Klick, Saint Xavier University

Anita Jo Kliewer, University of North Texas

Michelle LaRocque, Florida Atlantic University-Boca

Maribeth Lartz, Illinois State University

Yvette Latunde, Azusa Pacific University

Sheryl Leytham, Grand View College

Timothy Lillie, University of Akron

Jennifer Mahdavi, Sonoma State University

Teresa Montani, Fairleigh Dickinson University

Sheila Marie Trzcinka, Indiana University Northwest

Shataisha Winston, University of District of Columbia

Dawn Witt, California State University, Channel Islands

I would also like to thank the following people who participated in the video interviews that accompany the text.

Carol Allison
Anne Alvarez
Melissa Berenstein
Claudia Bishop
Lori Boehm
Jacqi Conlon
Kathy Heller
April Jacobsen
Kristen Lanning
Mary Murphy
Daniel Negrete
Betty Nelson
Julia Link Roberts
Mary Jean Sanspree
Nicole Santana
Bryce Schrader
Eric Schrader
Greg Shane
Christina Tam
Jordyn Thornton
Liz Thornton
Julie Tresback
Megan Tresback

I had the privilege of working with an outstanding and very talented team of professionals at SAGE Publications, who took my jumbled ideas, poor sentence structure, and sometimes inaccurate references and turned them into a superb and scholarly book. Thank you for your support, enthusiasm, and confidence in me.

I will always be grateful for the encouragement, creative vision, professionalism, and good humor of my editor, Diane McDaniel. Diane's enthusiasm for this project and her editorial creativity and competency are clearly evident throughout this book. Thanks as well to Sarah Quesenberry, Megan Krattlis, and Rachael Leblond for their hard work on the digital edition of the text. Terri Accomazzo served as my primary contact person throughout the evolution of this book. She helped me to maintain critical deadlines, answered countless questions, calmly dealt with my compulsiveness, and saw to it that this textbook actually made it to print. Melinda Masson is a peerless copy editor who always noticed the smallest inconsistency and sometimes glaring errors. It was a joy to work with someone with exceedingly high standards and a desire for perfection. Jenifer Kooiman is a proofreader par excellence. I also appreciate your attention to detail. Finally, a huge thank-you to Brittany Bauhaus, for producing a well-designed and especially attractive book. Your production team is outstanding.

So many other individuals, many of whom labored behind the scenes, also contributed to the development of a book of which I am very proud to be the author. I deeply appreciate the dedicated efforts of those who created the supplemental materials for the Instructor's Resources, including Ron Tinsley, Richard Stockton College of New Jersey, who created the classroom activities and discussion questions; Heather Garrison, East Stroudsburg University, who created the PowerPoint slides and lecture outlines; Laura E. Pierce, J. L. Gibson, Robert C. Pennington, Melinda Jones Ault, Ann Katherine Griffen, and Donald M. Stenhoff of the University of Kentucky, who created the test bank; Teresa Gardner, Jacksonville State University, who created the sample syllabi and suggested answers for the study questions; Ted Crumbley, who created the test bank for the fourth edition; Dewayne Bettag, University of Hawaii at Manoa, who provided video links for each chapter; and Lyle Barton, Kent State University, who created the web quizzes, web exercises, and researched web resources. Also critical were the efforts of those who worked on the student study site, including Terry Spigner and Charolette Myles-Nixon of the University of Central Oklahoma.

One other group of professionals whose contributions add a very practical perspective to this book are the educators who willingly shared their experiences and insights about working in inclusive settings: Brooke Bunn, Susan Brennan, Lisa Cranford, Catherine Davis, Erin de Haven, Astrid Freeman, Tonya Perry, Sarah Reynolds, Teresea Teaff, and Jennifer J. Tumlin. Thank you for sharing your expertise with the readers.

I would be remiss if I did not honor and praise those individuals who contributed to the First Person features and the chapter-opening vignettes. A very special thank-you for telling your story. The ability of each and every one of you to poignantly share an aspect of your lives added immensely to the "human side" of this text—a goal that I hope I achieved.

Finally, a very special acknowledgment is reserved for my family, who survived my 3:00 A.M. wake-up calls; struggled with my attempts at balancing the roles of husband, father, and author; and also understood why this book was personally so very important to me. Thank you. I love you dearly.

PART I

Foundations of Special Education

"Questioning is the door of knowledge."

—Irish Proverb

CHAPTER 1

Learning Objectives

After reading Chapter 1 you should be able to:

- Define exceptional children, disability, handicapped, developmentally delayed, at-risk, and special education.
- Identify the thirteen disability categories recognized by the federal government.
- Distinguish between prevalence and incidence.
- Describe the historical evolution of services for children and adults with disabilities.
- List the related services sometimes required by students with disabilities.
- Outline the differences between multi-, inter-, and transdisciplinary team models.
- Describe common instructional models of cooperative teaching.
- Identify key dimensions of universal design for learning.
- Explain the services typically available to infants/toddlers, preschoolers, adolescents, and adults with disabilities.

Special Education in Context

People, Concepts, and Perspectives

We are all different. It is what makes us unique and interesting human beings. Some differences are obvious, such as our height, the color of our hair, or the size of our nose. Other features are not so readily discernible, such as our reading ability or political affiliation. Of course, some characteristics are more important than others. Greater significance is generally attached to intellectual ability than to shoe size. Fortunately, appreciation of individual differences is one of the cornerstones of contemporary American society.

Although most people would like to be thought of as "normal" or "typical" (however defined), for millions of children and young adults this is not possible. They have been identified and labeled by schools, social service agencies, and other organizations as exceptional, thus requiring special educational services. This textbook is about these individuals who are exceptional.

You are about to embark on the study of a vibrant and rapidly changing field. Special education is an evolving profession with a long and rich heritage. The past few decades in particular have been witness to remarkable events and changes. It is truly an exciting time to study human exceptionality. You will be challenged as you learn about laws and litigation affecting students with special needs, causes of disability, assessment techniques, and instructional strategies, to mention only a few of the topics we will present. But perhaps more important than any of these issues is our goal to help you develop an understanding and appreciation for a person with special needs. We suspect that you will discover, as we have, that individuals with disabilities are more like their typically developing peers than they are different. People with disabilities and those without disabilities share many similarities. In fact, we believe that special education could rightly be considered the study of similarities as well as differences.

Finally, we have adopted a people-first perspective when talking about individuals with disabilities. We have deliberately chosen to focus on the person, not the disability or specific impairment. Thus, instead of describing a child as a "retarded student," we say a "pupil with mental retardation" or a "student with cognitive impairments." This style reflects more than just a change in word order; it reflects an attitude and a belief in the dignity and potential of people with disabilities. The children and adults whom you will learn about are first and foremost people.

Video Link 1.1
Watch more about changing language.

Definitions and Terminology

Teachers work with many different types of pupils. Let's take a look at some of the children in the fifth-grade class of Daniel Thompson, a first-year teacher. As in many other classrooms across the United States, most of his students are considered to be educationally typical; yet five youngsters exhibit special learning needs. Eleven-year-old Victoria, for instance, is a delightful young girl with a bubbly personality who is popular with most of her classmates. She has been blind since birth, however, as a result of a birth defect. Miguel is shy and timid. He doesn't voluntarily interact with many of his classmates. This is his first year at Jefferson Elementary. Miguel's family only recently moved into the community from their previous home in Mexico. Mr. Thompson tells us that one boy is particularly disliked by the majority of his classmates. Jerome is verbally abusive, is prone to temper tantrums, and on several occasions has been involved in fights on the playground, in the lunchroom, and even in Mr. Thompson's classroom despite the fact that his teacher is a former college football player. Mr. Thompson suspects that Jerome, who lives with his mother in a public housing apartment, might be a member of a local gang. Stephanie is teased by most of her peers. Although many of her classmates secretly admire her, Stephanie is occasionally called "a nerd," "a dork," or "Einstein." Despite this friendly teasing, Stephanie is always willing to help other students with their assignments and is sought after as a partner for group learning activities. The final student with special learning needs is Robert. Robert is also teased by his fellow pupils, but for reasons opposite to Stephanie. Robert was in a serious automobile accident when he was in kindergarten. He was identified as having cognitive delays in the second grade. Sometimes his classmates call him "a retard" or "Dumbo" because he asks silly questions, doesn't follow class rules, and on occasion makes animal noises that distract others. Yet Robert is an exceptional athlete. All his classmates want him on their team during gym class.

As future educators, you may have several questions about some of the students in Mr. Thompson's classroom:

- Why are these pupils in a general education classroom?
- Will I have students like this in my class? I'm going to be a high school biology teacher.
- Are these children called disabled, exceptional, or handicapped?
- What does *special education* mean?
- How will I know if some of my students have special learning needs?
- How can I help these pupils?

One of our goals in writing this textbook is to answer these questions as well as address other concerns you may have. Providing satisfactory answers to these queries is not an easy task. Even among special educators, confusion, controversy, and honest disagreement exist about certain issues. As you continue to read and learn, acquire knowledge and skill, and gain experience with individuals with disabilities, we hope you will develop your own personal views and meaningful answers.

Exceptional Children

Both general and special educators will frequently refer to their students as **exceptional children**. This inclusive term generally refers to individuals who differ from societal or community standards of normalcy. These differences may be due to significant physical, sensory, cognitive, or behavioral characteristics. Many of these children may require educational programs customized to their unique needs. For instance, a youngster with superior intellectual ability may require services for students identified as gifted; a child with a visual impairment may require textbooks in large print or Braille. However, we need to make an important point. Just because a pupil is identified as exceptional does not automatically mean that he or she will require a special education. In some instances, the student's educational needs can be met in the general education classroom by altering the curriculum and/or instructional strategies.

We must remember that exceptionality is always relative to the social or cultural context in which it exists. As an illustration, the concept of normalcy, which forms an important part of our definition of exceptionality, depends on the reference group (society, peers, family) as well as the specific circumstances. Characteristics or behaviors that might be viewed as atypical or abnormal by a middle-aged school administrator might be considered fairly typical by a group of high school students. Normalcy is a relative concept that is interpreted or judged by others according to their values, attitudes, and perceptions. These variables, along with other factors such as the culture's interpretation of a person's actions, all help to shape our understanding of what it is to be normal. Is it normal:

Children with disabilities are first and foremost children.

- To use profanity in the classroom?
- For adolescent males to wear earrings or shave their head?
- To run a mile in less than four minutes?
- To study while listening to the stereo?
- To always be late for a date?
- To stare at the floor when reprimanded by a teacher?
- To be disrespectful to authority figures?
- To wear overly large, yet stylish, clothes?

The answer, of course, is that it all depends.

Disability Versus Handicap

On many occasions, professionals, as well as the general public, will use the terms *disability* and *handicap* interchangeably. This is incorrect. These terms, contrary to popular opinion, are not synonymous but have distinct meanings. When talking about a child with a **disability**, teachers are referring to an inability or a reduced capacity to perform a task in a specific way. A disability is a limitation imposed on an individual by a loss or reduction of functioning, such as the paralysis of leg muscles, the absence of an arm, or the loss of sight. It can also refer to problems in learning. Stated another way, a disability might be thought of as an incapacity to perform as other children do because of some impairment in sensory, physical, cognitive, or other areas of functioning. These limitations only become disabilities when they interfere with a person's attainment of his or her educational, social, or vocational potential.

The term **handicap** refers to the impact or consequence of a disability, not the condition itself. In other words, when we talk about handicaps, we mean the problems or difficulties that a person with a disability encounters as he or she attempts to function and interact with the environment. We would like to extend this definition and suggest that a handicap is more than just an environmental limitation; it also can reflect attitudinal limitations imposed on the person with the disability by people without disabilities.

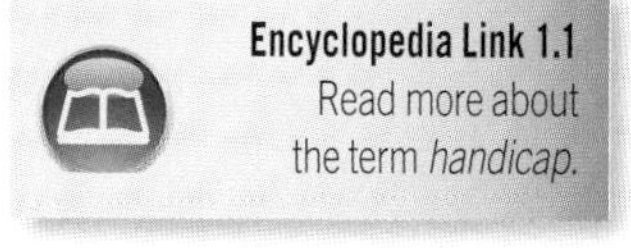

Individuals with disabilities often encounter various forms of discrimination in their daily lives, which frequently limits their full participation in society. As a result, some would suggest that these citizens are "marginalized and excluded from mainstream society" (Kitchin, 1998, p. 343). Sadly, in some ways, this is an accurate portrayal of contemporary life in America despite the ongoing efforts of activists and the disability rights movement, which seeks to end discrimination on the basis of disabilities. In fact, the term **handicapism** was coined more than three decades ago to describe the unequal and differential treatment experienced by those with a disability (Bogdan & Biklen, 1977).

A disability may or may not be a handicap, depending on specific circumstances and how the individual adapts and adjusts. An example should help clarify the differences between these two concepts. Laura, a ninth grader who is mathematically precocious, uses a wheelchair because of a diving accident. Her inability to walk is not a problem in her calculus class. Architectural barriers at her school, however, do pose difficulties for her. She cannot access the water fountain, visit the computer lab on the second floor, or use the bathroom independently. When describing Laura in these situations, we would be correct in calling her handicapped. It is important that professionals separate the disability from the handicap.

Gargiulo and Kilgo (2011) remind us that an individual with a disability is first and foremost a person, a student more similar to than different from his or her typically developing classmates. The fact that a pupil has been identified as having a disability should never prevent us from realizing just how typical he or she is in many other ways. As teachers, we must focus on the child, not the impairment; separate the ability from the disability; and see the person's strengths rather than weaknesses. The accompanying First Person feature provides an example of this thinking. Also see Suggestions for the Classroom (page 8) when writing about or discussing individuals with disabilities.

Developmentally Delayed and At-Risk

Before we can answer the question "What is special education?" we have two more terms to consider: *developmentally delayed* and *at-risk*. These labels are incorporated in federal legislation (PL 99–457 and PL 108–446, discussed in Chapter 2) and are usually used when referring to infants and preschoolers with problems in development, learning, or other areas of functioning. Although these terms are incorporated in our national laws, Congress failed to define them, leaving this responsibility to the individual states. As you can imagine, a great deal of diversity can be found in the various interpretations, and no one definition is necessarily better than another. The result is the identification of a very heterogeneous group of youngsters.

Each state has developed specific criteria and measurement procedures for ascertaining what constitutes a **developmental delay**. Many states have chosen to define a developmental delay quantitatively, using a youngster's performance on standardized developmental assessments. In one state, a child might be described as being delayed if her performance on a standardized test is at least 25 percent below the mean for children of similar chronological age in one or more developmental areas such as motor, language, or cognitive ability. In another state, the determination is made when a preschooler's score on an assessment instrument is two or more standard deviations below the mean for youngsters of the same chronological age. Each approach has its advantages and disadvantages. What is really important, however, is that the pupil be identified and receive the appropriate services (Gargiulo & Kilgo, 2011).

The use of the broad term *developmentally delayed* is also in keeping with contemporary thinking regarding the identification of young children with disabilities. Because of the detrimental effects of early labeling, the Individuals with Disabilities Education Act (PL 101–476), commonly referred to as IDEA, permits states to use the term *developmentally delayed* when discussing young children with disabilities. In fact, PL 105–17, the 1997 reauthorization of this law, allows the use of this term, at the discretion of the state and local education agency, for children ages 3 through 9. We believe, as other professionals do, that the use of a specific disability label for young children is of questionable value. Many early childhood special education programs offer services without categorizing children on the basis of a disability. We believe this approach is correct.

When talking about children who are **at-risk**, professionals generally mean individuals who, although not yet identified as having a disability, have a high probability of manifesting a disability because of harmful biological, environmental, or genetic conditions. Environmental and biological factors often work together to increase the likelihood

First Person: Elizabeth
Perceptions and Impressions

As a woman in my early 40s with cerebral palsy, I can readily reflect on how I am perceived by those who are not disabled. I was born with cerebral palsy, which affects my motor skills. I contend that it is much easier to be born with a disability than to acquire one later in life—I don't know what it is like to be "normal."

I am very blessed in being more independent than I ever dreamed would be possible! I drive an unadapted car, work part-time for a law firm, and live alone with help from a wonderful outside support team. I'm active in my church and in community affairs, serving on the board of the Independent Living Center, as well as in other activities. I'm a member of a local United Cerebral Palsy sports team. As you can see, not much grass grows under my feet!

Throughout my life, I have encountered many and varied reactions to my disability. Some people see me as a person who happens to be disabled. It is wonderful to be around them. They accept me as "Elizabeth." Yes, my speech is, at times, difficult to understand. Yes, I'm in constant motion. But these people see me first and can look beyond my disability, many times forgetting it. I am able to be myself!

When I do need assistance, all I have to do is ask. I have a strong family pushing me to be as independent as possible. I'm grateful to my stepfather, who said, "You can do it!" My mother, afraid I might fall, was hesitant but supportive. My siblings have been great encouragers. I have many friends who are able to see beyond my disability.

I have also met people who have not been around individuals with physical disabilities. I can easily spot those who are uncomfortable around me. Sometimes, after being around me for a while, they may get used to me and then feel quite comfortable. In fact, when people ask me to say something again, rather than nodding their heads pretending to understand me, it shows that they care enough about what I said to get it right.

From those who feel uncomfortable around me, I usually get one of two reactions: "Oh, you poor thing!" or "You're such an inspiration—you're a saint to have overcome cerebral palsy!" I realize people mean well, but I see right through their insecurities. Think about some of their comments. I'm not a "thing," I'm an individual. I have the same thoughts, dreams, and feelings as anyone else.

Many times I am perceived as being retarded, even though I have a college degree. When I'm in a restaurant, my friend may be asked, "What does she want?" One day I was getting into the driver's seat of my car, and a lady inquired, "Are you going to drive that car?" I kept quiet, but I thought, "No, it will drive itself!" Recently, while flying home from Salt Lake City, the flight attendant asked my friend if I understood how the oxygen worked. I chuckled to myself. I have been flying for over thirty years! Furthermore, my former roommate had lived with an oxygen tank for three years, and we were constantly checking the flow level. (In defense of airlines, I must say that I have been treated with great respect.)

For those who say I am an inspiration, I can respond in one of two ways. I can take the comment as a sincere compliment and genuinely say, "Thank you." On the other hand, I can see it as an off-the-cuff remark. Those who say that I inspire them may be thinking, "I'm glad I'm not like her" or "Boy, she goes through so much to be here." As I stated earlier, I do things differently, and it takes me longer. But I have learned to be patient and the importance of a sense of humor. I am very grateful to have accomplished as much as I have.

SOURCE: E. Ray, personal communication.

of a child's exhibiting disabilities or developmental delays. Exposure to adverse circumstances *may* lead to future difficulties and delays in learning and development, but it is not guaranteed that such problems will present themselves. Many children are exposed to a wide range of risks, yet fail to evidence developmental problems. Possible risk conditions include low birth weight, exposure to toxins, child abuse or neglect, oxygen deprivation, and extreme poverty, as well as genetic disorders such as Down syndrome or PKU (phenylketonuria).

Special Education

When a student is identified as being exceptional, a special education is sometimes necessary. Recall that just because the student has a disability does *not* mean that a

Suggestions for the Classroom

Suggestions for Communicating About Individuals With Disabilities

As a teacher, you are in a unique position to help shape and mold the attitudes and opinions of your students, their parents, and your colleagues about individuals with disabilities. Please consider the following points when writing about or discussing people with disabilities:

☑ **Do not focus on a disability** unless it is crucial to a story. Avoid tear-jerking human interest stories about incurable diseases, congenital impairments, or severe injury. Focus instead on issues that affect the quality of life for those same individuals, such as accessible transportation, housing, affordable health care, employment opportunities, and discrimination.

☑ **Do not portray successful people with disabilities as superhuman.** Even though the public may admire superachievers, portraying people with disabilities as superstars raises false expectations that all people with disabilities should achieve at this level.

☑ **Do not sensationalize a disability** by saying "afflicted with," "crippled with," "suffers from," or "victim of." Instead, say "person who has multiple sclerosis" or "man who had polio."

☑ **Do not use generic labels** for disability groups, such as *the retarded* or *the deaf.* Emphasize people, not labels. Say "people with mental retardation" or "people who are deaf."

☑ **Put people first,** not their disability. Say "woman with arthritis," "children who are deaf," or "people with disabilities." This puts the focus on the individual, not the particular functional limitation. Because of editorial pressures to be succinct, we know it is not always possible to put people first. If the portrayal is positive and accurate, consider the following variations: *disabled citizens, nondisabled people, wheelchair user, deaf girl,* and *paralyzed child. Crippled, deformed, suffers from, victim of, the retarded,* and *infirm* are never acceptable under any circumstances.

☑ **Emphasize abilities,** not limitations. For example, say "uses a wheelchair/braces" or "walks with crutches," rather than "is confined to a wheelchair," "is wheelchair-bound," or "is crippled." Similarly, do not use emotional descriptors such as *unfortunate* or *pitiful.*

☑ **Avoid euphemisms** in describing disabilities. Some blind advocates dislike *partially sighted* because it implies avoiding acceptance of blindness. Terms such as *handicapable, mentally different, physically inconvenienced,* and *physically challenged* are considered condescending. They reinforce the idea that disabilities cannot be dealt with up front.

☑ **Do not imply disease** when discussing disabilities that result from a prior disease episode. People who had polio and experience aftereffects years later have a "postpolio disability." They are not currently experiencing the disease. Do not imply disease with people whose disability has resulted from anatomical or physiological damage (such as a person with spina bifida or cerebral palsy). Reference to disease associated with a disability is acceptable only with chronic diseases, such as arthritis, Parkinson's disease, or multiple sclerosis. People with disabilities should never be referred to as "patients" or "cases" unless their relationship with their doctor is under discussion.

☑ **Show people with disabilities as active participants** in society. Portraying persons with disabilities interacting with nondisabled people in social and work environments helps break down barriers and open lines of communication.

SOURCE: Developed by the Research and Training Center on Independent Living, University of Kansas, Lawrence.

Contemporary thinking suggests that students with disabilities should be educated in the most normalized environment.

special education is automatically required. A special education is appropriate only when a pupil's needs are such that he or she cannot be accommodated in a general education program. Simply stated, a **special education** is a customized instructional program designed to meet the unique needs of an individual learner. It may necessitate the use of specialized materials, equipment, services, and/or teaching strategies. For example, an adolescent with a visual impairment may require books with larger print; a pupil with a physical disability may need specially designed chairs and work tables; a student with a learning disability may need extra time to complete an exam. In yet another instance, a young adult with cognitive impairments may benefit from a cooperative teaching arrangement involving one or more general educators along with a special education teacher. Special education is but one component of a complex service delivery system crafted to assist the individual in reaching his or her full potential.

A special education is not limited to a specific location. Contemporary thinking requires that services be provided in the most natural or normalized environment appropriate for the particular student. Such settings might include the local Head Start program for preschoolers with disabilities, a self-contained classroom in the neighborhood school for children with hearing impairments, or a special high school for students who are academically gifted or talented. Many times a special education can be delivered in a general education classroom.

Finally, if a special education is to be truly beneficial and meet the unique needs of students, teachers must collaborate with professionals from other disciplines who provide **related services.** Speech-language pathologists, social workers, and occupational therapists are only a few of the many professionals who complement the work of general and special educators. Related services are an integral part of a student's special education; they allow the learner to obtain benefit from his or her special education.

Before leaving this discussion on definitions and terminology, we believe it is important to reiterate a point we made earlier. Individuals with disabilities are more like their typical peers than they are different. Always remember to see the person, not the disability, and to focus on what people can do rather than what they can't do. It is our hope that as you learn about people with disabilities, you will develop a greater understanding of them, and from this understanding will come greater acceptance.

Categories and Labels

Earlier we defined a person with exceptionalities as someone who differs from a community's standard of normalcy. Students identified as exceptional may require a special education and/or related services. Many of these pupils are grouped or categorized according to specific disability categories. A **category** is nothing more than a label assigned to individuals who share common characteristics and features. Most states, in addition to the federal government, identify individuals receiving special education services according to discrete categories of exceptionality. Public Law (PL) 108–446 (the Individuals with Disabilities Education Improvement Act of 2004) identifies the following thirteen categories of disability:

- Autism
- Deaf-blindness
- Developmental delay
- Emotional disturbance
- Hearing impairments including deafness
- Mental retardation
- Multiple disabilities
- Orthopedic impairments
- Other health impairments
- Specific learning disabilities
- Speech or language impairments
- Traumatic brain injury
- Visual impairments including blindness

The federal government's interpretation of these various disabilities is presented in Appendix A. Individual states frequently use these federal definitions to construct their own standards and policies as to who is eligible to receive a special education.

Notably absent from the preceding list are individuals described as gifted or talented. These students are correctly viewed as exceptional, although they are not considered individuals with disabilities; nevertheless, most states recognize the unique abilities of these pupils and provide a special education.

In the following chapters, we will explore and examine the many dimensions and educational significance of each of these categories. It is important to remember, however, that although students may be categorized as belonging to a particular group of individuals, each one is a unique person with varying needs and abilities.

The entire issue of categorizing, or labeling, individuals with disabilities has been the subject of controversy. Labeling, of course, is an almost inescapable fact of life. How would you label yourself? Do you consider yourself a Democrat or a Republican? Are you overweight or thin, Christian or non-Christian, and liberal or conservative? Depending on the context, some labels may be considered either positive or negative. Labels may be permanent, such as *cerebral palsy*, or temporary, such as *college sophomore*. Regardless, labels are powerful, biasing, and frequently filled with expectations about how people should behave and act.

Labels, whether formally imposed by psychologists or educators or casually applied by peers, are capable of stigmatizing and, in certain instances, penalizing children. Remember your earlier school days? Did you call any of your classmates "a retard," "Four-Eyes," "Fatso," "a geek," or "a nerd"? Were these labels truly valid? Did they give a complete and accurate picture of the person, or did the teasing and taunting focus only on a single characteristic? The labels we attach to people and the names we call them can significantly influence how individuals view themselves and how others in the environment relate to them.

Special educators have been examining the impact of labels on children for many years; unfortunately, the research evidence is not clear-cut, and it is difficult to draw consistent conclusions (Bicard & Heward, 2010; Ysseldyke, Algozzine, & Thurlow, 1992). The information gleaned from a variety of studies is frequently inconclusive, contradictory, and often subject to methodological flaws. Kliewer and Biklen (1996) perhaps best capture this state of affairs when they note that labeling or categorizing certain youngsters is a demeaning process frequently contributing to stigmatization and leading to social and educational isolation; on the other hand, a label may result in a pupil's receiving extraordinary services and support.

Despite the advantages of labeling children (see Table 1.1), we, like many of our colleagues in the field of special education, are not ardent supporters of the labeling process. We find that labeling too often promotes stereotyping and discrimination and may be a contributing factor to exclusionary practices in the educational and social arenas. Hobbs (1975) commented, many years ago, that labeling erects artificial boundaries between children while masking their individual differences. Reynolds and his colleagues (Reynolds, Wang, & Walberg, 1987), who strongly oppose labeling pupils with special needs, astutely observe that "the boundaries of the categories [*intellectual disabilities* is a good illustration] have shifted so markedly in response to legal, economic, and political forces as to make diagnosis largely meaningless" (p. 396). Some professionals (Cook, 2001; Harry & Klingner, 2007) are of the opinion that labeling actually perpetuates a flawed system of identifying and classifying students in need of special educational services.

Audio Link 1.1
Listen to how labels affect children.

One of our biggest concerns is that the labels applied to children often lack educational relevance. Affixing a label to a child, even if accurate, is not a guarantee of better services. Rarely does a label provide instructional guidance or suggest effective management tactics. We are of the opinion that the delivery of instruction and services should be matched to the needs of the child rather than provided on the basis of the student's label. This thinking has led to calls for **noncategorical** programs constructed around student needs and common instructional requirements instead of categories of exceptionality. These programs focus on the similar instructional needs of the pupils rather than the etiology of the disability. Although noncategorical programs are gaining in popularity, it is still frequently necessary to classify students on the basis of the severity of their impairment—for example, mild/moderate or severe/profound.

TABLE 1.1 The Pros and Cons of Labeling Individuals With Special Needs

Advantages	Disadvantages
• Labels serve as a means for funding and administering education programs. • Teacher certification programs and the credentialing process are frequently developed around specific disability categories (e.g., intellectual disabilities, hearing impairment). • Labels allow professionals to communicate efficiently in a meaningful fashion. • Research efforts frequently focus on specific diagnostic categories. • Labels establish an individual's eligibility for services. • Treatments, instruction, and support services are differentially provided on the basis of a label (e.g., sign language for a student who is deaf, an accelerated or enriched curriculum for pupils who are gifted and talented). • Labels heighten the visibility of the unique needs of persons with disabilities. • Labels serve as a basis for counting the number of individuals with disabilities and thus assist governments, schools, agencies, and other organizations in planning for the delivery of needed services. • Advocacy and special interest groups, such as the Autism Society of America or the National Federation of the Blind, typically have an interest in assisting particular groups of citizens with disabling conditions.	• Labels can be stigmatizing and may lead to stereotyping. • Labeling has the potential of focusing attention on limitations and what a person cannot do instead of on the individual's capabilities and strengths. • Labels can sometimes be used as an excuse or a reason for delivering ineffective instruction (e.g., "Marvin can't learn his multiplication facts because he is intellectually disabled"). • Labels can contribute to a diminished self-concept, lower expectations, and poor self-esteem. • Labels are typically inadequate for instructional purposes; they do not accurately reflect the educational or therapeutic needs of the individual student. • Labeling can lead to reduced opportunities for normalized experiences in school and community life. • A label can give the false impression of the permanence of a disability; some labels evaporate upon leaving the school environment.

Prevalence of Children and Young Adults With Disabilities

How many children and adolescents are identified as exceptional and have special needs? This is, as we will shortly see, not an easy question to answer. We begin by clarifying two key terms frequently encountered when describing the number of individuals with disabilities.

Definitions and Difficulties

Handbook Link 1.1
Read more about youth and disability.

Statisticians and researchers often talk about *incidence* and *prevalence*. Technically speaking, **incidence** refers to a rate of inception, or the number of *new* instances of a disability occurring within a given time frame, usually a year. As an illustration, it would be possible to calculate the number of infants born with Down syndrome between January 1 and December 31, 2011, in a particular state. This figure would typically be expressed as a percentage of the total number of babies born within the prescribed period of time; for example, 20 infants with Down syndrome out of 15,000 births would yield an incidence rate of .133 percent. **Prevalence** refers to the *total* number of individuals with a particular disability existing in the population at a given time. Prevalence is expressed as a percentage of the population exhibiting this specific exceptionality—for instance, the percentage of pupils with learning disabilities enrolled in special education programs during the current school year. If the prevalence of learning disabilities is estimated to be 5 percent of the school-age population, then we can reasonably expect about 50 out of every 1,000 students to evidence a learning disability. Throughout this text, we will report prevalence figures for each area of exceptionality that we study. Of course, establishing

TABLE 1.2 Number of Students Ages 6–21 Receiving a Special Education During School Year 2008–2009

Disability	Number	Percent of Total
Specific learning disabilities	2,525,898	42.88
Speech or language impairments	1,121,961	19.05
Mental retardation	476,131	8.08
Emotional disturbance	418,068	7.09
Multiple disabilities	124,073	2.10
Hearing impairments	70,781	1.20
Orthopedic impairments	62,371	1.05
Other health impairments	648,398	11.00
Visual impairments	25,816	0.43
Autism	292,818	4.97
Deaf-blindness	1,745	0.02
Traumatic brain injury	24,866	0.42
Developmental delay	96,923	1.64
Total	5,889,849	100.00

NOTE: Table based on data from the fifty states, Puerto Rico, the District of Columbia, and outlying areas.

SOURCE: U.S. Department of Education. (2010). *IDEA data.* Retrieved April 14, 2010, from https://www.ideadata.org/PartBReport.asp

accurate estimates of prevalence is based on our ability to gather specific information about the number of individuals with disabilities across the United States. Obviously, this is not an easy job. Fortunately, the federal government has assumed this responsibility. Each year the Department of Education issues a report (*Annual Report to Congress on the Implementation of the Individuals with Disabilities Education Act*) based on data supplied by the various states.

Efforts at gathering meaningful prevalence figures, which tend to vary from state to state, are frequently hindered by several issues:

- The accurate identification and assessment of children and adolescents with special needs (estimates are only as valid as the criteria and evaluation procedures used)
- Variations across states in the definition of disabilities
- Changing rules and regulations affecting special education (for example, who is eligible to receive a special education)
- The time-bound nature of some disabilities (a youngster recognized as disabled in the primary grades may not be considered so later on)

In summary, reliable prevalence data are difficult to obtain, and we recommend that the figures be interpreted cautiously.

Number of Children and Young Adults Served

More than 5.8 million U.S. students (5,889,849) between the ages of 6 and 21 were receiving a special education during the 2008–2009 school year (U.S. Department of Education, 2010). The number of students in each of the thirteen disability categories

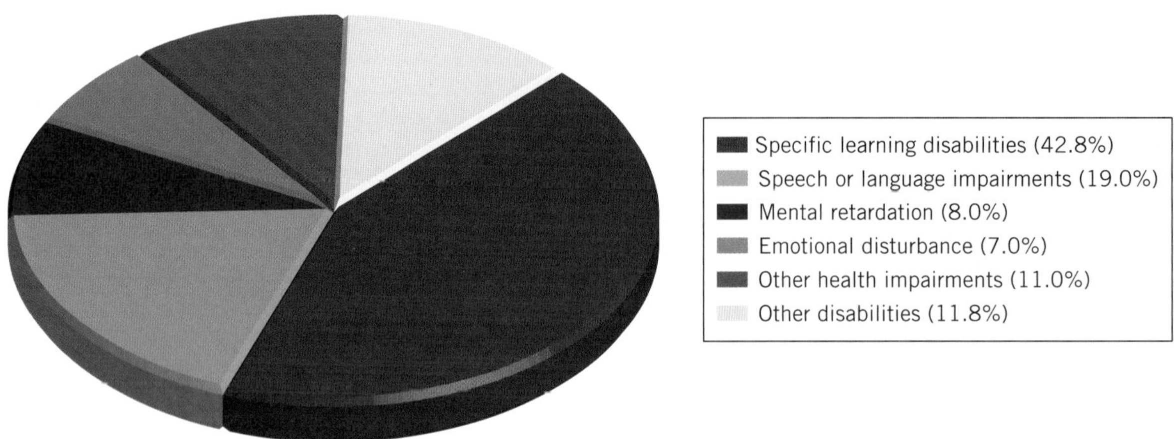

FIGURE 1.1 Distribution of Students Ages 6–21 Receiving a Special Education During School Year 2008–2009

NOTE: Percents based on data from the fifty states, Puerto Rico, the District of Columbia, and outlying areas.

Other disabilities include multiple disabilities, hearing impairments, orthopedic impairments, visual impairments, autism, deaf-blindness, traumatic brain injury, and developmental delay.

SOURCE: U.S. Department of Education. (2010). *IDEA data.* Retrieved April 14, 2010, from https://www.ideadata.org/PartBReport.asp

recognized by the federal government is recorded in Table 1.2 (see page 13). Learning disabilities account for slightly less than half of all pupils with disabilities (42.88%); students with dual sensory impairments (deaf-blindness) represent the smallest category of exceptionality (.02%). Figure 1.1 visually presents the percentages of students with various disabilities receiving a special education.

The growth in the number of students (ages 3–21) receiving a special education since the inception of PL 94–142 (now IDEA) in 1975 has been phenomenal. Each year the states typically report a continuously increasing number of individuals enrolled in special education programs. Since the 1976–1977 school year, the number of pupils being provided with a special education has increased by an astonishing 89 percent (3,485,088 versus 6,598,853). This remarkable growth is portrayed in Figure 1.2.

While the growth of special education over the past decades has truly been noteworthy, some areas of disability have grown faster than others. For instance, the population of students identified as learning disabled has grown dramatically since the inauguration of PL 94–142. In 1976, learning disabilities accounted for approximately 25 percent of the total population of students with disabilities; today, slightly less than half of all individuals enrolled in special education have learning disabilities. Another area that has shown tremendous growth is other health impairments (OHI). Children with attention deficit hyperactivity disorder (ADHD) have been eligible to receive a special education under this label since 1991. At that time, slightly more than 53,000 pupils were identified as other health impaired. Recent data indicate that more than 648,000 students were labeled OHI during the 2008–2009 school year. This represents an increase of over 1,100 percent. Experts (Lerner & Johns, 2009) believe that this increase is largely due to the inclusion of individuals with ADHD.

Figure 1.3 depicts the changes in distribution for select categories of exceptionality.

With the passage of PL 99–457 (the Education of the Handicapped Act Amendments of 1986, currently referred to as IDEA), services for infants, toddlers, and preschoolers with special needs have significantly increased. This first major amendment to PL 94–142 was enacted because more than half the states did not require special education services for preschoolers with disabilities (Koppelman, 1986). PL 99–457 remedied this situation by mandating that youngsters between 3 and 5 years of age receive the

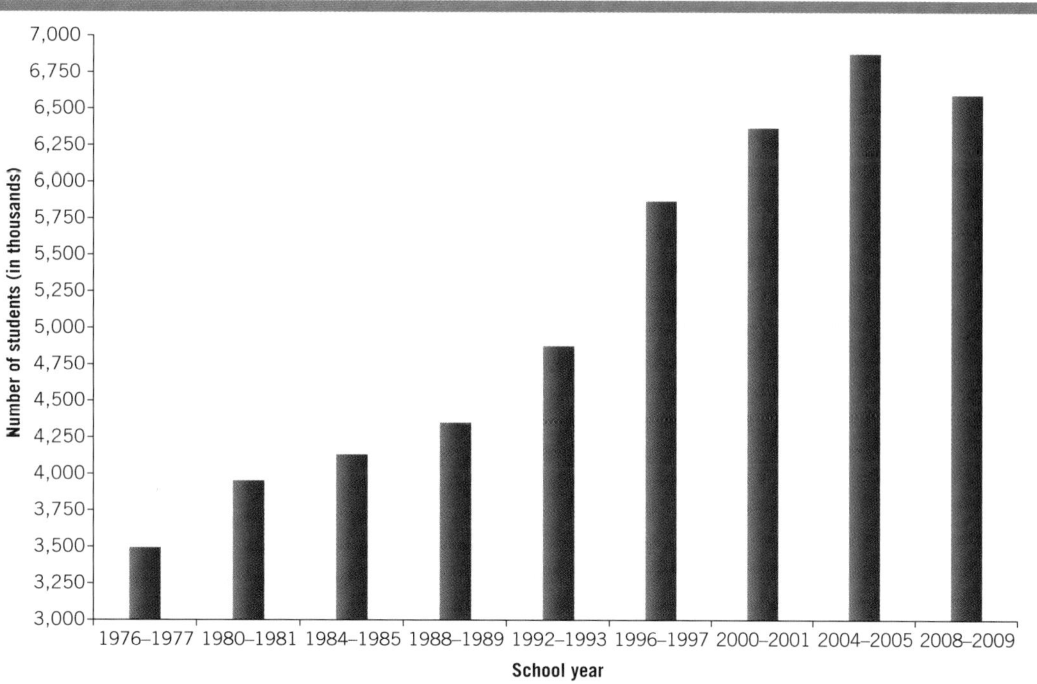

FIGURE 1.2 Growth in Number of Students Ages 3–21 Served in Special Education Programs in Select School Years: 1976–2008

NOTE: Figure based on data from the fifty states, Puerto Rico, the District of Columbia, and outlying areas.

SOURCE: U.S. Department of Education. (1992–2004). *Annual Reports to Congress on the Implementation of the Individuals with Disabilities Education Act.* Washington, DC: U.S. Government Printing Office.

U.S. Department of Education. (2010). *IDEA data.* Retrieved April 14, 2010, from https://www.ideadata.org/PartBReport.asp

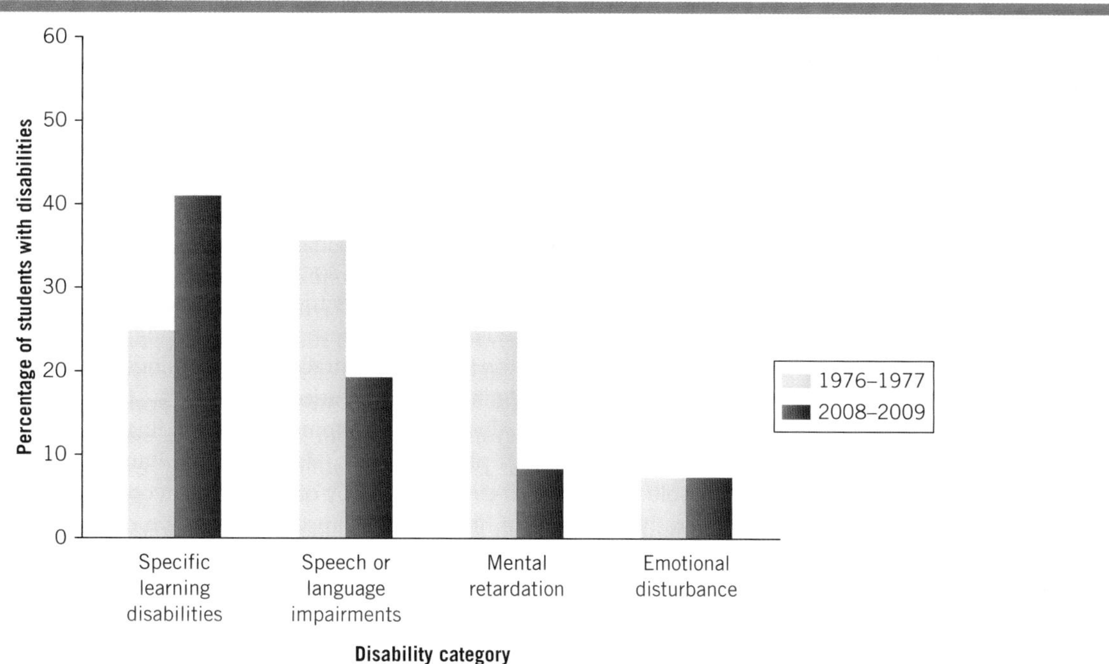

FIGURE 1.3 Changes in the Distribution of Students With Disabilities: 1976–1977 Versus 2008–2009

NOTE: Information based on children ages 6–21 served under IDEA.

SOURCE: U.S. Department of Education. (1992). *Fourteenth Annual Report to Congress on the Implementation of the Individuals with Disabilities Education Act.* Washington, DC: U.S. Government Printing Office. U.S. Department of Education. (2010). *IDEA data.* Retrieved April 14, 2010, from https://www.ideadata.org/PartBReport.asp

TABLE 1.3 Pioneering Contributors to the Development of Special Education

The Individuals	Their Ideas
Jacob Rodrigues Pereine (1715–1780)	Introduced the idea that persons who were deaf could be taught to communicate. Developed an early form of sign language. Provided inspiration and encouragement for the work of Itard and Seguin.
Philippe Pinel (1745–1826)	A reform-minded French physician who was concerned with the humanitarian treatment of individuals with mental illness. Advocated releasing institutionalized patients from their chains. Pioneered the field of occupational therapy. Served as Itard's mentor.
Jean-Marc Gaspard Itard (1774–1838)	A French doctor who secured lasting fame because of his systematic efforts to educate an adolescent thought to be severely mentally retarded. Recognized the importance of sensory stimulation.
Thomas Gallaudet (1787–1851)	Taught children with hearing impairments to communicate through a system of manual signs and symbols. Established the first institution in the United States.
Samuel Gridley Howe (1801–1876)	An American physician and educator accorded international fame because of his success in teaching individuals with visual and hearing impairments. Founded the first residential facility for the blind and was instrumental in inaugurating institutional care for children with mental retardation.
Dorothea Lynde Dix (1802–1887)	A contemporary of S. G. Howe, Dix was one of the first Americans to champion better and more humane treatment of the mentally ill. Instigated the establishment of several institutions for individuals with mental disorders.
Louis Braille (1809–1852)	A French educator, himself blind, who developed a tactile system of reading and writing for people who were blind. His system, based on a cell of six embossed dots, is still used today. This standardized code is known as Standard English Braille.
Edouard Seguin (1812–1880)	A pupil of Itard, Seguin was a French physician responsible for developing teaching methods for children with mental retardation. His training emphasized sensorimotor activities. After immigrating to the United States, he helped to found an organization that was the forerunner of the American Association on Intellectual and Developmental Disabilities.
Francis Galton (1822–1911)	Scientist concerned with individual differences. As a result of studying eminent persons, he believed that genius is solely the result of heredity. Those with superior abilities are born, not made.
Alexander Graham Bell (1847–1922)	Pioneering advocate of educating children with disabilities in public schools. As a teacher of students with hearing impairments, Bell promoted the use of residual hearing and developing the speaking skills of students who are deaf.
Alfred Binet (1857–1911)	A French psychologist who constructed the first standardized developmental assessment scale capable of quantifying intelligence. The original purpose of this test was to identify students who might profit from a special education and not to classify individuals on the basis of ability. Also originated the concept of mental age with his student Theodore Simon.
Maria Montessori (1870–1952)	Achieved worldwide recognition for her pioneering work with young children and youngsters with mental retardation. First female to earn a medical degree in Italy. Expert in early childhood education. Demonstrated that children are capable of learning at a very early age when surrounded with manipulative materials in a rich and stimulating environment. Believed that children learn best by direct sensory experience.
Lewis Terman (1877–1956)	An American educator and psychologist who revised Binet's original assessment instrument. The result was the publication of the Stanford-Binet Scale of Intelligence in 1916. Terman developed the notion of intelligence quotient, or IQ. Also famous for lifelong study of gifted individuals. Considered the grandfather of gifted education.

Special Education in the Public Schools

It was not until the second half of the nineteenth century and the early years of the twentieth century that special education classes began to appear in public schools. Services for children with exceptionalities began sporadically and slowly, serving only a very small number of individuals who needed services. Of course, during this era, even children without disabilities did not routinely attend school. An education at this time was a luxury; it was one of the benefits of being born into an affluent family. Many children, some as young as 5 or 6, were expected to contribute to their family's financial security by laboring in factories or working on farms. Being able to attend school was truly a privilege. It is against this backdrop that the first special education classes in public schools were established. Examples of these efforts are listed in Table 1.4.

At one time education was a privilege, not a right.

The very first special education classrooms were **self-contained**; students were typically grouped together and segregated from the other pupils. The majority of their school day was spent with their teacher in a classroom isolated from the daily activities of the school. In some instances, even lunch and recess provided no opportunity for interacting with typical classmates. This type of arrangement characterized many special education classrooms for the next fifty years or so.

After World War II, the stage was set for the rapid expansion of special education. Litigation, legislation, and leadership at the federal level, coupled with political activism and parental advocacy, helped to fuel the movement. Significant benefits for children with exceptionalities resulted from these efforts. In 1948, only about 12 percent of children with disabilities were receiving an education appropriate to their needs (Ballard, Ramirez, & Weintraub, 1982). From 1947 to 1972, the number of pupils enrolled in special education programs increased by an astonishing 716 percent, compared with an 82 percent increase in total public school enrollment (Dunn, 1973).

TABLE 1.4 The Development of Public School Classes for Children With Disabilities

Year	City	Disability Served
1869	Boston, MA	Deafness
1878	Cleveland, OH	Behavioral disorders
1896	Providence, RI	Mental retardation
1898	New York, NY	Slow learners
1899	Chicago, IL	Physical impairments
1900	Chicago, IL	Blindness
1901	Worcester, MA	Giftedness
1910	Chicago, IL	Speech impairment

Beginning in the mid-1970s and continuing to the present time, children with disabilities have secured the right to receive a free and appropriate public education provided in the most normalized setting. An education for these students is no longer a privilege; it is a right guaranteed by both federal and state laws and reinforced by judicial interpretation. We will talk about some of these laws and court cases in the next chapter. Special education over the past thirty years can perhaps best be seen as a gradual movement from isolation to participation, one of steady and progressive inclusion. (See the accompanying Insights feature.)

Professionals Who Work With Individuals With Exceptionalities

It is very common for teachers to work with professionals from other disciplines. A special education may require the expertise of other individuals outside the field of education. Recall our earlier definition of a special education, which incorporates this idea and the concept of related services. IDEA, in fact, mandates that educational assessments of a student's strengths and needs be multidisciplinary and that related services be provided to meet the unique requirements of each learner. Examples of related services include:

- Physical therapy
- Audiology
- Transportation
- Speech and language
- Psychology
- Recreational therapy
- Orientation and mobility
- Interpreting services
- Occupational therapy
- Nutrition
- Medical services
- Social work
- Vocational education
- Rehabilitation counseling
- Parent counseling
- School nurse services

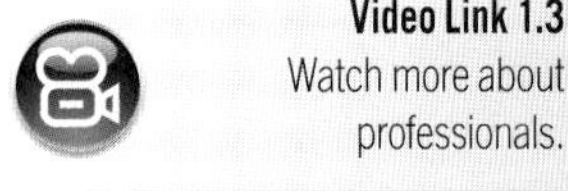

Video Link 1.3
Watch more about professionals.

Related services are neither complete nor exhaustive, and additional services—such as assistive technology devices or interpreters for pupils with hearing impairments—may be required if a student is to receive benefit from a special education. The issue of what constitutes a related service, however, has generated some controversy among educators and school administrators. Disagreements are also common as to what kinds of services should be provided by the public schools and which services are rightfully the responsibilities of the child's parent(s).

There is a growing recognition of the importance of professionals working together regardless of the different disciplines they may represent. No one discipline or profession possesses all of the resources or clinical skills needed to construct the appropriate interventions and educational programs for children and young adults with disabilities, a large number of whom have complex needs. Although the idea of professionals working together in a cooperative fashion has been part of special education since the enactment of PL 94–142 some thirty years ago, we have not always been successful in implementing this idea. Obstacles range from poor interpersonal dynamics, to concerns about professional turf, to the lack of planning time, to the absence of administrative support for this concept. However, we find that professionals are increasingly working together. Professional cooperation and partnership are the key to delivering services in an efficient and integrated manner. "Serving students with disabilities in inclusive settings depends greatly on effective collaboration among professionals" (Hobbs & Westling,

A Timeline of Key Dates in the History of Special Education in the United States

1817 Rev. Thomas Hopkins Gallaudet becomes principal of the American Asylum for the Education of the Deaf and Dumb, the first residential school in the United States.

1829 Samuel Gridley Howe establishes the New England Asylum for the Blind.

1834 Louis Braille publishes the Braille code.

1839 First teacher training program opens in Massachusetts.

1848 Samuel Gridley Howe establishes the Massachusetts School for Idiotic and Feeble Minded Children.

1848 Dorothea Dix calls attention to the shocking conditions of American asylums and prisons.

1869 First public school class for children with hearing impairments opens in Boston.

1876 Edouard Seguin helps to organize the first professional association concerned with disabilities (mental retardation), a predecessor to today's American Association on Intellectual and Developmental Disabilities.

1897 National Education Association establishes a section for teachers of children with disabilities.

1898 Elizabeth Farrell, later to become the first president of the Council for Exceptional Children, begins a program for "backwards" or "slow learning" children in New York City.

1904 The Vineland Training School in New Jersey inaugurates training programs for teachers of students with mental retardation.

1916 Lewis Terman publishes the Stanford-Binet Scale of Intelligence.

1920 Teachers College, Columbia University, begins training program for teachers of pupils who are gifted.

1922 Organization that later would become the Council for Exceptional Children (CEC) is founded in New York City.

1928 Seeing Eye dogs for the blind are introduced in the United States.

1936 First compulsory law for testing the hearing of school-age children is enacted in New York.

1949 United Cerebral Palsy (UCP) association is founded.

1950 Association for Retarded Children (ARC) is founded (known today as the Association for Retarded Citizens, or simply The Arc).

1953 National Association for Gifted Children is founded.

1963 Association for Children with Learning Disabilities (forerunner to Learning Disabilities Association of America) is organized.

1972 Wolf Wolfensberger introduces the concept of normalization, initially coined by Bengt Nirje of Sweden, to the United States.

1973 Public Law 93–112, the Vocational Rehabilitation Act of 1973, is enacted; Section 504 prohibits discrimination against individuals with disabilities.

1975 Education for All Handicapped Children Act (PL 94–142) is passed; landmark legislation ensures, among other provisions, a free and appropriate public education for all children with disabilities.

1986 Education of the Handicapped Act Amendments of 1986 (PL 99–457) are enacted; mandates a special education for preschoolers with disabilities and incentives for providing early intervention services to infants and toddlers.

1990 Americans with Disabilities Act (PL 101–336) becomes law; prohibits discrimination on the basis of disability.

1990 PL 101–476, the Individuals with Disabilities Education Act (commonly known as IDEA), is passed; among other provisions, emphasizes transition planning for adolescents with disabilities.

1997 Individuals with Disabilities Education Act (PL 105–17) is reauthorized, providing a major retooling and expansion of services for students with disabilities and their families.

2001 No Child Left Behind Act of 2001 (PL 107–110) is enacted; a major educational reform effort focusing on academic achievement of students and qualifications of teachers.

2004 Individuals with Disabilities Education Improvement Act of 2004 (PL 108–446) is passed; aligns IDEA legislation with provisions of the No Child Left Behind Act; modifies the individualized education program (IEP) process in addition to changes affecting school discipline, due process, and evaluation of students with disabilities.

2008 Americans with Disabilities Act Amendments of 2008 are enacted; expand statutory interpretation of a disability while affording individuals with disabilities greater protections.

SOURCE: Information partially based on data from the 75th Anniversary Issue, *Teaching Exceptional Children, 29*(5), 1997, pp. 5–49.

Effective programming for students with disabilities requires meaningful involvement of teachers, parents, and related service providers.

1998, p. 14). McLean, Wolery, and Bailey (2004) identify several reasons why collaboration is beneficial:

- Incorrect placement recommendations are likely to be reduced.
- There is a greater likelihood that assessments will be nondiscriminatory.
- More appropriate educational plans and goals are likely to result from professional teaming.

Collaboration is *how* people work together; it is a style of interaction that professionals choose to use in order to accomplish a shared goal (Friend & Cook, 2010). For collaboration to be effective, however, service providers must exhibit a high degree of cooperation, trust, and mutual respect and must share the decision-making process. Additional key attributes necessary for meaningful collaboration include voluntary participation and parity in the relationship, along with shared goals, accountability, and resources (Friend & Cook). A good example of the beneficial outcomes of these collaborative efforts can be found in the development of a student's **individualized education program**, or **IEP**, which necessitates a collaborative team process involving parents, teachers, and professionals.

Video Link 1.4
Watch more about working together.

Several models are available for building partnerships among related services personnel, general education teachers, and special educators. We have chosen to examine two different approaches: consultative services and service delivery teams.

Consultative Services

A growing number of school districts are developing strategies for assisting general educators in serving children with disabilities. This effort is part of a larger movement aimed at making the neighborhood school and general education classroom more inclusive. One effective support technique is to provide assistance to general educators through consultative services. **Consultation** is a focused, problem-solving process in which one individual offers expertise and assistance to another. The intent of this activity is to modify teaching tactics and/or the learning environment in order to accommodate the needs of the individual student with disabilities. Instructional planning and responsibility thus become a shared duty among various professionals. Assistance to the general education teacher may come from a special educator, the school psychologist, a physical therapist, or any other related services provider. A vision specialist, for example, may provide suggestions on how to use various pieces of mobility equipment needed by a student who is visually impaired; a school psychologist or behavior management specialist may offer suggestions for dealing with the aggressive, acting-out behaviors of a middle school student with emotional problems. Hourcade and Bauwens (2003) refer to this type of aid as indirect consultation. In other instances, services are rendered directly to the student by professionals other than the classroom teacher. In this situation, specific areas of weakness or deficit are the target of remediation. Interventions are increasingly being provided by related services personnel in the general education classroom. The general educator also typically receives instructional tips on how to carry out the remediation efforts in the absence of the service provider.

We should also point out that consultative services are equally valuable for special educators. The diverse needs of pupils with disabilities frequently require that special education teachers seek programming suggestions and other types of assistance from various related services personnel. It should be obvious that no one discipline or professional possesses all of the answers. The complex demands of today's classrooms dictate that professionals work together in a cooperative fashion.

According to Pugach and Johnson (2002), consultative services are an appropriate and beneficial strategy, a means whereby all school personnel can collaboratively interact as part of their commitment to serving *all* children. Meaningful collaborative consultation requires mutual support, respect, flexibility, and a sharing of expertise. No one professional should consider himself or herself more of an expert than others. Each of the parties involved can learn and benefit from the others' expertise; of course, the ultimate beneficiary is the student. We believe that the keys to developing effective collaborative practices are good interpersonal skills coupled with professional competency and a willingness to assist in meeting the needs of all children.

Service Delivery Teams

Another way that professionals can work together is to construct a team. Special education teachers seldom work completely alone. Even those who teach in a self-contained classroom function, in some way, as part of a team (Crutchfield, 1997). Simply stated, a team consists of a group of individuals whose purpose and function are derived from a common philosophy and shared goals. Obviously, educational teams will differ in their membership; yet individual professionals, who typically represent various disciplines, appreciate their interdependence and sense of common ownership of their objective (Gargiulo & Metcalf, 2010).

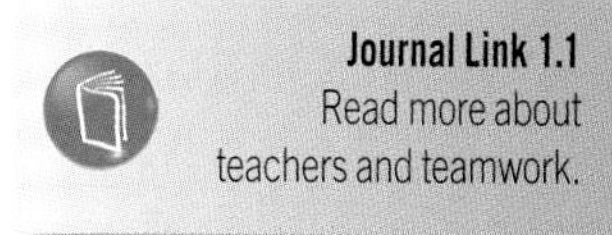

Besides having members from different fields, teams will also differ according to their structure and function. Such teams are often used in evaluating, planning, and delivering services to individuals with disabilities, especially infants and toddlers. The three most common approaches identified in the professional literature (McDonnell, Hardman, & McDonnell, 2003) are multidisciplinary, interdisciplinary, and transdisciplinary teams. These approaches are interrelated and, according to Giangreco, York, and Rainforth

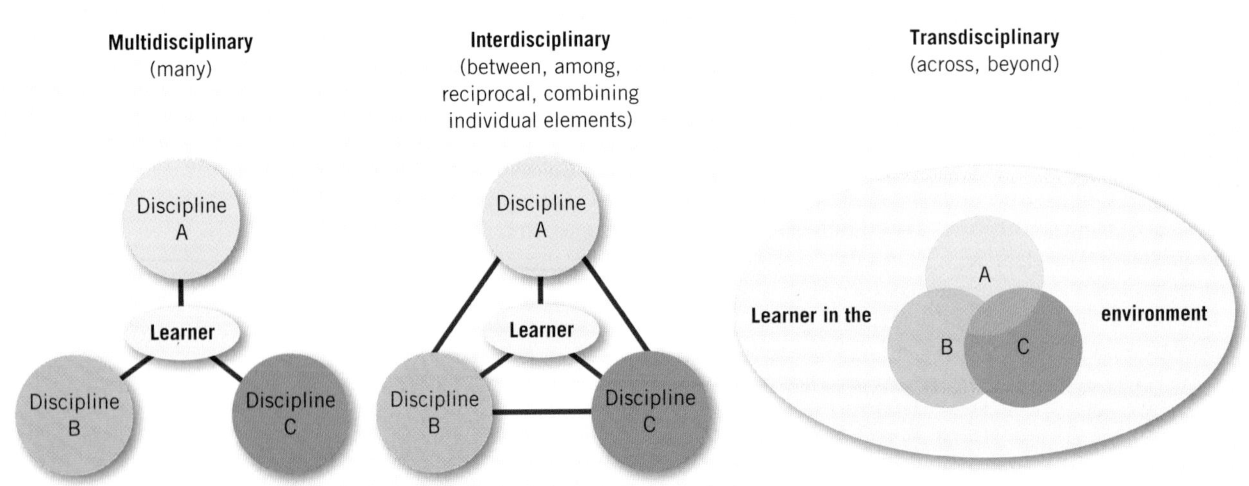

FIGURE 1.4 Multidisciplinary, Interdisciplinary, and Transdisciplinary Team Models

SOURCE: M. Giangreco, J. York, and B. Rainforth, "Providing Related Services to Learners with Severe Handicaps in Educational Settings: Pursuing the Least Restrictive Option," *Pediatric Physical Therapy, 1*(2), 1989, p. 57.

(1989), represent a historical evolution of teamwork. This evolutionary process can be portrayed as concentric circles, with each model retaining some of the attributes of its predecessor. Figure 1.4 illustrates these various configurations.

Multidisciplinary Teams

The concept of a **multidisciplinary** team was originally mandated in PL 94–142 and was recently reiterated in the 2004 reauthorization of IDEA (PL 108–446). This approach utilizes the expertise of professionals from several disciplines, each of whom usually performs his or her assessments, interventions, and other tasks independent of the others. Individuals contribute according to their own specialty area with little regard for the actions of other professionals. There is a high degree of professional autonomy and minimal integration. A team exists only in the sense that each person shares a common goal. There is very little coordination or collaboration across discipline areas. Friend and Cook (2010) characterize this model as a patchwork quilt whereby different, and sometimes contrasting, information is integrated but not necessarily with a unified outcome.

Parents of children with disabilities typically meet with each team member individually. They are generally passive recipients of information about their son or daughter. Because information flows to them from several sources, some parents may have difficulty synthesizing all of the data and recommendations from the various experts. Gargiulo and Kilgo (2011) do not consider the multidisciplinary model to be especially "family friendly."

Interdisciplinary Teams

The **interdisciplinary team** model evolved from dissatisfaction with the fragmented services and lack of communication typically associated with the multidisciplinary team model (McCormick, 2003). In this model of teaming, team members perform their evaluations independently, but program development and instructional recommendations are

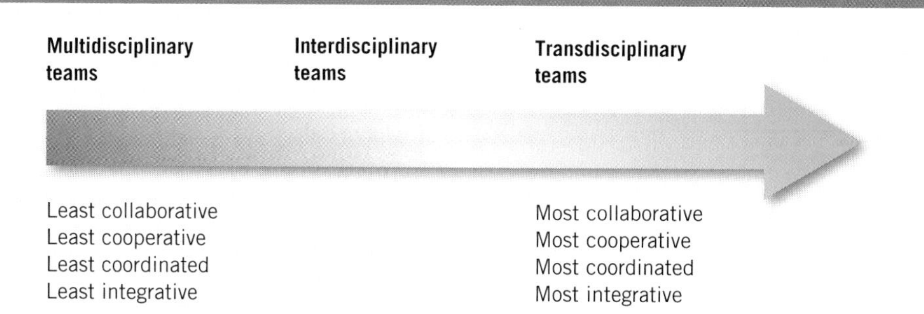

FIGURE 1.5 Characteristics of Teaming Models

SOURCE: From R. Gargiulo and J. Kilgo, *An Introduction to Young Children with Special Needs,* 3rd ed. ©2011 Wadsworth, a part of Cengage Learning, Inc. Reproduced by permission. www.cengage.com/permissions

the result of information sharing and joint planning. Significant cooperation among the team members leads to an integrated plan of services and a holistic view of the student's strengths and needs. Greater communication, coordination, and collaboration are the distinctive trademarks of this model. Direct services such as physical therapy, however, are usually provided in isolation from one another. Families typically meet with the entire team or its representative; in many cases, a special educator performs this role.

Transdisciplinary Teams

The **transdisciplinary team** approach to providing services builds upon the strengths of the interdisciplinary model. In this model, team members are committed to working collaboratively across individual discipline lines. The transdisciplinary model is distinguished by two additional and related features: role sharing and a primary therapist. Professionals from various disciplines conduct their initial evaluations and assessments, but they relinquish their role (role release) as service providers by teaching their skills to other team members, one of whom will serve as the primary interventionist. This person is regarded as the team leader. For many children and adolescents with special needs, this role is usually filled by an educator. This individual relies heavily on the support and consultation provided by his or her professional peers. Discipline-specific interventions are still available, although they occur less frequently.

Audio Link 1.2
Listen to more about inclusion.

"The primary purpose of this approach," according to Bruder (1994), "is to pool and integrate the expertise of team members so that more efficient and comprehensive assessment and intervention services may be provided" (p. 61). The aim of the transdisciplinary model is to avoid compartmentalization and fragmentation of services. It attempts to provide a more coordinated and unified approach to assessment and service delivery. Members of a transdisciplinary team see parents as full-fledged members of the group with a strong voice in the team's recommendations and decisions.

Figure 1.5 illustrates some of the characteristics of each team model as viewed by Gargiulo and Kilgo (2011).

Cooperative Teaching

Cooperative teaching, or co-teaching as it is sometimes called, is an increasingly popular approach for achieving inclusion (Gargiulo & Metcalf, 2010; Scruggs, Mastropieri, & McDuffie, 2007). With this strategy, general education teachers and special educators work together in a cooperative manner; each professional shares in the planning and delivery of instruction to a heterogeneous group of students. Hourcade and Bauwens (2003, p. 41) define **cooperative teaching** as

> direct collaboration in which a general educator and one or more support service providers voluntarily agree to work together in a co-active and coordinated fashion in the general education classroom. These educators, who possess distinct and complementary sets of skills, share roles, resources, and responsibilities in a sustained effort while working toward the common goal of school success for all students.

The aim of cooperative teaching is to create options for learning and to provide support to *all* students in the general education classroom by combining the content expertise of the general educator with the pedagogical skills of the special educator (Smith, Polloway, Patton, & Dowdy, 2008). Cooperative teaching can be implemented in several different ways. These arrangements, as identified by Friend and Cook (2010), typically occur for set periods of time each day or on certain days of the week. Some of the more common instructional models for co-teaching are depicted in Figure 1.6. The particular strategy chosen often depends on the needs and characteristics of the pupils, curricular demands, amount of professional experience, and teacher preference, as well as such practical matters as the amount of space available. Many experienced educators use a variety of arrangements depending on their specific circumstances.

One Teach, One Observe

In this version of cooperative teaching, one teacher presents the instruction to the entire class while the second educator circulates, gathering information (data) on a specific pupil, a small group of students, or targeted behaviors across the whole class such as productive use of free time. Although this model requires a minimal amount of joint planning, it is very important that teachers periodically exchange roles to avoid one professional being perceived as the "assistant teacher."

One Teach, One Support

Video Link 1.6
Watch more on cooperative teaching.

Both individuals are present, but one teacher takes the instructional lead while the other provides support and assistance to the students. It is important that one professional (usually the special educator) is not always expected to function as the assistant; rotating roles can help to alleviate this potential problem.

Station Teaching

In this type of cooperative teaching, the lesson is divided into two or more segments and presented in different locations in the classroom. One teacher presents one portion of the lesson while the other teacher provides a different portion. Then the groups rotate, and the teachers repeat their information to new groups of pupils. Depending on the class, a third station can be established where students work independently or with a "learning buddy" to review material. Station teaching is effective at all grade levels.

Parallel Teaching

Video Link 1.7
Watch more on parallel teaching.

This instructional arrangement lowers the teacher-pupil ratio. Instruction is planned jointly but is delivered by each teacher to one half of a heterogeneous group of learners. Coordination of efforts is crucial. This format lends itself to drill-and-practice activities or projects that require close teacher supervision. As with station teaching, noise and activity levels may pose problems.

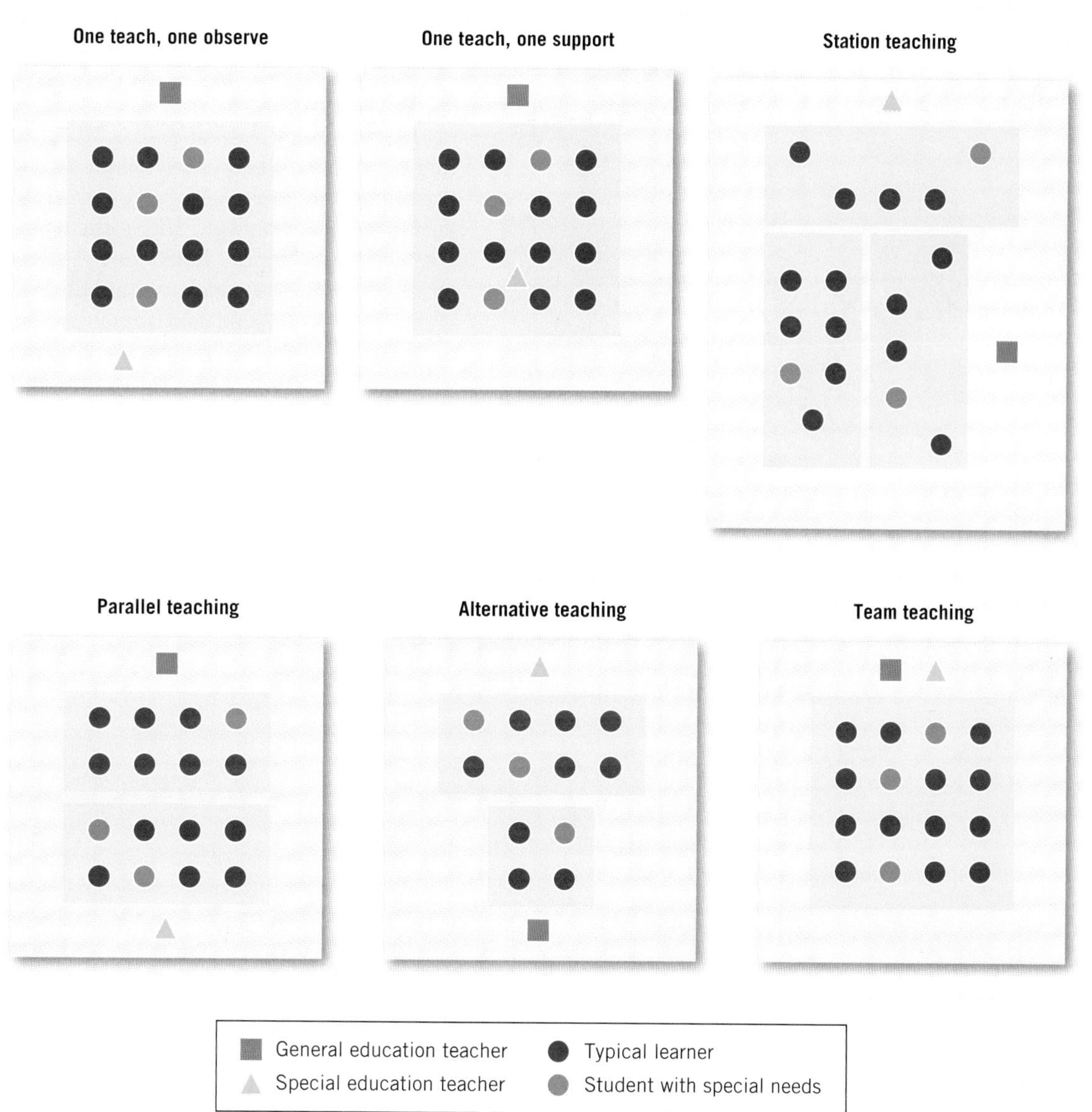

FIGURE 1.6 Cooperative Teaching Arrangements

SOURCE: Adapted from M. Friend and L. Cook, *Interactions: Collaboration Skills for School Professionals,* 6th ed. (Boston: Pearson Education, 2010), p. 142.

Alternative Teaching

Some students benefit from *small* group instruction; alternative teaching meets that need. With this model, one teacher provides instruction to the larger group while the other teacher interacts with a small group of pupils. Although commonly used for remediation purposes, alternative teaching is equally appropriate for enrichment activities and in-depth study. Teachers need to be cautious, however, that children with disabilities are not exclusively and routinely assigned to the small group; all members of the class should participate periodically in the functions of the smaller group.

Today's classrooms serve all children.

Team Teaching

In this type of cooperative teaching, both teachers share the instructional activities equally. Each teacher, for example, may take turns leading a discussion about the causes of World War II, or one teacher may talk about multiplication of fractions while the co-teacher gives several examples illustrating this concept. This form of cooperative teaching, sometimes called interactive teaching (Walther-Thomas, Korinek, McLaughlin, & Williams, 2000), requires a significant amount of professional trust and a high level of commitment.

Cooperative teaching should not be viewed as a panacea for meeting the multiple challenges frequently encountered when serving students with disabilities in general education classrooms; it is, however, one mechanism for facilitating successful inclusion. According to researchers (Rice, Drame, Owens, & Frattura, 2007; Scruggs et al., 2007), some of the key ingredients required for successful cooperative teaching include the following:

- Voluntary participation
- Adequate planning time
- Mutual respect
- Administrative support
- Flexibility and creativity
- Personal and professional compatibility
- Shared instructional philosophy

Video Link 1.8
Watch team teaching in action.

Teachers also need to openly address potential obstacles, such as workload and time management, if co-teaching is to be successful (Smith et al., 2008).

To ensure that co-teaching is efficient and effective, Reinhiller (1996) recommends that teachers address the following five questions:

- Why do we want to co-teach?
- How will we know whether our goals are being met?
- How will we communicate and document the collaboration?
- How will we share responsibility for the instruction of all students?
- How will we gain support from others? (p. 46)

Keefe, Moore, and Duff (2004) offer the following guidelines for creating and maintaining a successful co-teaching experience:

- *Know yourself*—recognize your strengths and weaknesses; acknowledge preconceived notions about teaching in an inclusive setting.
- *Know your partner*—foster a friendship; accept each other's idiosyncrasies; appreciate differences in teaching styles.
- *Know your students*—discover the students' interests; listen to their dreams; embrace acceptance.
- *Know your "stuff"*—share information and responsibility; jointly create IEPs; be knowledgeable about classroom routines.

Like Murawski and Dieker (2004), we believe that in the final analysis the key question that must be answered is "Is what we are doing good for the both of us and good for our students?"

TABLE 1.5 Advantages and Disadvantages of Cooperative Teaching Arrangements

Instructional Model	Advantages	Disadvantages
Team Teaching	• Provides systematic observation/data collection • Promotes role/content sharing • Facilitates individual assistance • Models appropriate academic, social, and help-seeking behaviors • Teaches question asking • Provides clarification (e.g., concepts, rules, vocabulary)	• May be job sharing, not learning enriching • Requires considerable planning • Requires modeling and role-playing skills • Becomes easy to "typecast" specialist with this role
Station Teaching	• Provides active learning format • Increases *small* group attention • Encourages cooperation and independence • Allows strategic grouping • Increases response rate	• Requires considerable planning and preparation • Increases noise level • Requires group and independent work skills • Is difficult to monitor
Parallel Teaching	• Provides effective review format • Encourages student responses • Reduces pupil-teacher ratio for group instruction or review	• Hard to achieve equal depth of content coverage • May be difficult to coordinate • Requires monitoring of partner pacing • Increases noise level • Encourages some teacher-student competition
Alternative Teaching	• Facilitates enrichment opportunities • Offers absent students "catch up" time • Keeps individuals and class on pace • Offers time to develop missing skills	• May select same low-achieving students for help • Creates segregated learning environments • Is difficult to coordinate • May single out students

SOURCE: From Chris Walther-Thomas, Lori Korinek, Virginia L. McLaughlin, and Brenda Toler Williams, *Collaboration for Inclusive Education: Developing Successful Programs,* 1st ed. Published by Allyn and Bacon, Boston, MA. Copyright © 2000 by Pearson Education. Reprinted by permission of the publisher.

Advantages and disadvantages of cooperative teaching are summarized in Table 1.5. An award-winning teacher's recommendations for facilitating successful co-teaching experiences are offered in Table 1.6.

Video Link 1.9
Watch educators share their strategies.

Universal Design for Learning

In today's climate of high-stakes testing and calls for greater student and teacher accountability, full access to the general education curriculum for students with disabilities is receiving growing attention. One way of ensuring access to, along with participation and progress in, the general education curriculum, as required by PL 108–446, is via the concept of universal design. Originally an idea found in the field of architectural studies, **universal design for learning** can be simply stated as "the design of instructional materials and activities that allows the learning goals to be achievable by individuals with wide differences in their abilities to see, hear, speak, move, read, write, understand English, attend, organize, engage, and remember" (Orkwis & McLane, 1998,

TABLE 1.6 Recommendations for Successful Co-teaching

For working with children with disabilities:	For working with general education teachers:
• When you construct your plan, think about how you can make it visual, auditory, tactile, and kinesthetic. You'll have a better chance of meeting different learning styles. • Think about what is the most important thing all students need to learn and then think about how you can break the task into smaller parts for some students and make it more challenging for students who are ready to move ahead. • Be keenly aware of student strengths, and plan to find a way for each student to be successful academically every day. • Working with a peer/buddy is often a helpful strategy. • Mix up your groups now and then. A student may need a different group for reading than for math. Try not to "label" anyone. • Children with disabilities (many children actually) need very clear, precise directions. Pair auditory with visual directions if possible. Students with more severe impairments may need to see objects. • It may be helpful to only give one direction at a time. This doesn't mean the pace has to be slow. In fact, a fast pace is often quite effective. Using signals (e.g., for getting attention, transitions) can also be very helpful. • Be consistent. • Notice students being "good"—offer verbal praise or perhaps a small positive note. • Have high expectations for *all* children.	• Find teachers who welcome your students and whom you enjoy working with if possible. It is helpful to find co-teachers who have different strengths so you can complement each other. • Faithfully plan ahead with these teachers—at least a week ahead. • Be willing to do more than your share at first if necessary to get a solid footing for the year. It will pay off. • Keep communication open and frequent. Use positive language with each other as much as possible. Brainstorm solutions to challenges together, and try different solutions. • Document the work you do with students. Help with assessment as much as possible. • Attend open houses, parent conferences, and other similar meetings so the parents view you as part of the classroom community. • Look for the good in the teacher(s) and students, and tell them when you see a "best practice." • If you don't know the answer to something, ask. If you don't know some of the content very well, study. Find out who does something well, and observe him or her if it is a skill you need to work on. • When you say you will do something, be sure you follow through.

SOURCE: D. Metcalf, H. B. Sugg Elementary School, Farmville, NC. The Council for Exceptional Children (CEC) 2004 Clarissa Hug Teacher of the Year.

p. 9). Universal design allows education professionals the flexibility necessary to design curriculum, instruction, and evaluation procedures capable of meeting the needs of *all* students (Hitchcock, Meyer, Rose, & Jackson, 2002). Universal design for learning is accomplished by means of flexible curricular materials and activities that offer alternatives to pupils with widely varying abilities and backgrounds. These adaptations are built into the instructional design rather than added on later as an afterthought. Universal design for learning provides equal access to learning, not simply equal access to information. It assumes that there is no one method of presentation or expression, which provides equal access for all learners. Learning activities and materials are purposely designed to allow for flexibility and offer various ways to learn (Scott, McGuire, & Shaw, 2003). Table 1.7 presents some of the many different ways in which a teacher could present a lesson.

Video Link 1.10
Watch more about universal design for learning.

Universal design for learning (UDL) is envisioned as an instructional resource, a vehicle for diversifying instruction in order to deliver the general education curriculum to each pupil. UDL does not remove academic challenges; it removes barriers to access. Simply stated, universal design for learning is just good teaching (Ohio State University Partnership Grant, 2010).

According to Wehmeyer, Lance, and Bashinski (2002), "universally designed curriculum takes into account individual student interests and preferences and individualizes representation, presentation, and response aspects of the curriculum delivery accordingly" (p. 230). It offers the opportunity for creating a curriculum that is sufficiently

TABLE 1.7 Multiple Methods of Presenting Instructional Content

Auditory	Visual	Tactile/Kinesthetic	Affective	Technology
Lecture	Video clips	Field trip	*Small* group work	Digitized video PalmPilot Video conferencing
Discussion	Sign language Speech reading	Sign language Gestures	Cross-age tutoring Peer-mediated instruction	Electronic discussion boards Online chat rooms
Song	Watch a play	Drawing	Role play	
Read aloud	Books	Braille books		Tape recorder iPod
Questioning	Graph, table, chart Slide show Transparency Whiteboard	Demonstration Role play Dance Games Manipulatives Build an object		Spreadsheet PowerPoint Overhead data projector

NOTE: Not an exhaustive list; some methods may fit more than one category.

flexible to meet the needs of all learners. Universal design provides a range of options for accessing, using, and engaging learning materials—explicitly acknowledging that no one option will work for all students (Gargiulo & Metcalf, 2010). Some of the beneficiaries of this strategy include, for example, individuals who speak English as a second language, pupils with disabilities, and students whose preferred learning style is inconsistent with the teacher's teaching style (Ohio State University Partnership Grant, 2010). There are three essential elements of universal design for learning that are often considered when developing curriculum for learners with diverse abilities. These components (see Figure 1.7) are multiple means of representation, engagement, and expression.

Exceptionality Across the Life Span

When we talk about special education, most people envision services for children of school age; yet the field embraces a wider range of individuals than students between the ages of 6 and 18. In recent years, professionals have begun to focus their attention on two distinct populations: infants/toddlers and preschoolers with special needs, and students with disabilities at the secondary level who are about to embark into adulthood. Meeting the needs of pupils at both ends of the spectrum presents a myriad of challenges for educators as well as related services personnel; however, professionals have a mandate to serve individuals across the life span.

Our purpose at this point is only to introduce some of the concepts and thinking about these two age groups. In later chapters, we will explore more fully many of the issues specific to young children with special needs as well as services for adults with disabilities.

Infants/Toddlers and Preschoolers With Special Needs

Prior to PL 94–142, services for infants, toddlers, and preschoolers with disabilities or delays were virtually unheard of. In many instances, parents had to seek out assistance

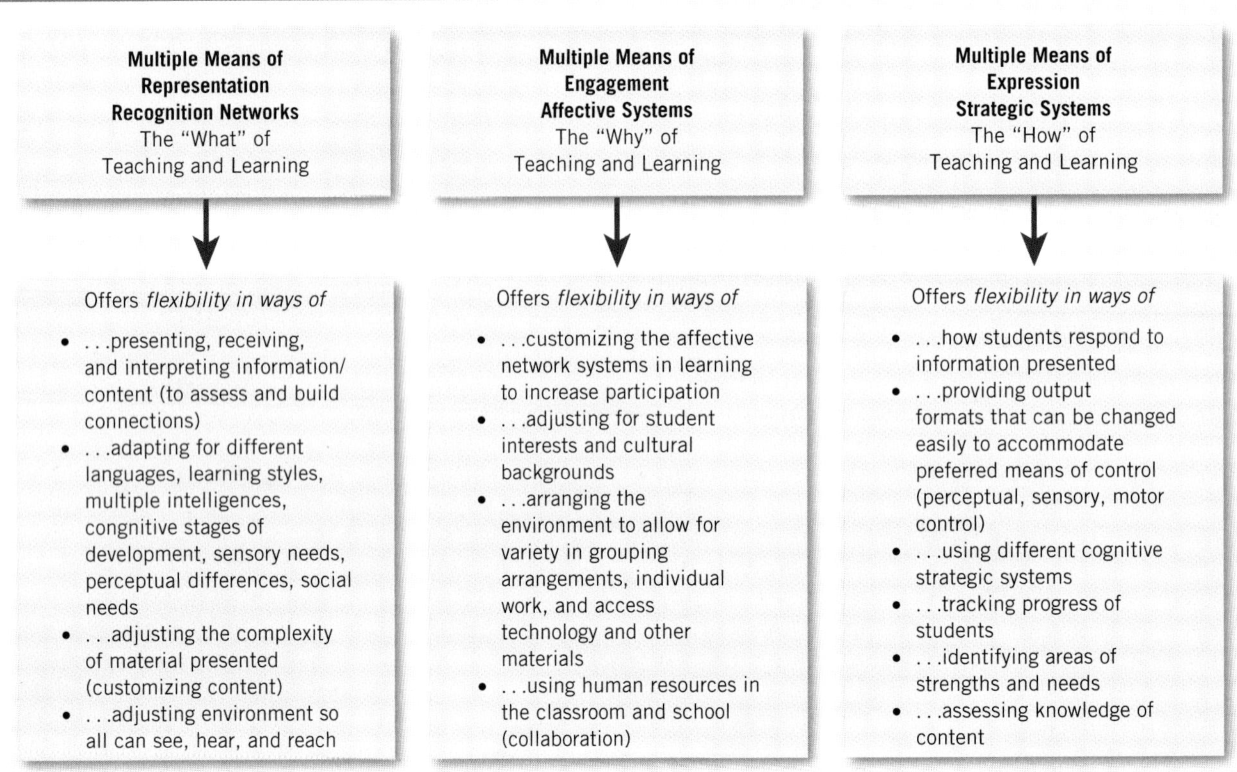

FIGURE 1.7 Three Essential Qualities of Universal Design for Learning

SOURCE: From R. Gargiulo and D. Metcalf, *Teaching in Today's Inclusive Classrooms,* 1st ed. © 2010. Wadsworth, a part of Cengage Learning, Inc. Reproduced by permission. www.cengage.com/permissions

on their own; public schools did not routinely offer early intervention or other supports. As we noted earlier in this chapter, even with the enactment of the Education for All Handicapped Children Act, more than half the states did not provide a special education for preschoolers with special needs. Today, professionals realize the importance and value of intervening in the lives of young children. In fact, the earlier that intervention is begun, the better the outcomes (Bruder, 2010; Sandall, Hemmeter, McLean, & Smith, 2005). "Without early intervention many [young] children with disabilities fall further and further behind their nondisabled peers, and minor delays in development often become major delays by the time the child reaches school age" (Bicard & Heward, 2010, p. 331). Providing services to our youngest citizens with disabilities or delays has become a national priority. Presently, more than 1 million children from birth to age 5 receive some form of intervention or special education (U.S. Department of Education, 2010).

Journal Link 1.2
Read more about young children and early intervention.

The Education of the Handicapped Act Amendments of 1986 (PL 99–457) are largely responsible for the rapid development of services for youngsters with disabilities or delays and those children who are at risk for future problems in learning and development. PL 99–457 is concerned with the family of the youngster with special needs as well as the child. This law clearly promotes parent–professional collaboration and partnerships. Parents are empowered to become decision makers with regard to programs and services for their son or daughter. We can see this emphasis in the **individualized family service plan**, or **IFSP** as it is commonly known. Similar to an IEP for older students with disabilities, the IFSP is much more family focused and reflective of the family's resources, priorities, and concerns. (Both of these documents will be fully discussed in Chapter 2.)

When professionals talk about providing services to very young children with disabilities or special needs, a distinction is generally made between two frequently used terms: *early intervention* and *early childhood special education*. **Early intervention** is typically used, according to Gargiulo and Kilgo (2011), to refer to the delivery of a coordinated and comprehensive package of specialized services to infants and toddlers (birth through age 2) with developmental delays or at-risk conditions and their families. **Early childhood special education** is used to describe the provision of customized services uniquely crafted to meet the individual needs of youngsters with disabilities between 3 and 5 years of age.

Young children with special needs greatly benefit from early intervention.

Early intervention represents a consortium of services, not just educational assistance but also health care, social services, family supports, and other benefits. The aim of early intervention is to affect positively the overall development of the child—his or her social, emotional, physical, and intellectual well-being. We believe that incorporating a "whole child" approach is necessary because all of these elements are interrelated and dependent on one another (Zigler, 2000).

Adolescents and Young Adults With Disabilities

Preparing our nation's young people for lives as independent adults has long been a goal of American secondary education. This objective typically includes the skills necessary for securing employment, pursuing postsecondary educational opportunities, participating in the community, living independently, and engaging in social/recreational activities, to mention only a few of the many facets of this multidimensional concept. Most young adults make this passage, or **transition**, from one phase of their life to the next without significant difficulty. Unfortunately, this statement is not necessarily true for many secondary students with disabilities. Full participation in adult life is a goal that is unattainable for a large number of citizens with disabilities. Consider the implications of the following facts gathered from various national surveys:

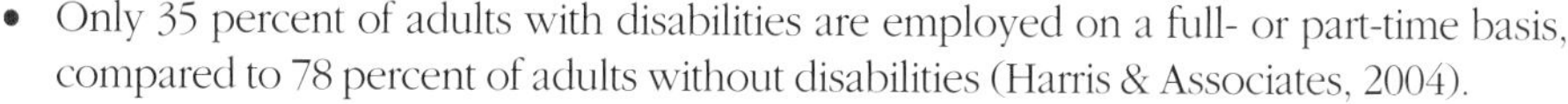

- Only 35 percent of adults with disabilities are employed on a full- or part-time basis, compared to 78 percent of adults without disabilities (Harris & Associates, 2004).
- Approximately one out of five adults with disabilities has less than a high school education; by way of comparison, only 11 percent of adults without disabilities lack a high school diploma (Harris & Associates, 2004).
- Only 57 percent of youths with disabilities are competitively employed after secondary school (National Longitudinal Transition Study 2, 2009).
- Three times as many individuals with disabilities live in poverty (incomes below $15,000) as compared to adults without disabilities (Harris & Associates, 2004).
- Approximately 31 percent of students with disabilities exit school by dropping out (U.S. Department of Education, 2009).
- About one out of three adults with disabilities is very satisfied with life in general compared to 61 percent of adults without disabilities (Harris & Associates, 2004).

The picture that the preceding data paint is rather bleak. For many special educators this profile is totally unacceptable and unconscionable. What do these statistics say about the job professionals are doing in preparing adolescents with disabilities for the adult world? Can we do better? Obviously, we need to. It is abundantly clear that a large percentage of young people with disabilities have difficulty in making a smooth transition from adolescence to adulthood and from high school to adult life in their community. With more than 633,000 students with disabilities exiting the educational system annually (U.S. Department of Education, 2010), what happens to them after they leave is a crucial question confronting professionals and parents alike. This issue of transition has become one of the dominant themes in contemporary special education. Rarely has one topic captured the attention of the field for such a sustained period of time. Transitioning from high school to the many dimensions of independent adulthood has become a national educational priority.

Transition Defined

Several different definitions or interpretations of transition can be found in the professional literature. One of the earliest definitions was offered by Madeleine Will (1984), Assistant Secretary of Education, Office of Special Education and Rehabilitative Services (OSERS). Will viewed transition as

> a period that includes high school, the point of graduation, additional postsecondary education or adult services, and the initial years in employment. Transition is a bridge between the security and structure offered by the school and the opportunities and risks of adult life. . . . The transition from school to work and adult life requires sound preparation in the secondary school, adequate support at the point of school leaving, and secure opportunities and services, if needed, in adult situations. (p. 3)

According to Will (1984), three levels of services are involved in providing for an individual to move successfully from school to adult employment. The top level, "no special services," refers to those generic services available to any citizen within the community, even if special accommodations may be necessary. An example of this form of support might be educational opportunities at a local community college or accessing state employment services. The middle rung of this model, "time-limited services," involves specialized, short-term services that are typically necessary because of a disability. Vocational rehabilitation services best illustrates this level of the model. "Ongoing services" constitutes the third level of this early model. This type of ongoing employment support system was not widely available in the early 1980s. However, it represented an integral component of Will's paradigm, and these services were promoted through federally funded demonstration projects (Halpern, 1992).

Commonly referred to as the "bridges model," Will's (1984) proposal sparked almost immediate debate and controversy from professionals who considered the OSERS interpretation of transition too restrictive or narrow (Brown et al., 1988; Clark & Knowlton, 1988; Halpern, 1985). Adult adjustment, they argued, must be viewed as more than just employment. We agree with this point of view. Halpern, for example, believes it is wrong to focus exclusively on employment. Instead, he proposes that the primary goal of transition be community adjustment, which includes "a person's residential environment and the adequacy of his or her social and interpersonal network. These two dimensions are viewed as being no less important than employment" (1985, p. 480). Thus, living successfully in the community should be the ultimate goal of transition. Halpern's reconfiguration of the OSERS model is portrayed in Figure 1.8.

Video Link 1.12
Watch more about planning for transitions.

Today, transition is viewed in much broader terms than Will (1984) originally proposed. This concept presently includes many different aspects of adult adjustment and participation in community life. Employment, personal competence, independent living, social interaction, and community adjustment are just some of the factors associated with the successful passage from school to adult life for secondary special education students.

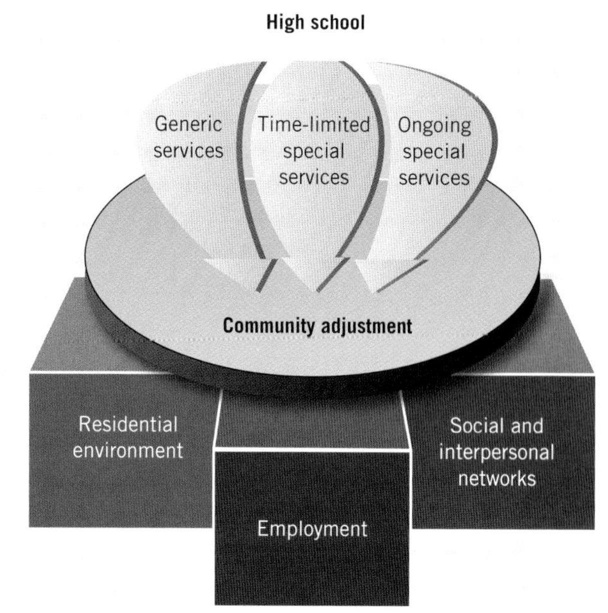

FIGURE 1.8 Halpern's Model of Transition Goals

SOURCE: From "Transition: A Look at the Foundations" by A. Halpern, *Exceptional Children, 51*(6), 1985, p. 481. Copyright © 1985 by the Council for Exceptional Children. Reprinted with permission.

Federal Definition of Transition Services

PL 108–446 (IDEA 2004) stipulates that each student with a disability is to receive **transition services**, which are defined as a coordinated set of activities for a student with a disability that

A. is designed within a results-oriented process, focused on improving the academic and functional achievement of the child with a disability to facilitate the child's movement from school to post-school activities, including post-secondary education, vocational training, integrated employment (including supported employment), continuing and adult education, adult services, independent living, or community participation;

B. is based upon the child's needs, taking into account the child's strengths, preferences, and interests; and

C. includes instruction, related services, community experiences, the development of employment and other post-school adult living objectives, and when appropriate, acquisition of daily living skills and functional vocational evaluation. [20 U.S.C. § 1401 (34)]

Individualized Transition Plan

To ensure that the mandate for transition services is met, IDEA 2004 requires that each student, beginning no later than age 16 (and annually thereafter), have a statement of transition services incorporated into his or her IEP. Commonly referred to in education circles as an **individualized transition plan (ITP)**, this document must include postsecondary goals as well as a statement of the linkages and/or responsibilities that various agencies such as employment services, vocational rehabilitation, and the school system will assume in order to move the individual smoothly from school to living and working in the community. The ITP must also include a statement of transition service needs and courses of study that are intended to enhance the student's postschool success. Simply stated, an ITP is an annually updated instrument of coordination and cooperation. It is a working document that identifies the range of services, resources, supports, and activities that each student may require during the transition process.

Transition Challenges

We conclude this introduction to transitioning adolescents from school to adult life by briefly examining two related areas of concern for professionals. The first issue is how to create a curriculum that prepares students to participate fully in all aspects of community life. Such a curriculum would need to address not only educational needs but also work behaviors, independent living skills, and recreational and leisure time activities. For some secondary students, the traditional high school curriculum is often inadequate for equipping them for life after school. As educators, we must increase the relevance of the curriculum. If we are to prepare students for successful post-school adjustment, then secondary programming for students with disabilities should reflect the basic functions of adult life—work, personal management, and leisure. The goal, according to McDonnell et al. (2003), is to link curricular content to the demands of living and working in the community as an independent adult. If we are to meet this challenge, our instructional strategies must change. Accompanying this shift from remedial academics to functional skills is the requirement that instruction occur in community-based settings—that is, in the natural environment where the skills are to be exhibited (Halpern, 1992). Research evidence (Hartman, 2009) supports the value and benefit of teaching skills in the actual environment in which they are to be performed.

The issue of curricular redesign must be balanced, however, by the increasing number of calls for greater emphasis on academic excellence. Thus, the second challenge for professionals is how to respond to the demands for higher standards while still preparing students for life after high school.

Beginning in the mid-1980s, various national reports strongly criticized the American educational system (Goodlad, 1984; National Commission on Excellence in Education, 1983). Major areas of concern included the declining academic achievement of U.S. students in comparison to youths from other industrialized nations, adult illiteracy, dropout rates, and readiness for school. These concerns were initially addressed in 1989 by the

Preparing young adults with disabilities to enter the workforce is an important role for schools.

nation's governors, meeting at the first-ever Education Summit. Several broad national goals emerged from this historic conference, establishing a blueprint for educational progress. In March 1994, Congress enacted Goals 2000: Educate America Act (PL 103–227), which translated these reform efforts into law. Similarly, in 2001, Congress reauthorized the Elementary and Secondary Education Act, popularly known as the No Child Left Behind Act of 2001 (PL 107–110). This legislation (to be discussed in Chapter 2) reflects President George W. Bush's commitment to educational reform and greater accountability. This ambitious law requires that eventually all pupils, including those in special education, be expected to demonstrate proficiency in reading and mathematics, with science eventually being included.

Consequently, one question now confronting educators, parents, and even students is "What is an appropriate curriculum for students with disabilities at the secondary level, given this climate of tougher academic standards and greater educational accountability?" Should the curriculum reflect an academic emphasis, should it focus on preparation for adult life, or is it possible to merge these two potentially conflicting points of view? Obviously, these are difficult questions, with no easy solution. What is best for one student may not be appropriate for another. Transition programs must be customized to the individual needs and desired outcomes of each young adult.

We believe an argument can be made that transitioning is for *all* students, not just those with disabilities. Transitioning can play a role in the overall educational reform movement. Many students, with and without disabilities, will require support and assistance as they cross the bridge from school to adult life in the community. Our job as educators is to make this journey as successful as possible for each and every one of our pupils.

CHAPTER IN REVIEW

Definitions and Terminology

Audio Link 1.3
Listen to a chapter summary.

- Exceptional children are individuals who resemble other children in many ways but differ from societal standards of normalcy. These differences may be due to physical, sensory, cognitive, or behavioral characteristics.
- When educators talk about a student with a disability, they are referring to an inability or incapacity to perform a particular task or activity in a specific way because of sensory, physical, cognitive, or other forms of impairment.
- The term *handicap* should be restricted to describing the consequence or impact of the disability on the person, not the condition itself.
- A special education can be defined as a customized instructional program designed to meet the unique needs of the pupil. A special education may include the use of specialized materials, equipment, services, or instructional strategies.

Categories and Labels

- The Individuals with Disabilities Education Improvement Act (PL 108–446) identifies thirteen disability categories.
- Empirical investigations fail to provide clear-cut answers to questions about the effects of labels on children and young adults with disabilities.

Prevalence of Children and Young Adults With Disabilities

- At the present time, more than 5.8 million students between the ages of 6 and 21 are receiving a special education. Of this total, about half are individuals with learning disabilities.
- Collectively, states are providing a special education to more than 6.9 million individuals from birth through age 21.

A Brief History of the Development of Special Education

- Historically speaking, the foundation of contemporary societal attitudes can be traced to the contributions of various reform-minded eighteenth- and nineteenth-century European educators, philosophers, and humanitarians.
- By the middle of the nineteenth century, several specialized institutions were established in the United States.
- It was not until the latter part of the nineteenth century and early years of the twentieth century that special education classes began to appear in public schools.

Professionals Who Work With Individuals With Exceptionalities

- Educators frequently work with a variety of other professionals representing several distinct disciplines. These individuals provide a wide variety of related services, ranging from occupational therapy to therapeutic recreation to psychological services and even transportation to and from school.
- Providing consultative services to both general and special educators is one way that school districts are attempting to meet the increasingly complex demands of serving students with disabilities.
- The three teaming models most frequently mentioned in the professional literature are multidisciplinary, interdisciplinary, and transdisciplinary teams.

Cooperative Teaching

- Cooperative teaching, or co-teaching as it is sometimes called, is an increasingly popular approach for facilitating successful inclusion.
- Cooperative teaching is an instructional strategy designed to provide support to all students in the general education classroom.
- Teachers can choose from multiple models of cooperative teaching depending on their specific circumstances.

Universal Design for Learning

- Universal design for learning is an instructional resource designed to meet the needs of all students; it provides equal access to learning.
- Universal design for learning allows for multiple means of representation, engagement, and expression.

Exceptionality Across the Life Span

- Twenty-five years ago, services for children with disabilities younger than age 6 were virtually unheard of. Today, however, over 1 million children younger than 6 receive some type of intervention or special education.
- The issue of transition has become one of the dominant themes in contemporary special education.
- Every high school student who is enrolled in a special education program is to have an individualized transition plan (ITP) as part of his or her individualized education program, or IEP.

STUDY QUESTIONS

1. How is the concept of normalcy related to the definition of children identified as exceptional?
2. Differentiate between the terms *disability* and *handicap.* Provide specific examples for each term.
3. What is a special education?
4. Name the thirteen categories of exceptionality presently recognized by the federal government.
5. Compare and contrast arguments for and against the practice of labeling pupils according to their disability.
6. How are the terms *prevalence* and *incidence* used when discussing individuals with disabilities?
7. Identify contributing factors to the growth of the field of special education.
8. Why do you think the federal government has not mandated special education for students who are gifted and talented?
9. What role did Europeans play in the development of special education in the United States?
10. What are related services, and why are they important for the delivery of a special education?
11. List the characteristics that distinguish multidisciplinary, interdisciplinary, and transdisciplinary educational teams. What are the advantages and disadvantages of each teaming model?
12. How can cooperative teaching benefit students with and without disabilities?
13. Explain how universal design for learning benefits all students.
14. Why is transitioning important for students with disabilities at the secondary level?
15. What challenges do professionals face as they prepare adolescents to move from school to adult life in the community?

KEY TERMS

exceptional children 4
disability 5
handicap 5
handicapism 5
developmental delay 6
at-risk 6
special education 9
related services 10
category 10
noncategorical 11
incidence 12
prevalence 12
self-contained 19
collaboration 22
individualized education program (IEP) 22
consultation 23
multidisciplinary 24
interdisciplinary team 24
transdisciplinary team 25
cooperative teaching 26
universal design for learning 29
individualized family service plan (IFSP) 32
early intervention 33
early childhood special education 33
transition 33
transition services 35
individualized transition plan (ITP) 35

LEARNING ACTIVITIES

1. Keep a journal for at least four weeks in which you record how individuals with disabilities are represented in newspapers, magazines, television commercials, and other media outlets. Are they portrayed as someone to be pitied, or as a superhero? Is "people-first" language used? Do your examples perpetuate stereotyping, or are they realistic representations of persons with disabilities? In what context was the individual shown? What conclusions might a layperson draw about people with disabilities?
2. Visit an elementary school and a high school in your community. Talk to several special educators at each location. Find out how students with disabilities are served. What related services do these pupils receive? Ask each teacher to define the term *special education.* How are regular and special educators collaborating to provide an appropriate education for each learner? What strategies and activities are secondary teachers incorporating to prepare their students for life after graduation?
3. Obtain prevalence figures for students enrolled in special education programs in your state. How do these data compare to national figures? Identify possible reasons for any discrepancies. Do the figures suggest any trends in

enrollment? Which category of exceptionality is growing the fastest?

4. Interview a veteran special educator (someone who has been teaching since the early 1980s). Ask this person how the field of special education has changed over the past decades. In what ways are things still the same? What issues and challenges does this teacher confront in his or her career? What is this person's vision of the future of special education?

5. Contact the office of disability support at your college or university. What types of services does it provide to students with disabilities? Volunteer to serve in this program.

REFLECTING ON STANDARDS

The following exercises are designed to help you learn to apply the Council for Exceptional Children (CEC) standards to your teaching practice. Each of the reflection exercises below correlates with a knowledge or skill within the CEC standards. For the full text of each of the related CEC standards, please refer to the standards integration grid located in Appendix B.

Focus on Instructional Strategies ***(CEC Content Standard #4 CC4S1)***
Reflect on what you have learned about co-teaching in this chapter. If you were to have a student with special needs in your class, which of these models (team teaching, station teaching, parallel teaching, or alternative teaching) would you want to integrate into your teaching? What would be the advantages and disadvantages to you and your class in incorporating these strategies?

Focus on Collaboration ***(CEC Content Standard #10 CC10K2)***
Reflect on what you have learned in this chapter about the importance of building partnerships to create students' individualized education programs. What collaborative skills do you have that will benefit you in this type of teamwork? What skills do you need to improve upon?

STUDENT STUDY SITE

Visit the Student Study Site at www.sagepub.com/gargiulo4emedia for these additional learning tools:

- Video links
- Media links
- Self-quizzes
- E-flashcards
- Full-text SAGE journal articles
- Web exercises

CHAPTER 2

Learning Objectives

After reading Chapter 2 you should be able to:

- Identify the court cases that led to the enactment of Public Law 94–142.
- Summarize the key components of the Individuals with Disabilities Education Act from 1974 to 2004.
- Describe the legislative intent of Section 504 of the Rehabilitation Act of 1973 and the Americans with Disabilities Act.
- Distinguish between inter- and intraindividual differences.
- Describe the difference between norm- and criterion-referenced assessments.
- Outline the steps in the referral process for the delivery of special education services.
- List the key components of an individualized education program (IEP) and an individualized family service plan (IFSP).
- Define mainstreaming, least restrictive environment, regular education initiative, and full inclusion.

Policies, Practices, and Programs

Many of the policies, procedures, and practices that are common in special education today have resulted from the interaction of a variety of forces, situations, and events. One example is the role that litigation and legislation have played in the development of the field. Coupled with this activity was the gradual realization by professionals that many of our earlier educational customs and methods were ineffective in meeting the needs of individuals with disabilities and their families. Several currently accepted practices, such as nondiscriminatory assessment, placement in a least restrictive environment, and meaningful parent involvement, reflect this correction in thinking.

The purpose of this chapter is to review a variety of contributions that have helped to shape contemporary special education. Besides the impact of national legislation and the courts, we will examine the identification and assessment of individual differences, instructional programming, and models of service delivery.

Video Link 2.1
Watch more about legislation.

Litigation and Legislation Affecting Special Education

Over the past several decades, the field of special education has been gradually transformed and restructured, largely as a result of judicial action and legislative enactments. These two forces have been powerful tools in securing many of the benefits and rights presently enjoyed by more than 6.5 million pupils with disabilities.

Securing the opportunity for an education has been a slowly evolving process for students with disabilities. What is today seen as a fundamental right for these children was, at one time, viewed strictly as a privilege. Excluding students with disabilities from attending school was a routine practice of local boards of education in the 1890s and early 1900s. In 1893, local school officials in Cambridge, Massachusetts, denied an education to one individual because this student was thought to be too "weak minded" to profit from instruction. In 1919, in Antigo, Wisconsin, a student of normal intelligence but with a type of paralysis attended school through the fifth grade but was subsequently suspended because "his physical appearance nauseated teachers and other students, his disability required an undue amount of his teacher's time, and he had a negative impact on the discipline and progress of the school" (Osborne, 1996, p. 4). In both instances, state supreme courts upheld the decisions of the school boards. Today, these actions would be seen as clear violations of the pupils' rights and a flagrant disregard for the equal protection clause of the Fourteenth Amendment to the U.S. Constitution. Still, almost four decades passed before students with disabilities had a legal means for acquiring educational rights.

Journal Link 2.1 Read more about litigation.

In the 1954 landmark school desegregation case, *Brown v. Board of Education of Topeka, Kansas* (347 U.S. 483), the U.S. Supreme Court reasoned that it was unlawful to discriminate against a group of individuals for arbitrary reasons. The Court specifically ruled that separate schools for black and white students were inherently unequal, contrary to the Fourteenth Amendment, and thus unconstitutional. Furthermore, education was characterized as a fundamental function of government that should be afforded to all citizens on an equal basis. Though primarily recognized as striking down racial segregation, the thinking articulated in *Brown* had major implications for children with disabilities. Much of contemporary litigation and legislation affecting special education is legally, as well as morally, grounded in the precedents established by *Brown*.

Audio Link 2.1 Listen to more about desegregration.

The movement to secure equal educational opportunity for children with disabilities was also aided by the U.S. civil rights movement of the 1960s. As Americans attempted to deal with issues of discrimination, inequality, and other social ills, advocates for individuals with disabilities also pushed for equal rights. Parental activism was ignited. Lawsuits were filed and legislation was enacted primarily as a result of the untiring, vocal, collaborative efforts of parents and politically powerful advocacy groups. The success of these tactics was felt at the local, state, and eventually national level.

It is exceedingly difficult to say which came first, litigation or legislation. Both of these forces have played major roles in the development of state and federal policy concerning special education. They enjoy a unique and almost symbiotic relationship—one of mutual interdependence. Litigation frequently leads to legislation, which in turn spawns additional judicial action as the courts interpret and clarify the law, which often leads to further legislation (see Figure 2.1). Regardless of the progression, much of special education today has a legal foundation.

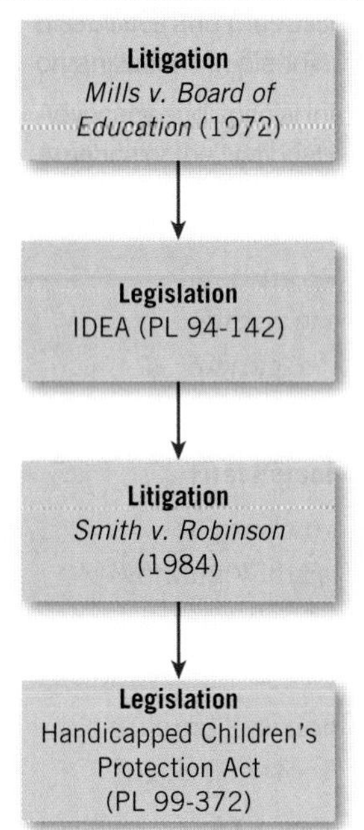

FIGURE 2.1 An Example of the Interrelationship Between Litigation and Legislation

SOURCE: Adapted from *The Law and Special Education,* 2nd ed., by M. L. Yell, © 2006, p. 15. Reprinted by permission of Pearson Education, Inc., Upper Saddle River, NJ.

Key Judicial Decisions

Since the 1960s and early 1970s, a plethora of state and federal court decisions have helped to shape and define a wide range of issues affecting contemporary special education policies and procedures. Although a thorough review of this litigation is beyond the scope of this chapter, Table 2.1 summarizes, in chronological order, some of the landmark cases affecting the field of special education. Several of the judicial remedies emanating from these lawsuits serve as cornerstones for both federal and state legislative enactments focusing on students with disabilities. Furthermore, many of today's accepted practices in special education, such as nondiscriminatory assessments and due process procedures, can trace their roots to various court decisions.

Individuals With Disabilities Education Act: 1975–1997

Federal legislative intervention in the lives of persons with disabilities is of relatively recent origin. Before the late 1950s and early 1960s, little federal attention was paid to citizens with special needs. When legislation was enacted, it primarily assisted specific groups of individuals, such as those who were deaf or mentally retarded. The past forty years, however, have witnessed a flurry of legislative activity that has aided the growth of special education and provided educational benefits and other opportunities and rights to children and adults with disabilities. Between 1827 and 1975, a total of 175 federal laws addressing individuals with disabilities were enacted; 61 of these laws were passed between March 1970 and March 1975 (Weintraub, Abeson, Ballard, & LaVor, 1976).

TABLE 2.1 A Synopsis of Selected Court Cases Influencing Special Education

Case	Year	Issue	Judicial Decision
Brown v. Board of Education of Topeka, Kansas	1954	Educational segregation	Segregation of students by race ruled unconstitutional; children deprived of equal educational opportunity. Effectively ended "separate but equal" schools for white and black pupils. Used as a precedent for arguing that children with disabilities cannot be excluded from a public education.
Hobson v. Hansen	1967	Classifying students	Ability grouping or "tracking" of students on the basis of nationally normed tests, which were found to be biased, held to be unconstitutional. Tracking systems discriminated against poor and minority children, thus denying them an equal educational opportunity. Equal protection clause of Fourteenth Amendment violated.
Diana v. State Board of Education	1970	Class placement	Linguistically different students must be tested in their primary language as well as English. Students cannot be placed in special education classes on the basis of IQ tests that are culturally biased. Verbal test items to be revised so as to reflect students' cultural heritage. Group-administered IQ tests cannot be used to place children in programs for individuals with mental retardation.
Pennsylvania Association for Retarded Children v. Commonwealth of Pennsylvania	1972	Right to education	State must guarantee a free public education to all children with mental retardation ages 6–21 regardless of degree of impairment or associated disabilities. Students to be placed in the most integrated environment. Definition of education expanded. Case established the right of parents to participate in educational decisions affecting their children. State to engage in extensive efforts to locate and serve ("child-find") all students with mental retardation. Preschool services to be provided to youngsters with mental retardation if local school district serves preschoolers who are not retarded.
Mills v. Board of Education, District of Columbia	1972	Right to education	Extended the Pennsylvania decision to include all children with disabilities. Specifically established the constitutional right of children with exceptionalities to a public education regardless of their functional level. Students have a right to a "constructive education" matched to their needs, including specialized instruction. Presumed absence of fiscal resources is not a valid reason for failing to provide appropriate educational services to students with disabilities. Elaborate due process safeguards established to protect the rights of the child, including parental notification of pending initial evaluation, reassignment, or planned termination of special services.
Larry P. v. Riles	1972, 1979	Class placement	A landmark case parallel to the *Diana* suit. African American students could not be placed in classes for children with mild mental retardation solely on the basis of intellectual assessments found to be culturally and racially biased. The court instructed school officials to develop an assessment process that would not discriminate against minority children. Failure to comply with this order resulted in a 1979 ruling that completely prohibited the use of IQ tests for placing African American students in classes for children with mild mental retardation. Ruling applies only to the state of California.
Wyatt v. Stickney	1972	Right to treatment	Individuals with mental retardation residing in a state institution have a right to appropriate treatment. Absence of meaningful education reduces opportunity for habilitation and thus may be considered unlawful detention. State mandated to ensure a therapeutic environment for residential population.

(Continued)

TABLE 2.1 (Continued)

Case	Year	Issue	Judicial Decision
Stuart v. Nappi	1978	Expulsion from school	Expulsion of a pupil with disabilities for disciplinary reasons without due process was disallowed. Expulsion was considered a change in placement and a denial of the opportunity for an appropriate education. School authorities, however, can temporarily suspend students with disabilities who are disruptive.
Armstrong v. Kline	1980	Extended school year	State's refusal to pay for schooling in excess of 180 days for pupils with severe disabilities is a violation of their rights to an appropriate education as required by PL 94–142. The court found that some children with disabilities will regress significantly during summer recess and have longer recoupment periods; thus, they are denied an appropriate education if not provided with a year-round education.
Tatro v. State of Texas	1980	Related services	U.S. Supreme Court held that catheterization qualified as a related service under PL 94–142. Catheterization was not considered an exempted medical procedure, as it could be performed by a health care aide or school nurse. Court further stipulated that only those services that allow a student to benefit from a special education qualify as related services.
Board of Education of the Hendrick Hudson Central School District v. Rowley	1982	Appropriate education	First U.S. Supreme Court interpretation of PL 94–142. Court addressed the issue of what constitutes an "appropriate" education for a student with hearing impairments making satisfactory educational progress. Supreme Court ruled that an appropriate education does not necessarily mean an education that will allow for the maximum possible achievement; rather, students must be given a reasonable opportunity to learn. Parents' request for a sign language interpreter, therefore, was denied. An appropriate education is not synonymous with an optimal educational experience.
Smith v. Robinson	1984	Recovery of attorney fees	U.S. Supreme Court ruled that parents cannot be reimbursed for legal expenses under PL 94–142. Issue subsequently addressed by Congress, which enacted PL 99–372 permitting such payment. Court also stipulated that claims cannot be filed simultaneously under PL 94–142 and Section 504 of PL 93–112; when available, IDEA is to be the exclusive avenue.
Honig v. Doe	1988	Exclusion from school	Children with special needs whose behavior is a direct result of their disability cannot be expelled from school for misbehavior. If behavior leading to expulsion is not a consequence of the exceptionality, pupil may be expelled. Short-term suspension from school not interpreted as a change in pupil's individualized education program (IEP).
Daniel R.R. v. State Board of Education	1989	Class placement	Fifth Circuit Court of Appeals held that a segregated class was an appropriate placement for a student with Down syndrome. Preference for integrated placement viewed as secondary to the need for an appropriate education. Court established a two-prong test for determining compliance with the least restrictive environment (LRE) mandate for students with severe disabilities. First, it must be determined if a pupil can make satisfactory progress and achieve educational benefit in the general education classroom through curriculum modification and the use of supplementary aids and services. Second, it must be determined whether the pupil has been integrated to the maximum extent appropriate.

TABLE 2.1 (Continued)

Case	Year	Issue	Judicial Decision
			Successful compliance with both parts fulfills a school's obligation under federal law. Ruling affects LRE cases in Louisiana, Texas, and Mississippi, but has become a benchmark decision for other jurisdictions as well.
Timothy W. v. Rochester (New Hampshire) School District	1989	Right to education	Reaffirmation of the principle of zero-reject education. First Circuit Court of Appeals established entitlement to a free and appropriate public education regardless of the severity of the child's disability. IDEA interpreted to mean all students; pupil need not demonstrate an ability to benefit from a special education. Education defined broadly to include instruction in functional skills.
Carter v. Florence County School District Four	1991	IEP goals, private school costs	Fourth Circuit Court of Appeals held that an IEP goal of four months' progress in reading during the school year was insufficient to allow the pupil to achieve academic progress. Absence of meaningful growth seen as evidence of an inappropriate IEP and thus failure to provide an appropriate education. Case was eventually heard on a related issue by the U.S. Supreme Court in 1993 (*Florence County School District Four v. Carter*). The Court ruled that, because of the school district's failure to comply with IDEA, the student's parents were eligible to receive reimbursement for unilaterally enrolling their daughter in a nonaccredited private residential school as long as the school was providing an appropriate education.
Oberti v. Board of Education of the Borough of Clementon School District	1992	Least restrictive environment	Placement in a general education classroom with supplementary aids and services must be offered to a student with disabilities prior to considering more segregated placements. Pupil cannot be excluded from a general education classroom solely because curriculum, services, or other practices would require modification. A decision to exclude a learner from the general education classroom necessitates justification and documentation. Clear judicial preference for educational integration established.
Agostini v. Felton	1997	Provision of services	U.S. Supreme Court reversed a long-standing ruling banning the delivery of publicly funded educational services to students enrolled in private schools. Interpreted to mean that special educators can now provide services to children in parochial schools.
Cedar Rapids Community School District v. Garret F.	1999	Related services	U.S. Supreme Court expanded and clarified the concept of related services. Affirmed that intensive and continuous school health care services necessary for a student to attend school, if not performed by a physician, qualify as related services.
Schaffer v. Weast	2005	Burden of proof	A U.S. Supreme Court ruling addressing the issue of whether the parent(s) or school district bears the burden of proof in a due process hearing. The specific question before the Court was whether the parent(s), acting on behalf of their son or daughter, must prove that their child's individualized education program (IEP) is inappropriate or whether the school district must prove that the IEP is appropriate. The court ruled that the burden of proof is placed upon the party seeking relief.

(Continued)

TABLE 2.1 (Continued)

Case	Year	Issue	Judicial Decision
Arlington Central School District Board of Education v. Murphy	2006	Recovery of fees	At issue in this U.S. Supreme Court case is whether or not parents are able to recover the professional fees of an educational consultant (lay advocate) who provided services during legal proceedings. The Court ruled that parents are not entitled to reimbursement for the cost of experts because only attorney fees are addressed in IDEA.
Winkelman v. Parma City School District	2007	Parental rights	One of the more significant Supreme Court rulings. The Court, by unanimous vote, affirmed the right of parents to represent their children in IDEA-related court cases. Ruling seen as an expansion of parental involvement and the definition of a free and appropriate public education. Decision also interpreted to mean that IDEA conveys enforceable rights to parents as well as their children.
Forest Grove School District v. T. A.	2009	Tuition reimbursement	A Supreme Court decision involving tuition reimbursement for a student with learning disabilities and attention deficit hyperactivity disorder as well as depression who was never declared eligible for a special education and never received services from the school district. Parents removed their child from school and unilaterally enrolled the child in a private school. Subsequently they sought reimbursement from the school district for expenses. In a 6-3 decision, the Court found that IDEA authorizes reimbursement for private special education services when a public school fails to provide a free and appropriate education and the private school placement is appropriate, regardless of whether the student previously received special education services from the public school.

SOURCE: Adapted from R. Gargiulo and J. Kilgo, *An Introduction to Young Children with Special Needs,* 3rd ed. (Belmont, CA: Wadsworth/Cengage Learning, 2011), pp. 33–36.

Given the multitude of public laws[1] affecting special education, we will focus on landmark legislation. We will examine six significant pieces of legislation that have dramatically affected the educational opportunities of infants, toddlers, preschoolers, school-age children, and young adults with disabilities. Our initial review will focus on PL 94–142, the Education for All Handicapped Children Act, or, as it is now called, the Individuals with Disabilities Education Act (IDEA). This change in legislative titles resulted from the enactment on October 30, 1990, of PL 101–476, which will be reviewed later.

Public Law 94–142

The Individuals with Disabilities Education Act is viewed as a "Bill of Rights" for children with exceptionalities and their families; it is the culmination of many years of dedicated effort by both parents and professionals. Like many other special educators, we consider this law to be one of the most important, if not the most important, pieces of federal

1. National legislation, or public law (PL), is codified according to a standardized format. Legislation is thus designated by the number of the session of Congress that enacted the law followed by the number of the particular bill. PL 94–142, for example, was enacted by the 94th session of Congress and was the 142nd piece of legislation passed.

legislation ever enacted on behalf of children with special needs. PL 94–142 may rightfully be thought of as the legislative heart of special education.

The purpose of this bill, which was signed into law by President Gerald Ford on November 29, 1975, is

> to assure that all handicapped children have available to them . . . a free appropriate public education which emphasizes special education and related services designed to meet their unique needs, to assure that the rights of handicapped children and their parents or guardians are protected, to assist States and localities to provide for the education of all handicapped children, and to assess and assure the effectiveness of efforts to educate handicapped children. [Section 601(c)]

In pursuing these four purposes, this legislation incorporates six major components and guarantees that have forever changed the landscape of education across the United States. Despite legislative and court challenges over the past three decades, the following principles have endured to the present day:

- **A free appropriate public education (FAPE).** All children, regardless of the severity of their disability (a "zero reject" philosophy), must be provided with an education appropriate to their unique needs at no cost to the parent(s)/guardian(s). Included in this principle is the concept of related services, which requires that children receive, for example, occupational therapy as well as other services as necessary in order to benefit from special education.

- **The least restrictive environment (LRE).** Children with disabilities are to be educated, to the maximum extent appropriate, with students without disabilities. Placements must be consistent with the pupil's educational needs.

- **An individualized education program (IEP).** This document, developed in conjunction with the parent(s)/guardian(s), is an individually tailored statement describing an educational plan for each learner with exceptionalities. The IEP, which will be fully discussed later in this chapter, is required to address (1) the present level of academic functioning (commonly referred to by school personnel as present level of performance); (2) annual goals and accompanying instructional objectives; (3) educational services to be provided; (4) the degree to which the pupil will be able to participate in general education programs; (5) plans for initiating services and length of service delivery; and (6) an annual evaluation procedure specifying objective criteria to determine if instructional objectives are being met. Many teachers and school administrators refer to this as progress monitoring.

- **Procedural due process.** The act affords parent(s)/guardian(s) several safeguards as it pertains to their child's education. Briefly, parent(s)/guardian(s) have the right to confidentiality of records; to examine all records; to obtain an independent evaluation; to receive written notification (in parents' native language) of proposed changes to their child's educational classification or placement; and to an impartial hearing whenever disagreements arise regarding educational plans for their son/daughter. Furthermore, the student's parent(s)/guardian(s) have the right to representation by legal counsel.

- **Nondiscriminatory assessment.** Prior to placement, a child must be evaluated by a multidisciplinary team in all areas of suspected disability by tests that are neither racially or culturally nor linguistically biased. Students are to receive several types of assessments, administered by trained personnel; a single evaluation procedure is not permitted for either planning or placement purposes.

- **Parental participation.** PL 94–142 mandates meaningful parent involvement. Sometimes referred to as the "Parent's Law," this legislation requires that parents participate fully in the decision-making process that affects their child's education.

Legislation has greatly benefited individuals with disabilities and their families.

Congress indicated its desire by September 1, 1980, to provide a free appropriate public education for all eligible children ages 3 through 21. The law, however, did not require services to preschool children with disabilities. Because many states were not providing preschool services to typical children, an education for young children with special needs, in most instances, was not mandated. Although this legislation failed to require an education for younger children, it clearly focused attention on the preschool population and recognized the value of early education.

PL 94–142 did contain some benefits for children under school age. It offered small financial grants (Preschool Incentive Grants) to the individual states as an incentive to serve young children with disabilities. It also carried a mandate for schools to identify and evaluate children from birth through age 21 suspected of evidencing a disability. Finally, PL 94–142 moved from a census count to a child count of the actual number of individuals with disabilities being served. The intent was to encourage the states to locate and serve children with disabilities.

Providing a special education to millions of students with disabilities is a very expensive proposition. Congress realized that many school districts would not have sufficient funds to provide the needed services without additional financial support from the federal government. It was the intent of Congress to pay 40 percent of the excess cost of educating pupils enrolled in special education programs. Unfortunately, federal support never achieved this level; over the years, actual appropriations have typically remained closer to 10 percent (Center for Special Education Finance, 2004). Thus, the bulk of the costs for educating children with special needs falls on the financial shoulders of state governments and local school districts. Annual costs for educating a student in special education are approximately twice the expenditure for a student enrolled in general education (Center for Special Education Finance). Of course, the costs vary tremendously depending on the nature and severity of the student's disability.

Many young children with developmental delays or disabilities have benefited from early intervention.

Public Law 99–457 (1986 Amendments to PL 94–142)

In October 1986, Congress passed one of the most comprehensive pieces of legislation affecting young children with special needs and their families—PL 99–457. This law changed both the scope and the intent of services provided to preschoolers with special needs and formulated a national policy for infants and toddlers at risk for and with identified disabilities.

As noted earlier, IDEA gave the states financial incentives to provide an education and related services to preschool children with disabilities. This was a permissive or voluntary element of the act, not a mandated requirement. Trohanis (1989) reported congressional data indicating that fewer than 80 percent of the estimated 330,000 youngsters with disabilities ages 3 to 5 were being served. An estimated 70,000 preschoolers were, therefore, unserved. PL 99–457, the Education of the Handicapped Act Amendments of 1986, was enacted to remedy this situation.

Simply stated, this law is a downward extension of PL 94–142, including all its rights and protections. This legislation does not require that preschoolers be identified with a specific disability label. It does demand that, as of the 1991–1992 school year, all preschoolers with special needs, ages 3 through 5 inclusive, are to receive a free and appropriate public education. This element of the law is a mandated requirement; states will lose significant amounts of federal preschool funding if they fail to comply. The goal of this legislation was finally accomplished in the 1992–1993 school year, when all states had mandates in place establishing a free and appropriate public education for all children with disabilities ages 3 through 5.

Title I of PL 99–457 created the Handicapped Infants and Toddlers Program (Part H), a new provision aimed at children from birth through age 2 with developmental delays or disabilities. This component of the legislation is voluntary; states are not compelled to comply. This part of the statute creates a discretionary program that assists states in implementing a statewide, comprehensive, coordinated, multidisciplinary, interagency program of services for very young children and their families who are experiencing developmental delays or who evidence a physical or mental condition that has a high probability of resulting in a delay, such as cerebral palsy or Down syndrome. (At the state's discretion, youngsters who are at risk for future delays may also be served.) As of September 30, 1994, all states had plans in place for the full implementation of Part H (U.S. Department of Education, 1995).

Eligible children and their families must receive a multidisciplinary assessment conducted by qualified professionals and a written individualized family service plan, or IFSP. An IFSP must be reviewed every six months (or sooner if necessary) to assess its continued appropriateness. The law requires that each infant or toddler be reevaluated

First Person: Lisa
Teaching in the Age of Accountability

Having taught for almost ten years, I can safely say there is a definite need for accountability in education, but teaching in the twenty-first century presents some unique challenges. Everyone is accountable to someone for something. Teachers, for example, are accountable for teaching curriculum in preparation for high-stakes assessments, delivering data-driven instruction, using research-based strategies, and meeting the demands and deadlines imposed by administrators, while also communicating with parents. Students, on the other hand, are accountable for passing the high-stakes assessments and responding to the data-based instruction and research-based instructional strategies, while making adequate progress at increasingly higher levels of performance. Each year it almost seems as though we have to surpass what was accomplished the previous year. The accompanying paperwork to prove this accountability doesn't get any less cumbersome either.

All this accountability comes from increasing concerns about the quality of our education. Yet, even with all this accountability, we see many students transfer with gaps in learning from not having been taught to the same high expectations. There are disparities from school system to school system that make it difficult to reach these ever increasing levels of accountability. This "achievement gap" affects what we have to work with; yet, we are still accountable to get these pupils to the academic level they need to be at. If there is one thing you can count on in teaching it is that change is constant.

Teaching is a balancing act, and educators have to be sure that they do not get lost in the "accountability jungle" or forget that one of the reasons we teach is to help our students become discoverers of their own learning, not simply to be able to pass a high-stakes assessment. As educators, our accountability goal should be how well our students apply and generalize the knowledge and information that we share with them, not how well they can regurgitate facts in order to pass an isolated test that only represents a small sample of what they have learned.

The school days are getting longer, lunchtimes are getting shorter, and weekends are often spent in a quiet classroom in preparation to teach in the coming week. It seems as though we are overly accountable to the point that we are losing valuable instructional time and focus. With all that said, accountability *is* important as long as we view it wisely.

General education teachers are now being required to prove that their students are being taught with research-based tools and that student performance is documented. No longer are student performance, methods of instruction, and teaching practices at the teacher's discretion. This new level of accountability for general education teachers is going to require them to rely more and more on the expertise of special education teachers not only for the students that have IEPs but also for all struggling learners. At the same time, the special educator is also held accountable for ensuring compliance with regulations, timelines, and mounting paperwork with increasingly larger caseloads. It is a constant battle to find the proper balance—the demands of paperwork, the needs of individual students, and communication with families and general education teachers are all under the accountability microscope. This balance is more difficult to find with each new law, mandate, and policy. Although I feel it is a privilege to work as a teacher, and more particularly as a special education teacher, working as an inclusive teacher in the age of accountability becomes increasingly difficult each year.

—*Lisa Cranford*
Instructional Support Teacher
Rocky Ridge Elementary, Hoover, Alabama

- School districts will be allowed, with parental consent, to develop comprehensive multiyear IEPs (not to exceed three years).
- The U.S. Department of Education is charged with developing and disseminating model IEP forms and model IFSP forms.

Identifying Students With Specific Learning Disabilities

Under IDEA 1997, when identifying an individual for a possible learning disability, educators typically looked to see if the student exhibited a severe discrepancy between achievement and intellectual ability. IDEA 2004 removed this discrepancy provision. School districts will now be able, if they so choose, to use a process that determines

Special educators are required to be highly qualified.

whether the pupil responds to empirically validated, scientifically based interventions—a procedure known as response to intervention (treatment). Under the new guidelines, rather than comparing IQ with performance on standardized achievement tests, general education teachers can offer intensive programs of instructional interventions. If the child fails to make adequate progress, a learning disability is assumed to be present, and additional assessment is warranted. (This concept will be discussed further in Chapter 6.)

Highly Qualified Special Education Teachers

The language contained in IDEA 2004 concerning who is considered a "highly qualified" special educator is complementary to the standards promulgated in the No Child Left Behind Act (NCLB) of 2001, PL 107–110.

- All special education teachers must hold at least a bachelor's degree and be fully certified or licensed in the field of special education to be deemed highly qualified. Special educators employed as of July 1, 2005, were required to meet this standard.
- Special educators who teach core subjects in elementary schools can obtain highly qualified status by passing their state's licensing or certification exam.
- Teachers of middle or high school–aged students with significant cognitive deficits—that is, pupils whose progress will be assessed via alternate achievement standards—may be considered highly qualified if they meet the NCLB standards for *elementary* school teachers. The effective date of this provision was December 3, 2004.
- Currently employed special educators who teach multiple core academic subjects exclusively to students with disabilities may be designated highly qualified after successfully passing "a single, high-objective uniform state standard of evaluation" (HOUSSE), which addresses multiple subjects.
- A special education teacher who is new to the field but already deemed highly qualified in a single core academic area (such as science, reading, language arts, mathematics, foreign languages, or history) may become highly qualified by successfully completing the HOUSSE requirement for the remaining subjects taught. This requirement must be fulfilled within two years of the teacher's hire date. This provision, like the preceding one, became effective on December 3, 2004.
- This legislation does not address "highly qualified" requirements for early childhood special educators.

Discipline

- PL 108–446 stipulates that when a student is removed from the current educational setting for more than ten days, the pupil is to continue to receive those services that enable him or her to participate in the general education curriculum and to ensure progress toward meeting his or her IEP goals.
- IDEA 1997 allowed school authorities to unilaterally remove a student to an interim alternative educational setting (IAES) for up to forty-five days for offenses involving weapons or drugs. IDEA 2004 now permits school officials to remove any pupil (including those with and without disabilities) to an IAES for up to forty-five days for inflicting "serious bodily injury."
- Removal to an IAES will now be for forty-five *school* days rather than forty-five calendar days.
- Behavior resulting in disciplinary action still requires a manifestation review; however, language requiring the IEP team to consider whether the pupil's disability impaired the ability to control his or her behavior or comprehend the consequences of his or her actions has been eliminated. IEP teams will now need to ask only two questions:

  1. Did the disability cause or have a direct and substantial relationship to the offense?
  2. Was the violation a direct result of the school's failure to implement the IEP?

- IDEA 2004 modifies the "stay put" provision enacted during an appeals process. When either the local education agency (LEA) or the parent requests an appeal of a manifestation determination or placement decision, the pupil is required to remain in the current IAES until a decision is rendered by the hearing officer or until the time period for the disciplinary violation concludes. A hearing must be held within twenty school days of the date of the appeal.

Due Process

• Parents will encounter a two-year statute of limitations for filing a due process complaint from the time they knew or should have known that a violation occurred. Alleged violations might involve identification, assessment, or placement issues or the failure to provide an appropriate education.

• A mandatory "resolution session" is now required prior to proceeding with a due process hearing. (The parents and school district may waive this requirement and directly proceed to mediation.) School districts must convene a meeting with the parents and IEP team members within fifteen days of receiving a due process complaint. If the complaint is not satisfactorily resolved within thirty days of the filing date, the due process hearing may proceed.

• Under provisions of IDEA 1997, parents who prevailed in due process hearings and/or court cases could seek attorney's fees from the school district. IDEA 2004 now permits school districts to seek attorney's fees from the parents' attorney (or the parents themselves) if the due process complaint or lawsuit is deemed frivolous, unreasonable, or without foundation or the attorney continues to litigate despite these circumstances. Reasonable attorney fees can also be awarded by the court if the complaint or lawsuit was filed for an improper purpose such as to harass, cause unnecessary delay, or needlessly increase the cost of litigation.

Evaluation of Students

- School districts will be required to determine the eligibility of a student to receive a special education and the educational needs of the child within a time frame of sixty calendar days. (This provision does not apply if the state has already established a timeline for accomplishing this task.) The sixty-day rule commences upon receipt of parental permission for evaluation.

- Reevaluation of eligibility for a special education may not occur more than once per year (unless agreed to by the school district and parent), and it must occur at least once every three years unless the parent and school district agree that such a reevaluation is unnecessary.
- IDEA 2004 modifies the provision pertaining to native language and preferred mode of communication. New language in the bill requires that evaluations are to be "provided and administered in the language and form most likely to yield accurate information on what the child knows and can do academically, developmentally, and functionally, unless it is not feasible to so provide or administer."
- School districts are not allowed to seek dispute resolution when parents refuse to give their consent for special education services. If parents refuse to give consent, then the school district is not responsible for providing a free and appropriate public education.

Assessment Participation

- PL 108–446 requires that *all* students participate in all state- and districtwide assessments (including those required under the No Child Left Behind Act, PL 107–110), with accommodations or alternative assessments, if necessary, as stipulated in the pupil's IEP. States are permitted to assess up to 1 percent of students (generally those pupils with significant cognitive deficits) with alternative assessments aligned with alternative achievement standards. This cap represents approximately 9 percent of all students with disabilities. IDEA 2004 further requires that assessments adhere to the principles of universal design when feasible.

The coming years will be ones of exciting opportunities and challenges as the entire educational community responds to the mandates of PL 107–110 and PL 108–446. These laws, like PL 94–142 more than thirty-five years ago, will dramatically change the educational landscape for both general education and special education.

Civil Rights Legislation

Section 504 of the Rehabilitation Act of 1973

The preceding pieces of legislation that we just examined are representative special education laws (the exception being PL 107–110). PL 93–112, the Rehabilitation Act of 1973, however, is a *civil rights* law. Section 504 of this enactment was the first public law specifically aimed at protecting children and adults against discrimination due to a disability. It said that no individual can be excluded, solely because of his or her disability, from participating in or benefiting from any program or activity receiving federal financial assistance, which includes schools (Council for Exceptional Children, 1997).

Unlike IDEA, this act employs a functional rather than categorical model for determining a disability. According to this law, individuals are eligible for services if they

1. have a physical or mental impairment that substantially limits one or more life activities;
2. have a record of such an impairment; or
3. are regarded as having such an impairment by others.

"Major life activities" are broadly defined and include, for example, walking, seeing, hearing, working, and learning.

To fulfill the requirements of Section 504, schools must make "reasonable accommodations" for pupils with disabilities so that they can participate in educational programs provided to other students. Reasonable accommodations might include modifications of the general education program, the assignment of an aide, a behavior management plan, or the provision of special study areas (Smith, 2002; Smith & Patton, 2007). Students may also receive related services such as occupational or physical therapy even if they are not receiving a special education through IDEA.

Because the protections afforded by this law are so broad, an individual who is ineligible for a special education under IDEA may qualify for special assistance or accommodations under Section 504. An adolescent with attention deficit hyperactivity disorder (ADHD) or a student with severe allergies, for example, would be eligible for services via Section 504 although unlikely eligible to receive services under IDEA (Council for Exceptional Children, 1997). All students who are eligible for a special education and related services under IDEA are also eligible for accommodations under Section 504; the converse, however, is *not* true.

Similar to IDEA, there is a mandate contained within Section 504 to educate pupils with special needs with their typical peers to the maximum extent possible. In addition, schools are required to develop an accommodation plan (commonly called a "504 plan") customized to meet the unique needs of the individual. This document should include a statement of the pupil's strengths and weaknesses, a list of necessary accommodations, and the individual(s) responsible for ensuring implementation. The purpose of this plan is to enable the student to receive a free, appropriate public education (Gargiulo & Metcalf, 2010).

Finally, unlike IDEA, which offers protections for students only between the ages of 3 and 21, Section 504 covers the individual's life span. See Table 2.2 for a comparison of some of the key provisions of IDEA and Section 504.

TABLE 2.2 A Comparison of Key Features of IDEA and Section 504

Provision	IDEA	Section 504
Purpose	Provides a free and appropriate public education to children and youth with specific disabilities.	Prohibits discrimination on the basis of a person's disability in all programs receiving federal funds.
Ages Covered	Individuals 3–21 years old.	No age restriction.
Definition of Disability	Twelve disabilities defined according to federal regulations plus state/local definition of *developmentally delayed.*	Broader interpretation of a disability than found in IDEA—a person with a physical or mental impairment that substantially limits a major life activity, who has a record of such impairment, or who is regarded as having such an impairment.
Funding	States receive some federal dollars for excess cost of educating students with disabilities.	Because this is a civil rights law, no additional funding is provided.
Planning Documents	Individualized education program (IEP).	Accommodation plan (commonly referred to as a "504 plan").
Assessment Provisions	A comprehensive, nondiscriminatory eligibility evaluation in all areas of suspected disability conducted by a multidisciplinary team; reevaluations every three years unless waived.	Eligibility determination requires nondiscriminatory assessment procedures; requires reevaluation prior to a "significant change" in placement.
Due Process	Extensive rights and protections afforded to student and parents.	Affords parents impartial hearing, right to inspect records, and representation by counsel. Additional protections at discretion of local school district.
Coordination	No provision.	School district required to identify a 504 coordinator.
Enforcement	U.S. Department of Education, Office of Special Education Programs.	Office for Civil Rights, U.S. Department of Education.

Public Law 101–336 (Americans With Disabilities Act)

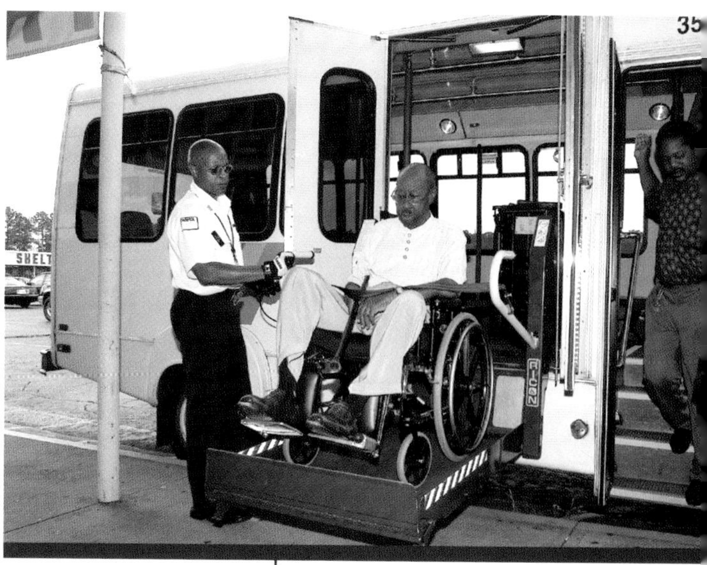

The Americans with Disabilities Act requires that mass transit systems be accessible to citizens with disabilities.

Probably the most significant civil rights legislation affecting individuals with disabilities, the Americans with Disabilities Act (ADA) was signed into law on July 26, 1990, by President George H. W. Bush, who stated, "Today, America welcomes into the mainstream of life all people with disabilities. Let the shameful wall of exclusion finally come tumbling down." This far-reaching enactment, which parallels Section 504 of PL 93–112, forbids discrimination against persons with disabilities in both the public and private sectors. Its purpose, according to Turnbull (1993), is to "provide clear, strong, consistent, and enforceable standards prohibiting discrimination against individuals with disabilities without respect for their age, nature or extent of disability" (p. 23).

The ADA goes far beyond traditional thinking of who is disabled and embraces, for instance, people with AIDS, individuals who have successfully completed a substance abuse program, and persons with cosmetic disfigurements. In fact, any person with an impairment that substantially limits a major life activity is covered by this legislation. It extends protections and guarantees of civil rights in such diverse arenas as private sector employment, transportation, telecommunications, public and privately owned accommodations, and the services of local and state government.

Examples of the impact of this landmark legislation include the following:

- Employers of fifteen or more workers must make "reasonable accommodations" so that an otherwise qualified individual with a disability is not discriminated against. Accommodations might include a Braille computer keyboard for a worker who is visually impaired or wider doorways to allow easy access for an employee who uses a wheelchair. Furthermore, hiring, termination, and promotion practices may not discriminate against an applicant or employee who has a disability.
- Mass transit systems, such as buses, trains, and subways, must be accessible to citizens with disabilities.
- Hotels, fast-food restaurants, theaters, hospitals, early childhood centers, banks, dentists' offices, retail stores, and the like may not discriminate against individuals with disabilities. These facilities must be accessible, or alternative means for providing services must be available.
- Companies that provide telephone service must offer relay services to individuals with hearing or speech impairments.

Think what this legislation means for the field of special education in general, and specifically for adolescents with disabilities as they prepare to leave high school and transition to the world of adulthood as independent citizens able to participate fully in all aspects of community life. Thanks to this enactment, the future of the almost 54 million Americans with disabilities is definitely brighter and more secure.

Public Law 110–325 (the Americans With Disabilities Act Amendments of 2008)

On September 25, 2008, President Bush signed into law the Americans with Disabilities Act Amendments. PL 110–325 became effective on January 1, 2009. Commonly called ADAA, this legislation revises the definition of a disability in favor of a broader interpretation, thereby extending protections to greater numbers of individuals. In fact, this law expressly overturns two Supreme Court decisions that had previously limited the meaning of the term disability. Additionally, ADAA expands the definition of "major life activities" by including two noninclusive lists, the first of which includes activities not expressly stipulated such as reading, concentrating, and thinking. The second list includes major bodily functions—for example, functions of the immune system or neurological functioning (U.S. Equal Employment Opportunity Commission, 2010). The act also states that the interpretation of "substantial limitation" must be made without regard to the ameliorative effects of mitigating measures like medication or medical equipment. (The only stated exception is eyeglasses or contact lenses.)

Changes incorporated in this legislation also apply to students eligible for protections under Section 504 of PL 93–112. According to Zirkel (2009), "the overall effect is obviously to expand the number and range of students eligible under Section 504" (p. 69). A pupil, however, cannot be "regarded as" having a disability if his or her disability is minor or transitory (a duration of six months or less). It is anticipated that the new ADAA eligibility standards will have a significant impact on special education. "IDEA eligibility teams will need to closely coordinate with Section 504 eligibility teams not only when determining that a student is ineligible for initial services under IDEA but also upon exiting the student from an IEP" (Zirkel, p. 71).

We see the overall intent of this enactment as ensuring that individuals with disabilities receive the protections and services to which they are legally entitled.

Identification and Assessment of Individual Differences

One of the distinguishing characteristics of our field is the individuality and uniqueness of the students we serve. There is considerable wisdom in the maxim "No two children are alike." Experienced educators will quickly tell you that even though students may share a common disability label, such as *learning disabled* or *visually impaired*, that is where the similarity ends. These pupils are likely to be as different as day and night. Of course, the individuality of our students, both typical and atypical, has the potential for creating significant instructional and/or management concerns for the classroom teacher. Recall from Chapter 1 the types of youngsters enrolled in Mr. Thompson's fifth-grade classroom. Today's schools are serving an increasingly diverse student population. At the same time, there is greater cooperation and more shared responsibility between general and special educators as they collectively plan appropriate educational experiences for all learners.

When teachers talk about the individuality of their students, they often refer to **interindividual differences**. These differences are what distinguish each student from his or her classmates. Interindividual differences are differences *between* pupils. Examples might include distinctions based on height, reading ability, athletic prowess, or intellectual competency. Some interindividual differences are more obvious and of greater educational significance than others.

Interindividual differences are frequently the reason for entry into special education programs. One child might be significantly above (or below) average in intellectual ability; another might exhibit a significant degree of hearing loss. Categorization and placement decision making by school personnel revolve around interindividual differences. Stated another way, school authorities identify, label, and subsequently place a student in an instructional program on the basis of the student's interindividual differences.

However, not all pupils in a given program are alike. Children also exhibit **intraindividual differences**—a unique pattern of strengths and weaknesses. Intraindividual differences are differences *within* the child. Instead of looking at how students compare with their peers, teachers focus on the individual's abilities and limitations. We should point out that this is a characteristic of all pupils, not just those enrolled in special education programs. For example, Victoria, who is the best artist in her eighth-grade class, is equally well known for her inability to sing. One of her classmates, Melinda, has a learning disability. Her reading ability is almost three years below grade level; yet she consistently earns very high grades in math.

Intraindividual differences are obviously of importance to teachers. A student's IEP (individualized education program) reflects this concern. Assessment data, derived from a variety of sources, typically profile a pupil's strengths and needs. This information is then used in crafting a customized instructional plan tailored to meet the unique needs of the learner.

Referral and Assessment for Special Education

"Evaluation [assessment] is the gateway to special education but referral charts the course to the evaluation process" (Turnbull, Turnbull, Erwin, & Soodak, 2006, p. 232). Litigation, IDEA requirements, and today's best practices serve as our road map as we travel along the evaluation pathway to providing appropriate educational experiences for students with disabilities. This journey from referral to assessment to the development of an IEP and eventual placement in the most appropriate environment is a comprehensive process incorporating many different phases. Figure 2.2 illustrates this process. In the following sections, we examine several of the key elements involved in developing individualized program plans.

Prereferral

Although evaluation may be the gateway to special education, a great deal of activity occurs prior to a student's ever taking the first test. Careful scrutiny of our model reveals an intervention strategy known as **prereferral intervention**, which occurs prior to initiating a referral for possible special education services. The purpose of this strategy is to reduce unwarranted referrals while providing individualized assistance to the student without the benefit of a special education. Although not mandated by IDEA, prereferral interventions have become increasingly common over the past two decades. In fact, IDEA 2004 permits the use of federal dollars to support these activities. Well over half of the states either require or recommend the use of this tactic with individuals suspected of having a disability (Buck, Polloway, Smith-Thomas, & Cook, 2003).

Prereferral interventions are preemptive by design. They call for collaboration between general educators and other professionals for the express purpose of developing creative, alternative instructional and/or management strategies designed to accommodate the particular needs of the learner. This process results in shared responsibility and joint decision making among general and special educators, related service providers, administrators, and other school personnel, all of whom possess specific expertise; the pupil's parents typically do not participate in this early phase. The child's success or failure in school no longer depends exclusively on the pedagogical skills of the general educator; rather, it is now the responsibility of the school-based intervention assistance team (also commonly known as teacher-assistance teams, instructional support teams, or child study teams) (Buck et al., 2003).

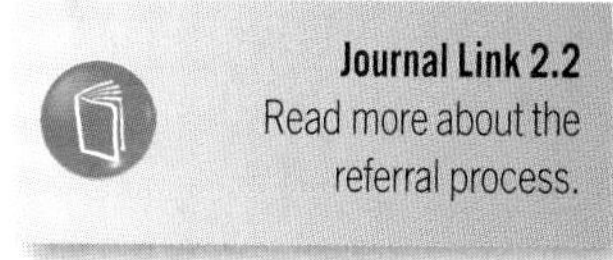

As beneficial as this strategy often is, it is not always successful. Detailed documentation of these intervention efforts provides a strong justification for the initiation of a formal referral.

Referral

A **referral** is the first step in a long journey toward receiving a special education. As we have just seen, a referral may start as a result of unsuccessful prereferral interventions, or it may be the outcome of **child-find** efforts (IDEA-mandated screening and identification of individuals suspected of needing special education).

Simply stated, a referral is a written request to evaluate a student to determine whether the child has a disability. Typically, a referral begins with a general educator; it may also be initiated by a school administrator, related services provider, concerned parent, or other individual. Referrals typically arise from a concern about the child's academic achievement and/or social/behavioral problems. In some instances, a referral may be

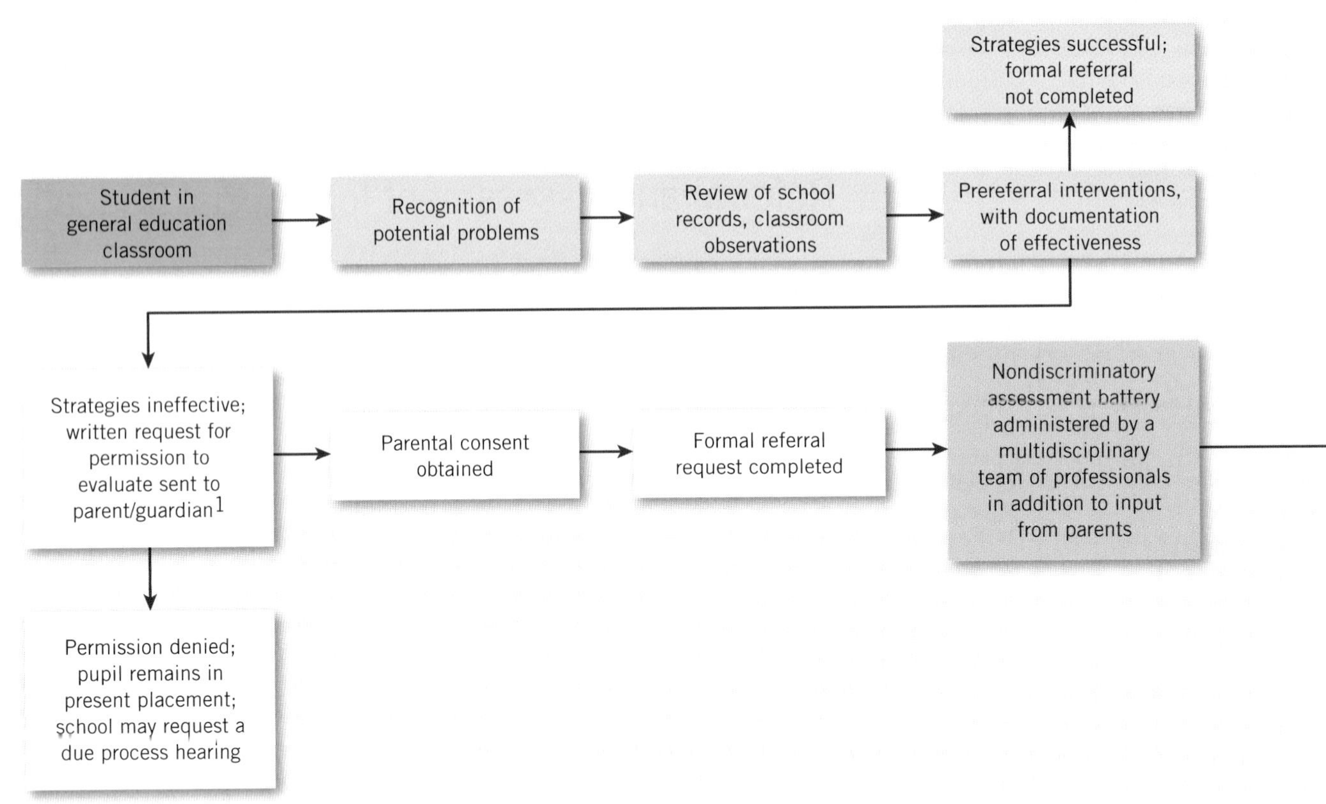

FIGURE 2.2 A Procedural Decision-Making Model for the Delivery of Special Education Services

1. IDEA does not mandate parental consent for referral but does require consent for evaluation.

2. Eligibility determination must occur within sixty days of referral.

initiated because of a pupil's cultural or linguistic background; it may even be the result of problems caused by inappropriate teacher expectations or poor instructional strategies. Thus, the reasons for the referral may not always lie within the student. This is one reason why prereferral intervention strategies are so important. Only about 75 percent of the referrals for special education services actually result in placement; the remaining children are found ineligible (Ysseldyke, 2001).

Referral forms vary in their format. Generally, in addition to student demographic information, a referral must contain detailed reasons as to why the request is being made. Teachers must clearly describe the pupil's academic and/or social performance. Documentation typically accompanies the referral and may include test scores, checklists, behavioral observation data, and actual samples of the student's work. Teachers need to paint as complete a picture as possible of their concern(s), as well as their efforts to rectify the situation.

In most schools, the information that has been gathered is then reviewed by a committee, often known as the child study committee, special services team, or other such name. The composition of this group of professionals varies but typically includes an administrator, a school psychologist, and experienced teachers. Other personnel may also be involved, depending on the nature of the referral. It is the job of this committee to review the available information and decide whether further assessment is warranted. If the team decides to proceed, a written request for permission to evaluate is sent to the child's parent(s). School authorities *must* obtain permission of the parent/guardian

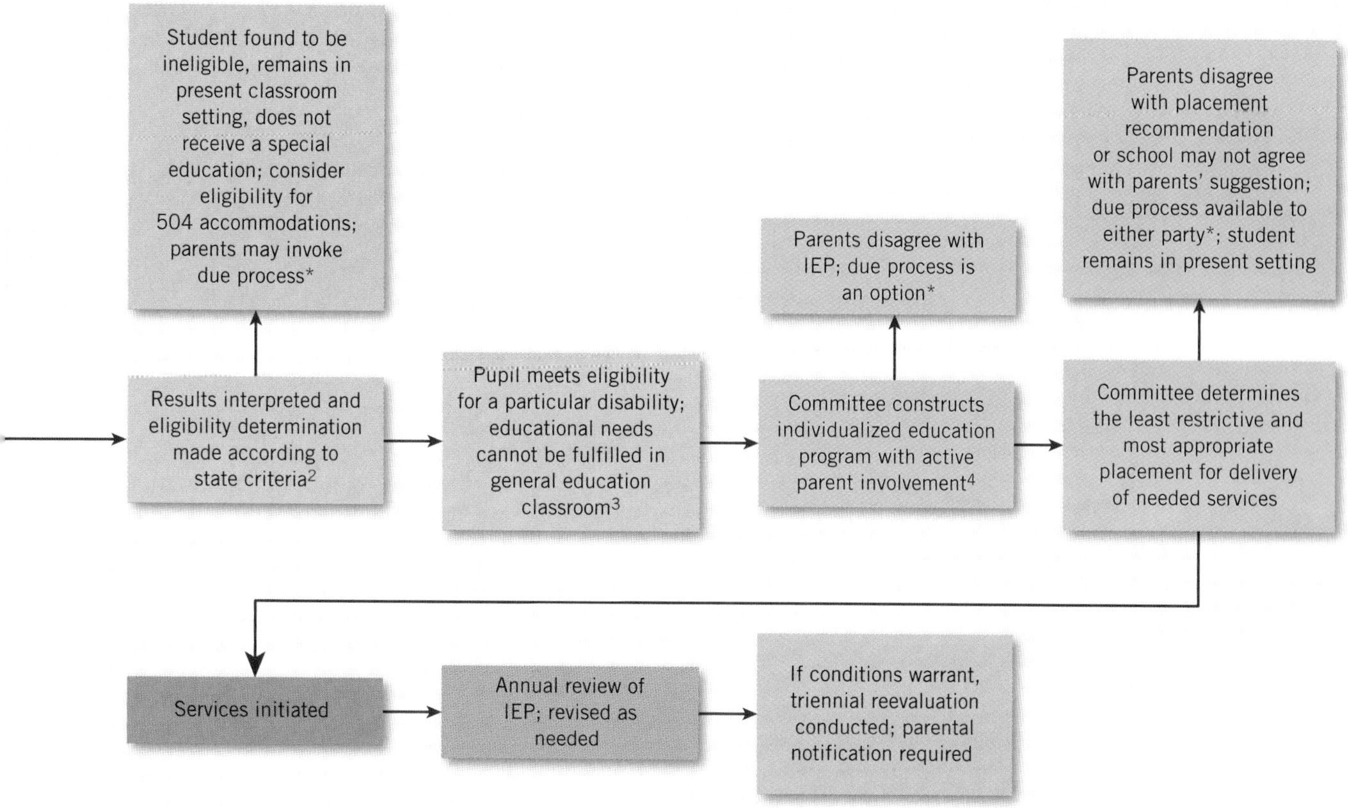

Student found to be ineligible, remains in present classroom setting, does not receive a special education; consider eligibility for 504 accommodations; parents may invoke due process*

Results interpreted and eligibility determination made according to state criteria[2]

Pupil meets eligibility for a particular disability; educational needs cannot be fulfilled in general education classroom[3]

Committee constructs individualized education program with active parent involvement[4]

Parents disagree with IEP; due process is an option*

Committee determines the least restrictive and most appropriate placement for delivery of needed services

Parents disagree with placement recommendation or school may not agree with parents' suggestion; due process available to either party*; student remains in present setting

Services initiated

Annual review of IEP; revised as needed

If conditions warrant, triennial reevaluation conducted; parental notification required

3. If parents refuse consent for a special education, school district is not responsible for providing a free and appropriate public education.

4. IEP must be developed within thirty days of eligibility determination.

*Mandatory resolution session required prior to a due process hearing.

before proceeding with a formal evaluation. Interestingly, IDEA does not require parental consent for referrals. We believe, however, that it is wise to notify parents that a referral is being initiated, explain the reasons for the referral, and solicit their input and cooperation in the referral process.

Assessment

The first step in determining whether a student has a disability, and is in need of a special education, is securing the consent of the child's parent(s)/guardian(s) for the evaluation. As noted previously, this step is mandated by IDEA as part of the procedural safeguards protecting the legal rights of parent(s)/guardian(s). Under the provisions of IDEA, school officials must notify the pupil's parent(s)/guardian(s), in their native language, of the school's intent to evaluate (or refusal to evaluate) the student and the rationale for this decision; they must explain the assessment process and alternatives available to the parent(s)/guardian(s), such as the right to an independent evaluation of their son or daughter. Many schools automatically send parent(s)/guardian(s) a statement of their legal rights when initial permission to evaluate is sought.

Assessment, according to Gargiulo and Metcalf (2010), is a generic term that refers to the process of gathering information about a pupil's strengths and needs. Educational assessment can rightly be thought of as an information-gathering and decision-making process.

Assessments can be conducted at a young age and must be individualized and comprehensive.

One of the goals of the assessment process is to obtain a complete profile of the student's abilities and his or her needs. By law (IDEA), this requires the use of a **multidisciplinary team** of professionals, of which one member must be a teacher. In practice, some school districts are fulfilling this mission by establishing inter- and transdisciplinary assessment teams. Regardless of the model adopted by the school district, the team is responsible for developing an individualized and comprehensive assessment package that evaluates broad developmental domains (cognitive, academic achievement) as well as the specific areas of concern noted on the referral, such as social/emotional problems or suspected visual impairments.

Successful accomplishment of this task dictates the use of both formal and informal assessment tools. Once again, IDEA is very clear about this issue: No one procedure may be used as the sole basis of evaluation; a multitude of tests is required. IDEA regulations further require that the evaluations be presented in the pupil's native language or, when necessary, via other modes of communication such as sign language or Braille for students who are sensory impaired. Additionally, the selection and administration of the assessment battery must accurately reflect the child's aptitude and achievement and not penalize the student because of his or her impairment in sensory, manual, or speaking skills. The accompanying Insights feature describes some accommodations that may be needed for accurate assessment.

School psychologists, educational diagnosticians, and other professionals responsible for evaluating the student have a wide variety of assessment instruments at their disposal. Evaluators attempt to gauge both inter- and intraindividual differences by using both norm- and criterion-referenced assessments. Simply stated, **norm-referenced assessments** are standardized tests and are linked to interindividual differences. Norm-referenced tests compare a pupil's performance with that of a representative sample of children, providing the evaluator with an indication of the pupil's performance relative to other individuals of similar chronological age. Data are typically presented in terms of percentile ranks, stanines, or grade equivalent scores. Data gleaned from norm-referenced tests provide limited instructional information. In contrast, **criterion-referenced assessments** are associated with intraindividual differences and can provide data that are useful for instructional planning. In this type of assessment procedure, a student's performance on a task is compared to a particular level of mastery. The criterion level is typically established by the classroom teacher. Criterion-referenced assessments are especially helpful, according to Gargiulo and Metcalf (2010), in pinpointing the specific skills that the pupil has mastered as well as determining what skills necessitate additional instruction. Teachers are concerned with the individual's pattern of strengths and needs rather than how the student compares with his or her classmates.

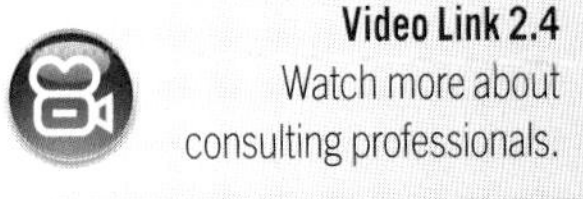

Video Link 2.4
Watch more about consulting professionals.

As mentioned earlier, evaluators must put together a complete educational portrait of the student's abilities. This frequently requires multiple sources of information, which typically include standardized tests, work samples, and observational data, among other forms of input. Table 2.3 summarizes some of the types of assessments increasingly being used by evaluation specialists to complement data derived from norm-referenced tests.

Instructional Programming and Appropriate Placement

When properly conducted, educational assessments lead to the development of meaningful IEPs and IFSPs. Measurable annual goals (and short-term objectives/benchmarks for pupils evaluated via alternate assessments) are crafted based upon data gleaned from

Assessment Accommodations

In order to accurately portray a pupil's abilities and needs, assessment accommodations are sometimes necessary. Accommodations are changes in how students access and demonstrate learning without changing the standards they are working toward. Accommodations must be individualized; not all pupils require them, nor do students with the same disability require the same type of accommodations. The need for accommodations may change over time; some individuals may require fewer accommodations while in other situations additional support is required. Listed below are examples of accommodations that IEP teams may find beneficial.

Presentation accommodations let students access assignments, tests, and activities in ways other than reading standard print. Students with print disabilities (inability to visually decode standard print because of a physical, sensory, or cognitive disability) may require a combination of these accommodations:

- Visual: large print, magnification devices, sign language, visual cues
- Tactile: Braille, Nemeth code, tactile graphics
- Auditory: human reader, audiotape or CD, audio amplification device
- Visual and auditory: screen reader, videotape, descriptive video, talking materials

Response accommodations allow students to complete assignments, tests, and activities in different ways or solve or organize problems using an assistive device or organizer. Response accommodations include:

- Different ways to complete assignments, tests, and activities: expressing responses to a scribe through speech, sign language, pointing, or an assistive communication device; typing on or speaking to a word processor, Brailler, or tape recorder; writing in a test booklet instead of on an answer sheet
- Materials or devices to solve or organize responses: calculation devices; spelling and grammar assistive devices; visual or graphic organizers

Timing and scheduling accommodations give students the time and breaks they need to complete assignments, tests, and activities and may change the time of day, day of the week, or number of days over which an activity takes place. These include:

- Extended time
- Multiple or frequent breaks
- Changing the testing schedule or order of subtests
- Dividing long-term assignments

Setting accommodations change the location in which a student receives instruction or the conditions of the setting. Students may be allowed to sit in a different location than the majority of students to:

- Reduce distractions
- Receive accommodations
- Increase physical access
- Use special equipment

SOURCE: Adapted from S. Thompson, "Choosing and Using Accommodations on Assessments," *CEC Today, 10*(6), 2004, pp. 12, 18.

these evaluations. But first, the multidisciplinary team must determine whether the student is eligible to receive special education services according to specific state criteria. Eligibility standards differ from state to state, but most are framed around IDEA criteria.

If team members, working in concert with the child's parent(s), determine that the student fails to qualify for a special education, we suggest developing intervention strategies and recommendations for accommodations to address the referral concerns. We believe this is necessary because the pupil will remain in his or her present

TABLE 2.3 Emerging Sources of Assessment Information

Source	Description
Naturalistic Observation	Documentation of qualitative as well as quantitative aspects of youngster's behavior in natural environment. Information may be recorded formally (rating scales, observational recording systems) or informally (anecdotal records, audio recordings). Data can be used to support or refute information gathered from other sources.
Interviews	Information obtained from significant individuals in student's life—parents, teachers, older siblings, or the pupil him- or herself. Interviews are a planned and purposeful activity whose purpose is to gain insight or perspective on specific areas of interest, such as the child's background or possible reasons for behavioral problems. Format may be formal (interviewer follows a predetermined set of questions) or informal (interview proceeds according to the individual's responses). Data may be gathered orally or in writing.
Work Samples	Evidence of a pupil's actual classroom performance, typically focused on particular skill development. Sometimes referred to as a permanent product. Spelling tests, arithmetic fact sheets, and handwriting samples are examples of this information source. Work samples are especially useful when planning instructional intervention and modification. Requires teacher to think diagnostically and look, for example, at error patterns or clarity of directions.
Portfolios	A type of authentic assessment, portfolios are an outgrowth of the familiar work folder concept. They include a wide range of examples of a student's emerging abilities and accomplishments over time. Qualitative and quantitative indicators of performance might include writing samples, audio/video recordings, worksheets, drawings, photographs, or other forms of evidence. Useful for student self-assessment.

placement—the general education classroom. Additionally, the team may wish to consider the pupil for a 504 accommodation plan if the student is eligible for such services. Parent(s)/guardian(s) must be sent written notification summarizing the evaluation and stating why their son or daughter is ineligible to receive a special education. If, however, it is determined that the pupil is eligible for a special education, the multidisciplinary team is then confronted with two monumental tasks: constructing the IEP/IFSP and determining the most appropriate placement for the student.

Designing Individualized Instructional Programs

According to IDEA, each student identified by a multidisciplinary child study team as disabled and in need of special education must have an individualized program plan of specially designed instruction that addresses the unique needs of the child and, in the case of infants and toddlers, the needs of the family as well. IEPs and IFSPs are guides to the design and delivery of customized services and instruction. They also serve as vehicles for collaboration and cooperation between parents and professionals as they jointly devise appropriate educational experiences.

Individualized Education Program

An individualized education program (IEP) is part of an overall strategy designed to deliver services appropriate to the individual needs of pupils ages 3 and older. By the time we reach the IEP stage, the appropriate permissions have been gathered, assessments have been conducted, and a disability determination has been made. We are now at the point where the IEP is to be developed, followed by placement in the most appropriate and least restrictive setting. Bateman and Linden (2006) make a very important point about *when* the IEP is to be developed. They believe that IEPs are often written at the wrong time. Legally, the IEP is to be developed within 30 days following the evaluation and determination of the child's disability, but *before* a placement recommendation is formulated. Placement in the least restrictive and most normalized setting is based on a completed IEP, not the other way around. An IEP should not be limited by placement options or the availability of services. We believe it is best to see the IEP as a management tool or planning vehicle that ensures that children with disabilities receive an individualized education appropriate to their unique needs. This focus is in concert with both the intent and the spirit of IDEA.

For an in-depth example of an IEP, visit the SAGE Study Site at www.sagepub.com/gargiulo4emedia.

IEPs are written by a team. At a minimum, participation must include a parent/guardian; the child's teachers, including a general education teacher and a special educator; a representative from the school district; and an individual able to interpret the instructional implications of the evaluation. When appropriate, the student, as well as other professionals who possess pertinent information or whose expertise is desired, may participate at the discretion of the parent or school. Parents have a legal right to participate meaningfully in this planning and decision-making process; they serve as the child's advocate. Although IDEA mandates a collaborative role for parents, it does not stipulate the degree or extent of their participation.

IEPs will vary greatly in their format and degree of specificity. Government regulations do not specify the level of detail considered appropriate, nor do they stipulate how the IEP is to be constructed—only that it be a written document. What is specified are the components (see the accompanying Insights feature).

Elements of a Meaningful IEP

Current Performance. A statement of the student's present levels of educational and functional performance, including how the pupil's disability affects his or her involvement and progress in the general education curriculum, or, for preschoolers, how the disability affects participation in age-appropriate activities.

Goals. A statement of measurable annual goals (both functional and academic) that address the student's involvement and progress in the general education curriculum as well as the student's other education needs; short-term objectives or benchmarks are required for pupils who take alternate assessments aligned to alternate achievement standards.

Special Education and Related Services. A statement of special education, related services, and supplementary aids and services (based on peer-reviewed research) to be provided, including program modifications or supports necessary for the student to advance toward attainment of annual goals; to be involved and progress in the general education curriculum, extracurricular activities, and nonacademic activities; and to be educated and participate in activities with other children both with and without disabilities.

Participation With Typical Students. An explanation of the extent, if any, to which the student will *not* participate in the general education classroom.

Participation in State- and Districtwide Assessments. A statement of any individual modifications needed for the student to participate in a state- or districtwide assessment; if a student will not participate, a statement of why the assessment is inappropriate and how the pupil will be assessed.

Dates and Places. Projected date for initiation of services; expected location, duration, and frequency of such services.

Transition Services. Beginning at age 16, a statement of needed transition services identifying measurable postschool goals (training, education, employment, and, if appropriate, independent living skills), including a statement of interagency linkages and/or responsibilities.

Measuring Progress. A statement of how progress toward annual goals will be measured and how a student's parents (or guardians) will be regularly informed of such progress.

Age of Majority. Information provided at least one year before reaching the age of majority regarding transfer of rights to the student upon reaching the age of majority.

As stated previously, an IEP is, in essence, a management tool that stipulates *who* will be involved in providing a special education, *what* services will be offered, *where* they will be delivered, and for *how long*. In addition, an IEP gauges *how successfully* goals have been met. Although the IEP does contain a measure of accountability, it is not a legally binding contract; schools are not liable if goals are not achieved. Schools are liable, however, if they do not provide the services stipulated in the IEP. IEPs are to be reviewed annually, although parents may request an earlier review. A complete reevaluation of the pupil's eligibility for special education must occur every three years. PL 108–446 waives this requirement, however, if both the parents and school officials agree that such a review is not necessary.

Audio Link 2.3
Listen to suggestions for IEP meetings.

IEPs are not meant to be so detailed or complete that they serve as the entire instructional agenda, nor are they intended to dictate what the individual is taught. They do have to be individualized, however, and address the unique learning and/or behavioral requirements of the student. It is for this reason that we find fault with the growing reliance on computer-generated goals and objectives. Although computer-managed IEPs may serve as a useful logistical tool, like Bateman and Linden (2006), we have grave doubts as to the educational relevancy of this procedure and question its legality. We hope teachers will use this resource only as a starting point for designing customized and individually tailored plans.

One of the challenges confronting the IEP team is ensuring that students have access to the general education curriculum as stipulated in both the 1997 and 2004

Parents play a crucial role in developing their child's individualized education program.

Suggestions for the Classroom

Suggested Individualized Education Program Meeting Agenda

- ☑ Welcome and introduction of participants and their respective roles
- ☑ Statement of purpose
- ☑ Review of previous year's IEP (except for initial placement) and accomplishments
- ☑ Discussion of student's present level of performance and progress:
  - Assessment information
  - Strengths and emerging areas
- ☑ Consideration of specific needs:
  - Instructional modifications and accommodations
  - Participation in state- and districtwide assessments
  - Related services
  - Assistive technology needs
  - Transition goals
  - Behavior intervention plan
  - Language needs for student with limited English proficiency
  - Braille instruction for student who is visually impaired
- ☑ Development of annual goals (and benchmarks if appropriate)
- ☑ Recommendations and justification for placement in least restrictive environment
- ☑ Closing comments, securing of signatures
- ☑ Copies of IEP to all team members

reauthorizations of IDEA. But what is the general education curriculum? In most instances, it is the curriculum that typical learners are exposed to, which is often established by individual state boards of education. The IEP must address how the pupil's disability affects his or her involvement in and ability to progress in the general education curriculum. The underlying assumption seems to be that even if a child is receiving a special education, he or she should engage the general education curriculum. Documentation is required if the team believes that this curriculum is inappropriate for a particular student.

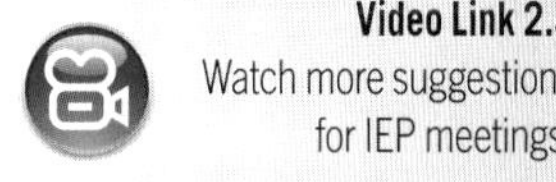
Video Link 2.5
Watch more suggestions for IEP meetings.

IDEA 2004 requires the IEP team to develop measurable annual goals while also emphasizing exposure to the general education curriculum. Goal statements are purposely broad. Their intent is to provide long-range direction to a student's educational program, not to define exact instructional tasks. Based on the pupil's current level of performance, goals are "written to reflect what a student needs in order to become involved in and to make progress in the general education curriculum" (Yell, 2006, p. 293). They represent reasonable projections or estimates of what the pupil should be able to accomplish within the academic year. They also answer the question "What should the student be doing?" Annual goals can reflect academic functioning, social behavior, adaptive behavior, or life skills. Regardless of their emphasis, goal statements should be positive, student-oriented, and relevant (Polloway, Patton, & Serna, 2008).

Measurable annual goals should include the following five components:

- The student . . . (the who)
- Will do what . . . (the behavior)
- To what level or degree . . . (the criterion)
- Under what conditions . . . (the conditions)
- In what length of time . . . (the time frame)

Quality IEPs largely depend on having well-written and appropriate goals (and objectives) that address the unique needs of the individual. IEPs are the primary means of ensuring that a specially designed educational program is provided. The accompanying Suggestions for the Classroom feature provides a sample agenda for an IEP team meeting.

Individualized Family Service Plan

For an in-depth example of an IFSP, visit the SAGE Study Site at www.sagepub.com/gargiulo4emedia.

The individualized family service plan (IFSP) is the driving force behind the delivery of early intervention services to infants and toddlers who are at risk or disabled. The IFSP was originally conceived to focus on children younger than age 3, but recent changes in thinking now allow this document to be used with preschoolers who require a special education. This change was initiated by the federal government in an effort to minimize the differences between early intervention and preschool special education services; the government is now encouraging states to establish "seamless systems" designed to serve youngsters from birth through age 5. As a result of this policy decision, states now have the authority to use IFSPs for preschoolers with special needs until the child enters kindergarten (Lipkin & Schertz, 2008).

Like an IEP, the IFSP is developed by a team consisting of professionals and the child's parents as key members. In addition, parents may invite other family members to participate, as well as an advocate. Typically, the service coordinator who has been working with the family, the professionals involved in the assessment of the youngster, and the service providers constitute the remainder of the group charged with the responsibility of writing the IFSP. The elements required for an IFSP, as stipulated in PL 108–446, are summarized in Table 2.4.

The IFSP was intentionally designed to preserve the family's role as primary caregiver. Well-constructed IFSPs, which are reviewed every six months, fully support the family and encourage their active and meaningful involvement. This thinking is in keeping with an empowerment model (Turnbull, Turnbull, Erwin, Soodak, & Shogren, 2011) that views families as capable (with occasional assistance) of helping themselves. It allows parents to retain their decision-making role, establish goals, and assess their own needs. It is also in keeping with our support of an ecological perspective (Gargiulo & Kilgo, 2011), which argues that one cannot look at a child without considering the various systems and spheres of influence that provide support—in this instance, the infant's or toddler's family and community.

Information obtained from the assessment of the family and data about the infant's or toddler's developmental status are used to generate outcome statements or goals for the child and his or her family. Practitioners are increasingly emphasizing real-life or authentic goals for children with special needs (Pretti-Frontczak & Bricker, 2004). These goals, which are based on the priorities and concerns of the family, are reflected in the IFSP's required outcome statements. Interventionists no longer teach skills in isolation; rather, goals are developed that are relevant to the daily activities of the youngsters and their families. These statements need to be practical and functional, reflecting real-life situations occurring in the natural environment.

TABLE 2.4 Comparable Components of an IEP and IFSP

Individualized Education Program	Individualized Family Service Plan
A statement of the child's present levels of academic achievement and functional performance, including involvement and progress in the general education curriculum	A statement of the infant's or toddler's present levels of physical, cognitive, communication, social/emotional, and adaptive development
No comparable feature	A statement of the family's resources, priorities, and concerns
A statement of measurable annual goals, including benchmarks or short-term instructional objectives for children who take alternate assessments aligned to alternate achievement standards	A statement of measurable results or outcomes expected to be achieved for the infant or toddler and the family
A statement indicating progress toward annual goals and a mechanism for regularly informing parents/guardians of such progress	Criteria, procedures, and timelines used to determine the degree to which progress toward achieving the outcomes or results is being made
A statement of specific special education and related services and supplementary aids and services, based on peer-reviewed research, to be provided and any program modifications	A statement of specific early intervention services, based on peer-reviewed research, necessary to meet the unique needs of the infant or toddler and the family
An explanation of the extent to which the child will not participate in general education programs	A statement of the natural environments in which early intervention services will appropriately be provided, or justification if not provided
Modifications needed to participate in state- or districtwide assessments	No comparable feature
The projected date for initiation of services and the anticipated duration, frequency, and location of services	The projected date for initiation of services and the anticipated duration of services
No comparable feature	The name of the service coordinator
At age 16, a statement of transition services needed including courses of study in addition to measurable postsecondary goals	The steps to be taken to support the child's transition to other services at age 3

SOURCE: Adapted from Individuals with Disabilities Education Improvement Act of 2004, Title 20 U.S. Code (U.S.C.) 1400 *et seq,* Part B Section 614 (d) (1) (A), and Part C Section 636 (d).

Service Delivery Options: Where a Special Education Is Provided

Now that the IEP/IFSP team has decided *what* will be taught, it must decide *where* special education services will be provided. The issue of appropriate placement of children with disabilities has generated considerable controversy and debate. In fact, it has been a point of contention among special educators for almost forty years. IDEA mandates that services be provided to students in the least restrictive setting—or, as Henry and Flynt (1990) call it, the most productive environment. The question confronting the team is "What is the most appropriate placement to achieve the goals (outcomes) of the IEP (IFSP)?" The chosen setting must allow the pupil to reach his or her IEP (IFSP) goals and work toward his or her potential.

It is at this point in our decision-making model that school authorities, in collaboration with the child's parent(s)/guardian(s), attempt to reach agreement about where the student will be served. The principle guiding this decision is known as the **least restrictive**

Designing Individualized Instructional Programs

- An individualized education program (IEP) is essentially a management tool that stipulates who will be involved in providing a special education, what services and instruction will be provided, where they will be delivered, and for how long. In addition, the IEP is designed to gauge whether or not goals are successfully achieved.
- The individualized family service plan (IFSP) is the driving force behind the delivery of early intervention services to infants and toddlers and their families.
- The IFSP is family focused and is designed to preserve the parent's role of primary caregiver and principal decision maker. It must address the concerns and priorities of the family while also acknowledging the resources and strengths of the family.

Service Delivery Options: Where a Special Education Is Provided

- According to the principle of least restrictive environment (LRE), services are to be provided in the setting that most closely approximates the general education classroom while still meeting the unique needs and requirements of the learner.
- Mainstreaming represents a popular interpretation of the principle of LRE.
- Implicit in the mandate of LRE is the notion of a continuum or cascade of service delivery options—a hierarchy of educational environments that allows for customized placement possibilities based on the needs of the individual pupil.
- Full inclusion seeks to place all students with disabilities, regardless of the type or severity of their impairment, in age-/grade-appropriate classrooms at neighborhood schools.
- The concept of full inclusion evolved from the regular education initiative, which sought a shared responsibility or partnership between general and special educators, resulting in greater collaboration and cooperation in meeting the needs of pupils with disabilities.

STUDY QUESTIONS

1. How have litigation and legislation influenced the field of special education?
2. What is the significance of the following cases?
   - *Brown v. Board of Education of Topeka, Kansas*
   - *Pennsylvania Association for Retarded Children v. Commonwealth of Pennsylvania*
   - *Larry P. v. Riles*
   - *Board of Education of the Hendrick Hudson Central School District v. Rowley*
   - *Daniel R.R. v. State Board of Education*
3. Name and describe the six major components and guarantees contained in PL 94–142.
4. What was the purpose of the Americans with Disabilities Act? List four areas where this law affects the lives of individuals who are disabled.
5. How did PL 108–446 modify PL 105–17?
6. Distinguish between interindividual and intraindividual differences.
7. How do prereferral interventions benefit the student suspected of requiring a special education?
8. How do norm-referenced and criterion-referenced tests differ?
9. List the key elements required of a meaningful IEP. Who is responsible for developing this document?
10. Compare the provisions and purpose of an IFSP with those of an IEP.
11. Define the following terms: ***mainstreaming***, ***least restrictive environment***, and ***regular education initiative***. How are these terms related to the mandate of providing services in the LRE?
12. Distinguish between a cascade of services delivery model and the philosophy of full inclusion. What do you see as the advantages and disadvantages of full inclusion?

KEY TERMS

interindividual differences 62
intraindividual differences 62
prereferral intervention 63
referral 63
child-find 63
assessment 65
multidisciplinary team 66
norm-referenced assessments 66
criterion-referenced assessments 66
least restrictive environment (LRE) 74
mainstreaming 76
regular education initiative (REI) 78
full inclusion 78

LEARNING ACTIVITIES

1. Interview an administrator of special education programs for your local school district. Find out how court decisions and legislative requirements have affected the delivery of special education services. Here are some suggested topics for discussion:
   - How has special education changed over the past several years as a result of judicial and legislative mandates?
   - What does the school district do to protect the rights of the students, involve parents, ensure due process, and assess in a nondiscriminatory manner?
   - How is the school district meeting the requirement of educating pupils with disabilities in the least restrictive environment?
   - What are the perceived advantages and disadvantages of IDEA at the local level?
2. Obtain a copy of your state's special education law. How do the requirements and provisions of the law compare with IDEA?
3. Obtain samples of several IEPs and IFSPs from different school districts in your vicinity. In what ways do the forms differ? How are they the same? Do they fulfill the requirements of the law as outlined in your textbook?
4. Visit several elementary and high schools in your area. What service delivery options are available for students with disabilities? Are children with different exceptionalities served in similar settings? Ask the teachers what they believe are the advantages and disadvantages of their particular environment.

REFLECTING ON STANDARDS

The following exercises are designed to help you learn to apply the Council for Exceptional Children (CEC) standards to your teaching practice. Each of the reflection exercises below correlates with a knowledge or skill within the CEC standards. For the full text of each of the related CEC standards, please refer to the standards integration grid located in Appendix B.

Focus on Foundations ***(CEC Content Standard #1 CC1K4)***
Reflect on what you have learned in this chapter about the rights of individuals with disabilities. What measures would you take in your classroom to make sure that your students were educated in the least restrictive environment possible?

Focus on Development and Characteristics of Learners ***(CEC Content Standard #2 CC2K6)***
Reflect on what you have learned in this chapter about understanding the uniqueness of each of your students. Pair up with another student and assess his or her intraindividual differences (unique patterns of strengths and weaknesses). If you were to create an individualized education plan for this "student," what unique needs would he or she have?

STUDENT STUDY SITE

Visit the Student Study Site at www.sagepub.com/gargiulo4emedia for these additional learning tools:

- Video links
- Media links
- Self-quizzes
- E-flashcards
- Full-text SAGE journal articles
- Web exercises

CHAPTER 3

Learning Objectives

After reading Chapter 3 you should be able to:

- Explain how cultural and linguistic diversity is affecting America's classrooms.
- Define culture, multiculturalism, multicultural education, and bilingual education.
- List six instructional options for teaching students who are bilingual.
- Outline the issues associated with the disproportional representation of culturally and linguistically diverse learners in special education.
- Describe the challenges confronting educators when assessing students from culturally and linguistically diverse groups.

Cultural and Linguistic Diversity and Exceptionality

The United States is an enormously diverse and pluralistic society—an amalgamation of different races, languages, folkways, religious beliefs, traditions, values, and even foods and music. As a nation, we greatly benefit from this cultural mixture; it is a defining characteristic of the United States and one of its great strengths. Perhaps nowhere else is this diversity more noticeable than in our schools.

Although in many instances we value and celebrate the richness of American diversity, all too often cultural differences result in prejudice and stereotypes as well as outright discrimination and unequal opportunities. Unfortunately, this statement is a valid characterization of some U.S. schools. In the opinion of various business leaders, policymakers, and educators, the educational environment encountered by many students from culturally and linguistically diverse backgrounds is inadequate, damaging, and openly hostile (Quality Education for Minorities Project, 1990). In some of our public schools, children from minority groups are seen as less than capable and/or difficult to teach. To our way of thinking, this situation is unacceptable and inexcusable. As educators working in increasingly cultural diverse environments, we need to model respect for and sensitivity to the cultural and linguistic characteristics represented by our students and their families.

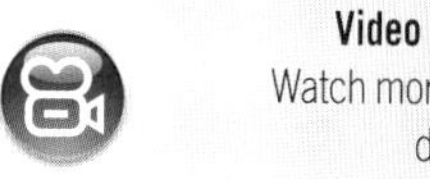

Video Link 3.1
Watch more about diversity.

The goal of this chapter is to examine the link between cultural and linguistic diversity and exceptionality. We will explore the historical patterns of American reaction to and acceptance of people from other lands. We will discuss issues of multicultural and bilingual education and consider the multitude of challenges confronting teachers who work with students with special needs from culturally and linguistically diverse backgrounds (see the accompanying Insights feature).

Cultural Diversity: The Changing Face of a Nation

The United States is made up of people from many different lands; in fact, only about 1 percent of Americans are native (U.S. Census Bureau, 2009a). A vast number of Americans are descended from the millions of immigrants who entered the United States through Ellis Island, located in lower New York Harbor, in the latter part of the nineteenth and the early decades of the twentieth century. Immigration to the United States has

children of immigrants into American culture as quickly as possible. There was a widely held belief that public education could unite the population and instill the ideals of American society in diverse groups of people. The goal of this assimilation or homogenizing process was to "Americanize" vast numbers of new citizens. They were expected to abandon their native languages, cultural heritage, beliefs, and practices. In their place would emerge a common American culture—*E pluribus unum* ("Out of many, one")—with an allegiance to the "American way of doing things." Metaphorically speaking, the United States was seen as a huge **melting pot**—a cauldron into which diverse people were dumped to melt away their differences, thus creating a citizenry who were very much alike (Tiedt & Tiedt, 2010).

For a variety of political and social reasons, Americans in the 1960s slowly began to question the wisdom of a melting pot theory as the country struggled with issues of civil rights and equal opportunity. Schools were no longer seen as the primary vehicle for homogenizing new citizens; instead, a student's ethnic heritage was to be valued and prized. Interest in cultural pluralism and multicultural education was ignited. As a result, a new set of metaphors evolved to counter the philosophy of America as a melting pot. The United States is now likened to a patchwork quilt, a floral bouquet, or a salad.

The notion of the United States as a melting pot society has gradually given way to **cultural pluralism** wherein cultural and ethnic differences are appreciated and respected. Cultural pluralism does *not* require cultural groups to relinquish or abandon their cultural heritage. Schools now value the richness that diversity brings to the classroom; diversity is seen as a strength rather than a weakness.

Terminology of Cultural Differences

Educators and other professionals in the field of education are confronted with a barrage of labels and terms used to describe the education of children from different cultural backgrounds. Sometimes this terminology contributes to inaccurate generalizations, stereotyping, and incorrect assumptions about certain individuals or groups of people. In some instances, it is even difficult to know how to correctly describe the youngsters themselves. Do we, for example, refer to some children as black or African American? Is it more appropriate to identify a student as Hispanic or Latino, and how about pupils from Asian cultures? Also, what is the difference between bilingual education and multicultural education? As you can see, the topic of cultural and linguistic diversity can easily become a source of confusion and controversy. Perhaps it is best to begin our discussion of key terminology by arriving at an understanding of what we mean by culture.

Culture

We define **culture** as the attitudes, values, belief systems, norms, and traditions shared by a particular group of people that collectively form their heritage. A culture is transmitted in various ways from one generation to another. It is typically reflected in language, religion, dress, diet, social customs, and other aspects of a particular lifestyle (Gargiulo & Kilgo, 2011). Siccone (1995) points out that culture also includes the way particular groups of people interpret the world; it provides individuals with a frame of reference or perspective for attaching meaning to specific events or situations, such as the value and purpose of education or the birth of a child with a disability.

Video Link 3.2
Watch more about attitudes.

Gargiulo and Kilgo (2011) caution educators to guard against generalizing and stereotyping when working with pupils from various cultural groups. Even within specific groups, each person is unique, even though all members of the group may share distinctively similar group characteristics. Two students from the same racial group will most likely perform quite differently in the classroom regardless of their shared cultural heritage.

Because of the increasing diversity of our society, the United States is now often likened to a floral bouquet or patchwork quilt.

Multiculturalism

We live in a multicultural society; yet **multiculturalism** is frequently a confusing and poorly understood concept. In its most basic interpretation, multiculturalism refers to more than one culture. It acknowledges basic commonalities among groups of people while appreciating their differences. Implicit within the concept of multiculturalism is the belief that an individual can function within more than one culture. Multiculturalism also provides us with a foundation for understanding multicultural education.

Multicultural Education

Multicultural education is an ambiguous and somewhat controversial concept. Sleeter and Grant (2009) characterize multicultural education as an umbrella concept involving issues of race, language, social class, and culture as well as disability and gender. Banks (2010) and Gollnick and Chinn (2009) portray multicultural education as an educational strategy wherein the cultural background of each pupil is valued, viewed positively, and used to develop effective instruction.

Bilingual Education

A term frequently associated with multicultural education is **bilingual education**, an equally controversial and somewhat confusing concept. The two are not synonymous, however. Multicultural education can be infused throughout the curriculum without the benefit of bilingual education. Simply defined, bilingual education is an educational strategy whereby students whose first language is not English are instructed primarily through their native language while developing their competency and proficiency in English. Teachers initially use the language that the child knows best (Baca & Baca, 2004b). Once a satisfactory command of English is achieved, it becomes the medium of instruction.

Describing Diversity

The clientele of U.S. schools is rapidly changing.

U.S. society is an amalgamation of many different cultures. The U.S. government, however, officially recognizes only five distinct racial groups. The federal government uses this classification scheme when reporting, for example, Head Start enrollment, poverty figures, high school graduation rates, and other such statistics. The Office for Civil Rights within the U.S. Department of Education (1987) identifies citizens as follows:

- **American Indian or Alaskan Native**. A person having origins in any of the original peoples of North America and who maintains cultural identification through tribal affiliation or community recognition.
- **Asian or Pacific Islander.** A person having origins in any of the original peoples of the Far East, Southeast Asia, the Pacific Islands, or the Indian subcontinent. This area includes, for example, China, India, Japan, Korea, the Philippine Islands, and Samoa.
- **Hispanic**. A person of Mexican, Puerto Rican, Cuban, Central or South American, or other Spanish culture or origin regardless of race.
- **Black (not of Hispanic origin).** A person having origins in any of the black racial groups of Africa.
- **White (not of Hispanic origin)**. A person having descended from any of the original peoples of Europe, North Africa, or the Middle East. (p. 37)

We should point out that the preceding descriptions are arbitrary and represent umbrella terms. This terminology camouflages immense cultural and racial variability while obscuring the richness of individual cultures. Regardless of how specific groups of people are described, the diversity and variation within each group are tremendous. Various cultural groups are anything but homogeneous; differences are likely to be found in language, ethnicity, social class, home country, and a host of other dimensions (Lustig & Koester, 2010). It is important for teachers to acknowledge and respect this heterogeneity. They must also guard against perpetuating ethnic and racial stereotypes. Educators frequently fail to use qualifiers such as *some*, *many*, or *most* when discussing various cultural groups. This insensitivity to individuality can easily result in students' receiving an erroneous, oversimplified, and possibly stereotypical impression of a particular racial group (Ryan, 1993).

Teachers must also guard against assuming that the behaviors, beliefs, and actions of their particular cultural group are the correct or only way of doing something. Such assumptions reflect **ethnocentrism**—viewing one's own cultural group characteristics as superior or correct and the ways of other groups as inferior or peculiar.

Multicultural Education, Bilingual Education, and Student Diversity

By now it should be apparent that multicultural education is closely intertwined with issues of student diversity. Because the clientele of American schools is rapidly changing, there has been much debate and controversy over how best to educate children with culturally and linguistically diverse backgrounds. It is axiomatic that all students are different and not all people learn in the same way; this is especially true for students who are culturally and linguistically diverse. It would be foolish for teachers to expect children (or adults, for that matter) to leave their values, traditions, beliefs, and even language at the schoolhouse door. Effective teachers are sensitive to the cultural heritage of each learner and attempt to provide educational experiences that are culturally relevant and culturally appropriate.

Multicultural Education: Concepts and Characteristics

Embedded within the concept of multicultural education is a belief that all students, regardless of their race, ethnicity, culture, and other characteristics such as social class or disability, should experience equal educational opportunities. Although no single recipe can accommodate all the facets of multicultural education, there are certain common ingredients. Figure 3.1 portrays six goals of multicultural education, as synthesized by Winzer and Mazurek (1998). These aims are broad and overlapping, supporting the authors' contention that multicultural education is an orientation and not a specific pedagogical technique.

Throughout this chapter, we have stressed the multicultural nature of U.S. society. At the heart of this society is a core national culture, identified as the **macroculture**, which represents a shared culture. Traits such as individualism, independence, competitiveness, and ambition are characteristic of the American macroculture (Gollnick & Chinn, 2009), along with values such as equality and fair play. Within this larger culture are several distinct subcultures, or **microcultures**, which, while sharing attributes of the macroculture, maintain their own distinct values, norms, and behaviors. The United States is composed of many different microcultures, as illustrated in Figure 3.2. According to Banks (2010), the various microcultures to which a person belongs are interrelated and interact with one another to collectively influence the individual's behavior. Membership in a particular group does not define a person's behavior, but it does make certain types of behavior more likely.

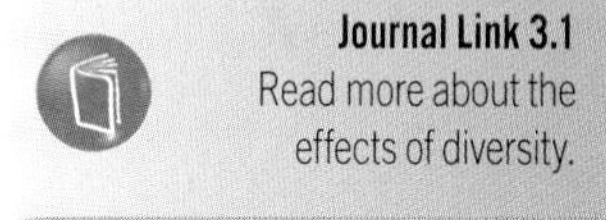
Journal Link 3.1
Read more about the effects of diversity.

Differences between the various microcultures and the macroculture are frequently a source of conflict and misunderstanding. A major goal of multicultural education, therefore, is for pupils to acquire the knowledge, attitudes, and skills needed to function effectively in each cultural setting (Banks, 2010). Banks argues that students in contemporary society should be able to function in their own as well as other microcultures, the macroculture, and the global community.

Bilingual Education: Concepts and Characteristics

As noted previously, multicultural education and bilingual education are not the same thing. Multicultural education can exist independently of bilingual education, but bilingual education cannot exist without multicultural education because it emphasizes the student's culture as well as language. As we have seen, approximately one out of five Americans, or almost 20 percent of the population, speaks a language other than English. The U.S. government estimates that there are almost 11 million school-age children whose primary language is not English (National Center for Education Statistics, 2009b). Yet controversy

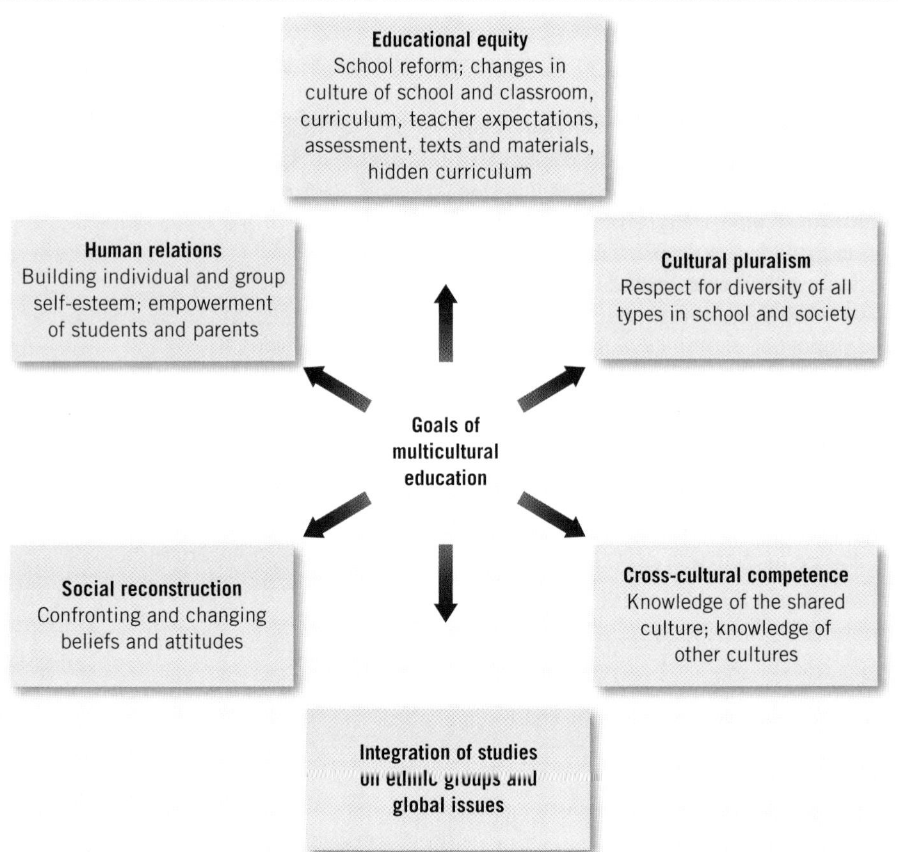

FIGURE 3.1 Goals of Multicultural Education

SOURCE: From *Special Education in Multicultural Contexts* by Winzer/Mazurek, © 1998. Reprinted by permission of Pearson Education, Inc., Upper Saddle River, NJ.

and debate continue over how best to meet the needs of these students. In many school districts, bilingual education provides one possible answer. Not everyone, however, agrees with this strategy. Thirty states have enacted legislation or passed constitutional amendments establishing English as the "official" language of their state (Crawford, 2004; U.S. English, 2010), and five states actually prohibit bilingual education in their schools (Baca & Baca, 2004a).

Students whose first language is not English represent a very heterogeneous group of individuals. Their competency in their primary language as well as in English may vary greatly. Some of these pupils may be identified as **limited English proficient (LEP)**, the term incorporated in IDEA 2004. Other professionals, however, prefer the label *English language learners*. The term *limited English proficient* refers to a reduced or diminished fluency in reading, writing, or speaking English. Typically, these students are unable to profit fully from instruction provided in English. *Limited English proficiency* is not a disparaging label. "It does not equate with lack of capacity or an inherent limitation," Winzer and Mazurek (1998) write, "but it is synonymous with the reality of children who speak another language and are not yet adept in English" (p. 51).

The primary purpose of bilingual education programs is to provide assistance to students with limited proficiency in English so that they can "function effectively in both their native language and English. . . . The student's native language and culture

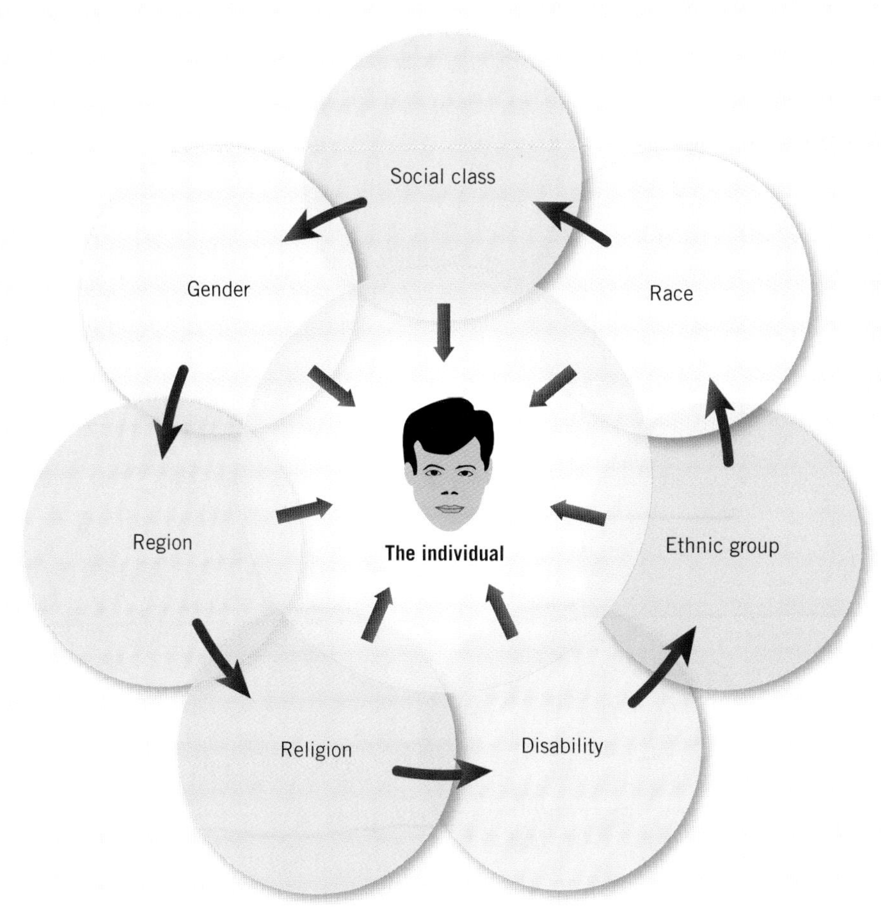

FIGURE 3.2 Influence of Microcultures on an Individual's Behavior

SOURCE: Adapted from J. Banks, *Cultural Diversity and Education,* 5th ed. (Needham Heights, MA: Allyn and Bacon, 2006), p. 77.

are taught concurrently with English and the dominant culture" (Gollnick & Chinn, 2006, p. 299). The result is that the pupil becomes bilingual and bicultural in the process. Similarly, Baca and Baca (2004b), authorities in the field of bilingual education, see the primary mission of bilingual education as providing instruction to pupils using the language they know best and then reinforcing this information through English, while also promoting cognitive as well as affective development and cultural enrichment. Although it is not explicitly stated, we believe that one of the principal goals of bilingual education is to provide increased educational opportunities for students whose native language is not English. It is interesting to note that, contrary to popular belief, the original aim of bilingual education was not to advocate bilingualism but rather to promote the acquisition of English language skills. Bilingual education was thought to be the quickest way for a non-English-speaking person to become literate in English (Janzen, 1994).

The research evidence on the effectiveness of bilingual education strongly suggests that bilingual education is the most appropriate approach for working with students with limited proficiency in English. Greater academic gains and improved language skills can be directly attributed to bilingual education (Winzer & Mazurek, 1998). Of course, the

Instructional Options for Students Who Are Bilingual

Approach	Strategies
1. Transitional programs	Students are instructed in academic content areas via their native language only until they are sufficiently competent in English, then transition to all-English classes. Primary goal of this program is to move students as quickly as possible to English-only classes. Many students exit after two to three years of instruction. Most common instructional model; bilingual education legislation favors this approach.
2. Maintenance (developmental) programs	Strong native language emphasis. Pupils maintain proficiency in first language while receiving instruction in English. A long-term approach with less emphasis on leaving program. Solid academic foundation is stressed.
3. Enrichment programs	Typically used with monolingual children, who are introduced to new language and culture.
4. Immersion programs	English language is the exclusive medium of instruction; first language and culture are not incorporated. A "sink or swim" philosophy.
5. English as a second language (ESL) programs	Not a true form of bilingual education. Children typically receive instruction in English outside the regular classroom. Goal is to quickly develop English proficiency in bilingual students. Exclusive emphasis on English for teaching and learning; native language not used in instruction. An assimilationist model with multiple variations.
6. Sheltered English	Students receive instruction in academic subjects exclusively in English; no effort is made to maintain or develop proficiency in first language. English instruction is continually monitored and modified to ensure pupil's comprehension. Simultaneous exposure to English language and subject content matter. Pupils who are culturally and linguistically diverse and disabled present unique challenges for teachers.

key to effective bilingual education is to match the instructional strategy to the specific needs and background of the student. Depending on the child's proficiency in his or her native language and English, different instructional models are used. The accompanying Insights feature summarizes some of the approaches typically used with students who are bilingual while the First Person feature describes one teacher's experiences working with English language learners.

Experts in the field of bilingual education disagree as to which pedagogical strategy is most effective for teaching students who are bilingual. There is general agreement, however, that the more opportunities individuals have to use their newly acquired language skills with classmates, friends, family members, and others, the more proficient they will become. In comparison to classroom settings, the natural environment seems to better facilitate language development.

Educators must consider carefully when they transition students with limited English proficiency to all-English classrooms. Many of these pupils' academic failures appear to be due to transitioning too quickly. Conversational fluency typically develops in children who are LEP after approximately two years of instruction. Teachers, therefore, assume that pupils are ready to move on because they appear to be proficient in English. However, according to investigators (Hoover, Klinger, Baca, & Patton, 2008; Salend & Salinas, 2003), the deeper and more complex language skills needed for academic success require an

First Person: Jenny
Teaching English Language Learners

I began my teaching career as a French and English teacher in a large school system in an urban high school. The majority of the student population was African American. In my first year of teaching I had a couple of students in my French class from Vietnam who were English language learners (ELLs). Perhaps because I was a language teacher, I was very interested in learning what instructional techniques I could use to help them. At that time, the school only offered an immersion program. I was very frustrated by this policy and wished that I spoke Vietnamese so that I could better support my students. After three years, I moved and began teaching in a middle-class suburban high school in a small school district. This high school has increased in its cultural and economic diversity during my twenty years of teaching there.

In my first years there, I sought opportunities to work with the few ELLs who were in the school. Initially, the ELLs included a variety of European, Asian, and African students who were the children of professionals, such as researchers and college professors. I developed the first English as a second language (ESL) program classes at the school, using my knowledge as a language teacher. I provided support to students with their assignments in content classes and collaborated with their teachers regarding accommodations and assessments. After a couple of years, our ESL program began assessing the English proficiency of the students and creating instructional plans. I think that being both an ESL teacher and a general education teacher helped me to collaborate with other general education teachers—we spoke the same language, and I had to do what I suggested my colleagues do.

Gradually our high school ELL population increased and changed. Currently, the majority of our students are Hispanic whose parents are employed in the service industry. I went back to school and completed a master's degree in special education and certification as an ESL teacher. As a result of my training and the changes in our ELL population, I coauthored curriculum for sheltered English courses to supplement our ESL classes. I also began to co-teach in some content-area classes. I still have the occasional opportunity to teach an English class, where I hone my skills at accommodation and have to practice what I ask other teachers to do. In addition, because of my degree in special education, I am a more effective advocate for the appropriate assessment of ELLs who might be eligible for special education services.

One of the biggest challenges my students face is acquiring English proficiency while meeting requirements for graduation—both earning credits and passing graduation exams. As older learners, my pupils have less time to acquire English proficiency and greater course requirements to master. Other challenges may include differences in learning styles and educational expectations. In addition, teachers of ELLs may have confusion about or resistance to differentiating instruction for ELLs. Most teachers never expected to also have to teach their students to speak English. They may also have strong feelings about teaching students who might be undocumented immigrants.

Addressing the challenges ELLs and their teachers face can be demanding; yet, being an ESL teacher is a highly rewarding job. I get to work with students and their families over a period of several years and to learn from them about their cultures. I observe them sharing their culture with other students and becoming successful in academic and extracurricular activities.

—*Jenny Harvey*
ESL Teacher
Homewood High School, Homewood, Alabama

additional five to seven years of instruction. Movement to a monolingual English class setting should occur only if the teacher is certain that the student possesses the requisite language skills to compete in an academic environment.

Bilingual Special Education: Concepts and Characteristics

Encyclopedia Link 3.1
Read more about bilingual special education.

Students who are culturally and linguistically diverse *and* disabled present significant challenges for educators. How do we meet the needs of this growing population of pupils? Currently, over 454,000 pupils or slightly fewer than 8 percent of individuals receiving a special education are recognized as limited English proficient (U.S. Department of Education, 2010). What is the most normalized environment for students experiencing "double jeopardy"—that is, linguistic differences and disability? Which area should teachers primarily focus on—the problems posed by the disability or the lack of English proficiency? These questions have no easy answers. One frequently mentioned solution is to place these pupils in classrooms with a special educator who is bilingual. In the majority of instances, however, this is not a feasible solution because of a severe shortage of qualified personnel (Council for Exceptional Children, 2010). What these students truly need is an instructional model known as **bilingual special education**. Baca, Baca, and de Valenzuela (2004) define this concept as

Journal Link 3.2
Read more about effective techniques with English language learners.

> the use of the home language and the home culture along with English in an individually designed program of special instruction for the student in an inclusive environment. Bilingual special education considers the child's language and culture as foundations upon which an appropriate education may be built. (p.18)

The main goal of these efforts is to assist the pupil in reaching his or her maximum potential. The student's primary language and culture are the vehicles for accomplishing this task.

One of the critical issues confronting professionals is how to merge two different programs, bilingual education and special education, into one cogent paradigm. The integration of these two programs requires a focus not only on the acquisition of English language proficiency but also on the construction of individualized educational interventions. The goal is the development of both academic and English language skills, which often requires a team approach. Meaningful instruction for pupils who are culturally and linguistically diverse and disabled entails a coordinated effort involving general educators, special education teachers, and bilingual educators (Gollnick & Chinn, 2009; Salend & Salinas, 2003).

Attempts at providing a special education to pupils who are LEP have frequently encountered a number of problems, including challenges obtaining an accurate diagnosis coupled with assessment difficulties, which often lead to an inappropriate placement. These issues are intricately interrelated and complementary and must be considered within a broader context. Most educators, according to Winzer and Mazurek (1998), recognize that disability and cultural and linguistic differences are related phenomena that play a significant role in a student's learning and development. Cultural and linguistic characteristics frequently coexist and interact with disability-related factors. Consider if you will Ramón, a 9-year-old boy identified as intellectually disabled and with limited English proficiency, whose parents are migrant workers. His family of six has an income below the federal poverty line. Ramón's special education program must address the interaction of these confounding variables. Winzer and Mazurek caution teachers to remember that pupils who are LEP do not give up their right to bilingual education when found to be eligible for special education services. Too often, however, these students fall between the cracks of both programs.

If special education services are to be truly inclusive and meet the unique requirements of learners who are culturally and linguistically diverse, then special educators must focus their attention on the following four areas identified by Garcia and Malkin (1993, p. 52):

1. Information about the language characteristics of learners with disabilities who are bilingual or have limited English proficiency that will assist in the development of a language use plan
2. Information about cultural factors that influence educational planning and services
3. Characteristics of instructional strategies and materials that are culturally and linguistically appropriate
4. Characteristics of a learning environment that promotes success for all students

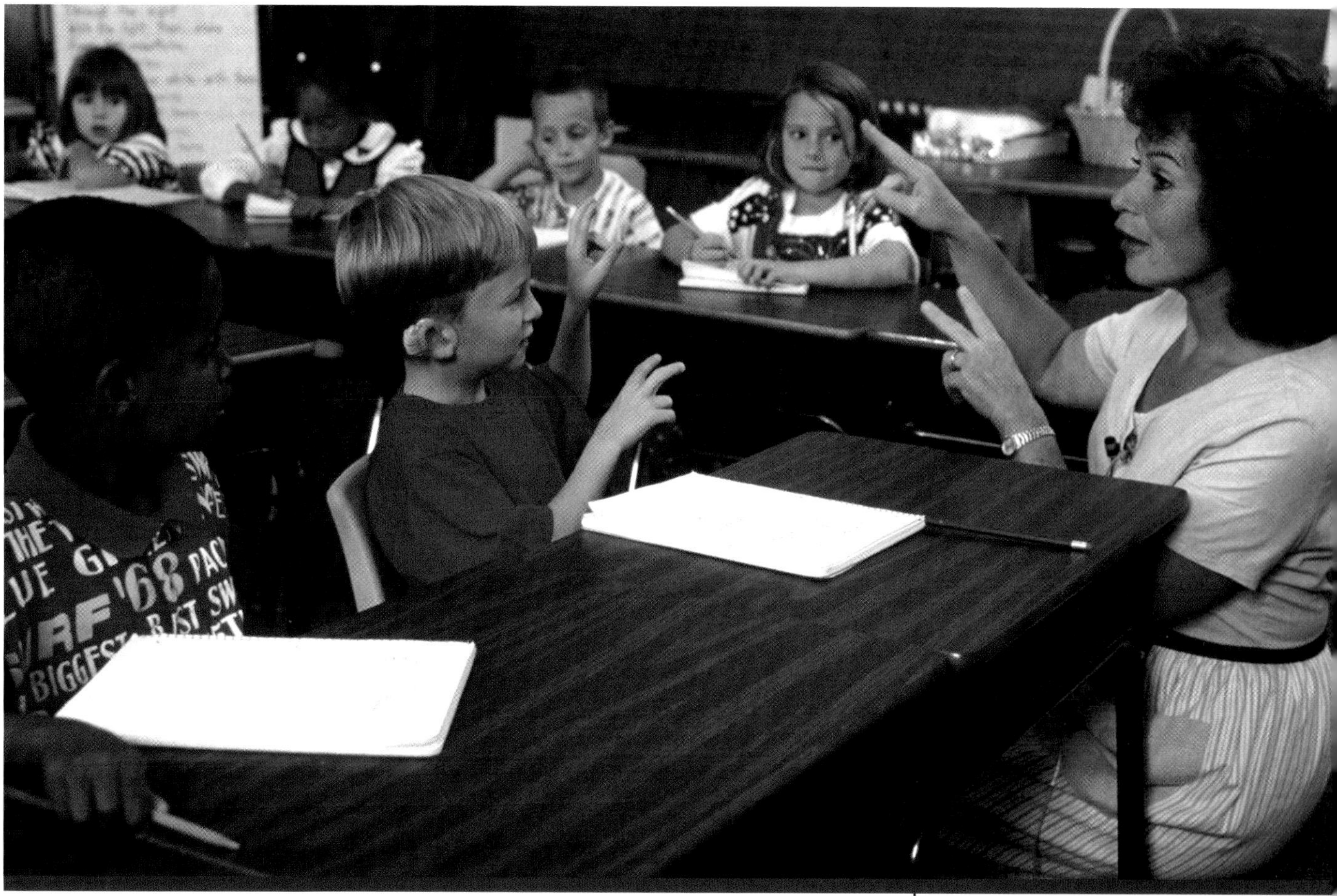

Pupils who are culturally and linguistically diverse and disabled present unique challenges for teachers.

PL 108–446 also speaks to the issue of appropriate programming for these children. A student *cannot* be considered eligible for special education services under this law if his or her educational difficulties are primarily the result of limited proficiency in English or poor instruction.

Disproportional Representation of Minority Students in Special Education Programs

The disproportionate presence of pupils from minority groups in special education programs has been a pressing and volatile concern of educators for more than four decades (Blanchett, Munford, & Beachum, 2005). The fact that greater numbers of children from minority groups are placed in special education programs than would be anticipated based on their proportion of the general school population is commonly referred to as **overrepresentation**. At the same time, there is a long-standing pattern of **underrepresentation** (fewer students in a particular category than one might expect based on their numbers in the school population) of African Americans, Native Americans, and Hispanics in programs for children and youth who are gifted and talented (Borland, 2004; Clark, 2008; Gollnick & Chinn, 2009). Asian American children and Pacific Islanders are typically underrepresented in special education classes but overrepresented in classes for students who are gifted and talented (Donovan & Cross, 2002; Ford, Grantham, & Whiting, 2008; U.S. Department of Education, 2009).

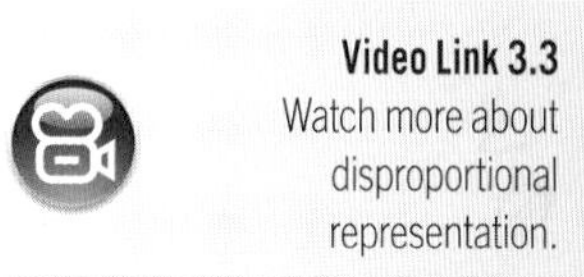

The fact that a disproportionate number of students from minority groups are enrolled in special education classrooms is a stinging indictment of the efficacy of the professional practices of special educators and a challenge to the concept of honoring diversity—presumably the cornerstone of our field (Meyer, Bevan-Brown, Park, & Savage, 2010). At the heart of the discussion about disproportional representation is the issue of inappropriate placement in special education programs. The primary concern is with false positives—when a pupil from a cultural or linguistic minority is identified as disabled when, in fact, he or she is *not* disabled and is therefore inappropriately placed in a class for students with disabilities. To ignore the gifts and talents of children from diverse backgrounds is equally damaging and denies them the opportunity to reach their full potential (Artiles & Zamora-Durán, 1997). Many complex factors and circumstances influence student placement; however, for those racially and ethnically diverse students who are misclassified and inappropriately placed or denied access to appropriate services, the outcomes are often serious and enduring (U.S. Department of Education, 1997).

It should be noted that the problem of overrepresentation does not occur across all categories of disabilities. The disproportionate presence of students from minority groups occurs only in those disability categories in which professional judgment and opinion play a role in the decision-making process, such as mild intellectual disabilities or behavior disorders. Overrepresentation is not a problem in disability areas that have a clear biological basis. For instance, sensory or motor impairments do not yield dramatically different proportions than one would anticipate on the basis of the ethnic composition of the general school population (Artiles, Kozleski, Trent, Osher, & Ortiz, 2010; Harry, 2008; Harry & Klinger, 2007; Skiba et al., 2008).

Office for Civil Rights Survey Data

The Office for Civil Rights (OCR) within the Department of Education has been concerned about over- and underrepresentation of minorities in special education programs since its creation in 1965. Since 1968, OCR has conducted biennial surveys of representative school districts across the United States in which enrollment patterns of children in special education classes are analyzed. Generally speaking, information gleaned from these surveys portrays "persistent patterns of minority students being disproportionately represented in special education programs and classes relative to their enrollment in the general school population" (U.S. Department of Education, 1997, p. I-42).

The classic Chinn and Hughes (1987) analysis of OCR reports for school years 1978, 1980, 1982, and 1984 reveals that the number of African American children in classes for students with mild intellectual disabilities (mental retardation) was approximately twice as large as one would expect on the basis of their percentage of the total school population. A similar pattern was found for the disability areas of behavior disorders and moderate intellectual disabilities. The representation of African American children in programs for learners who are gifted and talented, however, was disproportionately low. Native American students also had disproportionately high representation in classes for students with learning disabilities and disproportionately low representation in programs for the gifted and talented. In contrast, almost twice as many Asian and Pacific Islander children were attending classes for pupils identified as gifted and talented as would be expected on the basis of their proportion of total school enrollment; in almost every other category, this group was underrepresented. White students, too, were consistently underrepresented in classes for students with mild and moderate intellectual disabilities and overrepresented in classes for gifted and talented youth. The representation of Hispanic youngsters was disproportionately low across all categories of exceptionality.

The 1998–1999 school year was the first time that the states were required to report the race and ethnicity of students with disabilities served under IDEA. Table 3.1 presents recent information on the percentage and number of students receiving a special education in representative disability categories according to race. Although black students represent only about 20 percent of the total enrollment in special education programs, approximately 31 percent of the pupils in classes for students with mental retardation (intellectual disabilities) are African American. Interestingly, fewer black children are enrolled in programs for pupils with hearing impairments than one might expect based

TABLE 3.1 Number and Percentage of Students Ages 6–21 Receiving a Special Education in Select Disability Categories

Disability		American Indian/Alaskan Native	Asian/ Pacific Islander	Black	Hispanic	White	Total
Specific Learning Disabilities	*N*	44,791	47,226	529,064	620,018	1,372,496	2,613,595
	%	1.71	1.81	20.24	23.72	52.51	
Speech or Language Impairments	*N*	15,715	37,644	175,051	223,685	698,701	1,150,796
	%	1.37	3.27	15.21	19.44	60.71	
Mental Retardation	*N*	6,416	10,902	155,383	83,007	240,596	496,304
	%	1.29	2.20	31.31	16.73	48.48	
Emotional Disturbance	*N*	7,029	5,143	126,432	51,706	248,046	438,356
	%	1.60	1.17	28.84	11.80	56.59	
Hearing Impairments	*N*	862	3,826	11,529	17,401	38,365	71,983
	%	1.20	5.32	16.02	24.17	53.30	
Traumatic Brain Injury	*N*	370	585	3,877	3,231	15,734	23,797
	%	1.55	2.46	16.29	13.58	66.12	
All Disabilities	*N*	90,820	138,906	1,209,387	1,150,132	3,399,891	5,989,136
	%	1.52	2.32	20.19	19.20	56.77	

NOTE: Information is for the 2007–2008 school year.

Based on data from the fifty states, Puerto Rico, the District of Columbia, and outlying areas.

Due to rounding, percentages do not always add to 100 percent.

SOURCE: U.S. Department of Education. (2009). *IDEA data.* Retrieved August 10, 2009, from http://www.ideadata.org/PartBReport.asp

on their contribution to the total special education population. Additional representative comparisons can be found in the table.

Bicard and Heward (2010) wisely note that

> the fact that culturally [and linguistically] diverse students are identified as having disabilities is not in itself a problem. . . . Disproportionate representation is problematic, however, if students have been wrongly placed in special education, are segregated and stigmatized, or are denied access to special education because their disabilities are overlooked as a result of their membership in a racial or ethnic minority group. (pp. 333–334)

The entire issue of representational discrepancies is subject to debate and controversy. Harry (1992), for instance, does not believe that placement rates in special education programs for Native American and Hispanic students are suggestive of overrepresentation when examined nationally. At the individual state and local level, however, a different picture emerges. Like Benner (1998), she argues that placement statistics must be examined cautiously and kept in perspective. In the opinion of Benner and Harry, the larger the enrollment of pupils from minority groups within a school district, the greater their representation will be in special education classrooms. This is to be expected. Furthermore, the larger the education program, the greater the likelihood of disproportionate representation. Harry sees this phenomenon as a classic "chicken-and-egg" question. "While large numbers of minority children may lead to a perceived need for more special education programs, it may also be that the greater availability of programs encourages increased placement of minority children" (p. 66).

These precautionary observations notwithstanding, the misclassification and/or inappropriate placement of minority students in special education programs frequently leads to stigmatization and lower expectations. This is especially true when a pupil is removed from the general education setting and consequently denied access to the general education curriculum, which often results in limited postsecondary educational and employment opportunities. In some school systems, the disproportionate representation of these students also results in significant racial separation.

Factors Contributing to Over- and Underrepresentation

A myriad of explanations have been put forth to explain the problem of over- and underrepresentation of culturally diverse students in some categories of special education. No one explanation fully accounts for this situation; the various reasons are complex and frequently intertwined. Scholars (Artiles et al., 2010; Harry & Klinger, 2006) often see this problem as deeply rooted in the commingling of socioeconomic, sociocultural, and sociopolitical forces.

The overrepresentation of children of color is perhaps best understood as a relationship between family socioeconomic status and disability rather than between disability and minority group status per se. Individuals from minority groups typically populate urban centers and tend to be poor. Poverty and ethnicity are inextricably interwoven variables in American society (Artiles & Bal, 2008; Artiles et al., 2010; Donovan & Cross, 2002). Report after report and survey after survey routinely indicate an overrepresentation of minority groups living in poverty. According to the Children's Defense Fund (2008), over 13 million children, or nearly one out of every five youngsters, live in poverty.

Key Facts About America's Children

- A child is born into poverty every thirty-three seconds.
- 17 percent of children (12.5 million) receive food stamps.
- 62 percent of children under the age of six have both parents in the workforce.
- 11 percent of children (8.9 million) are without health insurance.
- 68 percent of fourth graders in public schools read below grade level.

SOURCE: Children's Defense Fund, *Children in the United States*, November 2008. Available at www.childrensdefense.org/

Poverty often means limited access to health care (especially prenatal care), poor nutrition, and adverse living conditions. All of these variables increase the probability of a child being at risk for learning and developmental difficulties. Cultural and language differences only exacerbate the student's vulnerability, increasing the likelihood of educational failure and his or her need for special education services (Gargiulo & Kilgo, 2011).

The evidence strongly suggests that socioeconomic status rather than ethnicity is one of the primary reasons that students from racially and ethnically diverse populations encounter persistent academic problems in the public schools (MacMillan & Reschly, 1998). Poverty, however, is not the only culprit contributing to the disproportional representation of minorities in some special education programs. Faulty identification procedures, ineffective prereferral strategies, test bias, and inappropriate assessment techniques may also account for some of the overrepresentation. The lack of standardized tests appropriate for use with students who have limited English proficiency is another contributing factor (Coutinho & Oswald, 2000; Voltz, 1998). Although, as Winzer and Mazurek (1998) point out, biased and discriminatory assessment instruments do play a role, these factors alone are insufficient to account for the misplacement and disproportionate representation of pupils from minority groups in special education classes. Other relevant variables include teacher bias, different behavioral and academic performance standards for students from minority populations, and incongruity or discrepancy between the child's home culture and school expectations. For example, behaviors considered adaptive in a student's home, such as nonassertiveness and cooperation, may conflict with expectations in the classroom, where independence and competition are valued.

Incongruity may also exist in instructional methodology. Research has demonstrated that children from minority groups learn differently than white youngsters. African

Poverty and ethnicity are inextricably interwoven aspects of American society.

American pupils, for example, tend to be **field dependent/sensitive** (relational, global) learners who approach learning intuitively rather than analytically and logically (Banks, 2010; Ford, 1998). These students perform better in social settings like those found in cooperative learning environments and group work (Gollnick & Chinn, 2009). In contrast, white students and Asian/Pacific Islanders are typically **field independent** (detail-oriented and analytically inclined) learners who thrive in competitive settings where achievement and individual accomplishment are prized.

White teachers, as a whole, are typically field independent, whereas educators from minority populations are more likely to be field dependent. The lack of congruency between the cognitive style of many culturally diverse students and that of their teachers is another possible reason for disproportional representation. Teachers often perceive pupils with cognitive styles different from their own in negative ways. This, of course, exacerbates the student's learning problems. This incongruity frequently causes teachers to overlook a youngster's strengths and abilities and increases the likelihood of a referral for special education services. By the same token, a teacher may fail to recognize the attributes of the brightest pupils and thus be less likely to refer them to programs for students with special gifts and talents.

The reasons for the underrepresentation of certain groups in programs for the gifted and talented are as varied as the explanations for overrepresentation in other programs. Benner (1998) suggests that relevant factors include the politics of race and social class, attitudinal bias, and pressure from peers not to excel academically. Ford (1998) cites problems related to screening and identification, low teacher expectations and negative perceptions of minority pupils, and a lack of teacher training in the area of gifted education.

Consequences of Disproportional Representation

The over- and underenrollment of racial and ethnic minorities in some special education programs often leads to unequal educational opportunities. In many instances, removal from the general education classroom and assignment to a special education classroom results in an inferior and ineffective educational experience for these children (Donovan & Cross, 2002; Harry & Klinger, 2007). The educational experiences of racially, ethnically, and culturally diverse pupils often put them at risk for underachievement and dropping out of school. In comparison to their white peers, students from ethnically and racially diverse backgrounds drop out of school at a much higher rate. In the 2007 school year, the dropout rate for Hispanic youth (19.9 percent) was over three times the rate for white pupils (6.1 percent). About 12 percent of African American students leave school before completing their education (National Center for Education Statistics, 2009b). Adolescents who fail to graduate are more likely to be unemployed and constitute a disproportionate percentage of the incarcerated population (Amos, 2008).

The disproportionately high representation of racial and ethnic minorities as well as culturally and linguistically diverse students in some special education classrooms is a problem that has plagued educators for more than thirty years. Unfortunately, the debate over disproportionate representation, inappropriate placement, and misclassification of minority pupils is far from being resolved. However, advocates, policymakers, researchers, educators, and parents have moved beyond the mere condemnation of this long-standing and complex problem to seek solutions. Yet solutions to the issue of greater educational opportunity and quality of education remain elusive. A multifaceted, broad-based attack is necessary. Attention needs to be focused on the identification and referral process, assessment bias, instructional factors, and teacher attitudes, as well as environmental factors impinging on the student and the interrelationships among these variables.

Issues in Assessing Students From Culturally and Linguistically Diverse Groups

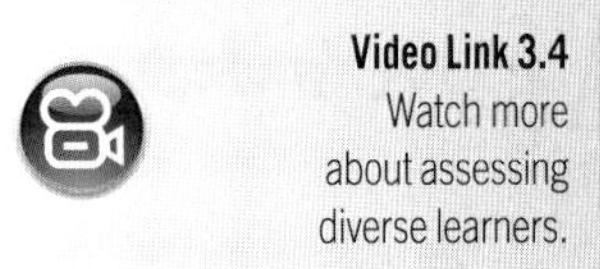

With the number of pupils from culturally and linguistically diverse backgrounds expected to grow to 40 percent of the projected school-age population in 2020 (National Center for Education Statistics, 2007b), teachers can expect to encounter an especially challenging and difficult task—accurately assessing children from diverse cultures for disabilities. The appropriate assessment of all students has been a long-standing concern among special educators, but it is an especially critical issue for youngsters from minority populations. Assessment is the primary vehicle through which access to services is determined and progress is evaluated, using a variety of formal and informal means. We consider assessment to be a dynamic, multifaceted, multipurpose decision-making process whose primary goal is to evaluate the academic and behavioral progress of a student. Table 3.2 identifies some of the outcomes of this process for children from diverse cultural backgrounds.

Assessment of students from culturally and linguistically diverse backgrounds is both controversial and problematic (Utley & Obiakor, 2001). Because of the inherent difficulties, assessment of these learners has been characterized as "random chaos" (Figueroa, 1989). The absence of best practice guidelines for evaluating language minority and

TABLE 3.2 Assessment Outcomes for Culturally and Linguistically Diverse Students

- An accurate appraisal of a child's level and mode of functioning within the context of the child's cultural experiences
- A focus on a child's strengths and abilities as a basis for the development of new skills
- Identification of a child's specific educational needs, including both first and second language acquisition
- Literacy and basic level skills evaluation, especially for students who lack educational experiences
- Identification of emotional difficulties
- Generation of data that may be used for placement decisions and the formulation of an individual education program, if necessary

SOURCE: M. Winzer and K. Mazurek, *Special Education in Multicultural Contexts* (Upper Saddle River, NJ: Prentice Hall, 1998), pp. 177–178.

culturally diverse pupils results in a complicated and confusing assignment for teachers and other service providers.

Inappropriate assessment measures and evaluation procedures are thought to be one of the primary reasons for the disproportionate representation of culturally and linguistically diverse students in various special education programs. Concerns focus mainly on the use of standardized testing with this population, especially standardized tests of intelligence. Recall from Chapter 2 that the *Larry P.* and *Diana* lawsuits centered around claims that IQ tests were inherently unfair to students from minority groups and thus resulted in the misidentification and inaccurate labeling of these pupils, resulting in an inappropriate education.

Standardized testing has frequently been criticized for its failure to consider the cultural and experiential background of culturally and linguistically diverse students. A disregard for the life experiences of these students results in an unfair evaluation and a depressed portrayal of their ability. Remember, not all children approach a testing situation with homogeneous backgrounds or a reservoir of similar life experiences. "A student who has no experience with an item presented on a test or has experienced it differently is apt to answer the question incorrectly" (Council for Exceptional Children, 1997, p. 9). For instance, a 10-year-old from Hawaii, a state where there are no snakes, may have difficulty answering a question about rattlesnakes, whereas a youngster from New Mexico is very likely to be familiar with this creature. Likewise, an adolescent from rural Alabama who is asked about ice fishing is much less likely to answer the question correctly than his cousin from northern Wisconsin. Gollnick and Chinn (2009) believe that the use of standardized tests with children from minority groups measures only their degree of cultural assimilation, not their intelligence.

life experience

Assessment Challenges

There are several roadblocks to the goal of achieving meaningful and valid assessments of students who are culturally and linguistically diverse. Foremost is the lack of measurement tools that provide an accurate assessment of these students' abilities. Many standardized tests are simply not available in languages other than English or in appropriate dialects. Coupled with this problem is the issue of bias in the assessment process. All tests are biased to some degree; it is an unavoidable artifact of psychometric evaluation. Yet some of these unwanted influences are of greater concern than others. As a result of bias, test scores are frequently rendered

Suggestions for the Classroom

Recommendations for Assessing Culturally and Linguistically Diverse Pupils

- ☑ Assessment of an individual's language competency in both English and his or her native language should be completed before administering other tests.
- ☑ In order to be eligible for a special education, a student must exhibit a disability when evaluated in his or her native language.
- ☑ Schools should incorporate ecological assessments that include not only multiple evaluation tools familiar to the examiner but also information gathered from the student's teachers, the student's parents, and the student.
- ☑ Evaluators should use evaluation techniques that are as unbiased as possible. For example, a bilingual professional, not an interpreter, should administer the test.
- ☑ If a bilingual professional is unavailable, an interpreter may be used if he or she is first trained in assessment principles and terminology.
- ☑ Parents and other stakeholders should be involved when developing alternative assessments.

suspect and may not reflect an accurate appraisal of the student's ability or skill. Linn, Miller, and Gronlund (2010) note that bias may involve extrinsic variables, such as the child's response style or the value attached to competitive behavior in the pupil's culture. Intrinsic bias factors are difficulties with the instruments themselves, such as culturally bound test items (recall our rattlesnake example) or normative sampling issues. Bias can also come from several other sources, some of which are external to the child and others internal, such as issues of test validity and reliability when tests are translated; a lack of test-taking skills such as performing under time constraints, motivation, and appropriate response selection strategies; and other issues in addition to the obvious concern of linguistic bias when the student's primary language is not English. Individually and collectively, these sources of bias often result in incorrect assumptions about a student's abilities and may lead, in turn, to an inappropriate educational placement.

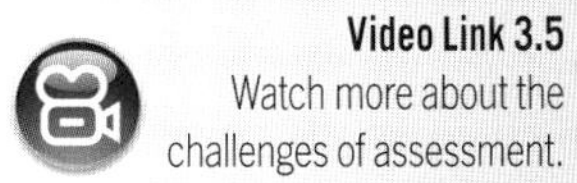

Video Link 3.5
Watch more about the challenges of assessment.

Assessment Safeguards

Professionals are fully aware of the importance of obtaining an accurate profile of an individual's strengths and weaknesses. To accomplish this goal and to minimize potential for abuses in the assessment process, PL 94–142 and its subsequent amendments contain several procedural safeguards. Realizing that nonbiased evaluations are crucial to special education, the framers of IDEA mandated **nondiscriminatory testing**. School districts are required to adopt

> procedures to assure that testing and evaluation materials and procedures utilized for the evaluation and placement of children with disabilities will be selected and administered so as not to be racially or culturally discriminatory. Such materials or procedures shall be provided and administered in the child's native language or mode of communication, unless it is clearly not feasible to do so, and no single procedure shall be the sole criterion for determining an appropriate educational program for a child. (20 U.S.C. § 1412 [5] [C])

In addition, students are to be assessed by trained personnel who are part of a multidisciplinary team that is responsible for the evaluation. Written communications with the pupil's parents are to be provided in the parents' native language.

Because of bias, test scores may be suspect and may not reflect an accurate appraisal of a child's disability.

Assessment Innovations

Professionals have long recognized that bias is a very real threat to the assessment process, especially for persons from culturally and linguistically diverse groups. Concern about this problem has resulted in efforts at minimizing test bias. Although a completely nonbiased or culture-fair assessment is unlikely, initial attempts at reducing bias focused on the instruments themselves. Many tests were revised in an effort to reduce the number of culturally specific test items (content bias) and the reliance on culturally specific language. Tests were also renormed, or restandardized, to reflect the growing diversity of American schoolchildren. Even the testing environment and the race of the examiner and his or her interactions with the student have come under scrutiny.

The primary purpose of these modifications has been to obtain a more accurate picture of a student's abilities, especially for pupils from culturally and linguistically diverse populations. The search for solutions to the problem of test bias has resulted in the development of pluralistic assessment techniques that are meant to be sensitive to the cultural and linguistic characteristics of children from minority groups. One example of this effort is the Kaufman Assessment Battery for Children (K-ABC) II designed by Kaufman and Kaufman (2004).

The K-ABC is used to assess children between 3 and 18 years of age. This instrument was normed on groups of white, Hispanic, African American, Native American, and Asian American children in addition to a population of individuals with disabilities. The K-ABC minimizes a student's verbal skills and abilities, thus enhancing its usefulness with children with limited English proficiency. A Spanish version is also available.

Concern about test bias has also resulted in an expanded understanding of the concept of intelligence. IQ tests have traditionally looked at intelligence in a somewhat narrow and restricted fashion, limiting the performance of many students. For instance, success in the classroom often depends on linguistic intelligence, an area in which many students from culturally and linguistically diverse backgrounds are deficient. Gardner (1983, 1993, 2006), however, argues for the concept of **multiple intelligences.** According to his theory, problem solving involves eight different, though somewhat related and interactive, intelligences:

- Verbal/linguistic
- Musical/rhythmic
- Bodily/kinesthetic
- Interpersonal

- Logical/mathematical
- Visual/spatial
- Intrapersonal
- Naturalist

His ideas have gained widespread acceptance among practitioners but, unfortunately, have received little attention from publishers of standardized tests (de Valenzuela & Baca, 2004). We believe that Gardner's theory has considerable merit. As educators, we need to stop thinking about how smart a student is and start asking, "*How* is the child smart?"

Contemporary Assessment Strategies

Many school districts are searching for better ways of assessing the growing population of students who are culturally and linguistically diverse. One particularly promising practice is the movement toward more authentic, performance-based assessment strategies such as **portfolio assessment** (Friend & Bursuck, 2009). This innovation could possibly help in resolving the problem of the over- and underrepresentation of language and ethnic minorities in some special education programs. This alternative assessment model is a relatively new idea for educators, although architects and graphic artists have been demonstrating their skills and competencies via work products for years.

Portfolio assessment is uniquely intriguing because it emphasizes the instructional environment and focuses on student performance and the outcomes of learning (McLoughlin & Lewis, 2008). Unlike infrequent or one-time standardized testing, performance-based assessment relies on the pupil's learning experiences and evaluates meaningful, real-world tasks using multiple performance indicators such as writing samples, speeches, artwork, videotapes, and work samples gathered over time and collected in a portfolio. Authentic assessments are relevant and culturally responsive assessments (Gargiulo & Metcalf, 2010).

Portfolios are able to document, in a tangible way, a student's developmental progress. They can pinpoint areas of strength and weakness, thus facilitating instructional intervention. It is our opinion that portfolio assessment has great potential for meeting the needs of students who are culturally and linguistically diverse, especially those with disabilities. Information gleaned from portfolios typically results in more numerous, more specific, and more detailed recommendations and judgments about a child than does information derived from traditional, standardized testing (Linn et al., 2010).

Portfolio assessment, of course, is not the complete solution to eliminating bias in the assessment of culturally and linguistically diverse children. Several questions and concerns about this performance-based measure remain unanswered. Does portfolio assessment result in a fairer and more accurate portrayal of students from minority groups? Do portfolio data generate decisions about these students that differ from those formulated around the results of traditional testing? What is the basis for our standards or benchmarks? Do teachers use individual standards, or are comparisons based on districtwide, statewide, or even national performance indicators? The answers to these and other questions await further research evidence.

We believe that portfolio assessment should be an integral component of the assessment process. It represents an exciting alternative to assessing learning and the funds of student knowledge.

Assessment Recommendations

Accurately assessing students from culturally and linguistically diverse backgrounds presents many challenges for professionals. Issues of language, test bias, and other such matters are of real concern because they affect assessment results, which in turn affect educational decision making. Completely fair and nonbiased assessments may not be possible, but professionals can at least minimize those variables that may influence performance outcomes. The recommendations (Council for Exceptional Children, 1997; Ortiz & Yates, 1988) in the accompanying Suggestions for the Classroom represent attempts at achieving authentic data and ensuring fairer, more accurate appraisals of culturally and linguistically diverse pupils and those with limited English proficiency.

Educational Programming for Students With Exceptionalities Who Are Culturally and Linguistically Diverse

Providing specific instructional strategies and tactics for students with disabilities who are culturally and linguistically diverse (and even pupils who are nondisabled) is an arduous, if not impossible, task. We can, however, offer some general suggestions for enhancing instructional effectiveness. Earlier we noted that effective teachers are sensitive to the cultural heritage of each student and attempt to provide educational experiences that are culturally relevant and appropriate. This is critically important. Our instructional practices must be culturally affirming, sensitive, and responsive. The pupil's cultural background should be seen as an instructional resource (Garcia & Ortiz, 2006; Shealey & Callins, 2007). A meaningful educational program must incorporate the individual's language and culture. The degree to which this integration occurs is a valid gauge of academic success.

A pupil's life experiences can be the building blocks or foundation for developing a curriculum that is authentic and culturally relevant. Programs and services for children who are culturally and linguistically diverse and exceptional should be crafted around the principles and purposes of multicultural education in an effort to create a supportive climate for learning (Gollnick & Chinn, 2009). Additionally, Hoover and Collier (2004) suggest that the instructional strategies identified in the IEP "exhibit culturally appropriate cues and reinforcements as well as culturally appropriate motivation and relevance" (p. 285). While attention to instructional strategies is crucial, effective programs for culturally and linguistically diverse students with exceptionalities must also consider the content (needed academic skills and knowledge), the instructional environment, and student behaviors, and how these elements reciprocally interact and are influenced by the pupil's linguistic and cultural heritage (Hoover & Patton, 2005; Voltz, Sims, Nelson, & Bivens, 2005). Meaningful IEPs for pupils with disabilities who also exhibit cultural and/or linguistic diversity should reflect goals and instructional strategies that are appropriate to the student's disability while also reflecting his or her language status.

Attainment of IEP goals depends, in part, on establishing a supportive learning environment. One way of enhancing the context in which teaching and learning occur is through the careful selection and evaluation of instructional materials. Materials that reflect the sociocultural, linguistic, and experiential backgrounds of the students increase the likelihood that children will respond to them in a positive manner (Gollnick & Chinn, 2009). The accompanying Suggestions for the Classroom feature presents several guidelines that educators should consider when evaluating materials for their classroom.

Effectively instructing students with exceptionalities who are also culturally and linguistically diverse requires that teachers provide experiences that are culturally appropriate and pertinent. Instructional success with children from diverse populations depends largely on the teacher's ability to construct meaningful pedagogical bridges that

Audio Link 3.1
Listen to how books show diversity.

Suggestions for the Classroom

Guidelines for Selecting and Evaluating Instructional Materials

- ☑ Are the perspectives and contributions of people from diverse cultural and linguistic groups—both men and women, as well as people with disabilities—included in the curriculum?
- ☑ Are there activities in the curriculum that will assist students in analyzing the various forms of the mass media for ethnocentrism, sexism, "handicapism," and stereotyping?
- ☑ Are men and women, diverse cultural/racial groups, and people with varying abilities shown in both active and passive roles?
- ☑ Are men and women, diverse cultural/racial groups, and people with disabilities shown in positions of power (i.e., the materials do not rely on the mainstream culture's character to achieve goals)?
- ☑ Do the materials identify strengths possessed by so-called underachieving diverse populations? Do they diminish the attention given to deficits, to reinforce positive behaviors that are desired and valued?
- ☑ Are members of diverse racial/cultural groups, men and women, and people with disabilities shown engaged in a broad range of social and professional activities?
- ☑ Are members of a particular culture or group depicted as having a range of physical features (e.g., hair color, hair texture, variations in facial characteristics and body build)?
- ☑ Do the materials represent historical events from the perspectives of the various groups involved or solely from the male, middle-class, and/or Western European perspective?
- ☑ Are the materials free of ethnocentric or sexist language patterns that may make implications about persons or groups based solely on their culture, race, gender, or disability?
- ☑ Will students from different ethnic and cultural backgrounds find the materials personally meaningful to their life experiences?
- ☑ Are a wide variety of culturally different examples, situations, scenarios, and anecdotes used throughout the curriculum design to illustrate major intellectual concepts and principles?
- ☑ Are culturally diverse content, examples, and experiences comparable in kind, significance, magnitude, and function to those selected from mainstream culture?

SOURCE: S. Garcia and D. Malkin, "Toward Defining Programs and Services for Culturally and Linguistically Diverse Learners in Special Education," *Teaching Exceptional Children, 26*(1), 1993, p. 55.

cross over different cultural systems (Garcia & Ortiz, 2006; Meyer et al., 2010). "When instruction and learning are compatible with a child's culture and when minority students' language and culture are incorporated into the school program, more effective learning takes place" (Winzer & Mazurek, 1998, p. vii).

CHAPTER IN REVIEW

Cultural Diversity: The Changing Face of a Nation

Audio Link 3.2
Listen to a chapter summary.

- Although the population of culturally and linguistically diverse students continues to grow, the diversity of the teaching workforce has failed to keep pace. About 80 percent of U.S. teachers are white, and it is projected that the teaching profession will become increasingly homogeneous over the next few years.
- The task of assimilating or "Americanizing" the children of immigrants was metaphorically described as a melting pot, whereby the various languages, beliefs, and customs of immigrants were melted away and replaced with a common American culture.
- In the latter part of the twentieth century, interest in cultural pluralism and multicultural education was sparked. U.S. society is now characterized metaphorically as a floral bouquet or patchwork quilt; cultural and ethnic differences are valued and respected.

Multicultural Education, Bilingual Education, and Student Diversity

- Multicultural education addresses issues of race, language, social class, and culture as well as disability and gender.
- Bilingual education is an educational strategy whereby students whose first language is not English are instructed primarily through their native language while developing competency and proficiency in English.
- *Limited English proficient* is a term used to describe individuals with a reduced fluency in reading, writing, or speaking English.
- Bilingual special education services embrace the use of the pupil's primary language and culture coupled with an individually tailored program of special instruction.

Disproportional Representation of Minority Students in Special Education Programs

- Historically, greater numbers of children from minority groups have been placed in special education classrooms than would be anticipated based on their proportion of the school population. This situation is commonly referred to as overrepresentation. Underrepresentation in certain programs, or fewer students than one would anticipate based on their numbers in the school population, is also a problem.
- The overrepresentation of children of color is perhaps best understood as a relationship between socioeconomic status and disability rather than between minority group membership and disability.
- Test bias, teacher expectations and bias, and incongruity in instructional methodology and cognitive styles may also account for this phenomenon.

Issues in Assessing Students From Culturally and Linguistically Diverse Groups

- Some of the barriers to achieving meaningful and valid assessments of students from culturally and linguistically diverse backgrounds are the lack of appropriate measurement tools and bias in the assessment process.
- Federal law requires that professionals use nondiscriminatory testing practices when evaluating pupils for possible special education placement.
- Some professionals have expanded their understanding of the notion of intelligence and argue for the concept of multiple intelligences.
- Another attempt at meaningful assessment of students from culturally and linguistically diverse backgrounds is a movement toward authentic, performance-based assessment techniques such as portfolio assessment.

Educational Programming for Students With Exceptionalities Who Are Culturally and Linguistically Diverse

- The child's cultural and linguistic heritage must be reflected in his or her IEP if instructional strategies are to be effective. The instructional materials should also mirror the sociocultural, linguistic, and experiential backgrounds of the students.

STUDY QUESTIONS

1. What do the terms *culture* and *cultural diversity* mean to you?
2. At one time, the United States was described as a melting pot. Why? Metaphorically speaking, American society is now characterized as a floral bouquet or patchwork quilt. What factors contributed to this change in thinking?
3. Define the following terms: *cultural pluralism, multicultural education*, and *bilingual education*.
4. Why is bilingual education a controversial topic?
5. Compare and contrast the various instructional models used with students who are bilingual.
6. Explain why pupils from minority groups experience disproportional representation in some special education programs.
7. What are the consequences of disproportional representation?
8. Why is the assessment of culturally and linguistically diverse students perceived to be problematic? How might these difficulties be corrected?
9. Define portfolio assessment. Identify the advantages of this strategy for evaluating the performance of children who are culturally and linguistically diverse.

KEY TERMS

melting pot 88
cultural pluralism 88
culture 88
multiculturalism 89
multicultural education 89
bilingual education 89
ethnocentrism 90
macroculture 91
microcultures 91
limited English proficient (LEP) 92
bilingual special education 96
overrepresentation 97
underrepresentation 97
field dependent/sensitive 101
field independent 101
nondiscriminatory testing 104
multiple intelligences 105
portfolio assessment 106

LEARNING ACTIVITIES

1. Talk to a school psychologist, an educational diagnostician, or another assessment specialist about strategies and procedures used when evaluating students from a culturally or linguistically diverse background. What types of modifications, if any, does he or she use? Does he or she have any concerns about the validity of the assessment process? What is his or her opinion about alternative assessments such as portfolios?
2. Visit several different schools in your area. Interview administrators or teachers about services available for pupils from culturally and linguistically diverse groups. Is there a problem of over- and underrepresentation in special education classes? What types of modifications are available to meet the needs of these pupils? How are parents and other family members involved in the school? Is multicultural education reflected in the school environment?
3. Attend various functions sponsored by ethnic groups in your community. Activities may include musical programs, art exhibitions, festivals, religious celebrations, school functions, and other ceremonies. How did you feel about participating in these activities? What did you learn as a result of your involvement? Were your personal viewpoints and stereotypes challenged as a result of this experience?

REFLECTING ON STANDARDS

The following exercises are designed to help you learn to apply the Council for Exceptional Children (CEC) standards to your teaching practice. Each of the reflection exercises below correlates with a knowledge or skill within the CEC standards. For the full text of each of the related CEC standards, please refer to the standards integration grid located in Appendix B.

Focus on Learning Environments and Social Interactions ***(CEC Content Standard #5 CC5S1)***
Reflect on your own culture and how you interact with people of other cultures. In what ways would you share your cultural background with your students? What strategies would you use to help your students appreciate their own cultural background and value the cultural diversity of others?

Focus on Professional and Ethical Practice ***(CEC Content Standard #9 CC9K1)***
Reflect on what personal cultural biases you have. How might these biases affect your teaching? If possible, find an assessment to help you understand what hidden cultural biases you might have. Talk to colleagues, family, and friends to try and understand what biases you have that might hinder your teaching.

STUDENT STUDY SITE

Visit the Student Study Site at www.sagepub.com/gargiulo4emedia for these additional learning tools:

- Video links
- Media links
- Self-quizzes
- E-flashcards
- Full-text SAGE journal articles
- Web exercises

Answer Key to Cultural and Linguistic Diversity Quiz on p. 86

1. True
2. True
3. False
4. False
5. False
6. False
7. True
8. True
9. False
10. True
11. True
12. True

CHAPTER 4

Learning Objectives

After reading Chapter 4 you should be able to:

- Outline the evolution of parent–professional partnerships.
- Describe the four key elements of a family systems model for understanding the impact of a disability on the family constellation.
- List the emotional responses associated with the stages of parents' reaction to their child's disability.
- Summarize the effects of an individual with a disability on family members.
- Explain how a family's cultural and linguistic background influences its reaction to a disability.

Parents, Families, and Exceptionality

The family is our most fundamental social institution, the cornerstone of our society. It is also the primary arena in which an individual, whether disabled or not, is socialized, educated, and exposed to the beliefs and values of his or her culture. This crucial responsibility is generally assumed by the youngster's parents, who serve as principal caregivers and the child's first teachers. In this chapter, when we refer to a parent, we mean any adult who fulfills these essential caregiving duties and responsibilities for a particular child.

Video Link 4.1
Watch more about family.

Being a parent of a child with a disability is not a role most parents willingly choose for themselves. Generally speaking, few individuals ever ask to be a parent of a person with special needs, and most parents are never fully prepared for this tremendous responsibility. Parenting a child with a disability can be a difficult, demanding, and confusing job; yet we believe it is a role that can also be filled with joy, triumphs, and satisfaction.

Although exceptionality can certainly change the ecology of the family and the interactions that occur within it, the role of the family, and of the parents in particular, remains essentially the same. Stated another way, although each family is unique, in the majority of instances professionals are primarily working with just another family—not a family that is dysfunctional. We believe it is important for teachers and other service providers to focus on the strengths and the resources of the family and not concentrate solely on the challenges and stresses that are sometimes experienced by families with a child who has a disability.

Video Link 4.2
Meet the parent of a child with special needs.

The purpose of this chapter is to more fully explore the issue of parent–professional partnerships and to examine the interactive relationship of exceptionality and its impact on the family. We have adopted a family systems approach to guide us on our journey. We will also explore the topic of cultural and linguistic diversity as it pertains to families and exceptionality. We conclude with suggestions for facilitating parent–professional partnerships.

Parent–Professional Relationships: Changing Roles

Many teachers believe that parental involvement is crucial to the success of the educational experience, especially for children with disabilities. Parents are a valuable resource for professionals; in comparison to teachers and other service providers, parents

TABLE 4.3 Emotional Responses of Children Toward Siblings With a Disability

Resentment	Perhaps the most common reaction experienced by typical siblings is resentment. It is a natural by-product of being angry about having a brother or sister with a disability. Resentment may develop because the child with special needs may require a disproportionate amount of the parents' attention. This sibling may also prohibit the family from participating in certain experiences or excursions. Special treatments and/or therapy may contribute to family financial hardship. Older siblings may resent having to babysit, or having social constraints placed upon them by their younger brother or sister who is disabled.
Jealousy	Resentment can easily develop into jealousy, especially if the typical sibling perceives that he or she has lost "favor" with the parents. The brother or sister with a disability may become a rival or competitor for the parents' attention and affection. Often the typical sibling will engage in behaviors designed to secure parental attention, such as having academic or behavioral problems in school, telling lies, or exhibiting unusual mischievousness.
Hostility	From feelings of jealousy often comes hostility, which is a perfectly natural reaction. Unlike objective adults, children are subjective and consider events in terms of how they are personally affected. They may view their brother or sister with special needs, rather than the disability, as the source of all their problems. Therefore, feelings of hostility are usually aimed toward their sibling. These feelings may manifest themselves in physical aggression or verbal harassment and ridicule. In some instances, hostility is directed toward the parents through acts of disobedience or impertinence.
Guilt	Siblings without disabilities frequently evidence feelings of guilt; however, these reactions differ from the parents'. Their guilt may stem from the negative feelings they have about their brother or sister, or it may be a consequence of having mistreated their sibling. Furthermore, when viewing their sibling who has an impairment, some children experience guilt because of their own good fortune to be thought of as typical.
Grief	Siblings frequently grieve for their brother or sister who is disabled. Their grief is often a reflection of their parents' sorrow. They grieve not for what they have lost, but for what will possibly be denied to their sibling.
Fear	Typical siblings may also experience fear. They may be fearful of acquiring a disability or of their own future children being disabled. A further worry is that someday they may have to assume total responsibility for the care of their sibling.
Shame and embarrassment	Shame and embarrassment are common emotional responses of typical siblings. A child may be ashamed of his brother or sister who is intellectually disabled, embarrassed to have friends visit, or embarrassed to be seen in public with his or her sibling.
Rejection	In some families, siblings who are typical may reject their brother or sister with a disability. They may reject the reality of the impairment. More commonly, however, rejection is shown by withholding affection or ignoring the sibling's existence.

SOURCE: Adapted from R. Gargiulo, *Working with Parents of Exceptional Children: A Guide for Professionals* (Boston: Houghton Mifflin, 1985), pp. 51–52.

investigation of siblings of children with mental retardation notes such benefits as greater tolerance toward others, increased compassion, and higher levels of empathy and altruism as a result of growing up with a brother or sister with a disability. Meyer's (2009) more recent work also poignantly validates the many positive aspects experienced by siblings of individuals with special needs.

Siblings typically exhibit a myriad of feelings toward a brother or sister with special needs. The accompanying First Person feature vividly captures some of these emotions. Table 4.3 gives examples of some of the reactions and feelings sustained by brothers and sisters of children with disabilities.

First Person: Mindy
The Other Children

I first remember having a sense of special responsibility for my deaf sister when I was 3. It was my duty to keep her out of danger and mischief—a seemingly normal responsibility for an older sister. But the responsibility has at times felt unbearably heavy. As a 2-year-old, Mindy was not only typically rambunctious, she lived in a bizarre and often dangerous world all her own—separated from the rest of us by her deafness and her inability to communicate. It was a world of fascinating objects to handle, of races with Mother, Daddy, and big sister—a world, even, of nocturnal romps in the street while the rest of the family slept. And once, it was a world of pretty colored pills in the bathroom medicine cabinet.

"Second Mother" to Mindy

When Daddy spent a year in Korea, I became Mother's sole helper. My role as a second mother to Mindy held some prestige and much responsibility. It took away from play time with children my own age. And, just as a mother serves as an example for her children, I was expected to be an exceptionally "good" little girl. The high standards my mother set for my behavior, though, had not only to do with my setting an example; her reasons were also practical. Mindy's impetuous behavior left her with little patience, energy, or time to put up with shenanigans from me. As I got older, problems resulting from my having a deaf sister increased. My mother began to attend college, and the new pressures and demands caused her to be demanding and dependent upon me. I did not understand why I would be severely chastised for the same behavior that Mindy, who embodied the behavior problems of three children, "couldn't help." My friends' parents seemed less critical of their children than my parents were of me. Mother and Daddy "expected more" from me, but it seemed to me that they gave me less. The responsibility I felt for Mindy was tremendous. One year, when my "baby-sitting" duties involved periodic checking on my sister, Mindy wandered away between checks. After a thorough but fruitless search of the neighborhood, my mother hysterically told me that if anything happened to Mindy I would be to blame. I felt terrified and guilty. I was 7.

Competition and Rivalry

Mindy's achievements always met with animated enthusiasm from our parents. In contrast, it seemed, Mother and Daddy's response to my accomplishments were on the pat-on-the-back level. I was expected to perform well in every circumstance. I wanted my parents to be enthusiastic about my accomplishments too. I didn't want to have to beg for praise. I didn't want to be taken for granted. I wanted to be noticed.

Babysitter and Manager

When I was not baby-sitting, there was my role of "fetch and carry"—sometimes literally. Mindy's deafness prevented my parents from calling to her so I was appointed official messenger. "Go tell Mindy to come to dinner." "Go tell Mindy to come inside." "Go tell Mindy to clean up her room." At first I probably gloried a bit in my "authority." But that soon grew stale. I was expected to stop whatever I was doing and bear some message to Mindy. And I discovered that like the royal messengers of old, bearers of orders or bad tidings are not cordially received. In retaliation against the inconvenience and hostile receptions, I made a point of being as bossy in my deliveries as possible—which resulted in acute mutual aggravation.

Love and Respect

In my junior year of high school, Mindy and I began to grow close as sisters. Our increased maturity and the circumstances of our father's being away in Vietnam caused us to turn to one another for companionship and comfort. In the process, we began to discover one another as individuals. We took time to understand our mutual antagonisms and to forgive each other a little. Mindy now understands that as a child my responsibility for her was immense and often intolerable, and that she thoughtlessly made it more difficult for me. She has forgiven me for the hurt and resentment I caused her. Differences between us will always exist, but Mindy and I now understand and respect each other's needs without resentment. The impact a disabled child has upon the other children in a family is tremendous—in both a positive and negative sense. Parents must not expect sainthood from their "other children." Most likely many years will pass before their nondisabled children fully understand why their sister or brother "couldn't help it," why they were expected to be model children, why attention from their parents was rationed, and why their parents sometimes seemed unduly critical and impatient. Until the "other children" do understand, their reactions may be "thoughtless" or "unfair." Before love can replace misunderstanding and intolerance, resentment must be recognized and accepted as a legitimate and even inevitable part of the struggle of growing up together.

SOURCE: V. Hayden, "The Other Children," *Exceptional Parent, 4*, 1974, pp. 26–29.

Disability and the Family

- The entire family constellation is affected by the presence of a child with a disability. The various subsystems and individual family members are uniquely impacted. No two families are likely to deal with an exceptionality in quite the same way.

Working With Families Who Are Culturally and Linguistically Diverse

- If the values, traditions, and beliefs of caregivers from culturally and linguistically diverse backgrounds are not addressed, then the development of optimal relationships will very likely be hindered.
- Teachers must exhibit culturally sensitive behavior when working with families whose backgrounds differ from their own.

Suggestions for Facilitating Family and Professional Partnerships

- In order to establish meaningful and effective alliances with families with children who are disabled, it is recommended that professionals create partnerships built around the principles of honesty, trust, and respect.
- Service providers must be genuine and exhibit a caring attitude, using active listening when communicating with family members and other significant adults.

STUDY QUESTIONS

1. How has the relationship between parents and professionals changed over the years? What circumstances have aided this process?
2. What was the purpose of the eugenics movement, and how did it affect relationships between professionals and parents?
3. Why do professionals currently believe that efforts should be directed toward working with families of children with special needs instead of just parents?
4. Define the term *collaboration* as it pertains to professionals and parents.
5. What is the rationale behind a family systems model?
6. Identify the four key components of the Turnbull family systems framework. Explain the characteristics of each of these elements.
7. How does the concept of cohesion differ from adaptability in the Turnbull model?
8. What are the stages of emotional response that many parents go through when informed that their child has a disability? Give examples of the types of behavior typically exhibited at each stage.
9. What cautions does Gargiulo stress when applying a stage theory model to parents of children with disabilities?
10. In what ways might a child with a disability affect his or her family?
11. What does the research literature suggest about the impact of childhood disability on marital relationships, mothers, fathers, siblings, and grandparents of children with special needs?
12. Name five emotional responses typically exhibited by siblings of children with disabilities.
13. Why are an awareness of and sensitivity to cultural and linguistic differences important for professionals when working with families of children with disabilities?
14. Describe what you believe to be key personal characteristics of professionals who work with families of individuals with disabilities.

KEY TERMS

eugenics movement 114
family systems model 117
family characteristics 117
family interactions 118
cohesion 118
adaptability 118
family functions 119
family life cycle 119
transition 119
stage theory 121
respite care 124
cultural sensitivity 129
active listening 131

LEARNING ACTIVITIES

1. Talk to family members of a person with a disability. Learn how the family adapted to the person's exceptionality and how the family as a whole and individual members were or still are affected by the disability. Be certain to ask sensitive questions and ensure confidentiality.
2. Attend a support group meeting for family members of a person with a disability. What kinds of information were presented, and how was it delivered? In your opinion, did those in attendance benefit from the experience?
3. Develop a list of resources and supports in your community aimed at assisting individuals with disabilities and their families. Share your list with your classmates. Examples of resources and supports might include recreational opportunities, religious programs, support groups, respite care, local chapters of national parent/advocacy groups, and health care professionals who work with people with disabilities.
4. Discuss with two general educators and two special education teachers the strategies and techniques they use to establish parent–professional partnerships. What activities seem to be most effective for ensuring meaningful participation? How do these professionals ensure the involvement of parents from culturally and linguistically diverse backgrounds?
5. Volunteer to work for an organization that provides respite care for families of children with disabilities. Keep a journal about your experiences.
6. Interview parents or other family members from diverse cultural backgrounds as a means of learning about their perspectives on disabilities and the educational system, as well as any culturally specific behaviors and values such as child-rearing practices and communication styles.

REFLECTING ON STANDARDS

The following exercises are designed to help you learn to apply the Council for Exceptional Children (CEC) standards to your teaching practice. Each of the reflection exercises below correlates with a knowledge or skill within the CEC standards. For the full text of each of the related CEC standards, please refer to the standards integration grid located in Appendix B.

Focus on Professional and Ethical Practice ***(CEC Content Standard #9 CC9S6)***
Reflect on a time when you have negatively stereotyped someone because of his or her culture, language, religion, gender, disability, socioeconomic status, or social orientation. How might stereotyping a student or his or her family negatively affect your teaching? What strategies might you want to put in place in your classroom to avoid stereotyping?

Focus on Collaboration ***(CEC Content Standard #10 CC10S3)***
Reflect on the various ways your family was involved in your education. What are the advantages to fostering meaningful partnerships with your students' families? How will you want to involve families in your classroom?

STUDENT STUDY SITE

Visit the Student Study Site at www.sagepub.com/gargiulo4emedia for these additional learning tools:

- Video links
- Media links
- Self-quizzes
- E-flashcards
- Full-text SAGE journal articles
- Web exercises

P A

A Study of Individuals With Special Needs

"It is not enough to give the handicapped life. They must be given a life worth living."

—Helen Keller (1880–1968)

CHAPTER 5

Learning Objectives

After reading Chapter 5 you should be able to:

- Summarize the key elements of the AAIDD definitions of intellectual disability from 1961 to 2010.
- Describe the concepts of intellectual ability and adaptive behavior.
- Explain four ways of classifying individuals with mental retardation.
- Provide examples of pre-, peri-, and postnatal causes of intellectual disabilities.
- Outline society's reaction to and treatment of individuals with intellectual disabilities.
- Identify representative learning and social/behavioral characteristics of persons with mental retardation.
- Define functional curriculum, functional academics, and community-based instruction.
- List the key features of the following instructional strategies: task analysis, cooperative learning, and scaffolding.
- Describe the goals of early intervention for young children with intellectual disabilities.
- Characterize contemporary services for adults with mental retardation.

Individuals With Intellectual Disabilities or Mental Retardation

LAUREN'S STORY

Our daughter, Lauren, is an extraordinary child. But she is certainly not an easy child. Sometimes people use the word *exceptional* to describe a child like Lauren who has Down syndrome.

Jason and I were married when we were both 33 and were ready to have children. I was pregnant with Lauren by the time we celebrated our first anniversary. The delivery of our baby was long and difficult, with some concerns about an irregular heartbeat and a possible emergency C-section. Finally, she was born on a Monday afternoon around 5:00. As exhausted as I felt, I was excitedly anticipating holding my new baby. I noticed a nurse looking at the baby and whispering into the doctor's ear. My doctor looked at me and said, "We think the baby has Down's," as they passed Lauren to me. I was stunned for a moment and then asked, "Is it a boy or a girl?" I was only allowed to see my baby girl very briefly, before my husband and the nurse took her to the special care nursery. It was not the moment of joy we had been expecting at the birth of our child. Instead, we were both shocked and divided into our own private worlds of grief.

Video Link 5.1
Watch more about intellectual disabilities.

Even though I was familiar with Down syndrome (due to my training as a special educator), I suddenly felt like I knew nothing. I wanted to be able to hold Lauren because I felt it would help me to make a connection with her. Nothing about her delivery had gone the way we expected, and then I realized that in all the conversations we had before she was born, not one time had we discussed or considered the possibility of a birth defect or any problems.

Lauren's health was a critical issue as I began an endless series of doctor visits with her, making sure to check each possible health complication associated with Down syndrome. Our pediatrician saw Lauren frequently and guided us through the process step by step. Lauren had a very mild heart defect, but it did not require surgery or even medication. Her hearing and vision were normal, except for nystagmus—Lauren's eyes waver from side to side constantly as if she were reading. The ophthalmologist told us this would never go away but it would become less obvious and improve with time. We talked with a geneticist who explained the characteristics of Down syndrome, and we met with a developmental pediatrician who assessed Lauren's development. We were grateful for their help and recommendations.

Soon after Lauren was home I began to call agencies in the area that assisted parents of children with special needs. We were directed to a federally funded agency that provides assistance to parents of developmentally delayed children from birth to 3 years of age. At 6 weeks old Lauren was the focus of a group assessment conducted in our home by a team of professionals including a speech therapist, an occupational therapist, a physical therapist, a special education teacher, and a service coordinator to assist with all the paperwork. Lauren was lying on the floor, the center of our attention. She was already smiling and holding her head up. We all identified goals for us to work on and set up regular visits by her teacher and therapist. I felt more confident that I was taking the right steps to help Lauren develop to her full potential. It seems incredible how many people were involved in our lives during those early years.

I will always remember Lauren learning to walk; it's one of my favorite memories. She has to work so hard to do things that can be so easy for other children. Our physical therapist would visit us once a month. She advised us not to encourage Lauren to walk because she was developing upper body strength by crawling. So that kind of relieved us of one more concern. By 13 or 14 months Lauren did start walking. And she loved it. You could see it in her facial expression just how exciting it must have felt; she was so proud of herself. I can still see her walking across the yard. She would take a few steps, fall down, and get up over and over again. You could hear her laughing the whole time. Lauren is certainly not a timid child; she does the things she enjoys with enthusiasm.

Because of Lauren's excellent motor development we expected her other milestones would continue to be close to a typical progression. Unfortunately, Lauren's speech progress was very slow. She said her first word around 15 months, which was *ba* for ball. She really didn't refer to Jason or me with any words, even though she was making the sounds *mama* and *dada*. We insisted she begin receiving speech therapy at 2 years old. Everything I read told me that children with Down syndrome have trouble developing language, and I was seeing it firsthand.

Currently I am enrolled in a sign language class because Lauren communicates better with signs and visual prompts. I am looking forward to the day she and I can have our first conversation. She communicates in any way that she is able, which is a combination of words, signs, and gestures. She and I deal with many frustrating moments struggling to understand each other. It may take some time, but I cannot wait to hear her express her thoughts and feelings to me with words.

Lauren is now in elementary school, where she participates in an inclusion class for most of the school day and attends a resource class for direct speech instruction and some academics for about one hour a day. We love having her included with her typical peers in a general education classroom.

Lauren's progress is exciting to witness. When we went to a local restaurant for lunch recently, the hostess looked at her and said, "How are you?" and Lauren looked at her and clearly responded "Good" with the sign. She loves greetings and will ask others, "How are you?" This is a welcome change from that awkward feeling you have as a parent when you feel as though you have to "talk" for your child.

Lauren's behavior is the biggest obstacle for our family. The days when we could scoop her up and move on as we managed to calm her down are over. She currently weighs 80 pounds, and she is next to impossible to move when she decides she isn't going anywhere. Transitions are difficult for her, and flexibility isn't Lauren's style. Although it is helpful to have a routine to structure her day, it just isn't realistic to always follow routines, especially on weekends.

We feel fortunate that we have neighbors, teachers, friends, and family who accept and celebrate Lauren's accomplishments with us. They don't mind singing "Happy Birthday" and blowing out the candles just because there is a cake, even when it isn't anyone's birthday. My dream is for Lauren to form lasting friendships with peers, develop her own personal interests, and achieve her academic potential. I believe meeting these goals will help Lauren live a full and meaningful life.

—D. Shipman

Mental retardation is a very powerful term. It is also an emotionally laden label, one that conjures up various images of people with intellectual disabilities. What do you think of when someone says "mental retardation"? Do you immediately think of the character from the movie *Radio*, *The Other Sister*, or *I Am Sam*? Maybe you recall meeting a young girl with Down syndrome when you volunteered to help during last year's Special Olympics, or perhaps you recollect how you felt when a group of adults with intellectual disabilities sat by you in a restaurant. Often our images of individuals with intellectual disabilities are based on stereotypes resulting from limited contact and exposure. Consequently, many of us are susceptible to inaccuracies, misconceptions, and erroneous beliefs about this population. As a result, people with intellectual disabilities frequently encounter prejudice, ignorance, and, in some instances, outright discrimination simply because society has identified them as being "different." Yet despite the diversity represented by this group, we firmly believe that children and adults with intellectual disabilities are first and foremost people who are more like their typically developing peers than they are different. In fact, very few ever fit the images and stereotypes commonly portrayed by the media.

Partly as a result of the pejorative nature of the term *mental retardation*, and the accompanying negative connotations and stereotyping, the term *intellectual disabilities* is gaining in popularity. The acceptance of this new terminology has been championed by the premier professional organization in the field—the American Association on Intellectual and Developmental Disabilities. Founded in 1876, the association itself has undergone several name changes. In the late 1800s it was originally known as the Association of Medical Officers of American Institutions for Idiotic and Feebleminded Persons. Later, in 1906, the designation was changed to the American Association for the Study of the Feebleminded, while in 1933 it became the American Association on Mental Deficiency (AAMD). In 1987 another name change occurred. AAMD became the American Association on Mental Retardation (Luckasson & Reeve, 2001). In January 2007 the association changed its name once again and is now known as the American Association on Intellectual and Developmental Disabilities.

The term *intellectual disabilities* is preferred by many policymakers, advocates, parents, service providers, teachers, and scholars. It is generally less offensive to persons with this disability and is also consistent with contemporary Canadian and European terminology. The term *mental retardation*, however, is still widely used. It is used for citizenship and many legal services, health care, income support, and housing, among other areas (American Association on Intellectual and Developmental Disabilities, 2010b). In fact, it is the term of choice for the U.S. Department of Education and is found in IDEA 2004. Because of this dual status we have chosen to use both terms interchangeably.

The goal of this chapter is to examine basic issues and concepts necessary for understanding the field of intellectual disabilities and individuals identified as intellectually disabled. In this chapter, we will look at historical foundations, evolving definitions and classification models, causes of intellectual disabilities, characteristics of persons with intellectual disabilities, contemporary educational practices, and trends in service delivery along with related concepts. We have adopted a life span perspective for exploring the concept of intellectual disabilities. This chapter, and those that follow, will therefore address topics and issues pertaining to infancy through adulthood.

Defining Intellectual Disabilities or Mental Retardation: An Evolving Process

Mental retardation is a complex and multifaceted concept. Intellectual disabilities have been studied by psychologists, sociologists, educators, physicians, and many other professionals. This multidisciplinary interest in and investigation of mental retardation, while beneficial, has significantly contributed to problems of conceptual and definitional clarity (Drew & Hardman, 2007). Yet, by their very nature, intellectual disabilities cannot be studied independently of other disciplines. We fully agree with Drew and his colleague that there is considerable merit in a multidisciplinary approach; however, we must not lose sight of what should be our central focus, the individual with mental retardation.

1961 AAIDD Definition

The American Association on Intellectual and Developmental Disabilities (AAIDD) has been a tremendous help in advancing our understanding of the concept of mental retardation. AAIDD's sixth definition appeared in 1961 and was widely adopted. This slightly revised version of a 1959 manual on terminology and classification describes mental retardation as "subaverage general intellectual functioning which originates during the developmental period and is associated with impairments in adaptive behavior" (Heber, 1961, p. 3). Let us analyze the meaning of these phrases. *Subaverage general intellectual functioning* is defined as an intelligence quotient (IQ) greater than one **standard deviation (SD)** (a statistic describing variance from the mean or average score of a particular group) below the mean for a given age group. In 1961, this was interpreted to be an IQ below 85 or 84 depending on which standardized IQ test was used. The *developmental period* extended from birth to approximately age 16. The criterion of *impairments in adaptive behavior* is a critical and unique aspect of this definition. The inclusion of this factor establishes dual criteria for identifying someone as mentally retarded (Scheerenberger, 1987). **Adaptive behavior**, which Heber first introduced, refers to an individual's ability to meet the social requirements of his or her community that are appropriate for his or her chronological age; it is an indication of independence and social competency. Thus, according to Heber's definition, a person with an IQ of 79 who did not exhibit significant impairment in adaptive behavior would not be identified as mentally retarded. (See Figure 5.1.)

Adaptive behavior	Intellectual functioning: Low	Intellectual functioning: High
Low	Mentally retarded	Not mentally retarded
High	Not mentally retarded	Not mentally retarded

FIGURE 5.1 Relationship Between Intellectual Functioning and Adaptive Behavior

NOTE: Classification of an individual as intellectually disabled requires both low intellectual functioning and deficits in adaptive behavior.

The association's definition, though widely used, was not without its critics. Professional concern focused on the lack of appropriate assessment instruments for measuring adaptive behavior as well as a belief that the definition was overly inclusive—almost 16 percent of the population could have an IQ within the range thought to indicate mental retardation. These concerns and others led to a revised definition in 1973.

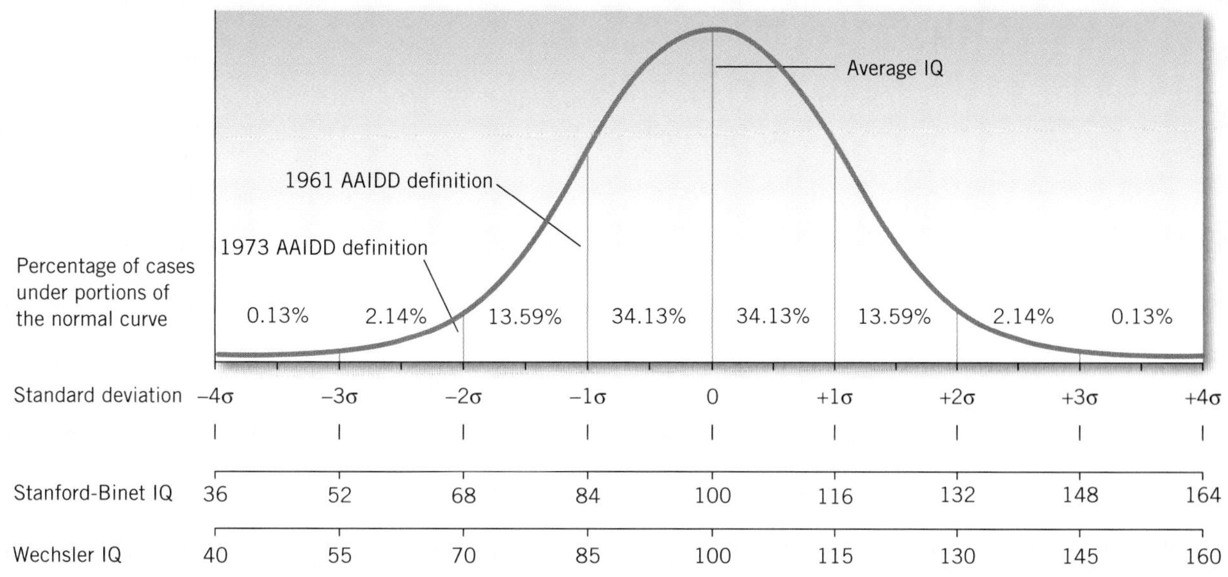

FIGURE 5.2 The Normal Curve: A Theoretical Distribution of Intelligence

NOTE: The 1961 AAIDD definition defines mental retardation as an IQ lower than 85 (84) on a standardized measure of intelligence. The 1973 AAIDD definition defines intellectual disabilities as an IQ lower than 70 (68). Later versions allow for professional judgment when considering intellectual performance.

1973 AAIDD Definition

Herbert Grossman chaired a committee charged with revising the 1961 AAIDD definition. Grossman's (1973) definition viewed mental retardation as "significantly subaverage general intellectual functioning existing concurrently with deficits in adaptive behavior, and manifested during the developmental period" (p. 11). Though paralleling its predecessor, the Grossman definition is conceptually distinct. First, the 1973 definition refers to significantly subaverage intellectual ability. Operationally, intellectual disability was psychometrically redefined as performance at least two standard deviations below the mean. This more conservative approach considered the upper IQ limit to be 70 or 68 (again, depending on whether the Stanford-Binet Intelligence Scale [SD = 16 points] or the Wechsler Intelligence Scale for Children [SD = 15 points] was used). Statistically speaking, this represents the lower 2.27 percent of the population instead of the approximately 16 percent included in the Heber definition. (See Figure 5.2.) Adopting this standard eliminated the classification of "borderline" mental retardation incorporated in Heber's conceptual scheme.

Audio Link 5.1
Listen to individuals talk about labels and definitions.

The Grossman definition also sought to clarify the relationship between adaptive behavior and intellectual functioning. This definition attempted to focus greater attention on adaptive behavior and described it as the ability of an individual to meet "the standards of personal independence and social responsibility expected of his [or her] age and cultural group" (Grossman, 1973, p. 11). Adaptive behavior was to be considered within the context of the person's age and sociocultural group. Grossman's work attempted to strengthen the link between IQ and adaptive behavior in an effort to reduce the number of pupils identified as mentally retarded solely on the basis of their IQ. The 1973 definition also extended the concept of the developmental period to age 18 to more accurately reflect when most people complete their education.

Although the 1973 Grossman definition, incorporated into IDEA 2004 (PL 108–446), represented a conceptual advancement over the work of Heber, shortcomings remained.

As an illustration, many educators were concerned that lowering the IQ threshold to 68 (70) would deny special education services to many students who otherwise would have been eligible for placement in programs serving individuals with mild mental retardation. It was feared that these children would be misclassified and inappropriately placed and thus "drown in the mainstream" (Scheerenberger, 1987). MacMillan (1989) echoed this concern. He characterized these students as "residing in a no-man's land," roughly equivalent to an educational demilitarized zone, ineligible for special education services. Once again, AAIDD revised its definition of intellectual disabilities to achieve greater clarity and a contemporary focus.

1983 AAIDD Definition

In 1983, AAIDD published yet another revision to its manual on terminology and classification. Once again, Grossman led the organization's efforts. This eighth edition, mirroring its 1973 predecessor, describes intellectual disabilities as "significantly subaverage general intellectual functioning resulting in or associated with concurrent impairments in adaptive behavior and manifested during the developmental period" (Grossman, 1983, p. 1).

Though very similar in wording to the 1973 definition, this version contains some important changes. The 1983 Grossman edition suggests using a range of 70–75 when describing the upper limits of intellectual performance on a standardized measure of intelligence rather than a strict cutoff of 70. An IQ score of 70 is intended only as a guideline. Flexibility is the key to understanding the operation of this definition. The clinical judgment of the professional plays an important role when making a diagnosis of mental retardation.

The 1983 AAIDD definition was generally well accepted by the professional community. Like all definitions, however, it was time-bound. As our knowledge base and ideas about intellectual disabilities change, so do our definitions. In 1992, AAIDD issued yet another version of its thinking about mental retardation.

1992 AAIDD Definition

In May 1992 Ruth Luckasson and her colleagues crafted a new definition of intellectual disabilities, which was published in *Mental Retardation: Definition, Classification, and Systems of Support*. According to this manual,

> Mental retardation refers to substantial limitations in present functioning. It is characterized by significantly subaverage intellectual functioning, existing concurrently with related limitations in two or more of the following applicable adaptive skill areas: communication, self-care, home living, social skills, community use, self-direction, health and safety, functional academics, leisure, and work. Mental retardation manifests before age 18. (p. 5)

Application of this definition requires careful consideration of the following four essential assumptions:

1. Valid assessment considers cultural and linguistic diversity as well as differences in communication and behavioral factors.
2. The existence of limitations in adaptive skills occurs within the context of community environments typical of the individual's age peers and is indexed to the person's individualized needs for supports.
3. Specific adaptive limitations often coexist with strengths in other adaptive skills or other personal capabilities.
4. With appropriate supports over a sustained period, the life functioning of the person with mental retardation will generally improve. (Luckasson et al., 1992, p. 5)

The 1992 AAIDD definition is a highly functional definition. It portrays mental retardation as a relationship among three key elements: the individual, the environment, and the type of support required for maximum functioning in various settings. It essentially reflects the "fit" between the person's capabilities and the structure and expectations of the environment. This ninth version also represents a conceptual shift away from viewing intellectual disabilities as an inherent trait to a perspective that considers the person's present level of functioning and the supports needed to improve it. The interaction among the individual, the environment, and support is depicted in Figure 5.3. The framers of the 1992 definition selected an equilateral triangle to represent their thinking because it shows the equality among the three elements.

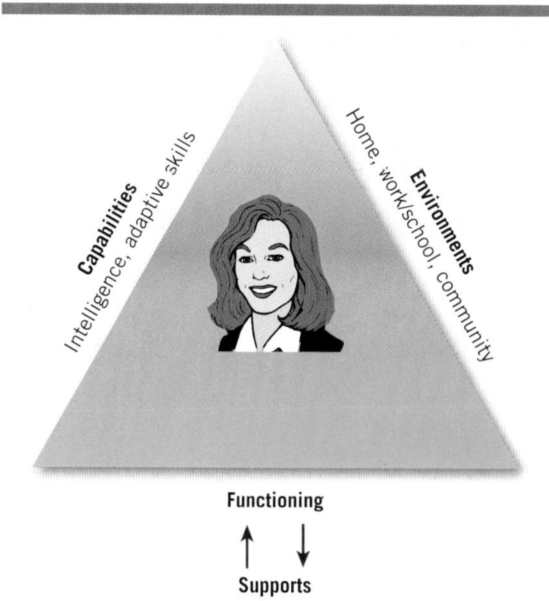

FIGURE 5.3 General Structure of the 1992 AAIDD Definition of Intellectual Disabilities

SOURCE: *Mental Retardation: Definition, Classification, and Systems of Supports*, 9th ed. (Washington, DC: American Association on Mental Retardation, 1992), p. 10. Reprinted with permission.

The 1992 AAIDD description of intellectual disabilities stresses functioning in one's community rather than just focusing on the clinical aspect of the individual such as IQ or adaptive behavior (Smith, Polloway, Patton, & Dowdy, 2008). This definition is an optimistic one; it assumes that a person's performance will improve over time when appropriate supports are provided. Though certainly a unique portrayal of mental retardation, this definition, like its predecessors, retains an emphasis on intellectual performance coupled with impairments in adaptive skills.

The 1992 version of the AAIDD definition of intellectual disabilities has proven to be fairly controversial, and not all professionals in the field are embracing it (Conyers, Martin, Martin, & Yu, 2002; Detterman & Gabriel, 2006; Polloway, 2004), possibly because it represents a paradigm shift from a deficiency-based model of mental retardation to a support-based model. The purpose of this definition, according to Reiss (1994), a member of the committee that crafted it, is to encourage people to change their thinking about intellectual disabilities and to serve as a cornerstone for contemporary public policy. Research (Denning, Chamberlain, & Polloway, 2000; Polloway, Lubin, Smith, & Patton, 2010) suggests that this reformulated description of intellectual disabilities is having minimal influence on changing guidelines used by individual states for identifying students with mental retardation. Currently, thirty-four states still follow the federal (IDEA) definition of mental retardation (Polloway, Patton, Smith, Antoine, & Lubin, 2009). Recall that this definition mirrors the 1973 Grossman definition of intellectual disabilities.

Questions and concerns raised in various professional circles about the 1992 definition led to yet another interpretation of mental retardation. In 2002 AAIDD offered a reformulated description of intellectual disabilities.

2002 AAIDD Definition

The AAIDD definition reformulated by Luckasson et al. in 2002 represented another effort in our evolving understanding of intellectual disabilities. The purpose of the tenth edition was to "create a contemporary system of diagnosis, classification, and systems of support for the disability currently known as mental retardation" (Luckasson et al., p. xii).

This definition states that "mental retardation is a disability characterized by significant limitations both in intellectual functioning and in adaptive behavior as expressed in conceptual, social, and practical adaptive skills. This disability originates before age 18" (Luckasson et al., 2002, p. 1).

Accompanying this description are five assumptions considered essential when applying this definition:

- Limitations in present functioning must be considered within the context of community environments typical of the individual's age, peers, and culture.
- Valid assessment considers cultural and linguistic diversity as well as differences in communication and sensory, motor, and behavioral factors.
- Within an individual, limitations often coexist with strengths.
- An important purpose of describing limitations is to develop a profile of needed supports.
- With appropriate personalized supports over a sustained period, the life functioning of the person with mental retardation will generally improve. (Luckasson et al., 2002, p. 1)

Like the ninth edition developed ten years earlier, the 2002 AAIDD definition retains a positive perspective toward individuals with intellectual disabilities while continuing to acknowledge the significance of adaptive behavior and systems of support. It also preserves the idea that mental retardation is a "function of the relationship among individual functioning, supports, and contexts" (Wehmeyer, 2003, p. 276). This conceptualization of intellectual disabilities, while not flawless, represents a logical step in the continuing challenge of advancing our understanding of the concept of intellectual disabilities.

2010 AAIDD Definition

The eleventh AAIDD definition (Schalock et al., 2010) both reiterates and strengthens key concepts found in the 2002 definition of intellectual disabilities. Developed by a committee of eighteen medical and legal scholars as well as policymakers, educators, and other professionals, the 2010 definition emphasizes the abilities and assets of individuals with intellectual disabilities rather than their deficits or limitations.

Intellectual disability is viewed as a state of functioning rather than an inherent trait. As in earlier definitions, one of the goals of the 2010 definition is to maximize support services so as to allow persons with intellectual disabilities to participate fully in all aspects of daily life.

The description of intellectual disabilities in the 2010 manual mirrors the wording found in the tenth edition, as do the five accompanying assumptions. The eleventh edition also retains the emphasis on adaptive behavior while stressing systems of support. The term *mental retardation,* however, is replaced by the more contemporary label, *intellectual disabilities.* This term is less pejorative while also reflecting a social-ecological understanding of disability (Schalock, 2010). The committee notes, however, that despite the change in terminology, the term *intellectual disabilities* refers to the same population of individuals who were recognized previously as being mentally retarded (Schalock et al., 2010).

The latest AAIDD definition reflects best practices and new thinking about classifying individuals with intellectual disabilities. Rather than using intellectual functioning as a basis for classifying persons with cognitive limitations, the 2010 definition encourages professionals and service providers to classify on the basis of various dimensions of human functioning—intellectual abilities, adaptive behavior, health, participation, and context (see Figure 5.4). *Human functioning* is essentially viewed as "an umbrella term for all life activities and encompasses body structures and functions, personal activities, and participation, which in turn are influenced by one's health and environmental or contextual factors" (Schalock et al., 2010, p. 15). This multidimensional perspective allows one to classify depending on the questions being asked (for example, "Is this person competent to be a self-advocate, maintain a bank

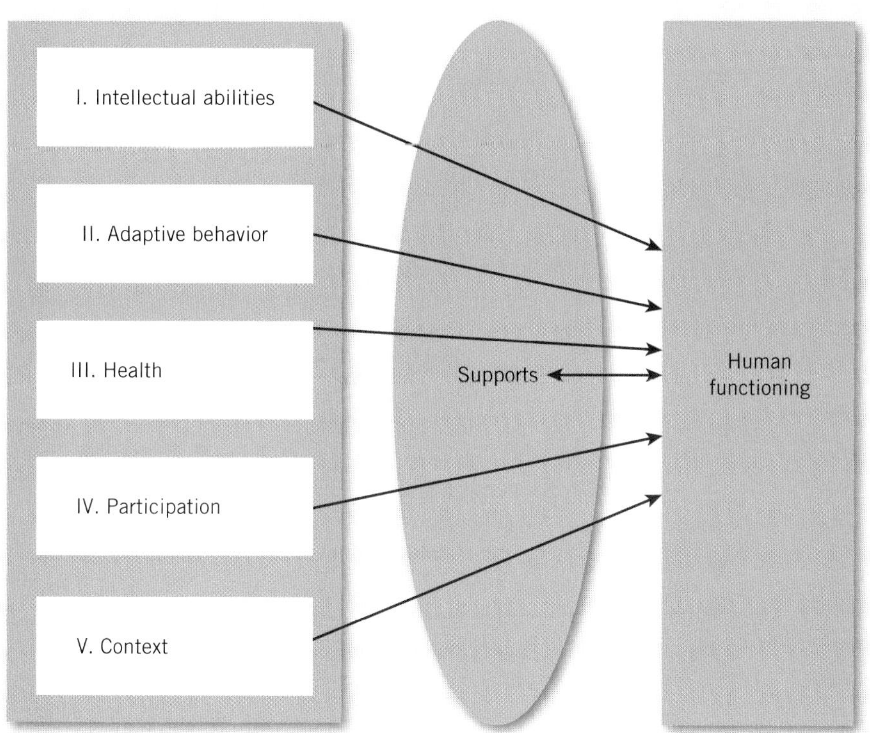

FIGURE 5.4 A Conceptual Framework of Human Functioning

SOURCE: *Intellectual Disabilities: Definition, Classification, and Systems of Support,* 11th ed. (Washington, DC: American Association on Intellectual and Developmental Disabilities, 2010), p. 15.

account, or have sexual relations?") and the specific purpose of the classification system. Classification is then linked to personalized systems of support for that individual (Schalock, 2010).

Assessing Intellectual Ability and Adaptive Behavior

The constructs of intelligence and adaptive behavior play key roles in our understanding of the concept of mental retardation. Yet both of these terms are somewhat difficult to define and assess. For the sake of clarity we will discuss each concept separately; but remember they are intricately interrelated and provide the foundation for contemporary thinking about intellectual disabilities.

Intellectual Ability

The question of what constitutes intelligence and how to describe it has challenged educators, psychologists, and thinkers throughout the years. Even today there is disagreement among professionals as to the meaning of this term and the best way of measuring intelligence. Intelligence is perhaps best thought of as a construct or theoretical abstraction; it is not a visible entity but rather a human trait whose existence

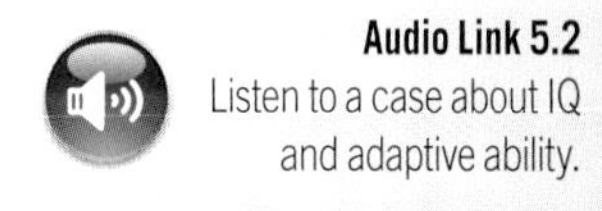

Audio Link 5.2
Listen to a case about IQ and adaptive ability.

Persons with intellectual disabilities can be taught how to live independently.

is inferred based on a person's performance on certain types of cognitive tasks. Because no one has ever seen intelligence and we have only deduced its presence, professionals have come to the realization that they are "attempting to explain one of the most complex and elusive components of human functioning" (Beirne-Smith, Patton, & Kim, 2006, p. 95).

These difficulties notwithstanding, a great amount of effort has been expended on trying to accurately assess intellectual functioning. The most common way of determining an individual's cognitive ability is through an IQ or intelligence test. Two of the more widely used individually administered IQ measures are the Wechsler Intelligence Scale for Children (4th ed.), or WISC-IV (Wechsler, 2003), and the fifth edition of the original work of Binet and Simon from the early twentieth century, the Stanford-Binet Intelligence Scale (Roid, 2003). As noted in Chapter 3, some psychologists and psychometrists rely on the Kaufman Assessment Battery for Children (Kaufman & Kaufman, 2004), especially when evaluating youngsters from culturally and linguistically diverse backgrounds.

Data gleaned from the WISC-IV, the Stanford-Binet V, and similar measures are thought to represent a sample of an individual's intellectual skills and abilities. These data are usually summarized as an IQ score. Originally an IQ was defined as a ratio between the person's mental age (MA or developmental level) and chronological age (CA) multiplied by 100. For instance, a student whose chronological age is 10 but who performs on an IQ test like a typical 5-year-old would have an IQ of 50; if accompanied by deficits in adaptive behavior, this individual would very likely be identified as intellectually disabled. Today, deviation IQs or standard scores have replaced intelligence quotients in most professional circles. A standard score is nothing more than an expression of how far a particular raw score deviates from a specific reference point such as the test mean. Standard scores are often expressed as standard deviations.

If large numbers of people were assessed with an IQ test, their performance would reflect a distribution of scores represented as a bell-shaped curve, or normal curve (see Figure 5.2). In this theoretical statistical distribution, an average IQ score is designated as 100 (representing equivalence between MA and CA). Most people cluster around the center of the curve, with fewer individuals at the extremes of the distribution. Variance from the mean or average score occurs in a predictable fashion and is referred to in terms of standard deviations. One standard deviation (SD) on both the Stanford-Binet V and the WISC-IV is equivalent to 15 IQ points. Both tests have a mean IQ of 100.

Although IQ testing is very common in schools, the issue of assessing someone's intelligence, especially if a special education placement may result, is somewhat controversial. Cautionary flags and reasons for concern tend to focus on these issues:

- **Potential for cultural bias.** Intellectual assessments are often criticized because of their highly verbal nature and reflection of middle-class Anglo standards.

- **Stability of IQ.** An IQ test only reports a person's performance at a particular point in time; intelligence is not static but capable of changing, and in some cases, the change can be significant.
- **Overemphasis on IQ scores.** An IQ score is not the sole indicator of an individual's ability, nor is it a measure of the person's worth; yet IQ is often stressed at the expense of other factors such as motivation or adaptive skills.

Despite the various criticisms and concerns, IQ testing does a good job of predicting how well a student will do in school—in other words, his or her potential for academic success. Still, educators should not overly rely on a single IQ score as a predictor of performance in the classroom; an IQ score should only be one piece of the diagnostic puzzle. With increasing frequency, professionals are looking at alternative or supplemental indicators of performance and are gathering information using a holistic approach, including work samples, parent–teacher interviews, behavior checklists, and classroom observation. Collectively, these sources of data can provide a more realistic and valid picture of the child's performance and potential.

Adaptive Behavior

The notion of adaptive behavior was first introduced in the 1973 AAIDD definition of mental retardation. It was retained in the 1983 description of intellectual disabilities and is the underpinning of the most recent AAIDD definitions. Adaptive behavior is seen as "the degree to which, and the efficiency with which, the individual meets the standards of maturation, learning, personal independence, and/or social responsibility that are expected for his or her age level and cultural group" (Grossman, 1983, p. 11). In continuing this thinking, the 2002 AAIDD definition by Luckasson et al. describes adaptive behavior as "the collection of conceptual, social, and practical skills that have been learned by people in order to function in their everyday society" (p. 73). Stated another way, it is how well a person copes with the everyday demands and requirements of his or her environment. The idea of context is important for understanding the concept of adaptive behavior. Because behavior is strongly influenced by cultural factors, age and situation appropriateness must always be considered within the setting in which it occurs. For example, a teenage girl who uses her fingers while eating might be viewed as exhibiting inappropriate behavior; however, this behavior is only maladaptive when considered within the context of Western cultures.

The 1992, 2002, and 2010 AAIDD definitions, like earlier formulations, stress adaptive behavior, but now it is more clearly articulated. In earlier versions, adaptive behavior was described globally; in the Luckasson et al. (2002) configuration, it is seen as significant limitations in the expression or performance of conceptual, social, and practical adaptive skills. Table 5.1 illustrates these three areas and provides examples of the skills.

It is not always easy to assess adaptive behavior. It is usually measured by direct observation, structured interviews, or standardized scales. Informants may include parents, teachers, caregivers, or other professionals. One of the more widely used instruments for assessing adaptive behavior is the AAMR Adaptive Behavior Scale—School (Lambert, Nihira, & Leland, 1993), which provides a comprehensive assessment of an individual's competency over a wide range of behaviors. The school version assesses performance in the areas of personal responsibility and daily living skills, along with social adaptation and maladaptive behavior. Another form is available for evaluating individuals with mental retardation who reside in community and residential settings: the AAMR Adaptive Behavior Scale—Residential and Community (Nihira, Leland, & Lambert, 1993). Like its companion scale, this instrument is norm referenced and individually administered and contains two main sections: personal independence and social adaptation.

TABLE 5.1 2002 AAIDD Adaptive Skill Areas

Skill Area	Examples of Behavior
Conceptual	• Language (receptive and expressive) • Reading and writing • Money concepts • Self-direction
Social	• Interpersonal • Responsibility • Self-esteem • Gullibility (likelihood of being tricked or manipulated) • Naiveté • Follows rules • Obeys laws • Avoids victimization
Practical	• Activities of daily living: – Eating – Transfer/mobility – Toileting – Dressing • Instrumental activities of daily living: – Meal preparation – Housekeeping – Transportation – Taking medication – Money management – Telephone use • Occupational skills • Maintains safe environments

SOURCE: Adapted from *Mental Retardation: Definition, Classification, and Systems of Support*, 10th ed. (Washington, DC: American Association on Mental Retardation, 2002), p. 42.

AAIDD is currently developing the Diagnostic Adaptive Behavior Scale (DABS) as a standardized measure of adaptive behavior. Based on the three adaptive skill areas identified in Table 5.1, this new instrument is being normed on individuals *without* intellectual disabilities in the chronological age range of 4–21 years old. Designed as a diagnostic test, the DABS seeks to provide a precise cutoff point for persons deemed to have "significant limitations" in adaptive behavior (American Association on Intellectual and Developmental Disabilities, 2010a). Recall that such limitations are one of the key components of the 2002 and 2010 AAIDD definitions of intellectual disabilities.

Classification of Individuals With Intellectual Disabilities or Mental Retardation

A classification system is a convenient way for differentiating among individuals who share a common characteristic—in this instance, mental retardation. Of course, we must remember that there is a great degree of variability among members of this population despite the fact that they share a common label. Because intellectual disabilities exist along a continuum, there have been numerous proposals on how to classify people with this disability. Many years ago, Gelof (1963) reported the existence of almost two dozen classification schemes. Like definitions of mental retardation, classification models tend to vary according to a particular focus. We will examine several systems—some vintage ones along with the most contemporary thinking in this area. Types of classification systems include grouping individuals with intellectual disabilities according to etiology or cause of the disability, severity of the condition, and educational expectations. Finally, the current strategy classifies on the basis of levels of support.

An Etiological Perspective

Traditionally, individuals with intellectual disabilities have been classified based on known or presumed medical/biological causes. This etiological orientation assumes that mental retardation is a consequence of a disease process or biological defect. Examples include intellectual disabilities that are due to infections such as rubella (German measles) or maternal syphilis, chromosomal abnormalities such as Down syndrome, or metabolic disorders such as phenylketonuria (PKU). (These examples and others will be more fully explored in a later section of this chapter.) Although useful for physicians and other health care workers, this classification scheme has limited applicability for nonmedical practitioners.

Intellectual Deficits

A long-standing and popular classification scheme among psychologists and educators is one based on the severity of intellectual impairment as determined by an IQ test. This model is one of the most widely cited in the professional literature and, until recently, reflected the position of AAIDD dating back to the 1973 Grossman definition of mental retardation. According to this system, deficits in intellectual functioning and related impairments in adaptive behavior result in individuals being classified into one of four levels of mental retardation—mild, moderate, severe, or profound—with *mild* representing the highest level of performance for persons thought to be intellectually disabled and *profound* the lowest. Intellectual competency is often the primary variable used in constructing these discriminations; Table 5.2 presents the IQ ranges typically used.

An Educational Perspective

Another classification system popular with educators since the 1960s is to classify students with intellectual disabilities on the basis of expected or anticipated educational accomplishments. Generally speaking, special education teachers classified children

TABLE 5.2 Classification of Intellectual Disabilities According to Measured Intelligence

Classification Level	Measured IQ	SD Below Mean
Mild retardation	55–70	2 to 3
Moderate retardation	40–55	3 to 4
Severe retardation	25–40	4 to 5
Profound retardation	Under 25	More than 5

NOTE: IQ scores are approximate.

SD = standard deviation.

TABLE 5.3 Classification of Intellectual Disabilities According to Intensities of Support

Support Level	Description	Examples
Intermittent	Supports on an as-needed or episodic basis. Person does not always need the support(s), or person needs short-term supports during life span transitions. When provided, intermittent supports may be of high or low intensity.	• Loss of employment • Acute medical crisis
Limited	Supports characterized by consistency over time, time-limited but not intermittent; may require fewer staff and less cost than more intense levels of support.	• Job training • Transitioning from school to adult status
Extensive	Supports characterized by regular involvement (e.g., daily) in at least some environments (such as work or home) and not time-limited.	• Ongoing home living assistance
Pervasive	Supports characterized by their constancy and high intensity; provided across all environments, potential life-sustaining nature. Pervasive supports typically involve more staff and intrusiveness than extensive or time-limited supports.	• Chronic medical situation

SOURCE: Adapted from *Mental Retardation: Definition, Classification, and Systems of Supports,* 10th ed. (Washington, DC: American Association on Mental Retardation, 2002), p. 152.

into two groups: **educable mentally retarded (EMR)** or **trainable mentally retarded (TMR).** These designations are roughly equivalent to the AAIDD labels of *mild* and *moderate mental retardation*, with IQs ranging from about 50–55 to 70–75 and 35–40 to 50–55, respectively. (Before the enactment of PL 94–142, public schools rarely served individuals with IQs lower than 35; therefore, these youngsters were not labeled according to this system.) As you might expect, the term *educable* implies that a youngster has some, albeit limited, academic potential; *trainable* implies that a child is incapable of learning but possibly could be trained in nonacademic areas. Over the years, professionals have learned that these prognostic labels, which represent an "educability quotient," are inaccurate and present a false dichotomy; we affirm that all children are capable of learning when presented with the appropriate circumstances. The notion of presumed academic achievement has slowly fallen out of favor in professional circles. These terms are currently considered pejorative and tend to perpetuate stereotypical and prejudicial attitudes.

Levels of Support

In the early nineties, AAIDD (Luckasson et al., 1992), in a dramatic and controversial maneuver, shifted from a classification model based on severity of intellectual impairment to one based on the type and extent of needed supports. This scheme, retained in the 2002 definition by Luckasson et al., classifies individuals with intellectual disabilities according to the **level of support**—intermittent, limited, extensive, or pervasive—needed to effectively function across adaptive skill areas in various natural settings, rather than according to their deficits. In fact, AAIDD recommends abandoning references to the severity of retardation. Table 5.3 describes the four classification levels endorsed by AAIDD.

The aim of this approach is to explain an individual's functional (rather than intellectual) limitations in terms of the amount of support he or she requires to achieve optimal growth and development at home, at school, at the workplace, and in other community settings (Beirne-Smith et al., 2006). This model, which represents more than a mere substitution for the previous AAIDD IQ-based classification scheme, extends the concept of support beyond the intensity of needed support to include the type of support system required. **Natural supports** typically include family members, friends, teachers, and coworkers. **Formal supports** are usually thought of as government-funded social programs like Social Security payments or health care programs, habilitation services, and even the advocacy efforts of groups like the Council for Exceptional Children or The Arc, a national organization on mental retardation. It is probably too early to tell how professionals, school systems, and other groups will respond to this new way of thinking about classifying people with intellectual disabilities.

In January 2004 AAIDD published the Supports Intensity Scale (SIS) by Thompson et al. This new assessment instrument assesses the practical support requirements of the individual with intellectual disabilities across fifty-seven life activities and twenty-nine behavioral and medical areas. The SIS measures the support needs of the adult with cognitive impairments in the domains of home living, community living, lifelong learning, employment, health and safety, social activities, and protection and advocacy. Rather than focusing on the skills the individual lacks, the SIS looks at the individual's needs in areas considered important for leading an independent life. Data are gathered by interviewing the individual with intellectual disabilities as well as those who are well acquainted with the person. A version appropriate for children with intellectual disabilities is under development.

A Brief History of the Field

It is generally believed that individuals thought to be mentally retarded have been present in all societies throughout the ages. Historically speaking, the field of mental retardation resembles an ever-changing mosaic influenced by the sociopolitical and economic climate of the times. Attitudes toward and understanding of intellectual disabilities have also affected the treatment of people with mental retardation. Mental retardation is a field that is continually evolving—from the ignorance of antiquity to the highly scientific and legal foundations of the early twenty-first century. Along this pathway, people with intellectual disabilities have had to endure and battle myths, fear, superstition, attempts at extermination, and educational and social segregation before arriving at today's policy of normalization and inclusion.

Early Civilizations

Early written records from the era of the Greek and Roman empires make reference to citizens who were most likely mentally retarded. In some instances, these accounts date back to almost 1550 B.C. (Lindman & McIntyre, 1961). In many ways, the Greek and Roman societies were highly advanced and civilized, but the treatment of infants with disabilities would be judged cruel and barbaric by today's standards. Scheerenberger's (1983) detailed account of the history of mental retardation reveals, for example, that in the city-state of Sparta, which placed a premium on physical strength and intellectual ability, eugenics and infanticide were common, everyday occurrences. Only the brightest and strongest of citizens were encouraged to have children. Newborns were examined by a council of inspectors, and babies thought to be defective or inferior were thrown from a cliff to die on the rocks below.

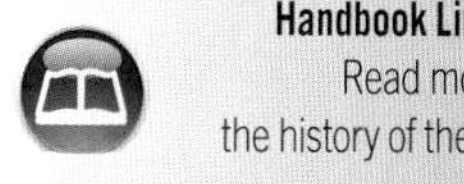

Handbook Link 5.1
Read more on the history of the field.

The early days of the Roman Republic mirrored the practices of the Greeks. Deformed infants were routinely allowed to perish—but only during the first eight days of life. Fathers held complete control over their children and could do whatever they wished, including selling or killing them. This doctrine of *patria potestas* is unparalleled in any other society.

The Middle Ages

From the fall of the Roman Empire in A.D. 476 to the beginning of the Renaissance in the 1300s, religion became a dominant social force, heralding a period of more humane treatment of individuals with disabilities. Churches established monasteries and asylums as sanctuaries for persons with intellectual disabilities. Children with mental retardation were often called *les enfants du bon Dieu* ("the children of God"). Infanticide was rarely practiced because the largely agrarian societies required many workers in the fields. In some instances, individuals thought to be mentally retarded found their way into castles where, though protected and shown favor, they served as buffoons and court jesters entertaining the nobility (Gargiulo, 1985). King Henry II of England enacted a policy in the twelfth century, *de praerogativa regis* ("of the king's prerogative"), whereby "natural fools" became the king's wards (Drew & Hardman, 2007).

At the same time, it was an era in which fear and superstition ran rampant. People with mental retardation were frequently thought to be "filled with Satan" and to possess demonic powers, which often led to torture and death for practicing witchcraft. It was not uncommon for individuals with intellectual disabilities to be sent to prison and kept in chains because they were perceived to be a danger to society and their behavior was seen as unalterable.

Early Optimism

The "modern" period in the history of mental retardation traces its roots to the early nineteenth century. It was during this period that the groundbreaking work of Jean-Marc Gaspard Itard (1774–1838) occurred. Recall from Chapter 1 that his pioneering efforts with Victor, the so-called *homme sauvage* or "wild man," earned him the title *Father of Special Education*. His systematic attempts at educating Victor, whom he believed to be a victim of social/educational deprivation, signals the start of the notion that individuals with mental retardation are capable of learning—however limited it may be.

Edouard Seguin (1812–1880) was inspired by the work of his mentor, Itard. Based on his religious convictions, Seguin advocated fervently for the education of children with intellectual disabilities. In 1837, Seguin established the first school in Paris for the education of children with mental retardation. Because of the political turmoil in France in the mid-1800s, Seguin immigrated in 1848 to the United States, where he played a principal role in helping to establish residential facilities for persons with mental retardation in several states. In 1876, the Association of Medical Officers of American Institutions for Idiotic and Feebleminded Persons was established, with Seguin serving as its first president. Recall that this association was the forerunner of today's American Association on Intellectual and Developmental Disabilities.

Protection and Pessimism

The late nineteenth and early twentieth centuries witnessed the development of large, geographically isolated institutions for the mentally retarded. The focus of these facilities changed as the invigorating optimism of the early 1800s generally gave way to disillusionment, fear, and pessimism (Morrison & Polloway, 1995). Institutions were overcrowded and understaffed. Their mission shifted from one of education and rehabilitation, as espoused by Seguin and others, to a new custodial role. Caring concern was slowly replaced by an unjustified concern with protecting society from individuals with intellectual disabilities.

One of the unfortunate consequences of this shift in societal attitude was that institutions became permanent residences for people with mental retardation; thus, they were no longer prepared for their eventual return to society (Drew & Hardman, 2007). Education and training functions virtually disappeared, and only the most rudimentary care was provided. Over time, these institutions deteriorated, becoming warehouses for society's unwanted citizens. Living conditions were harsh and often deplorable. This situation was poignantly captured by Blatt and Kaplan (1966) in their classic photographic essay on institutional life, *Christmas in Purgatory*.

Beginning in the 1960s, a highly visible call for more humane and normalized living arrangements for people with intellectual disabilities was issued. Initiated in Sweden by Nirje (1969), the principle of **normalization** emphasizes "making available to the mentally retarded patterns and conditions of everyday life which are as close as possible to the norms and patterns of the mainstream of society" (p. 181). In the United States, the idea that persons with mental retardation have a right to culturally normative experiences was championed by Wolfensberger (1972). This concept, coupled with a renaissance of societal concern for the mentally retarded, helped to facilitate a movement, beginning in the 1970s, toward **deinstitutionalization** and more community-based services for individuals with intellectual disabilities. Today, legislative as well as legal action has resulted in more normalized lifestyles and greater access to all aspects of society for our fellow citizens with intellectual disabilities.

The Emergence of Public Education for Students With Intellectual Disabilities

Although institutions were firmly established as part of the American social fabric in the late 1800s, public education for children with mental retardation was virtually nonexistent. The first public school class for "slow learning" youngsters was formed in Providence, Rhode Island, at the very end of the nineteenth century. You might remember that these programs were largely segregated or self-contained classes and would remain so for the better part of the twentieth century. Classes for higher-functioning pupils with intellectual disabilities began to grow, in part as a result of the popularizing of IQ testing. Scheerenberger (1983) reports that by 1930, sixteen states had enacted either mandatory or permissive legislation regarding special classes for children with mental retardation. By 1952, forty-six of the forty-eight states provided an education to children with intellectual disabilities. Youngsters with severe or profound mental retardation, however, were largely excluded from public education.

The 1960s and 1970s marked the beginning of an era of national concern for the rights of individuals, a focus that continues today. People with intellectual disabilities would benefit from this attention. Aided by the actions of President Kennedy, who had a sister with mental retardation, enlightened social policies, new educational programs, and a national research agenda were all forthcoming. At the same time, advances in the field of psychology and education demonstrated that, to some degree, all individuals with intellectual disabilities are capable of learning. Professionals also began a movement toward less restrictive and more integrated educational placements for students with mental retardation—an emphasis with a very contemporary flavor. But perhaps the principal legacy of this era, which is foundational to today's educational programming, is a greater acceptance of persons with intellectual disabilities and their right, as fellow citizens, to live their lives in the most normalized fashion.

Prevalence of Intellectual Disabilities or Mental Retardation

How many people in the United States are intellectually disabled? Although this may seem a relatively straightforward and factual question, in reality, it is somewhat difficult to answer. According to data from the U.S. Department of Education (2010), 476,131 children between the ages of 6 and 21 were identified as mentally retarded and receiving a special education during the 2008–2009 school year. These students represent approximately 8 percent of all pupils with disabilities and about 1 percent of the total school-age population. Although a figure of approximately 476,000 may seem large, over the

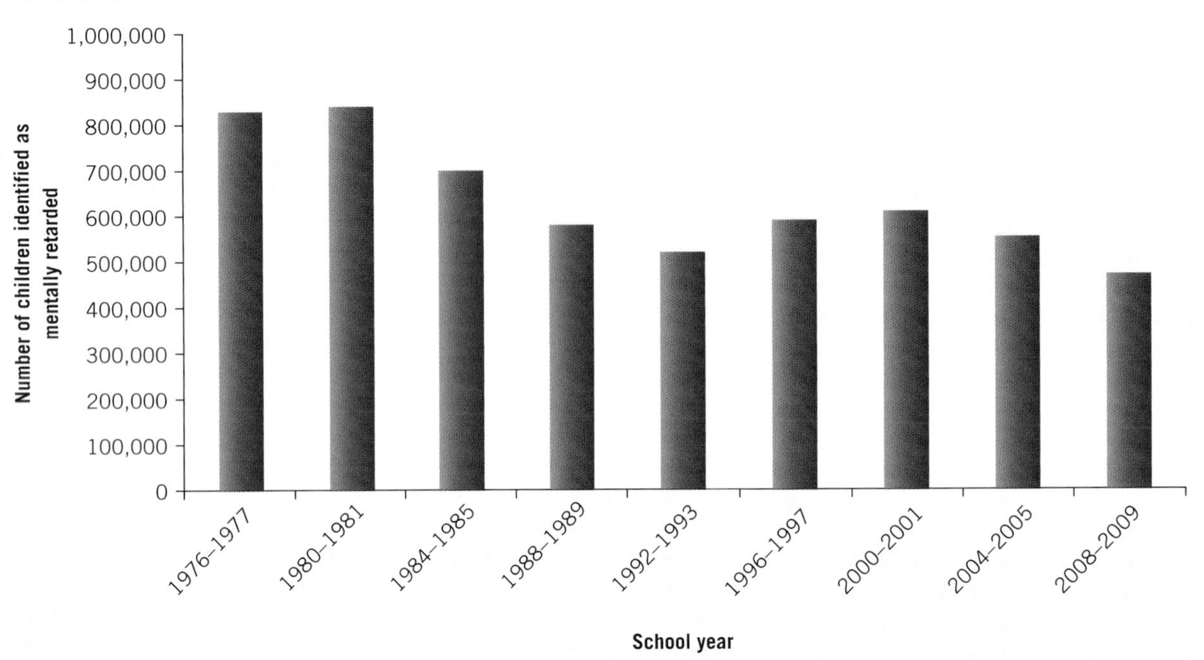

FIGURE 5.5 Changes in the Approximate Number of Children Classified as Intellectually Disabled in Representative Years

NOTE: Enrollment figures represent children ages 6–21 served under Part B and Chapter 1

SOURCE: Various U.S. Department of Education Annual Reports to Congress on the Implementation of IDEA.

years the number of students classified as mentally retarded has decreased significantly. Since the enactment of PL 94–142 in 1975, almost 344,000 fewer pupils are being served in classes for individuals with intellectual disabilities, representing a decrease of about 42 percent. Figure 5.5 documents this dramatic reduction.

The federal government, for the first time since the 1987–1988 school year, is now requiring states to report the number of preschoolers receiving a special education according to their disability label. This requirement represents a shift away from allowing states to use the term *developmentally delayed* when reporting preschoolers with disabilities. According to the U.S. Department of Education (2010), more than 12,400 preschoolers are recognized as being mentally retarded. This figure represents 1.7 percent of all youngsters with a disability.

There are several reasons for this downward shift in the number of school-age children classified as intellectually disabled. Prevention and early intervention efforts have certainly played a role in decreasing the number of children identified as mentally retarded. Other plausible explanations include changes in the definition of mental retardation, the impact of litigation (for example, *Diana v. State Board of Education* [1970]; *Larry P.* [1972]), changes in referral tactics, and the placement of higher-functioning students with intellectual disabilities into programs for pupils with learning disabilities. But perhaps the most compelling reason for the gradual reduction in the number of children classified as intellectually disabled is a growing reluctance on the part of professionals to identify (or misidentify) youngsters as mildly mentally retarded, especially if they are from minority groups (Beirne-Smith et al., 2006; Oswald, Coutinho, Best, & Nguyen, 2001).

For many years, the federal government estimated the prevalence of intellectual disabilities in the general population to be about 3 percent. According to the President's Committee for People with Intellectual Disabilities (2010), approximately 7 million to 8 million people in the United States have mental retardation, a figure that has not substantially changed in several decades. Intellectual disabilities directly affect one out of ten American families. Researchers, however, have serious questions about the accuracy of the 3 percent prevalence figure. Most contemporary thinking suggests a prevalence figure closer to 1 percent of the general population (Beirne-Smith et al., 2006).

Within the population of individuals considered intellectually disabled, persons with mild mental retardation constitute the largest proportion. It is estimated that approximately 90 percent of people with intellectual disabilities function, to use a familiar term, at the mild level (IQ 50–70/75). The remaining 10 percent are classified as exhibiting moderate, severe, or profound mental retardation (Drew & Hardman, 2007).

As you can see, the answer to our original question, "How many people in the United States are intellectually disabled?" is truly a difficult one. An objective answer to this query depends on many variables, suggesting that a definitive answer will likely remain elusive.

Etiology of Intellectual Disabilities or Mental Retardation

Determining the cause, or **etiology**, of intellectual disabilities is a difficult process. An individual may be mentally retarded for a multitude of reasons, and often the cause is unknown. In fact, in only about half of all cases of intellectual disabilities can a specific cause be cited (American Association on Intellectual and Developmental Disabilities, 2010b). Generally speaking, the less severe the retardation, the greater the likelihood that a particular cause cannot be determined.

Although scientists and other researchers are unable to determine the etiology of mental retardation in every instance, we do know a great deal about what causes intellectual disabilities or is at least implicated as a possible etiological factor. Investigators have designed several different schemes or models for classifying known and/or suspected causes of intellectual disabilities. For the purpose of this discussion, we have adopted the AAIDD (Luckasson et al., 2002) format for categorizing etiological factors typically associated with mental retardation. The 2002 AAIDD model and the 2010 conceptualization designate three main sources of possible causes of intellectual disabilities, based on the time of onset: **prenatal** (occurring before birth), **perinatal** (occurring around the time of birth), and **postnatal** (occurring after birth). Table 5.4 identifies some of the variables that often lead to intellectual disabilities.

Prenatal Contributions

Even a quick glance at Table 5.4 suggests that many different factors, of various origins, contribute to the possibility that a developing fetus may be at risk for intellectual disabilities. In some instances, mental retardation will be an inescapable fact; in other cases, it is highly probable. Fortunately, researchers are making great strides in the areas of detection and prevention of certain types of intellectual disabilities.

Chromosomal Abnormalities

Down syndrome, the most common and perhaps best-known genetic disorder, was first described by Dr. John Langdon Down in 1866; however, it was not until 1959 that Down syndrome was linked to a chromosomal abnormality (Lejune, Gautier, & Turpin, 1959). Most people have forty-six chromosomes arranged in twenty-three pairs; people with Down syndrome have forty-seven. Chromosomes are rod- or threadlike bodies that carry the genes that provide the blueprint or building blocks for development. About 5 percent of all people with mental retardation have Down syndrome (Beirne-Smith et al., 2006). The most common type of Down syndrome, accounting for approximately 90 percent of cases, is known as trisomy 21. In this instance, an extra chromosome becomes attached to the twenty-first pair, with the result that there are three (tri) chromosomes at this particular site.

TABLE 5.4 Possible Causes of Intellectual Disabilities

Prenatal Factors	Examples	Perinatal Factors	Examples	Postnatal Factors	Examples
Chromosomal abnormalities	• *Down syndrome* • *Fragile X syndrome* • *Turner syndrome*	Gestational disorders	• *Low birth weight* • *Prematurity*	Infections and intoxicants	• *Child abuse/ neglect* • *Head trauma* • *Malnutrition* • *Environmental deprivation*
Metabolic and nutritional disorders	• *Phenylketonuria* • *Tay-Sachs disease* • *Galactosemia* • *Prader-Willi syndrome*	Neonatal complications	• *Hypoxia* • *Birth trauma* • *Seizures* • *Respiratory distress* • *Breech delivery* • *Prolonged delivery*	Environmental factors	• *Lead poisoning* • *Encephalitis* • *Meningitis* • *Reye's syndrome*
Maternal infections	• *Rubella* • *Syphilis* • *HIV (AIDS)* • *Cytomegalovirus* • *Rh incompatability* • *Toxoplasmosis*			Brain damage	• *Neurofibromatosis* • *Tuberous sclerosis*
Environmental conditions	• *Fetal alcohol syndrome* • *Illicit drug use*				
Unknown influences	• *Anencephaly* • *Hydrocephalus* • *Microcephaly*				

Scientists are uncertain as to exactly what causes Down syndrome. Thyroid problems, drugs, and exposure to radiation are all suspected, but there appears to be a strong link between maternal age and Down syndrome. It is estimated that at age 25, the incidence of Down syndrome is about 1 out of 1,250 births; at age 30, it is 1 in 1,000 births; at age 35, it is 1 in 400 births; at age 40, it is 1 in 100 births; and at age 45, the risk is about 1 out of 30 births (March of Dimes, 2009a; Roizen, 2007). It is important to note that age itself does *not* cause Down syndrome, only that there is a strong correlation. Down syndrome affects all racial and socioeconomic groups equally.

Down syndrome most often results in mild to moderate mental retardation. In some instances, however, individuals may be severely retarded, and in others, near normal intelligence is possible. Besides intellectual disabilities, this chromosomal aberration frequently results in other health concerns such as heart defects, hearing loss, intestinal malformations, vision problems, and an increased risk for thyroid difficulties and leukemia (March of Dimes, 2009a).

People with Down syndrome have distinctive physical characteristics. Among the most commonly observed features are an upper slant of the eyes, short stature, a flat nose, somewhat smaller ears and nose, an enlarged and sometimes protruding tongue, short fingers, reduced muscle tone, and a single crease (simian crease) across the palm of the hand (people without Down syndrome have parallel lines). Most individuals with Down syndrome will exhibit some, but not all, of these identifying characteristics.

Down syndrome most often results in mild to moderate mental retardation.

Life expectancies for people with Down syndrome have increased dramatically. In the 1920s and 1930s, the life span for a child with Down syndrome was generally less than ten years; today, thanks to advances in medicine and health care, large numbers of individuals with Down syndrome are living well into their upper 50s (March of Dimes, 2009a). With advancing chronological age, however, individuals with Down syndrome face a greater risk for developing Alzheimer's disease (National Down Syndrome Society, 2010).

Fragile X syndrome is one of the more recently identified conditions linked to mental retardation. This syndrome affects approximately 1 in 4,000 males and at least half as many females, making it one of the leading inherited causes of intellectual disabilities (March of Dimes, 2007; Taylor, Brady, & Richards, 2005). Because of the involvement of the X chromosome, this condition, which is caused by an abnormal or defective gene, predominantly affects males, although females can be carriers of the gene that causes it.

Individuals who have this disorder have a deficiency in the structure of the X chromosome of the twenty-third pair. Under a microscope, one of the "arms" of the X chromosome appears pinched or weakened and thus fragile. Females, who have two X chromosomes, are less susceptible to the defective gene; males, who have one X and one Y chromosome, are substantially at risk.

Typical characteristics associated with this syndrome include cognitive deficits of varying degrees, a long narrow face, large ears, a prominent forehead, and a large head circumference. At puberty, enlarged testicles are present (Meyer, 2007). Behaviorally, individuals with fragile X syndrome typically exhibit attention disorders, self-stimulatory behaviors, and speech and language problems. Meyer reports that about one third of girls with this disorder have mild mental retardation or learning disabilities. The fragile X syndrome also appears to be associated with other disabilities such as autism and disorders of attention (Beirne-Smith et al., 2006).

Metabolic and Nutritional Disorders

Phenylketonuria, more commonly known by its acronym, **PKU,** is an example of an inborn error of metabolism. It is a recessive trait, meaning that both parents have to be carriers of the defective gene. When this occurs, there is a 25 percent chance that the infant will be born with PKU. There is an equal probability, however, that the baby will be healthy (and a 50 percent chance it will be an asymptomatic carrier). PKU appears in about 1 out of every 25,000 births and is most common among Northern European and Native American ethnic groups (March of Dimes, 2008b).

PKU affects the way an infant's body processes or metabolizes protein. Affected babies lack the liver enzyme needed to process phenylalanine, which is common in many high-protein foods such as milk. As a result of this deficiency, phenylalanine accumulates in the bloodstream and becomes toxic. This metabolic malfunction, if not promptly treated, leads to brain damage and mental retardation, which is often severe.

Elevated levels of phenylalanine can be detected in the blood and urine of newborns within the first few days of life. All states now routinely screen for this disorder, although it is not a mandatory procedure in all instances. If unusually high levels of phenylalanine are found, the infant is placed on a special diet, reducing the intake of protein. Researchers have found that if dietary restrictions are introduced shortly after birth, the devastating consequences of PKU are significantly minimized and normal developmental milestones are usually achieved (Channon, German, Cassina, & Lee, 2004; March of Dimes, 2008b). It is unclear, however, how long the dietary restrictions must be maintained. As individuals with PKU get older, dietary control becomes more difficult. Of particular concern are women of childbearing age who have PKU. The metabolic imbalances within these women can cause serious consequences to the developing fetus. In more than 90 percent of these pregnancies, babies are born with intellectual disabilities and heart defects, and they are usually of low birth weight. However, returning to an individualized, restricted diet prior to pregnancy and maintaining it throughout pregnancy usually results in a healthy baby (March of Dimes). Awareness of this concern has resulted in warning labels on many popular food items such as diet soft drinks and some low-fat foods ("Caution: product contains phenylalanine").

Galactosemia is another example of an inborn error of metabolism. In this disorder, infants are unable to process galactose, a form of sugar, typically found in milk and other food products. Manifestation of this condition in newborns typically includes jaundice, liver damage, heightened susceptibility to infections, failure to thrive, vomiting, and cataracts, along with impaired intellectual functioning (Drew & Hardman, 2007). If galactosemia is detected early, a milk-free diet can be started, which substantially reduces the potential for problems and delays.

Maternal Infections

Viruses and infections often cause intellectual disabilities and a host of other problems. While pregnant, a woman and her developing child are very susceptible to a wide variety of potentially damaging infections. Exposure during the first trimester of pregnancy usually results in severe consequences. **Rubella** (German measles) is a good example of this type of infection. This mild but highly contagious illness has been linked to mental retardation, vision and hearing defects, heart problems, and low birth weight. Rubella is one of the leading causes of multiple impairments in children. With the introduction of a rubella vaccine in 1969, instances of rubella-related disabilities have substantially decreased.

Sexually transmitted diseases such as gonorrhea and **syphilis** are capable of crossing the placenta and attacking the central nervous system of the developing fetus. In contrast to rubella, the risk to the unborn child is greater at the later stages of fetal development.

Acquired immune deficiency syndrome (AIDS), which is attributed to the human immunodeficiency virus (HIV), is another probable cause of mental retardation and other developmental delays. Generally transmitted via unprotected sexual intercourse with an infected person or the sharing of hypodermic needles, HIV crosses the placenta and affects the central nervous system while also damaging the immune system, leaving the fetus substantially at risk for opportunistic infections. Pediatric AIDS is suspected of being a leading infectious cause of intellectual disabilities. At the same time, HIV is the single most preventable cause of infectious mental retardation.

Maternal–fetal **Rh incompatibility**, although technically not an infection, is another potential cause of intellectual disabilities. At one time, this disease was a leading cause of mental retardation, affecting approximately 16,000 infants annually. Since 1968, there has been a dramatic reduction in the number of cases of Rh disease, thanks to the development of a treatment that usually prevents its occurrence (March of Dimes, 2009b). Simply stated, Rh disease is a blood group incompatibility between a mother and her unborn child. This discrepancy is the result of the Rh factor, a protein found on the surface of red blood cells. Rh-positive blood contains this protein; Rh-negative blood cells do not (Beirne-Smith et al., 2006).

Rh incompatibility often leads to serious consequences such as intellectual disabilities, cerebral palsy, epilepsy, and other neonatal complications. The problem arises when an

Rh-negative mother carries an Rh-positive baby, which causes her to produce antibodies against any future Rh-positive fetus. For this reason, Rh-negative women today generally receive an injection of Rh immune globulin within 72 hours of delivering an Rh-positive baby. In the vast majority of cases, this procedure prevents the production of antibodies, thus preventing problems in any future pregnancies.

Toxoplasmosis is a further example of maternal infection that typically poses grave risks to an unborn child. Toxoplasmosis is contracted through exposure to cat fecal matter; it is also present in undercooked or raw meat and raw eggs. If the mother is exposed to this parasitic infection during pregnancy, especially in the third trimester, it is very likely that fetal infection will occur. Infected infants may be born with intellectual disabilities, cerebral palsy, damaged retinas leading to blindness, microcephaly (unusually small head), enlarged liver and spleen, jaundice, and other very serious complications. Antibiotics seem to provide some defense for both mother and child.

Our final illustration of maternal infections is **cytomegalovirus (CMV)**, an especially common virus that is part of the herpes group. Most women have been exposed to this virus at some time in their lives and thus develop immunity. If initial exposure occurs during pregnancy, however, the fetus may be severely affected. CMV often leads to brain damage and thus mental retardation, blindness, and hearing impairments.

Environmental Contributions

Many unsafe maternal behaviors—among them, smoking, illicit drug use (for example, cocaine, heroin), and the consumption of alcohol before and during pregnancy—have been linked to impaired fetal development. The use of alcohol, in particular, has captured the attention of scientists and researchers for many years. In 1973, the term **fetal alcohol syndrome**, or **FAS**, was first coined (Jones, Smith, Ulleland, & Streissguth, 1973). Currently, FAS is one of the leading causes of mental retardation in the United States (Davidson & Myers, 2007). Each year approximately 40,000 babies are born with some degree of alcohol-associated damage or defect (March of Dimes, 2008a).

Alcohol can damage the central nervous system of the unborn child, and brain damage is not uncommon. FAS is characterized by a variety of physical deformities, including facial abnormalities, heart defects, low birth weight, and motor dysfunctions. In addition to mild to moderate intellectual disabilities, attention disorders and behavioral problems are usually present. Less severe and subtler forms of alcohol-related damage are recognized as **fetal alcohol effect (FAE)**. The effects of excessive alcohol consumption last a lifetime; yet this condition is entirely preventable.

Unknown Influences

Several types of cranial malformations are the result of unknown prenatal factors. **Anencephaly** is but one illustration. In this condition, the entire brain or a large portion of it fails to develop properly, with devastating consequences for the infant. A more common condition is **microcephaly**, characterized by an unusually small head and severe retardation. **Hydrocephalus** is a disorder associated with the interference or blockage of the flow of cerebrospinal fluid, resulting in an accumulation of excess fluid that typically leads to an enlarged cranial cavity and potentially damaging compression on the brain. Doctors can surgically implant shunts that remove the excess fluid, thereby minimizing the pressure on the infant's brain and consequently the severe effects of this condition.

Video Link 5.3
Watch the story of twins.

Perinatal Conditions

Gestational Disorders

The two most common problems associated with gestational disorders are **low birth weight** and **premature birth**. Prematurity is generally defined as a birth that occurs prior to thirty-seven weeks of gestation. Low birth weight is defined as less than 5 pounds,

8 ounces (2,500 grams), and very low birth weight as less than 3 pounds, 5 ounces (1,500 grams). In the majority of instances, but not all, low-birth-weight infants are premature. Not all babies with gestational disorders will have a disability or encounter future difficulties in school. However, some of these children may develop subtle learning problems, some may have intellectual disabilities, and still others may have sensory and motor impairments.

Neonatal Complications

Complications surrounding the birth process may cause intellectual disabilities and other developmental delays. One common example is **anoxia** (oxygen deprivation) or **hypoxia** (insufficient oxygen). Anoxia may occur because of damage to the umbilical cord or as a result of a prolonged and difficult delivery. Obstetrical or **birth trauma**, such as the improper use of forceps, may cause excessive pressure on the skull, which in turn may damage a portion of the infant's brain. A **breech presentation** is another illustration of a neonatal problem. In a breech delivery, the infant exits the birth canal buttocks first instead of the more typical headfirst presentation. This fetal delivery position raises concerns about the possibility of damage to the umbilical cord and a heightened threat of injury to the baby's head because of the greater intensity and frequency of uterine contractions later in the birth process. Worries about the infant's skull also arise when a **precipitous birth** (one lasting less than two hours) occurs. The gentle molding of the skull may not take place during a precipitous birth, thus increasing the risk of tissue damage and intellectual disabilities (Drew & Hardman, 2007).

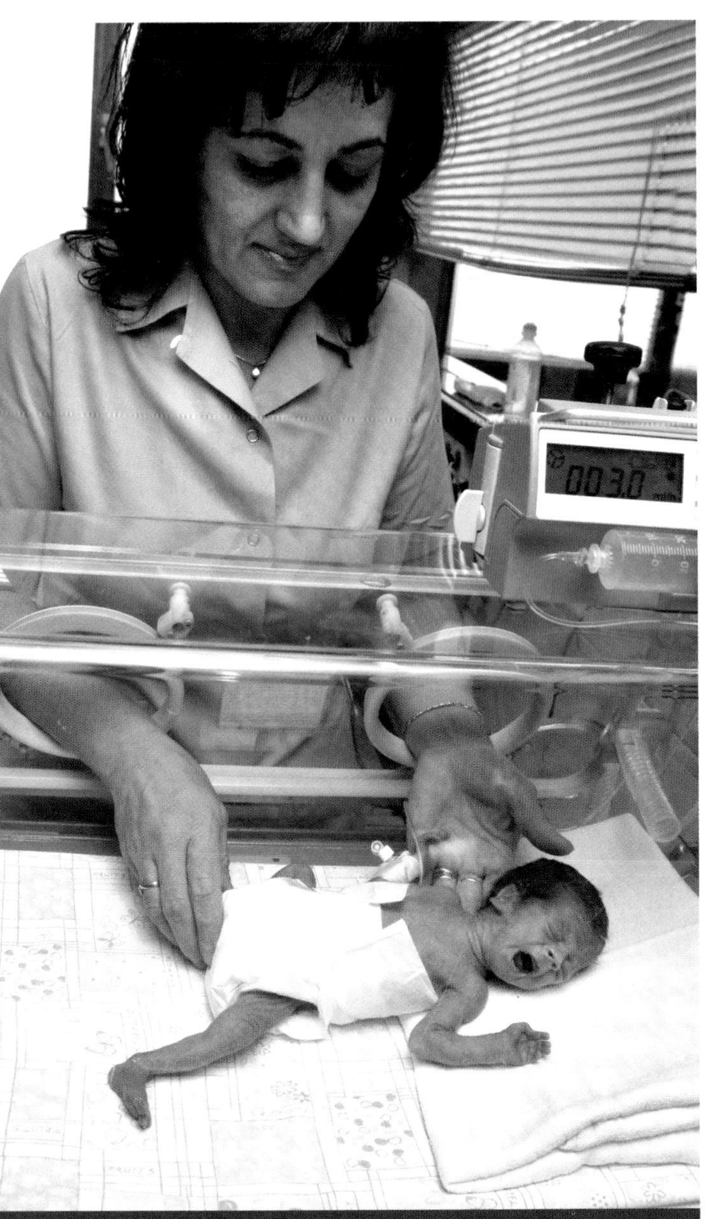

Complications surrounding the birth process may cause intellectual disabilities and other developmental delays.

Postnatal Factors

Infections and Intoxicants

Lead and mercury are two examples of environmental toxins that can cause intellectual disabilities. **Lead poisoning** is a serious public health problem. Because of its highly toxic nature, lead is no longer used in the manufacturing of gasoline or paint. But even though it is no longer commercially available, some youngsters are still at risk for lead poisoning. Children who live in older homes or apartments may ingest lead by eating peeling paint chips containing lead. Lead poisoning can cause seizures, brain damage, and disorders of the central nervous system.

Infections represent another source of concern for young children. **Meningitis**, a viral infection, causes damage to the covering of the brain known as the meninges. Meningitis may result from complications associated with typical childhood diseases such as mumps, measles, or chicken pox. Because it is capable of causing brain damage, mental retardation is a distinct possibility. Equally devastating is **encephalitis**, which is an inflammation of the brain tissue. Encephalitis may cause damage to the central nervous system and can result from complications of infections typically associated with childhood such as mumps or measles.

Environmental Factors

A wide variety of environmental or psychosocial influences are often associated with intellectual disabilities, especially instances of mild mental retardation. Debilitating factors may include nutritional problems, adverse living conditions, inadequate health care, and a lack of early cognitive stimulation. Many of these factors are associated with lower socioeconomic status. Child abuse and neglect along with head trauma resulting from automobile accidents or play-related injuries are also potential contributing factors. Of course, not all children exposed to these traumatic postnatal situations become intellectually disabled. These illustrations represent only evidence correlated with, but not necessarily causes of, mental retardation. It is perhaps best to think of these variables as interacting risk factors, with some children being more vulnerable than others. Fortunately, most children exposed to these unfavorable circumstances develop normally.

Although a large portion of mental retardation is attributed to environmental factors, contemporary thinking suggests that intellectual disabilities associated with psychosocial influences are the result of interaction between environmental and genetic or biological contributions. Stated another way, a youngster's genetic endowment provides a range of intellectual opportunity that is then mediated by the environment to which that individual is exposed.

As you can see, the question "What causes intellectual disabilities?" is indeed a difficult one to answer. Many variables must be considered, and in many cases, we just don't know why a particular child is mentally retarded. Perhaps the more intriguing question to ask is "Can we prevent intellectual disabilities?"

Prevention of Intellectual Disabilities or Mental Retardation

Prevention of intellectual disabilities has been a goal of scientists, medical researchers, and a host of other professionals for several decades. In many instances, unfortunately, the cause of mental retardation is still unknown. Let us focus our attention, however, on the accomplishments. Each year, thanks to advances in medical research, we prevent approximately

- 250 cases of intellectual disabilities due to PKU because of newborn screening and dietary intervention;
- 1,000 cases of mental retardation due to congenital hypothyroidism, also as a result of newborn screening and the use of thyroid hormone replacement therapy;
- 1,000 cases of mental retardation by using Rh immune globulin (RhoGAM) to prevent Rh disease and severe jaundice;
- 5,000–7,000 cases of intellectual disabilities caused by Hib meningitis by using the Hib vaccine; and
- 4,000 cases of mental retardation resulting from measles, largely due to vaccination efforts and greater public awareness.

Other examples of successful preventive efforts include the removal of lead, a highly toxic substance, from gasoline and paint. Additionally, legislation mandating the use of car seats or seat belts and encouraging children to wear bicycle helmets has helped to reduce the incidence of head trauma as a possible cause of mental retardation (The Arc, 2005). Obviously, the more we know about the etiology of intellectual disabilities, the better our chances are of preventing it.

Researchers typically identify three levels of prevention: primary, secondary, and tertiary. According to Graham and Scott (1988), **primary prevention** refers to eliminating the problem before its onset or occurrence; **secondary prevention** aims at minimizing or eliminating a potential risk factor; and **tertiary prevention** seeks to limit the adverse consequences of an existing problem while maximizing a person's potential. From a different perspective, Luckasson et al. (1992) write that

> primary prevention efforts are directed toward the parents of the person with mental retardation or the person who might otherwise develop a condition which would result in mental retardation. Secondary prevention efforts are directed toward the person who is born with a condition that might otherwise result in mental retardation. Tertiary prevention efforts are directed toward the person who has mental retardation. (p. 72)

An example of primary prevention would be heightening the awareness of pregnant women about the potential dangers of smoking and alcohol use while pregnant. Good prenatal health care, prevention of child abuse, and genetic counseling prior to conception also illustrate primary prevention tactics. After a child is conceived, the fetus can be analyzed for genetic or chromosomal abnormalities through medical procedures known as **amniocentesis, chorionic villus sampling (CVS)**, and a noninvasive test, **ultrasound**. All three tests are viewed as primary prevention measures.

Chorionic villus sampling is a diagnostic procedure usually performed at about ten to twelve weeks of gestation. With this procedure, which has only been available since 1983, chorionic tissue or placenta material is sampled for chromosomal or genetic birth defects. Although CVS is slightly more risky than amniocentesis, detection of defects occurs earlier in fetal development.

In the vast majority of instances, these prenatal biochemical analyses do not reveal the presence of a disorder or defect. When the results are positive, however, and indicate that the fetus has, for example, Down syndrome, parents are confronted with a decision as to whether to terminate the pregnancy (called an elective or **therapeutic abortion**) or to begin planning and preparation for an infant who will most likely be disabled. These are very difficult and often painful decisions involving a variety of moral and ethical dilemmas.

Finally, ultrasound is a mapping or imaging of the fetus accomplished by a procedure much like sonar. This test can be done anytime during the pregnancy and without risk to the baby. Ultrasound is useful for detecting hydrocephalus, defects in the development of limbs, and, in some cases, central nervous system defects such as **spina bifida**.

The screenings of newborns for PKU and galactosemia shortly after birth are representative of secondary prevention. PKU screening, which has been available since 1957, is a relatively inexpensive test that allows health care professionals to establish dietary controls and thus halt the effects of this inherited genetic disorder. Surgical implantation of a shunt to remove excess fluid around the brain in instances of hydrocephalus also illustrates secondary prevention efforts.

Tertiary prevention strategies are aimed at maximizing the quality of life for a person with intellectual disabilities. Early intervention for a toddler with Down syndrome, inclusive education programs for school-age children with mental retardation, and comprehensive community-based services for adults with intellectual disabilities are examples of tertiary efforts across the life span.

Research holds the key to new opportunities for preventing various types of intellectual disabilities. Two promising areas are fetal treatments, involving in utero intervention for certain defects, and gene therapy, which is designed to correct genetic flaws. Only time will tell how successful we will be in preventing some forms of mental retardation.

Characteristics of Individuals With Intellectual Disabilities or Mental Retardation

When discussing characteristics common to people with intellectual disabilities, it is important to remember that although, as a group, they may exhibit a particular feature, not all individuals identified as mentally retarded will share this characteristic. Persons with intellectual disabilities are an especially heterogeneous population; interindividual differences are considerable. Many factors influence individual behavior and functioning—among them, chronological age, the severity and etiology of the disability, and educational opportunities. We caution you to remember that the following descriptions represent generalizations and are only useful for framing this discussion. Finally, in several ways, individuals with intellectual disabilities are more like their typically developing counterparts than they are different, sharing many of the same social, emotional, and physical needs.

Some students with intellectual disabilities experience difficulty learning because they fail to attend to the relevant attributes of the task.

Learning Characteristics

The most common defining characteristic of someone identified as intellectually disabled is impaired cognitive functioning, which, you may recall, can vary greatly. Investigators are typically not concerned with the person's intellectual ability per se but rather are concerned with the impact that lower IQ has on the individual's ability to learn, acquire concepts, process information, and apply knowledge in various settings such as school and community. Scientists do not yet fully understand the complexity of the learning process in human beings. Learning is a difficult concept to define—in many ways, it is unique to the individual—and is composed of many interrelated cognitive processes. Learning, then, is not a unitary variable. We have chosen, therefore, to briefly examine several of the characteristics that researchers believe influence learning.

Attention

Attention, which is a multidimensional concept, plays a key role in learning. Many of the learning difficulties of individuals with mental retardation are thought to be due to attentional deficits. Before learning a task, a person must be able to attend to its relevant attributes. Tomporowski and Tinsley (1997) theorize that individuals who are mentally retarded experience difficulty focusing their attention, maintaining it, and selectively attending to relevant stimuli. They also have less attention to allocate. It may well be that children with intellectual disabilities perform poorly on certain learning tasks because they do not know how to attend to the relevant aspects or dimensions of the problem.

Memory

Memory, which is an important component of learning, is often impaired in children with intellectual disabilities. Generally speaking, the more severe the retardation, the greater the deficits in memory (Drew & Hardman, 2007; Owens, 2010). Early investigators researching memory processes of individuals with mental retardation frequently distinguished between short-term memory (STM)—data recalled after a few seconds or hours—and long-term memory (LTM)—the retrieval of information days or months later. Early experiments suggested that persons who are intellectually disabled experience difficulty with STM learning tasks (recalling directions in sequence) (Ellis, 1963); however, when LTM is assessed (recalling their telephone number or address), individuals with mental retardation perform comparably to their typically developing peers (Belmont, 1966). Unfortunately, many of these early investigative efforts were plagued by methodological flaws, making interpretation of the results difficult. Contemporary researchers have shifted their attention away from an LTM-versus-STM model to one that considers memory as an important component of an information-processing model.

Researchers have identified several factors that may contribute to the memory difficulties of persons with intellectual disabilities. Among them are problems attending to relevant stimuli (Westling & Fox, 2009), inefficient rehearsal strategies, and an inability to generalize skills to novel settings or tasks (Tomporowski & Tinsley, 1997).

Academic Performance

As you might anticipate, students with intellectual disabilities encounter difficulties in their academic work. Generally, this deficiency is seen across all subject areas, but reading appears to be the weakest area, especially reading comprehension (Katims, 2000). Pupils identified as mentally retarded are also deficient in arithmetic, but their performance is more in line with their mental age (Drew & Hardman, 2007). Remember, just because a student is academically unsuccessful does not mean that he or she cannot excel in other school endeavors such as athletics or the arts.

Motivation

Despite their importance for understanding individuals who are intellectually disabled, motivational factors have not received the attention they deserve (Morrison & Polloway, 1995). Yet these variables are crucial for understanding the discrepancy that often exists between an individual's performance and his or her actual ability. It is not unusual for children with mental retardation to approach a learning situation with heightened anxiety. A history of failure in earlier encounters contributes to this generalized feeling of apprehension; consequently, pupils seem to be less goal oriented and lacking in motivation.

Past experiences with failure typically lead individuals with intellectual disabilities to exhibit an **external locus of control**; that is, they are likely to believe that the consequences or outcomes of their behavior are the result of circumstances and events beyond their personal control, rather than their own efforts. Repeated episodes of failure also give rise to a related concept, **learned helplessness** (Drew & Hardman, 2007)—the perception that no matter how much effort they put forth, failure is inevitable. ("No matter how hard I try, I won't be successful!") This expectancy of failure frequently causes students with mental retardation to stop trying, even when the task is one they are capable of completing. Educators sometimes refer to this behavior as the "pencil down syndrome."

Accumulated experiences with failure also result in a style of learning and problem solving characterized as **outer-directedness**, or a loss of confidence and trust in one's own abilities and solutions and a reliance on others for cues and guidance (Bybee & Zigler, 1998). While not solely limited to individuals with intellectual disabilities, this overreliance on others contributes to a lack of motivation and increased dependence. Once again, the origin of this behavior can be traced to the debilitating effects of repeated failure.

Generalization

Video Link 5.4
Watch suggestions for instructional strategies.

It is not unusual for individuals with intellectual disabilities to experience difficulty in transferring or **generalizing** knowledge acquired in one context to new or different settings. In a large number of instances, learning in someone who is mentally retarded is situation specific; that is, once a particular skill or behavior is mastered, the individual has difficulty duplicating the skill when confronted with novel circumstances—different cues, different people, or different environments (Taylor et al., 2005). For example, an adolescent with intellectual disabilities who can successfully determine correct change from a purchase in the school cafeteria might experience difficulty when counting his or her change at a grocery store or a restaurant. Therefore, teachers must systematically plan for generalization; typically it does not occur automatically. Generalization of responses can be facilitated, for example, by using concrete materials rather than abstract representations, by providing instruction in various settings where the strategies or skill will typically be used, by incorporating a variety of examples and materials, or by simply informing the pupils of the multiple applications that are possible.

Language Development

Speech and language development are closely related to cognitive functioning. In fact, speech and language difficulties are more common among individuals with mental retardation than in their typically developing counterparts (Warren & Yoder, 1997). Given the association between intellectual ability and speech and language, it is not surprising that students with intellectual disabilities experience a great deal of difficulty with academic tasks, such as reading, that require verbal and language competency.

Speech disorders are common among individuals with mental retardation. These may include errors of articulation such as additions or distortions, fluency disorders (stuttering), and voice disorders such as hypernasal speech or concerns about loudness. In fact, researchers have found that speech and language difficulties are a fairly common secondary disability among students with intellectual disabilities (Beirne-Smith et al., 2006).

Despite the prevalence of speech disorders, language problems are receiving increased attention from professionals because deficits in this arena are highly debilitating. There is a strong correlation between intellectual ability and language development—the higher the IQ, the less pervasive the language disorder. Although children with mental retardation, especially those with higher IQs, acquire language in the same fashion as their typically developing peers, development occurs more slowly, their vocabulary is more limited, and grammatical structure and sentence complexity are often impaired (Owens, 2010). Yet language is crucial for the independent functioning of the individual with intellectual disabilities. Deficits in this area represent one of the greatest obstacles hindering the integration of people with mental retardation into the mainstream of society (Owens, 2009).

Social and Behavioral Characteristics

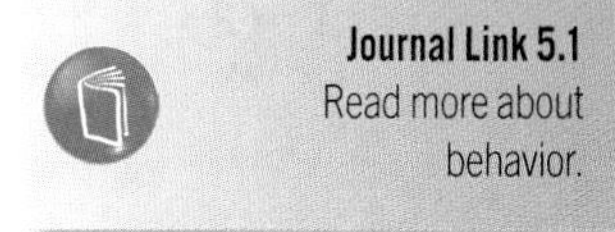

The ability to get along with other people is an important skill; and it is just as significant for individuals who are intellectually disabled as it is for those who are not mentally retarded. In fact, in some situations, social adeptness or proficiency may be as important as, if not more important than, intellectual ability. In the area of employment, for example, when workers with intellectual or other developmental disabilities experience difficulty on the job, it is frequently due to problems of social interactions with coworkers and supervisors rather than job performance per se (Hendricks & Wehman, 2009).

Individuals with intellectual delays often exhibit poor interpersonal skills and socially inappropriate or immature behavior; as a result, they frequently encounter rejection by peers and classmates. It is not unusual for individuals with mental retardation to lack the social competency necessary to establish and maintain friendships with coworkers and others (Wehman, 2006). Friend and Bursuck (2009) note that the success or failure of students with intellectual disabilities who are placed in general education classrooms is often determined by their social skills. This lack of social ability can pose significant difficulties as increasing numbers of individuals with intellectual disabilities are seizing the opportunity to participate in more normalized environments. Direct social skill instruction is one way of enhancing the social development of persons who are mentally retarded. Behavior modification techniques can reduce inappropriate social behaviors while establishing more desirable and acceptable behaviors. The modeling of the appropriate behavior of classmates is another way that students with intellectual disabilities can acquire more socially attractive behaviors, which in turn can lead to greater peer acceptance.

Table 5.5 presents a summary of selected learning and behavioral characteristics of individuals with intellectual disabilities.

TABLE 5.5 Representative Learning and Behavioral Characteristics of Learners With Intellectual Disabilities

Dimension	Associated Attributes and Features
Attention	• Inability to attend to critical or relevant features of a task • Diminished attention span • Difficulty ignoring distracting stimuli
Memory	• Deficits in memory correlated with severity of intellectual disability • Limitations in ability to selectively process and store information • Inefficient rehearsal strategies • Difficulty with short-term (working) memory is common—recalling directions in sequence presented seconds earlier • Long-term retrieval (recalling telephone number) is similar to that of peers without mental retardation
Motivation	• History of and a generalized expectancy for failure—learned helplessness—effort is unrewarded; failure is inevitable • Exhibit external locus of control—belief that outcomes of behavior are the result of circumstances (fate, chance) beyond personal control rather than own efforts • Evidence outer-directedness, a loss of confidence and a distrust of own abilities, reliance on others for cues and guidance
Generalization	• Difficulty applying knowledge or skill to new tasks, situations, or settings • Problem in using previous experience in novel situations • Teachers must explicitly plan for generalization; typically it does not automatically occur
Language Development	• Follow same sequence of language acquisition as typical individuals, albeit at a slower pace • Strong correlation between intellectual ability and language development—the higher the IQ, the less pervasive the language difficulty • Speech disorders (articulation errors, stuttering) more common than in peers without intellectual disabilities • Vocabulary is often limited • Grammatical structure and sentence complexity are often impaired
Academic Development	• Generally exhibit difficulties in all academic areas with reading being the weakest • Problem-solving difficulties in arithmetic
Social Development	• Typically lacking in social competence • Rejection by peers and classmates is common—poor interpersonal skills • Frequently exhibit socially inappropriate or immature behavior—difficulty establishing and maintaining friendships • Diminished self-esteem coupled with low self-concept

SOURCE: Adapted from R. Gargiulo and D. Metcalf, *Teaching in Today's Inclusive Classrooms* (Belmont, CA: Wadsworth/Cengage Learning, 2010), p. 60.

Educational Considerations

Educators and other professionals no longer consider students with intellectual disabilities to be ineducable. Children who are retarded are capable of learning. To be successful, however, they require an instructional program that is individualized to meet their unique needs. Additionally, the instruction provided to these learners must be comprehensive and functional, equipping them, to the maximum extent possible, with the experiences they need to live and work in their respective communities, both now and in the future. As with other pupils, our goal as teachers should be one of developing independence and self-sufficiency. Obviously, for this population of children, this objective dictates that an education be interpreted broadly and not construed solely as academic learning. As we explore the issue of educational opportunities for individuals who are mentally retarded, you will discover that the concepts of individualization and appropriateness are of paramount importance.

In this part of the chapter, we will explore the various educational options available to children who are intellectually disabled and where these services are delivered. Our focus here is on school-age individuals; preschool and adult programming will be addressed in later sections.

Where Are Students With Intellectual Disabilities or Mental Retardation Educated?

Despite the contemporary trend toward educating children with disabilities in more normalized settings, pupils with mental retardation are more than three times as likely as other students with exceptionalities to be educated in a separate class. Only 15.3 percent of all individuals with disabilities were educated in self-contained classrooms during the 2007–2008 school year, but 48.8 percent of youngsters with intellectual disabilities were placed in this environment (U.S. Department of Education, 2009). Historically speaking, this administrative arrangement has characterized the delivery of educational services to pupils who are intellectually disabled. Over the years, the U.S. Department of Education has chronicled this national trend. In 1991, for example, it found that only about 6 percent of students identified as mentally retarded were educated in the general education classroom, with an additional 22 percent being served in a resource room. A separate classroom was the placement of choice for more than half (59 percent) of these pupils, and 10 percent were receiving services in a separate school. A 1995 Department of Education survey found a similar, albeit improving, placement pattern. Approximately 7 percent of students with intellectual disabilities were assigned to the general education classroom, and some 27 percent attended a resource room. Thus, about one third of the youngsters with intellectual disabilities spent at least part of their educational day in the general education classroom, but more than 57 percent of these students received services in a self-contained classroom and 8 percent attended a separate school. More recent national data (see Figure 5.6) reflect greater opportunities for participation in more normalized placements, but in the eyes of many authorities and advocates, much still needs to be done toward having children with mental retardation educated in less restrictive settings.

Educational Programming Options

Generally speaking, educational programming for pupils who are intellectually disabled reflects a marriage of various emphasis areas or focal points. Among these concentrations are functional academic skills, vocational training, community living, and self-help skills, along with a growing emphasis on exposure to the general education curriculum. Of course, the individual needs of the student must dictate how a specific educational program is constructed. Remember, children with mental retardation represent an especially heterogeneous population of learners with a wide range of skills and abilities. The curriculum designed for these pupils must be individualized, functional, and comprehensive (Beirne-Smith et al., 2006). In addition, instructional programming for the intellectually disabled must be forward looking, giving due consideration to these students' current needs and future life goals.

Video Link 5.5
Watch more about educational considerations.

We cannot stress enough the importance of individually crafted instructional programs. A "one size fits all" approach for instructing individuals with intellectual disabilities is inappropriate. An effective curriculum must not only be individualized, emphasizing

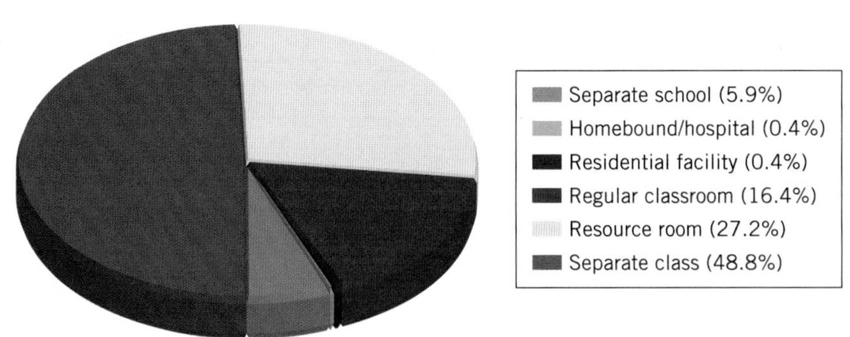

FIGURE 5.6 Educational Placements of Students With Intellectual Disabilities

NOTE: Figure represents percentage of enrollment of students with intellectual disabilities during the 2007–2008 school year.

SOURCE: U.S. Department of Education. (2009). *IDEA data.* Retrieved September 5, 2009, from https://www.ideadata.org/PartBReport.asp

academic as well as adaptive skills; it must also be comprehensive (Drew & Hardman, 2007). A comprehensive curriculum for learners with cognitive limitations (Polloway, Patton, & Serna, 2008) should, among other things,

- be responsive to the needs of the individual student at the current time;
- provide maximum interaction with nondisabled peers and access to the general education curriculum, while also attending to specific curricular needs missing in the general education curriculum;
- be based on a realistic assessment of adult outcomes; and
- be sensitive to diploma requirements and graduation goals.

Functional Curriculum

A **functional curriculum** is one that instructs pupils in the life skills they require for successful daily living and prepares them for those situations and environments they will encounter upon leaving school. In a functional curriculum, academic skills are applied to everyday, practical life situations—for example, making change, following directions in a cookbook, reading washing instructions, or completing a job application. Known as **functional academics**, these skills are often the core of instructional programs for some individuals with mild or moderate mental retardation. Additionally, these students are exposed to curriculum content focusing on personal hygiene, independent living skills, community resources, and other issues that, collectively, are designed to enhance their current and future independence and successful adjustment (Johnson, 2005).

Several approaches are available for teaching functional academics. Two of the most commonly used strategies are functional, generalized skills useful for life routines and embedded academic skills appropriate to specific life situations. In some situations, however, it may be necessary to simply bypass academic instruction (Browder & Snell, 2000). Browder and Snell recommend that the IEP team consider the following six factors when selecting an instructional approach:

1. The student's preferences
2. The parent's preferences
3. The student's chronological age or number of years left in school
4. The student's current and future settings
5. The student's rate of learning academic skills
6. The student's other skill needs (p. 500)

A functional curriculum may be appropriate for some students with intellectual disabilities.

Table 5.6 provides an example of the application of these instructional options.

A functional curriculum is concerned with the application of skills to real-life situations. This requires that instruction occur as much as possible in natural settings, using actual items rather than mere representations in simulated settings. This instructional technique, known as **community-based instruction**, is most appropriate for individuals with mental retardation. This strategy eliminates many of the difficulties that pupils with intellectual disabilities have when attempting to transfer and generalize skills learned in the classroom to other settings in which the skill is to be used. Simulated experiences, though useful, are often ineffective with this population. For example, reading a menu or shopping for groceries can easily be simulated in the classroom; however, it is generally more effective when these particular skills occur in vivo, or in the actual environment. Research suggests that students with mental retardation learn more efficiently and retain more if skill instruction occurs in a natural setting (Hartman, 2009; Wehman, 2006; Wehmeyer & Sailor, 2004).

Variations of a functional curriculum are also appropriate for individuals identified as moderately mentally retarded and, in some cases, for students with severe intellectual disabilities. As with their higher-functioning counterparts, areas of emphasis—or domains, as they are sometimes called—are individualized based on the current and future needs of the student. Typical domains include self-help skills, socialization, communication, and vocational training, along with using community resources and exposure to very basic or "survival" academics. An example of this last domain might include functional or environmental reading of survival words and phrases such as *danger, exit, on, off, gentlemen, detour, fire escape, don't walk, keep out, beware of dog*, and other key

TABLE 5.6 Approaches for Teaching Functional Academics

Academic Approach	Learning Outcomes	Examples
Functional, generalized skills usable across life routines	Student will learn some pivotal skills (e.g., useful word and number recognition and counting) and use them in home, school, and community activities.	Sharon is mastering generalized counting skills. She can count dollars to make a purchase, objects to do simple addition in math class, and ingredients when cooking with her mother. She not only learns sight words related to daily activities, such as following her schedule, but also learns high-frequency words that she uses in reading and other academic subjects.
Embedded academic skills usable in specific life routines	Student will acquire an academic response as part of a daily life routine (e.g., use money to buy school lunch; use time and word schedule to organize day).	Juan has a sight word vocabulary of five words. He uses each of these words in a specific way. For example, he finds his name on a set of job cards at his work site. He can select a sweatshirt that has the name of his school to wear on school spirit day.
Adaptations to bypass academic skills	Student will learn to use adaptations that avoid the need for an academic skill (e.g., money envelopes, bus passes).	Because it is difficult for Lauren to count money, her teacher helps her use a predetermined amount of money to make purchases (e.g., a dollar for a soda).

SOURCE: Adapted from M. Snell and F. Brown, *Instruction of Students with Severe Disabilities,* 5th ed. (Upper Saddle River, NJ: Prentice Hall, 2000), p. 498.

protective vocabulary. Equally useful are career and vocational terms identified by Schilit and Caldwell (1980). Their list of a hundred important terms includes words such as *boss*, *wages*, *tools*, *break*, and *first aid*. Arithmetic concepts might stress quantitative concepts such as big/little or more/less, telling time, learning telephone numbers and addresses, calendar activities, money recognition, and other types of functional numerical concepts. As noted previously, instruction should occur in the community using natural settings to maximize the meaningfulness and relevancy of the instruction and to allow for the integration of skills from other domains (Thoma, Bartholomew, & Scott, 2009). An illustration of this type of activity would be a trip to a local grocery store, where several different functional skills could be practiced. The goal of these activities, and others like them, is to decrease the students' dependence on others and to enhance their ability to live and work independently in their community.

Standards-Based Curriculum

In some instances, a functional curriculum approach may not be appropriate. The needs of some individuals with intellectual disabilities may best be served by exposure to both traditional academic subjects—in other words, the general education curriculum—and life skills, depending on the needs of the student and the wishes of the parents. As children get older and progress through school, however, there is often a sense of urgency to incorporate a life skills curriculum in preparation for adulthood. Yet one perplexing challenge confronting both general and special educators is how to blend or integrate the standards-based general education curriculum with a life skills curriculum (Hoover & Patton, 2004; Snell & Brown, 2006).

In many ways a functional curriculum runs counter to the basic tenets of the philosophy of full inclusion with its emphasis on age- and grade-appropriate placement. Does this philosophy mean that a student with intellectual disabilities should enroll, for example, in a geometry or foreign language class? In some instances, the answer might be yes; in other cases, this would be an inappropriate recommendation. We believe that all students with intellectual disabilities should be integrated, to the maximum extent possible,

Suggestions for the Classroom

Characteristics of Effective Teachers

- ☑ Effective special educators have high expectations for their students; they expect their pupils to learn and succeed. Effective teachers establish realistic goals, monitor progress carefully and frequently, provide feedback, and reward successes.
- ☑ Skilled instructors individualize their instruction to meet the unique needs of each child, teaching the child how to learn as well as what to learn. Students are actively engaged and participate in the learning process. Teachers explicitly communicate why a particular skill or concept is important, when it is to be used, and how it should be applied. New learning is anchored to previously learned material. Lessons are well planned and carefully conceived so as to enhance student achievement. Positive academic outcomes are the result of instructional clarity.
- ☑ Effective teachers involve all children and interact frequently with them. Their teaching tactics are many and varied, designed to maintain pupil attention and elicit correct responses. Student performance is evaluated frequently, using multiple procedures. Data are used to assess student understanding of the material and to plan future lessons.

in classrooms and activities with their same-age peers who are not disabled. The general education classroom, however, is not necessarily the appropriate learning environment for all pupils who are mentally retarded. Some pupils will achieve greater educational benefit from instruction in settings outside of school. The key to an appropriate education for students with intellectual disabilities is individualization. Just as all students in the general education classroom do not learn the same material, pupils who are mentally retarded must have their instructional program developed around their unique characteristics and specific educational requirements.

Instructional Methodology

Once a decision is made about what to teach, educators are then confronted with the question of how best to instruct their students. These important issues are interrelated. Decisions that professionals make about what and how to teach pupils who are mentally retarded are crucial for the students' success in school (Beirne-Smith et al., 2006). Here we will briefly examine representative instructional strategies that have proven effective with individuals who are intellectually disabled. But first we offer some general instructional suggestions (Christenson, Ysseldyke, & Thurlow, 1989; Gargiulo & Metcalf, 2010) that have been shown to positively affect children's learning and performance in the classroom. (See the accompanying Suggestions for the Classroom.)

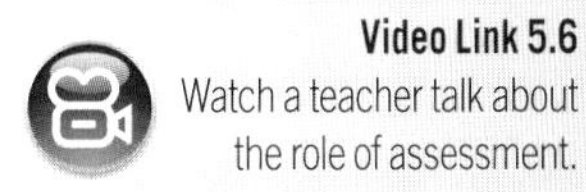

Video Link 5.6
Watch a teacher talk about the role of assessment.

Instructional methodologies and accommodations that are often used with pupils who are mentally retarded are the same ones that make learning successful for all

Cooperative learning is a popular instructional strategy for teaching pupils with intellectual disabilities in inclusive settings.

students (Friend & Bursuck, 2009). Friend and Bursuck believe that general educators are capable of reasonably accommodating in their classrooms most students with special needs, including pupils with intellectual disabilities. To accomplish this goal, they recommend the following seven steps, which they call INCLUDE:

- Identify classroom demands.
- Note student learning strengths and needs.
- Check for potential areas of student success.
- Look for potential problem areas.
- Use information to brainstorm ways to differentiate instruction.
- Differentiate instruction.
- Evaluate student progress (p. 154).

This generic model is applicable to a variety of classroom settings. It is based on the assumption that student performance is a result of the interaction between the learner's characteristics and the instructional environment. By skillfully analyzing the student's learning needs and the requirements of the classroom, teachers are often able to maximize student success and accomplishment.

Similarly, Smith and his colleagues (2008) recommend that teachers consider the following teaching and learning adaptations, which are designed to improve learning outcomes for students with mental retardation:

- Ensure attention to relevant task demands.
- Teach ways to learn content while teaching content itself.
- Focus on content that is meaningful to the students, to promote learning as well as to facilitate application.
- Provide training that crosses multiple learning and environmental contexts.
- Offer opportunities for active involvement in the learning process. (p. 233)

In our opinion, these suggestions are applicable to all pupils, not just individuals with intellectual disabilities.

Task Analysis

We begin with an approach known as **task analysis**, which is often identified with a functional or life skills curriculum. A functional curriculum is a highly individualized, individually referenced model (Hickson, Blackman, & Reis, 1995) in which the teacher crafts each pupil's curriculum based on the skills and abilities that are part of the student's repertoire. In task analysis, which is part of a behavioral approach to instruction, a complex behavior or task is broken down and sequenced into its component parts (Alberto & Troutman, 2009). Task analysis, according to Alberto and Troutman, is the foundation for teaching complex functional and vocational skills to individuals with disabilities.

Alberto and Troutman (2009) offer working guidelines that define the basic steps for conducting a task analysis:

- Define target behavior or task.
- Identify the prerequisite skills for learning the task: "What does the student need to know?"
- Identify needed materials to perform the task.
- Observe a competent person performing the task, and list the steps necessary for successful task completion in sequential order.

We believe that an additional component is necessary. Teachers must take steps to ensure that the student is capable of generalizing the particular skill to other settings. Recall that this is part of the reasoning for teaching functional skills in the student's natural setting.

Over the years researchers have used task analysis to teach a wide variety of daily living and vocational skills to individuals with varying degrees of cognitive impairment. Examples of these successful efforts include teaching food preparation skills to elementary students with moderate to severe intellectual disabilities (Fiscus, Schuster, Morse, & Collins, 2002), teaching functional counting skills to young children with moderate to severe mental retardation (Xin & Holmdal, 2003), teaching laundry skills to high school students with moderate mental retardation (Taylor, Collins, Schuster, & Kleinert, 2002), and teaching leisure time activities to adults with intellectual disabilities (Jared, Frantino, & Sturmey, 2007).

Cooperative Learning

Cooperative learning is another instructional intervention that educators frequently employ, especially when teaching pupils with intellectual disabilities in inclusive or integrated settings. This strategy is growing in popularity and is considered a promising instructional approach (McMaster & Fuchs, 2002). Unlike most of today's classrooms, which tend to emphasize competition among students, cooperative learning encourages

EFFECTIVE INSTRUCTIONAL PRACTICES Teaching Pupils With Intellectual Disabilities

Steps to Good Teaching

Students with intellectual disabilities, like other pupils, typically respond to well-planned instructional strategies. The following mnemonic (CLOCS-RAM) identifies eight steps that are characteristic of good teaching.

C = Clarity	The student must know exactly what to do (i.e., have no doubt about what is expected).
L = Level	The student must be able to do the task with a high degree of accuracy (i.e., be able to get at least 80 percent correct), but the task must be challenging (i.e., the student should not easily get 100 percent correct repeatedly).
O = Opportunities	The student must have frequent opportunities to respond (i.e., be actively engaged in the task a high percentage of the time).
C = Consequences	The student must receive a meaningful reward for correct performance (i.e., the consequences of correct performance must be frequent and perceived as desirable by the student).
S = Sequence	The tasks must be presented in logical sequence so that the student gets the big idea (i.e., steps must be presented and learned so that the knowledge or skill is built on a logical progression or framework of ideas, which is a systematic curriculum).
R = Relevance	The task must be relevant to the student's life and, if possible, the student understands how and why it is useful (i.e., the teacher attempts to help the student see why the task is important in the culture).
A = Application	The teacher helps the student learn how to learn and remember by teaching memory and learning strategies and applying knowledge and skills to everyday problems (i.e., teaches generalizations, not just isolated skills, and honors the student's culture).
M = Monitoring	The teacher continuously monitors student progress and always knows and can show what the student has mastered and the student's place or level in a curriculum or sequence of tasks.

SOURCE: J. Kauffman, M. Mostert, S. Trent, and P. Pullen, *Managing Classroom Behavior,* 4th ed. (Boston: Allyn and Bacon, 2006), p. 17.

Making Inclusion Work

As an eighth-grade English language arts teacher with over a decade of teaching experience, I find teaching to be a new adventure every day.

I strive to enhance the learning opportunities for all of my students. Many of my current students are struggling writers, as identified by teachers from previous years. Keeping these students involved, interested, and yearning to learn, but at the same time making sure that every child is challenged and thriving, can sometimes be a difficult task. But I have asked for this setting because I want to rise to the occasion and see my students succeed.

Inclusive Education Experience

Working in an inclusive classroom takes careful planning. First, I make sure that I know my students' abilities and weaknesses. I make the classroom inclusive of all learners, which builds a positive community. I have had students in my regular English classes who are visually impaired, students who are in wheelchairs, and students who are self-contained in another teacher's room except for reading class. I have come to understand the importance of community and peer support. The teacher in any classroom, but especially the inclusive classroom, becomes the coach or facilitator of learning. Since the children come to school at multiple levels of learning, the teacher must meet the student where he or she is in the learning process and build from that point.

The challenge lies in assisting each child at his or her level and moving him or her along in the learning process. With one teacher and a class of twenty-five learners, moving around the class to help every child is difficult. The student–teacher ratio is high in the regular education class. Another challenge is keeping up with the paperwork that informs the teacher of the accommodations or modifications in the child's IEP. Third, a child who is too challenged or is not challenged enough can become frustrated, which may lead to other disruptive classroom issues. Finally, having all of the students involved in learning at the same time with material that everyone can understand is a challenge. Some students may feel comfortable reading lower-level books while others need more advanced materials. As their teacher, I am responsible for teaching them all.

I am constantly working on resolutions for my dilemmas, however, and I come closer to my answers every day. I rely on my colleagues for ideas that work in their classes. We have an idea exchange at team meetings as we discuss pedagogy and students. I learn from reading professional articles and books. I have always individualized my instruction, but I have learned to do it more effectively.

Strategies for Inclusive Classrooms

Collaboration with special education teachers is a must. They have teaching tips that work well with all students.

- Accommodate instruction and assignments as needed to ensure success for all students, not just those with IEPs; however, only modify assignments for those students who have IEPs. Simple accommodations include providing a word bank for vocabulary quizzes, a study guide before a test, rubrics before a project, a copy of class notes, a book on audiotape, and the use of a computer. Testing or quizzing accommodations include reading a quiz or test aloud to a student, allowing the student to read the quiz or test aloud, explaining directions or language, reducing the number of choices but covering the same objectives, extending the time permitted, allowing the student to dictate his or her answers, allowing mistakes to be corrected for extra points, or allowing a test to be retaken for an average of both scores.
- Understand the importance of presentation. Type assignment directions, activity sheets, quizzes, and tests in a larger font size such as 14 point to make the print easier to read. Be sure the print is clear and legible for the student. Allow students to use a note card to read line-by-line multiple-choice answers separately. Allow for white space around directions so the students will not confuse the directions with the actual test or quiz questions.
- Teach students that organization is pertinent to learning success. Allow a peer to help a student organize his or her notebook. Often a student has difficulty studying because he or she lacks the organizational skills needed to prepare for tests or quizzes.
- Realize that students are often embarrassed to ask for help during class. Periodically monitor students' progress throughout class by individually inquiring with each

Video Link 5.7
Watch more on inclusion.

student about his or her progress. Be available before and after school for study sessions and in between classes for additional assistance.

- Make sure students are on-task by walking around their desks and prompting them to return to the task at hand if they are not working diligently.
- Elicit the aid of parents in a three-way partnership among student, parents, and teacher. Communicate the progress of the student through the student's daily assignment agenda. For example, have the student record any special assignments or daily homework in an agenda. This teaches the student the responsibility of finding out the daily requirements expected of him or her. As a teacher, read the student's agenda and clarify any mistakes or omissions the student may have made, record any newly earned grades, and comment on the student's progress. At night, parents also check the student's agenda and communicate any questions or comments by writing in the student's agenda for the teachers to read the following day.

Working With Parents and Families

Parents want to be informed. When a student does not do well on an assignment or seems to fall behind in class, contact the parents via e-mail, phone, or note or in person to inform them of their child's progress or any concerns. Parents also enjoy seeing samples of their child's class work. For instance, sending home a portfolio during each grading period gives parents an opportunity to see growth in writing skills or progress in reading comprehension. A commentary sheet requesting parents and child to analyze the enclosed work is an excellent means of feedback for teachers. This process of commenting on favorite pieces of writing and selecting a writing piece for publication in a contest or school literary magazine also causes the child to reflect on his or her improvements.

Hosting parent seminars as a team of teachers once a semester on topics such as "Boosting Your Child's Study Habits," "Interpreting SAT-9 Scores" with an emphasis on building on strengths and improving weaknesses, and "Improving Reading Comprehension With Reading Strategies" provides an avenue for improving students' learning with the collaboration of students, parents, and teachers. Parents often desire to help their child at home but are not always equipped with the necessary tools to do so. Through parent seminars, parents learn strategies they can use at home to reinforce the learning that takes place at school. Parents learn of these seminars and other events through team newsletters that are distributed with report cards or progress reports during each grading period.

Each effort at communication through phone calls, notes, person-to-person contact, or e-mail is recorded in my communication log, including the name of the person with whom I spoke, the means of communication, the time and date, and a brief description of the conversation. This helps me to remember the conversation's details in case I need to follow up with the student and parent in the future.

Advice for Making Inclusion and Collaboration Work

My advice to new teachers working in inclusive settings would be to learn as much as possible not only about a special-needs student's academic performance and needs but also about the individual. Sometimes just knowing about a student's personal interests can be a catalyst to help him or her improve learning. Learn about the student's academic performance and needs by talking with the special education teacher and reviewing last year's report card, standardized test scores, and portfolio. Learn about the student's personal interests by having the student complete a reading and writing questionnaire, participate in book talks or reading/writing conferences, and observe the student interacting with other students. Use the knowledge that you have gained to improve students' learning progress.

Knowing a child's learning styles, weaknesses, and strengths allows you to approach the child's difficulties and challenges with new insight. This also shows the student that you care about him or her as an individual and not just as a member of a class. Finally, do not be afraid to continue to elicit the help of parents, special education teachers, other team teachers, counselors, administrators, and other education professionals who work directly with the child. Sharing ideas and collaborating with others will greatly benefit all involved.

—*Tonya Perry*
Former middle school language arts teacher
Alabama State Teacher of the Year 2001
One of the four national finalists,
National Teacher of the Year 2001
Assistant Professor, University of
Alabama at Birmingham

Suggestions for the Classroom

Using Scaffolding in the Classroom

- ☑ **Introduce the concept.** List all of the steps in the strategy using concrete illustrations. Teacher then models the strategy.
- ☑ **Regulate difficulty during guided practice.** Strategy is presented one step at a time using simplified situations. Pupils are guided through the process with the teacher providing assistance.
- ☑ **Provide varying contexts for student practice.** Students initially practice the strategy using authentic problems under the guidance of their teacher. Pupils eventually conduct practice sessions in small group settings.
- ☑ **Provide feedback.** Instructor provides constructive feedback. Evaluative checklists are available so students can self-evaluate their performance.
- ☑ **Increase student responsibility.** Students are required to use the strategies independently. As pupils become increasingly proficient, supports are gradually decreased. Teacher evaluates for student mastery.
- ☑ **Provide independent practice.** Students are provided with extensive opportunities for practice and apply the steps to novel situations. (Friend & Bursuck, 2009)

pupils with varying strengths and abilities to work together toward achieving a common goal. **Cooperative learning** can be defined as an instructional technique in which small, heterogeneous groups of learners are actively involved in jointly accomplishing an activity or assignment. The teacher structures the task in such a fashion that each pupil significantly contributes to the completion of the activity according to his or her ability. Although recognition and rewards are based on group performance, the success of each individual directly affects the accomplishments of his or her classmates (Johnson, Johnson, & Holubec, 1998, 2002).

Cooperative learning, which can take many different forms, can be used with any subject area; however, it requires careful planning and consideration of the needs and abilities of each team member. Pupils with disabilities may require special preparation and support in order to allow for their maximum participation and benefit (Johnson et al., 1998). Teachers, for instance, may have to review certain social skills with their students who are mentally retarded. One of the keys to successfully involving students with cognitive delays in the general education setting is providing the necessary and appropriate supports.

Cooperative learning has been shown to increase the opportunities for students with disabilities to experience success in school (Lewis & Doorlag, 2011). Cooperative learning benefits all pupils, contributes significantly to student achievement, enhances the self-esteem of individuals with special needs, and increases the acceptance and understanding of children with disabilities (Smith et al., 2008).

Scaffolding

Our final example is a teaching strategy called **scaffolding**. This technique is especially applicable to students with intellectual disabilities, who are often characterized as "inactive" or "passive" learners. The aim of this approach is to help pupils become independent, proficient problem solvers. Scaffolding is a cognitive approach to instruction. In this teacher-directed strategy, various forms of support are provided to students as they initially engage in learning a new task or skill. As the student becomes increasingly competent, the supports or "scaffolds" are gradually removed.

Vaughn and Bos (2009) describe scaffolding as a way of

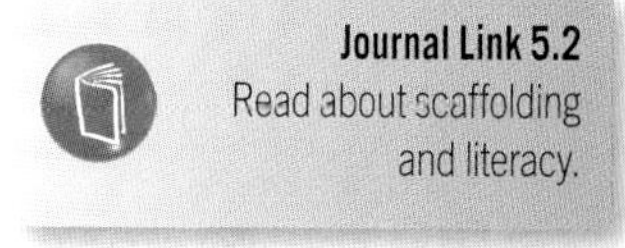

> adjusting and extending instruction so that the student is challenged and able to develop new skills. The teacher can scaffold instruction to meet the needs of the students by manipulating the task, materials, group size, pace, presentation, and so on. The metaphor of a scaffold captures the idea of an adjustable and temporary support that can be removed when it is no longer needed. (p. 22)

This instructional method begins with what the pupil already knows and attempts to connect new information with previously learned material. New information is presented in a logical sequence, building on the student's knowledge base. Pupils are then given the opportunity to apply and practice what they have learned. Suggestions for using this instructional technique can be found in the accompanying Suggestions for the Classroom (page 178).

These three examples are by no means the only instructional models appropriate for students with intellectual disabilities. Other approaches, such as direct instruction and learning strategies (discussed in Chapter 6), are also useful.

Services for Young Children With Intellectual Disabilities or Mental Retardation

The importance of early intervention for young children identified as, or suspected of being, mentally retarded cannot be overestimated. Early intervention can be defined as the services and supports rendered to children age 3 and younger with disabilities, or those who evidence risk factors, and their families. Early intervention represents a consortium of services—not just educational assistance but also health care, social services, family supports, and other benefits. The aim of early intervention is to affect positively the overall development of the child—his or her social, emotional, physical, and intellectual well-being. Thanks to the work of social scientists from various disciplines, federally funded research projects, and the impact of legislation such as PL 99–457 (the Education of the Handicapped Act Amendments of 1986), significant advancements have occurred in this arena. As a result, the quality of life for countless youngsters with intellectual disabilities and other impairments has been improved.

Hickson et al. (1995) describe two main goals of early intervention for young children with intellectual disabilities. The focus of these efforts varies, depending on the severity of the impairment. For preschoolers considered to have moderate or greater degrees of retardation, the main emphasis is on furthering their development by reducing delays in reaching significant developmental and cognitive milestones such as walking or talking. (Similar programs that focus on infants with intellectual disabilities, such as babies with Down syndrome, are frequently identified as **infant stimulation** programs.) Some youngsters may also profit from programs that stress functional objectives centered on activities of daily living. Children thought to be mildly mentally retarded and those considered to be at risk will benefit from programs whose chief aim is to prepare these young students for successful academic experiences upon entering school. These experts go on to state that the primary objectives of early intervention for young children with less severe cognitive limitations are (1) "to minimize and, if possible, reverse the impact of delays or deficits in normal cognitive development on later school performance; and (2) to support family efforts to achieve desired intellectual, vocational, and social outcomes" (p. 223). The second goal, in our opinion, seems to be appropriate for all individuals with intellectual disabilities regardless of their age or severity of impairment.

To these two laudable goals we would like to add a third objective: prevention of intellectual disabilities. You may remember that in Chapter 1 we reviewed the benefits of early intervention for young children who were at increased risk of delayed development and possibly mental retardation due to environmental factors such as poverty and related conditions. Gargiulo and Kilgo (2011) identify these children as being **environmentally at-risk**. Other intervention programs target different audiences. Children who are at risk or highly vulnerable for cognitive impairments include youngsters with **established risk**—that is, children with a diagnosed medical disorder of known etiology and a predictable outcome or prognosis, such as Down syndrome or fragile X syndrome. In other cases, infants, toddlers, and preschoolers who are **biologically at-risk** for intellectual delays and deficits because of low birth weight, prematurity, fetal alcohol syndrome, or HIV infection often profit from their involvement with early intervention activities.

It is important to keep in mind that early intervention programs for youngsters with intellectual disabilities, regardless of the severity of cognitive impairment, are not designed as "anti–mental retardation vaccinations"; rather, they are a first step in a comprehensive, coordinated, and ongoing effort aimed at enhancing the child's potential in all areas of development. Combating the deleterious effects of intellectual disabilities will require a coordinated effort among parents, professionals, advocates, and government officials.

Today, many early intervention programs are structured around a concept known as **family-centered early intervention**. Although the needs of young children with disabilities are an important intervention focus, early interventionists and other service providers are becoming increasingly aware that the needs of youngsters are often inseparable from those of their family. Young children with special needs frequently require a constellation of services based not only on their specific needs but also on the differential needs of the family unit. Family-centered early intervention embraces a positive view of the youngster's family; professionals now talk about enabling and empowering families rather than viewing the child and his or her family as having deficits that necessitate intervention to "fix" the problem. This movement away from a deficit model reflects contemporary thinking (Gargiulo & Kilgo, 2011).

An emphasis on family-centered early intervention characterizes many early childhood special education programs, but it is important to remember that the delivery of services is customized to meet the unique needs of the child as well as the family. Besides the importance attached to individualization, effective programs are comprehensive, normalized, and outcome based, and provide for interaction between disabled and nondisabled youngsters. These benchmarks are appropriate regardless of the curriculum orientation adopted. Typical approaches include a developmental model based largely on the theorizing of Jean Piaget, an operant or behavioral approach consistent with the work of B. F. Skinner, the Montessori method, and a functional curriculum representing a hybrid of the first two approaches. Beirne-Smith et al. (2006) note that no one approach has been shown to be clearly superior to the others and stress that "curriculum should be chosen based on the individual needs of the child and the family" (p. 340).

Transition Into Adulthood

Adolescence is a time of transition and, for individuals with mental retardation, one that is often difficult and stressful. Edgar (1988) characterizes this period of movement from student to independent adulthood as one of "floundering." For many young adults with intellectual disabilities, this journey is not a successful one. Becoming a productive, self-sufficient, and independent adult frequently remains an elusive goal.

The graduates of special education programs, according to Drew and Hardman (2007), do not yet participate fully in the economic and social mainstream of their communities. Today, unfortunately, many individuals with mental retardation either are underemployed or remain unemployed. Besides employment difficulties, researchers have found that for many citizens with intellectual disabilities, independent living is an objective not yet attained (Harris & Associates, 2004; National Longitudinal Transition

Study 2, 2009). The preceding evidence suggests that professionals must do a better job of planning timely transitioning experiences for adolescents with intellectual disabilities if they are to reach their full potential as adults.

Transition planning is a shared responsibility of educators and other school personnel, adult service providers from the community, family members, and, perhaps most important, the student. It is a comprehensive and collaborative activity focusing on adult outcomes that are responsive to the adolescent's goals and vision for adulthood (Sitlington, Neubert, & Clark, 2010). Thoma (1999) believes that meaningful transition planning requires that adult team members listen to and respect the desires and preferences of the student for his or her own adult lifestyle. You may also remember that transition services are mandated by federal law.

Video Link 5.8
Watch more about transitions.

Successful adjustment as an independent adult requires careful planning commencing long before graduation from high school. Public Law 108–446, which recently reauthorized IDEA, requires that transition services begin no later than the first IEP in effect when the student turns 16 (and be updated annually). This legislation also established a new requirement for postsecondary goals pertaining to appropriate education, training, employment, and independent living skills.

In earlier chapters, we reviewed the requirements for effective transition planning and the key elements of an individualized transition plan or ITP. Here we focus on the area that is probably preeminent in transition planning for adolescents with mental retardation: employment.

For most individuals, with or without intellectual disabilities, work is an important part of daily life. Work is often used as a gauge of social status, financial success, and personal fulfillment, and is a vehicle for opportunities to participate in one's community. Oftentimes uninformed persons believe that individuals with mental retardation are incapable of obtaining and holding a job. This is simply not true, even though employment rates for adults with intellectual disabilities are dismal—especially for young women who are mentally retarded (Harris & Associates, 2004; National Longitudinal Transition Study 2, 2009). Generally speaking, with appropriate training, individuals with mental retardation are able to secure and maintain meaningful and gainful employment. Persons who are intellectually disabled make good employees. In those cases where they are unsuccessful on the job, it is frequently due not to their skill level or job performance but to a lack of interpersonal and social behaviors appropriate to the workplace.

Training is often the key to successful employment, and it begins during the transition period. Historically speaking, early job training programs centered on a model known as a **sheltered workshop**. At one time this was a very popular training option, particularly for individuals with moderate or severe retardation, who typically require long-term and intense support. Sheltered workshops are generally large facilities that provide job training in a segregated environment. Clients, as the workers are called, typically work on contract jobs that are often repetitive in nature and require low skill level—for instance, sorting "junk mail" inserts. Typically, these jobs are of short duration and offer the clients minimal job training. Placement in a sheltered workshop may, in some cases, be transitional to obtaining employment in the community, but it is more likely to be a permanent position.

In recent years, sheltered workshops have come under fire. Critics (Migliore, Mank, Grossi, & Rogan, 2007; Murphy, Rogan, Handley, Kincaid, & Royce-Davis, 2002; Simmons & Flexer, 2008) have focused their attention on the low wages paid to workers, the segregated work setting, the absence of meaningful training, and the failure to move clients into competitive employment. This dissatisfaction, coupled with the contemporary movement toward more integrated and normalized experiences for individuals with mental retardation, has given rise to the notion of **supported competitive employment**. In this model, which has proven effective in preparing adolescents for employment in community settings, an individual with intellectual disabilities is placed on a competitive job site alongside other workers who are not disabled. A **job coach** or employment specialist provides on-the-job assistance and support to the worker with intellectual disabilities. This person's role is to train the adolescent with mental retardation on the specific job requirements and then, hopefully, to decrease support services as the employee becomes more proficient.

Many adults with intellectual disabilities are capable of working successfully in the community.

Job coaches are also usually responsible for locating the job and matching the needs of the employer to the abilities of the student (worker).

The use of a supported competitive employment model has grown significantly over the past decade; it has been shown to be a cost-effective strategy with benefits accruing to both employer and employee (Beirne-Smith et al., 2006; Simmons & Flexer, 2008). Researchers have found that individuals with intellectual disabilities who are prepared using this approach tend to function better in competitive employment settings than persons who only have experience in sheltered workshops (McDonnell, Hardman, & McDonnell, 2003), in addition to reporting higher job satisfaction (Test, Carver, Evers, Haddad, & Person, 2000). Employment opportunities typically range from entry-level custodial or food service positions to jobs in various high-technology industries.

Although this model is in keeping with contemporary thinking regarding self-determination (discussed in the next section of this chapter), supportive competitive employment has its limitations. Some of the drawbacks include excessive dependence on the job coach, disruption of the work environment by the presence of the job coach, and differential performance when the job coach is on-site (Simmons & Flexer, 2008). These disadvantages have contributed to the idea of using coworkers as natural supports (Mank, Cioffi, & Yovanoff, 2003). These individuals typically function as mentors and friends, offering valuable assistance and encouragement as needed to workers with intellectual disabilities.

For many young adults with intellectual disabilities, competitive employment is a realistic goal. By providing early and carefully crafted transitioning experiences, schools can maximize the probability that students who are mentally retarded will have successful postschool adjustment, not only in the area of employment but in other domains as well.

Adults With Intellectual Disabilities or Mental Retardation

Over the past several years, professionals and advocates alike have devoted increased attention to the needs of adults with intellectual disabilities. For some of these individuals, successful adjustment to the community is an appropriate and achievable objective. For all intents and purposes, they are no different from most other adults without disabilities, although at times they may require (as others sometimes do) support and assistance from family members, friends, coworkers, or social service agencies. Here we will focus on the community adjustment of adults with intellectual disabilities who require more intense and ongoing support.

Video Link 5.9
Watch more about adulthood.

Earlier in this chapter, we introduced the principle of normalization, defined as "making available to the mentally retarded patterns and conditions of everyday life which are as close as possible to the norms and patterns of the mainstream of society" (Nirje, 1969, p. 181). The principle of normalization attempts "to establish and/or maintain personal behaviors which are as culturally normative as possible" (Wolfensberger, 1972, p. 28). The overarching philosophy is that individuals with mental retardation (and other disabilities) should be integrated, to the greatest extent possible, in all aspects of daily life such as employment, recreation, living arrangements, and other areas of community life.

The principle of normalization has given rise to the belief that individuals with intellectual disabilities, especially those with more severe cognitive impairments, have a right to make their own choices and decisions in life and to become as independent as possible—in short, to have some degree of personal control over their own lives. These decisions may be as simple as what to watch on television, what time to go to bed, or

Persons with intellectual disabilities are seeking greater control over their lives and fuller participation in all aspects of society.

which dress to wear, or they may involve more profound choices such as where to live and with whom. This decision-making capacity is often referred to as **self-determination** or, to use AAIDD terminology, self-direction. Self-direction is often seen as a crucial component for success in later adult life for individuals with intellectual disabilities (Hughes, Washington, & Brown, 2008). Although self-determination is a critical adaptive skill, educators should bear in mind that self-determination reflects North American and Western European ideals and beliefs; other cultures may not value independence and personal decision making as highly as European Americans. Teachers, therefore, are strongly encouraged to consider the cultural preferences and heritage of their pupils when formulating instructional strategies for developing skills in self-determination (Turnbull, Turnbull, Erwin, Soodak, & Shogren, 2011).

Because free choice is typically a restricted activity for large numbers of adults with mental retardation, **self-advocacy** is gaining in both popularity and importance. People with intellectual disabilities are encouraged, via self-help groups, to speak out on issues of personal importance such as living arrangements and personal relationships. The purpose of self-advocacy is for individuals with mental retardation to gain greater personal control over their lives and to foster their own independence. Self-advocacy empowers people and helps them to assertively state their needs, wants, and desires.

Of course, successfully adjusting to life in one's community requires more than skills in self-determination and self-advocacy; it is also predicated on acceptance and support from the general public. Several other variables besides community acceptance that are likely to influence success in community living are illustrated in Figure 5.7.

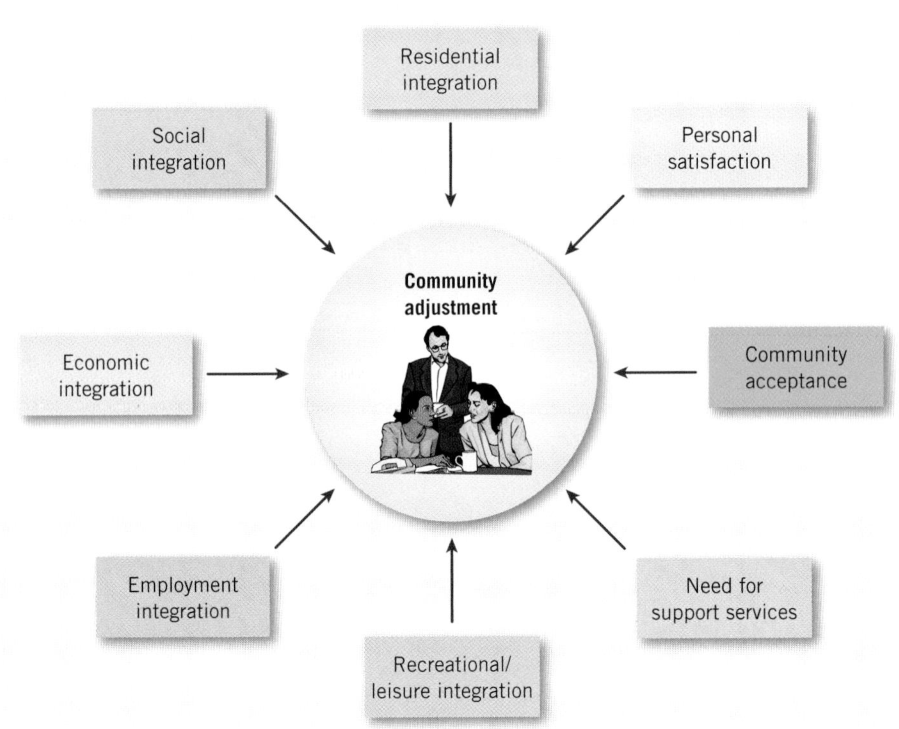

FIGURE 5.7 Variables Affecting Successful Community Living of Adults With Intellectual Disabilities

SOURCE: Adapted from M. Beirne-Smith, J. Patton, and S. Kim, *Mental Retardation,* 7th ed. (Upper Saddle River, NJ: Pearson Education, 2006).

Family Issues

A child with mental retardation (or any other disability) typically elicits a wide range of emotional responses, which can vary from anger and denial to awareness and acceptance. Additionally, parents may worry about financial obligations, educational concerns, the impact of the disability on siblings, long-term care requirements, and a host of other fears. These families often require understanding, assistance, and support. The importance of a natural support network, which may include coworkers, neighbors, friends, aunts and uncles, and other family members, should not be underestimated (McDonnell et al., 2003). For many parents of children with disabilities, these individuals, and not professionals, serve as the "first line of defense" in dealing with a child who is recognized as being mentally retarded. Other parents of youngsters with Down syndrome, for example, can often provide sensitive assistance and serve as a valuable resource on community services for infants with special needs. Long-term and mutually sustaining relationships are frequently established between parents of children with intellectual disabilities because of this common connection. Support is necessary because a child with mental retardation may significantly affect the structure, function, and overall development of the entire family constellation (Gargiulo & Kilgo, 2011). In this case, valuable assistance is available from The Arc, a national organization on intellectual disabilities, which offers information and support not only to parents but also to siblings and other family members such as grandparents.

It is impossible to predict how a family will respond to a child with intellectual disabilities. This term means different things to different families. As a society, we must value all families and should not overlook the potential benefits that an individual with

intellectual disabilities brings to his or her family. See the accompanying First Person feature written by a young adult with Down syndrome.

Issues of Diversity

A long-standing concern exists among special educators about the misclassification and/or inappropriate placement of students from minority backgrounds in special education programs. All too often, diversity is incorrectly linked with disability. It is indeed unfortunate that children from minority groups are frequently seen as deviant or disabled.

First Person: Meredith In Her Own Words

What can you tell us about yourself and your family?

I am Meredith, age 22, and I live with my parents in Alabama. I have a younger brother named Zach. One of my favorite childhood memories is dressing up at Halloween. Zach was Captain Hook and I was Peter Pan, and another time he was a cowboy and I was an Indian. We also had fun at Christmas, which is my favorite holiday to celebrate. My family has many traditions I enjoy. One is getting an ornament each year to remind us of our interests, like my Barbie Doll collection, and my two former dogs, Scamper and Misha.

What do you like to do in your free time?

For fun, I go out with my boyfriend, Matthew, or my girlfriends. Matthew and I usually go out to dinner and a movie. We take turns having dinner at each other's house and we love watching the Three Stooges videos. I'm also involved with People First, a self-advocacy group for people with disabilities. I am the chaplain and open the meeting with words of encouragement about having a positive attitude. At church I help out in the fourth-grade Religious Education classroom. I also volunteer for the North Shelby County Library and Alabama Wildlife Rehabilitation Center.

What can you tell us about your experience at school?

I graduated from Oak Mountain High School. During high school, I was nominated for the Homecoming Court, and was voted Best Choral Student. I really enjoyed high school because it had a great atmosphere and I had many friends. My favorite subjects were government, choir, and environmental science. I also liked our pep rallies and football games. My least favorite subject was math. My best high school memory is getting to be in the Macy's Thanksgiving Day parade. We walked three miles singing and dancing in New York City where it was very cold. Some of the challenges were trying to be smart and independent. While in high school I joined the Special Olympics Rhythmic Gymnastics Team and I still compete today. I also am on a Special Olympics bowling team.

What can you tell us about your work background?

During my senior year, I started to get work experience. I got to work at a video store, a card shop, a restaurant, and Jefferson State Community College. My first real job was at a department store where I helped organize and fold clothes. I don't have a job right now, but am working with my job coach to find one. I'd like to work in an office or clothing store.

What do you see yourself doing in the future?

My dream for the future is to have a job, live in my own place, and maybe one day get married. My grandmother, who was very sweet, is my role model. She was a very strong woman and never complained even though she had diabetes for over fifty years. She always encouraged me to be healthy and take care of myself.

What is one thing you want people to remember about you?

I would like people to know that I love my life.

❖

When our daughter, Meredith, was born with Down syndrome, we faced numerous medical, social, and educational challenges. We had no way of knowing that very soon we would become partners with doctors; speech, physical, and occupational therapists; early interventionists; teachers; job coaches; and other advocates who value the rights and dignity of individuals with disabilities. This partnership has created lasting bonds of friendship, changed attitudes, strengthened inclusive educational practices, and allowed Meredith to achieve many goals.

Meredith's literary abilities have far exceeded our earliest expectations. She is an excellent reader with incredible spelling and comprehension skills. Her passion for learning and wanting to educate herself is remarkable. Meredith is a delightful, self-confident young woman with a sense of humor; knows no prejudice; and loves unconditionally. Meredith is an extraordinary person trying to live an ordinary life, and we are blessed to be her parents.

The issue of cultural diversity is intricately interwoven into the fabric of American special education. It is related to discussions of identification, psychoeducational assessment, etiology, educational placement, and intervention. The overrepresentation of children of color is particularly relevant to a discussion on intellectual disabilities. The U.S. Department of Education (2006) reports, for example, that African American youth constitute 15 percent of the public school population, yet about one out of every three pupils in classes for the mentally retarded are from this group (U.S. Department of Education, 2009). Drew and Hardman (2007) observe that individuals are often misdiagnosed as intellectually disabled when, in fact, their behavior is more a reflection of cultural differences than an indication of reduced or impaired functioning.

We know that the overrepresentation of minorities in special education classes, especially programs for children with intellectual disabilities, is a multifaceted problem. Contributing factors range from culturally biased assessment instruments to the insidious role of poverty to teacher bias and expectation. The challenge that continually confronts educators and other professionals is how to combat this problem. The answer to this perplexing issue has eluded special educators for much too long.

Technology and Individuals With Intellectual Disabilities or Mental Retardation

Technology holds significant promise for improving the quality of life for individuals with mental retardation. It also has great potential for assisting teachers in providing a high-quality and appropriate education to students with disabilities, including those who are intellectually disabled. Lewis and Doorlag (2011) note that there are two types of technology to consider when talking about pupils with disabilities: instructional technology and assistive technology. **Instructional technology** is any device that supports the teaching/learning process, such as a computer or television. **Assistive technology** is technology that is specially designed to assist persons with disabilities. Assistive technology is defined in federal law.

Clearly, students with mental retardation can benefit from the application of technology in the classroom. Thanks to the reauthorization of IDEA, technology is a viable mechanism for expanding access to the general education curriculum. Increasingly, technology is being recommended to assist pupils with cognitive impairments achieve in more challenging curriculums. Table 5.7 illustrates how various types of technology may benefit students with intellectual disabilities as well as other pupils.

Trends, Issues, and Controversies

As we conclude this chapter, we hope that you have gained an understanding of and appreciation for the many complex and often related issues surrounding the subject of intellectual disabilities. Topics such as amniocentesis and the accompanying question of abortion, test bias and the overrepresentation of minorities in programs for the mentally retarded, concerns about appropriate placements, and thoughts about the quality of life of persons with intellectual disabilities are only some of the many issues that have captured the attention of parents, educators, policymakers, advocates, legislators, and a host of other concerned individuals.

Like others, we too are concerned about where we have been, where we are today, and what the future holds for the field of intellectual disabilities. Understanding the present state of affairs is often beneficial when contemplating where we might be headed. In fact, the past is often seen as a prologue to the future. With this in mind, we must point out that although individuals who are mentally retarded will most likely benefit from advances in technology, medical breakthroughs, new legislation, and a host of other beneficial

TABLE 5.7 Application of Technology to Students With Intellectual Disabilities

	Application	Purposes
Reading Tools	Text and screen reading programs	Translate a variety of text-based documents to speech.
	Scan-and-speak programs and tools	Translate printed information into digital text that can be read by text-to-speech functions.
	Tools for organizing content-area information	Help students organize a variety of information to facilitate comprehension and to aid studying for tests and other evaluations.
Writing Tools	Word processors	Support the writing process by easing the logistical burdens of creating and, in many cases, reading text to facilitate editing and revising.
	Spell checkers and electronic writing supports	Support students' writing by providing feedback about accurate spelling and by providing information such as synonyms, definitions, and translations from one language to another.
	Word prediction software	Supports those who have difficulty typing or spelling by predicting a user's words and offering a selection of possible words from which to choose.
	Prompted writing tools	Scaffold the writing process by offering directions, cues, guidance, or pictures that can prompt users' background knowledge, guide them in various types of writing, and promote revision.
	Speech recognition programs	Permit users to dictate their compositions by transcribing their dictation into written text.

SOURCE: Adapted from C. Okolo, "Technology and Individuals with Mild Disabilities," In J. Lindsey (Ed.), *Technology and Exceptional Individuals,* 4th ed. (Austin, TX: Pro-Ed, 2008), p. 329.

developments, attitudinal change is frequently the precursor to a change in the delivery of services and the recognition of the rights of our fellow citizens with disabilities.

Attempting to anticipate where the field of intellectual disabilities is going is perhaps best left to the futurist or the clairvoyant. This disclaimer notwithstanding, our vision of the future includes the following:

- More community-based activities will be available across several domains, including employment, education, and residential options.
- There will be a growing emphasis on the application of assistive technology to meet the needs of the person with mental retardation; to varying degrees, individuals with intellectual disabilities will join the information age.
- Quality of life and normalization across the life span will become increasingly prominent national advocacy issues.
- Human services providers as well as communities will be confronted with a growing geriatric population with intellectual disabilities.
- Biomedical research and well-designed psychosocial interventions will lead to a reduction in the number of people identified as mentally retarded.
- More inclusive educational placements will be the norm for students with significant cognitive impairments, requiring intensive supports.
- Greater attention will be paid across all age groups to fostering self-advocacy and self-determination, as persons with intellectual disabilities seek greater control over their lives and fuller participation in all aspects of society.

Overall, we foresee significant improvement in the coming years in both the quality and the quantity of programs and services for persons with intellectual disabilities.

CHAPTER IN REVIEW

Defining Intellectual Disabilities or Mental Retardation: An Evolving Process

Audio Link 5.3
Listen to a chapter summary.

- Contemporary practice considers intellectual disabilities to be the result of interactions among the person, the environment, and those supports required to maximize the individual's performance in particular settings or environments.

Assessing Intellectual Ability and Adaptive Behavior

- Intelligence is a theoretical construct whose existence can only be inferred on the basis of a person's performance on certain types of cognitive tests that only represent a sample of the person's intellectual skills and abilities.

Classification of Individuals With Intellectual Disabilities or Mental Retardation

- Some models group persons with intellectual disabilities according to the etiology or cause of the disability; others label persons according to the severity of their cognitive impairment, such as mildly or severely mentally retarded.
- Educators sometimes label students with intellectual disabilities as educable mentally retarded (EMR) or trainable mentally retarded (TMR).
- The 2002 AAIDD definition classifies individuals with intellectual disabilities on the basis of the extent or levels of support they require to function effectively across adaptive skill areas in various natural settings, such as home, school, or job.

Prevalence of Intellectual Disabilities or Mental Retardation

- Currently, approximately 8 percent of all students with disabilities, or about 1 percent of the total school-age population, are recognized as being mentally retarded.
- The vast majority of persons with intellectual disabilities have an IQ between 50 and 70–75.

Etiology of Intellectual Disabilities or Mental Retardation

- One way of categorizing etiological factors is on the basis of time of onset: before birth (prenatal), around the time of birth (perinatal), or after birth (postnatal).

Characteristics of Individuals With Intellectual Disabilities or Mental Retardation

- Common behaviors of persons with mental retardation include attention deficits, or difficulty focusing and attending to relevant stimuli, and memory problems.
- Past experiences with failure frequently lead individuals who are intellectually disabled to doubt their own abilities and thus exhibit an external locus of control.
- Recurring episodes of failure also give rise to learned helplessness. These accumulated instances of failure frequently result in a loss of confidence and trust in one's own problem-solving abilities and a reliance on others for direction and guidance. This behavior is identified as outer-directedness.
- Individuals with intellectual impairments also often exhibit poor interpersonal skills and socially inappropriate or immature behaviors.

Educational Considerations

- Students with intellectual disabilities are more than three times as likely as other children with disabilities to be educated in a self-contained classroom.

- Many students with intellectual disabilities are exposed to a functional curriculum, whose goal is to equip these children with the skills they require for successful daily living both now and in the future.
- Best practice dictates that instruction occur as much as possible in natural settings rather than simulated environments. This instructional concept is known as community-based instruction.
- Task analysis is frequently used with persons who are mentally retarded.
- Cooperative learning is another instructional intervention that educators often employ. This strategy is especially useful when teaching pupils with intellectual disabilities in inclusive or integrated classrooms.
- Scaffolding, which is a cognitive approach to instruction, is a teacher-directed strategy in which various forms of support are provided to students as they engage in learning a new task or skill.

Adults With Intellectual Disabilities or Mental Retardation

- The principle of normalization currently guides the delivery of services to individuals with intellectual disabilities. This notion suggests that persons who are mentally retarded should have a lifestyle that is as culturally normative as possible.
- The principle of normalization has also given rise to the belief that individuals who are intellectually disabled should have a right to make their own choices and decisions about various aspects of their lives. This decision-making capacity is often referred to as self-determination.

Technology and Individuals With Intellectual Disabilities or Mental Retardation

- Instructional technology is any piece of equipment that facilitates the teaching/learning process.
- Assistive technology is any apparatus or equipment that is used to enhance or maintain the functional capabilities of individuals with mental retardation and other disabilities.

STUDY QUESTIONS

1. How has the definition of intellectual disabilities changed over the past several decades?
2. Identify the three key elements of the 1992 AAIDD definition of mental retardation. How are they conceptually interrelated?
3. Why is the assessment of intelligence such a controversial issue?
4. What is adaptive behavior, and how is it assessed?
5. List four different strategies for classifying individuals with intellectual disabilities.
6. How have society's view and understanding of persons who are intellectually disabled changed over the centuries?
7. What factors have contributed to the gradual reduction in the number of individuals classified as mentally retarded?
8. Mental retardation is often the result of various etiological factors. List seven possible causes of intellectual disabilities. Give an example of each.
9. How do learned helplessness, outer-directedness, and generalizing affect learning in students with intellectual disabilities?
10. Define the term *functional academics.* How are functional academics related to the concept of community-based instruction?
11. What is cooperative learning, and why is it a popular instructional technique?
12. List and describe the necessary steps for effectively using scaffolding with students with intellectual disabilities.
13. How has family-centered early intervention influenced programming activities for young children with intellectual disabilities?
14. Distinguish between a sheltered workshop for adults with mental retardation and the contemporary practice of supported competitive employment.
15. What is assistive technology, and how might it benefit individuals who are intellectually disabled?

KEY TERMS

standard deviation (SD) 142
adaptive behavior 142
educable mentally retarded (EMR) 152
trainable mentally retarded (TMR) 152
level of support 152
natural supports 153
formal supports 153
normalization 155
deinstitutionalization 155
etiology 157
prenatal 157
perinatal 157
postnatal 157
Down syndrome 157
fragile X syndrome 159
phenylketonuria (PKU) 159
galactosemia 160
rubella 160
syphilis 160
acquired immune deficiency syndrome (AIDS) 160
Rh incompatibility 160
toxoplasmosis 161
cytomegalovirus (CMV) 161
fetal alcohol syndrome (FAS) 161
fetal alcohol effect (FAE) 161
anencephaly 161
microcephaly 161
hydrocephalus 161
low birth weight 161
premature birth 161
anoxia 162
hypoxia 162
birth trauma 162
breech presentation 162
precipitous birth 162
lead poisoning 162
meningitis 162
encephalitis 162
primary prevention 163
secondary prevention 163
tertiary prevention 163
amniocentesis 164
chorionic villus sampling (CVS) 164
ultrasound 164
therapeutic abortion 164
spina bifida 164
external locus of control 166
learned helplessness 166
outer-directedness 166
generalizing 166
functional curriculum 170
functional academics 170
community-based instruction 171
task analysis 174
cooperative learning 178
scaffolding 178
infant stimulation 179
environmentally at-risk 180
established risk 180
biologically at-risk 180
family-centered early intervention 180
sheltered workshop 181
supported competitive employment 181
job coach 181
self-determination 183
self-advocacy 183
instructional technology 186
assistive technology 186

LEARNING ACTIVITIES

1. Make arrangements to visit classrooms serving students with intellectual disabilities. What differences did you observe between elementary and secondary programs? Did the instructional program differ for students with severe or profound cognitive impairments in comparison to pupils with mild or moderate mental retardation? What pedagogical techniques or teaching strategies did the teachers use? How did the other children interact with and relate to their classmates with intellectual disabilities? Was a particular curriculum incorporated? What was your overall impression of the program; what specific features stood out?
2. Visit several businesses in your community that employ individuals with intellectual disabilities. Interview the employer or supervisor. Find out how successful these individuals have been. What type of training do workers with mental retardation require? How have customers and/or coworkers accepted these individuals? Why did the company hire people who are mentally retarded (financial reasons, corporate policy, public relations)? Are they good employees? Have the workers with intellectual disabilities posed any special challenges or problems for the employer?
3. Visit various residential facilities in your area that serve individuals with intellectual disabilities. Interview the caregivers. Discover what the daily routine is like for individuals with mental retardation. Do the various facilities allow for different degrees of independence and decision making on the part of the residents? What is your opinion of the quality of life of these individuals? How has the community accepted its neighbors with intellectual disabilities? What supports and services are made available to the residents? Do the individuals with mental retardation participate in the life of the community—attend special events and festivities; utilize community recreational facilities such as parks, museums, or the zoo; or make purchases in local shops?
4. Involve yourself with various community agencies and organizations that focus on individuals with mental retardation. Attend a meeting of The Arc or a parent support group. Volunteer to work at the Special Olympics, become a Best Buddy, or assist in programs offering respite care to parents of children with intellectual disabilities.

5. Prepare a multimedia presentation for your class on an aspect of intellectual disabilities that personally interests you. Here are some possible topics:
   - Assistive technology
   - Prenatal diagnostic screening
   - Supported competitive employment
   - Group homes
   - Causes and prevention of intellectual disabilities
   - Overrepresentation of minorities in classes for the mentally retarded
   - Assessment of intelligence
   - Early intervention

REFLECTING ON STANDARDS

The following exercises are designed to help you learn to apply the Council for Exceptional Children (CEC) standards to your teaching practice. Each of the reflection exercises below correlates with a knowledge or skill within the CEC standards. For the full text of each of the related CEC standards, please refer to the standards integration grid located in Appendix B.

Focus on Individual Learning Differences ***(CEC Content Standard #3 CC3K1)***
Reflect on an individual with intellectual disabilities that you have known. How has that individual made an impact on his or her family, friends, teachers, and/or community? What struggles did that individual have as a result of his or her differences? What did you learn from this person about individuals with disabilities?

Focus on Instructional Planning ***(CEC Content Standard #7 CC7S7)***
Reflect on what you have learned in this chapter about students with intellectual disabilities. If you were to have a student with Down syndrome in your class, how would you need to modify your teaching to integrate affective, social, and life skills within your day-to-day curriculum?

ORGANIZATIONS CONCERNED WITH INTELLECTUAL DISABILITIES OR MENTAL RETARDATION

The Arc (formerly the Association for Retarded Citizens of the United States)
1660 L Street, NW
Suite 301
Washington, DC 20036
(800) 433-5255
(202) 534-3731 (Fax)
http://www.thearc.org

American Association on Intellectual and Developmental Disabilities
501 Third Street N.W.
Suite 200
Washington, DC 20001
(800) 424-3688
(202) 387-2193 (Fax)
http://www.aamr.org

National Down Syndrome Congress
1370 Center Drive
Suite 102
Atlanta, GA 30338
(800) 232-6372
(770) 604-9898 (Fax)
http://www.ndsccenter.org

National Down Syndrome Society
666 Broadway
Suite 810
New York, NY 10012
(800) 221-4602
(212) 979-2873 (Fax)
http://ndss.org

STUDENT STUDY SITE

Visit the Student Study Site at www.sagepub.com/gargiulo4emedia for these additional learning tools:

- Video links
- Media links
- Self-quizzes
- E-flashcards
- Full-text SAGE journal articles
- Web exercises

CHAPTER 6

Learning Objectives

After reading Chapter 6 you should be able to:

- Summarize the key components of the IDEA definition of learning disabilities.
- Outline the four phases in the development of the field of learning disabilities.
- Identify possible causes of learning disabilities.
- List representative learning and social/emotional characteristics of individuals with learning disabilities.
- Explain the concept of response to intervention.
- Describe the following instructional approaches: cognitive training, direct instruction, and learning strategies.
- Summarize educational services for persons with learning disabilities across the life span.

Individuals With Learning Disabilities

WHAT'S A MOTHER TO DO?

"What's a mother to do?" I moped silently. I knew that there was something slightly wrong. Was Ryan just lazy? His seventh-grade teachers had just told us so in the parent conference. As I painfully replayed the conference in my mind, I reflected on my son's school experiences.

Ryan had a very successful elementary school experience up until the fifth grade. In fifth grade things got a bit more difficult. His disorganization and his lack of ability to do written work began to destroy his confidence and academic success. Grades dropped from mostly As to Cs and Ds. Ryan's teacher and his classmates loved him; but he failed at least one subject each grading period—usually a different one each time. He never brought assignments home, frequently did the wrong homework—if he did it at all—and forgot to turn in finished homework. His teacher said that he had trouble getting his books, pen, and paper out at the beginning of class. She said that he was, therefore, behind before he even got started. His fifth-grade penmanship looked like that of a much younger child. He could not spell. His backpack was a mess of wadded-up papers. We all thought Ryan was just a typical boy. Neither we nor the teachers ever mentioned the possibility of a learning disability.

Video Link 6.1
Watch more about learning disabilities.

Then we were in middle school. Ryan was still one of the most popular kids in the class—sociable, handsome, and clearly the class "stud"—but his grades were gradually deteriorating. We asked for a parent–teacher conference. At the conference, my husband and I were attacked by his team of teachers. They seemed to think we were bad parents. "Why don't you make Ryan do his work?" they asked.

Ryan's seventh-grade test scores clearly showed a large discrepancy. Spelling was at the third-grade level while all other skills were at or above a twelfth-grade level. His reading comprehension was excellent, and his vocabulary was extensive; yet he did not read for pleasure. He passed most classes with only average grades. His teachers told us he was lazy. Once again, not one teacher mentioned the possibility of a learning disability.

I did not know what to do with this smart yet obviously learning-disabled child. I finally asked for help when our son was in the eighth grade. I agree that being classified as a special education student gives a child a certain unfavorable stigma; but I did not know any other way to help my child. Ryan somehow survived middle school, thanks largely to the efforts of his special education teacher.

That summer we moved to a larger city about two hours away. As a family, we decided not to seek special education services for Ryan as he began his freshman year in high school. We did not want him to carry the stigma of special education into this new environment. His grades always ranged from As to Fs. I had to constantly help him with his written work. He composed very well, but sometimes I had to type as he "wrote" his work orally. He had to go to summer school every summer to keep up, but somehow he managed to pass almost all of his classes and eventually graduate.

After a few years of successful employment Ryan was ready for college. He began by taking a history class at a nearby university and, with Mom's help on all papers, made a B in that class. He joined a fraternity. It was great fun. In the fall, he took a full load and quickly landed on academic probation. At that point I started looking for help from the university, only to find out that he could not get financial help until he got off academic probation. Ryan was still ambivalent about letting his professors know that he had a learning disability and would not ask the office of disability support services to contact his professors. So, again, he was in school depending on his mother to be his personal "special education" resource. He is now a third-semester freshman. He composes beautifully, but we are still writing orally while I or his girlfriend types his papers. He forgets to go to class sometimes and usually runs late to his part-time job or the pool where he coaches swim teams. His notebooks and his car are full of school supplies, athletic equipment, and miscellaneous stuff that is wildly disorganized.

I want my child to get a college degree and not have to work night shifts in the retail world for the rest of his life. We are now borrowing money to send him to school, hoping that he will pass every class, and worrying what will happen with his health insurance when he turns 24 and our policy no longer covers him. The financial burden is killing us, and I'm still in a quandary. What's a mother to do?

—*Anonymous*

Persons with learning disabilities are a very heterogeneous group. We will learn about children and adults who typically have normal intelligence but, for some reason, fail to learn as easily and efficiently as their classmates and peers. The idea that some individuals might possess a hidden or invisible disability is of relatively recent origin. The notion of learning disabilities is only about five decades old, but it has quickly grown and today represents the largest category of children and youth enrolled in special education.

The study of learning disabilities involves professionals from many different disciplines. Our knowledge base about this perplexing field has been greatly enriched by the contributions of investigators and practitioners from psychology, medicine, speech and language, and education, as well as other disciplines. Despite this solid multidisciplinary foundation, individuals with learning disabilities are often an enigma to their parents, teachers, and researchers, and the field itself has generated significant controversy, confusion, and debate.

In reality, most individuals have imperfections and, to some degree, experience difficulty in learning, but in some instances these problems are more pronounced than in others. For large numbers of people, these learning difficulties are chronic and will persist throughout life. It would be wrong to assume, however, that these individuals are incapable of accomplishments and a life of quality. Some of the most distinguished individuals and brightest minds the world has ever known had extreme difficulty in learning and could easily be considered learning disabled. These eminent people include Leonardo da Vinci, Auguste Rodin, Albert Einstein, Thomas Edison, Woodrow Wilson, Winston Churchill, and Ernest Hemingway. Other noted personalities include Walt Disney, George Patton, Nelson Rockefeller, Tom Cruise, Charles Schwab, and Bruce Jenner (Lerner & Johns, 2009; Smith, Polloway, Patton, & Dowdy, 2008). By all accounts, the preceding individuals are very successful persons, but they are exceptions. The vast majority of children and adults with learning disabilities will be frequently misunderstood and experience ongoing challenges and frustrations in their daily lives.

In this chapter, we will explore several issues and attempt to answer a number of questions related to learning disabilities. What is a learning disability? How many individuals are thought to be learning disabled? Can we cure it? What instructional strategies work best for students who are learning disabled? How do professionals determine if someone has a learning disability? Of course, there are many other questions about this puzzling field of study, and some for which we do not have complete answers. We begin our exploration of learning disabilities by examining various definitions.

Defining Learning Disabilities

Students with learning disabilities have always been in our classrooms, but professionals have often failed to identify these pupils and recognize their special needs. These children have been known by a variety of confusing and sometimes controversial labels, including *neurologically impaired*, *perceptually disordered*, *dyslexic*, *slow learner*, *remedial reader*, and *hyperactive*. Almost forty years ago, Cruickshank (1972) published a list of some forty terms used to describe students known today as learning disabled. Deiner's (1993) more recent analysis found more than ninety terms used in the professional literature to characterize individuals with learning disabilities. It is easy to see why controversy and confusion surround this population of learners. Part of the problem is the many different disciplines involved in serving these students. Based on their professional training, physicians, speech–language pathologists, educators, and psychologists each describe persons with learning disabilities in their own unique way. Over the years, however, the various terms have been consolidated into the concept now known as learning disabilities. Today, this term enjoys wide acceptance among educators and the general public.

Defining the term *learning disability* has proven to be problematic. At one time, Vaughn and Hodges (1973) identified thirty-eight different definitions. Hammill (1990) notes that eleven definitions have enjoyed varying degrees of official status in the field. Defining what a learning disability is has thus been an evolving process over the past forty years.

The term *learning disabilities* was initially used by Samuel Kirk in 1963 at a meeting of parents and professionals concerned about children with various learning difficulties. His proposed label was enthusiastically received and helped to unite the participants into an organization known as the Association for Children with Learning Disabilities, the forerunner of today's Learning Disabilities Association of America. Although the term was coined in 1963, Kirk had defined the concept a year earlier. His definition of **learning disabilities** was

> a retardation, disorder, or delayed development in one or more of the processes of speech, language, reading, writing, arithmetic, or other school subject resulting from a psychological handicap caused by a possible cerebral dysfunction and/or emotional or behavioral disturbances. It is not the result of mental retardation, sensory deprivation, or cultural and instructional factors. (Kirk, 1962, p. 263)

A learning disability is an umbrella concept covering a wide range of difficulties.

As you will see, elements of this definition, which is an umbrella concept encompassing a multitude of educational "sins," appear in many of the later definitions of learning disabilities, including subaverage academic performance, processing disorders, and the exclusion of certain etiological possibilities.

National Advisory Committee on Handicapped Children

In the late 1960s, Congress was considering the funding of various programs that would benefit individuals with learning disabilities. As part of this process, the U.S. Office of Education was requested to craft a definition of learning disabilities. A committee was established with Kirk as its chair. Its discussions resulted in the following definition, which was subsequently incorporated in the Specific Learning Disabilities Act of 1969 (PL 91–230):

> Children with special (specific) learning disabilities exhibit a disorder in one or more of the basic psychological processes involved in understanding or in using spoken and written language. These may be manifested in disorders of listening, thinking, talking, reading, writing, spelling or arithmetic. They include conditions which have been referred to as perceptual handicaps, brain injury, minimal brain dysfunction, dyslexia, developmental aphasia, etc. They do not include learning problems that are due primarily to visual, hearing, or motor handicaps, to mental retardation, emotional disturbance, or to environmental disadvantage. (U.S. Office of Education, 1968, p. 34)

It is not surprising, given the fact that Kirk spearheaded this task force, that there is a high degree of similarity between Kirk's initial description and the committee's definition. Nonetheless, three differences are evident:

1. An emphasis on children
2. The addition of thinking disorders as an example of learning disabilities
3. The addition of emotional disturbance as an exclusionary etiological contribution (Hammill, 1990)

This definition proved to be immensely popular and was later, with slight modifications, incorporated in PL 94–142. In fact, by 1975 more than thirty states were using some version of the committee's definition as their state definition of learning disabilities (Mercer, Forgnone, & Wolking, 1976).

Federal Definition of Learning Disabilities

After the Education for All Handicapped Children Act was enacted in 1975, the U.S. Office of Education spent two years developing the accompanying rules and regulations for identifying and defining individuals with learning disabilities. The following official federal definition of learning disabilities was published in the *Federal Register* in December 1977:

> "Specific learning disability" means a disorder in one or more of the basic psychological processes involved in understanding or in using language, spoken

> or written, which may manifest itself in an imperfect ability to listen, speak, read, write, spell, or to do mathematical calculations. The term includes such conditions as perceptual handicaps, brain injury, minimal brain dysfunction, dyslexia, and developmental aphasia. The term does not include children who have learning disabilities which are primarily the result of visual, hearing, or motor handicaps, or mental retardation, or emotional disturbance, or of environmental, cultural, or economic disadvantage. (U.S. Office of Education, 1977, p. 65083)

This definition was retained in the Individuals with Disabilities Education Act (PL 101–476), commonly called IDEA, and is incorporated, with a few word changes, in both the 1997 and 2004 reauthorizations of IDEA (PL 105–17, PL 108–446).

In the same issue of the *Federal Register*, the U.S. Office of Education issued the regulations and operational guidelines that were to be used by professionals as the criteria for identifying pupils suspected of being learning disabled. These regulations required that

> (a) A team may determine that a child has a specific learning disability if:
> 1. The child does not achieve commensurate with his or her age and ability levels in one or more of the areas listed in paragraph (a) (2) of this section, when provided with learning experiences appropriate for the child's age and ability levels; and
> 2. The team finds that a child has a severe discrepancy between achievement and intellectual ability in one or more of the following areas:
>   i. Oral expression;
>   ii. Listening comprehension;
>   iii. Written expression;
>   iv. Basic reading skill;
>   v. Reading comprehension;
>   vi. Mathematics calculation; or
>   vii. Mathematics reasoning. (U.S. Office of Education, 1977, p. 65083)

This definition of learning disabilities and its accompanying regulations describe a syndrome rather than a particular student. Like the other definitions we have examined, the federal interpretation is useful for classifying children but provides little information on how to instruct these pupils.

The IDEA definition contains two key elements worthy of additional attention. One central component is the idea of a **discrepancy** between the student's academic performance and his or her estimated or assumed ability or potential. This discrepancy would not be anticipated on the basis of the pupil's overall intellectual ability—generally average to above-average IQ. This discrepancy factor is considered by many professionals to be the *sine qua non* of the definition of learning disabilities. It explains how, for instance, a 10-year-old with above-average intelligence reads at a level a year or more below expectations for his chronological age. Generally speaking, in most instances, a discrepancy of two years or more below expected performance levels in one academic area is necessary for a designation of learning disabilities. Unfortunately, the federal government failed to stipulate what was meant by "a severe discrepancy." Early on, it attempted to quantify the notion of a discrepancy by offering several formulas, but its efforts only led to criticism and confusion (Council for Learning Disabilities, 1986; Reynolds, 1992). Thus, the rules and regulations were published without a method for quantifying a severe discrepancy.

You may recall from Chapter 2 that IDEA 2004 removed this discrepancy provision. While PL 108–446 does not prohibit the use of a discrepancy approach for identifying pupils suspected of being learning disabled (Cortiella, 2006), it does give educators another way of discovering whether a student has a learning disability. School districts will now be able, if they so choose, to use a process that determines if the pupil responds to empirically validated, scientifically based interventions—a procedure known as **response to intervention**, or **RTI**. We will have much more to say about this new way of thinking later in this chapter.

The 1977 federal interpretation also specifies that a learning disability cannot be due primarily to sensory impairments, mental retardation, emotional problems, or environmental, cultural, or economic disadvantage. This language has come to be known as the **exclusionary clause**. This concept has generated considerable concern in some circles because it seems to suggest that students with other impairments cannot be considered learning disabled as well. Mercer and Pullen (2009), however, believe that the word *primarily* suggests that a learning disability can coexist with other exceptionalities. We believe that what is important is that professionals recognize that a youngster is experiencing learning difficulties, regardless of their etiology, and thus is in need of some form of intervention.

Association for Children With Learning Disabilities

The federal definition of learning disabilities has had its share of criticism and accompanying controversy. As a result, in 1986 the Association for Children with Learning Disabilities (now known as the Learning Disabilities Association of America) proposed a definition that incorporates several key elements not found in the IDEA definition. This substitute definition stresses the lifelong aspect of learning disabilities, addresses issues of socialization and self-esteem, eliminates the exclusionary language, and suggests that adaptive behaviors (daily living skills) may also be compromised by this disability. This group's definition is as follows:

> Specific Learning Disabilities is a chronic condition of presumed neurological origin which selectively interferes with the development, integration, and/or demonstration of verbal and/or nonverbal abilities. Specific Learning Disabilities exists as a distinct handicapping condition and varies in its manifestations and in degree of severity. Throughout life, the condition can affect self-esteem, education, vocation, socialization, and/or daily living activities. (Association for Children with Learning Disabilities, 1986, p. 15)

The Continuing Debate

After reading all of these definitions, you may believe that the field of learning disabilities is in a continual state of confusion and raucous debate over what a learning disability is. You may be partly correct. Some of the confusion is due to the different theoretical orientations of professionals working in the field. Remember, this is a multidisciplinary field that embraces sometimes competing viewpoints as to the very nature of the construct and its etiology. As noted earlier, it is perhaps best to envision learning disabilities as a family or syndrome of disabilities affecting a wide range of academic and/or behavioral performance. The key elements of the various definitions are summarized in Table 6.1.

TABLE 6.1 Common Components of Definitions of Learning Disabilities

- Intellectual functioning within normal range
- Significant gap or discrepancy between a student's assumed potential and actual achievement
- Inference that learning disabilities are not primarily caused by other disabilities or extrinsic factors
- Difficulty in learning in one or more academic areas
- Presumption of central nervous system dysfunction

A Brief History of the Field

Learning disabilities is an evolving and ever-changing field. Over the years, it has been influenced and significantly shaped by eminent individuals, various movements, governmental policies, research findings, and theoretical debates and has benefited from the activities of various advocacy/interest groups. The collective outcome of these sometimes competing efforts has been the present-day concept of learning disabilities.

The origins of the field of learning disabilities are international, multicultural, and multidisciplinary (Hallahan, Kauffman, & Lloyd, 1999). In fact, according to Hallahan et al., over the past century several different groups and professions have been involved, to varying degrees, in influencing the growth of the field. These influences include medicine, law, education, psychology, and advocacy groups, among others.

Lerner and Johns (2009) divide the development of the field into four distinct historical periods spanning almost two hundred years. These phases, illustrated in Figure 6.1, are discussed in the following sections.

Foundation Phase

Although the modern-day concept of learning disabilities traces its origin to an address given by Samuel Kirk in 1963, the roots of this concept lie in the studies of brain functions conducted in the nineteenth and early twentieth centuries. Neurologists and other physicians of this era were interested in detecting which areas of the brain control specific activities such as speech or reading. By investigating adults with brain damage, these early pioneers were able to identify regions of the brain that appeared to be associated with particular cognitive impairments such as aphasia (inability to speak). James Hinshelwood, for example, was a Scottish medical researcher who was intrigued by a young boy's inability to learn to read. Despite apparently normal intelligence and vision, this child exhibited a severe reading disability that Hinshelwood called "word blindness." He attributed this problem to a defect in a specific area of the boy's brain.

These pioneering efforts paved the way for later scientists such as Kurt Goldstein, a physician who studied soldiers suffering from traumatic brain injuries acquired during World War I. He noticed that many of these young men exhibited perceptual impairments; they were highly distractible, unable to attend to relevant stimuli, and overly meticulous. He hypothesized that these behavioral and perceptual impairments were the consequence of damage to the brain. Goldstein's theorizing was later expanded on by Alfred Strauss, a neuropsychiatrist, and his colleague Heinz Werner, a developmental psychologist. Both men fled Nazi Germany and joined the research staff at the Wayne County Training School in Michigan, where they studied children thought to have brain injury and intellectual disabilities. Interestingly, they observed that these students exhibited

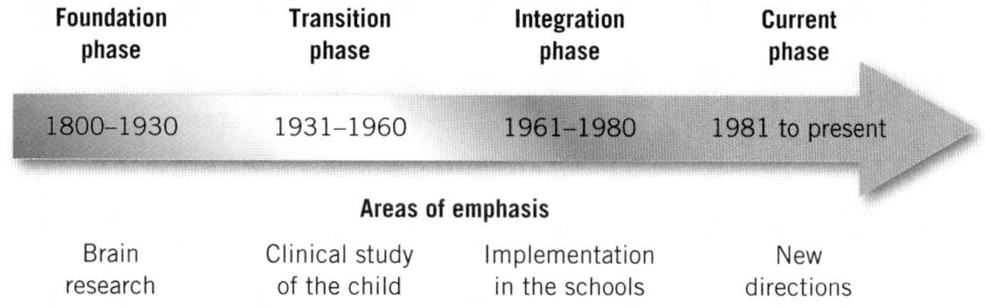

FIGURE 6.1 Phases in the Development of the Field of Learning Disabilities

SOURCE: Adapted from J. Lerner and B. Johns, *Learning Disabilities and Mild Disabilities,* 11th ed. (Belmont, CA: Wadsworth/Cengage Learning, 2009), p. 30.

characteristics similar to those identified by Goldstein, although they had not suffered any obvious head injuries. Werner and Strauss speculated that the pupils' intellectual disabilities could be attributed to brain damage resulting from nongenetic factors. They developed a list of behavioral characteristics that distinguished between individuals with and without brain injury and suggested instructional tactics that could benefit students with learning disabilities.

Transition Phase

Beginning in the 1930s, teachers, reading specialists, psychologists, and others began to apply the scientific research evidence to children with learning problems. During this period, various individuals from different professional backgrounds played key roles in developing assessment instruments and remediation strategies designed to ameliorate academic difficulties (Lerner, 2003). Among the important theorists and contributions of this period are the following:

- Samuel Orton, a specialist in neurology, hypothesized that language disorders in children were due to the absence of cerebral dominance. He also devoted considerable energy to working with pupils with severe reading disorders, whom he called dyslexic. He speculated that their reading difficulties were due to neurological problems. The Orton Dyslexia Association, now the International Dyslexia Association, was named in honor of his contributions in this area.
- Grace Fernald, an educator who worked at the laboratory school at the University of California, Los Angeles, established a clinic for children who were experiencing significant learning difficulties despite their normal intellect. Over the years, she perfected various remedial reading and spelling programs. One of her tactics was a visual-auditory-kinesthetic-tactile (VAKT) approach to learning. This technique is the foundation of today's multisensory approach to instruction.
- Newell Kephart, a colleague of Strauss at the Wayne County Training School, pioneered a perceptual–motor development theory of learning. He advocated movement and physical exercises, among other corrective activities, as a means of remediating learning problems, which he attributed to deficiencies in perceptual–motor integration.
- Marianne Frostig was another early worker in the field of learning disabilities. She believed that a youngster's academic difficulties, especially poor reading, were a consequence of poorly developed visual perceptual skills. Assessment and remediation efforts, therefore, centered on specific aspects of visual perception. Frostig constructed her Developmental Test of Visual Perception as a means of pinpointing areas of weakness. Deficits were remediated by means of specially prepared exercises in hopes of improving visual perceptual abilities and thus the student's performance in reading. Her approach, like Kephart's, remained popular for many years but eventually fell out of favor among professionals for lack of empirical evidence documenting its effectiveness.

Integration Phase

In the latter part of the twentieth century, learning disabilities became an established disability area in schools across the United States (Lerner & Johns, 2009). As mentioned earlier, it was Samuel Kirk who initially popularized the term *learning disabilities*. This new term was welcomed by parents whose children had previously been identified as neurologically impaired, perceptually handicapped, brain damaged, and other pejorative labels. When schools elected to serve these students, many of whom were experiencing significant academic difficulties, they were often incorrectly placed in classes for pupils with intellectual disabilities or, in some instances, in settings for children with emotional problems; others received services from remedial reading specialists. Some pupils were denied help because school authorities were unable to classify them using the then current disabilities categories necessary for placement in a special education program.

The integration era witnessed the enactment of PL 91–230, the Specific Learning Disabilities Act of 1969, soon followed by the landmark "Bill of Rights" for children with disabilities, PL 94–142, now referred to as IDEA. Other milestones included the establishment of the Association for Children with Learning Disabilities in 1964, followed four years later by the birth of the Division for Children with Learning Disabilities (DCLD) as part of the Council for Exceptional Children (CEC). In 1982, a group of DCLD members withdrew from CEC over policy issues and created an independent association also concerned about individuals with learning disabilities, the Council for Learning Disabilities. Also in 1982, other former DCLD members began a new division under the auspices of CEC, the Division for Learning Disabilities.

Current Phase

It is hard to pinpoint the end of the integration phase and the beginning of the current phase. Beginning in the last decades of the twentieth century, however, the field of learning disabilities has been affected by several, sometimes controversial, forces. Some special educators believe that the field is embarking on a period of turbulent transition (Hallahan & Mercer, 2002). Mercer and Pullen (2009) predict that the field will be buffeted by a variety of social, political, economic, and professional forces. The question is "How will the field respond to these challenges?" Some of the emerging challenges or issues identified by Lerner and Johns (2009) include concerns about the movement toward full inclusion, how best to serve culturally and linguistically diverse learners, and the impact of assistive technology, along with issues of high-stakes assessment, response to intervention, and several other matters. Many of these topics will be addressed elsewhere in this chapter.

Prevalence of Learning Disabilities

It is difficult to ascertain the percentage of students with learning disabilities because of variations used in determining eligibility for services. Current estimates range from 1 to 30 percent of the school population (Lerner & Johns, 2009). Recent statistics compiled by the federal government suggest that approximately 2.52 million pupils ages 6 to 21 are identified as learning disabled (U.S. Department of Education, 2010). Thus, learning disabilities is by far the largest category of special education, accounting for slightly less than one half (42.8 percent) of all individuals receiving services in the 2008–2009 school year.

The growth of the field of learning disabilities is nothing short of phenomenal. During the 1976–1977 school year, the initial year of federal reporting, the number of pupils identified as learning disabled was slightly lower than 800,000; over the next thirty-two years, this figure gradually increased to well over 2.5 million youngsters, an increase of approximately 215 percent.

This dramatic increase is obviously cause for concern. Critics assert that the number has grown because the concept itself is ill defined (Hallahan, Lloyd, Kauffman, Weiss, & Martinez, 2005), and because it is extremely difficult to distinguish between underachieving pupils and those diagnosed as learning disabled (Kavale, 2002). However, not all professionals are convinced that the growth is unwarranted. Several valid reasons could account for the spiraling growth rate. According to Lerner and Johns (2009), the rapid increase is an artifact of (1) greater public awareness of the disability, resulting in more referrals for services; (2) improved diagnostic and assessment procedures; and (3) higher social acceptance of the label and less accompanying stigma.

The number of pupils identified as learning disabled varies by age. The number of children receiving services increases steadily between the ages of 6 and 9 (from approximately 22,000 to about 173,000), which is not too surprising considering the increasing academic demands of the elementary school curriculum. The bulk of students served (48 percent), however, are between the ages of 10 and 14 (U.S. Department of Education, 2010).

Finally, the federal government now counts preschoolers with learning disabilities. The U.S. Department of Education (2010) reports in excess of 14,000 youngsters with learning disabilities. This number represents 1.9 percent of all preschoolers with a disability.

Etiology of Learning Disabilities

Despite intense research activity over the years, pinpointing the precise cause or causes of learning disabilities has remained an elusive goal. In fact, researchers have been unable to offer much in the way of concrete evidence as to the etiology of learning disabilities (Hallahan et al., 2005). Many of the proposed causal factors remain largely speculative. In the vast majority of instances, the cause of a person's learning disability remains unknown. Just as there are many different types of learning disabilities, there appear to be multiple etiological possibilities. We should point out that the cause of an individual's learning difficulties is often of little educational relevance. In other words, knowing why a particular pupil is learning disabled does not necessarily translate into effective instructional strategies and practices. Nonetheless, investigators posit four basic categories for explaining the etiology of learning disabilities: acquired trauma, genetic/hereditary influences, biochemical abnormalities, and environmental possibilities (Mercer & Pullen, 2009).

Neurological dysfunction is suspected as a cause of some learning disabilities.

Acquired Trauma

The medical literature uses the term *acquired trauma* when describing injury or damage to the central nervous system (CNS) that originates outside the person and results in learning disorders. Depending on when the damage occurs, the trauma is identified as prenatal (before birth), perinatal (during birth), or postnatal (after birth). These traumas, according to Mercer and Pullen (2009), have been linked to learning problems in children.

One example of an acquired trauma that may manifest itself pre-, peri-, or postnatally is **brain injury.** Historically speaking, professionals have long presumed CNS dysfunction as a probable cause of learning disabilities (Hallahan & Mercer, 2002), and for some students this is a valid assumption. Spivak (1986) estimates that as many as 20 percent of children identified as learning disabled have had a prior brain injury. (Of course, this also means that eight out of ten youngsters do not evidence brain damage.) The belief that injury to the CNS is a likely cause of learning disabilities is common in some professional circles. Advances in neuroimaging techniques such as magnetic resonance imaging (MRI), positron emission tomography (PET), and other computerized neurological measures have allowed researchers, in some instances, to establish the importance of neurological dysfunction as a cause of learning disabilities. In the majority of cases, however, there is no definitive evidence of brain damage. In the absence of clear clinical evidence, it is perhaps best to view these data as speculative and inferential. For this reason, professionals, especially physicians, often use terms such as *assumed brain injury* and *presumed CNS dysfunction* when talking about learning disabilities.

Brain injury is certainly one type of acquired trauma that can occur before, during, and after birth, but a number of other factors have also been implicated as possible causes of learning disabilities:

Prenatal Causes

- Smoking
- Illicit drugs
- Use of alcohol

Perinatal Causes

- Prolonged and difficult delivery
- Anoxia
- Prematurity/low birth weight
- Trauma caused by medical instruments such as forceps

Postnatal Causes

- Strokes
- Concussions
- Meningitis/encephalitis
- High fever
- Head injury resulting from falls or accidents (Mercer & Pullen, 2009)

Audio Link 6.1
Listen to more about causes of learning disabilities.

Genetic/Hereditary Influences

Do learning disabilities "run" in families? Researchers investigating this question believe that some learning problems are indeed inherited. Over the years, a fairly strong link has been established between heredity and some types of learning disabilities (Galaburda, 2005; Isles & Humby, 2006; Shapiro, Church, & Lewis, 2007). Raskind (2001) notes, for instance, that reading and spelling deficits are substantially inherited. **Familiality studies**, which examine the tendency of certain conditions to occur in a single family, suggest that reading difficulties and certain types of speech and language impairments are family related (Lewis, 1992). Familiality does not clearly prove heritability, however; learning problems may occur in certain families for environmental reasons, such as child-rearing practices. We recommend, therefore, that the findings of familiality studies be interpreted cautiously.

Although it is difficult to control for the effect of environmental influences on learning, **heritability studies** enable investigators to more clearly answer the question "Are learning disabilities inherited?" In this investigative technique, scientists compare the school performance of monozygotic twins (identical twins, developing from the same egg with identical genetic characteristics) with that of dizygotic twins (fraternal twins, developing from two different eggs with different genetic makeup). The research evidence generally supports the hypothesis that certain types of learning problems, including reading and math disabilities, are more common among identical twins than fraternal twins (Shalev, 2004; Wadsworth & DeFries, 2005; Wood & Grigorenko, 2001).

Biochemical Abnormalities

In some youngsters, biochemical conditions are suspected of causing learning disabilities. Over the years, several different theories have enjoyed varying degrees of popularity among parents and professionals. In the mid-1970s, Feingold (1975, 1976) championed the view that allergic reactions to certain artificial colorings, flavorings, and additives contained in many food products contribute to children's learning problems and hyperactive behavior. He recommends that parents restrict the consumption of foods containing natural salicylates, including apples, oranges, and some types of berries; ban products containing artificial colors and flavors; and limit the intake of certain other products such as toothpaste and compounds containing aspirin. The scientific community, however, has found little support for Feingold's theory (Kavale & Forness, 1983).

Another popular theory of this era was megavitamin therapy, whose chief advocate was psychiatrist Alan Cott. Cott (1972) theorizes that learning disabilities can be caused by the inability of a person's blood to synthesize a normal amount of vitamins. In an effort to treat learning disabilities, large daily doses of certain vitamins are recommended to counteract the suspected vitamin deficiency. Again, scientific research (Arnold, Christopher, Huestis, & Smeltzer, 1978) has failed to substantiate the benefit of this treatment.

We suspect that, in some instances, an individual's biochemical makeup may affect his or her learning and behavior. The current research evidence, however, cannot definitively support this hypothesis.

Environmental Possibilities

Another school of thought attributes the etiology of learning disabilities to a host of environmental factors such as low socioeconomic status, malnutrition, lack of access to health care, and other variables that may contribute to neurological dysfunction (Hallahan et al., 2005). Although the IDEA definition and others specifically exclude these conditions as etiological possibilities, many educators believe that these risk factors indirectly contribute to the learning and behavioral difficulties of some pupils.

Another variable implicated as causing learning disabilities is the quality of instruction that students receive. Simply stated, some children are identified as learning disabled as a result of poor teaching. Engelmann (1977) estimates that the vast majority of students labeled as learning disabled "have been seriously mistaught. Learning disabilities are made, not born" (p. 47). Recently, during a visit to a foreign country, your author was told by a veteran special educator of a slogan in her country that speaks directly to this issue: "There are no bad students, only poor teachers." Lyon et al. (2001) also contend that learning disabilities may result from poor teachers and inadequate instruction. While implying that the quality of the learning environment contributes to learning disabilities, researchers also note that learning problems can often be remediated by exposure to individualized and high-quality instructional practices.

Characteristics of Individuals With Learning Disabilities

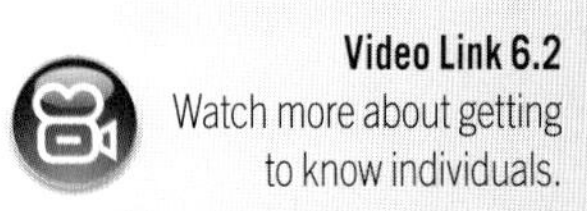

Video Link 6.2
Watch more about getting to know individuals.

There is probably no such entity as a "typical" person with learning disabilities; no two students possess the identical profile of strengths and weaknesses. The concept of learning disabilities covers an extremely wide range of characteristics. One pupil may have deficits in just one area while another exhibits deficits in several areas; yet both will be labeled as learning disabled. Some children will experience cognitive difficulties, others may have problems with motor skills, and still others may exhibit social deficits.

Over the years, parents, educators, and other professionals have identified a wide variety of characteristics associated with learning disabilities. One of the earliest profiles, developed by Clements (1966), includes the following ten frequently cited attributes:

- Hyperactivity
- Perceptual–motor impairments
- Emotional lability
- Coordination problems
- Disorders of attention
- Impulsivity

- Disorders of memory and thinking
- Academic difficulties
- Language deficits
- Equivocal neurological signs

Parents of children with learning disabilities (Ariel, 1992) have described many of the same behaviors. Lerner and Johns's (2009) recent list includes the following learning and behavioral characteristics of individuals with learning disabilities:

- Disorders of attention
- Poor motor abilities
- Psychological process deficits and information-processing problems
- Lack of cognitive strategies needed for efficient learning
- Oral language difficulties
- Reading difficulties
- Written language problems
- Quantitative disorders
- Social skills deficits

Not all students with learning disabilities will exhibit these characteristics, and many pupils who demonstrate these same behaviors are quite successful in the classroom. It is often the frequency, intensity, and duration of the behaviors that lead to problems in school and elsewhere. Furthermore, in some instances, the characteristics are contradictory. One youngster, for example, is rambunctious and "always on the go" (hyperactive) while a classmate who is also learning disabled may be overly lethargic and inactive (hypoactive). The way deficits are manifested also varies according to grade level. A language disorder may exhibit itself as delayed speech in a preschooler, as a reading problem in the elementary grades, and as a writing difficulty at the secondary level (Lerner & Johns, 2009).

Gender differences also play a role in the recognition of learning disabilities. Boys are four times as likely as girls to be identified as learning disabled. Lerner and Johns (2009) synthesize several lines of research suggesting that, in actuality, there are not fewer girls with learning disabilities, but girls are not as readily identified—perhaps because of differences in the kinds of disabilities they exhibit. These experts note that "boys tend to exhibit more physical aggression and loss of control . . . [while] girls with learning disabilities tend to have more cognitive, language, and social problems, and to have severe academic achievement deficits in reading and math" (p. 16).

Learning disabilities encompass a broad range of characteristics beyond those associated primarily with academic problems. Mercer and Pullen (2009), for instance, believe that cognitive and social/emotional factors are also key elements (see Figure 6.2). Common cognitive disorders include deficits in attention, metacognition, memory, and perception. Social and emotional difficulties include hyperactive behaviors, low self-esteem, and learned helplessness.

In the past, professionals concerned with learning disabilities have typically focused on the elementary school–age child; in recent years, however, the field has adopted a life span approach. We now realize that learning disabilities may manifest themselves

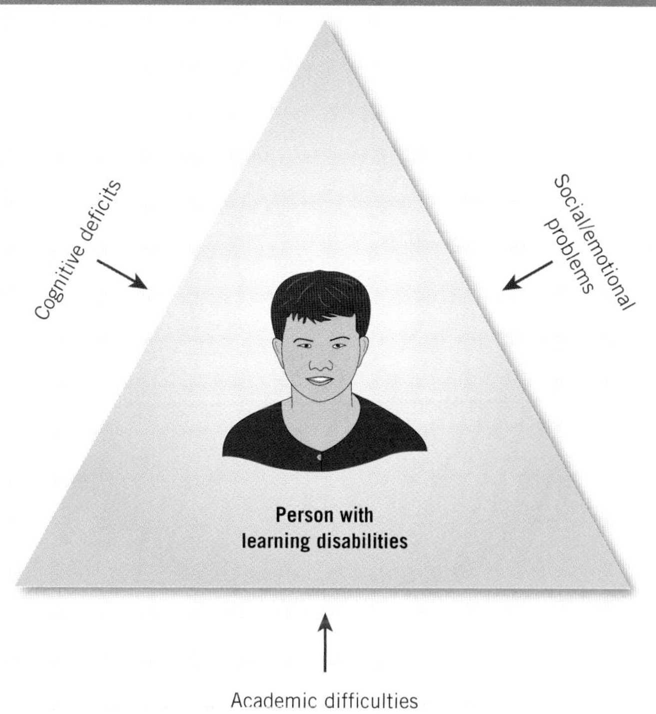

FIGURE 6.2 Broad Characteristics Associated With Learning Disabilities

at different stages of life and that problems present themselves in different ways depending on the age of the individual (Lerner & Johns, 2009).

Learning Characteristics

Most professionals agree that the primary characteristics of students with learning disabilities are deficits in academic performance. A learning disability does not exist without impairments in academic achievement. These deficits may involve several different categories of school performance.

Reading

Well over half of all students identified as learning disabled exhibit problems with reading (Bender, 2008; Lerner & Johns, 2009). The difficulties experienced by these youngsters are as varied as the children themselves. Some pupils have trouble with reading comprehension; others evidence word recognition errors; still others lack word analysis skills or are deficient in oral reading. Table 6.2 lists several areas of reading difficulty common among students with learning disabilities. Deficits in reading are thought to be a primary reason for failure in school; they also contribute to a loss of self-esteem and self-confidence (Polloway, Patton, & Serna, 2008).

TABLE 6.2 Common Reading Problems of Students With Learning Disabilities

	Problem Areas	Observations
Reading Habits	Tension movements	Frowning, fidgeting, using a high-pitched voice, lip biting
	Insecurity	Refusing to read, crying, attempting to distract the teacher
	Loses place	Losing place frequently (often associated with repetitions)
	Lateral head movements	Jerking head
	Holds material close	Deviating extremely (from 15 to 18 inches)
Word Recognition Errors	Omissions	Omitting a word (e.g., *Tom saw [a] cat*)
	Insertions	Inserting words (e.g., *The dog ran [fast] after the cat*)
	Substitutions	Substituting one word for another (e.g., *The house ~~horse~~ was big*)
	Reversals	Reversing letters in a word (e.g., *no* for *on, was* for *saw*)
	Mispronunciations	Mispronouncing words (e.g., *mister* for *miser*)
	Transpositions	Reading words in the wrong order (e.g., *She away ran* for *She ran away*)
	Unknown words	Hesitating for 5 seconds at words they cannot pronounce
	Slow, choppy reading	Not recognizing words quickly enough (20 to 30 words per minute)
Comprehension Errors	Cannot recall basic facts	Unable to answer specific questions about a passage (e.g., *What was the dog's name?*)
	Cannot recall sequence	Unable to tell sequence of the story that was read
	Cannot recall main theme	Unable to recall the main topic of the story
Miscellaneous Symptoms	Word-by-word reading	Reading in a choppy, halting, and laborious manner (no attempt to group words into thought units)
	Strained, high-pitched voice	Reading in a pitch higher than conversational tone
	Inadequate phrasing	Inappropriately grouping words (e.g., *The dog ran into [pause] the woods*)
	Ignored or misinterpreted punctuation	Running together phrases, clauses, or sentences

SOURCE: C. Mercer and P. Pullen, *Students with Learning Disabilities,* 6th ed. (Upper Saddle River, NJ: Prentice Hall, 2005), p. 195. Reprinted by permission of Pearson Education, Inc., Upper Saddle River, NJ.

One term frequently heard when discussing reading problems is **dyslexia**. Simply stated, dyslexia is a type of reading disorder in which the student fails to recognize and comprehend written words—a severe impairment in the ability to read. It is generally thought that this problem results from difficulties with **phonological awareness**—a lack of understanding of the rules that govern the correspondence between specific sounds and certain letters that make up words (Lyon, Shaywitz, & Shaywitz, 2003; Simmons, Kame'enui, Coyne, & Chard, 2007). In other words, letter–sound recognition is impaired.

Phonemic awareness, or understanding that words are constructed of small units of sounds known as **phonemes**, is another important element of learning to read. Some pupils, for example, may experience reading problems because they are unable to decode the word *cat* into three distinct phonemes —/c/ /a/ /t/—while other students might experience difficulty isolating beginning, middle, and ending sounds. For example, "What is the first sound in the word *rabbit*?" (Simmons et al., 2007).

Mathematics

Researchers estimate that about one out of every four pupils with learning disabilities receives assistance because of difficulties with mathematics (Lerner & Johns, 2009). Students who experience this problem are unique; not all children exhibit the same deficiency or impairment. In some instances, pupils may have difficulty with computational skills, word problems, spatial relationships, or writing numbers and copying shapes. Other classmates may have problems with telling time, understanding fractions and decimals, or measuring. Problems that begin in elementary school generally continue through high school and may have debilitating consequences in adulthood.

Written Language

Many individuals with learning disabilities exhibit deficits in written language, including spelling, handwriting, and composition (Hallahan et al., 2005). Researchers (Jennings, Caldwell, & Lerner, 2010) speculate that a link exists between these areas of deficiency and a person's reading ability. The association between reading and writing impairments should not be too surprising, as both may arise from a lack of phonological awareness.

Poor penmanship may be due to the absence of the requisite fine motor skills needed for legible handwriting and/or a lack of understanding of spatial relationships (for example, up, down, bottom), which may contribute to difficulties with letter formation and spacing between words and sentences (see Figure 6.3).

Children's writing changes as they mature. According to Hallahan et al. (1999), the focus of a youngster's writing "shifts from (1) the process of writing (handwriting and spelling) to (2) the written product (having written something) to (3) communication with readers (getting across one's message)" (p. 396). Early on, pupils focus on becoming competent in mastering the mechanical aspects of composition—spelling and handwriting; in later grades, they learn to organize and present their ideas in a lucid and logical fashion. Children who are learning disabled, however, lag behind their nondisabled peers. Investigators have observed that individuals with learning disabilities use less complex sentence structure, incorporate fewer ideas, produce poorly organized paragraphs, and write less complex stories (Hallahan et al., 2005).

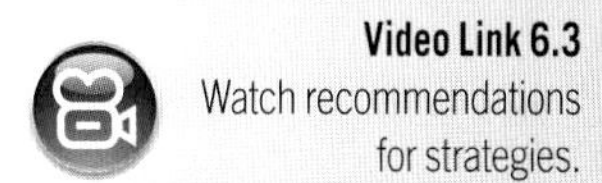

Spelling is another problem area for students with learning disabilities. They may omit certain letters or add incorrect ones. Auditory memory and discrimination difficulties are thought to be part of the reason for their problem.

Spoken Language

Persons with learning disabilities frequently experience difficulties with oral expression—a problem that can affect both academic performance and social interactions. Problems with appropriate word choice, understanding complex sentence structures, and responding to questions are not uncommon. Specific mechanical deficits may involve syntax (rule

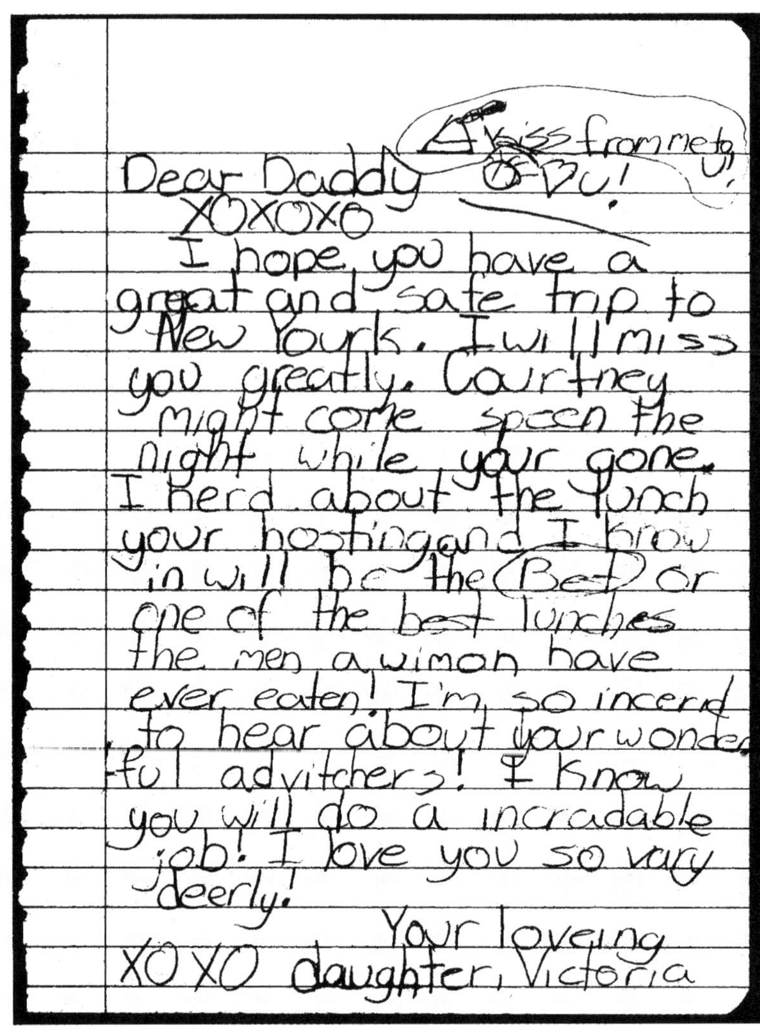

A kiss from me to U!

Dear Daddy
XOXOXO
I hope you have a great and safe trip to New Yourk. I will miss you greatly. Courtney might come speen the night while your gone. I herd about the lunch your hostingand I know in will be the (Best) or one of the best lunches the men a wimon have ever eaten! I'm so incerd to hear about your wonderful advitchers! I know you will do a incradable job! I love you so vary deerly!

Your loveing
XOXO daughter, Victoria

FIGURE 6.3 Writing Sample of a 10-Year-Old Girl

Dear Daddy

A kiss from me to you!

XOXOXO

I hope you have a great and safe trip to New York. I will miss you greatly. Courtney might come spend the night while you are gone. I heard about the lunch you are hosting and I know it will be the best or one of the best lunches the men and women have ever eaten! I'm so interested to hear about your wonderful adventures! I know you will do a incredible job! I love you so very dearly.

XOXO

Your loving daughter, Victoria

systems that determine how words are organized into sentences), semantics (word meanings), and phonology (sound formation and blending of sounds to form words). One aspect of oral expression that is receiving increased attention is **pragmatics**—the functional use of language in social situations. Researchers note that children with learning disabilities sometimes experience communication problems in social settings (Pearl & Donahue, 2004). Participating in conversations with friends can be especially troublesome for someone who is learning disabled. The ebb and flow that is characteristic of conversations may elude him or her, and nonverbal language clues may also be overlooked. In short, many individuals with learning disabilities are not good conversationalists.

Memory

It is well documented that children and adolescents with learning disabilities have significant difficulties remembering both academic and nonacademic information, such as doctor appointments, homework assignments, multiplication facts, directions, and telephone numbers. Teachers frequently comment that, with these students, it seems to be "in one ear and out the other," which can be highly aggravating for teachers as well as parents.

Research evidence suggests that many students with learning disabilities have problems with short-term memory as well as working memory (Swanson, Cooney, & McNamara, 2004; Swanson & Jerman, 2007). **Short-term memory** tasks typically involve the recall, in correct order, of either aurally or visually presented information (such as lists of digits or pictures) shortly after hearing or seeing the items several times. **Working memory** requires that an individual retain information while simultaneously engaging in another cognitive activity. Working memory is involved, for example, when we try to remember a person's address while also listening to directions on how to arrive there (Swanson, 2005).

Students with learning disabilities, in contrast to their typical peers, apparently do not spontaneously use effective learning strategies (such as rehearsal or categorizing of items) as an aid in recall. Deficits in memory, particularly working memory, often translate into difficulties in the classroom. Success with reading and math seems to depend more on working memory than on short-term memory (Council for Exceptional Children, 2003). Working memory also appears to be crucial for word recognition and reading comprehension.

Reading difficulties are very common among students with learning disabilities.

Metacognition

It is not unusual for persons with learning disabilities to exhibit deficits in **metacognition**—the ability to evaluate and monitor one's own performance. Students who are learning disabled often lack an awareness of their own thinking process. Metacognitive skills typically consist of several key components: (1) a recognition of task requirements—that is, the strategies and resources needed to perform effectively; (2) implementation of the appropriate process; and (3) monitoring, evaluating, and adjusting one's performance to ensure successful task completion. Competency as a learner requires that students exhibit these metacognitive skills (Meltzer & Krishnan, 2007).

The reading problems of some children with learning disabilities may be due to deficiencies in metacognition. Reading comprehension difficulties, for example, may be due to deficits in the following skills:

- **Clarifying the purpose(s) of reading:** Pupils do not adjust their reading styles to accommodate the difficulty of the text.
- **Focusing attention on important goals:** Youngsters with reading problems experience difficulty in selecting the main ideas of a paragraph.
- **Monitoring one's level of comprehension:** Inefficient readers do not recognize that they are failing to understand what they are reading.
- **Rereading and scanning ahead:** Children with learning disabilities do not go back and reread portions of previously read text, nor do they scan upcoming material as an aid to comprehension.
- **Consulting external sources:** Ineffective readers do not utilize external sources like dictionaries and encyclopedias. (Hallahan et al., 2005)

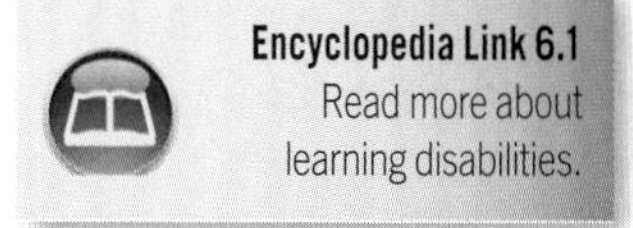

Encyclopedia Link 6.1
Read more about learning disabilities.

Fortunately, as you will learn later, metacognitive skills can be taught.

Many individuals with learning disabilities believe that no matter how hard they try, they will still fail.

Attributions

What individuals believe about what contributes to their success or failure on a task is known as *attribution*. Many students with learning disabilities attribute success not to their own efforts but to situations or events beyond their control, such as luck. These pupils are identified as being outwardly directed.

Chronic difficulties with academic assignments often lead children with learning disabilities to anticipate failure; success is seen as an unattainable goal no matter how hard they try. Youngsters who maintain this attitude frequently give up and will not even attempt to complete the task. Friend and Bursuck (2009) identify this outlook as **learned helplessness**. Loss of self-esteem and a lack of motivation are common consequences of this phenomenon.

Because of their propensity for academic failure, individuals with learning disabilities tend to become passive or inactive learners. They are not actively involved or engaged in their own learning and often fail to demonstrate initiative in the learning process. When confronted with a task, persons with learning disabilities typically use less effective strategies; they have a deficiency in strategic learning behavior (Deshler, Ellis, & Lenz, 1996). These pupils are often characterized as inactive or inefficient learners (Hallahan et al., 2005). In some cases, attributions can be altered through the use of various reinforcement and motivational strategies that attempt to demonstrate to the pupil the link between his or her own efforts and success (Sexton, Harris, & Graham, 1998).

Social and Emotional Problems

Research suggests that some students with learning disabilities, in comparison to their typical peers, have lower self-esteem (Manning, Bear, & Minke, 2006; Pearl & Donahue, 2004; Vaughn, Sinagub, & Kim, 2004) and a poor self-concept, most likely due to frustration with their learning difficulties (Mercer & Pullen, 2009). Shapiro and his colleagues (2007) observe that "these individuals are less likely to take pride in their successes and more likely to be overcome by their failures" (p. 374).

Investigators are now beginning to realize that deficits in social skills are a common characteristic among many, but not all, individuals with learning disabilities (Kavale & Mostert, 2004; Wiener, 2004). Many of these students are deficient in social cognition; they are inept at understanding and interpreting social cues and social situations, which can easily lead to impaired interpersonal relationships. The social–emotional difficulties of persons with learning disabilities may be the result of social imperceptiveness—a lack of skill in detecting subtle affective cues. Students with learning disabilities often experience rejection by nondisabled peers and have difficulty making friends, possibly because they misinterpret the feelings and emotions of others (Lerner & Johns, 2009; Shapiro et al., 2007).

Attention Problems and Hyperactivity

Individuals who are learning disabled frequently experience difficulty attending to tasks, and some exhibit excess movement and activity, or hyperactive behavior. It is not unusual for educators to mention these characteristics when describing students with learning disabilities. Teachers note that some pupils have difficulty staying on task and completing assignments, following directions, or focusing their attention for a sustained period of time—they are easily distracted. In other instances, children are perceived to be overly active and fidgety, racing from one thing to another as if driven. Problems with inattention, distractibility, and hyperactivity can easily impair and impede an individual's successful performance in the classroom, at home, and in social situations.

The term usually heard when discussing this condition is **attention deficit hyperactivity disorder (ADHD)**, typical in the language of medical professionals and psychologists. This label is derived from the *Diagnostic and Statistical Manual of Mental Disorders—Text Revision,* revised in 2000 by the American Psychiatric Association and commonly referred to as DSM-IV-TR. Although hyperactivity and attention disorders are fairly common among persons with learning disabilities, with estimates ranging from about 25–40 to possibly 80 percent of children with learning disabilities displaying characteristics of ADHD (Bender, 2008; Lerner & Johns, 2009; Mercer & Pullen, 2009), the terms are *not* synonymous—not all students with learning disabilities have ADHD, and vice versa. The exact relationship between learning disabilities and ADHD is not fully understood, but scientists and researchers are now beginning to unravel this complex phenomenon.

Assessment of Learning Disabilities

Federal law dictates that individuals being considered for possible placement in a program for children with learning disabilities receive a multidisciplinary evaluation that is conducted by a team of professionals in a nondiscriminatory fashion. Recall that this evaluation process will only occur if the recommended prereferral strategies have proven ineffective. IDEA requires, among other regulations, that

- tests be administered by trained individuals;
- tests be reliable and valid and appropriate for the purpose for which they are being used;
- tests be neither racially nor culturally discriminatory;
- tests be administered in the student's native language or preferred means of communication; and
- no single measure be used as the basis for determining a pupil's eligibility.

Once the evaluation is completed, the team determines the youngster's eligibility for placement in a learning disabilities program in light of their state's definition of learning disabilities and federal guidelines.

Assessment Decisions

At the heart of assessing a student for possible placement in a program for individuals with learning disabilities is determining whether the student exhibits a severe discrepancy between estimated or perceived ability and actual educational achievement. This discrepancy is typically established by comparing a student's performance on a standardized achievement test with a measure of cognitive abilities or intelligence. Frequently used measures of intellectual performance (mentioned in Chapter 5) include the Wechsler Intelligence Scale for Children (4th ed.), the Stanford-Binet Intelligence Scale (5th ed.), and the more recently developed Kaufman Assessment Battery for Children. A wide variety of achievement tests are available to educational diagnosticians. Comprehensive batteries designed to measure overall academic achievement include the well-known Iowa Test of Basic Skills, the Stanford Achievement Test, and the Wechsler Individual Achievement Test. Many other achievement tests assess a student's abilities in content areas such as math, reading, and language arts. Several states use the concept of a severe discrepancy to identify individuals with learning disabilities.

A variety of complicated mathematical formulas are used to arrive at a discrepancy score. Unfortunately, there is no nationally agreed-upon mechanism for determining a discrepancy; different states use different formulas and even different tests in an effort to quantify the gap between potential and performance. As a result, a child identified as learning disabled in one state may be ineligible for services if the family relocates to another state.

Researchers, parents, and practitioners alike are now questioning the educational validity of identifying youngsters as learning disabled solely on the basis of a discrepancy formula and are calling for the use of alternative strategies such as relying on professionals' clinical judgment and experience in addition to assessing discrepancies among various cognitive and academic skills (Lerner & Johns, 2009).

Response to Intervention

Video Link 6.5
Watch more about response to intervention.

Recently, with the reauthorization of IDEA 2004, some of these concerns were addressed. States and local school districts now have the option of choosing between the achievement–ability discrepancy model and making eligibility decisions on the basis of how a pupil responds to scientific, research-based educational interventions. This strategy is commonly referred to as response to intervention (RTI) or response to treatment.

There is no formal definition of RTI, nor is there one model or strategy that is widely accepted by researchers or educators (Bradley, Danielson, & Doolittle, 2007; Cortiella, 2006; Fuchs, Fuchs, & Stecker, 2010). Generally speaking, RTI is a procedure whereby a pupil is exposed to increasingly intensive tiers or levels of instructional intervention with ongoing progress monitoring. The fidelity or integrity of RTI is predicated upon two crucial elements: (1) the use of evidence-based or scientifically validated instructional practices, and (2) the frequent and systematic assessment of the individual's performance, known as **progress monitoring**. Essentially, RTI is an instructional and dynamic assessment process based on rigorous scientific research (Kame'enui, 2007) and is typically portrayed as a multitiered model of prevention generally consisting of three levels. One such conceptualization is illustrated in Figure 6.4. This configuration is thought to best serve the early intervention and identification aims of RTI (Fuchs & Fuchs, 2005).

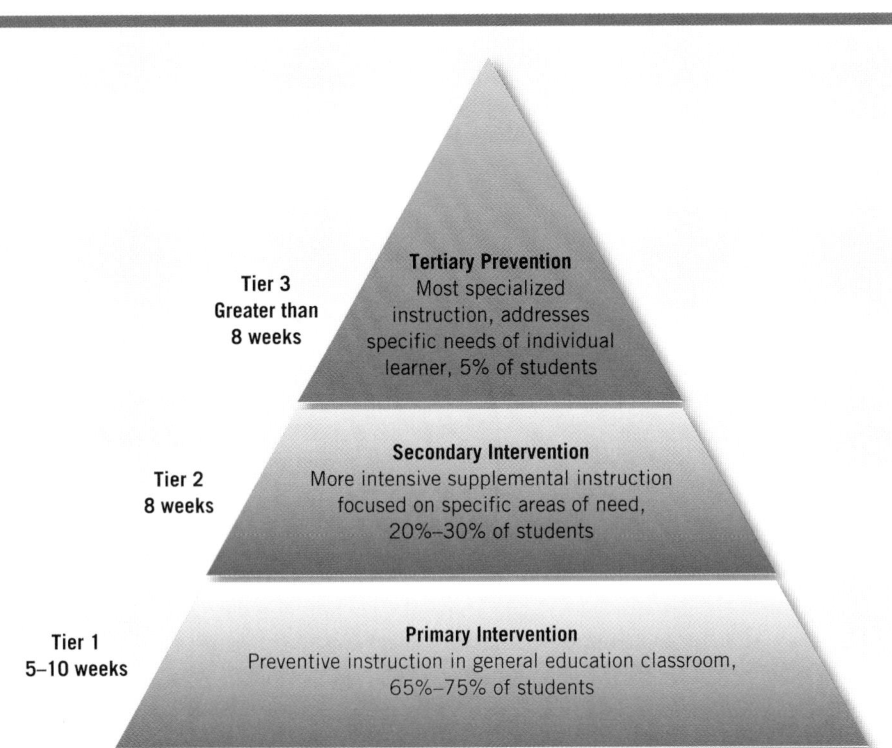

FIGURE 6.4 A Response to Intervention Model

NOTE: Percentage of students participating at each level is approximate.

Duration of intervention is approximate.

Students may move between tiers as individual needs dictate.

The student initially receives research-based instruction in the general education classroom. If the child fails to demonstrate "responsiveness" after receiving increasingly individualized and intensive instruction, a learning disability is presumed to be present and a referral for special education services is usually initiated. Using reading instruction as an example, Table 6.3 highlights the differences, according to one RTI model, among primary, secondary, and tertiary interventions.

The RTI model represents a significant conceptual shift in thinking from a "wait to fail" approach to one that emphasizes early identification and possible prevention (Bradley et al., 2007; Vaughn & Bos, 2009). This approach to determining whether a pupil

Video Link 6.6
Watch more about the RTI model.

TABLE 6.3 A Response to Intervention Model: Tiers of Instruction

	Tier 1 (Primary)	Tier 2 (Secondary)	Tier 3 (Tertiary)
Definition	Reading instruction and programs, including ongoing professional development and benchmark assessments (3 times per year)	Instructional intervention employed to supplement, enhance, and support Tier 1; takes place in small groups	Individualized reading instruction extended beyond the time allocated for Tier 1; groups of 1–3 students
Focus	All students	Students identified with reading difficulties who have not responded to Tier 1 efforts	Students with marked difficulties in reading or reading disabilities who have not responded adequately to Tier 1 and Tier 2 efforts
Program	Scientifically based reading instruction and curriculum emphasizing the critical elements	Specialized, scientifically based reading instruction and curriculum emphasizing the critical elements	Sustained, intensive, scientifically based reading instruction and curriculum highly responsive to students' needs
Instruction	Sufficient opportunities to practice throughout the school day	• Additional attention, focus, support • Additional opportunities to practice embedded throughout the day • Preteach, review skills; frequent opportunities to practice skills	Carefully designed and implemented, explicit, systematic instruction
Interventionist	General education teacher	Personnel determined by the school (classroom teacher, specialized reading teacher, other trained personnel)	Personnel determined by the school (e.g., specialized reading teacher, special education teacher)
Setting	General education classroom	Appropriate setting designated by the school	Appropriate setting designated by the school
Grouping	Flexible grouping	Homogeneous small-group instruction (e.g., 1:4, 1:5)	Homogeneous small-group instruction (1:2, 1:3)
Time	Minimum of 90 minutes per day	20–30 minutes per day in addition to Tier 1	50-minute sessions (or longer) per day depending upon appropriateness of Tier 1
Assessment	Benchmark assessments at beginning, middle, and end of academic year	Progress monitoring twice a month on target skill to ensure adequate progress and learning	Progress monitoring at least twice a month on target skill to ensure adequate progress and learning

SOURCE: Adapted from S. Vaughn and G. Roberts, "Secondary Interventions in Reading," *Teaching Exceptional Children, 39*(5), 2007, p. 41.

has a learning disability eliminates poor or inadequate teaching as a possible reason for low achievement. It also places greater instructional responsibility on the shoulders of general educators.

While most of the early attention of RTI has focused on its application to reading, several benefits are recognized. Some of the advantages include a reduction in the number of inappropriate referrals for special education, interventions linked to ongoing assessment, greater collaboration between general and special educators, a reduction in the number of students recognized as having a learning disability, and less stigma placed on the learner (Klingner & Edwards, 2006; Marston, Muyskens, Lau, & Canter, 2003; Speece, Case, & Molloy, 2003).

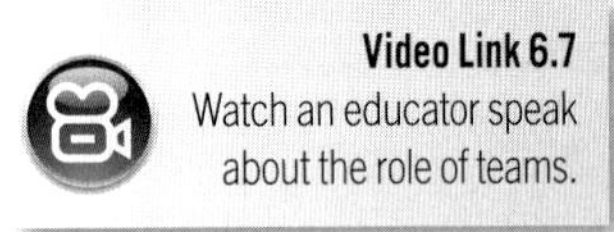

Although support for this process is growing in some educational circles, the research evidence is limited, and some professionals still adhere to the traditional discrepancy model (Kavale, Holdnack, & Mostert, 2005), while others remain somewhat skeptical of its use (Burns, Jacob, & Wagner, 2008). Many educators view RTI as a "promising practice" while acknowledging that several issues need to be addressed, for instance

- its application to other content areas such as mathematics;
- how responsiveness to intervention is determined;
- what the most effective duration of intervention is; and
- how many tiers or levels of intervention are required before a student is identified as learning disabled (Fuchs, Mock, Morgan, & Young, 2003; Stecker, 2007; Vaughn & Fuchs, 2003).

We suspect that these and other issues will be successfully resolved in the coming years. It will be interesting to see how individual states and local school districts respond to the RTI option for identifying pupils suspected of having a learning disability. In one national survey of state departments of education (Hoover, Baca, Wexler-Love, & Saenz, 2008), forty-four states indicated that they were either currently using RTI or in the planning stages of implementing this model. Caution was raised, however, that additional information is needed on the ability of RTI to accurately identify students with learning disabilities. A more recent national survey (Zirkel & Thomas, 2010) found significant fluidity in individual state practices regarding the adoption of RTI as a means of identifying pupils with a learning disability. It seems safe to say that this particular issue may best be characterized as a "work in progress."

Assessment Strategies

Traditionally, standardized tests have played a major role in the evaluation of students thought to be learning disabled. These instruments are also known as **norm-referenced assessments** because an individual's performance is compared to that of a normative group of peers (for example, all sixth graders in their state or a national sample of sixth graders) who have taken the same test. Standardized assessment requires rigid adherence to directions for administering, scoring, and interpreting the results. Teachers and psychologists rely heavily on standardized tests when assessing for learning disabilities. Norm-referenced tests provide a great deal of statistical information, allowing professionals to *compare* a particular student's performance with that of other pupils in the normative group. **Criterion-referenced assessments**, on the other hand, *describe* a youngster's performance. Criterion-referenced tests measure a student's abilities against a predetermined criterion or mastery level. In other words, the child's performance is compared with a standard expectation (100 percent knowledge of multiplication facts), not with the performance of others. Criterion-referenced tests, also commonly called teacher-made tests, offer a means of educational accountability, in that a teacher can demonstrate that a student has learned specific skills. It is a bit more difficult to show improvement in terms of percentile rankings or even grade-level scores (Lerner & Johns, 2009).

Although standardized testing is a useful component of a nondiscriminatory evaluation and provides meaningful information for identification purposes, norm-referenced tests are weak in providing instructional direction. Teacher-made tests are perhaps better suited for guiding instruction. One of the chief benefits of criterion-referenced tests is that they can help in instructional planning and decision making and in monitoring progress toward educational goals. Individualized educational programs (IEPs) are often constructed around data gleaned from various types of criterion-referenced tests.

Assessment strategies should always fit the question we are asking about a particular student. Professionals must also pay careful attention to the purpose of the assessment and how the data will be used (Aiken & Groth-Marnat, 2006).

Curriculum-Based Assessment

One frequently voiced concern about standardized testing is that the test items do not necessarily reflect or represent the content of the curriculum that a student has been exposed to. **Curriculum-based assessment (CBA)**, on the other hand, is a form of criterion-referenced assessment in which test items are based on objectives found in the local school curriculum. In this model, a pupil's performance, usually in the areas of math and reading, is evaluated several times a week with test items mirroring the daily instructional tasks. The student's performance is then charted or graphed so that his or her progress toward specific educational goals is easily recognized. The frequent and systematic sampling of a child's performance provides teachers with evidence of the effectiveness of their teaching tactics and may suggest the need for changes in instructional strategies. According to Lerner (2003), CBA is widely used in special education and is most useful for students with learning disabilities because it reinforces the important link between assessment and instruction.

Portfolio Assessment

Disillusionment with traditional testing has contributed, in some educational circles, to a movement toward alternative assessment procedures. One form of alternative assessment is **authentic assessment**, which is believed to paint a more accurate or genuine picture of what a pupil can and cannot accomplish in real-life situations such as in the classroom or at home. An example of an authentic procedure is **portfolio assessment**. A portfolio is a collection of samples of a student's best work gathered over a period of time (Taylor, 2009). According to Paulson, Paulson, and Meyer (1991), "a portfolio is a purposeful collection of student work that exhibits the student's effort, progress, and achievements in one or more areas" (p. 60). Mercer and Pullen (2009) see portfolio assessment as an attempt to improve the evaluation process and enhance instructional decision making.

One of the critical issues in portfolio assessment is knowing what to include in the portfolio and how to evaluate the person's efforts. A portfolio should have a specific purpose; without direction, it can easily become a mere collection of products.

A wide variety of student-generated products can be included in a portfolio. The teacher must first consider the goals of the instructional program and then select samples to match its intent. Using goals from the child's IEP is one strategy the teacher may wish to employ in determining what to include (Lerner & Johns, 2009). Examples of the diverse work products that might be part of a portfolio include audio recordings of oral reading samples, summaries of science experiments, poems, art projects, book reports, excerpts from journals, weekly quizzes, and math worksheets. Because portfolios reflect student progress, Salend (1998) recommends that they be used during parent–teacher conferences.

Educational Considerations

As noted elsewhere, individuals with learning disabilities are an especially heterogeneous population whose disabilities range from mild to severe. These students require a diversity of educational interventions and teaching strategies designed to meet their unique academic, social, and behavioral needs.

Where Are Students With Learning Disabilities Educated?

The educational placement of children with special needs is currently one of the most controversial issues in the field of special education, and children with learning disabilities are not immune to this debate. Where students receive instruction can significantly affect their attitude, achievement, and social development (Mercer & Pullen, 2009).

From a historical perspective, the resource room has been one of the most common service delivery models for serving children with learning disabilities. Since the mid-1990s, however, there has been a subtle shift away from this option—most likely reflecting the trend toward more inclusive programs. For example, during the 1992–1993 school year, more than half (54 percent) of all pupils identified as learning disabled received instruction in a resource room (U.S. Department of Education, 1994). In this model, students leave the regular classroom on a regularly scheduled basis and travel to another classroom where they receive individualized instruction from a special educator. At the conclusion of their assigned time, students return to the general education classroom. More recent statistics indicate, however, that the regular classroom is currently the more popular placement. During the 2007–2008 school year, well over half (59.5 percent) of all youngsters with learning disabilities received services in the regular classroom, and almost 30 percent were assigned to a resource room (U.S. Department of Education, 2009). This means that about nine out of every ten individuals with learning disabilities spend some, most, or all of their school day in a regular classroom (see Figure 6.5).

Researchers and others, however, argue against full inclusion as the placement option for all pupils with learning disabilities (Klingner, Vaughn, Hughes, Schumm, & Elbaum, 1998; National Joint Committee on Learning Disabilities, 2003; Swanson, 2000; Vaughn, Elbaum, & Boardman, 2001). The environment that is most appropriate for individuals with learning disabilities is the setting that is most enabling; inclusion must be done on a responsible basis and meet the unique needs of each child.

An individualized placement recommendation can only occur if there is a continuum of options from which to choose. Federal legislation does not require that pupils with learning disabilities be served only in the regular classroom. Legal scholars (Bateman & Linden, 2006; Osborne, 1997; Yell, 2006) note that the principle of least restrictive environment does not allow educators to presume that a single educational setting is appropriate for all youngsters with a particular type of disability. Such a notion would clearly be at odds with current federal law (Gargiulo & Kilgo, 2011). The contemporary controversy surrounding the question of where to educate pupils with special needs is a good example of where one size does not fit all; placing all students with learning disabilities in the general education classroom essentially ignores and disregards the concept

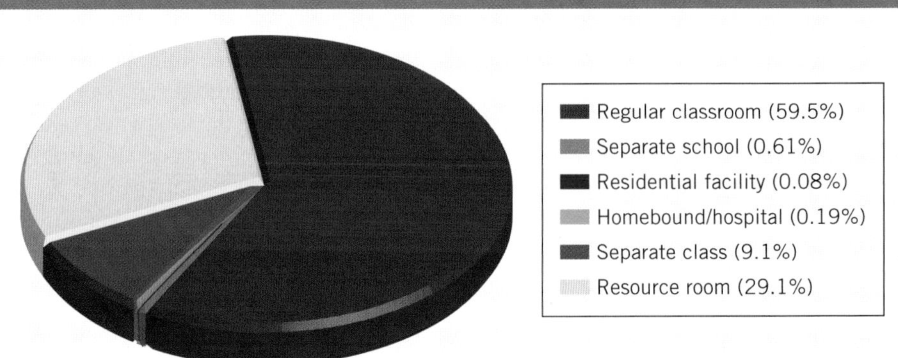

FIGURE 6.5 Educational Placements of Students With Learning Disabilities

NOTE: Figure represents percentages of enrollment of students with learning disabilities during the 2007–2008 school year.

SOURCE: U.S. Department of Education. (2009). *IDEA data.* Retrieved October 22, 2009, from https://www.ideadata.org/PartBReport.asp

of individualized planning (Crockett & Kauffman, 2001). Like Mercer and Pullen (2009), we are of the opinion that issues of placement must be evaluated on a case-by-case basis and decided based on the needs of the student rather than being directed by trends or philosophies that are insensitive to the uniqueness and individuality of each learner.

Instructional Approaches

There is no one "best" or "correct" way to teach individuals with learning disabilities. Just as we saw with the issue of educational placement, no single size or approach fits all. Individualization is the key to meeting the instructional needs of pupils with learning disabilities. Teachers often find that a wide variety of accommodations and modifications are necessary if the student is to experience success in the classroom. Some children will need additional time for testing or ask that a learning task be broken into smaller and more manageable segments; other pupils may require the privacy provided by a study carrel; some youngsters may need assistance in developing effective learning strategies; still others will benefit from additional drill and practice. What works for one student will not necessarily be appropriate for another.

Video Link 6.9
Watch other strategies.

EFFECTIVE INSTRUCTIONAL PRACTICES Teaching Reading

Phonic Analysis

Many students with learning disabilities experience difficulty with reading. A skill deficit often encountered is phonic analysis. Phonic analysis is a vital component of early reading instruction. Students must establish a strong understanding of letter-sound combinations and correspondence. They must also be able to recognize word parts. The following teaching strategies can help struggling readers learn to decode using phonic analysis skills.

- **Instructional content**: Teach letter-sound correspondence in a logical order. Most useful initially are the consonants *b, c, d, f, g, h, k, l, m, n, p, r, s,* and *t,* and the vowels. Present continuous letter sounds (e.g., *s* and /*sss*/, *m* and /mmm/, *n* and /nnn/) before stop letter sounds (*p* and /p/, *k* and /k/). Select letters that represent sounds found in decodable text that students will read.
- **Instructional content**: Introduce the most common sounds of the letters first. Lowercase letters should be taught before uppercase ones.
- **Instructional content**: Teach the letter combinations that most frequently occur in text.
- **Instructional content**: Avoid teaching letter-sound correspondence and letter combinations that sound similar and may confuse students. For instance, /m/ and /n/ and /sh/ and /ch/ should not be taught together. Letter combinations with the same sound, such as /ir/ and /ur/ and /ee/ and /ea/, can be taught at the same time.
- **Instructional content**: Teach phonograms containing letter-sound correspondences that have been introduced. Phonograms or rimes (which are parts of a word to which consonants or blends are added to make a word) such as *ap, at, ip, it, un,* and *et* paired with initial consonants or onsets provide opportunities to segment and blend sounds to make words. These words should be featured in the decodable text that students will read.
- **Instructional delivery**: Teach students to blend the letter sounds together in a seamless fashion. For instance, students should be taught to say *mmmaaannn* rather than separating the sounds /m/ /a/ /n/.
- **Instructional materials**: Have students read decodable texts—texts that contain words with the sounds and patterns you have previously taught and students have mastered.
- **Connections to spelling**: Have students spell the words so that their phonics instruction can be reinforced. Spelling and reading are closely related skills. Here are some examples of ways to make connections to spelling:
  - Introduce letter-sound correspondences for spelling as they are being introduced and taught in reading.
  - Have students sort words into spelling patterns.
  - Have students identify words from their text with patterns that match what they are learning in phonics.

SOURCE: D. Bryant, D. Smith, and B. Bryant, *Teaching Students with Special Needs* (Boston: Allyn and Bacon, 2008), pp. 404–405.

In this section, we look at some of the various pedagogical strategies for teaching students with learning disabilities. Educators have a broad array of instructional approaches and strategies at their disposal, some of them more effective than others. We recommend that teachers select their instructional tactics only after carefully considering the research evidence. The field of learning disabilities has a history of "hopping on the bandwagon" and vigorously advocating a particular instructional approach or strategy; unfortunately, in some cases, these procedures were lacking in empirical support. One example was the allegiance of many teachers to perceptual motor training, which was eventually shown to be ineffective (Hammill & Larsen, 1974; Kavale, 1990). Professionals must validate the effectiveness of their interventions.

We have chosen to examine three broad approaches to teaching academic skills: cognitive training, direct instruction, and learning strategies. Keep in mind that there is no "silver bullet" or magic formula for teaching students with learning disabilities; in most instances, it is a matter of matching the needs of the student to a particular instructional model.

Cognitive Training

Cognitive training is an umbrella approach covering a variety of educational procedures. It seeks to manipulate or modify a student's underlying thought patterns to effect observable changes in performance. Proponents of this approach believe that what occurs internally in the learner during the learning process is just as important as what happens externally. The pupil is seen as the critical agent in determining how information is processed—that is, identified, interpreted, organized, and utilized (Mercer & Pullen, 2009). Self-instruction and the use of mnemonic strategies are two instructional techniques frequently associated with cognitive training.

Developed by Meichenbaum (1977; Meichenbaum & Goodman, 1971), **self-instruction** is a strategy whereby students initially talk to themselves out loud while performing a task—children verbalize instructions necessary to complete the activity and then verbally reward themselves for success. Self-instruction makes the pupil aware of the various steps used in problem solving and then gradually brings these strategies under covert verbal control. According to Hallahan et al. (2005) and Lerner and Johns (2009), the following six steps are typically used during cognitive training:

1. Student observes the teacher perform a task while verbalizing aloud.
   a. Questions about the activity
   b. Instructions on how to perform the task
   c. A self-evaluation of performance
2. Pupil performs the task with teacher providing verbal directions.
3. Child performs the activity while verbalizing aloud.
4. Student performs the task while whispering instructions.
5. Pupil performs the activity while using covert or inner speech.
6. Child monitors and self-evaluates own performance (for example, "I did a good job" or "I need to work faster").

The goal of cognitive training, considered by some authorities to be a form of cognitive behavior modification, is not only to modify the pupil's behavior but also to increase the learner's awareness of the behavior and the thinking process affiliated with it (Lerner & Johns, 2009). Cognitive training has proven to be a beneficial strategy for remediating a wide variety of academic difficulties typically encountered by individuals with learning disabilities (Hallahan et al., 2005). Table 6.4 provides a list of suggestions for teachers using cognitive training strategies.

Mnemonic strategies are tools for helping students recall facts and relationships. Teachers frequently help their students transform abstract material into a more concrete form by constructing personally meaningful representations of the information—that is,

TABLE 6.4 Principles of Effective Cognitive Training Programs

Teach a few strategies at a time	Rather than bombard children with a number of strategies all at once, teach them just a few. In this way, there is a better chance that the students can learn the strategies in a comprehensive and not a superficial fashion.
Teach self-monitoring	It is helpful if students keep track of their own progress. When checking their own work, if they find an error, they should be encouraged to try to correct it on their own.
Teach them when and where to use the strategies	Many students with learning disabilities have problems with the metacognitive skill of knowing when and where they can use strategies that teachers have taught. Teachers must give them this information as well as extensive experience in using the strategies in a variety of settings.
Maintain the students' motivation	Students need to know that the strategies work. Teachers can help motivation by consistently pointing out the benefits of the strategies, explaining how they work, and charting students' progress.
Teach in context	Students should learn cognitive techniques as an integrated part of the curriculum. Rather than using cognitive training in an isolated manner, teachers should teach students to employ cognitive strategies during academic lessons.
Don't neglect a nonstrategic knowledge base	Sometimes those who use cognitive training become such avid proponents of it that they forget the importance of factual knowledge. The more facts children know about history, science, math, English, and so forth, the less they will need to rely on strategies.
Engage in direct teaching	Because the emphasis in cognitive training is on encouraging students to take more initiative in their own learning, teachers may feel that they are less necessary than is actually the case. Cognitive training does not give license to back off from directly teaching students. Students' reliance on teachers should gradually fade. In the early stages, teachers need to be directly in control of supervising the students' use of the cognitive strategies.
Regard cognitive training as long term	Because cognitive training often results in immediate improvement, there may be a temptation to view it as a panacea or a quick fix. To maintain improvements and have them generalize to other settings, however, students need extensive practice in applying the strategies they have learned.

SOURCE: Adapted from D. Hallahan, J. Lloyd, J. Kauffman, M. Weiss, and E. Martinez, *Learning Disabilities,* 3rd ed. (Needham Heights, MA: Allyn and Bacon, 2005), p. 239. Reprinted with permission.

a picture or pattern of letters. For example, one trick frequently used by beginning music students to help recall the treble staff is the saying "Every good boy does fine," which represents the notes e, g, b, d, and f.

Direct Instruction

Unlike cognitive training with its emphasis on the uniqueness of each learner, **Direct Instruction (DI)** focuses on the characteristics or components of the task or concept to be learned. The aim of DI is to produce gains in specific academic skills without worrying about possible processing deficits. "The key principle in Direct Instruction," Gersten, Carnine, and Woodward (1987) write, "is deceptively simple. For all students to learn, both the curriculum materials and teacher presentation of these materials must be clear and unambiguous" (pp. 48–49).

Based on the pioneering work of Bereiter and Engelmann (1966) in the 1960s, DI represents a highly organized instructional approach. Proponents of this model emphasize controlling details of instruction so as to actively engage students' involvement in learning. Drill and practice are stressed. DI lessons, which are teacher-directed, are precisely scripted, fast paced, and typically presented to small groups of children, usually five to ten. Teachers lead their students using a "script" or precisely worded lesson in an effort to ensure consistency and quality of instruction. Teachers elicit student response via hand

Learning strategies help pupils become more actively engaged in their own learning.

signals or cues (such as clapping or snapping the fingers), which results in choral or unison responding by the group. This technique is designed to maintain the pupils' attention. Correct answers are immediately praised, and incorrect responses receive corrective feedback.

According to Friend and Bursuck (2009), DI consists of six key components:

1. An explicit step-by-step strategy
2. Development of mastery at each step in the process
3. Strategy (or process) corrections for student errors
4. Gradual fading from teacher-directed activities toward independent work
5. Use of adequate, systematic practice with a range of examples
6. Cumulative review of newly learned concepts

The effectiveness of this skills training instructional model is well documented. Students exposed to DI methods demonstrate significant gains in academic learning (Marchand-Martella, Slocum, & Martella, 2004; Vaughn & Linan-Thompson, 2003; Walker, Shippen, Alberto, Houchins, & Cihak, 2005). Several different types of commercial programs based on DI teaching principles are available in the areas of reading, language, mathematics, social studies, and science.

Learning Strategies

Some authorities believe it is not enough to teach specific academic skills to pupils with learning disabilities. These students tend to be inefficient learners because they often lack systematic strategies and plans for remembering, monitoring, and directing their own learning. In contrast to proficient learners, individuals with learning disabilities haven't learned the "tricks of the trade"—the secrets to being a successful student (Lerner & Johns, 2009). A **learning strategies** approach to instruction focuses on teaching students *how* to learn—how to become a more purposeful and efficient learner.

Unlike other instructional methodologies, which focus on learning a particular task or academic content, learning strategies are seen as the "techniques, principles, or rules that facilitate the acquisition, manipulation, integration, storage, and retrieval of information across situations and settings" (Alley & Deshler, 1979, p. 13). In other words, learning strategies are the tools that individuals use to help themselves learn and recall new material. The goal of this approach is to help students become more actively engaged and involved in their own learning.

Learning strategies are skills for learning. Probably the most widely used model for teaching these skills, which has evolved after years of research, is the Strategies Intervention Model (SIM) developed by scholars at the University of Kansas (Deshler et al., 1996; Lenz, Ellis, & Scanlon, 1996). Recently renamed the Strategic Instruction Model, this approach is one of the field's most comprehensive models for providing strategy instruction. It can, according to one authority, "be used to teach virtually any strategic intervention" (Sturomski, 1997, p. 7).

Most often used with adolescents who are learning disabled, the SIM can be applied to all areas of curriculum typically encountered by middle school and high school students. This pedagogical technique emphasizes the cognitive aspects of learning rather than focusing on mastering specific subject content (Lenz & Deshler, 2004).

Success has been demonstrated across a wide range of academic areas, including essay writing, study skills, reading comprehension, math problems, and science (Bender,

Video Link 6.10
View more suggestions.

Suggestions for the Classroom

Suggestions for Teaching Students With Learning Disabilities

- ☑ Capitalize on the student's strengths.
- ☑ Provide high structure and clear expectations.
- ☑ Use short sentences and a simple vocabulary.
- ☑ Provide opportunities for success in a supportive atmosphere to help build self-esteem.
- ☑ Allow flexibility in classroom procedures (for example, allowing the use of tape recorders for note taking and test taking when students have trouble with written language).
- ☑ Make use of self-correcting materials that provide immediate feedback without embarrassment.
- ☑ Use computers for drill and practice and teaching word processing.
- ☑ Provide positive reinforcement of appropriate social skills at school and home.

SOURCE: National Dissemination Center for Children with Disabilities, *Fact Sheet No. 7: Learning Disabilities* (Washington, DC: Author, 1998, 2004).

2008). A learning strategies approach is especially relevant for today's classroom. As more emphasis is placed on exposure to the general education curriculum, this model can assist students in meeting this demand. With its emphasis on mastering cognitive strategies and empowering the student, a learning strategies model is a natural complement to the general classroom curriculum.

We believe, as others do, that no one instructional approach can meet the vast and complex needs of all individuals with learning disabilities. Teachers need to have an array of interventions at their disposal. Success in the classroom often depends, in part, on the match between learner characteristics and the teaching techniques used.

The accompanying Suggestions for the Classroom feature offers instructional recommendations that have been found to be effective with some students who are learning disabled.

Services for Young Children With Learning Disabilities

Determining whether a young child is learning disabled, or at risk for learning disabilities, is a difficult task. Many professionals believe that the earlier we identify a child as such, the sooner intervention can be initiated; of course, prevention is always preferable to remediation. Yet the notion of a preschool child having a learning disability is controversial. Testing at this age is mainly for purposes of prediction, not identification. The challenge confronting educators is determining which factors are truly indicative of future learning difficulties and which are simply manifestations of variation in growth and development. It is not uncommon for professionals to talk about a young child's being at risk for problems in learning and development. Because of their exposure to adverse circumstances, some youngsters experience greater vulnerability and have a heightened potential for future problems in the classroom. Factors that *may* place a child at risk (Gargiulo & Kilgo, 2011; National Joint Committee on Learning Disabilities, 2006), include the following:

- Maternal alcohol and drug abuse
- Home environment lacking adequate stimulation
- Chronic poverty
- Oxygen deprivation
- Accidents and head trauma
- Inadequate maternal and infant nutrition
- Prematurity
- Rh incompatibility
- Low birth weight
- Prolonged or unusual delivery

Remember, these factors do not guarantee that problems will arise; they only set the stage. Many young children are subject to a wide variety of risks yet never evidence any problems in school (Gargiulo & Kilgo, 2011).

A related controversy is the application of the *learning disability* label to preschoolers. The regulations accompanying the current federal definition of learning disabilities

Making Inclusion Work

My training in the field of special education began many years ago in South America where it was common practice to teach children with disabilities in self-contained classrooms. After transferring to the United States and earning a degree in special education, the range of possibilities for educating children with disabilities was a welcomed change. Starting out as a resource room teacher and eventually becoming an inclusion specialist has been an interesting and rewarding educational experience.

Inclusive Education Experience

Evolving into an inclusion teacher from a resource room teacher has definitely been an interesting journey. In the beginning it was challenging, although I welcomed the opportunity to serve my students in their least restrictive environment. It was difficult, however, for some general education teachers. This was especially true of the veteran teachers who did not understand the purpose of having students with disabilities in their classroom as well as having another educator in "their room." When the time came to implement the accommodations stated in the students' IEP, some teachers had difficulty understanding the need for the accommodations. A few made comments relating to the fact that the children should be able to do the work if they were being served in the regular classroom, while others alluded to the fairness to the other children. Working through this process was trying at times. This was especially true when working with students with learning disabilities—mainly because their disability is not readily obvious. Often, general educators could not figure out why these children were not performing like the rest of the class. Many times these children were labeled lazy or they were simply misunderstood. It took the general education teachers some time to appreciate the benefits of inclusion for *all* students in the class. It took some convincing and collaboratively working with them on a daily basis to make it successful.

Through the years I have seen tremendous changes toward the acceptance of children with disabilities. General educators have become more knowledgeable about pupils with disabilities thanks, in part, to working collaboratively with special educators. Working together as a team has proven to be the most productive and effective way to teach students with special needs.

Strategies for Inclusive Classrooms

The support of the school administration is the backbone of any solid inclusion program. It takes a great deal of time to effectively plan for students in an inclusive class. I would say considers deficits in academic performance and a discrepancy between a child's ability and academic achievement when identifying a pupil as learning disabled. How appropriate is this label when most preschoolers have not been exposed to academic work? Academic tasks are typically not introduced until the first grade, although a growing number of kindergartens and some preschools are stressing preacademic skills. Fuchs et al. (2007) describe the use of a discrepancy approach for identifying a learning disability in young children as a "wait and fail" method for ascertaining who may be eligible for special educational services. We believe that the needs of the young child are best served when professionals focus on the antecedents of learning disabilities. These precursors are often noted by simply observing the child engage in a variety of age-appropriate tasks such as cutting and coloring, imaginary play, or various gross motor activities such as running, hopping, or skipping. Table 6.5 identifies some of these warning signs. These indicators are simply that—warnings; they do *not* mean that learning problems will automatically appear later on.

There is a growing reluctance among some educators to label young children as having a learning disability. Instead, the more generic, and less stigmatizing, noncategorical label *developmentally delayed* is finding increasing favor in some professional circles. The reauthorization of IDEA in 1997 (PL 105–17) allowed states to use this descriptor for children ages 3 through 9 who require a special education and related services. Unfortunately, there is no federal definition of this term; each state is responsible for determining what the label means. The absence of federal guidance has resulted in significant variations in definition. Some states use various quantitative descriptions and

Video Link 6.11
Watch more about inclusion.

this is one of the most important aspects of an inclusion model. It is crucial that the general education teacher has time to meet and plan with the special education teacher. It is important to communicate openly about students' needs. It is necessary to evaluate the effectiveness of the various instructional strategies used in the classroom and to be sure that the needs of all learners are being met. It is vitally important that related service providers, paraprofessionals, and other individuals working with these students be informed of their progress or the problems that sometimes arise.

Successful Collaboration

Successful collaboration entails a wide variety of options. In my opinion, one of the most important things that special educators can do is to earn the trust of the teacher(s) they work with on a daily basis. When there is trust in the relationship, collaboration will naturally fall into place. It is important that the special educator and general education teacher share responsibilities for all students. Together they plan and implement strategies that will benefit not only students with IEPs, but all children in the class. Each teacher brings his or her own strengths, skills, and knowledge to the classroom in an effort to serve all students. It is important that if problems ever develop, both the special educator and the general education teacher support each other and work together in problem solving.

Working With Parents and Families

Parent and family involvement is crucial. Parents' input during the development of the individualized education program is extremely important since they work with the child on a daily basis outside of school. It is necessary that they share their concerns with the team in order to better serve their son or daughter. Parents need to become "educators" and help their child continue the learning process at home. Additionally, it is important that parents communicate openly with their child's teachers and provide feedback. Together parents and school personnel can provide an effective inclusive environment that meets the unique needs of the child.

Advice for Making Inclusion and Collaboration Work

Making inclusion and collaboration work entails a wide array of strategies. It is not an easy task and takes hours of planning to successfully implement, but the results are worth it. Yet, even when school personnel and parents have their hearts in the right place, difficulties may arise that make the process extremely frustrating. This is when all concerned need to focus on the common goal of what is best for the child. Administrative support, teachers working together for the good of all children, and active parent involvement often result in a successful inclusive environment benefiting all students.

—*Astrid Freeman*
Oak Mountain Middle School
Shelby County (Alabama) Schools

TABLE 6.5 Common Characteristics of Preschoolers at Risk for Being Identified as Learning Disabled

"He knocks into building blocks, bumps into doors, falls out of his chair, and crashes into his playmates."	• Inability to negotiate his body through his environment • Poor depth perception • Sitting in double-jointed fashion • Toe walking • Lurches while walking
"She's so smart yet has the attention span of a flea—she flits from one thing to another, and sometimes speaks like a broken record."	• Distractibility • Short attention span • Impulsiveness (impulsivity) • Hyperactivity • Preservation (doing the same thing over in the same way)
"She can talk about topiary trees, but she can't pull up her zipper or draw a circle, and hates putting toys and puzzles together."	• Poor motor coordination • Difficulty coordinating hand–eye maneuvers • Clumsiness
"He understands everything I say to him, but he does not express himself well like his brother and sister."	• Delayed speech • Uses sounds/words out of sequence: *aminals, Home I ran* • Limited vocabulary • Inappropriate use of words • Disorganized phrases
"He looks at everything but doesn't seem to see anything in particular. His hands seem to see better than his eyes."	• Difficulty focusing • Problems distinguishing shapes and color • Difficulty remembering what he sees • Problems remembering the order of things he sees • Difficulty making sense of what he sees
"She's four years old but acts much younger."	• Immature behavior/appearance • Immature speech • Immature coordination/movement • Immature choice and use of toys
"Her eyes look at me so intently, and she listens. But it just doesn't seem to get through."	• Problems understanding what she hears • Difficulty remembering what she hears • Problems remembering sequences of sounds • Difficulty following simple directions • Overreaction to noise • Does not enjoy being read to aloud
"He overreacts or underreacts to everything—it's like his emotion thermostat is malfunctioning."	• Indiscriminate or catastrophic reactions • Laughing one moment, crying the next • Very low or very high threshold of pain • Dislike of being touched or cuddled • No reaction or overreaction to being touched
"He never seems to be 'put together' right, and yet I spend so much more time and energy helping him than I do the other kids."	• Disorganized movement • Disorganized language • Disorganized appearance

SOURCE: *Learning Disabilities Fact Sheet—Early Childhood.* Learning Disabilities Association of America. Available at http://www.paec.org/david/ese/early.pdf

others use a variety of qualitative approaches when deciding if a youngster is developmentally delayed. Despite this drawback, this label suggests a developmental status and not a disability category, which hopefully will result in more inclusive models of service delivery (Gargiulo & Kilgo, 2011).

When preschoolers are found to be in need of a special education, teachers can choose from among several different curriculum models, including a developmental/cognitive model, a behavioral model, and a functional curriculum approach. We will briefly describe the major tenets of these models, drawing upon the work of Gargiulo and Kilgo (2011).

The **developmental/cognitive model** is based on the theorizing of Piaget, who sees cognitive development as resulting from maturation coupled with the youngster's active interaction and involvement with the environment. Instructional activities are designed according to Piaget's stages of cognitive development with an emphasis on stimulating a pupil's cognitive abilities (language, memory, concept formation).

A **behavioral curriculum model** is based on learning principles derived from behavioral psychology—particularly reinforcement theory. Curricula based on a behavioral approach emphasize direct instruction following a precise and highly structured sequence of instructional activities.

The **functional curriculum** approach stresses behaviors that have immediate relevance for students as they confront the demands of their natural environment. Developmental age is of less importance than the individual's proficiency in acquiring age-appropriate skills. Rather than emphasizing developmental sequences or preacademic skills, this model is oriented toward activities of daily living. Functional, age-appropriate skills needed in various natural settings are task-analyzed into a sequence of observable and measurable subskills. Learning to perform these skills enables youngsters with disabilities to function with greater independence while also increasing their chances of being successfully included in normalized settings.

Teachers who work with young children rarely adhere strictly to one particular model. Rather, they use a combination of approaches, selecting strategies that are most appropriate for meeting the needs of their students.

Transition Into Adulthood

Adolescence is a difficult period for many young persons, but especially for students with learning disabilities. These individuals frequently have a history of failure at academic tasks, a diminished self-concept, a lack of motivation, and some degree of social ineptness. The daily demands encountered in high school often make it extremely difficult for adolescents with learning disabilities to succeed. Mercer and Pullen (2009) identify some of the many challenges confronting these pupils:

- Gaining information from lectures and written materials
- Working independently with little feedback
- Demonstrating knowledge through tests
- Interacting appropriately
- Exhibiting motivation and sustained effort

Only recently have professionals become cognizant of the unique requirements facing students with learning disabilities in secondary schools. For many years, educators incorrectly assumed that children with learning disabilities would simply "outgrow" them. As a result, adolescents with learning disabilities have received less attention than their younger counterparts. What professionals failed to realize is that problems with attention and memory, deficits in planning and organizing, and difficulties with problem solving often continue well into adolescence and beyond (see the accompanying First Person feature on page 226).

First Person: Christopher In His Own Words

What can you tell us about yourself and your family?

My name is Christopher. I am a freshman at Oak Mountain High School. I am dyslexic and have a hard time reading and spelling. I have to get audio books or friends and family to help me with reading. I enjoy hands-on activities like building and drawing. I play football, lacrosse, and I also wrestle.

I have a brother and a sister who are also into sports and, like me, enjoy playing video games. My brother is visually impaired (around 20/600) from cone and rod dystrophy. I have to help him a lot with simple tasks at home and wherever we go. He helps me with spelling and math because he is really smart. He would help me more with reading if he could see better. My sister loves animals and rides English style in horse shows.

We go up to Pennsylvania once a year during Thanksgiving or Christmas to visit my relatives on my mom's side. All of my relatives on my dad's side live in Alabama so I get to see them a lot.

What do you like to do in your free time?

I spend most of my free time playing sports and video games. For football, I play on the defensive line (noseguard) and started last fall for the Oak Mountain freshman team.

I also wrestle for Oak Mountain High School. Although my weight (194 pounds) is in the bottom of the 215-pound weight division, I sometimes have to wrestle in the heavyweight division (up to 285 pounds) for junior varsity because there is no one else that size on our team. This means that I sometimes wrestle people who are up to 90 pounds heavier than I am!

This is my first year to play lacrosse. I play for the Altamont Knights because my high school does not yet have a lacrosse team. I play "attack," which is the offensive side that is trying to score goals on the other team's defense.

When not playing sports, I like to play on my Xbox 360. I especially enjoy playing online with all my friends. My favorite game is Call of Duty: Modern Warfare 2.

I also enjoy traveling during breaks from school. I have gone to Australia and Europe with an organization called People to People Student Ambassadors. I also go on a lot of fun trips with my family like to Las Vegas, New York, or the beach.

I also volunteer with Special Equestrians where I help kids with physical and mental challenges ride horses. I really enjoy it and have made many new friends.

What can you tell us about your experience at school?

I go to school like every other normal 15-year-old. I take the same classes that everyone else takes except I have a help period where I get extra time for tests and have teachers read the tests to me. My favorite thing about school is seeing all of my friends and talking with them. My least favorite thing about school is homework because it takes me two times longer to do it than regular kids. I also count studying as homework. Unlike all of my friends (my friends don't consider studying homework and don't study!), I will study for several hours, sometimes staying up late at night and waking up very early in the morning before school.

One of my favorite memories of school is yelling my lungs out with my football friends at the pep rallies. My favorite subjects in school are science and history. I have all As in school.

What can you tell us about your work background?

The only work experience I really have is refereeing soccer games. I started refereeing when I was 12 years old. Unlike other jobs, I get to pick my own schedule, and the pay is good. I enjoy working with other referees I have gotten to know. I usually referee four or five games a week when I don't have a conflict.

What do you see yourself doing in the future?

I am not exactly sure what kind of job I want, but I know I want to do something hands-on. I plan on going to college, but I am not sure what my major would be at this time. As a part of my IEP, I will be researching possible career opportunities next year.

What is one thing you want people to remember about you?

I want people to remember that I am a hard worker and will do whatever it takes to get the job done.

❖

It was quite shocking to discover that our son Christopher had dyslexia. It was difficult to know what we could do for him. We kept him at a Montessori school through sixth grade because we believed that the small class and school size would benefit him. However, the Montessori school full-sized classes ended at sixth grade. Also, after sixth grade, we knew his sports opportunities would be severely limited if he did not attend a public school. So, the decision was made to transfer Christopher to Oak Mountain Middle School.

I was pleasantly surprised at how well Christopher was able to fit into the school and how accommodating the faculty was. He worked hard, and his grades have been exceptional. In addition to his great academic work, Christopher won a character award from the school's faculty, presented to him and a few other students at a schoolwide assembly. We are as proud of that award as we are of his grades.

I am not sure what the future holds for Christopher, but I feel good about it knowing the character and work ethic that Christopher has!

Adolescence can be an especially difficult time for students with learning disabilities.

One of the purposes of an education is to prepare individuals to lead independent and productive lives as adults—to become contributing members of society. Unfortunately, our educational system has a less than stellar record of success with secondary students who are learning disabled. Recent statistics compiled by the U.S. Department of Education (2010) indicate that only 39 percent of students with learning disabilities graduate from high school, and almost 14 percent drop out of school. One can only conclude that our schools are failing to appropriately serve the vast number of these students.

One means of remedying this situation is through the development of a customized **transition plan**. PL 108–446 mandates that a transition plan be part of each adolescent's IEP. The purpose of this document is to develop goals and activities that are individually tailored to fulfill the student's postschool aspirations. Developing a meaningful ITP is a team effort requiring the active involvement of professionals, parents, and, perhaps most important, the student—after all, it is his or her life goals that the document addresses. Transition planning typically focuses on several different streams or options, including vocational training, preparation for postsecondary educational opportunities, or various employment possibilities.

Careful transition planning is crucial for successful adjustment later in life. The secondary school curriculum must not only prepare adolescents with learning disabilities academically, but it should also focus on preparation for future challenges such as independent living, employment options, and postsecondary schooling. Additionally, we believe that transition plans, after considering the individual needs of the student, should also focus on self-determination, social skills, and assistance with understanding and adjusting to one's lifelong disability.

Adults With Learning Disabilities

The needs of adults with learning disabilities have traditionally received little attention; only recently have professionals begun to focus on this group. In many instances, however, a learning disability is a lifelong problem; many of the characteristics of learning disabilities persist into adulthood (Ewen & Shapiro, 2008; Hudson, 2006). Adults with learning disabilities sometimes have great difficulty "finding their niche in the world" (Lerner & Johns, 2009, p. 313). A learning disability typically interferes with living independently, obtaining and maintaining employment, maintaining social relationships, and experiencing satisfaction with life in general (Tymchuk, Lakin, & Luckasson, 2001; Witte, Philips, & Kakela, 1998).

One should not necessarily paint a bleak picture for adults with learning disabilities. Many of these individuals achieve success and enjoy a life of quality. Successful adults establish goals, work hard, and exhibit a high degree of perseverance while also acknowledging their limitations (Raskind, Goldberg, Higgins, & Herman, 2002). Table 6.6 identifies some of the characteristics exhibited by successful and unsuccessful adults with learning disabilities.

Audio Link 6.2
Listen to more about adults with learning disabilities.

Postsecondary educational opportunities are becoming increasingly common for adults with learning disabilities. Researchers estimate that about 16 percent of students with learning disabilities are enrolled in four-year colleges or universities; an additional 35 percent attend two-year institutions such as community colleges while 22 percent are enrolled in vocational/technical schools (Newman, Wagner, Cameto, & Knokey, 2009). These figures may appear small, but they represent a dramatic increase in the number of

TABLE 6.6 Characteristics of Successful and Unsuccessful Adults With Learning Disabilities

Successful Adults	Unsuccessful Adults
Maintain perseverance in dealing with life events	Do not understand or accept their learning disability
Develop coping strategies and know how to reduce stress	Fail to take control of their lives
Maintain emotional stability	Maintain a sense of learned helplessness and fail to assume responsibility
Have and use support systems	Seek and promote dependent relationships
Demonstrate motivation and persistence	Exhibit a lack of drive and motivation
Pursue careers that maximize their strengths and minimize their weaknesses	Fail to establish social support systems
Develop creative ways to compensate and problem-solve	Drop out of secondary school
Maintain a positive attitude toward learning	

SOURCE: Adapted from C. Mercer, *Students with Learning Disabilities,* 5th ed. (Upper Saddle River, NJ: Prentice Hall, 1997), p. 400. Reprinted by permission of Pearson Education, Inc., Upper Saddle River, NJ.

college-bound students with learning disabilities. Although this growth is laudable, many students with learning disabilities do not fully consider postsecondary options (Mull, Sitlington, & Alper, 2001). Section 504 of PL 93–112 prohibits discrimination against individuals with disabilities and requires institutions to offer reasonable accommodations to students with learning disabilities (and other impairments). Hallahan et al. (2005) offer several examples of accommodations appropriate for students with learning disabilities:

Adjustment in Course Requirements and Evaluation

- Giving extra time on exams
- Allowing students to take exams in a distraction-free room
- Allowing students to take exams in a different format (for example, substituting an oral exam for a written one)

Modifications in Program Requirements

- Waiving or substituting certain requirements (for example, a foreign language)
- Allowing students to take a lighter academic load

Auxiliary Aid

- Providing tape recordings of textbooks
- Providing access to a Kurzweil Reading Machine (a computer that scans text and converts it into auditory output)
- Recruiting and assigning volunteer note-takers for lectures (p. 180)

Success in college obviously requires more than just course accommodations. Students must exhibit appropriate social skills, learn time management and organization skills, and develop self-discipline, effective study habits, and, perhaps most important, self-advocacy. Most institutions have an office of disability support services that provides students with disabilities with an array of special services designed to meet their unique requirements and enhance their chances of earning a degree. See the Insights feature for a related discussion provided by students with learning disabilities who are successfully attending college.

Young Adults With Learning Disabilities Speak Out: The Truth About Having a Learning Disability

Having a learning disability leads to serious psychological, emotional, and social consequences, according to the testimony of several students with learning disabilities who are successfully enrolled in college. The students' remarks made note of the fact that their success was due largely to their acceptance of their disability and an acknowledgment that life would be harder for them than for their nondisabled counterparts.

The Emotional Impact

Students said having a learning disability causes extreme damage to their self-esteem. The cumulative effects of the disability include behavior problems, anger, depression, job failure, and poor interpersonal relationships. In some cases, the students even cited their disability as contributing to drug, alcohol, and sexual abuse as well as suicidal tendencies.

The students vividly remember school experiences that reinforced their negative self-concept, such as teachers making them feel they were bad because they had difficulty understanding concepts, being called lazy or careless, having their skills underestimated, rarely being asked to think, and having their faults emphasized while their areas of success were ignored.

Coming to Grips With Having a Learning Disability

For students with learning disabilities to succeed, they must accept their learning problem, said the students. In this process, the students went through different stages. First may be denial. Then they must learn how to understand their own problem. At this point, students may feel "blessed and cursed" by their disability. From there, they must realize that while their disability is only a part of who they are, it will be a force they must accept and deal with on many levels, including socially and academically. Then, they must accept that many facets of life will be more difficult for them than others; therefore, they must develop coping strategies. Finally, students with disabilities must learn to lead a balanced life, recommended the students.

What Teachers Can Do to Help

Teachers play a vital role in helping students with disabilities, said the students. They pleaded with teachers to understand their learning and emotional problems and to care. They said "bad" teaching lives a long time, dashing hopes and dreams as well as demeaning their self-esteem in small cumulative steps. Having a good attitude toward students with learning problems is important, as is having high expectations of those students. They asked that teachers not let them get out of work they can do but help them find alternate ways to do the work.

Additionally, the students said it would be helpful if teachers or counselors would tell them what their life will be like with a learning disability, so they will know what is in store for them academically and socially. The students further recommended that school personnel help parents develop a realistic understanding of a learning disability. That way, the students will not have to fight with their parents to understand their difficulties or take the necessary steps to help them achieve their dreams.

SOURCE: From *CEC Today, 5*(9), p. 10. Copyright © 1999 by the Council for Exceptional Children. Reprinted with permission.

Family Issues

A learning disability is a family affair; it affects not only the individual but, in many instances, parents, siblings, grandparents, and extended family members. Parents pay a heavy emotional toll as they deal, on a daily basis, with their son's or daughter's learning and behavioral difficulties. Yet most families of children with learning disabilities are not dysfunctional but well adjusted (Dyson, 1996).

Brothers and sisters of an individual with learning disabilities may also be affected by their sibling's disability. Feelings of embarrassment, anger, and resentment are not unusual. Although in some families siblings are adversely affected, in others brothers and sisters adjust well and seem to positively benefit from their relationships (Dyson, 1996). Positive sibling adjustment appears to be associated with parental acceptance of the child with a disability.

In keeping with the idea that parents are crucial to the well-being and adjustment of the family, Lerner and Johns (2009) offer the following recommendations for parents:

- Become an informed consumer—educate yourself about learning disabilities.
- Be an assertive advocate—protect your child's legal rights while also seeking appropriate programs in the community as well as schools.
- Be firm yet empathetic in managing the child's behavior.
- Devote time and attention to other family members.
- Make a life for yourself.

A potentially rich resource for individuals with learning disabilities and their parents is the Internet. We urge caution, however, as the accuracy of information on the Internet cannot always be guaranteed.

Issues of Diversity

Currently, approximately four out of every ten U.S. students is African American, Hispanic, or Asian American (National Center for Education Statistics, 2009). Researchers believe that by the year 2020, students of color will represent about half of the entire school population in the United States (Gollnick & Chinn, 2009). Given immigration patterns and differential birthrates among various ethnic groups, demographers expect this trend to continue. Many of these children live in poverty in large urban centers. Poverty can have a deleterious effect on school performance. In fact, some educational researchers believe that the vast majority of individuals attending urban schools who are classified as learning disabled are not truly learning disabled; rather, they are students whose performance in the classroom is adversely affected by the ravages of poverty (Blair & Scott, 2002).

Teachers are confronted with significant challenges in their attempts to meet the educational needs of these pupils, especially when these students have limited English proficiency. One major issue for professionals who work with culturally and linguistically diverse students is distinguishing between learning problems that may arise from cultural differences and those that are due to learning disabilities. It is crucial that teachers make every effort to differentiate between differences and disabilities; cultural and linguistic differences must not be interpreted as a disability.

More than 1.24 million culturally and linguistically diverse children have a learning disability (U.S. Department of Education, 2009). Data compiled by the federal government on culturally and linguistically diverse students who are learning disabled are presented in Table 6.7. Because of long-standing concerns about disproportionate

TABLE 6.7 Students Ages 6–21 With Learning Disabilities, by Race/Ethnicity

Group	Number of Students	Percentage of Students
White	1,372,496	52.51
Black	529,064	20.24
Hispanic	620,018	23.72
American Indian/Alaskan Native	44,791	1.71
Asian/Pacific Islander	47,226	1.81
Total	2,613,595	100.00

NOTE: Data are for the 2007–2008 school year. Due to rounding, percentages do not add to 100 percent.

SOURCE: U.S. Department of Education. (2009). *IDEA data.* Retrieved October 22, 2009, from https://www.ideadata.org/PartBReport.asp

representation of racial and ethnic minorities in special education, Congress now requires that states maintain records according to race and ethnicity for enrollment, educational placement, school exiting status, and discipline. This information will help Congress to monitor disproportionate representation and, if necessary, suggest corrective revisions to current policies, practices, and procedures. Of course, attention must also focus on the broader issues of child poverty and its effect on school performance.

Technology and Individuals With Learning Disabilities

With the enactment of PL 105–17 and continuing with IDEA 2004, educators are now required to consider the appropriateness of **assistive technology** as a tool or intervention for every student with an IEP. Assistive technology refers to any technological device, regardless of sophistication, that enables the user to increase, maintain, or improve his or her functional capabilities. Students with learning disabilities are increasingly using assistive technology to compensate for barriers to learning. In fact, some see technology acting as a "cognitive prosthesis" allowing individuals with learning disabilities to become more effective and efficient learners (Bryant & Bryant, 2003). Innovative ways of delivering instruction to pupils with learning disabilities include DVDs, CD-ROMs, and, of course, the Internet. Another common application is word processing, which Lerner and Johns (2009) characterize as a "boon for students with learning disabilities who have difficulties with handwriting, spelling, and written composition" (p. 40). The writing skills of individuals with learning disabilities benefit from the use of word processing programs. Revisions are easily accomplished, poor handwriting is no longer a concern, and spelling and grammar checks improve the quality of the written product (Graham, Harris, & Larsen, 2001; MacArthur, 2000).

Researchers (Bender, 2008) have found that the use of hypermedia (interactive computer programs that incorporate various media) enhances the mathematical problem-solving abilities of students with learning disabilities. Improved performance in spelling is another area where computer-assisted instruction has aided children with learning disabilities (Belson, 2003).

Trends, Issues, and Controversies

The field of learning disabilities abounds with issues and controversies. We have chosen to briefly examine two contemporary issues confronting the field: the inclusion movement and efforts at educational reform.

Challenges in Service Delivery: The Full Inclusion Movement

The subject of full inclusion for students with learning disabilities is certainly one of the most controversial issues confronting the field of learning disabilities today. Parents, policymakers, educators, and administrators alike continue to wrestle with the various emotionally charged dimensions of this topic. For some, according to Mercer (1997),

> the inclusion movement represents a reduction of essential instructional services to students with learning disabilities and a threat to the existing area of learning disabilities within the educational structure. To others, inclusion represents an opportunity for students with learning disabilities to function successfully in a community of diverse learners without the stigmatization of being segregated. (p. 64)

The issue of full inclusion is sometimes portrayed as one of equity—a belief that individuals with disabilities have a right to participate in normalized educational experiences and should not be excluded from this opportunity simply on the basis of their impairment(s). Some advocates (Peterson & Hittie, 2010) argue that students with learning disabilities deserve to be educated in the general education setting.

As we saw earlier in this chapter, the regular classroom is currently the most popular placement for serving students with learning disabilities. Advocates of full inclusion believe that full-time placement in the general education classroom will result in enhanced academic performance, greater acceptance by typical peers, and better coordination between regular and special educators. However, those who advocate maintaining a continuum of service delivery options point out that pupils with learning disabilities are often poorly served in general education settings (McLeskey, Hoppery, Williamson, & Rentz, 2004; Vaughn et al., 2001; Zigmond, 2003). Zigmond and others (Schumm, Moody, & Vaughn, 2000; Swanson, 2000) note that the research evidence fails to support the efficacy of full inclusion for students with learning disabilities, at least as it pertains to achievement outcomes. Concerns about a lack of individualization of instruction (Zigmond & Baker, 1996) and apprehension about the appropriateness of exclusive exposure to the general education curriculum (Kauffman, 1999; Martin, 2002) are among the reasons that some special educators do not fully embrace full inclusion. Many of the professional associations concerned with learning disabilities have adopted policy statements opposing full inclusion. The accompanying Insights feature presents one such position paper.

We believe that a balanced approach to this controversy is appropriate. With skillful planning, equitable allocation of resources, a clear delineation of responsibilities, and careful attention to what will be taught and how it will be evaluated, full inclusion is not only feasible but also beneficial for some students with learning disabilities (Hallahan et al., 2005). However, we strongly encourage educators and other professionals to keep in mind the principle of individualization, which is the benchmark of special education. One size (program) does not fit all; it is a matter of a "goodness of fit." This means that for some children with learning disabilities, full inclusion is appropriate, but others may be better served in a resource room or possibly a self-contained classroom. Perhaps as we enter the twenty-first century, our energy and attention should focus on improving the quality of our instructional practices for all learners, with an emphasis on the individual needs of the student and not the place or location that services are provided.

A Reaction to Full Inclusion: A Reaffirmation of the Right of Students With Learning Disabilities to a Continuum of Services

The National Joint Committee on Learning Disabilities (NJCLD) supports many aspects of school reform. However, one aspect of school reform that the NJCLD cannot support is the idea that all students with learning disabilities must be served only in regular classrooms, frequently referred to as full inclusion. The NJCLD believes that full inclusion, when defined this way, violates the rights of parents and students with disabilities as mandated by the Individuals with Disabilities Education Act (IDEA).

Because each student with learning disabilities has unique needs, an individualized program must be tailored to meet those needs. For one student, the program may be provided in the regular classroom; yet for another student, the regular classroom may be an inappropriate placement. Therefore, the NJCLD supports the use of a continuum of services and rejects the arbitrary placement of all students in any one setting.

SOURCE: Adapted from the National Joint Committee on Learning Disabilities. (2003). Retrieved March 21, 2010, from http://www.ldonline.org/?module=uploads&func=download&fileId=589

Educational Reform Movement

Over the past several years, a number of reports have sharply criticized the U.S. educational system, especially when achievement outcomes of U.S. pupils are compared with those of their European and Asian counterparts. These reports have led to calls for higher academic standards in the United States. One early by-product of this pursuit of educational excellence was the enactment in March 1994 of PL 103–227. Commonly referred to as the Goals 2000: Educate America Act, this law seeks, among other provisions, to raise academic standards and increase high school graduation rates.

Although many professionals laud the provisions of this legislation, it is notably silent as far as addressing students with disabilities. In fact, there is genuine concern in some educational circles that with more rigorous standards of academic competency and stringent evaluation requirements, students with disabilities, including learning disabilities, may be shortchanged in their drive toward obtaining a high school diploma. In response to the mandates contained in PL 103–227, several states have instituted higher graduation standards, and there is a growing national trend toward greater teacher accountability for student performance. (Recall, for example, the emphasis on accountability found in the No Child Left Behind Act, PL 107–110.) This push poses some interesting challenges for both general and special educators because many students with learning disabilities experience difficulty fulfilling current academic expectations, let alone the newer performance guidelines.

The impact of the Goals 2000: Educate America Act of 1994 can be seen in the 1997 IDEA reauthorization. Possibly in reaction to Goals 2000, PL 105–17 contains several requirements that speak to the overall intent of the law. For instance, each pupil's IEP must now contain a statement that addresses the extent to which the student will be involved in and progress in the general education curriculum. IDEA 2004 maintains this requirement. An implication of this standard is that general educators will be held increasingly accountable for the performance of individuals with learning disabilities and other impairments. The 2004 version of IDEA, like its predecessor, also requires the inclusion of children with disabilities in state- and districtwide assessments (using appropriate accommodations) in an attempt to gauge their educational progress. Previously, these students were routinely excluded from testing programs most likely because their anticipated weak performance would reflect poorly on the school in ratings or rankings relative to other schools.

As we just mentioned, another chapter in the latest educational reform movement is the No Child Left Behind Act of 2001, which we initially examined in Chapter 2. Recall that all states are currently engaged in standards-based school reform efforts. *Accountability* is the buzzword as PL 107–110 stresses outcomes, as measured by academic achievement, for all learners, including pupils with disabilities. High-stakes testing is now commonplace for students, teachers, and administrators. Our concern, however, is with those individuals who fail to meet performance standards. Will we see an increase in referrals for special education services? Are we destined to have more children identified as learning disabled as schools continue to focus on high standards and accountability (Brooks, 2002)? Will IEP goals become more closely aligned with the content standards of the general education curriculum? Will students with learning disabilities simply drop out of school as a result of the growing emphasis on accountability and academic performance? Obviously, the No Child Left Behind Act has important implications for special education, especially for pupils recognized as learning disabled.

The current educational reform movement, with its clarion call for greater accountability and higher academic standards, will certainly affect students with learning disabilities. We anticipate that in the short term the quest for academic excellence will raise more questions than it answers; it is probably too early to assess the overall impact of these legislative endeavors. As the repercussions become clearer and researchers provide answers and suggestions for change, we believe that the vast majority of learners will see benefit from this movement.

CHAPTER IN REVIEW

Defining Learning Disabilities

- Persons with learning disabilities are a diverse group of individuals who, despite normal intelligence, fail to learn as easily and efficiently as their classmates and peers.
- The current IDEA definition contains two key concepts: (1) a discrepancy between the student's academic performance and his or her estimated or assumed ability or potential and (2) the proviso that a learning disability cannot be due primarily to factors such as sensory impairments, mental retardation, emotional problems, or environmental, cultural, or economic disadvantage (the exclusionary clause).

Prevalence of Learning Disabilities

- Learning disabilities is the largest category within special education, accounting for slightly less than half of all individuals receiving services.
- Government figures indicate that about 2.52 million pupils are identified as learning disabled.

Etiology of Learning Disabilities

- In the vast majority of instances, the cause of a person's learning disability is unknown.
- Researchers offer four possible factors for explaining the etiology of learning disabilities: injury or damage to the central nervous system (CNS), heredity, biochemical abnormalities, and environmental factors.

Characteristics of Individuals With Learning Disabilities

- Persons with learning disabilities are a very heterogeneous population.
- The primary characteristics of students with learning disabilities are deficits in academic performance.
- Reading is the most common problem encountered by children identified as learning disabled.
- Some individuals who are learning disabled have difficulty attending to tasks, and some exhibit excess movement and activity or hyperactive behavior. This condition is often identified as attention deficit hyperactivity disorder (ADHD).

Assessment of Learning Disabilities

- State and local school districts now have the option of making eligibility decisions on the basis of how a pupil responds to research-based educational interventions, a process known as response to intervention or RTI.
- Norm-referenced assessments compare an individual's performance to that of a normative group of peers.
- Criterion-referenced assessments provide educators with a description of the student's abilities, measured against a predetermined mastery level.
- Curriculum-based assessment is a type of criterion-referenced assessment.

Educational Considerations

- About nine out of every ten students with learning disabilities spend at least part of their day in the general education classroom.
- There is no one best or correct way to teach individuals with learning disabilities.
- Cognitive training is an approach concerned with the manipulation or modification of a student's underlying thought patterns; self-instruction and mnemonic strategies are examples of cognitive training.

- Direct Instruction (DI) focuses on analyzing the characteristics or components of the task to be learned and actively involving the student in the learning process.
- Learning strategies focus on teaching students how to learn by meaningfully involving them in the instructional process.

STUDY QUESTIONS

1. Developing a definition of learning disabilities has proven to be problematic. Describe three reasons why this process has been so challenging.
2. What are the main components of most definitions of learning disabilities?
3. Identify the four historical phases and their respective contributions to the development of the field of learning disabilities.
4. List four possible causes of learning disabilities. Give an example of each.
5. Identify and describe five learning and behavioral characteristics common to individuals with learning disabilities. In your opinion, which one of these deficits is most debilitating? Why?
6. What is RTI? Describe the intervention process typical of most RTI models.
7. Distinguish between norm-referenced and criterion-referenced assessments. What type of information does each test provide?
8. What is the current trend in educational placement of students with learning disabilities? Do you agree with this trend? Why or why not?
9. Identify the major components of the following instructional approaches used with students who are learning disabled: cognitive training, direct instruction, and learning strategies. What are the advantages and disadvantages of each approach?
10. Why is it difficult to determine if a preschooler is learning disabled?
11. What unique problems confront secondary students with learning disabilities? How can public schools help adolescents meet these challenges?
12. Describe the variables that contribute to the successful adjustment of adults with learning disabilities.
13. In what ways might an individual with learning disabilities affect his or her family?
14. Why is it difficult to distinguish between cultural/linguistic differences and a learning disability?
15. How can technology be used to benefit individuals with learning disabilities?
16. Describe two contemporary issues confronting the field of learning disabilities. How will these challenges affect programs for children and adolescents with learning disabilities?

KEY TERMS

learning disabilities 195
discrepancy 197
response to intervention (RTI) 197
exclusionary clause 198
brain injury 202
familiality studies 203
heritability studies 203
dyslexia 207
phonological awareness 207
phonemic awareness 207
phonemes 207
pragmatics 208
short-term memory 209
working memory 209
metacognition 209
learned helplessness 210
attention deficit hyperactivity disorder (ADHD) 211
progress monitoring 212
norm-referenced assessments 214
criterion-referenced assessments 214
curriculum-based assessment (CBA) 215
authentic assessment 215
portfolio assessment 215
self-instruction 218
mnemonic strategies 218
Direct Instruction (DI) 219
learning strategies 220
developmental/cognitive model 225
behavioral curriculum model 225
functional curriculum 225
transition plan 227
assistive technology 231

LEARNING ACTIVITIES

1. Obtain a copy of the definition of learning disabilities from your state department of education, and compare it with the IDEA definition. In what ways are these definitions similar and dissimilar? Pay particular attention to eligibility criteria. How would you improve your state's definition?
2. Interview a school psychologist or educational diagnostician and inquire about the assessment and identification procedures used to determine if a student is learning disabled. Ask about the strengths and weaknesses of the various assessment instruments. Do the evaluation procedures differ depending on the grade level of the pupil? How is a discrepancy between intelligence and achievement determined? What strategies does this professional use to gather information from parents and teachers? How are children from culturally and linguistically diverse backgrounds assessed?
3. Visit an elementary school, a middle school, and a high school in your community that serve individuals with learning disabilities. Observe in the classrooms, and interview the general educators and special educators who work with these students. What instructional approaches are used? How are the students evaluated? Does the delivery system vary according to grade level? How do the general and special educators work together? In your opinion, are the children with learning disabilities accepted by their classmates? Identify strengths and weaknesses of the learning disabilities program at each site. Would you want to be a teacher in these schools? Why or why not?
4. Interview a college student with learning disabilities. What types of supports and services does the college/university provide to students with learning disabilities? What academic and/or social areas pose the greatest challenge for this individual? What learning strategies work best for him or her? Ask the person to identify areas of strength both in and out of school. Does the individual require accommodations in the workplace? If so, what types of modifications are necessary? Inquire about the person's postschool plans and the availability of support services in the community.
5. Attend a local chapter meeting of a sibling and/or parent group for individuals with learning disabilities. What issues and concerns were addressed at this meeting? Determine what types of services and supports are available in your community for individuals with learning disabilities across the life span. Ask siblings and/or parents about the challenges and rewards of living with a person with a learning disability.

ORGANIZATIONS CONCERNED WITH LEARNING DISABILITIES

Council for Learning Disabilities (CLD)
11184 Antioch Road
Box 405
Overland Park, KS 66210
(913) 491-1011
(913) 491-1012 (Fax)
http://www.CLDinternational.org

Division for Learning Disabilities, Council for Exceptional Children
1110 North Glebe Road
Suite 300
Arlington, VA 22201-5704
(888) 232-7733
(866) 915-5000 (TTY)
(703) 264-9494 (Fax)
http://www.teachingLD.org

International Dyslexia Association
40 York Road
Fourth Floor
Baltimore, MD 21204
(410) 296-0232
(410) 321-5069 (Fax)
http://www.interdys.org

Learning Disabilities Association of America (LDA)
4156 Library Road
Pittsburgh, PA 15234-1349
(412) 341-1515
(412) 344-0224 (Fax)
http://www.ldanatl.org

National Center for Learning Disabilities
381 Park Avenue South
Suite 1401
New York, NY 10016
(888) 575-7373
(212) 545-9665 (Fax)
http://www.ncld.org

REFLECTING ON STANDARDS

The following exercises are designed to help you learn to apply the Council for Exceptional Children (CEC) standards to your teaching practice. Each of the reflection exercises below correlates with a knowledge or skill within the CEC standards. For the full text of each of the related CEC standards, please refer to the standards integration grid located in Appendix B.

Focus on Individual Learning Differences ***(CEC Content Standard #3 CC3K1)***
Reflect on a time when you weren't able to learn a skill or concept as quickly as you wanted to (for example, playing a sport or musical instrument or a particular subject in school). How did you feel about yourself? How did people treat you? What did you learn from that experience that will help you as you work with individuals who have learning disabilities?

Focus on Instructional Planning ***(CEC Content Standard #7 CC7K4)***
Reflect on what you have learned in this chapter about students with learning disabilities. If you were to have a student with a learning disability in your general education class, how might you utilize technology to meet the various demands of your learning environment?

STUDENT STUDY SITE

Visit the Student Study Site at www.sagepub.com/gargiulo4emedia for these additional learning tools:

- Video links
- Media links
- Self-quizzes
- E-flashcards
- Full-text SAGE journal articles
- Web exercises

CHAPTER 7

Learning Objectives

After reading Chapter 7 you should be able to:

- Define attention deficit hyperactivity disorder (ADHD).
- Describe the historical evolution of the concept of ADHD.
- List possible etiological factors associated with ADHD.
- Identify learning characteristics and social–emotional issues typical of persons with ADHD.
- Explain how ADHD is diagnosed.
- Define multimodal intervention.
- Outline instructional and environmental modifications typically used with pupils who have ADHD.
- Describe the role of stimulant medication in treating individuals with ADHD.
- Summarize the impact of ADHD on adolescents and adults.

Individuals With Attention Deficit Hyperactivity Disorder

A "BUFFER BOY" WITH A PH.D.

Video Link 7.1
Watch more about ADHD.

I am Rick Parsons. By title I am a professor of counseling and educational psychology at West Chester University outside Philadelphia, Pennsylvania; a licensed psychologist with a practice in suburban Philly; and an author of more than twenty books and fifty professional articles. From a brief review of my professional accomplishments one might conclude that I have had a relatively successful career. I should also tell you that in my childhood I was a student with undiagnosed attention deficit hyperactivity disorder (ADHD).

I went to a Catholic grade school at a time when those with unique learning needs were neither recognized nor diagnosed, nor did they receive services. The idea of ADHD was not a mainstay in the early to late 1950s. Children who were easily distracted, impulsive, often engaging and annoying of classmates, and most often itchy or squirmy were viewed as bad, out of control, or having strange diseases. The "treatment" of the day was most often of a punitive nature—detention, suspension, and even expulsion. Yet, I was one of the "lucky" ones. I was not suspended or expelled.

I can remember to this day the report cards. The grades were always mediocre, mostly 80s and a few 90s. The comments always pointed to how I could do better if I did my homework. There was always the direction that I needed to work on my *self-control and think before I acted!* You see I was, and still can be, a bit impulsive.

In the first few years of school I struggled with reading, being unable to really focus and attend. As a result, I was put in the slow reading group, believing I wasn't very bright. In later years, as we would stand for recitation or spelling bees, I would often become the object of the teacher's negative attention because of my talking in line, goofing around, and most often simply moving. At times I could be in constant motion—moving my hands, swaying back and forth, tapping and drumming with my fingers, and moving to the distraction and sometimes entertainment of those near me, almost always to the frustration of the teacher attempting to run the class.

Back then the teachers employed various "interventions." I was publicly reprimanded and sent to the principal. I had notes sent home to my parents, and I even was put in time-out. Time-out for me often took the form of simply being asked to sit in the back of the class, the very back; or if need be, I could take up temporary residence in the coat closet, and even once under the teacher's desk.

Video Link 7.2
Meet the parent of a child with ADHD.

Yes, the experience was one in which the message was clear. There was something wrong with this boy. After all, he came from a nice family that was actively involved in the parish, he had an older sister and brother who were excellent students, and even he had his moments in which he would shine. But this child completely lacked self-control; he was a red C student.

The poor attention and impulsive behavior were not restricted to school or bounded by the classroom. My parents had to deal with a 5-year-old who took a bus trip to the local town—just because. They parented me through years of behaviors such as climbing onto the rooftops of local stores, helping myself to penny candy, and never watching where I was going or what I was doing and therefore constantly having accidents, breaking things, or simply appearing to be a klutz. The words *pay attention, stand still, slow down,* and *watch what you're doing* became my mantra and the directive from most who knew me. And these messages took their toll.

Experience after experience had me doubt my educational abilities, my social acceptability, my emotional maturity, and even my fundamental goodness. That all changed when I met a wonderful nun, my seventh-grade teacher, Sister Mary. Without formal training in special education—simply having a respect for all of life and its uniqueness—Sister Mary helped me to understand that I wasn't bad, or immature, or ill; rather I just had a different way of learning and lots of energy to channel. It was during this seventh grade that "buffing" became more than a possible future career. Sister Mary structured my seat work so that as soon as I finished my work, and if I could wait patiently while she checked my work and assuming it was correct, I could exit the class and operate the buffing machine. Running the buffer became a way to release energy. Operating that machine became a statement of personal competence. The fact that running the buffer was contingent on successfully completing my work helped me to attend to my work, increase my success, and eventually believe in my academic abilities.

And even though today I can still easily be distracted by external stimuli, the unconditional guidance from teachers like Sister Mary has helped me accept that it's okay to be me—it's just a challenge.

—*Rick Parsons*

Attention deficit hyperactivity disorder (ADHD) is believed to affect about 3 to 5 percent of the school-age population (American Psychiatric Association, 2000; National Institute of Mental Health, 2006). Despite the relatively high estimate of prevalence, ADHD is not recognized as a separate disability category under the current IDEA legislation. However, youngsters who have ADHD may still be eligible for a special education. In response to the lobbying efforts of parents, professionals, and advocates, in 1991 the U.S. Department of Education issued a memorandum directed to state departments of education, stating that pupils with ADHD could receive a special education and related services under the disability category *other health impairments* (OHI). In fact, the regulations that accompany PL 108–446 specifically mention ADHD as a condition that renders an individual eligible for services under the rubric *other health impairments*. Children with ADHD are also eligible for accommodations in general education classrooms under the protections of Section 504 of the Rehabilitation Act of 1973 (PL 93–112).

Because of the high degree of overlap or **comorbidity** among ADHD, learning disabilities, and emotional disorders (Brown, 2006; U.S. Department of Education, 2008b), and the academic and social difficulties frequently experienced by individuals with ADHD, we have chosen to explore this topic in greater detail in a separate chapter while acknowledging that ADHD is not identified by the federal government as a discrete disability category. We believe, however, it is important for educators and other professionals to be able to recognize these students and offer services, supports, and accommodations regardless of how they might (or might not) be labeled.

ADHD is frequently misunderstood; it is a disability plagued by misconceptions and myths. The behavior of individuals with ADHD is also often misinterpreted, with their actions being seen as indicators of laziness, disorganization, and even disrespect (Smith, Polloway, Patton, & Dowdy, 2008). Some people even question the legitimacy of this disability, believing that it has only been created to absolve parents (and teachers) of any responsibility for the child's conduct (Cohen, 2006).

The goal of this chapter is to examine several concepts and issues associated with ADHD. We will answer a variety of questions, such as "What is ADHD and what causes it?" "How can I help students with ADHD?" and "What role does medication play in the treatment of ADHD?" We begin our examination by defining the term *attention deficit hyperactivity disorder*.

ADHD affects males more than females.

Defining Attention Deficit Hyperactivity Disorder

Because IDEA does not define ADHD, we use the definition put forth by the American Psychiatric Association (2000), which describes this condition as "a persistent pattern of inattention and/or hyperactive impulsivity that is more frequent and severe than is typically observed in individuals at a comparable level of development" (p. 85). This description, derived from the *Diagnostic and Statistical Manual of Mental Disorders* (4th ed., text rev.), commonly referred to as DSM-IV-TR, also contains criteria to assist professionals, mainly physicians, in determining whether a child has ADHD. These guidelines are listed in Table 7.1. In examining the table, you may recognize yourself (we are all forgetful at times and occasionally easily distracted); but in individuals with ADHD, it is the chronic nature of the characteristics and their duration that often lead to impaired functioning in activities of daily living.

Video Link 7.3
Watch more about ADHD.

The American Psychiatric Association (2000) definition recognizes three subtypes of ADHD based on the individual's unique profile of symptoms: (1) ADHD, predominantly inattentive type; (2) ADHD, predominantly hyperactive–impulsive type; and (3) ADHD, combined type. The vast majority of individuals with ADHD exhibit the combined type (Barkley, 2006).

A Brief History of the Field

Individuals with attention deficit hyperactivity disorder have been recognized for more than a hundred years. In 1902, George Still, a London physician, described a group of youngsters who had average or above-average intelligence yet were disobedient toward

TABLE 7.1 Diagnostic Criteria for Attention Deficit Hyperactivity Disorder

Six (or more) of the following symptoms of inattention and/or hyperactivity-impulsivity that have persisted for at least 6 months to a degree that is maladaptive and inconsistent with developmental level:

Inattention	• Often fails to give close attention to details or makes careless mistakes in schoolwork, work, or other activities • Often has difficulty sustaining attention in tasks or play activities • Often does not seem to listen when spoken to directly • Often does not follow through on instructions and fails to finish schoolwork, chores, or duties in the workplace (not due to oppositional behavior or failure to understand instructions) • Often has difficulty organizing tasks and activities • Often avoids, dislikes, or is reluctant to engage in tasks that require sustained mental effort (such as schoolwork or homework) • Often loses things necessary for tasks or activities (e.g., toys, school assignments, pencils, books, or tools) • Is often easily distracted by extraneous stimuli • Is often forgetful in daily activities
Hyperactivity	• Often fidgets with hands or feet or squirms in seat • Often leaves seat in classroom or in other situations in which remaining seated is expected • Often runs about or climbs excessively in situations in which it is inappropriate (in adolescents or adults, may be limited to subjective feelings of restlessness) • Often has difficulty playing or engaging in leisure activities quietly • Is often "on the go" or often acts as if "driven by a motor" • Often talks excessively
Impulsivity	• Often blurts out answers before questions have been completed • Often has difficulty awaiting turn • Often interrupts or intrudes on other (e.g., butts into conversations or games)

Also, some hyperactive-impulsive or inattentive symptoms were present before age 7.

The symptoms must be present in two or more settings (e.g., at school [or work] and at home).

Clear evidence of clinically significant impairment in social, academic, or occupational functioning must be demonstrated.

The symptoms do not occur exclusively during the course of a pervasive developmental disorder, schizophrenia, or other psychotic disorder and are not better accounted for by another mental disorder (e.g., mood disorder, anxiety disorder, dissociative disorder, or a personality disorder).

SOURCE: Adapted from American Psychiatric Association, *Diagnostic and Statistical Manual of Mental Disorders*, 4th ed., text rev. (Washington, DC: Author, 2000), pp. 92–93.

adults, acted impulsively, and exhibited inattention along with hyperactivity (Still, 1902). He identified these children as manifesting "defective moral conduct." Still speculated that there was a hereditary foundation to their condition and that these children had neurological impairments. In the late 1930s it was discovered that administering stimulant medication to individuals with characteristics similar to those described by Dr. Still decades earlier had a calming effect on their behavior (Bradley, 1937).

Our early understanding of persons with ADHD was also aided by the work of Heinz Werner and Alfred Strauss, who had worked with children with intellectual disabilities in Germany. These scientists, having left Germany and immigrated to the United States, observed that some institutionalized children with mental retardation exhibited behavior patterns of distractibility and hyperactivity not unlike those attributed to persons with brain injury. In a series of experiments comparing the performance of supposedly brain-injured children with intellectual disabilities to that of youngsters who were mentally retarded but without brain injury, Werner and Strauss found that children with brain injury were more likely to focus on background objects than on the target stimulus (Strauss & Werner, 1942; Werner & Strauss, 1941). Their "figure–ground" investigations, although methodically flawed, offered evidence of the detrimental effects that distractibility and hyperactivity can have on a child's cognitive performance. Youngsters who displayed high levels of distractibility and hyperactivity were commonly referred to as exhibiting the **Strauss syndrome**.

The work of Werner and Strauss was replicated several years later by Cruickshank and his colleagues. These investigators (Cruickshank, Bice, & Wallen, 1957) extended the earlier figure–ground research of Werner and Strauss to children with cerebral palsy. Conceptually, this was an important extension. The youngsters in the Werner and Strauss study were assumed to have brain damage, whereas the children in the Cruickshank experiment all had cerebral palsy—a disability characterized by motor impairments resulting from brain damage (see Chapter 13). Additionally, the individuals evaluated by Werner and Strauss were mentally retarded, but the Cruickshank et al. subjects primarily exhibited normal or near-normal intellectual ability. The finding of hyperactivity and inattention in children without intellectual disabilities was important because it established a link between attentional difficulties and learning problems (Hallahan, Lloyd, Kauffman, Weiss, & Martinez, 2005).

Cruickshank extrapolated his findings into educational recommendations for students who today would likely be recognized as exhibiting ADHD. He called for reducing nonessential classroom stimuli, following a highly structured teacher-directed program, and enhancing the stimulus value of instructional materials (Cruickshank, Bentzen, Ratzeburg, & Tannhauser, 1961). Although these suggestions form the nucleus of many of today's interventions for pupils with ADHD, there is a lack of scientific support for their efficacy (Barkley, 2006).

In the 1950s and 1960s, **minimal brain injury** was the label typically used to describe individuals with distractible, impulsive, and/or hyperactive behavior but no discernible neurological abnormalities. Use of this term soon faded because professionals believed that the designation *minimal* depreciated the difficulties experienced by these individuals. Additionally, in many instances, there was insufficient neurological evidence that the brain tissue was actually damaged (Hallahan et al., 2005).

The 1960s were known as the "Golden Age of Hyperactivity" (Barkley, 1998). During this era the label **hyperactive child syndrome** came into vogue, replacing *minimal brain injury* as the term of choice. Professionals favored this description because it focused attention on observable behaviors rather than relying on speculative indicators of brain injury. Eventually, during the 1980s, the *hyperactive child syndrome* label lost its position of prominence as investigators focused their interest on the inattention component of ADHD as the major deficit exhibited by children with ADHD (Hallahan et al., 2005).

Prevalence of Attention Deficit Hyperactivity Disorder

As we noted earlier, ADHD is believed to affect approximately 3 to 5 percent of the school-age population (American Psychiatric Association, 2000; Barkley, 2006), or an estimated 1.5 million to 2.5 million children (U.S. Department of Education, 2008b). According to Lerner and Johns (2009), ADHD represents one of the most common chronic conditions of childhood. Nationally, almost 8 percent of children 4 to 17 years of age exhibit ADHD, with significant variation found among the states. In Colorado, for instance, only 4.9 percent of youth were diagnosed with ADHD while Alabama reports a prevalence of over 11 percent (Centers for Disease Control and Prevention, 2010). It is obvious that the number of individuals with ADHD continues to grow, most likely

Students with ADHD frequently exhibit other academic and behavioral difficulties.

because of greater awareness and improved diagnostic procedures.

Recall that ADHD is not one of the thirteen disability categories recognized by the federal government; these pupils may be served, however, under the label *other health impairments*. During the 2008–2009 school year, over 648,000 students were identified as having OHI. In the past decade this category has seen an increase of over 425,000 children, or an astonishing 193 percent increase (U.S. Department of Education, 2000, 2010). Of course, not all of this gain can be attributed to pupils with ADHD. We suspect, however, that individuals with ADHD are largely responsible for the dramatic growth of this category. In fact, because of this growth, some authorities in special education now consider OHI to be a high-incidence disability.

The research literature generally suggests that ADHD is more readily identified in males than in females. This condition is diagnosed four to nine times more often in boys than in girls (U.S. Department of Education, 2008b), although other estimates suggest a ratio of three to one (DuPaul & White, 2004). These statistics suggest the possibility of a gender bias in identification and diagnosis: Boys may be overidentified and girls underidentified. We believe that this situation exists because ADHD manifests itself differently in males and females. Boys are more likely to exhibit disruptive, hyperactive behavior, thus being more noticeable to teachers. Girls, on the other hand, are more likely to be withdrawn and exhibit inattention; consequently, they are less likely to be identified (Vaughn, Bos, & Schumm, 2011). Though gender bias may explain part of the discrepancy between males and females, scientific evidence points to actual biological differences as the primary contributing factor (Barkley, 2006).

Etiology of Attention Deficit Hyperactivity Disorder

The precise cause of attention deficit hyperactivity disorder is unknown. To date, no single etiological factor has been discovered, although researchers are exploring several possibilities including neurological foundations, hereditary contributions, and environmental conditions. As scientists learn more about ADHD, it is likely that multiple causes will be identified.

Neurological Dysfunction

Audio Link 7.1
Listen to more ADHD and neurology.

Research suggests that neurological dysfunction plays a key role in individuals with ADHD. Anatomical differences and imbalances in brain chemistry are being closely examined as etiological possibilities (Moore et al., 2006; Salend & Rohena, 2003; Weyandt, 2006, 2007). In recent years, neuroscientists have been able to advance our understanding of the functioning of the human brain—particularly as it relates to individuals with ADHD. Aided by advances in neuroimaging technology, researchers are using scans of the brain such as positron emission tomography (PET) and magnetic resonance imaging (MRI) procedures, as well as other techniques, to learn about brain structure and activity. Several regions of the brain, specifically the frontal lobes, parts of the basal ganglia, and the cerebellum, appear to consistently exhibit abnormalities in persons with

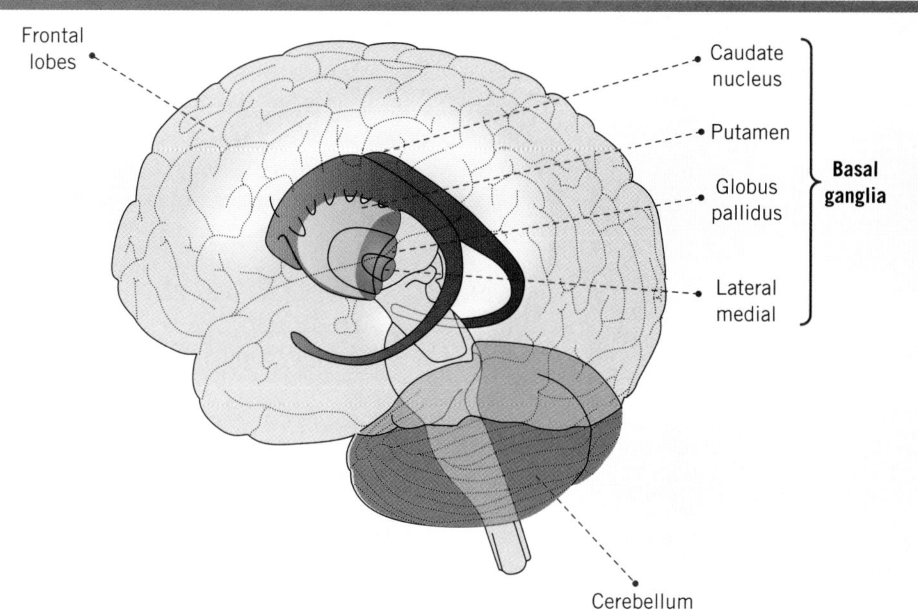

FIGURE 7.1 Areas of the Brain Suspected of Affecting Attention Deficit Hyperactivity Disorder

ADHD (Barkley, 2006; Brown, 2006; Glanzman & Blum, 2007, 2008). See Figure 7.1 for regions of the brain thought to be affected.

The prefrontal and frontal lobes, located in the far forward region of the brain, are responsible for control of **executive functions**—behaviors such as self-regulation, working memory, inner speech, and arousal levels, among other dimensions. The basal ganglia, consisting of several parts (caudate and globus pallidus), is responsible for control and coordination of motor behavior. The cerebellum is also involved in controlling motor behavior (Hallahan et al., 2005). Disorganization and inattention, frequently implicated with ADHD, are believed to be associated with impairments in the prefrontal and frontal cortex, whereas hyperactive behavior is thought to be due to abnormalities in the cerebellum and/or basal ganglia (Glanzman & Blum, 2008).

Scientists are also exploring the possibility of chemical abnormalities in the brain as a reason for ADHD. Although the neurological basis for ADHD is not fully comprehended, a deficiency or imbalance in one or more of the neurotransmitters in the brain is suspected. Simply stated, neurotransmitters are the chemicals that transport electrical impulses (messages) from one brain cell or neuron to another across tiny gaps known as the synaptic cleft. Current thinking suggests that ADHD results from a deficiency or dysfunction of the neurotransmitter dopamine in the regions of the brain that control activity and attention (Mill et al., 2006; Volkow et al., 2007). Although the precise nature of the defect is not known, investigators believe that the level of dopamine is too low in the frontal cortex, thereby interfering with aspects of executive functioning, and elevated in the basal ganglia region, contributing to impulsive and hyperactive behavior (Castellanos, 1997).

Hereditary Factors

There is strong evidence of the role of heredity in contributing to ADHD. Hereditary factors are believed to account for a large percentage of hyperactive–impulsive behavior

Pupils with ADHD are typically served in the general education classroom.

(Daley, 2006; Glanzman & Blum, 2007, 2008). Approximately one out of three persons with ADHD also has relatives with this condition (Barkley, 2006). Family studies further reveal that a child who has ADHD is much more likely to have parents who exhibit ADHD (Levy, Hay, & Bennett, 2006). Additionally, researchers investigating monozygotic (identical) and dizygotic (fraternal) twins have consistently found a higher concordance of ADHD in identical twins than in fraternal twins, strongly suggesting a genetic link (Larsson, Larsson, & Lichtenstein, 2004; Martin, Levy, Pieka, & Hay, 2006).

Environmental Factors

Various pre-, peri-, and postnatal traumas are also implicated as contributing to ADHD (Barkley, 2006; U.S. Department of Education, 2008a). Examples of environmental factors include maternal smoking and alcohol abuse, lead poisoning, low birth weight, and prematurity. Many of these factors are also suspected as leading to mental retardation and learning disabilities.

Research (Hallahan et al., 2005; U.S. Department of Education, 2008a) has discounted many other environmental explanations. Among the popular myths regarding suspected causes of ADHD, but lacking in scientific support, are too much/too little sugar, food additives/coloring, yeast, fluorescent lighting, bad parenting, and too much television.

Characteristics of Individuals With Attention Deficit Hyperactivity Disorder

Characteristics of persons with attention deficit hyperactivity disorder vary considerably. This disorder generally manifests itself early in a child's life. In fact, some precursors have been noted in infancy (Barkley, 2000). It would not be uncommon for behaviors associated with ADHD to be exhibited as early as kindergarten or first grade (Vaughn et al., 2011). Though many young children are sometimes inattentive, fidgety, or somewhat impulsive, the developmental features that distinguish ADHD from typical patterns of behavior in young children include the following:

- Chronic over time
- Generally pervasive behaviors across situations
- Deviant from age-based standards
- Increased likelihood of having another difficulty such as a learning or psychiatric disorder (Vaughn et al., pp. 163–164)

Audio Link 7.2
Listen to other characteristics of ADHD.

ADHD presents itself in many different ways. In some students, inattention is the primary deficit. These pupils have difficulty concentrating on a specific task; they are forgetful and easily distracted. Students who exhibit hyperactive–impulsive disorder are constantly in motion; racing from one activity to another, they have difficulty sitting still or playing quietly. Individuals with a combined type of ADHD manifest aspects of both types. Table 7.2 provides examples of characteristics typical of students with ADHD. (See the accompanying First Person feature.)

First Person: Helen
Good Things Come in Small Packages

Video Link 7.4
Watch more from a parent's perspective.

Like any expectant first-time mom, I was thrilled at the thought of becoming a parent. My joy, however, quickly turned to fear when I went into premature labor. My concerns were multiplied when I developed pulmonary edema and could barely breathe. The only thing that kept me sane was the constant, rhythmic heartbeat of my baby girl coming through loud and clear on the fetal monitor. My family knew how serious my condition was, but I was in a total fog—completely unaware that the doctor had addressed the possibility of my husband having to choose between my life and that of our unborn child. Six days after entering the hospital, and four days after our life-threatening ordeal, our daughter Helen was born.

Five weeks premature and weighing only 4 pounds, 12 ounces, she made a feisty entrance into the world. My husband and I were able to take her home just two days later. With the exception of developing jaundice, she had no health problems whatsoever. Developmental milestones such as rolling over, sitting alone, and pulling up were reached well within normal limits. She even took her first step on her first birthday. Although she was tiny, we had no concerns for her physical development.

Helen's intellectual and emotional growth initially appeared right on track as well; sometimes she was even ahead of the norm. She talked at a very young age. She used simple but complete sentences by the time she was 18 months old and could carry on a decent conversation by age 2.

When the time came for her to start kindergarten, we had some reservations about her beginning school; but at the time, her starting public school was the best option for our family. Helen was one of the youngest children in her class and was definitely the smallest. Our first hint of trouble came during this year. She struggled with reading and math, but her teacher had no worries about her moving on to first grade. She saw no problem that a little maturity couldn't fix.

Helen made great strides in first grade but still struggled. Approximately one month before the year was over, the light seemed to turn on—she got it! Her teacher lamented the fact that she could not keep her another six weeks. Much as in kindergarten, my husband and I discussed the possibility of either having her tested for a learning disability or repeating the grade, but her teacher believed she would be fine.

Second grade was a repeat of first. No problems at the beginning of the school year, then increasing struggles as the year progressed, and of course the "eureka" moment near the end of the year. As in both kindergarten and first grade, Helen's teacher strongly recommended against holding her back, citing the social stigma of repeating while crediting many of her problems to her immaturity. Yet again, a referral for special education was discouraged.

It was not until third grade that we had a major turning point. The work was becoming more difficult, and her frustration was growing. The final straw came one evening when, after a long and confusing homework session, Helen put her head down on the table and began to cry. When I asked her what was wrong, she began to sob uncontrollably, then threw herself into my arms and pleaded with me, "Mommy, why can't I learn like everybody else?" I honestly don't remember what I told her. All I could really think of was getting to school the next day to talk with her teacher. Thus began the long saga of figuring out exactly where the problems were and how we would address them.

After multiple tests to determine her eligibility for special education, all the assessments indicated "normal" results. But thank goodness the principal, the counselor, and her teacher saw past the scores and into the eyes and heart of a little girl who was quickly losing any belief in herself. We hired a tutor, we made modifications in the classroom, and Helen took more diagnostic tests—still nothing that would qualify her for services under special education. About two thirds of the way through the school year, Helen's pediatrician diagnosed her with ADHD; thus, she was eligible to receive a special education under the label *other health impairments*. She began taking Ritalin, and we saw a gradual improvement in her schoolwork.

The improvement we saw did not come without a price. Helen was very angry with her father and me when she realized why she was taking medication every day. She was truly terrified of not having any friends if they found out she had ADHD.

About halfway through fourth grade, we decided to try the extended release form of her medication. We did this in hopes that she would not feel as though she was being "watched" by her classmates when she had to go take medicine in the middle of the day, and also to help with her homework in the late afternoon and early evening. Unfortunately, coming off the medication in the evening turned into a "crash and burn" event most nights. Helen even began to have suicidal ideation and one night did not eat dinner because, as she put it, she "could control herself" (in reference to living

(Continued)

(Continued)

or dying). We of course changed medications, and the emotional outbursts tapered off. The remainder of fourth and fifth grade was an up-and-down roller coaster, ending with yet another twist in the ride. Helen's younger sister was identified as gifted, thus creating a new set of struggles with self-confidence and self-esteem.

Currently, as a seventh grader (but the size of a third grader), she is developing new friends and her own sense of style and self. Academics continue to be a daily struggle. She tends to get lost in lengthy operations and has a great deal of trouble focusing attention and identifying pertinent information. Helen has a tremendous problem with spelling and grammar. She also has trouble transferring and assimilating knowledge from one situation to another. Helen is very rules oriented and desperately needs structure, but she cannot provide that structure for herself. She tends to vacillate from overly focused to airhead. At times, Helen appears almost belligerent—she is unable to "shift gears" as circumstances change. We frequently see this with her schoolwork. She continues to make the same mistakes over and over again because of her unwillingness (inability) to adopt a different strategy—because, in her eyes, her way is the correct way.

Her father and I continue to try to instill the idea of effort being more important than grades, but she holds herself to a higher standard. I am not sure what the next eight to ten years hold. Helen is a very hard worker, but at this point in time a four-year college degree may or may not be in her future. Our biggest concern is that she find something she enjoys and that she can excel in. Our goal is not for her to make the honor roll or be rich, but for Helen to be a self-confident and fulfilled young woman.

—Anonymous

TABLE 7.2 Representative Characteristics of Pupils With Attention Deficit Hyperactivity Disorder

Inattention	Hyperactivity	Impulsivity
• Making careless mistakes • Having difficulty sustaining attention • Seeming not to listen • Failing to finish tasks • Having difficulty organizing • Avoiding tasks requiring sustained attention • Losing things • Becoming easily distracted • Being forgetful	• Fidgeting • Being unable to stay seated • Moving excessively (restless) • Having difficulty engaging quietly in leisure activities • Being "on the go" • Talking excessively	• Blurting answers before questions are completed • Having difficulty awaiting turn • Interrupting/intruding upon others

SOURCE: Adapted from M. Wolraich and A. Baumgaertel, "The Practical Aspects of Diagnosing and Managing Children with Attention Deficit Hyperactivity Disorder," *Clinical Pediatrics, 36*(9), 1997, pp. 497–504.

Behavioral Inhibition and Executive Functioning

Contemporary thinking suggests that problems with **behavioral inhibition** are the primary characteristic of persons with ADHD (Barkley, 2006). Behavioral inhibition consists of three elements that affect the ability to (1) withhold a planned response, (2) interrupt a response that has already been initiated, and (3) protect an ongoing activity from competing or distracting stimuli (Barkley; Lawrence et al., 2002). Problems with behavioral inhibition can lead to a variety of difficulties in the classroom. According to Hallahan et al. (2005), students may have trouble, for example, waiting their turn, resisting distractions, delaying immediate gratification, or interrupting a faulty line of thinking.

Both Barkley (2006) and Brown (2006, 2007) note that individuals with ADHD also often have difficulty with executive functions. Recall from our earlier discussion of the etiology of ADHD that executive functions involve a number of self-directed behaviors such as self-regulation, working memory, inner speech, and arousal levels, among other dimensions. Impaired executive functioning in children with ADHD affects a wide range of performance. Difficulty following rules or directions, forgetfulness, and a lack of emotional control are just a few of the ways that students are affected.

Social and Emotional Issues

Social problems and emotional difficulties are not uncommon among individuals with ADHD. Children with ADHD often experience difficulty making friends and maintaining appropriate relationships with peers (Chronis, Jones, & Raggi, 2006; Glanzman & Blum, 2007). Diminished self-confidence, low self-esteem, and feelings of social isolation/rejection are fairly typical in some individuals with ADHD (Friend & Bursuck, 2009). In some instances, in their attempts to be popular and gain friends, students with ADHD, because of their impaired impulse control, actually wind up aggravating peers and further ostracizing themselves from the very individuals with whom they are attempting to establish relationships.

Persons with ADHD may manifest a wide variety of emotional difficulties. Some individuals may exhibit aggression and antisocial behaviors; in others, withdrawn behavior, depression, and anxiety disorders are typical (Brown, 2006; National Institute of Mental Health, 2008). A majority of parents of children with recognized emotional disorders report that their child also exhibits ADHD (U.S. Department of Education, 2008b).

Comorbidity

Students with ADHD frequently have other academic and behavioral difficulties. Learning disabilities, for example, are very common among individuals with ADHD (Bender, 2008; Pierce, 2003). In an interesting distinction, Silver (1990) observes that a learning disability affects the brain's *ability* to learn whereas ADHD interferes with a person's *availability* to learn. On the other hand, pupils who are gifted and talented (see Chapter 14) are also frequently recognized as having ADHD. Some of these students, in fact, exhibit intense curiosity, creativity, and concentration (Dodson, 2002; Honos-Webb, 2005). Additionally, researchers have found that children with ADHD have coexisting psychiatric disorders at a much higher rate than their peers without ADHD (Atkins & Mariñez-Lora, 2008; Stein & Shin, 2008). Unfortunately, at the present time, investigators are unable to fully explain the reasons for the high degree of overlap between ADHD and other impairments.

Assessment of Attention Deficit Hyperactivity Disorder

Identifying pupils with attention deficit hyperactivity disorder is not always easy, although many teachers will say "you know it when you see it." Valid and reliable assessment of ADHD is difficult; there is no single, definitive medical or psychological test that clearly distinguishes these children from others. Identifying a child as having ADHD is a multidimensional process. Typical strategies for assessing this condition involve direct observation of the youngster and the use of behavior rating scales and other types of observation instruments completed by parents, teachers, and other professionals. Teachers, in particular, represent a valuable source of information about the child as they are involved with this student in a variety of academic and social situations.

Assessment and diagnosis of ADHD is a multifaceted endeavor involving the gathering of specific medical, behavioral, and educational data (U.S. Department of Education, 2008a). The intent of these efforts is to glean as much useful information as possible in order to accurately assess the child's condition.

Medical Evaluation

Generally speaking, a medical evaluation is designed to rule out medical conditions that might be contributing to the pupil's hyperactivity and/or inattention. Examples of these conditions include epilepsy, thyroid problems, and brain tumors (Hallahan et al., 2005; National Institute of Mental Health, 2006). Knowledge of a child's health status can also assist the health care professional in deciding which type of medication to prescribe, should that be a treatment option.

Professionals confronted with making a diagnosis of ADHD can also seek guidance from guidelines disseminated by the American Academy of Pediatrics (2000). These guidelines, crafted around DSM-IV-TR criteria, include the following six recommendations:

- In a child 6 to 12 years old who presents with inattention, hyperactivity, impulsivity, academic underachievement, or behavior problems, primary care clinicians should initiate an evaluation for ADHD.
- The diagnosis of ADHD requires that a child meet *DSM-IV* criteria.
- The assessment of ADHD requires evidence directly obtained from parents or caregivers regarding core symptoms of ADHD in various settings, the age of onset, duration of symptoms, and degree of functional impairment.
- The assessment of ADHD requires evidence directly obtained from the classroom teacher (or other school professional) regarding core symptoms of ADHD, duration of symptoms, degree of functional impairment, and coexisting conditions.
- Evaluation of the child with ADHD should include assessment for coexisting conditions.
- Other diagnostic tests are not routinely required to establish a diagnosis of ADHD. (pp. 1158–1170)

An interesting phenomenon is sometimes observed during the clinical interview. In novel and structured situations, such as a physician's office, it is not unusual for the child to be symptom-free of characteristics typically associated with ADHD—much to the bewilderment of his or her parents or caregivers. This phenomenon, recognized many years ago, is commonly referred to as the **doctor's office effect** (Cantwell, 1979).

Behavioral/Educational Evaluation

Rating scales provide another important source of information about the student suspected of having ADHD. Evaluation of the child's performance in the classroom and his or her behavior at home will assist professionals in establishing a complete picture of the pupil's condition and ensure that the data are as accurate as possible. Although behavioral rating scales can accurately distinguish between children with and without ADHD (U.S. Department of Education, 2008a), their usefulness and accuracy are largely dependent upon raters' knowledge of the individual and their perception of his or her behavior. Despite the standardized nature of these instruments, bias is a real concern.

One example of a reliable and valid assessment measure is the ADHD Rating Scale—IV (DuPaul, Power, Anastopoulos, & Reid, 1998). Similar to other rating indices, informants rate an individual's performance using a Likert scale (*never or rarely*, *sometimes*, *often*, or *very often*). The Conners' Teachers Rating Scale—Revised (Conners, 1997) is another representative example of a commonly used standardized rating scale. This instrument allows the evaluator to rate a variety of ADHD characteristics on the basis of how closely the statement portrays the student. Some assessment instruments primarily assess symptoms of ADHD; other scales are multidimensional. Table 7.3 shows sample test items from one such measure. This instrument, which is typically completed by teachers, evaluates the impact of ADHD on cognitive processes, social–emotional behaviors, and impulsivity–hyperactivity.

TABLE 7.3 Sample Test Items From the "Strengths and Limitations Inventory: School Version"

		Never Observed	Sometimes Observed	Often Observed	Very Often Observed
Attention/ Impulsivity/ Hyperactivity	Exhibits excessive nonpurposeful movement (can't sit still, stay in seat).				
	Does not stay on task for appropriate periods of time.				
	Verbally or physically interrupts conversations or activities.				
	Does not pay attention to most important stimuli.				
Reasoning/ Processing	Makes poor decisions.				
	Makes frequent errors.				
	Has difficulty getting started.				
Memory	Has difficulty repeating information recently heard.				
	Has difficulty following multiple directions.				
	Memory deficits impact daily activities.				
Executive Function	Has difficulty planning/organizing activities.				
	Has difficulty attending to several stimuli at once.				
	Has difficulty monitoring own performance throughout activity (self-monitoring).				
	Has difficulty independently adjusting behavior (self-regulation).				
Interpersonal Skills	Has difficulty accepting constructive criticism.				
	Exhibits signs of poor self-confidence.				
Emotional Maturity	Inappropriate emotion for situation.				
	Displays temper outbursts.				
	Does not follow classroom or workplace "rules."				

SOURCE: C. Dowdy, J. Patton, T. Smith, and E. Polloway, *Attention Deficit/Hyperactivity Disorder in the Classroom* (Austin, TX: Pro-Ed, 1998), pp. 112–113.

Educational Considerations

How does a teacher assist the student who exhibits attention deficit hyperactivity disorder? With an estimated 2 million school-age children exhibiting this disorder (U.S. Department of Education, 2008b), this is an important issue for many classroom teachers and parents. Many pupils with ADHD experience significant difficulty in school, where attention and impulse control are prerequisites for success. In fact, academic underachievement is one of the most salient features of this disability. Many students with ADHD are at risk for chronic school failure (McKinley & Stormont, 2008).

Video Link 7.5
Watch more about accommodations.

Most children with ADHD respond to a structured and predictable learning environment where rules and expectations are clearly stated and understood, consequences are predetermined, and reinforcement is delivered immediately (National Dissemination Center for Children with Disabilities, 2004). Of course, environmental modifications alone are not the key to success. Educational researchers believe that **multimodal interventions**, or concurrent treatments, are generally more effective for individuals with ADHD than any one particular strategy (Brown, 2006; Evans et al., 2006; Mercer & Pullen, 2009; MTA Cooperative Group, 1999a, 1999b). Instructional adaptations, behavioral interventions, home–school communication, medication, and counseling represent some of the available intervention options for individuals with ADHD. We have chosen to highlight four of these treatment approaches, including a concluding examination of the role of medication in the treatment of ADHD. But first we look at the issue of the educational setting that is most appropriate for pupils with ADHD.

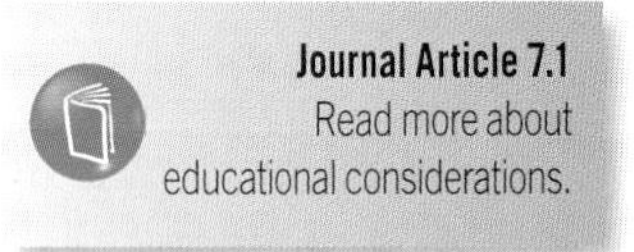

Where Are Students With Attention Deficit Hyperactivity Disorder Educated?

Because the federal government does not recognize attention deficit hyperactivity disorder as a discrete disability, information usually provided by the U.S. Department of Education on the educational settings in which these pupils are served is unavailable. Individuals with ADHD who qualify for a special education are eligible for services under the category *other health impairments*. It is not possible, however, to distinguish which students in this group have ADHD.

Given our current educational climate of emphasizing inclusionary placement for individuals with disabilities, it is safe to assume that large numbers of students with ADHD receive services in the general education classroom. Mercer and Pullen (2009) offer support for this assumption, citing evidence that the majority of students with ADHD are appropriately served in the general education classroom. Sometimes this placement involves general education teachers and special educators working together as a collaborative team. Of course, the most appropriate setting for a student with ADHD must be decided on a case-by-case basis.

Recall that not all students with ADHD qualify for special education services under IDEA (PL 108–446). These individuals will most likely receive accommodations in the general education classroom through the protections afforded them under Section 504 of PL 93–112. See the accompanying Suggestions for the Classroom feature for a list of accommodations appropriate for designing 504 plans (and IEPs too).

Teachers who are successful in working with children with ADHD, regardless of the educational setting in which they are served, typically incorporate a three-pronged strategy. They begin by identifying the unique needs of the child. For example, the teacher determines how, when, and why the pupil is inattentive, impulsive, and hyperactive. The teacher then selects different educational practices associated with academic instruction, behavioral interventions, and classroom accommodations that are appropriate to meet the child's needs. Finally, the teacher combines these practices into an IEP or other individualized plan and integrates this program with educational activities provided to other students. The three steps, which summarize this strategy, are as follows:

- Evaluate the child's individual needs and strengths.
- Select appropriate instructional practices.
- Integrate practices within the IEP if the student is receiving a special education.

"Because no two children with ADHD are alike, it is important to keep in mind that no single educational program, practice, or setting will be best for all children" (U.S. Department of Education, 2008b, p. 4).

We will now examine several different treatment approaches typically used to meet the unique needs of students with ADHD.

Video Link 7.6
Watch for additional suggestions.

Suggestions for the Classroom

Accommodations to Help Students With Attention Deficit Hyperactivity Disorder

Children and youth with attention deficit hyperactivity disorder (ADHD) often have serious problems in school. Inattention, impulsiveness, hyperactivity, disorganization, and other difficulties can lead to unfinished assignments, careless errors, and behavior that is disruptive to oneself and others. Through the implementation of relatively simple and straightforward accommodations to the classroom environment or teaching style, teachers can adapt to the strengths and weaknesses of students with ADHD. Small changes in how a teacher approaches the student with ADHD or in what the teacher expects can turn a losing year into a winning one for the child. Examples of accommodations that teachers can make to adapt to the needs of students with ADHD are grouped below according to areas of difficulty.

Inattention

- ☑ Seat student in quiet area.
- ☑ Require fewer correct responses for grade.
- ☑ Seat student near good role model.
- ☑ Reduce amount of homework.
- ☑ Seat student near "study buddy."
- ☑ Instruct student in self-monitoring using cueing.
- ☑ Increase distance between desks.
- ☑ Pair written instructions with oral instructions.
- ☑ Allow extra time to complete assigned work.
- ☑ Provide peer assistance in note taking.
- ☑ Shorten assignments or work periods to coincide with span of attention; use timer.
- ☑ Give clear, concise instructions.
- ☑ Break long assignments into smaller parts so student can see end of work.
- ☑ Seek to involve student in lesson presentation.
- ☑ Assist student in setting short-term goals.
- ☑ Cue student to stay on task (i.e., private signal).
- ☑ Give assignments one at a time to avoid work overload.

Impulsiveness

- ☑ Ignore minor inappropriate behavior.
- ☑ Acknowledge positive behavior of nearby students.
- ☑ Increase immediacy of rewards and consequences.
- ☑ Seat student near role model or near teacher.
- ☑ Use time-out procedure for misbehavior.
- ☑ Set up behavior contract.
- ☑ Supervise closely during transition times.
- ☑ Instruct student in self-monitoring of behavior (i.e., hand raising, calling out).
- ☑ Use "prudent" reprimands for misbehavior (i.e., avoid lecturing or criticism).
- ☑ Call on only when hand is raised in appropriate manner.
- ☑ Attend to positive behavior with compliments, etc.
- ☑ Praise when hand raised to answer question.

Motor Activity

- ☑ Allow student to stand at times while working.
- ☑ Supervise closely during transition times.
- ☑ Provide opportunity for "seat breaks" (run errands, etc.).
- ☑ Remind student to check over work product if performance is rushed and careless.
- ☑ Provide short breaks between assignments.
- ☑ Give extra time to complete tasks (especially for students with slow motor tempo).

(Continued)

(Continued)

Academic Skills

- ☑ If reading is weak: Provide additional reading time; use "previewing" strategies; select text with less on a page; shorten amount of required reading; avoid oral reading.
- ☑ If written language is weak: Accept nonwritten forms for reports (i.e., displays, oral reports); accept use of typewriter, word processor, tape recorder; do not assign large quantity of written work; test with multiple-choice or fill-in questions.
- ☑ If oral expression is weak: Accept all oral responses; substitute a display for an oral report; encourage student to tell about new ideas or experiences; pick topics easy for student to talk about.
- ☑ If math is weak: Allow use of calculator; use graph paper to space numbers; provide additional math time; provide immediate corrective feedback and instruction via modeling of the correct computational procedure.

Organization Planning

- ☑ Ask for parental help in encouraging organization.
- ☑ Allow student to have extra set of books at home.
- ☑ Provide organization rules.
- ☑ Give assignments one at a time.
- ☑ Encourage student to have notebook with dividers and folders for work.
- ☑ Assist student in setting short-term goals.
- ☑ Provide student with homework assignment book.
- ☑ Do not penalize for poor handwriting if visual–motor defects are present.
- ☑ Supervise writing down of homework assignments.
- ☑ Encourage learning of keyboarding skills.
- ☑ Send daily/weekly progress reports home.
- ☑ Allow student to tape-record assignments or homework.
- ☑ Regularly check desk and notebook for neatness; encourage neatness rather than penalize sloppiness.

Compliance

- ☑ Praise compliant behavior.
- ☑ Supervise student closely during transition times.
- ☑ Provide immediate feedback.
- ☑ Seat student near teacher.
- ☑ Ignore minor misbehavior.
- ☑ Set up behavior contract.
- ☑ Use teacher attention to reinforce positive behavior.
- ☑ Implement classroom behavior management system.
- ☑ Use "prudent" reprimands for misbehavior (i.e., avoid lecturing or criticism).
- ☑ Instruct student in self-monitoring of behavior.
- ☑ Acknowledge positive behavior of nearby students.

Mood

- ☑ Provide reassurance and encouragement.
- ☑ Make time to talk alone with student.
- ☑ Frequently compliment positive behavior and work product.
- ☑ Encourage social interactions with classmates if student is withdrawn or excessively shy.
- ☑ Speak softly in nonthreatening manner if student shows nervousness.
- ☑ Reinforce frequently when signs of frustration are noticed.
- ☑ Review instructions when giving new assignments to make sure student comprehends directions.
- ☑ Look for signs of stress build-up and provide encouragement or reduced workload to alleviate pressure and avoid temper outburst.
- ☑ Look for opportunities for student to display leadership role in class.
- ☑ Spend more time talking to students who seem pent up or display anger easily.
- ☑ Conference frequently with parents to learn about student's interests and achievements outside of school.
- ☑ Provide brief training in anger control: encourage student to walk away; use calming strategies; tell nearby adult if getting angry.
- ☑ Send positive notes home.

Socialization

- ☑ Praise appropriate behavior.
- ☑ Encourage cooperative learning tasks with other students.
- ☑ Monitor social interactions.
- ☑ Provide small group social skills training.
- ☑ Set up social behavior goals with student and implement a reward program.
- ☑ Praise student frequently.
- ☑ Prompt appropriate social behavior either verbally or with private signal.
- ☑ Assign special responsibilities to student in presence of peer group so others observe student in a positive light.

—*Harvey C. Parker*

SOURCE: A.D.D. Warehouse, 304 Northwest 70th Avenue, Plantation, FL 33317; (800) 233-9273. Available online at http://www.addwarehouse.com

Functional Behavioral Assessment

Behavioral strategies are an effective intervention technique for students with ADHD. One example of this approach is the use of **functional behavioral assessment**. A functional behavioral assessment focuses on determining the purpose or function that a particular behavior serves. This process entails, according to Alberto and Troutman (2006), "detailed observation, analysis, and manipulation of objects and events in a student's environment to determine what is occasioning and maintaining the [inappropriate] behaviors" (p. 62). Once this analysis is completed, the goal is to construct interventions that modify the antecedent or triggering behaviors and/or the consequences that are reinforcing and maintaining the undesirable performances.

Self-Regulation/Monitoring

Self-regulation is a behavioral self-control strategy drawn from the early work of Glynn, Thomas, and Shee (1973) on self-monitoring. It is a highly recommended intervention strategy for students with ADHD (Daly & Ranalli, 2003; Harris, Friedlander, Saddler, Frizzelle, & Graham, 2005; Weiss & Illes, 2006). "Self-regulation requires students to stop, think about what they are doing, compare their behavior to a criterion, record the results of their comparison, and receive reinforcement for their behavior if it meets the criterion" (Johnson & Johnson, 1999, p. 6). Self-monitoring includes all of the preceding steps with the exception of dispensing reinforcement. Self-regulation techniques can be used across all grade levels and are appropriate for youngsters served in special education settings and general education classrooms alike.

Self-regulatory strategies are frequently used to modify common classroom behaviors such as working independently, staying on task, completing assignments, or remaining at one's desk. Five sequential steps form the basis of self-regulation, which should focus on a positive target behavior (Johnson & Johnson, 1999). After the teacher determines the student's current level of performance, the student follows these steps:

1. **Self-observation**—looking at one's own behavior, given a predetermined criterion
2. **Self-assessment**—deciding if the behavior has occurred, through some form of self-questioning activity
3. **Self-recording**—recording the decision made during self-assessment on a private recording form
4. **Self-determination of reinforcement**—setting a criterion for success, and selecting a reinforcer from a menu of reinforcers
5. **Self-administration of reinforcement**—administering a reinforcer to oneself

Before allowing students to follow these steps independently, it is recommended that teachers teach self-reinforcement strategies by first demonstrating the necessary steps through modeling or guided practice. Self-monitoring of behavior has been shown to increase academic productivity and on-task behavior of students in both elementary and secondary classrooms (Hallahan et al., 2005; Weyandt, 2007).

Self-regulation is a common intervention strategy used with students with ADHD.

Home–School Collaboration

Home–school collaboration is essential for all pupils, but especially for those with ADHD; it is an important ingredient for promoting their success at school (Jones & Teach, 2006).

EFFECTIVE INSTRUCTIONAL PRACTICES Managing Students With ADHD

Classwide interventions are time-efficient strategies for managing students with ADHD without singling out or stigmatizing the child. They also have the advantage of benefiting *all* pupils, not just the pupil with ADHD. Classwide interventions can have a positive effect on the academic and behavioral difficulties frequently associated with ADHD. Some of these instructional options are listed below.

	Intervention	Key Features	Pros	Cons	Behavior Outcomes	Academic Outcomes
Behavioral	Contingency Management	Positively state rules Clear expectations and guidelines Identify reinforcers and punishers	Effective Flexible Adaptive Engaging, fun	Requires consistency to be effective Setup time	↓ Hyper-activity, inattentive, disruptive behavior ↑ Compliance, time on task	↑ Work accuracy and completion
	Therapy Balls	Replacing child's seat with a gym ball	Effective Socially valid Simple to implement	Costly ($$) May not be practical for whole class	↑ In-seat behavior	↑ Written work
	Self-Monitoring	Identity target behavior Explicitly teach rating scale Decisions on when and how to monitor the behavior	Teaches autonomy and responsibility One-to-one teacher attention Inexpensive	Setup time Gradual shift toward positive behavior	↑ Time on task ↓ Inattentive and inappropriate behaviors	
	Peer Monitoring	Outline appropriate and inappropriate behaviors Practice system before use Clear guidelines and rules	Focus on prosocial behaviors Use of peers to improve behavior	Requires vigilance and practice to prevent peer rejection	↓ Talking out	
	Instructional Choice	Teacher-developed menu of assignments or tasks Student choice of task	Simple to implement Inexpensive	Preparation Possible student expectancy	↓ Behavior problems	↑ Academic engagement
Academic	Classwide Peer Tutoring	Pair students together Alternate tutor–learner roles	Teacher can monitor whole class	Setup time Initial training period	↑ Time on task ↓ Disruptive behavior	↑ Performance in math, reading, and spelling

	Intervention	Key Features	Pros	Cons	Behavior Outcomes	Academic Outcomes
		Provides immediate corrective feedback	Peer attention Immediate feedback Self-selected pace Inexpensive			
	Instructional Modification	Altering the assignment	Personalized to target students' needs	Time-consuming Challenging to find adequate modifications	↓ Disruptive behavior ↑ Task engagement	↑ Performance in reading and writing
	Computer-Assisted Instruction	Use of computer programs to supplement instruction Align with curriculum	Provides additional instruction Fun, engaging Builds fluency	Expensive Need computer access Some programs may not be appropriate	↑ Time on task	↑ Math performance

NOTE: ↑ indicates increase, ↓ indicates decrease.

SOURCE: Adapted from J. Harlacher, N. Roberts, and K. Merrell, "Classwide Interventions for Students with ADHD," *Teaching Exceptional Children, 39*(2), 2006, pp. 6–12.

As illustrated in Figure 7.2 (page 258), this partnership must be "ongoing, reciprocal, mutually respectful, and student centered" (Bos, Nahmias, & Urban, 1999, p. 4).

Video Link 7.7
Watch more about parent–teacher collaboration.

Parents have played a key role in their children's education ever since the enactment of PL 94–142 in 1975. Their involvement has recently been expanded, however, as part of IDEA 2004 (PL 108–446), and input from parents is now solicited during prereferral and eligibility meetings as well as when planning positive behavioral interventions. Bos et al. (1999) note that home–school collaboration can be used in many areas of school life, but it is especially appropriate for students with ADHD when parents and teachers communicate about monitoring medication effects, completing homework assignments, establishing goals and rewards, assessing intervention effectiveness, and developing behavior management plans. The communication techniques themselves can range from simple (daily checklists or rating scales) to more sophisticated strategies such as weekly journals or traveling notebooks (communication folders). What is important is not the method used but that consistent and meaningful communication occur. Parents and teachers should use whatever strategies work best for them.

Instructional Modification

As noted earlier, environmental modifications are often crucial if the student with ADHD is to succeed in the classroom. Instructional adaptations coupled with modifications of the learning environment are powerful tools that can help the pupil sustain attention

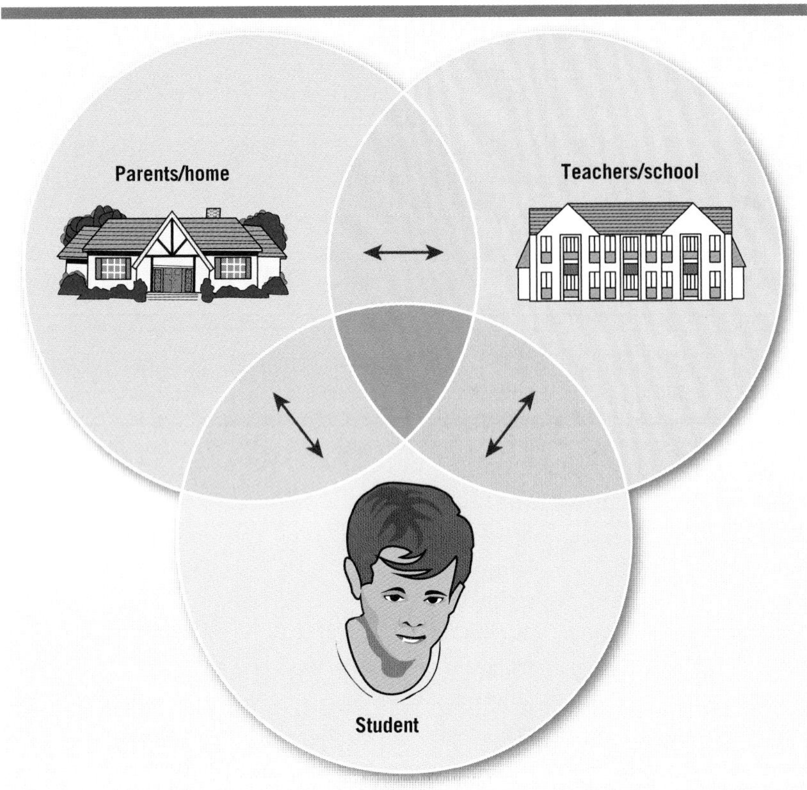

FIGURE 7.2 Components of Effective Home–School Collaboration

SOURCE: From "Targeting Home-School Collaboration for Students with ADHD" by C. Bos, M. Nahmias, and M. Urban, *Teaching Exceptional Children, 31*(6), p. 4. Copyright © 1999 by the Council for Exceptional Children. Reprinted with permission.

while cultivating a climate that fosters learning and encourages the child to control his or her behavior. The following list of adaptations may benefit the individual with ADHD, regardless of educational placement.

As noted earlier in this chapter, even if a student is ineligible for a special education, general educators are required, under Section 504 of PL 93–112, to accommodate individual differences and learning styles of children who exhibit an impairment (such as ADHD) that substantially limits a major life activity such as learning. Lerner and Lowenthal (1993) offer the following suggestions for teachers:

1. Place the youngster in the least distracting location in the class. This may be in front of the class, away from doors, windows, air conditioners, heaters, and high-traffic areas. It may be necessary for the child to face a blank wall or be in a study carrel to enable the child to focus attention.
2. Surround the student with good role models, preferably peers that the child views as significant others. Encourage peer tutoring and cooperative learning.
3. Maintain a low pupil–teacher ratio whenever possible through the use of aides and volunteers.
4. Avoid unnecessary changes in schedules and monitor transitions because the child with ADHD often has difficulty coping with changes. When unavoidable disruptions do occur, prepare the student as much as possible by explaining the situation and what behaviors are appropriate.
5. Maintain eye contact with the student when giving verbal instructions. Make directions clear, concise, and simple. Repeat instructions as needed in a calm voice.
6. Combine visual and tactile cues with verbal instructions since, generally, multiple modalities of instruction will be more effective in maintaining attention and increasing learning.
7. Make lists that help the student organize tasks. Have the student check them off when they are finished. Students should complete study guides when listening to presentations.
8. Adapt worksheets so that there is less material on each page.
9. Break assignments into small chunks. Provide immediate feedback on each assignment. Allow extra time if needed for the student to finish the assignment.
10. Ensure that the student has recorded homework assignments each day before leaving school. If necessary, set up a home–school program in which the parents help the child organize and complete the homework.
11. If the child has difficulty staying in one place at school, alternate sitting with standing and activities that require moving around during the day.

12. Provide activities that require active participation such as talking through problems or acting out the steps.
13. Use learning aids such as computers, calculators, tape recorders, and programmed learning materials. They help to structure learning and maintain interest and motivation.
14. Provide the student opportunities to demonstrate strengths at school. Set up times in which the student can assist peers. (pp. 4–5)

Medication

Many professionals believe that medication, particularly **psychostimulants**, can play an important role in the treatment of ADHD. It is our opinion that the use of medication should always be in conjunction with educational and behavioral interventions; medication represents only one part of a total treatment package and should not be seen as a panacea for dealing with ADHD. In fact, instructional and environmental accommodations should always be the first intervention tactic used to assist pupils with ADHD (U.S. Department of Education, 2008a, 2008b). Although medication may play a vital role in treating ADHD, teachers should *never* recommend to parents that their son or daughter needs to be on medication. Only the child's health care professional can make such a determination. Interestingly, despite the importance of medication in helping children with ADHD, few educators are knowledgeable about ADHD and the use of stimulant medication (Snider, Busch, & Arrowood, 2003). (See the accompanying Insights feature on page 261 on the myths and misunderstandings surrounding stimulant medication.)

One of the more popular stimulant medications is Ritalin, with Dexedrine and Adderall also commonly prescribed. See Table 7.4 for an overview of these and other

TABLE 7.4 Examples of Psychostimulant Medication Typically Used in Treating Attention Deficit Hyperactivity Disorder

Brand Name	Generic Name	Approved Age of Use	Onset of Effectiveness	Duration of Effectiveness	Comments
Ritalin	Methylphenidate	6 and older	Less than 30 minutes	Approximately 4 hours	Most frequently prescribed. Excellent safety record.
Dexedrine	Dextroamphetamine	3	Less than 30 minutes	Approximately 4–5 hours	Must be administered frequently. Excellent safety record.
Focalin	Dexmethylphenidate	6 and older	Approximately 30 minutes	Approximately 5 hours	Potential adverse side effects.
Adderall	Dextroamphetamine sulfate	3	Approximately 30 minutes	Approximately 4–6 hours	Requires only one daily dose.
Concerta	Methylphenidate HCL	6	Approximately 30 minutes	Approximately 12 hours	One daily dose. Minimal side effects.
Strattera	Atomoxetine HCL	6 and older	Usually within 24 hours; therapeutic level reached in 3–4 weeks	Approximately 20 hours	Typically one daily dose. Only medication clinically proven effective for adults with ADHD.

SOURCE: Adapted from J. Lerner and B. Johns, *Learning Disabilities and Related Mild Disabilities, 11th ed.* (Belmont, CA: Wadsworth/Cengage Learning, 2009), p. 228.

Making Inclusion Work

I recall seeing a cartoon once where a student with attention deficit hyperactivity disorder (ADHD) was portrayed as a tornado sitting in a desk (something a student with ADHD can possibly relate to). A tornado is something that gets a lot of attention, but all of it is negative. As I enter my tenth year of teaching, I reflect back on those students I worked with and the varying degrees of attention deficit hyperactivity disorder I encountered. I clearly remember one particular student and parent. This child was new to our school, but not new to special education. His mother finally admitted in December that she had no insurance but wanted desperately to fill her son's prescription because by this time he was constantly in trouble. After we helped her locate free medical insurance, she quickly took him to his pediatrician.

Medication helped him control his impulsiveness, and he made more than a year's progress in the few short months left in school that year. The child didn't return the following year, and I've always wondered how he was doing. Then there are the parents that I've known who have ADHD themselves. Despite facing the same issues, many of these parents still did not know how to help their child. I also recall interacting with my colleagues, wondering how some teachers can be so understanding while others are absolutely oblivious to the effects that this disability has on the educational performance of their pupils. I realized then that it was going to be my job, as a special educator, to educate my fellow teachers as well as the students.

Inclusive Education Experience

Including students with ADHD in the general education classroom is just the right thing to do. A pull-out or resource room setting typically does not benefit these students. Best practices, accommodations, and a great deal of patience are all that is usually required. Depending on the severity of the disorder, behavioral interventions may be necessary, but these too are best done in the least restrictive environment. At the same time, the least restrictive environment can become overly restrictive if traditional self-control, self-direction, and adherence to inflexible classroom rules are required of the learner with ADHD. The extent to which the student's needs are matched to the teacher's expectations is important to success; and the extent to which home and school expectations mirror each other builds on that positive inclusive experience. Typically, you are not going to change the child to fit the learning environment; rather, the classroom needs to accommodate the learner's unique needs and learning style.

Strategies for the Inclusive Classroom

Most classroom strategies that can be used for pupils with ADHD are good for all students. Having an example of an organized notebook with all the required assignments in it, for instance, is a great way to give students a means of organizing themselves. Assigning a dependable peer to help with this activity will ensure that the student with ADHD stays organized while also giving him or her ownership of the task. That same notebook can help children who were absent be sure they get everything they missed.

Another classroom practice that may benefit all students is repeating instructions or assignments several times, simplifying instructions, or giving directions in multiple ways.

Most kids today love technology; therefore, teachers should incorporate what the children love. Today's technologies such as iPods, audiobooks, and computers that give constant/instant stimulation or feedback are great ways for teachers to supplement their instruction.

Successful Collaboration

To make collaboration a success it is important to appreciate the challenges frequently encountered by the general educator who works with pupils with ADHD. Co-teaching is but one example of a collaborative activity that may provide the general education teacher with the opportunity to focus on the particular needs of the student with ADHD while the special educator instructs the entire class. On the other hand, the special educator may work with a small group of children

without parental permission, communication between teachers and caregivers is essential. Parent–teacher communication can take many forms—telephone calls, notes, or having teachers complete checklists and rating scales.

We encourage schools to establish written policies regarding the administration and storage of any medication given to pupils by school personnel. We also recommend

Video Link 7.8
Watch more on this inclusion.

while the general education teacher delivers whole group instruction. Cooperative learning groups of specifically chosen peers is another way of engaging students with ADHD. The keys to a successful collaborative relationship are listening, acknowledging the teacher's concerns, meeting the teacher's needs as well as those of the students, and doing all of this in a timely manner.

Working With Parents and Families

A close relationship with the parents and families of students with ADHD is vital to the child's success at school. Recently I e-mailed a parent about extreme changes in her son's behavior. The classroom teacher first brought it to my attention, and the paraprofessional who works with him noticed the changes as well. I also observed the changes, but working with this student for only fifteen minutes each day I failed to put it all together. I simply informed his mother that we had seen some changes and wanted to address them with her before it began to affect his progress and ultimately his grade. Later that same day she stopped by my classroom and said she had brought him his medicine. It seems that she had simply stopped giving her son his medication and wanted to see if we would notice any changes. While medication should not be the first line of defense in dealing with ADHD, for many students medication is a necessity. Some parents, however, do not believe in the benefits of medication for their child. It is important for teachers to realize that this is a very personal decision, and they must respect the wishes of the parent. Parents who feel that their voice is not being heard are more likely to become defensive and uncooperative when problems do arise.

Follow-through and consistency of routines across environments are crucial for the child with ADHD. At home there should be a schedule similar to the one used at school. There should be consequences and rewards that mirror what is done in the classroom. A clear understanding of expectations that are consistent across environments will often enhance success.

Homework is often a huge source of frustration for both parents and the child. Teachers can usually suggest ways to minimize frustration. For example, it may not always be necessary to complete each and every homework problem if the student is able to demonstrate an understanding of the concept. Breaking homework into manageable chunks or giving due dates for assignments early will allow parents additional time to help their child and possibly keep the student from feeling overwhelmed. Sometimes students are good at certain parts of an assignment, and these can possibly be omitted. A student, for instance, who is great at computation facts but weak at deciphering word problems may be required only to determine the equation but not expected to work it out. The bottom line is two-way communication. It is important that parents and teachers view each other as a team.

Advice for Making Inclusion Work

Special educators often assist the general education teacher as much as they do the student. Being available when assistance is required and serving as a source of effective instructional and behavioral interventions are very important for making inclusion work. I often send my colleagues useful articles and short weekly e-mails with instructional suggestions. I also remind them that ADHD is real and that the child is not trying to drive them crazy.

Students with ADHD lack the ability to focus and are distracted by anything overly stimulating, so finding ways to make learning fun is a key component of success. In an inclusive setting the special educator has to help the general education teacher find ways to make the learning environment less stimulating and his or her teaching more stimulating. Again, this works for *all* students, not just the child with ADHD. Be sure that you facilitate open lines of communication between home and school. View inclusion as a partnership among the general education teacher, the special educator, and the family for the benefit of all, but especially the student with ADHD.

—*Lisa Cranford*
Instructional Support Teacher
National Board Certified Teacher
2009 Alabama CEC Special Education Teacher of the Year
Hoover (Alabama) City Schools

that any adult who administers medication to a child complete a daily medication log; at a minimum, this log should include the medication name, dosage, time, and signature of the person administering the drug. Finally, parents and teachers need to be careful that they do not send a message to the student that medication is a substitute for self-responsibility and self-initiative; nor does the use of psychostimulants absolve the

CHAPTER 8

Learning Objectives

After reading Chapter 8 you should be able to:

- Outline the issues surrounding our understanding of emotional or behavioral disorders.
- Define socially maladjusted and conduct disorders.
- Distinguish between clinically derived and statistically derived systems for classifying emotional or behavioral disorders.
- Explain how society has historically dealt with persons with emotional or behavioral disorders.
- Identify biological and psychosocial risk factors of emotional or behavioral disorders.
- List the learning and social characteristics typical of students who exhibit emotional or behavioral disorders.
- Describe contemporary approaches for assessing pupils with emotional or behavioral disorders.
- Provide examples of academic and behavioral interventions often used with individuals with emotional or behavioral disorders.
- Define time management, transition management, proximity and movement management, classroom arrangement, and classroom ambience.
- Summarize educational services for persons with emotional or behavioral disorders across the life span.

Individuals With Emotional or Behavioral Disorders

MIKE

Video Link 8.1
Watch more about emotional disorders.

Mike was a happy baby who was constantly moving—not running all over the place, but he would rock when he played or sat or rode in a car. He even rocked himself to sleep on his hands and knees as a baby in his crib. Mike appeared to be very bright and very verbal. He could converse better than most children his age. The problem we had was that he couldn't sit still.

By the time he was in kindergarten, he was diagnosed with ADHD. He was prescribed Ritalin, and then Clonidine was added because he had such emotional mood swings. His kindergarten teacher was wonderful about communicating with us and working with him. I don't know how we'd have managed without her. I felt she had his best interest at heart in all that she did, and she treated him with love and kindness, but Mike was held back in kindergarten due to his immaturity. The school convinced us it would be the best thing for him. Yet, I had no idea how devastating this would be for Mike's self-esteem.

During his second year of kindergarten, he began having thoughts he couldn't control. His teacher called us because he told her he was having thoughts of killing his brother with a knife and said he would never do that but couldn't stop thinking about it. This was the beginning of his obsessive thoughts. During the next two to three years of school, Mike developed frequent outbursts of anger that were incredible to see in a child so small. He would fly into a rage over the least thing, rant and rave loudly, occasionally throw things, and then suddenly be as calm as a kitten. He frequently blamed all of his problems on the fact that he "failed" kindergarten and was stupid. His schoolwork began to suffer drastically. Mike's obsessive thoughts included burning down the house, killing his beloved cat, and a fear that someone was going to break into the house and kill him.

By the third grade, Mike was exhibiting eye twitches, grunts, sniffing, and throat clearing. He would pull his hair when he became frustrated, and when he couldn't do

---

Written by Lou Anne Worthington, University of Alabama at Birmingham, and Richard M. Gargiulo

We each view behavior through personal lenses that reflect our own standards, values, and beliefs. What appears to you as abnormal behavior may appear to another person as within the range of normal human behavior (Rosenberg, Wilson, Maheady, & Sindelar, 2004; Webber & Plotts).

Four Dimensions of Behavior

At least four dimensions of behavior are common to most definitions of emotional or behavioral disorders: (1) the frequency (or rate) at which the behavior occurs, (2) the intensity of the behavior, (3) the duration of the behavior, and (4) the age-appropriateness of the behavior (Webber & Plotts, 2008; Wicks-Nelson & Israel, 2009). Frequency of behavior indicates how often a behavior occurs. For example, many students talk out in class from time to time; however, the student who talks out thirty times during a class period may be engaging in atypical behavior. Intensity refers to the severity of behavior. Temper tantrums, for example, can range from whining that is irritating to others to more serious acts of physical aggression. Duration refers to the length of time a behavior occurs. For example, out-of-seat behavior can range from relatively brief (and mildly problematic) episodes to substantially longer episodes that create major disruptions in classroom learning. Finally, age-appropriateness must be considered. For example, sexual acting-out behavior among adolescents may be disturbing to many adults, but it is a fairly common, if problematic, behavior at this age. At the preschool and early elementary levels, however, sexual acting-out behavior is of much greater concern. It is important for teachers to remember that behavior viewed as problematic at one developmental level may be fairly typical or common at another age (Wicks-Nelson & Israel).

Disturbed and Disturbing Behavior

In 1981, James Kauffman, a noted authority in the field of emotional or behavioral disorders, made a critical distinction between *disturbed* behavior and *disturbing* behavior. He noted that some behaviors are inappropriate in some instances and not in others, simply because of differences in setting expectations. For example, the use of profanity may be within the range of acceptable behavior to a group of adolescents out "cruising" on a Saturday night, but most teachers would find such language unacceptable in the classroom. Likewise, drinking alcohol during adolescence is relatively common and is highly influenced by one's peers. This behavior, while disturbing to many adults, may not constitute disordered behavior. According to Kauffman, these behaviors are *disturbing* because they occur in a certain place and time and in the presence of certain individuals. In contrast, *disturbed* behavior occurs in many settings, is habitual, and is part of the individual's behavior pattern. For example, stealing, if it occurs in many settings over a long period of time, may be indicative of disordered behavior.

Transient Nature of Problematic Behavior

The transient nature of problematic behavior has been the focus of research for many years. For example, a landmark study by Rubin and Balow (1971) found that more than 50 percent of all school-age children were perceived by their teachers to have behavior problems at some point during their elementary years. In this same study, 7.5 percent of school-age children were consistently perceived by their teachers to exhibit problematic behavior. These findings suggest that it is common for children and youth (as well as adults) to have periods in their lives that are characterized by conflict, crisis, depression, stress, and ineffective decision making. These difficult periods may occur at vulnerable points in an individual's life—for example, when a family member or friend has died. The resulting acting-out behavior, though disturbing, may be transient and may disappear altogether after sufficient time to grieve has elapsed (Newcomer, 2003).

Typical and Atypical Behavior

Some children with emotional or behavioral disorders exhibit unusual, or qualitatively different, behaviors—behaviors that are not typical at *any* age. For example, children and youth with **Tourette's syndrome** exhibit peculiar behaviors such as uncontrollable motor movements (tics) and inappropriate vocalizations such as barking, profanity, or other socially inappropriate comments that are not developmentally typical at any age. These atypical behaviors are considered by some professionals to be disordered or disturbed. See the accompanying First Person feature.

Encyclopedia Link 8.1
Read more about Tourette's syndrome.

First Person: My Eagle Scout

We are at my son's Eagle recognition ceremony, an accomplishment that so few young men ever achieve. He has been in scouting since first grade, before we knew there were issues in his life that might make getting to this point a problem for him. He is sitting on the opposite side of this very large church, waiting to be called forward to receive his award. I am standing near the wall, poised to take his picture and thinking that he has no idea where I am. But in true fashion, he spies me and acknowledges my presence, just like he does at all his functions. We are connected, he and I. He is not embarrassed to be seen with his mom. What a joy he is—gentle, kind, loving, and totally uninhibited in his expression of joy or excitement. I tell my other children that while I love them all, I like him the best. For what is there about him that you wouldn't like? At 15 he is tall and handsome, a musician, an Eagle Scout, an avid Bama fan, a good student, a young man of faith, and a friend to anyone who will simply give him a chance. At times like this I often pause to reflect on how blessed we are to have him in our lives. Life has not been easy for him academically or, perhaps more important, socially. He has severe learning disabilities in some major areas such as math and reading, which impact every aspect of learning. He also has Tourette's syndrome, which impacts him socially, and this is perhaps what hurts him the most.

Having a child diagnosed with anything that means his or her life is going to be more difficult is a blow to a family. Hearing a doctor or a group of educators tell you that your child will likely not have the academic skills to go on to college is hard to hear. Watching peers shun and make fun of your child because of his speech and social skills is even more painful, and you are left trying to figure out how to proceed. How to help your child achieve his or her goals? It is like trying to negotiate a complex maze. You don't know where to go or what to do, and you often have no one in particular to ask about what to do or where to go. Parents often have to learn as they travel this course, and having educators who are willing to work with them can make all the difference in the outcome.

Reflecting back fifteen years, there was nothing unusual about my son's birth or development—well, for the most part. As a young child he was always a bit intense. He would pick up and put away everything he got out—not a bad habit, but unusual for a 2-year-old. He would try and clean the glass doors if he saw they needed it. He was extremely sensitive to loud noises and to light. Once he was even called an ugly name by an adult because he began to cry while in the gym at our church when the noise level had become unbearable to him.

So up until he was around 2 years old we thought, "Great, a child that will just move on easily." He was sweet and gentle and developing in a normal fashion. Then we began to notice that his speech was not coming along as it should. I was not blind. I was the mom of three kids, one of whom already had problems, and I was not about to wait to see if everything would turn out okay. So we began our struggle to find out what was going on.

Speech therapy was first. This was when the educational system first began to help. Therapy was provided by the school system, and he improved. But kindergarten started, and concerns began to surface. His reading was slow. He had difficulty making eye contact with his peers. He overreacted to being touched and didn't seem to know how to respond when socializing with his classmates. If his hands were dirty or sticky, he simply had to wash them and could not focus on anything else until that task was complete. In fact, if he got something in his mind that had to be done, then it had to be done before he could move on to the next thing.

In first grade he was tested by his school, and indeed, what we suspected was true. There were some issues with academics. But it seemed to be more than this. At this point I should say that the school was wonderful. It was at this time I realized just what an ally a good school system could be. Over time, more tests, outside consultations, and meetings were held until, finally, a diagnosis of Asperger syndrome was given. This diagnosis, however, never seemed to fit. As a parent, I continued to try and figure out if the experts were

(Continued)

(Continued)

right. As it turns out, they were not. Around 7 years of age, my son was diagnosed with Tourette's syndrome. Subsequently, he was diagnosed with a severe reading and math disability. This made sense and finally fit what we had been seeing. In every other aspect of his life, though, he did fine.

As a parent, it was like being hit in the stomach. I was sad for my child, and irritated at others around me who had children that seemed to be developing fine and who seemed unwilling to give my child a chance. I was angry with adults who wouldn't invite him over or include him in activities. Even relatives who thought he acted strange were the subjects of my irritation. You just want others to see in your child what you see. You find yourself defensive and trying to prevent your child, at least initially, from seeing himself as different. And then the work began with the school—the place he was to spend the majority of his life until age 18.

I have to say that my involvement with our school system has been, for the most part, excellent but, at times, very frustrating. As a parent, I was a bit intimidated by my son's teachers and by the administrative staff. While I trusted the school system, I wasn't about to sit back and let it totally direct his education. We had him evaluated outside the school system by a private therapist and had him seen by a pediatric neuropsychologist, who subsequently came to the school to meet with the faculty. I attended all meetings and read everything I could get my hands on. I volunteered for everything so I could be nearby, and I even acted as his aide in math class. His teachers were more than happy to have me, and I always felt welcomed by them in the classroom.

By educating myself I was able to be a key member of his educational team and not just a bystander, letting others call the shots. Because the educational team members knew I was involved, they made every effort to include me and to keep me completely informed. We did not always agree, however, on the direction his education should take, but it was not just academics that were at issue here.

I learned early on that sometimes academics had to come second to activities that allowed him a social outlet. Our son had difficulty understanding social cues. He had trouble with peer relationships. He wanted so much to have friends, but for the most part his peers had little to do with him. He was made fun of, laughed at, and rarely included in social events such as spend-the-night gatherings, parties, or even groups on the playground. You see, he had a hard time understanding and learning the rules of games, such as football. The light hurt his eyes, and the noises hurt his ears. He has trouble even now remembering information. He does not feel the passage of time and cannot tell you how many days there are in a year or a month, nor can he easily figure out how to divide something in half. Yet, he presents to the world as being very "normal." Everyone expects him to be able to do those things, and when he can't, they laugh and call him names. He has been bullied in the halls, at lunch, out in public, and on the Internet to the point where we had to threaten to bring charges against some of his peers.

The school has been an ally for us. Teachers and administrators have been available to answer my questions and to advocate for him. They have made sure that tests and study guides are appropriate and, when they are not, have allowed him extra time to study or to retake tests. They have provided guidance to me so that I can help from home, and I think, most important, they recognize that he is trying and that he does the best he can. They have, on many occasions, tried to educate other students about how to treat others and have allowed me time to talk to his peers about Tourette's syndrome in an attempt to educate them.

It hasn't always been easy. There have been times that I have had to go to war over him. Middle school was particularly hard. Part of the difficulty may have been because we had such a good experience in elementary school. Going from the protected environment of elementary school to middle school where he knew so few of the children in his class, where he was made fun of in the halls, and where he had so many different teachers was extremely difficult to deal with. But he survived, and things are better now that we are in high school.

For now at least, my son is doing well. He has made the transition to high school and has found his niche. He is in the marching band and loves it. He no longer has to participate in classes that are so over his head as to be embarrassing for him. He has a case coordinator who works well with him and who helps us with his class schedule. Because he will graduate with a diploma that is vocational in nature, he takes classes that are geared to his individual needs and not college prep courses. Vocational rehabilitation will start working with him, and he will soon begin to decide what kind of job he wants and begin training toward that goal. His teachers are very helpful and have shown tremendous flexibility with him.

As his parents, we are still protective and still very much involved in his life. But even I am having to back off a bit. He is a teenager now and will soon be driving (he just got his permit), which is bit scary, but I realize he is growing up and must learn to stand on his own. He will do well. After all, school is the only time in your life where you are expected to be good at everything. He will soon start choosing his path in life. I find that my anger has finally begun to subside and that I am growing more comfortable all the time with the outlook for his future. He has friends, particularly those at church, who love him. He has siblings who watch out for him. He is growing up quite nicely and is truly a young man with a mind and faith of his own. I could not be more proud.

— *Anonymous*

Variability in Cultural and Social Standards of Behavior

Kauffman and Landrum (2009) observe that only a few behaviors are universally recognized as abnormal in every cultural group and across all social strata. Examples of behaviors that appear to deviate from nearly all cultural norms are muteness, serious self-injury, eating one's feces, and murder. In contrast, the majority of behaviors considered to be disordered are labeled as such because they violate standards that are specific to an individual's culture and social milieu. Hitting others, swearing, sexual behavior, and physical aggression are but a few of the behaviors in which normative standards vary markedly across cultures.

Excluding students thought to be socially maladjusted from the IDEA definition of emotional disturbance is controversial.

Federal Definition

The Individuals with Disabilities Education Improvement Act (IDEA), or PL 108–446, uses the term **emotional disturbance** to describe the population referred to in this chapter as those with emotional or behavioral disorders. The federal definition of emotional disturbance, modeled after one proposed by Eli Bower (1960), is as follows:

> The term means a condition exhibiting one or more of the following characteristics over a long period of time and to a marked degree that adversely affects a child's educational performance:
>
> - An inability to learn that cannot be explained by intellectual, sensory, or health factors.
> - An inability to build or maintain satisfactory interpersonal relationships with peers and teachers.
> - Inappropriate types of behavior or feelings under normal circumstances.
> - A general pervasive mood of unhappiness or depression.
> - A tendency to develop physical symptoms or fears associated with personal or school problems.
>
> The term includes schizophrenia. The term does not apply to children who are socially maladjusted, unless it is determined that they have an emotional disturbance. [34 C.F.R. § 300.8(c)(4)]

Since the passage of Public Law 94–142 in the mid-1970s, only two changes have been made to this definition: (1) Autism, originally included in this category, became a separate disability category in 1990. (2) Prior to 1997, the term used was *serious emotional disturbance*.

In contrast to the current federal definition, Bower's (1960, 1981) definition did *not* exclude students considered to be **socially maladjusted.** Rather, Bower intended for the five components of the definition to be indicators of social maladjustment (Bower, 1982). Although there is much professional disagreement regarding the definition of social maladjustment, the following one is typical:

> [Students who are socially maladjusted] are those whose social, not emotional, behaviors inhibit meaningful normative growth and development. Specifically, they disregard or defy authority, refuse to meet minimal standards of conduct required in regular schools relating to society's normative expectations. . . . They are chronic social offenders. (Raiser & Van Nagel, 1980, p. 519)

Social maladjustment is often equated with **conduct disorders**, one of the most common psychiatric disorders among children and youth, and there have been many attempts to exclude these children and youth from special education and related services (Jensen, 2005). In your classroom, you may have a difficult time understanding why these students may not qualify for special education and related services, as you will probably perceive them as being very disabled by their behavior. You will not be alone in this perception. The Council for Children with Behavioral Disorders (CCBD) and others have been most vocal and active in advocating for the inclusion of students with conduct disorders in the federal definition (Council for Children with Behavioral Disorders, 1990; Forness & Kavale, 2000).

Subsequent research has supported neither the five criteria nor the "socially maladjusted" exclusionary clause in the current federal definition (Cullinan, 2007). Many have argued that this definition is not sufficient for identifying the full range of emotional or behavioral disorders found among children and youth (Crundwell & Killu, 2007; Newcomer, 2003). Other criticisms have targeted the ambiguity of such terms as *a long period of time, to a marked degree, inability to learn*, and *pervasive* (Forness & Kavale, 2000; Kerr & Nelson, 2010). The phrase *adversely affects a child's educational performance* has been criticized because at times it has been narrowly interpreted to mean only academic performance and not performance related to critical behavioral, social, and vocational skills. Rosenberg et al. (2004) criticize the phrase *inability to learn* because it may give the impression that children and youth with emotional or behavioral disorders do not have the capacity to learn—a conclusion that is simply untrue.

Contemporary Terminology and Definitions

In 1990, more than thirty special education advocacy and professional organizations began to collaborate with professionals in mental health fields in an attempt to establish a more workable and functional definition. This group of professionals, known as the Mental Health and Special Education Coalition, has been most active in advocating for changes in the federal definition (Forness & Kavale, 2000). One of its recommendations was to change the term *serious emotional disturbance* to *emotional or behavioral disorder*. The latter term is generally accepted in the field today because it (1) has greater utility; (2) is more representative of the students who experience problems with their emotions, their behavior, or both; and (3) is less stigmatizing than *emotional disturbance*.

The definition proposed by this coalition is as follows:

> The term *emotional or behavioral disorder* means a disability that is
>
> - characterized by behavioral or emotional responses in school programs so different from appropriate age, cultural, or ethnic norms that the responses adversely affect educational performance, including academic, social, vocational, and personal skills;
> - more than a temporary, expected response to stressful events in the environment;
> - consistently exhibited in two different settings, at least one of which is school-related; and
> - unresponsive to direct intervention applied in general education, or the condition of the child is such that general education interventions would be insufficient.

> The term includes such a disability that co-exists with other disabilities.
>
> The term includes a schizophrenic disorder, affective disorder, anxiety disorder, or other sustained disorder of conduct or adjustment, affecting a child if the disorder affects educational performance as described [above]. (McIntyre & Forness, 1996, p. 5)

Despite the many advantages of this proposed definition, little progress has been made to date toward incorporating it into federal law. Opponents have argued that it would result in an enormous influx of students with behavioral problems, severely straining the financial resources of federal and state governments (Webber & Plotts, 2008). Research, however, suggests this may not be the case, and many special educators support the integration of this definition into federal legislation (Forness & Kavale, 2000).

Classification of Individuals With Emotional or Behavioral Disorders

The term *emotional or behavioral disorders* encompasses a wide range of disorders. When a student is given this broad label, educators know very little about the specific nature or characteristics of the student's disability. To provide greater clarity and specificity, educators and mental health professionals have attempted to classify the many different types of emotional or behavioral disorders. Thus, for example, if a student is identified as having a conduct disorder, educators can anticipate that the student's behavior will be characterized by acting-out, aggressive, and rule-violating behavior. This pattern can be distinguished from schizophrenia, which is characterized by disturbances in thought processes, hallucinations, and bizarre behavior.

Two widely used classification systems are pertinent to the field of education. **Clinically derived classification systems** have been developed by psychiatrists and mental health professionals to describe childhood, adolescent, and adult mental disorders. The most widely used psychiatric, or clinically derived, classification system in the United States is the *Diagnostic and Statistical Manual of Mental Disorders* (4th ed., text rev., or DSM-IV-TR), which was revised by the American Psychiatric Association (APA) in 2000. **Statistically derived classification systems** are developed using sophisticated statistical techniques to analyze the patterns or "dimensions" of behaviors that characterize children and youth with emotional or behavioral disorders.

Clinically Derived Classification Systems

In general, there are no "tests" available to medical professionals to diagnose emotional or behavioral disorders among children and youth. For many years, psychiatrists and other mental health professionals have relied on clinically derived classification systems, such as the DSM-IV-TR, to assist them in making psychiatric diagnoses. These systems group behaviors into diagnostic categories and provide criteria useful for making diagnoses. Clinically derived systems also include descriptions of symptoms, indicators of severity, prevalence estimates, and information about variations of disorders. To make a diagnosis, psychiatrists and other mental health professionals may observe an individual's behavior over time and across different settings and then compare these behaviors to diagnostic criteria provided in a classification system.

Although such systems in the past have focused primarily on adult disorders, in recent years they have increasingly included disorders found among children (House, 2002; Wicks-Nelson & Israel, 2009), including attention deficit hyperactivity disorder, conduct disorder, pervasive developmental disorders, schizophrenia, anxiety disorders, depressive disorders, mood disorders, psychoactive substance abuse disorders, dissociative disorders, and adjustment disorders. A psychiatric diagnosis does not mean, however, that a child will qualify for special education and related services (Forness, Walker, & Kavale, 2003). Although many students with psychiatric diagnoses are eligible for special education, such eligibility is independent of, and uses criteria different from, those criteria found in a clinically derived classification system (Kauffman & Landrum, 2009).

Statistically Derived Classification Systems

Some researchers use sophisticated statistical techniques to establish categories, "dimensions," or patterns of disordered behavior that appear to be common among children and youth with emotional or behavioral disorders. Using these methods, researchers have been able to develop normative standards across a variety of dimensions to assist in making important decisions, such as eligibility for special education and related services.

Audio Link 8.1
Listen to more about depression.

Two global dimensions that have been consistently identified are **externalizing disorders** and **internalizing disorders** (Achenbach & Edelbrock, 1978, 2001). Externalizing disorders, sometimes referred to as "undercontrolled" disorders, are characterized by aggressiveness, tempter tantrums, acting out, and noncompliant behaviors. Externalizing disorders are disturbing to others and generally result in considerable disruption in the classroom. In contrast, internalizing disorders, sometimes referred to as "overcontrolled" disorders, are characterized by social withdrawal, depression, compulsions, and anxiety. Children and youth with internalizing disorders are far less likely to be identified by their teachers and families as having an emotional or behavioral disorder because they do not create the "chaos" that often characterizes children and youth with externalizing disorders. These internalizing disorders, however, are equally serious; if left untreated, they

TABLE 8.1 Quay and Peterson's Dimensions of Problem Behaviors

Conduct Disorder	This dimension is characterized by physical aggression, difficulty controlling anger, open disobedience, and oppositionality.
Socialized Aggression	This dimension includes behaviors similar to conduct disorders except that children and youth display these behaviors in the company of others. Behaviors include stealing and substance abuse in the company of others, truancy from school, gang membership, stealing, and lying.
Attention Problems/ Immaturity	This dimension is often associated with attention deficit disorder. It includes behaviors such as short attention span, diminished concentration, distractibility, and impulsivity, as well as behaviors such as passivity, undependability, and childishness.
Anxiety/Withdrawal	This dimension is related to internalizing disorders. It includes behaviors related to poor self-confidence and self-esteem, hypersensitivity to criticism and rejection, generalized fearfulness and anxiety, and reluctance to try new behaviors because of fear of failure.
Psychotic Behavior	This dimension includes psychotic symptoms such as speech disturbance, bizarre ideation, delusions, and impaired reality testing.
Motor Tension Excess	This dimension is characterized by overactivity, including restlessness, tension, and "jumpiness."

SOURCE: Adapted from H. Quay and D. Peterson, *Manual for the Revised Behavior Problem Checklist* (Odessa, FL: Psychological Assessment Resources, 1996), p. 1. Reproduced by special permission of the publisher, Psychological Assessment Resources, Inc., 16204 North Florida Avenue, Lutz, Florida 33549, from the *Revised Behavior Problem Checklist* by Herbert Quay, Ph.D. Copyright 1983, 1996 by PAR, Inc. Further reproduction is prohibited without permission of PAR, Inc.

can lead to a variety of negative long-term outcomes, including suicide (U.S. Department of Education, 2000). In general, males tend to be at more risk for developing externalizing disorders, whereas females appear to be at greater risk for developing internalizing disorders (Webber & Plotts, 2008). However, when females with externalizing disorders are identified, their problems may be more severe than those of their male counterparts (Nelson et al., 2003).

Other dimensions have also emerged from statistically derived procedures. Perhaps the best-known dimensions are those reported by Quay and Peterson (1996), reflected in the six scales of their Revised Behavior Problem Checklist (see Table 8.1). This behavioral rating scale is used by many educators to identify children and youth with emotional or behavioral disorders.

Some interesting findings in current research suggest that children and youth with emotional or behavioral disorders rarely exhibit problems along only one dimension. Rather, they often have elevated levels along two or more dimensions (Forness, 2003). In fact, researchers (Forness, Kavale, & Davanzo, 2002; Nelson et al., 2003) note that the co-occurrence of disorders may be the norm rather than the exception. For example, a student may have both a conduct disorder and attention problems. The fact that disorders often co-occur means that the students in your classroom will often present very complex behaviors, frequently requiring multifaceted interventions designed to address a wide range of behaviors.

A Brief History of the Field

The inclusion of students with emotional or behavioral disorders in public schools is a relatively recent phenomenon. Throughout history, the nature of this disability has frequently resulted in stigma and ostracism by society in general, and exclusion from education in particular. Even today, as we have seen, there is debate and controversy regarding whether or not these students should be educated in our public schools.

The historical roots of the field of emotional or behavioral disorders are intertwined with the history of other fields of study—most notably, intellectual disabilities, psychiatry, and psychology (Kauffman & Landrum, 2009). Not until 1886 was a legal distinction made between "insanity" and "feeblemindedness" (Hayman, 1939). This distinction was an important one, as it marked the separation of emotional or behavioral disorders from mental retardation. Differentiating the history of emotional or behavioral disorders from that of mental retardation before that time is difficult. Because this common history has been detailed in the chapter on intellectual disabilities, this historical review begins with the twentieth century. Unless otherwise noted, the historical account that follows is based on a synthesis of several substantive resources: Despert (1965), Kauffman & Landrum, Lewis (1974), Rie (1971), and Safford and Safford (1996).

The Mental Hygiene Movement

In 1909, Ellen Key published *The Century of the Child,* a most prophetic work in that much progress was made in educating and treating children and youth with emotional or behavioral disorders during the twentieth century. The first teacher training program in special education appeared in Michigan in 1914, and school psychology as a specialized field began to emerge.

Many other events of the first two decades of the century helped promote more effective treatment of individuals with *emotional disturbance*, a term that first began to be used around 1910. In 1908, Clifford Beers published *A Mind That Found Itself,* in which he described his nervous breakdown and subsequent maltreatment in a mental hospital. This book profoundly influenced public opinion, and Beers collaborated with two prominent leaders in mental health, Adolf Meyer and William James, to establish the National

Committee for Mental Hygiene in 1909. The founding of this committee began the mental hygiene movement, which focused on efforts such as detection, prevention, and rehabilitation in the schools.

The mental hygiene movement was greatly influenced by Sigmund Freud's work on infant sexuality and psychosocial development. Because of Freud's emphasis on early childhood experiences, children and youth became a major focus of study and research. Freud's work formed the foundation for many of the first attempts to formally educate children and youth with emotional or behavioral disorders during the first several decades of the twentieth century. Psychiatrist William Healy and psychologist Grace Fernald, founders of the Juvenile Psychopathic Institute in Chicago in 1909, used Freudian or psychodynamic methods. Similarly, the National Committee for Mental Hygiene established several children's clinics in the United States, each of which adopted Freudian theory as its treatment approach.

Near the end of this period, a very different body of research began to emerge, one that would profoundly influence special educators throughout the remainder of the twentieth century. John Watson introduced behaviorism to North America in his 1913 essay "Psychology as a Behaviorist Views It."

Early Research on Emotional or Behavioral Disorders

In the 1920s and 1930s, numerous longitudinal studies were undertaken on child development. This knowledge base led to the development of more effective educational programs for children and youth with emotional or behavioral disorders. Additionally, several prominent organizations were formed in the 1920s, including the American Orthopsychiatric Association and the Council for Exceptional Children. The first psychiatric hospital was founded in Rhode Island in 1931, and schools that specialized in the treatment of children and youth with emotional or behavioral disorders, especially those with psychotic disorders, were established. For example, Loretta Bender began her pioneering work with children with schizophrenia at her school located at the Bellevue Psychiatric Clinic in New York City in 1934. Bellevue School subsequently became a fertile training ground for many future leaders in the field of special education. In 1935, Leo Kanner published *Child Psychiatry,* the first textbook on child psychiatry published in the United States. Finally, in the 1930s, Dr. Karl Menninger's work stressed the importance of addressing the "total environment" when treating individuals with emotional or behavioral disorders, and his work greatly influenced psychiatry in the coming decades.

The Birth of a Specialized Field of Study

The years 1940–1960 marked the birth of special education for children and youth with emotional or behavioral disorders as a specialized field of study. Many experimental educational programs were established at this time. In the 1940s, the state of New York opened a number of schools for youths considered to be emotionally disturbed. Also in the 1940s, Fritz Redl and David Wineman established the Pioneer House for delinquent and disturbed youth in Detroit. These educators pioneered the "Life-Space Interview," a technique that influenced subsequent generations of special educators.

The Depression and World War II hampered funding for research and education for children and youth with emotional or behavioral disorders. At the same time, however, these world events brought to the United States several Europeans who would become leaders in special education. In the field of emotional or behavioral disorders, perhaps the most notable of these individuals was Bruno Bettelheim, who became a prominent leader in educational methods based on psychoanalytic theory. Although experimental programs for educating children and youth with emotional or behavioral disorders were developed from 1940 to 1960, many children and youth with emotional or behavioral disorders were still being denied a public education.

TABLE 8.2 Conceptual Models of Emotional or Behavioral Disorders

Model	Approach
Behavioral	Based on the work of B. F. Skinner and other behavioral psychologists, this model assumes that behavior is a function of environmental events. Maladaptive behaviors are thought to be learned and maintained by the environment. Seeks to establish a replicable cause–effect relationship. Uses systematic observations and data collection procedures. Behavior can be modified by changing antecedent or consequent events. Frank Hewett's "engineered" classroom, described in his book *The Emotionally Disturbed Child in the Classroom* (1968), was constructed around a behavioral approach.
Psychodynamic	Based on the thinking of Sigmund Freud and his followers, this model proposes that disturbed behaviors are symptomatic of underlying conflict between hypothetical mental functions (id, ego, superego) that are in dynamic interaction. Unconscious motivation for behavior must be understood in order for intervention to be successful. Individual psychotherapy for the student (and sometimes the parents) is frequently used to uncover deep-rooted problems typically originating in the child's past. A permissive classroom environment and an accepting teacher are also called for.
Psychoeducational	Like the psychoanalytic model, this approach emphasizes unconscious motivations and underlying conflicts, but it is balanced by the realistic demands of functioning at home, at school, and in the community. Teachers attempt to gain an understanding of the child's unconscious motivation for problem behaviors through therapeutic conversations (Life-Space Interviews) and try to help the student gain insight and acquire self-control through planning and reflection. *Conflict in the Classroom* (1965) by Nicholas Long, William Morse, and Ruth Newman offers a perspective on the psychoeducational model.
Ecological	This model attributes behavioral problems to the student's interactions in the family, at school, and in the community. Problematic behavior results from a lack of a "goodness of fit" between the student and the particular social milieu. Intervention attempts to alter the social settings and the transactions occurring therein. Project Re-ED, a residential treatment program established by Nicholas Hobbs in 1961, is an example of this approach.
Humanistic	This model, arising from the social-political movement of the 1960s and 1970s, stresses self-direction, self-fulfillment, and self-evaluation. Pupils are encouraged to be free and open. It is assumed that children are capable of generating their own solutions to their problems when provided with a caring and supportive environment where teachers are nonauthoritarian.
Biogenic	Underlying this model is a belief that emotional or behavioral disorders, such as depression or hyperaggression, are the result of physiological flaws. Treatments, therefore, may consist of drug therapy, biofeedback, dietary management, or even surgery. The Feingold diet, popular in the 1970s as a treatment for hyperactivity, is an example of this model.

SOURCE: J. M. Kauffman, *Characteristics of Emotional and Behavioral Disorders of Children and Youth,* 8th ed., © 2005. Adapted with permission of Pearson Education, Inc., Upper Saddle River, NJ.

The Emergence of Conceptual Models

In the 1960s, research on classroom programs, practices, and curricula for children and youth with emotional or behavioral disorders appeared in the professional literature for the first time. These publications presented a variety of conceptual models that had evolved during the preceding decades, many of which remain prominent in special education programs today. The emergence of these models, representing various theoretical approaches with differing assumptions and strategies, was one of the most significant developments in the field. (See Table 8.2 for a brief description of some of these models.) Educators now had a variety of approaches to use with pupils who exhibited emotional or behavioral disorders. As Kauffman and Landrum (2009) point out, practitioners are seldom guided exclusively by a single model; in many instances, teachers incorporate a number of different viewpoints in their work.

Besides the emergence of these conceptual models, several other important events occurred between 1960 and 1980. Substantial progress was made in the identification and assessment of students with emotional or behavioral disorders. Specifically, the works of Bower (1960) and Quay and Peterson (1975) provided assessment tools for identifying this population of students and also increased our understanding of the nature of emotional and behavioral disorders. In 1964, the Council for Children with Behavioral Disorders (CCBD) was formed, creating one of the world's largest professional organizations in this field of study. Public funding was generated to prepare teachers to work with children with emotional or behavioral disorders in 1963 through the enactment of PL 88–164. Finally, the passage of PL 94–142 in 1975 led to the formal inclusion of these students in public education for the first time.

Prevalence of Emotional or Behavioral Disorders

How prevalent are emotional and behavioral disorders among school-age children and youth? The answer to this question is not a simple one; prevalence estimates for this population vary widely. Among the reasons for this variance are conflicting definitions and a lack of consensus on what constitutes acceptable behavior.

From a historical perspective, the percentage of public school students receiving special education under this category grew from 0.5 percent in the mid-1970s to 1.0 percent in the mid-1980s. Since that time, however, growth in this category, unlike many other IDEA disability categories, has been negligible or even negative (Kauffman & Landrum, 2009). The number of students being served under this category is far lower than the original federal estimate of 2 percent (U.S. Department of Education, 1980). Moreover, this estimate is considered extremely conservative by many professionals in the field (Cullinan, 2007). Students with emotional or behavior disorders are considered to be the most underidentified of all IDEA disability categories (Landrum, Katsiyannis, & Archwamety, 2004).

The U.S. Department of Education (2010) reports that during the 2008–2009 school year, 418,068 students ages 6–21 were receiving a special education and related services because of an emotional disturbance. This number represents 7.0 percent of the total number of students served in special education, making this the fifth largest disability category for students in this age range.

At the preschool level, the U.S. Department of Education (2010) reports that only 3,488 children ages 3–5 were identified as emotionally disturbed during the 2008–2009 school year. This low level of identification may be due to at least two factors. First, because there is an emphasis on noncategorical labeling at the preschool level and in the early elementary grades, many students who ultimately are identified as emotionally disturbed may be labeled as developmentally delayed during the early childhood years. Second, school personnel may be hesitant to identify a youngster as emotionally disturbed during the early childhood years (Cullinan, 2007).

Although less than 1 percent of the school-age population currently receives special education services for emotional or behavioral disorders (U.S. Department of Education, 2010), credible studies in the United States indicate that at least 3 percent to 6 percent of children and youth exhibit serious and persistent problems (Blanchard, Gurka, & Blackman, 2006; Kauffman & Landrum, 2009). Numerous reasons have been offered for the underidentification of students with emotional or behavioral disorders. One major reason is the marked variability across states in identifying pupils with emotional or behavioral disorders (Kauffman & Landrum). The range of students receiving a special education during the 2007–2008 school year varies from a low of .13 percent in Arkansas to a high of 1.45 percent in Minnesota (U.S. Department of Education, 2009). Recall that IDEA allows states to adopt their own definitions, provided that state definitions identify an equivalent group of students. In fact, state definitions vary so widely that identification may be more a function of where an individual lives than of any other factor. Kauffman and Landrum believe that social policy and economic factors also play critical roles in underidentification.

Etiology of Emotional or Behavioral Disorders

Our understanding of the causes of emotional or behavioral disorders has increased substantially in recent years. A major milestone was the publication in the late nineties of a national report, *Mental Health: A Report of the Surgeon General* (Satcher, 1999). For the first time in history, the country's most prominent health care leader, the surgeon general, recognized that addressing the needs of both children and adults with mental illness is a pressing national concern.

This report describes the research regarding many of the risk factors associated with mental disorders of childhood. These risk factors often interact in a synergetic fashion; as the number of risk factors increases, so do the chances of negative outcomes such as emotional or behavioral disorders.

Biological Risk Factors

Although most professionals agree that the development of emotional or behavioral disorders is due to both biological and environmental factors, there has been increased consensus that biological factors are particularly influential in the etiology of several disorders. These emotional or behavioral disorders can be the result of either genetic influences or biological insults. Disorders that most likely have a genetic influence include autism, bipolar disorder, schizophrenia, social phobia, obsessive-compulsive disorder, and Tourette's syndrome. Biological insults such as injury, infection, lead poisoning, poor nutrition, or exposure to toxins (including intrauterine exposure to alcohol, illicit drugs, or cigarette smoke) may also influence the development of emotional or behavioral disorders.

Numerous studies suggest that infant temperament (that is, an infant born with a "difficult" temperament) may precede the development of emotional or behavioral disorders (Rosenblum, Dayton, & Muzik, 2009; Shaw, Gilliom, & Giovannelli, 2005; Webber & Plotts, 2008). Despite the early research in this area, more recent studies indicate that "difficult" infant temperament can be mediated to some extent by the environment (Kauffman & Landrum, 2009).

Research indicates that as many as 50 percent of students with emotional or behavioral disorders have additional disabilities (National Institute of Mental Health, 2008). For example, some students with conduct disorders are also depressed; in fact, these children often have a family history of depression (National Institute of Mental Health, 2010). Parental depression also increases the risk of children and youth developing anxiety disorders, conduct disorder, and alcohol dependency.

Suicide among depressed children and youth is a major concern in our society. Studies suggest that more than 90 percent of children and adolescents who have committed suicide had an apparent, though not identified, emotional or behavioral disorder before their deaths. Table 8.3 lists some of the warning signs of an impending suicide. As an educator, you need to be especially alert to these warning signs and be sure to report them to parents, counselors, administrators, and other appropriate professionals.

Psychosocial Risk Factors

Research suggests that conduct disorders have both biological and environmental components, with substantial psychosocial risk factors involved in their development. Environmental factors such as parental discord, a parent's mental illness or criminal behavior, overcrowding in the home, and large family size may result in conditions conducive to the development of conduct disorders—especially if the child or youth does not have a loving, nurturing relationship with at least one parent. Other risk factors include early maternal rejection and family neglect and abuse.

Poverty has been shown to be a significant risk factor for the development of emotional or behavioral disorders, as it often translates into increased family stress, poor health care, underachievement, and other negative outcomes. The United States has one

TABLE 8.3 Behavioral Suicide Warning Signs

Behavior	Manifestations
Quiet, withdrawn, few friends	Often not recognized because the individual is not noticed and makes no obvious trouble.
Changes in behavior	Personality changes—e.g., from friendliness to withdrawal, lack of communication, and sad and expressionless appearance, or from a quiet demeanor to acting out and troublemaking.
Increased failure or role strain	Often pervasive in school, work, home, friends, and love relationships, but often manifested clearly in school pressures for young people.
Recent family changes	Illness, job loss, increased consumption of alcohol, poor health, etc.
Recent loss of a family member	Death, divorce, separation, or someone leaving home.
Feelings of despair and hopelessness*	Shows itself in many forms, from changes in posture and behavior to verbal expression of such feelings.
Symptomatic acts	Taking unnecessary risks, becoming involved in drinking and drug abuse, becoming inappropriately aggressive or submissive, giving away possessions.
Communication*	Such statements as "Life is not worth living," "I'm finished," "Might as well be dead," or "I wish I were dead."
Presence of a plan*	Storing up medication, buying a gun.

*To be viewed with heightened concern.

SOURCE: Adapted from the Crisis Center, *Ten Behavioral Suicide Warning Signs* (Birmingham, AL: n.d.).

of the highest poverty rates of all developed countries (Children's Defense Fund, 2010). Although emotional and behavioral disorders occur among all socioeconomic classes, children who live in poverty may be at especially high risk (Kauffman & Landrum, 2009).

One important finding in recent years is that biological and environmental factors often are not mutually independent influences in the development of emotional or behavioral disorders; that is, one may directly influence the other (Rutter, 2006). For example, attention deficit hyperactivity disorder may have biological origins, but the difficult behaviors of children and youth with ADHD often influence and change their relationships with significant others in their lives (Wicks-Nelson & Israel, 2009). In these exchanges, coercive interactions may occur, thus creating a negative environment that may worsen the condition. Consider, for example, the following scenario:

> Jesse, a fourth grader with attention deficit hyperactivity disorder, genuinely dislikes completing his math worksheets. During this time, he often talks out, gets out of his seat, and is noncompliant and disrespectful to his teacher to avoid completing these tasks. His noncompliant and disruptive behavior often escalates to the point that he is sent to the office. Consequently, Jesse is negatively reinforced as his avoidance behavior is reinforced. Additionally, his teacher may be negatively reinforced if he or she views Jesse's noncompliant and disrespectful behavior as aversive. This means that both individuals are more likely in the future to engage in the same behavior, creating a coercive cycle that strengthens the behaviors of both Jesse and his teacher.

As a teacher, you need to be aware of the coercive nature of these interactions and how you may be able to disrupt coercive cycles. By understanding that the function of Jesse's behavior is escape or avoidance, you can respond to him in more productive ways. For example, you could reinforce Jesse's on-task behavior and not engage in exchanges that allow him to escape or avoid his assignments. Additionally, you have the power to change the nature of the assignment (worksheets) to one that is less aversive for him (for example, allowing him to use drill-and-practice software).

The role of **child maltreatment** in the development of a number of emotional or behavioral disorders is well established (Kauffman & Landrum, 2009). Child maltreatment has been associated with such problems as depression, conduct disorder, posttraumatic stress disorder, delinquency, and attention deficit hyperactivity disorder. Child maltreatment includes neglect, physical abuse, sexual abuse, and emotional abuse; Table 8.4 describes these four main types of child maltreatment. As a teacher, your role is critical in identifying and reporting your suspicions of child maltreatment to law enforcement and social service agencies.

It is important to remember that no one cause is thought to exclusively contribute to the development of emotional or behavioral disorders; rather a complex and multifactored interaction of various risk factors may lead to the development of maladaptive and other challenging behaviors. The greater the number of risk factors and the longer the child is exposed, the greater the likelihood of long-term destructive consequences (Sprague & Walker, 2000). Still, we caution that "causality in the world of emotional and behavioral disorders is rarely linear; it rarely proceeds unambiguously from event A to outcome B" (Oswald, 2003, p. 202). Figure 8.1 portrays one possible pathway to long-term and destructive outcomes.

Children who live in poverty may be at especially high risk for developing emotional or behavioral disorders.

TABLE 8.4 Four Main Types of Child Maltreatment

- **Physical abuse** is characterized by the infliction of physical injury as a result of punching, beating, kicking, biting, burning, shaking, or otherwise harming a child. The parent or caretaker may not have intended to hurt the child; rather, the injury may have resulted from overdiscipline or physical punishment.
- **Child neglect** is characterized by failure to provide for the child's basic needs. Neglect can be physical, educational, or emotional.
  - **Physical neglect** includes refusal or delay in seeking health care, abandonment, expulsion from the home or refusal to allow a runaway to return home, and inadequate supervision.
  - **Educational neglect** includes the allowance of chronic truancy, failure to enroll a child of mandatory school age in school, and failure to attend to a special educational need.
  - **Emotional neglect** includes such actions as marked inattention to the child's need for affection, refusal or failure to provide needed psychological care, spousal abuse in the child's presence, and permission of drug or alcohol use by the child.

This assessment of child neglect requires consideration of cultural values and standards of care as well as recognition that the failure to provide the necessities of life may be related to poverty.

- **Sexual abuse** includes fondling a child's genitals, intercourse, incest, rape, sodomy, exhibitionism, and commercial exploitation through prostitution or the production of pornographic materials. Many experts believe that sexual abuse is the most underreported of child maltreatment because of the "conspiracy of silence" that so often characterizes these cases.
- **Emotional abuse (psychological abuse/verbal abuse/mental injury)** includes acts of omission by the parents or other caregivers that have caused, or could have caused, serious behavioral, cognitive, emotional, or mental disorders. In some cases of emotional abuse, the acts of parents or other caregivers alone, without any harm evident in the child's behavior or condition, are sufficient to warrant Child Protective Services intervention.

SOURCE: Based on 42 U.S.C. § 5101 *et seq.* Child Abuse Prevention and Treatment Act. Public Law 101–36, 2003.

TABLE 8.5 Common Assessment Strategies Used to Evaluate Students With Emotional or Behavioral Disorders

Strategy	Description/Purpose	Advantages and Disadvantages
Interviews with student, parents, and teachers	**Description:** Lists of specific questions presented by an interviewer to elicit responses from an informant. **Purpose:** To provide a picture of the student's presenting problems as perceived by the informant; provide information about the environmental context in which the problem behavior is occurring; provide important developmental, historical information about the student. Results are used to formulate assessment questions and subsequent assessment strategies.	**Advantages:** Can guide assessment process and address concerns of all those involved with the student, as well as the student. **Disadvantages:** Reliability and validity are difficult to establish; informants may provide inaccurate information; interviewer bias may occur.
Examination of student records	**Description:** Inspection of cumulative records, disciplinary history, and other records of school achievement/performance. **Purpose:** To provide documentation that problems have existed over time and give some indication of whether the student's behavior may be affecting learning.	**Advantages:** Provides information on whether other factors (e.g., excessive absences, frequent school changes) may explain the behavior; documents behavior over time; addresses impact on learning. **Disadvantages:** Records may be incomplete or inaccurate.
Parent, teacher, and student rating scales	**Description:** Typically comprised of items that an informant rates in terms of severity (e.g., mild, moderate, severe) or frequency of occurrence (e.g., never, seldom, often). **Purpose:** Rating scales may be formal or informal. Formal rating scales are often used to determine eligibility, as they provide normative comparisons regarding children's behavior. Informal scales serve many purposes, such as identification of particular points in the day when problematic behavior occurs.	**Advantages:** Allow for normative comparisons that enable school personnel to make decisions regarding eligibility; enable educators to assess the student across informants (e.g., parents, teacher, students); are easy, quick, and inexpensive. **Disadvantages:** Possible rater bias and subjectivity. Also, many rating scales adopt a deficit-based, as opposed to a strength-based, assessment approach.
Observations in natural settings	**Description:** Anecdotal observations are narrative recordings (i.e., a written, running record) of student behavior; they are often used to identify the possible functions or purposes of student's behavior. Systematic observations reflect quantified accounts of student's behavior (e.g., how many times and for how long a student is out of seat). **Purpose:** To provide a picture of the student's spontaneous behavior in everyday settings; provide a systematic record of the student's behavior that can be used for intervention; provide verification of teacher and parent reports about the child's behavior.	**Advantages:** Provide an objective, quantifiable assessment of observable behavior; allow for a functional assessment of the student within the context of the natural environment (most systematic observations are sensitive to intervention effects). **Disadvantages:** Can be time-consuming; may not be representative or reflect behavior typical of the student; most lack normative data; may not be sensitive to variations in classroom normative standards.
Medical evaluations	**Description:** Psychiatric and other medical evaluations designed to diagnose emotional or behavioral disorders and/or other medical problems. **Purpose**: To rule in or out emotional or behavioral disorders and/or other medical conditions; may include identification of appropriate medical interventions, such as medication.	**Advantages:** Help ensure that a student's behavior is not the result of a medical condition unrelated to an emotional or behavioral disorder (e.g., allergic reaction, infection). **Disadvantages:** May not have much value in terms of educational interventions; are expensive and can be time-consuming.

Strategy	Description/Purpose	Advantages and Disadvantages
Standardized, norm-referenced assessments of intelligence, academics, and other areas of concern	**Description:** Measures of intelligence, academics (reading, math, writing), communication, motor skills, etc. **Purpose:** To rule in or out other areas of suspected disability; to provide normative comparisons of student abilities and performance; to assist in eligibility determination.	**Advantages:** Provide objective and normative comparisons of student abilities and performance levels; assist with eligibility decision making. **Disadvantages:** May not provide relevant information for intervention purposes; typically provide global, nonspecific information about student's abilities and performance levels.
Functional behavioral assessment	**Description:** Incorporates a variety of techniques and strategies to identify the causes (functions) of behavior; focus is on identifying biological, social, affective, and environmental factors that trigger and maintain the problematic behavior. **Purpose:** By determining the function of the behavior, interventions can be developed and implemented by manipulating antecedents to, and consequences following, the problematic behavior; designed to teach student more appropriate, alternative behavior and to prevent the behavior from occurring by providing positive behavioral supports.	**Advantages:** Is directly tied to intervention; helps teach the student more positive and appropriate behavior; serves as the foundation for positive behavior support; identifies environmental and other factors that may be contributing to the problematic behavior; provides a method for ongoing monitoring of the student's behavioral progress. **Disadvantages:** Requires considerable teacher training and can be time-consuming; may not always address important factors such as distorted cognitions and thought patterns and other nondirectly observable variables that contribute to problematic behavior.
Other informal assessment strategies such as examination of work samples, criterion-referenced tests, and curriculum-based assessment	**Description:** Include error analysis, analysis of instructional and curriculum variables that need to be considered when planning curriculum and instruction. **Purpose:** To identify specific strengths and needs of the student within the context of the general education (or independence) curriculum.	**Advantages:** Are directly tied to curriculum and instruction; provide considerable guidance for IEP development and implementation; provide a method for ongoing monitoring of the student's academic progress. **Disadvantages:** May be time-consuming and require teacher training.

too difficult, tedious and laborious assignments, or unclear expectations. By identifying the antecedents to a student's problematic behavior, the teacher can then take a preventive or proactive approach to intervention. For example, by knowing that assignments are too difficult for a student, the teacher can provide appropriate adaptations to facilitate the student's success and prevent acting-out behavior from ever occurring.

The consequences that follow a student's behavior are also important factors to consider when choosing appropriate interventions for children and youth with emotional or behavioral disorders. A student who finds work too difficult, for example, may act out in an effort to avoid or escape the task. If the student is successful in avoiding the task, he or she is reinforced for this acting-out behavior. Examples of consequences that may increase the likelihood of continued misbehavior include sensory stimulation, avoidance/escape, and attention. As a teacher, you need to be aware of your own possible role in the maintenance or escalation of a student's misbehavior. The consequences that follow a student's misbehavior may inadvertently reinforce the very behaviors you want to decrease.

Making Inclusion Work

Think back, if you will, and try to pinpoint the moment that you knew you wanted to be a teacher. For me, that moment came while standing on the tarmac of the outdoor basketball court in third grade. Each day, a very fair blonde girl just my age arrived by yellow school bus. She came to our school each day only for recess. She was nearly blind and stood on the court each day, staring at the sun and waving her hand in front of her eyes. I was saddened as to why she would not talk to me or play like the other kids. I told my mother that I wanted to learn more about this girl and what was wrong with her. She had a form of autism and, despite my efforts, I was unable to form a friendship with her. Teachers and students just left her alone, and I knew she must feel alone.

There are few things I remember about third grade except a very fair teacher, a teacher who yelled at me one time, and the girl I wanted so desperately to befriend. For those very reasons, I decided and declared during the middle of that year that I wanted to be a teacher—a teacher who would be fair and could help students with disabilities. Certainly, I would not be a teacher who yelled. It was important to me that all students felt included in everything about school. I felt so strongly that I never changed my mind or career path in twenty-plus years.

One of the benefits of spending many years in special education has been the opportunity to vicariously ride the swinging pendulum regarding the inclusion of students with special needs. As a teacher, counselor, and coordinator, all in the field of special education, I have seen and experienced the continuum of inclusion from the worst of times to what I consider the beginning of the best of times. What a great opportunity we have to grant each and every student the right to success they so desperately desire and deserve.

My very first job, some twenty-two years ago, was teaching students with emotional/behavioral disorders (E/BD) attending a separate special education school. Fourteen students, eleven boys and three girls, were brought by bus to our county school and somewhat thrown together in a self-contained classroom. The students' ages ranged from 14 through 21 and, although they were diagnosed as having E/BD, the disabilities and needs varied greatly. As a first-year teacher, survival was my objective, not teaching anyone to read or divide. Unfortunately, it was a terrifying, difficult year. As a teacher, I did not have the training or support needed to properly meet the needs of the students in my classroom. Students already typically deficient in social skills and academics were given scant opportunity for practice or success. In addition, there were virtually no positive peer role models within the classroom. I was discouraged because I knew we were letting these students down by separating them from the rest of the children. Needless to say, progress was minimal.

Fast-forward twenty-two years. I thankfully work in a society with an educational and legal system that now recognizes the benefits and need for inclusion of all students. It is a pleasure and honor to work with students and teachers preparing the way for meaningful inclusion of students. Not only do I get to work as a counselor and behavior interventionist with many students who have special needs, but I also teach at the

may influence student behavior. The teacher's desk should have a barrier-free view of all students and be positioned to allow the teacher to move quickly if a situation necessitates (Salend, 2011).

For students who need a quiet, distraction-free place to study, the use of study carrels may be helpful. If study carrels are used, teachers should make sure their use is continuously monitored and be cautious not to overuse them as they may isolate or stigmatize students if used excessively (Salend, 2011).

Classroom ambience, according to Di Giulio (2007), refers to the feeling one gets on entering a classroom. Some classrooms, when you enter them, just seem to have a sense of orderliness and pleasantness in terms of lighting, sound, visual appeal, temperature, and odor. As reported by Savage (1999), studies indicate that attractive classrooms influence students' behavior in positive ways. In contrast, unattractive classrooms have been associated with student reports of headaches, fatigue, and discomfort and with increased instances of teacher control statements and student conflicts. The implications of this research are that teachers should endeavor to make their classroom environments as attractive as possible.

Video Link 8.4
Watch additional strategies.

university level, training preservice general education and special education teachers. Whether I am in a public school or university classroom, I seize the occasion to champion the benefits of inclusion for students and teachers alike.

A predominant concern teachers have shared with me over the years is that they are willing to welcome most children with special needs into their classrooms if they are told how to include the students and what to do! The exception, however, is usually students with E/BD. The majority of these students want to be in a safe environment, and they crave structure, consistency, and predictability. An attitude geared toward welcoming any student into a safe learning environment is half of the formula for successful inclusion. Students will know if they are welcome in your classroom. They will likely feel welcomed and safe if you are clear about your expectations, are consistent, and are well prepared. Avoid assuming the worst and that students "can't." Assume they "can" with careful planning and preparation. Say what you mean and always mean what you say—follow through.

Preparation is so very important and may include modification of the curriculum, teaching styles, and classroom management procedures and practices. Does this mean you must change everything you do for one student? Absolutely not. It does mean that having students with special needs in your classroom should give you cause to reflect on your personal teaching style, strategies, tolerance levels, expectations, procedures, and behavior management style. Reflection on your practices as a teacher will shed light on your readiness to include all students, and you will be well on your way to making preparations for special-needs students.

Although this may all sound a bit overwhelming, the best news is that you are not alone. Collaboration may very well be the biggest key to successful inclusion. You will have access to a host of wisdom, knowledge, and experience from the professionals with whom you work. Take advantage. Be proactive with teachers and parents and learn as much about each student as possible. Access the special educators in your building and seek their knowledge regarding the special needs of your students. You may need to take the first step and ask for help. The special educator in your building may be hesitant as well, for fear of stepping on your turf. It is also important to establish your own relationship with the parents and well worth the effort to do so before the need arises to discuss a problem. Time spent getting to know each student personally is possibly the best investment. Once you know what interests a student, meaningful engagement in academics is more likely, and building of relationships will be easier. Collaborating and preplanning for the arrival of a student with special needs may mean the difference between success and failure for everyone. A favorite quote of mine comes from a third-grade student included for the very first time. After his first day in a general education class, I inquired how his day went and he responded, "Good. I got to be a real person today."

—*Teresa (Tracy) Teaff*
Formerly behavior interventionist, Arlington (Texas) Independent School District
Currently interim Provost and Vice President for Academic and Student Affairs
Texas A&M University–Central Texas

Academic and Instructional Interventions

Positive behavioral supports include providing effective academic content and instruction to students with emotional and behavioral disorders (Scheuermann & Hall, 2008). Although there has been much research on effective social–emotional behavioral interventions for students with emotional or behavioral disorders, the research on effective academic curriculum and instructional practices for these students has been limited.

The paucity of research on academic and instructional interventions is unfortunate given the high rates of academic failure experienced by these students. One significant way in which educators can help to minimize these negative long-term outcomes is through the provision of a sound academic program. There is a strong correlation between poor academic achievement and juvenile delinquency (Allen-DeBoer, Malmgren, & Glass, 2006). The hope is that if educators can design academic programs that strengthen the achievement levels of this population, delinquency rates will decrease. Academic achievement may serve as a critical protective or preventive factor for students with emotional or behavioral disorders.

Attractive classrooms influence students' behavior in positive ways.

Several researchers (Barton-Arwood, Wehby, & Falk, 2005; Lane, Little, Redding-Rhodes, Phillips, & Welsh, 2007) recommend a primary focus on academic interventions rather than social–emotional–behavioral interventions. Effective academic interventions may result not only in higher academic achievement but also in improved behavior (Nelson et al., 2004; Wehby, Falk, Barton-Arwood, Lane, & Cooley, 2003). Research suggests, however, that interventions that focus solely on improving behavior are not always accompanied by simultaneous improvement in academics. It is difficult for a student to be academically successful while simultaneously engaging in inappropriate behavior. To be effective, academic intervention must address two areas of concern: academic curriculum and instructional delivery. Academic curriculum includes the instructional programs or materials used by classroom teachers to teach specific content; instructional delivery refers to teaching skills or strategies that exist independently of instructional materials (Stein & Davis, 2000).

Academic Curriculum

In many respects, the academic curriculum for students with emotional or behavioral disorders mirrors that of students without disabilities. This population varies widely, however, in achievement and ability levels, and educators must adapt or modify the curriculum accordingly. PL 108–446 mandates that, to the maximum extent appropriate, students with disabilities have access to the general education curriculum. For students with emotional or behavioral disorders, this may necessitate appropriate supports and curriculum modifications. By incorporating students' interests into the curriculum, educators can enhance both the behavior and the academic engagement of these students. Thus, teachers should endeavor to design a curriculum that is both relevant and motivating for students with emotional and behavioral disorders.

Instructional Delivery

One important finding from research on students with emotional or behavioral disorders is that student–teacher instructional interactions are often very low, particularly when students are aggressive (Wehby, Symons, Canale, & Go, 1998). As a teacher, you must make an effort to engage often and substantively when providing instruction to students with emotional or behavioral disorders.

What limited research is available suggests that students with emotional or behavioral disorders benefit from certain teaching strategies (Scheuermann & Hall, 2008). Five strategies are discussed briefly here: effective instructional cycles, teaching mnemonics, self-monitoring strategies, curriculum-based measurement, and content enhancements.

Components of an **effective instructional cycle** include the following:

- Beginning each lesson with a statement of goals
- Beginning each lesson with a review of previous, prerequisite learning
- Presenting new material in small steps, with student practice following each step
- Providing active and sufficient practice for all students
- Asking many questions, checking frequently for student understanding, and obtaining responses from all students
- Providing systematic feedback and corrections to students
- Providing explicit instruction and practice for seatwork activities and, when necessary, actively monitoring students during these activities
- Continuing to provide practice until students are independent and confident (Rosenshine & Stevens, 1986)

Mnemonic strategies are tools for helping students recall facts and relationships. Mnemonic strategies have been found to be extremely effective in promoting academic achievement among students with disabilities, including those with emotional or behavioral disorders (Scruggs & Mastropieri, 2000). There are many different types of mnemonic strategies; a few of these are illustrated in Figure 8.5.

Self-monitoring strategies, such as assignment checklists and self-monitoring checklists, can be used to assist students with emotional or behavioral disorders. These strategies help students by providing the cues necessary to complete a task successfully. You may want to incorporate these strategies for all your students, not just those with emotional or behavioral disorders. See Figure 8.6 for an example of an academic self-monitoring checklist.

Curriculum-based measurement (CBM), according to Deno (1998), "is a standardized set of observational procedures for repeatedly measuring growth in core reading, writing, and arithmetic skills" (p. 12). By incorporating curriculum-based measurement into instructional delivery efforts, teachers can ensure that there is a close match between the content being presented and students' levels of achievement.

Content enhancements include graphic organizers, content diagrams, semantic maps, advance organizers, guided notes, and study guides. Content enhancements help students understand major concepts, ideas, and vocabulary in a manner that is conducive to knowledge acquisition, organization, and retrieval. These enhancements make explicit the content to be learned, link concepts together, and help students link new content to previously learned content.

Behavioral and Cognitive–Behavioral Interventions

Researchers (Cooper, Heron, & Heward, 2007) have identified two broad-based intervention approaches that have substantial support: behavior modification and

Transition Into Adulthood

Throughout this chapter, much emphasis has been placed on the negative long-term outcomes experienced by children and youth with emotional or behavioral disorders. Numerous studies indicate that the presence of emotional or behavioral disorders is a very accurate predictor of school failure, delinquency, adult psychiatric problems, and substance abuse (Lane et al., 2007). Youth with externalizing problems, such as conduct disorders, are at very high risk for psychiatric hospitalization, incarceration, and under- and unemployment (Wagner, Cameto, & Newman, 2003). Youth with internalizing disorders, such as anxiety and depression, are at heightened risk for negative long-term outcomes as well.

A particularly alarming statistic is that approximately 50 percent of students with emotional or behavioral disorders leave school before graduation—the highest dropout rate among all categories of students with disabilities (Kemp, 2006; Wagner, Newman, Cameto, Garza, & Levine, 2005). An equally disturbing finding is that the majority of students with emotional or behavioral disorders are not identified and served until their adolescent years. In stark contrast to students in other disability categories, who are identified and served at much earlier ages, the U.S. Department of Education (2009) reports that almost two thirds of all students receiving special education and related services because of emotional or behavioral disorders are adolescents. During the 2007–2008 school year, the peak age for placement of these students was 16 years of age. Clearly, educators need to work more aggressively to identify and serve this population at earlier ages and to implement effective dropout prevention and transition programs.

Relative to students with other types of disabilities, there is a conspicuous absence of research on effective transition programming for adolescents with emotional or behavioral disorders (Corbett, Clark, & Blank, 2002). This lack of research, coupled with the dismal findings on long-term outcomes for students with emotional or behavioral disorders, emphasizes the need for effective vocational training for students with emotional or behavioral disorders (U.S. Department of Education, 2003).

To plan effectively for the transition of adolescents with emotional or behavioral disorders from school to adulthood, educators need to understand that these students have a developmental disability that will require intervention throughout their life span. This means that transition planning needs to be comprehensive and broad-based. Transition services need to go well beyond just preparing these students for employment. Rather, there is a need to view transition in terms of postsecondary educational opportunities, independent living choices, and community participation in addition to vocational possibilities. Middle school and secondary school educators need to provide instruction in such diverse areas as personal management, personal health, leisure skills, citizenship, and social skills (Sabornie & deBettencourt, 2009). Effective transition planning includes vocational training, parental and student involvement, interagency collaboration, paid work experience, follow-up employment services, community-based instruction, and community-referenced curriculum.

One promising approach is a **wraparound plan**, which should begin in the elementary years and continue throughout the secondary years and adulthood. *Wraparound* refers to an approach that "wraps" services and supports around the student and his or her family. This network of coordinated interagency services is provided in natural school, home, and community environments (Eber, Breen, Rose, Unizycki, & London, 2008; Eber & Keenan, 2004). Such a plan allows for the coordinated involvement of multiple agencies to facilitate the successful transition from school to adulthood for adolescents with emotional or behavioral disorders. Such wraparound plans may be essential for adolescents because many do not have access to the many critical services offered in their communities.

Adults With Emotional or Behavioral Disorders

Once a student with emotional or behavioral disorders leaves secondary education and enters postsecondary education or employment, the protections offered by IDEA no longer apply. Two other legislative acts protect these young adults in the areas of education and employment: Section 504 of the Rehabilitation Act of 1973 (PL 93–112) and the Americans with Disabilities Act (ADA) (PL 101–336). Both Section 504 and ADA guarantee individuals with disabilities "equal access" to postsecondary programs if they are "otherwise qualified." This does not mean that individuals with disabilities are automatically guaranteed access to postsecondary institutions; they must meet the admission criteria for the institution to which they apply. It does mean that postsecondary institutions cannot deny admission simply because the individual has a disability. If an individual with a disability is admitted to a federally funded postsecondary institution, he or she is entitled to "reasonable accommodations." These accommodations might include extended time on assignments, texts on audiotapes, and peer tutoring.

Postsecondary institutions cannot deny admission simply because a student has a disability.

CHAPTER IN REVIEW

Defining Emotional or Behavioral Disorders

Audio Link 8.2
Listen to a chapter summary.

- There is no universally accepted definition of emotional or behavioral disorders.
- Terms used to describe individuals with emotional or behavioral disorders are very diversified and compounded by the variability in our understanding of what constitutes "normal" behavior.
- The current IDEA definition of emotional disturbance is controversial.

Classification of Individuals With Emotional or Behavioral Disorders

- Clinically and statistically derived classification systems are frequently used to classify the many different types of emotional or behavioral disorders.
- Externalizing disorders are sometimes referred to as "undercontrolled" behaviors, and internalizing disorders are sometimes referred to as "overcontrolled" behaviors.

Prevalence of Emotional or Behavioral Disorders

- Students with emotional or behavioral disorders represent an underidentified population. Currently, fewer than 1 percent of all pupils in public schools are recognized as having emotional or behavioral disorders.

Etiology of Emotional or Behavioral Disorders

- Most professionals believe that the development of emotional or behavioral disorders is related to both biological and psychosocial risk factors.

Prevention of Emotional or Behavioral Disorders

- Positive behavioral support is a schoolwide approach designed to prevent problem behaviors from occurring and, if they do occur, to intervene early to prevent escalation. It represents a proactive rather than reactive approach to dealing with problematic behaviors.

Characteristics of Children and Youth With Emotional or Behavioral Disorders

- Research indicates that pupils with emotional or behavioral disorders typically score in the low-average range on measures of intelligence.
- Perhaps the most salient characteristic of students with emotional or behavioral disorders is their difficulty in building and maintaining satisfactory relationships with peers and adults.

Assessing Students With Emotional or Behavioral Disorders

- Person-centered planning, strength-based assessment, and functional behavioral assessment are representative of the contemporary trends in assessment of pupils with emotional or behavioral disorders.
- A behavioral intervention plan is mandated by PL 108–446 for those individuals who exhibit problematic behaviors in school.

Educational Considerations

- Students with emotional or behavioral disorders are the most likely of all pupils with disabilities to be educated in self-contained classrooms or in programs outside the public school system.

- Effective management of the physical environment includes proactively addressing such areas as time management, transition management, proximity and movement management, classroom management, and classroom ambience.
- Mnemonic and self-monitoring strategies, curriculum-based measurement, and content enhancements are examples of effective academic and instructional strategies designed to assist students with emotional or behavioral disorders to access the general education curriculum.
- At the classroom level, educators can tap an array of interventions including social skills training, interpersonal problem solving and conflict resolution, and crisis prevention and management programs.

Transition Into Adulthood

- Students with emotional or behavioral disorders have the highest dropout rate among all categories of pupils with disabilities.
- To improve the outcomes for both adolescents and adults with emotional or behavioral disorders, recent research suggests that wraparound planning and systems of care are necessary. These approaches incorporate a family-centered approach designed to actively involve the student and his or her family in planning integrated services.

STUDY QUESTIONS

1. Explain why each of the following factors should be taken into consideration when defining emotional or behavioral disorders:
    a. Dimensions of behavior (frequency, intensity, duration, age-appropriateness)
    b. "Disturbed" versus "disturbing" behavior
    c. Transient nature of problematic behavior
    d. "Typical" versus "atypical" behavior
    e. Variability in cultural and social standards of behavior
2. Why is the federal definition of emotional disturbance controversial? How does this definition differ from the one proposed by the Mental Health and Special Education Coalition? Discuss the pros and cons of each definition.
3. Compare and contrast clinically and statistically derived classification systems. Give examples of each.
4. Define externalizing and internalizing disorders. Give an example of behaviors reflecting each of these two dimensions.
5. Describe the various conceptual models in the field of emotional or behavioral disorders.
6. List four causes of, and risk factors associated with, emotional or behavioral disorders.
7. How does a positive behavioral support model differ from traditional disciplinary methods?
8. What are some of the significant learning, social, and language/communication characteristics of children and youth with emotional or behavioral disorders?
9. List five strategies that are typically used to assess students with emotional or behavioral disorders.
10. What is a functional behavioral assessment?
11. Describe how you would use the following intervention strategies with students with emotional or behavioral disorders: social skills training, interpersonal problem solving and conflict resolution, counseling and school health services, and crisis prevention and management programs.
12. How can a teacher manipulate the physical environment to assist students with and without emotional or behavioral disorders?
13. List five academic and instructional interventions that are effective with pupils with emotional or behavioral disorders.
14. Provide an argument for providing early intervention services for students who have, or who are at risk for developing, emotional or behavioral disorders.
15. What does research say about the long-term outcomes for students with emotional or behavioral disorders?
16. What issues need to be considered when planning for the transition of adolescents with emotional or behavioral disorders?
17. Why is disproportionate representation an issue for students with emotional or behavioral disorders?
18. Define the terms *wraparound planning* and *systems of care*.

KEY TERMS

mentally ill 273
emotional or behavioral disorders 273
Tourette's syndrome 275
emotional disturbance 277
socially maladjusted 277
conduct disorders 278
clinically derived classification systems 279
statistically derived classification systems 279
externalizing disorders 280
internalizing disorders 280
child maltreatment 287
positive behavioral support 289
primary prevention 290
secondary prevention 290
tertiary prevention 290
person-centered planning 293
strength-based assessment 293
functional behavioral assessment 293
behavioral intervention plan 296
time management 297
transition management 298
proximity and movement management 298
classroom arrangement 299
classroom ambience 300
effective instructional cycle 303
mnemonic strategies 303
self-monitoring strategies 303
curriculum-based measurement (CBM) 303
content enhancements 303
social skills training 306
interpersonal problem solving 308
conflict resolution 308
crisis prevention and management programs 309
wraparound plan 310
family-centered approach 312
systems of care model 315

LEARNING ACTIVITIES

1. Break into small groups to debate whether or not Mike is "socially maladjusted" as defined by the current federal definition of emotional disturbance.
2. Visit a local mental health center and interview a counselor, psychologist, or social worker. Determine the extent to which this mental health center has created linkages with the public schools.
3. Work with a group to develop a presentation on promoting resiliency among children and youth.
4. Visit a local school. Investigate the extent to which a positive behavioral support model is being implemented. Identify ways in which such a model might be integrated into the school at the primary, secondary, and tertiary levels of prevention.
5. Interview a special educator who teaches students with emotional or behavioral disorders. Ask him or her to describe the types of assessment strategies typically used with this population in the school setting.
6. Prepare a class presentation on one of the following:
   a. Conduct disorders
   b. Schizophrenia
   c. Obsessive-compulsive disorder
   d. Depression and/or suicide

ORGANIZATIONS CONCERNED WITH EMOTIONAL OR BEHAVIORAL DISORDERS

Council for Children With Behavioral Disorders (CCBD), Council for Exceptional Children
1110 N. Glebe Road
Suite 300
Arlington, VA 22201–5704
(888) 232-7733
(866) 915-5000 (TTY)
(703) 264-9494 (Fax)
http://www.cec.sped.org

Federation of Families for Children's Mental Health
9605 Medical Center Drive
Suite 280
Rockville, MD 20850
(240) 403-1901
(240) 403-1909 (Fax)
http://www.ffcmh.org

Mental Health America
2000 N. Beauregard Street
Sixth Floor
Alexandria, VA 22311
(800) 969-6642
(703) 684-5968 (Fax)
http://www.nmha.org

American Psychological Association
750 First Street N.E.
Washington, DC 20002–4242
(800) 374-2721
(202) 336-6123 (TDD/TTY)
http://www.apa.org

American Psychiatric Association
1000 Wilson Boulevard
Suite 1825
Arlington, VA 22209–3901
(703) 907-7300
http://www.psych.org

REFLECTING ON STANDARDS

The following exercises are designed to help you learn to apply the Council for Exceptional Children (CEC) standards to your teaching practice. Each of the reflection exercises below correlates with a knowledge or skill within the CEC standards. For the full text of each of the related CEC standards, please refer to the standards integration grid located in Appendix B.

Focus on Learning Environments and Social Interactions ***(CEC Content Standard #5 CC5S10)***
Reflect on what you have learned about behavior management in this book thus far. Based on what you have learned, how would you establish your classroom rules? What kinds of rules do you think are important to have in your class? How do you plan to assess which classroom rules are best suited for your particular students?

Focus on Instructional Planning ***(CEC Content Standard #7 CC7S12)***
Reflect on a teacher you have had who used his or her instructional time in class effectively. Why was he or she effective? How did he or she schedule the instructional time in class to make things flow well? What steps do you plan to take in your instructional planning to make sure to use instructional time wisely?

STUDENT STUDY SITE

Visit the Student Study Site at www.sagepub.com/gargiulo4emedia for these additional learning tools:

- Video links
- Media links
- Self-quizzes
- E-flashcards
- Full-text SAGE journal articles
- Web exercises

CHAPTER 9

Learning Objectives

After reading Chapter 9 you should be able to:

- Define autism spectrum disorders.
- List the five categories associated with pervasive developmental disorders.
- Describe the changing perspectives on the causes of autism spectrum disorders.
- Provide examples of etiological possibilities for autism spectrum disorders.
- Outline the behavioral, social, and communication characteristics typically associated with individuals with autism spectrum disorders.
- Explain how autism spectrum disorders are diagnosed.
- Describe instructional strategies often used with students with autism spectrum disorders.
- Summarize services for young children with autism spectrum disorders.
- Characterize adult services for individuals with autism spectrum disorders.
- Explain how low-tech and high-tech devices are used to facilitate communication in pupils with autism spectrum disorders.

Individuals With Autism Spectrum Disorders

AUTISM FROM A PERSONAL PERSPECTIVE: A TRUE STORY OF BEATING THE ODDS AND WINNING

I would like to begin by dedicating my story to my parents, who never gave up, and to the loving memory of my grandmother, who would become a very instrumental person in my life. May her legacy live on through my words and testimony.

When I was 18 months old, a military psychiatrist diagnosed me with early childhood autism. My parents and I were living in Germany while my dad was serving in the army. My parents were told that the military could not provide any treatment or intervention, but if it found a program that I could benefit from that was located near a military base, the army would take care of relocating us. We came back to Anniston (Alabama), which is my hometown, and we lived with my grandmother for a few months until we knew what to do and where we were going. My first symptoms started with being nonverbal, rocking, sound sensitivity, and resistance to change.

Video Link 9.1 Watch more about autism.

However, I had some special abilities such as drawing, and I loved music. I'm also visually impaired, which has bothered me since birth but never had anything to do with autism. This was a disability I already had. I got my first pair of glasses after I turned a year old. I no longer drive because of my extremely low vision. I currently use public transportation services to get around town. After coming home from Germany, my mother started taking me to see some doctors, which did little good. Some would say, "Well, he's just a baby going through some phases, and he'll come out of it soon." Well, that wasn't enough for my mother. She knew there was something more wrong with me, and nobody was listening yet. I still wasn't talking, and I kept to myself a lot. My grandmother took this pretty hard because the last time she saw me, I was only a few months old. Now I was already walking and playing.

Original chapter contribution by Karen Bowen Dahle, University of Alabama at Birmingham

A lack of appropriate social skills is a common problem among individuals with autism spectrum disorders.

with social exchanges. They may fail to take social norms or the listener's feelings into account. They may rely exclusively on limited conversational strategies or stereotyped expressions, elaborating on some idiosyncratic interest or echoing a previous statement. For example, an individual with ASD may tell someone she smells whenever the person wears a particular perfume to work. Another individual may only talk to you if you talk about his favorite topic—pizza! The individual shows relatively little interest in others unless he or she needs help or responds to questions; there is little or no reciprocal social communication. An individual with these deficits will not ask you how you are feeling or seem to notice if there has been a change in mood. Social impairments in persons with autism spectrum disorders significantly affect their involvement with others in educational, vocational, and social settings (National Education Association, 2006).

Communication Symptoms

A lack of speech has long been considered a hallmark of autism spectrum disorders. In individuals with ASD who do speak, "their speech may not be functional or fluent and may lack communicative intent" (Johnson & Myers, 2007, p. 1192). Typical communication deficits include a delay in spoken language development, marked impairment in conversational skills, stereotyped and repetitive use of language, and a lack of spontaneous age-appropriate make-believe or social imitative play in addition to echolalia, or "parroting" the speech of others (American Psychiatric Association, 2000; Johnson & Myers; Owens, 2010).

The speech of individuals with ASD is clearly abnormal in rhythm, has an odd intonation or inappropriate pitch, and may sound toneless or mechanical. Deficits in the pragmatic or social use of language are also common (Owens, 2010; Volkmar & Pauls, 2003). Approximately 25 to 30 percent of youngsters with autism spectrum disorders begin to use words and then suddenly cease to speak, often between 15 and 24 months of age (Johnson & Myers, 2007).

The development of speech by age 5 or 6 is viewed as a positive sign for a good outcome (Nordin & Gillberg, 1998). Some of the early prespeech deficits that may facilitate an early diagnosis and thus early intervention include

- lack of recognition of mother's (or father's or consistent caregiver's) voice;
- disregard for vocalizations (e.g., lack of response to name), yet keen awareness of environmental sounds;
- delayed onset of babbling past 9 months of age;
- decreased or absent use of prespeech gestures (waving, pointing, showing);
- lack of expressions such as "oh oh" or "huh"; [and]
- lack of interest [in] or response of any kind to neutral statements (e.g., "Oh no, it's raining again!"). (Johnson & Myers, 2007, p. 1192)

Many individuals with autism spectrum disorders engage in stereotypical and repetitive behaviors.

Repetitive and Restrictive Behaviors

Repetitive and restrictive behaviors (see Table 9.2, p. 332) include preoccupation with at least one stereotyped and restricted pattern of interest to an abnormal degree, inflexible adherence to nonfunctional rituals or routines, stereotyped and repetitive motor mannerisms, and preoccupation with parts of objects. Individuals with ASD may

- play with toys in the same manner;
- be rigid about routines or object placements;
- eat few foods or only foods with a certain texture;
- smell food;
- be insensitive to pain;
- be unaware of danger;
- show unusual attachment to inanimate objects; and
- exhibit repeated body movements (hand flapping, rocking, finger licking, etc.).

Many professionals are now considering whether these actions represent a distinct diagnostic category or are manifestations of coexisting psychiatric disorders such as attention deficit hyperactivity disorder or obsessive–compulsive disorder (Johnson & Myers, 2007; Tsai, 2007). If the latter, this may explain why some individuals receive various diagnoses prior to being identified as having autism spectrum disorder.

Video Link 9.7
Watch more about characteristics.

Other Characteristics

In addition to the three primary characteristics of autism spectrum disorders, symptoms that can co-occur include problems with concentration, attention, and activity level; anxiety disorders; affective or mood disorders; and learning difficulties. These behaviors are briefly summarized in Table 9.3.

TABLE 9.3 Associated Characteristics of Individuals With Autism Spectrum Disorders

Areas of Concern	Behaviors
Concentration and Attention	• Hyperactivity • Short attention span • Impulsivity • Stimulus overselectivity (selective attention)
Anxiety Disorders	• Self-injurious behaviors • Excessive scratching or rubbing • Limiting diet to a few foods • Eating inedible items (pica) • Obsessive–compulsive disorders
Affective Disorders	• Abnormalities of mood or affect (giggling or crying for no apparent reason) • Sleeping problems (difficulties falling asleep, frequent awakening, early morning awakening) • Bed-wetting • Depression, suicidal ideation
Learning Difficulties	• Uneven achievement • Impaired executive functioning • Poor reading comprehension • Inadequate receptive/expressive language skills • Difficulty generalizing skills or information

Assessment of Autism Spectrum Disorders

The assessment of an individual with autism spectrum disorders is confounded by the fact that the very behaviors necessary for proper testing—the ability to sit still, pay attention, follow directions, and respond verbally—are often difficult for the individual with ASD. Some professionals believe that these deficits render persons with ASD untestable, and generally disregard the results of formal cognitive and achievement tests. However, most researchers believe that intellectual assessments and achievement tests can be administered effectively and used in planning programs for individuals with ASD. Behavioral assessments and rating scales can generate additional information about the individual with autism spectrum disorders, without the problems associated with a formal testing situation.

Intellectual Assessment

One of the common myths about autism spectrum disorders is that inside each child is a genius. This myth may have arisen because of the uneven nature of these children's skills, often referred to as "splinter" skills (see the accompanying Insights feature). Despite these unusual abilities, many individuals with ASD exhibit significant cognitive deficits (Bowler, 2006; Hyman & Towbin, 2007; Levy, Hyman et al., 2008). The exact prevalence, however, of intellectual disabilities in persons with autism spectrum disorders is somewhat controversial (Edelson, 2006).

For all individuals with ASD, we know that the severity of the symptoms affects the individual's overall level of functioning, particularly in the areas of language and

Examples of "Splinter Skills"

John noticed the sequence of numbers as he turned the pages of books (usually cookbooks illustrated with colored photographs of food). Soon he was writing the numbers on walls or on a chalkboard. From the car speedometer, he learned how to count by tens. From the binding on a set of books, he learned Roman numerals.

Numbers meant so much to him that if one was missing from the pages of a book it caused him to cry, but he resolved his unhappiness by writing in the number by hand. In instances where a publisher had inserted pages of illustrations in a book without numbering them in sequence with the pages of the text, John wrote numbers in by hand and then renumbered the pages of the text to keep the sequence correct.

If page 1 was preceded by unnumbered introductory pages, he numbered backward into the numbers below zero. If lowercase Roman numerals were used in the introductory pages of a book, he would write in negative Roman numerals, numbering backward until he came to the front cover.

All this was before he learned to talk . . .

Barry amazed people because at 7 months he was echoing sounds from the TV set. By the time he was a year-and-a-half old, he could recite from memory substantial passages from phonograph records, and he knew his ABCs. Barry's accomplishments of rote memory were not matched by conceptual understanding, however. It took years of work when he was a school-age child to learn the meaning of such concepts as *up and down* and *above and below* [italics added]. It wasn't until he was past the age of 8 that he began to be able to speak his own thoughts. Developing that ability was a long, slow process. The realization that the image in photos and in the mirror was himself did not come until he was more than 10 years old.

SOURCE: B. Sposato, *A Little about Autism and Some People Who Are Autistic* (Nebraska Chapter of the National Society for Children and Adults with Autism, 1986), pp. 1–3.

social skills. What is most important is not the individual's IQ, but his or her ability to function independently in society. Nevertheless, intellectual assessments are important components in determining an individual's eligibility for special education services, in making psychiatric diagnoses, and often in placement for group homes or vocational settings. Therefore, tests measuring intellectual ability as well as checklists assessing adaptive levels of functioning are typically administered as part of an overall assessment battery.

Screening and Diagnosis

There is no specific test to diagnose autism spectrum disorders. Physicians look for behavioral symptoms to make a diagnosis. These symptoms may be noticeable within the first few months of life, or they may appear anytime prior to age 3. In some instances, it is not unusual to find characteristics being recognized later primarily because they were likely confused with the symptoms of other disorders.

In the past decade, researchers have identified several characteristics that are helpful in making an early diagnosis of ASD. It has been shown that a diagnosis of autism spectrum disorders at age 2 is reliable, valid, and stable (Levy, Hyman et al., 2008; Lord et al., 2006).

The diagnosis of ASD should include two steps. The first step is a developmental screening (a brief assessment designed to identify youngsters who should receive a more thorough evaluation) and surveillance (a process whereby health care professionals monitor children who may have a developmental disability). It is recommended that screening tests be given to *all* children during their well-child visits at 9, 18, 24, and 30 months of age. Additional screening is warranted if the youngster is at high risk (for example, has a sibling or parent with ASD) or presents characteristics suggestive of autism spectrum disorders.

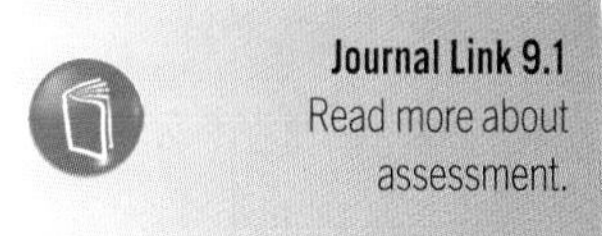

Transition Planning: Questions to Address

When thinking about transition from high school, sometimes it is helpful to start the process with a list of questions to act as a springboard for discussion. Below is a list of questions composed by a mother whose son has autism spectrum disorders. Some parents like to hold family meetings with siblings and the individual with ASD so that they can all share in the planning. You may want to share this list with the parents you work with to help them start planning for their child's transition.

- What does your child like to do?
- What can your child do?
- What does your child need to explore?
- What does your child need to learn to reach his or her goals?
- What about college (four-year, community), vocational education, or adult education?
- How about getting a job (competitive or supportive)?
- Where can your child go to find employment and training services?
- What transportation will your child use?
- Where will your child live?
- How will your child make ends meet?
- Where will your child get health insurance?

Many people think of adulthood in terms of getting a job and living in a particular area, but having friends and a sense of belonging in a community are also important. To address these areas, a few additional questions have been added:

- What about friendship? Are supports needed to encourage friendships?
- Do people in the community know your son or daughter?
- Are supports needed to structure time for recreation? Exercise?
- Does your child have any special interests that others may share as a hobby?
- Can you explore avenues for socializing such as religious affiliation or volunteer work?

It is also important that the transition process involve taking action. After identifying areas of interests and setting goals, one must take some active steps to meet those goals. For example, a student with autism spectrum disorders with particularly sharp computer skills is dismissed from school early a few days a week to work with an aide at a data processing office. This position was acquired through the vocational rehabilitation office, and it continues to provide needed support. Before beginning this job, the student was taught appropriate office social skills and important office procedures such as using a time clock.

Another student who prefers to be outdoors is more suited to work with a community cleanup project than in an office. Again, this emphasizes the need to develop a plan tailored to each individual's skills and preferences. Many professionals and families believe that three or four different experiences can be helpful in assessing a student's desires and capabilities while he is still in high school. The bottom line for all students is to prepare them for their lives after high school, whether that involves employment or further education.

SOURCE: Adapted from Autism Society of America, *Thinking about Transition.* (2010). Available at http://www.autism-society.org/site/DocServer/Transition_Across_Grade_Levels.pdf?docID=10621

For those individuals who are not able to live independently, families—and the individual, if capable—have many decisions to make, ranging from day treatment programs to residential care placements to employment options. Residential care may include traditional institutional and group home settings, as well as supervised apartment living. As adults with autism spectrum disorders age, their families often become unable to care for them, particularly if aggressive or self-injurious behaviors are present. Parents also worry about their adult child's future when the family is no longer there to provide care. Some of the common residential and employment options are reviewed here.

Some adults with autism spectrum disorders live in group homes located in residential neighborhoods.

Supervised Group and Apartment Living

Some adults with autism spectrum disorders are able to live independently with support services from community agencies. Services usually involve helping problem-solve issues such as money management, medication management, and transportation, and assisting individuals in interacting within their communities.

Supervised group homes are usually located in a residential setting. The homes are staffed with trained professionals who assist the residents based on their individual level of need. Typically, residents participate in sheltered workshops, supported employment, or day treatment programs. In the evenings, staff members assist residents with their personal care, housekeeping, and meal preparation, and implement behavior management programs.

A supervised apartment may be the choice for an individual who would prefer to live with fewer people but still requires some supervision and assistance. A staff person usually checks on the resident intermittently and provides agreed-upon services. These resources and supports may include the following:

- Home helpers to assist with household duties
- Case managers to help locate and coordinate various services
- Financial assistance to help with extra costs such as medical services
- Adaptive equipment, counseling, or necessary home modifications

Research (Hendricks & Wehman, 2009) suggests that integrated or residential living arrangements for adults with ASD often result in increased community participation and greater independent functioning along with a higher quality of life.

High-Tech Devices

VOCAs are electronic devices that can be programmed to produce synthetic speech. These devices can be as simple as programming *yes* or *no* response keys or as complex as producing multiple words, sentences, and social comments. An overlay with pictures or icons enables the child to choose what he or she would like to say or respond to by pressing the appropriate response. Some of these devices require little training on the part of the user; however, most users are dependent on a communication partner to change the overlays for them when the topic changes because it is often beyond their physical abilities. The efficacy of these devices with individuals with ASD has received little attention in the literature (Blishak & Schlosser, 2003), although there is some evidence that nonverbal individuals with autism spectrum disorders "benefit from exposure to high-tech AAC devices" (Paul & Sutherland, 2005, p. 956).

Low-Tech Devices

Visual strategies involve the use of pictures and sign language to communicate. In most picture exchange programs, the individual hands the instructor a picture of what he or she wants or needs as a form of communication. Bondy and Frost (1998) have pioneered a system known as the Picture Exchange Communication System (PECS), illustrated in Figure 9.3. Pictures can be grouped together by topic, such as how to get dressed or

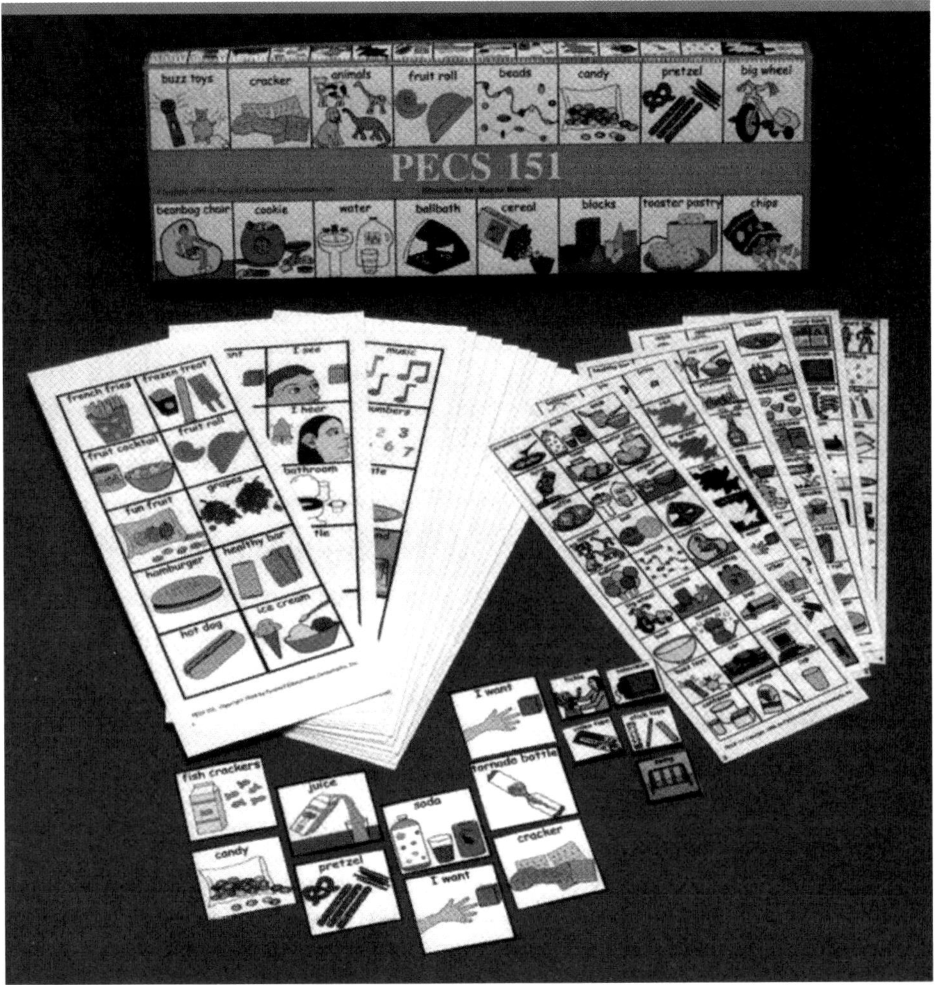

FIGURE 9.3 Picture Communication Aids

SOURCE: Courtesy Pyramid Educational Products, Inc.

how to wash your hands, or arranged as a discussion board. An advantage of pictures is the reduction of auditory instruction and a reliance on the visual strengths of individuals with autism spectrum disorders. PECS has been shown to spontaneously generalize to different settings for children with ASD (Kravits, Kamps, Kemmerer, & Potucck, 2002), to increase spontaneous communication skills, and to improve social interactions and decrease problem behaviors (Charlop-Christy, Carpenter, Le, LeBlanc, & Kellet, 2002). In addition to the empirical evidence, anecdotal reports also support the effectiveness of PECS with children with autism spectrum disorders (Paul & Sutherland, 2005).

Research suggests that the introduction of AAC systems to nonverbal children with autism spectrum disorders does not interfere with the acquisition of speech (Myers & Johnson, 2007; Paul & Sutherland, 2005); in fact, there is some evidence that it may actually stimulate the development of speech (Millar, Light, & Schlosser, 2006).

Trends, Issues, and Controversies

Parents of individuals with autism spectrum disorders are exposed to a variety of treatments that promise dramatic improvement or "cures" for their child. With so many possible causes of ASD, there are likely as many possible treatments that may help the family in caring for its child. Unfortunately, research has not advanced to the point that the cause can always be matched to an appropriate treatment. Families often rely on anecdotal reports of treatments rather than waiting for the research to support the claims of improvement. Who can blame them? As long as the treatment does not harm the child, some families do not believe they can wait for science to catch up and miss an opportunity that could make a difference in the life of their child. Many parents stay up-to-date on treatment methodologies and current debates using the Internet. Unfortunately, these parents frequently "become susceptible to the promotions of specific therapies that usually have little to offer other than hope" (Marcus et al., 2005, p. 1058).

In the language of the ASD community, unproven techniques and therapies fall under the heading of complementary and alternative medicine (CAM) (Myers & Johnson, 2007; Volkmar & Wiesner, 2009). A multitude of treatment options, both biological and nonbiological, are considered CAM therapies, including, for example, dietary and vitamin treatments, hormone injections, facilitated communication, music therapy, and auditory integration training, along with optometric training. While case reports and anecdotal evidence lend credence to the popularity of these interventions, the scientific literature, which requires the use of a randomized, double-blind, placebo-controlled study, does not support these treatments (Challman, Voigt, & Myers, 2008; Hyman & Towbin, 2007; Levy, Kruger et al., 2008). What is regrettably lacking in the field of autism spectrum disorders are "large-scale, rigorously designed, replicated intervention studies that compare the major autism intervention approaches" (Marcus et al., 2005, p. 1059). Until this evidence is available, parents and professionals alike need to carefully evaluate treatment options for individuals with autism spectrum disorders. Families should be especially cautious of a treatment strategy or intervention if they encounter

Audio Link 9.2
Listen to more about controversies.

- treatments that are based on overly simple scientific theories;
- therapies that claim to be effective for multiple, unrelated conditions or symptoms;
- claims that children will respond dramatically and some will be cured;
- use of case reports or anecdotal data rather than carefully designed studies to support claims for treatment;
- lack of peer-reviewed references or denial of the need for controlled studies; or
- treatments that are said to have no potential or reported adverse effects. (Myers & Johnson, 2007, p. 1173)

Parents and professionals alike can locate current information about autism spectrum disorders by visiting the Healing Thresholds website (http://autism.healingthresholds.com). Here you will find the latest scientific research on ASD explained in terms understandable by a layperson.

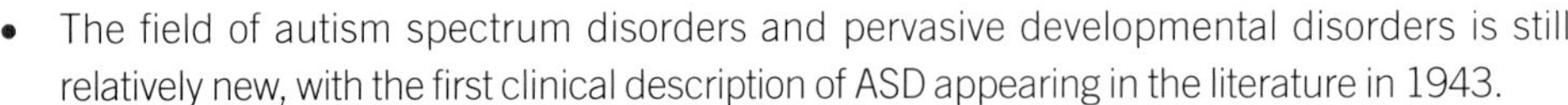

CHAPTER IN REVIEW

Audio Link 9.3
Listen to a chapter summary.

Defining Autism Spectrum Disorders: An Evolving Process

- The field of autism spectrum disorders and pervasive developmental disorders is still relatively new, with the first clinical description of ASD appearing in the literature in 1943.
- Autism spectrum disorders were not described as a separate clinical category until 1977.

Classification of Individuals With Autism Spectrum Disorders

- The most current DSM-IV-TR includes autism as one of five distinct disorders in a category called pervasive developmental disorders.
- Individuals with Asperger syndrome are now recognized by professionals as distinctly different from persons with high-functioning autism.
- IDEA included autism as a separate diagnostic category in 1990. The definition of autism in IDEA 2004 is fairly consistent with the description in the DSM-IV-TR.

Prevalence of Autism Spectrum Disorders

- According to the federal government, more than 337,000 pupils ages 3–21 were identified as having autism during the 2008–2009 school year.
- Prevalence rates vary considerably.

Etiology of Autism Spectrum Disorders

- We do not know the cause of autism, and we do not know how to prevent it.
- Current research is looking for biological markers; in general, any injury to the neurological system is suspect. This includes genetic contributions and structural abnormalities of the brain.

Characteristics of Individuals With Autism Spectrum Disorders

- Three cardinal characteristics define autism spectrum disorders: (1) social interaction deficits, (2) communication deficits, and (3) repetitive and restricted interests by age 3.
- Additional symptoms frequently reported in individuals with ASD include problems with concentration and attention, anxiety disorders, affective disorders, and learning difficulties.

Assessment of Autism Spectrum Disorders

- A good clinician will evaluate the presence of ASD symptoms using several diagnostic observation scales and inventories.
- Functional assessments of individuals with autism spectrum disorders help to identify emerging skills. It is not uncommon to find that an individual with autism spectrum disorders has splinter skills because of the uneven nature of his or her cognitive development.

Educational Considerations

- Almost 40 percent of all school-age students with autism spectrum disorders currently receive services in a self-contained classroom.

- Structured educational approaches are consistently identified as the most appropriate for individuals with ASD. Behavior modification strategies are often used to achieve this structure.

Services for Young Children With Autism Spectrum Disorders

- Early educational intervention makes a positive difference in the life of an individual with autism spectrum disorders.
- The major focus of most early intervention programs is to address the communication deficits and behavioral problems of very young children.

STUDY QUESTIONS

1. Describe the DSM-IV-TR system and compare it to the IDEA classification system.
2. Name and describe the other pervasive developmental disorders (excluding ASD).
3. Prior to the acknowledgment of the genetic and neurological causes of autism spectrum disorders, what were the prevailing theories and treatments?
4. Why is the prevalence of ASD increasing?
5. List three possible causes of autism spectrum disorders.
6. What does the term *autistic savant* mean?
7. Name the three cardinal characteristics of ASD.
8. Detail the characteristics of the most common interventions used to educate individuals with autism spectrum disorders.
9. What are the key issues related to transitioning into adulthood for individuals with ASD?
10. Describe the issues that families typically have to deal with when they have a child with autism spectrum disorders.
11. How can technology be used with individuals with ASD?
12. What is complementary and alternative medicine? Describe the type of research that is needed to rigorously evaluate treatment options for individuals with autism spectrum disorders.

KEY TERMS

autism spectrum disorders 323
pervasive developmental disorders 324
schizophrenia 324
multiaxial system 326
Rett's disorder 326
childhood disintegrative disorder 326
Asperger syndrome 326
pervasive developmental disorder, not otherwise specified (PDD, NOS) 326
autistic savant 328
psychogenic theories 329
applied behavior analysis (ABA) 329
theory of mind 333
self-determination 345
job coach 348
augmentative or alternative communication (AAC) 349
voice output communication aid (VOCA) 349

LEARNING ACTIVITIES

1. If possible, observe a student with autism spectrum disorders in a special education setting and in an inclusive setting. What are the advantages and disadvantages of both educational settings? What kinds of educational interventions did you observe? What kind of educational environment would you want if this were your child or sibling?
2. Consider participating in a local support group for individuals with autism spectrum disorders and listen to the families' concerns and needs. Is there something you or your friends could do to help, such as providing respite care? Have you ever considered extending your friendship to an adult with ASD? Contact an organization in your area and offer to be a friend to an adult with autism spectrum disorders.

ORGANIZATIONS CONCERNED WITH AUTISM SPECTRUM DISORDERS

Autism Society of America
4340 East–West Highway
Suite 350
Bethesda, MD 20814
(800) 328-8476
http://www.autism-society.org

Autism Speaks
2 Park Avenue
11th Floor
New York, NY 10016
(212) 252-8584
(212) 252-8676 (Fax)
http://www.autismspeaks.org

Indiana Resource Center for Autism (IRCA)
Indiana Institute on Disability and Community
Indiana University
2853 E. Tenth Street
Bloomington, IN 47408–2696
(812) 855-6508
(812) 855-9396 (TTY)
(812) 855-9630 (Fax)
http://www.iidc.indiana.edu/index.php?pageId=32

Kennedy Krieger Institute
707 N. Broadway
Baltimore, MD 21205
(888) 554-2080
(443) 923-2645 (TTY)
http://www.kennedykrieger.org

Ohio Center for Autism and Low Incidence
470 Glenmont Avenue
Columbus, OH 43214
(866) 886-2254
(614) 262-1070 (Fax)
http://www.ocali.org

REFLECTING ON STANDARDS

The following exercises are designed to help you learn to apply the Council for Exceptional Children (CEC) standards to your teaching practice. Each of the reflection exercises below correlates with a knowledge or skill within the CEC standards. For the full text of each of the related CEC standards, please refer to the standards integration grid located in Appendix B.

Focus on Learning Environments and Social Interactions ***(CEC Content Standard #5 CC5S4)***
Reflect on what you have learned about the social interaction difficulties individuals with autism spectrum disorders sometimes have. If you were to have a student with autism spectrum disorders in your class, how might you encourage him or her to participate in group and one-on-one interactions with other students? How might you modify assignments to allow for positive social interaction?

Focus on Instructional Planning ***(CEC Content Standard #7 CC7S7)***
Reflect on what you have learned about inclusion of students with autism spectrum disorders in a general education classroom. If you were to teach at a school where students with autism spectrum disorders received services in a self-contained special education classroom, how might you coordinate with the special education teacher to involve his or her students in your classroom? How might you be able to involve students with autism spectrum disorders to help them learn affective, social, and life skills while working with general education students?

STUDENT STUDY SITE

Visit the Student Study Site at www.sagepub.com/gargiulo4emedia for these additional learning tools:

- Video links
- Media links
- Self-quizzes
- E-flashcards
- Full-text SAGE journal articles
- Web exercises

CHAPTER 10

Learning Objectives

After reading Chapter 10 you should be able to:

- Define speech, language, and communication.
- Identify the five components of language.
- List three different types of speech impairments and five forms of language disorders.
- Define central auditory processing disorder.
- Distinguish between functional and organic causes of speech and language impairments.
- Explain the differences between receptive and expressive language impairments.
- Describe procedures used for assessing speech and language impairments.
- Explain the function of augmentative or alternative communication devices.

Individuals With Speech and Language Impairments

A PARENT'S STORY

Adam's life started with my pregnancy. It was a normal pregnancy with no complications. I had a caesarean section when Adam was a week overdue. He weighed 9.5 pounds, a very healthy baby. Adam reached all of his developmental milestones at normal times. He crawled at 6 months, walked at 10 months, and said his first word at 12 months. His speech and language continued to develop at a normal pace.

Video Link 10.1
Watch more about speech impairments.

When it was time to eat solid foods, we had a problem. Adam had a strong gag reflex and did not seem to want to eat any foods that were not pureed. I came to the conclusion that he was not just picky. In addition, Adam drooled a great deal until he turned 3. I knew this was a lot longer than normal. I talked to the pediatrician about the eating and drooling. He said it was probably from teething and told me to keep introducing foods—eventually Adam would eat them.

When Adam was about 2 years old, I noticed that he could not pronounce *n, t, d, l,* and *s* correctly. I knew that *l* and *s* were not supposed to be mastered until the age of 4. I just thought he would master these by the time he was 4.

My husband, Rick, and I started to notice a great deal of frustration in Adam, who was now 3. What was the cause of it? We did not know and assumed it was age related. He did not seem to understand punishment. We would ask him why he was on his "thinking bench," and he could never answer. He would get more upset and answer something inappropriate. We would go to the pool during the summer. Adam would ask at least ten times, "Where are we going?" I would answer and could tell he just did not understand. I would try to rephrase, and sometimes this would help. Adam did not seem to understand simple directions, question words (*why, how*), sequencing, verb tense, and common language concepts. All of these things were very subtle, and other people did not notice. He was not acquiring language concepts that children learn without formal teaching, and his pronunciation was not getting better.

Suggestions for the Classroom

Video Link 10.4
Watch additional suggestions.

Educational and Treatment Approaches for Central Auditory Processing Problems

One approach focuses on training certain auditory and listening skills, such as auditory discrimination (for example, telling the difference between *peas* and *bees*), localization of sound, sequencing sounds, or identifying a target sound in a noisy background. Training these skills in isolation, however, may not help a child understand complex language, such as a teacher's instructions. Therefore, another approach concentrates on teaching more functional language skills (vocabulary, grammar, conversational skills) and uses strategies (visual aids, repeating directions) to facilitate the processing of language.

Changes at home and in the classroom can also help a child with central auditory processing problems.

- **Seating:** To help the child focus and maintain attention, select seating that is away from auditory and visual distractions. A seat close to the teacher and the blackboard and away from the window and the door may be helpful.
- **Setting:** Reduce external visual and auditory distractions. A large display of posters or cluttered bulletin boards can be distracting. A study carrel in the room may help. Earplugs may be useful to block distracting noise from a heater or air conditioner, the pencil sharpener, or talking in the hallway. Check with an audiologist to find out if earplugs are appropriate and which kind to use. Placing mats and cloth poster boards on classroom walls has been shown to decrease the reverberation of noise. A structured classroom setting may be more beneficial than an open classroom situation.

To improve the listening environment, an audiologist may recommend the use of a device that transmits the teacher's voice directly to the student's ear while blocking out background noise. The audiologist can provide recommendations on the potential benefit of available options based on the child's individual needs.

Speaking:

- ☑ Gain the child's attention before giving directions.
- ☑ Speak slowly and clearly, but do not overexaggerate speech.
- ☑ Use simple, brief directions.
- ☑ Give directions in a logical, time-ordered sequence. Use words that make the sequence clear, such as *first, next,* and *finally.*
- ☑ Use visual aids and write instructions to supplement spoken information.
- ☑ Emphasize key words when speaking or writing, especially when presenting new information. Pre-instructions with emphasis on the main ideas to be presented may also be effective.
- ☑ Use gestures that clarify information.
- ☑ Vary loudness to increase attention.
- ☑ Check comprehension by asking the child questions or asking for a brief summary after key ideas have been presented.
- ☑ Paraphrase instructions and information in shorter and simpler sentences rather than just repeating them.
- ☑ Encourage the child to ask questions for further clarification.
- ☑ Make instructional transitions clear.
- ☑ Review previously learned material.

- ☑ Recognize periods of fatigue and give breaks as necessary.
- ☑ Avoid showing frustration when the child misunderstands a message.
- ☑ Avoid asking the child to listen and write at the same time. For children with severe central auditory processing problems, ask a buddy to take notes, or ask the teacher to provide notes. Tape-recording classes is another effective strategy.

Central auditory processing problems can affect learning, particularly in areas such as spelling and reading. It is important to identify problems early and help the child acquire adaptive strategies to compensate. If your student is a "poor" listener, frequently misunderstands speech, and has difficulty following directions, direct his or her parents to consult an audiologist or speech–language pathologist to determine if a problem exists.

SOURCE: Adapted from D. Kelly, *Processing Problems in Children* (San Antonio, TX: Communication Skills Builders, 1995), p. 25.

children with central auditory processing disorders. These suggestions are valid for many other speech and language disorders discussed in this chapter and provide a good beginning when planning.

Where Are Students With Speech and Language Impairments Served?

The majority of children with speech and language impairments are served in the regular or general classroom setting. Figure 10.4 graphically represents the educational placements typically used with pupils who have a speech or language impairment.

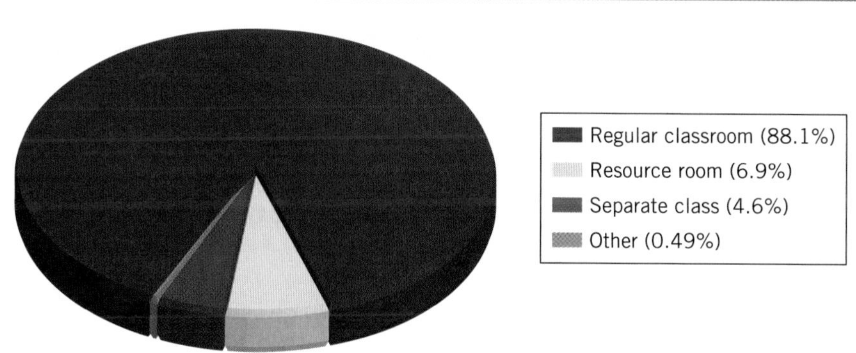

FIGURE 10.4 Educational Placement of Students With Speech and Language Impairments

NOTE: This figure represents the percentages of enrollment of students with speech and language disorders during the 2007–2008 school year.

Other placements include separate schools, residential facilities, and homebound/hospital settings.

SOURCE: U.S. Department of Education. (2009). *IDEA data.* Retrieved November 21, 2009, from https://www.ideadata.org/PartBReport.asp

The sooner early intervention begins for a youngster with communication disorders, the more promising the outcomes.

How families interact with their children and the prelinguistic skills that develop from these interactions vary considerably across cultures (Johnson & Wong, 2002). Observations of non-Western cultural groups make it clear that the large literature on child-directed talk primarily describes Western parent–child interaction patterns. When working with children from culturally and linguistically diverse populations, the speech–language pathologist may draw teaching materials directly from the children's homes and communities, capitalizing on whatever communication skills they have, regardless of whether they are verbal or nonverbal, in English or another language.

Over the past few years, the descriptor for individuals who are second-language learners has been changing. The term *limited English proficient* (LEP) is popular in some educational circles. Equally common, however, is the label *English language learner* (ELL). It is not unusual to find these terms used interchangeably (de Cohen & Clewell, 2007). Both IDEA 2004 and the No Child Left Behind Act use the descriptor *limited English proficient* when addressing the needs of students whose primary language is not English.

The lack of reliable and valid tests often makes it extremely difficult to identify speech and language impairments in children from culturally and linguistically diverse populations (Turner, 2008). There is always the issue of whether speech and language variations are due to a disorder or to the child's development in the second language (Bunce, 2003). Too often LEP children are mistakenly placed in special education classes based on test scores that are normed on English-speaking students. Many of these students are misdiagnosed and labeled as having intellectual disabilities or learning disabilities.

Intervention for LEP children who have language impairments depends on age, severity of the disability, attitude and goals of the family, resources and available social interactions, and vocational expectations (Bunce, 2003). Most intervention programs incorporate a variety of techniques similar to those used with monolingual children with language impairments, combined with techniques for second-language learners. The former focus on the different components of language—phonology, morphology, syntax, semantics, and pragmatics. Additional techniques for second-language learners include (1) teaching vocabulary and syntax in the context of ongoing activities, (2) allowing time for comprehension to develop before insisting on production, (3) using predictable books, (4) using peer buddies, and (5) incorporating parents and other family members as teaching partners.

Technology and Individuals With Speech and Language Impairments

Symbols, aids, strategies, and techniques used to enhance the communication process are commonly known as **augmentative or alternative communication (AAC).** This includes sign language and various communication boards, both low-tech and high-tech devices, that are used by individuals with impaired oral motor skills.

Kangas and Lloyd (2006) define an augmentative communication strategy as one that aids, enhances, or supplements the individual's residual speech skills. On the other hand, alternative communication completely supplants typical communication, such as a device with computerized speech output. The use of AAC systems and devices has been shown to be of significant benefit to pupils with communication challenges (Desch, 2008; Millar, Light, & Schlosser, 2006). These devices provide a means for children with speech and language impairments to interact and communicate with family members, teachers, friends, classmates, and other individuals (Kangas & Lloyd).

Technology has opened a world of opportunity for children who are nonverbal to access and use alternative and augmentative communication devices. Under IDEA, these devices are classified as assistive technology. Children who may benefit from AAC include children with autism spectrum disorders who are nonverbal, children with cerebral palsy, and students with intellectual disabilities. The most basic AAC devices can be nonelectronic or electronic. Most beginners use a form of nonelectronic AAC called a communication board. This low-tech device usually starts with a limited number of choices (two to four). Choices can be represented by real items, pictures of items, or symbols for items (printed words or Bliss symbols, for example). Having children express a choice regarding foods or activities (concrete choices that can be implemented immediately) is a typical beginning activity. As the AAC user makes gains in his or her ability and desire to express concrete preferences and connects the use of the communication board to the desired response, the communication board options grow in the number of possible selections. The use of high-tech electronic AAC devices begins in the same way. The added feature is that the AAC selections can include voice capabilities. Some of the most basic electronic AAC devices (for example, Cheap Talk) can be fitted for as few as one or as many as eight selections per template used. DynaVox, another popular AAC device for school-age children, can be programmed for as few as two selections and expanded over time to handle all of the communication needs of an adult. One of the more sophisticated systems available is the Liberator. Theoretical physicist and Nobel Prize winner Stephen Hawking has used a Liberator for communication because of the effects of amyotrophic lateral sclerosis (ALS) on his oral motor function.

Most advanced high-tech AAC devices have voice selection capabilities. This allows the user to have a voice of the same gender and age range as herself or himself. For children with significant motor challenges, many electronic AAC devices are now made single-switch accessible.

Although the history of AAC spans only a little more than four decades, the sum of its accomplishments is impressive. In the early 1970s, there were fewer than a dozen published reports of hearing individuals with severe communication disability using manual signs, communication boards, or modified typewriters to augment or replace speech. Today there are hundreds of books, chapters, periodicals, and newsletters devoted exclusively to AAC information and research reports. Most university personnel preparation programs now have at least one AAC course, and there is a professional organization (International Society for Augmentative and Alternative Communication) for people interested in the AAC field that publishes a quarterly journal (*Augmentative and Alternative Communication*).

Electronic communication boards are an example of an alternative or augmentative communication device.

Trends, Issues, and Controversies

Speech and language impairments represent a *high-incidence disability*—an impairment that has far-reaching and pervasive effects. Advances in the areas of early intervention, genetic research, and enhanced assistive technology continue to improve the prognosis for those with speech and language disorders. As research data confirm the merits of early intervention for children with communication disorders, particularly language disorders (Lipkin & Schertz, 2008), medical and educational professionals have become increasingly aware of the urgent need for early and accurate diagnosis and timely, well-designed provision of services.

Both medical and educational assessment techniques are the subject of ongoing review and modification. With the advent of sophisticated neurodiagnostic procedures such as brain mapping, the base of knowledge regarding the causes of many speech and language impairments is expanding rapidly. More effective management strategies will surely follow the acquisition of such understanding. As the Human Genome Project unlocks the complexities of the genetic code, the incidence of syndromes and disorders with a hereditary component may be reduced as medical intervention concurrently becomes more effective.

Cultural diversity, dialects, and nonstandard English have come to the forefront in political and educational arenas because of their implications for linguistic performance.

Common tools for assessing speech and language ability will continue to be reviewed for their adequacy in measuring linguistic skills of populations that are increasingly multicultural.

Controversy certainly persists regarding the etiologies of various speech and language disorders, such as CAPD and stuttering. With increased understanding of the underlying neurophysiological basis of such problems, educational management strategies for these and other disorders continue to improve. Digital technology has certainly enlarged the array of electronic devices that increase message redundancy or offer viable alternatives to conventional methods of communication. Such assistive technology provides avenues for communication that did not previously exist.

Inclusion of family members as partners in remediation efforts is currently viewed as best practice. Particularly for the young children, parental attitude toward and involvement in the intervention process is crucial (Gargiulo & Kilgo, 2011).

Rapid technological change is a hallmark of contemporary society. Biomedical innovations and increasingly sophisticated interventions and assessment strategies should encourage individuals and families dealing with speech and language impairments and hold promise for continued progress for those professionals who endeavor to assist them.

CHAPTER IN REVIEW

The Nature of Speech, Language, and Communication

- Speech is the expression of language with sounds—essentially, the oral modality for language.
- Language is a code whereby ideas about the world are represented through a conventional system of arbitrary signals for communication.
- Language has five components—phonology, morphology, syntax, semantics, and pragmatics—that are present at both the receptive and expressive levels.
- Communication is the exchange of ideas, information, thoughts, and feelings. It does not necessarily require speech or language.

Defining Speech and Language Impairments

- The most common speech problem is an articulation disorder, which includes substitutions, omissions, distortions, and additions.
- Stuttering and cluttering are examples of fluency disorders.
- Voice disorders are associated with the larynx. Phonation and resonance are illustrations of this disorder.
- Apraxia of speech involves both speech and language disorders. It results from the inability to position speech muscles necessary to produce speech sounds.
- Central auditory processing disorder (CAPD) is a problem in the processing of sound not attributed to hearing loss or intellectual ability.

Prevalence of Speech and Language Impairments

- About 20 percent of children receiving special education services are receiving services for speech and language impairments.

Etiology of Speech and Language Impairments

- Speech and language problems can result from functional (without an obvious physical basis) or organic (associated physiological deficit) etiologies.

- Disorders may be congenital or the result of an acquired insult.
- Aphasia is the loss or impairment of language functions.

Characteristics of Speech and Language Impairments

- The ability to understand what is meant by spoken communication is known as receptive language; the production of language that is understood by and meaningful to others is identified as expressive language.

Assessing Speech and Language Impairments

- Identifying speech and language impairments frequently involves collaborative teams using formal and informal performance measures.

Educational Considerations

- The vast majority (almost 87 percent) of pupils with speech or language impairments receive services in the general education classroom.

Technology and Individuals with Speech and Language Impairments

- Augmentative or alternative communication (AAC) devices include symbols, aids, strategies, and techniques used as a supplement or alternative to oral language. Sign language and communication boards, both manual and electronic, are two examples of these devices.

STUDY QUESTIONS

1. What are the two main categories of communication disorder?
2. How does IDEA define speech and language impairments?
3. List the three broad categories of speech disorders, and give an example of each.
4. Define language, and explain how it is different from speech.
5. List several factors that cause or contribute to voice disorders.
6. At what age should a child be pronouncing all sounds correctly? What course of action should be taken if he or she is not?
7. List the five rules that must be learned for successful language acquisition to occur.
8. Define central auditory processing disorder. What types of intervention strategies are most effective with this population?
9. Describe the evolution of the role of the speech–language pathologist during the twentieth century.
10. How does a developmental disorder differ from one that is acquired?
11. How has family-centered early intervention influenced remediation strategies for young children with speech and language impairments?
12. List an age-appropriate developmental milestone for a child 2 to 3 years of age.
13. Define expressive and receptive language.
14. Describe an effective informal measure of communication skills for the young child.
15. What difficulties are inherent to assessment of speech and language skills in a culturally diverse population?
16. Define AAC, and describe its use by children with speech and language impairments.

KEY TERMS

speech 359
language 359
phonology 362
morphology 362
syntax 362
semantics 362
pragmatics 362
communication 363
articulation disorders 364

omissions 364
substitutions 364
distortions 364
additions 364
fluency disorders 366
stuttering 366
cluttering 367
voice disorders 369
phonation 369
resonance 369
hypernasality 369
hyponasality 369
phonological disorder 369
apraxia of speech 370
morphological disorder 370
syntactical deficits 370
semantic disorders 370
pragmatic difficulties 370
central auditory processing disorder (CAPD) 370
functional 373
organic 373
aphasia 373
cleft lip 374
cleft palate 374
developmental language delay 375
receptive language 376
expressive language 376
family-directed assessment 380
language sample 381
prelinguistic 381
augmentative or alternative communication (AAC) 388

LEARNING ACTIVITIES

1. Visit an educational setting serving students with speech and language impairments. How was the students' classroom performance affected by their communication difficulty? How were their social interactions with other students and teachers affected? Were any special teaching techniques used or classroom modifications made to enhance their performance? Was therapy given outside of the general education classroom? Was this arrangement positive or negative? How did intervention differ for older children? What was your overall impression of the services provided?

2. Visit a clinic or hospital in your community providing services to persons with speech and/or language impairments. Interview the speech–language pathologist. What types of disorders are served? Are there special challenges in assessment techniques? What types of intervention strategies are used? What interaction does this professional have with the community at large? With area schools? Is there a team approach in use? Is there a family-centered remediation model for implementing therapy?

3. Prepare a resource book for your class that describes common types of speech and language impairments and their characteristics. Include appropriate assessment, referral, and remediation strategies. Provide information on causes and prevention, assistive technology, need for early intervention, and classroom strategies. Provide some websites of interest for each disorder.

4. Compile a list of local agencies (public and private), medical facilities, civic groups, and educational settings that provide services to persons with speech and language impairments. Be sure to include contact information as well as a brief description of services provided.

5. Visit a local preschool program for children at risk for language delay. Interview a staff member. Find out how young children are screened for speech and language problems, and describe the process. Volunteer to help with screenings if possible. What types of language stimulation activities are used? How are families included in this process? What is your opinion regarding the effectiveness of the program?

ORGANIZATIONS CONCERNED WITH SPEECH AND LANGUAGE IMPAIRMENTS

Alliance for Technology Access
1119 Old Humboldt Road
Jackson, TN 38305
(800) 914-3017
(731) 554-5284 (TTY)
(731) 554-5283 (Fax)
http://www.ataccess.org

American Speech-Language-Hearing Association (ASHA)
2200 Research Boulevard
Rockville, MD 20850
(800) 638-8255
(301) 296-5650 (TTY)
(301) 296-8589 (Fax)
http://www.asha.org

Cleft Palate Foundation
1504 E. Franklin Street
Suite 102
Chapel Hill, NC 27514
(919) 933-9044
(919) 933-9604 (Fax)
http://www.cleftline.org

Division for Communicative Disabilities and Deafness (DCDD), Council for Exceptional Children
1110 N. Glebe Road
Suite 300
Arlington, VA 22201–5704
(888) 232-7723
(866) 915-5000 (TTY)
(703) 264-9494 (Fax)
http://www.dcdd.us

National Craniofacial Association
P.O. Box 11082
Chattanooga, TN 37401
(800) 332-2373
http://www.faces-cranio.org

National Easter Seals Society
233 South Wacker Drive
Suite 2400
Chicago, IL 60606
(800) 221-6827
(312) 726-4258 (TTY)
(312) 726-1494 (Fax)
http://www.easterseals.com

National Dissemination Center for Children with Disabilities
1825 Connecticut Avenue N.W.
Suite 700
Washington, DC 20008
(800) 695-0285 (Voice/TTY)
(202) 884-8441 (Fax)
http://www.nichcy.org

REFLECTING ON STANDARDS

The following exercises are designed to help you learn to apply the Council for Exceptional Children (CEC) standards to your teaching practice. Each of the reflection exercises below correlates with a knowledge or skill within the CEC standards. For the full text of each of the related CEC standards, please refer to the standards integration grid located in Appendix B.

Focus on Foundations ***(CEC Content Standard #1 CC1K5)***
Reflect on what you have learned about how students with speech and language impairments are diagnosed. If you had a student in your class with a culturally or linguistically diverse background who exhibited signs of speech or language impairments, what kinds of issues might you have in defining and identifying if he or she had exceptional learning needs? How might you need to work with families and school personnel to make sure to address the student's learning needs?

Focus on Individual Learning Differences ***(CEC Content Standard #3 CC3K1)***
Reflect on what you have learned about students with speech and language impairments. If you were to have a student in your class who needed to daily meet with a speech–language pathologist, how might you support the student's attendance at therapy? How do you think the student might feel about standing out from his or her peers? How might his or her exceptional learning needs affect his or her relationships with peers? What can you, as a teacher, do to help alleviate any discomfort for the student?

STUDENT STUDY SITE

Visit the Student Study Site at www.sagepub.com/gargiulo4emedia for these additional learning tools:

- Video links
- Media links
- Self-quizzes
- E-flashcards
- Full-text SAGE journal articles
- Web exercises

CHAPTER 11

Learning Objectives

After reading Chapter 11 you should be able to:

- Define hearing impairment, deaf, and hard of hearing.
- Distinguish between conductive and sensorineural hearing loss.
- Explain the various assessment procedures used to measure hearing loss.
- Describe the difference between prelingual and postlingual hearing impairments.
- Outline the historical evolution of educational services for children and youth with hearing impairments.
- List possible causes of hearing loss.
- Identify representative academic, social, and language characteristics of individuals with hearing impairments.
- Distinguish among oral, manual, and total communication approaches for instructing students with hearing impairments.
- Describe the concept of the Deaf culture.
- Summarize educational services for persons with hearing impairments across the life span.
- Explain how technology benefits individuals with hearing impairments.

Individuals With Hearing Impairments

A PARENT'S STORY

We didn't think we would ever have a child. We were married for eleven years before the magic day. Christine is our little miracle child. Preparing for parenthood was lots of fun. We decorated a nursery, went shopping for furniture and clothes, and set up a college fund. Baby showers and teas were an exciting end to an uneventful pregnancy. My pregnancy was normal with no complications. The delivery was induced since my blood pressure was rising at the end. I had natural childbirth. She was beautiful . . . two eyes, one nose, one mouth, ten fingers, ten toes, and all in the right places. All the early checkups were routine, with no problems.

Video Link 11.1
Watch for more on hearing impairment.

I didn't start to worry until Christine was about 6 months of age. My pediatrician listened to my concerns. At an office visit, Christine was playing with the paper on the exam table when the doctor came in. He clapped his hands loudly. I almost jumped out of my skin, but our little girl never knew he was in the room. He examined her ears and found nothing wrong. He sent us to an ENT (ear, nose, and throat specialist).

Video Link 11.2
Watch a parent's perspective.

The first ENT said that there must be fluid behind her eardrums, so we got tubes. That didn't seem to make any difference. That ENT sent us to another ENT. The second ENT told me I was a hypochondriac and there was nothing wrong with my child. Finally, we were sent to another ENT, who diagnosed Christine as being hearing impaired, but because of her age, he was not sure of the severity. Let the grieving begin . . . no one plans on having a child with a disability. All our hopes and dreams popped like a balloon. What were we going to do? Where do we find help?

Written by Betty Nelson, University of Alabama at Birmingham

Video Link 11.3
Meet a child with hearing impairment.

We started reading and calling, talking to everyone. Christine got her first set of hearing aids before her first birthday, but they were not strong enough. Each time we got bigger and more powerful hearing aids. At age 1, she was finally diagnosed as profoundly hearing impaired. We wanted her to talk. We wanted her to be independent. I didn't want to send her to a special school, isolated from society.

We started auditory–verbal therapy. We made it a part of our daily life. It was once told to us that auditory–verbal therapy was living your life but narrating everything you see and do. After about six months with the most powerful hearing aids made, we didn't see any or very much progress.

Being in the medical profession, we started reading and talking to people about cochlear implants. That would be the next step. We talked to several surgeons in Georgia, Texas, and Tennessee, and here at home in Alabama. Christine was implanted at 2 years, 4 months of age, and the implant was turned on the first of November. It was a frightening time for all of us. She was our little miracle child, and we had waited so very long for her. Christine's and our lives began again after her implant was stimulated. It worked! The first month was very hard on all of us, with lots of tears from us all. It was a new world with sound. Christine was turning to her name within two weeks. We worked with her every day, all waking hours. We sang, talked, and babbled.

Christine was enrolled in a church preschool with normally hearing kids. We pushed her out there, but we were always right behind her all the way. Currently, Christine is in a mainstreamed elementary school with a sound field system in the classroom. She gets some help from a teacher of the hearing impaired when she needs it. We are there to help with anything she might not understand and to reinforce what is taught in the classroom. She is making straight As so far. Christine enjoys dancing competitively. We don't know how she does it.

If you were to sit and talk to her today, you would never know she had a disability. She has beautiful speech with great inflections in her voice. We were at a company party, and there were a lot of people we didn't know and who didn't know us. The kids were all swimming in the lake. I overheard one little boy ask his mother why Christine didn't talk to him, as she did earlier that day. I interrupted and asked the little boy if she had her back to him while he was talking. We told him she was deaf and could not hear him without her processor on. All the other parents were astonished. "But she talks so well—she doesn't sound deaf or sign," people said. We had to tell them all about cochlear implants and what a huge change it made in our life. Christine sounds like any other normally hearing child. That made us feel great. Strangers couldn't tell she was hearing impaired.

Video Link 11.4
Meet a child with hearing impairment.

If we can tell anyone about cochlear implants, it would be to say that it was the best thing that happened to us. It is worth looking into and doing. It is a lot of hard work. As a family, we have dedicated many hours and much money to the rehabilitation of Christine.

We are very grateful for having a child like her. She is a joy to be with, and watching her now . . . all the hard work we did early on has paid off. Granted, she will never have normal hearing and has to work harder than anyone in her classes, but we wouldn't change a thing. She is a great example of what a cochlear implant at an early age can do for someone.

—Kitty McBride

For most people, hearing is an automatic process. The ability to hear allows individuals to gain information about themselves and the world around them through development of communication skills and identification of environmental auditory clues. Language, the central communication skill in humans, is learned by interacting with the environment and associating stimuli in numerous ways (Allen & Cowdery, 2009). Typically, an individual's language is refined and speech is developed through a series of activities: observing, listening, understanding, imitating others, hearing oneself, and comparing and perfecting speech and language components of the communication process. Parts of these activities and the development of language and speech may be difficult for individuals with hearing impairments.

Definitions and Concepts in the Field of Hearing Impairment

Hearing impairment is a general term used to describe disordered hearing. We should point out that the use of this term is offensive to some individuals who are deaf and hard of hearing because the word *impairment* implies a deficiency. Although we acknowledge this viewpoint, the label *hearing impairment* is preferred by the federal government when describing this disability category. We have chosen to be consistent with the terminology used by the U.S. Department of Education.

Hearing sensitivity loss refers to a specific aspect of hearing impairment, and is ordinarily described as ranging in severity from mild to profound. The term **deaf** is often overused and misunderstood, and may be applied inappropriately to describe the various types of hearing loss. It can be defined as referring to those for whom the sense of hearing is nonfunctional for the ordinary purposes of life. The federal definition (PL 108–446) describes deafness as a hearing loss that adversely affects educational performance and is so severe that the child is impaired in processing linguistic information (communication) through hearing, with or without amplification (hearing aids). Deafness precludes successful processing of linguistic information through audition, with or without a hearing aid (Kuder, 2008). The term *Deaf*, used with a capital *D*, refers to those individuals who want to be identified with Deaf culture. It is inappropriate and misleading to use the term *deaf* in reference to any hearing loss that is mild or moderate in degree.

Persons who are hearing impaired but possess enough **residual hearing** (remaining usable hearing) to hear and understand speech may be described as **hard of hearing**. Hard of hearing individuals are those in whom the sense of hearing, although defective, is functional either with or without a hearing aid. For these persons, the use of a hearing aid is frequently necessary or desirable to enhance residual hearing (Kuder, 2008).

Minimal hearing loss (MHL), although not currently classified as a hearing impairment, is gaining significant attention. Persons with MHL have difficulty hearing spoken language at a distance or in the presence of background noise. Both of these conditions are present in classrooms and can significantly affect the ability of a child with MHL to learn language and succeed academically (Kaderavek & Pakulski, 2002; Kuder, 2008). The extent to which persons with hearing impairment have difficulty in developing speech and language, as well as the degree of auditory communication difficulty they experience, is heavily influenced by the degree of hearing loss.

The Anatomy of the Auditory System

The ear is divided into four connected sections: the **outer ear** (also known as the auricle), the **middle ear**, the **inner ear**, and the **central auditory nervous system** (see Figure 11.1). The outer ear functions to protect the middle ear, direct sound into the ear canal, and enhance sound localization. In addition, the outer ear serves to enhance the intensity of sounds in the midfrequency range where the sound spectrum of speech is located.

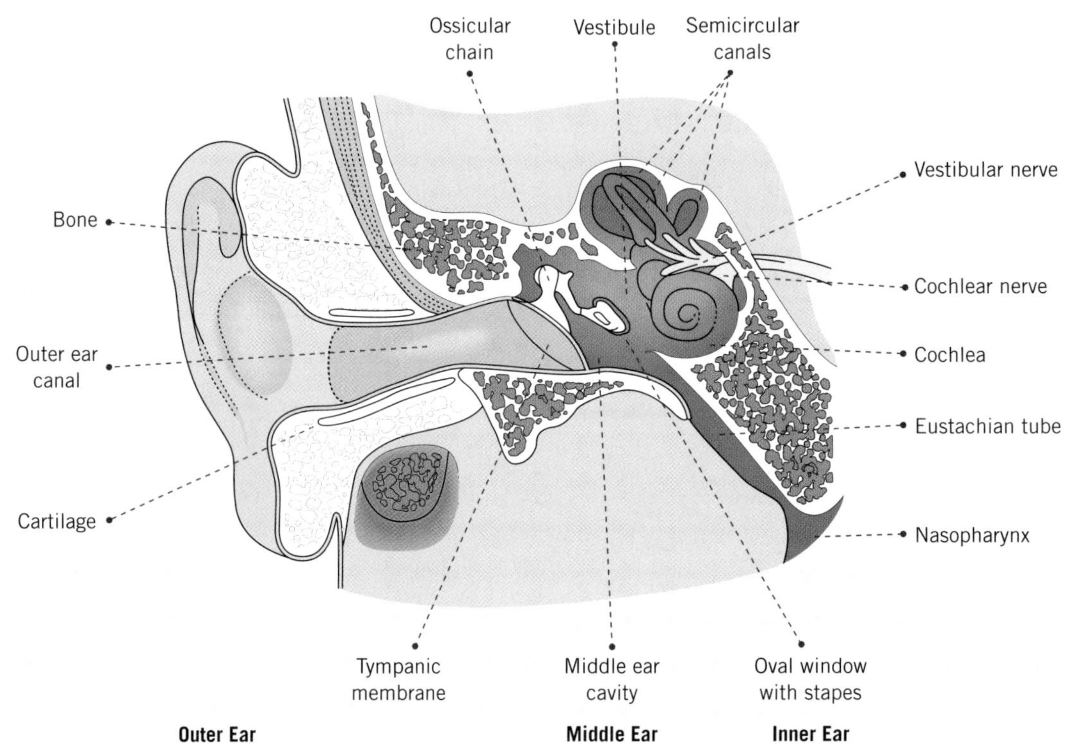

FIGURE 11.1 A Cross Section of the Human Ear

SOURCE: Redrawn from J. Northern, *Hearing Disorders,* 3rd ed. (Boston: Allyn and Bacon, 1996), p. 16.

Sound waves enter the outer ear and travel through the ear canal to the **tympanic membrane** (eardrum), causing a vibrating action. The tympanic membrane is attached to one of three of the smallest bones in the body, the **malleus** (hammer), through which the sound vibrations are transmitted to the second and third of the smallest bones, the **incus** (anvil) and the **stapes** (stirrup). These three bone structures form the **ossicular chain**, a bridge of bones across which sound vibrations travel to the inner ear. Together with the tympanic membrane, the ossicles convert airborne sound waves into mechanical (vibratory) energy and transfer this to the inner ear.

The footplate of the stapes, the smallest of the three middle ear bones, fits into the **oval window**, an opening into the inner ear. The vibratory motion of the stapes footplate in the oval window transmits mechanical energy to fluid-filled channels within the snail-like structure of the **cochlea** (inner ear). The cochlea houses the end organ of hearing, called the **organ of Corti.** Waves set up in the cochlear fluid, the result of vibratory energy from the tympanic membrane and ossicular chain, stimulate nearly 20,000 tiny hair cells in the organ of Corti arrayed along the length of the cochlea. This mechanical energy is transformed into electrical nerve impulses. The hair cells near the oval window respond to high-frequency energy, and those in the middle and at the apex of the cochlea respond to low-frequency energy. The resultant nerve impulses course through the auditory nervous system pathways to the auditory cortex, located in the temporal lobe of the brain, for message decoding (Herer, Knightly, & Steinberg, 2007).

Classifications of Hearing Loss

The classification or type of hearing loss refers primarily to the site of disorder in the auditory system causing the hearing impairment. A **conductive hearing loss** is caused by a blockage or barrier to the transmission of sound through the outer or middle ear. It is referred to as a conductive loss because sound is not conducted normally through the mechanical sound-conducting mechanisms in the disordered outer or middle ear (Stach, 2010). As a result, sounds are soft or attenuated in some way for the listener, but clearly heard when loud enough. Common causes of a conductive loss include inflammation, infection of the middle ear (**otitis media**), objects in the ear, or malformations of the outer or middle ear. Typically, a conductive loss can be reversed by medical or surgical intervention.

A **sensorineural hearing loss** is caused by disorders of the inner ear (cochlea), the auditory nerve that transmits impulses to the brain, or both. In this type of hearing loss, there is not only a loss of hearing sensitivity, but sounds are usually distorted to the listener and speech often is not heard clearly. This type of hearing loss may be congenital or may occur as a result of accident, illness, or disease. Although a small percentage of sensorineural hearing losses can be medically or surgically treated, most cannot be and are permanent in nature (Bess & Humes, 2008).

A **mixed hearing loss** is a combination of both a conductive and a sensorineural loss. In many cases, the conductive portion of the hearing loss may respond to medical or surgical treatment. Typically, however, the listener continues to experience the effects of the residual sensorineural impairment and may be a candidate for a hearing aid (Bess & Humes, 2008).

A **central hearing disorder** is one resulting from disorder or dysfunction in the central auditory nervous system between the brain stem and the auditory cortex in the brain. A hearing loss may or may not accompany this type of hearing impairment. The listener with this impairment may be able to hear, but cannot make sense of or understand speech. Additional problems, such as short- and long-term auditory memory and reading comprehension disability (Salvia, Ysseldyke, & Bolt, 2010), may also be present. This impairment may be referred to as a central auditory processing disorder, as described in Chapter 10 (Stach, 2010).

A similar type of hearing loss is **auditory neuropathy/auditory dys-synchrony**. In this type of hearing loss, the cochlea is functioning normally, but there is an absence of neural function. A relatively recent area of research, auditory neuropathy/auditory dys-synchrony is estimated to be present in one of every ten children with a hearing impairment and three of every thousand high-risk neonates. The effect of this type of loss is highly variable, and its eventual outcome is unpredictable (Scott, 2003).

A final, much less common type of hearing loss is **functional or nonorganic hearing loss**. Persons with this disorder typically demonstrate a loss of hearing that is inconsistent with **audiometric test** findings (Roeser, Valente, & Hosford-Dunn, 2008). In most cases, some organic hearing loss actually exists in these persons, but they may exaggerate the loss at the time of the audiometric evaluation. In some cases, test results show no organic hearing loss at all, although the individual may claim a hearing deficit.

Persons with hearing loss caused by a disorder in the brain or auditory nerve can be expected to have more difficulty processing sound and developing speech and language than those with hearing impairments caused by readily treatable factors such as ear infection. The type and degree of hearing loss often have significant implications for treatment and education.

Degree of Hearing Loss

The severity of auditory and speech communication disorders is often directly related to the degree or severity of hearing loss. Although there are individual differences in the effects associated with a given degree of hearing loss, listeners with mild hearing impairments generally experience less difficulty in auditory communication interactions than persons with a severe or profound degree of hearing loss. Persons with no hearing at all in one ear but normal hearing in the other experience some specific hearing deficits, but do not lose half of their hearing.

Accurate assessment of a hearing loss is important for determining its impact on communication.

Measurement of Hearing Impairment

An **audiologist** is an independent professional who holds certification and/or licensure and provides evaluation, rehabilitation, and prevention services to persons with hearing impairments. Audiologists are the primary specialists in evaluating hearing loss and determining the extent to which that loss constitutes an impairment and disability. Typically, the assessment of hearing begins with the goal of accurately measuring hearing threshold levels. If a hearing loss exists, the audiologist uses test and measurement procedures to determine the extent of the deficit, the impact on communication function, whether the hearing loss can be treated medically or surgically, and whether the use of hearing aids or other amplification systems is indicated.

Auditory threshold measures obtained by the audiologist during a hearing evaluation are plotted on a graph called an **audiogram** (see Figure 11.2, page 402). The horizontal axis of an audiogram is divided into octave intervals corresponding to the principal test frequencies of interest during the evaluation. The **frequency** of a particular sound is a measure of the rate at which the sound source vibrates and is measured in **hertz (Hz)**, so named in honor of a German scientist. The frequency of sounds can be precisely measured electronically. Pitch is the psychological correlate of frequency and cannot be measured as precisely because it is perceived differently from one person to the next. But in general, as the frequency of a sound increases, a listener perceives the sound as having increased in pitch. The audiogram typically displays a range of frequencies from about 250 Hz to 8,000 Hz. Most sounds important to human beings fall between 125 and 8,000 Hz, with most of the energy in human speech concentrated in the range of 500 to 3,000 Hz (Berk, 2008).

The vertical axis of the audiogram displays hearing threshold levels (HTLs) in increments of 10 **decibels (dB)**, with 0 dB at the top (representing no hearing loss). As the hearing loss increases, the hearing thresholds are plotted lower down on the audiogram. Decibels are units of sound pressure. Sound pressure is a physical measure that can be precisely determined. It is associated with the psychological sensation of loudness, which is not perceived identically by all persons. In general, as sound pressure in decibels increases, the sensation of loudness increases. Human speech normally ranges between a 40- and 60-dB sound pressure level; any sound above a 130-dB sound pressure level, such as large electrical turbines (145 dB), can be extremely painful and damaging (Bess & Humes, 2008). Table 11.1 presents the decibel levels of everyday sounds from our environment.

During the basic hearing evaluation process, **pure-tone audiometry** is conducted through earphones or other means to obtain an audiogram. Stimuli are delivered to the listener until a test signal of a particular frequency is barely audible 50 percent of the time. It is then presented to the person being evaluated, and a hearing threshold level for that signal can be plotted on the audiogram. This is a convenient and well-accepted measurement technique permitting an efficient determination of hearing threshold levels across the frequency range most important for hearing and understanding speech and environmental sounds. Ordinarily, pure-tone audiometry will be conducted in two modes, air conduction and bone conduction. **Air-conduction audiometry** is carried out with earphones or speakers and reflects hearing thresholds measured through the outer, middle, and inner ears. In contrast, **bone-conduction audiometry** is carried out with a small vibrator placed on the forehead or on the bone behind the ear, stimulating the inner

TABLE 11.1 Decibel Levels of Common Environmental Sounds

Noise levels are measured in decibels (dB). The higher the decibel level, the louder the noise. Sounds louder than 80 decibels are considered potentially hazardous. The noise chart below gives an idea of average decibel levels for everyday sounds around you.

Painful	• 150 dB = rock music peak • 140 dB = firearms, air raid siren, jet engine • 130 dB = jackhammer • 120 dB = jet plane takeoff, amplified rock music at 4–6 feet, car stereo, band practice
Extremely Loud	• 110 dB = rock music, model airplane • 106 dB = timpani and bass drum rolls • 100 dB = snowmobile, chain saw, pneumatic drill • 90 dB = lawnmower, shop tools, truck traffic, subway
Very Loud	• 80 dB = alarm clock, busy street • 70 dB = busy traffic, vacuum cleaner • 60 dB = conversation, dishwasher
Moderate	• 50 dB = moderate rainfall • 40 dB = quiet room
Faint	• 30 dB = whisper, quiet library

SOURCE: Adapted from the American Speech-Language-Hearing Association. Available at http://www.asha.org/public/hearing/disorders/noise.htm

ear directly. This reflects hearing sensitivity as measured primarily from the inner ear, not from the conductive mechanism in the outer and middle ears. A comparison of air- and bone-conduction hearing threshold levels forms the basis of determining the type of hearing loss present.

For example, Panel A in Figure 11.2 (page 402) shows a conductive hearing loss. When the audiogram is examined closely, the bone-conduction hearing threshold levels (HTLs) can be seen to be clustered around the 0-dB level, suggesting no hearing loss for these stimuli. On the other hand, Os, representing air-conduction HTLs, cluster around the 40-dB hearing level. These results suggest that, when the inner ear is stimulated directly by bone conduction, hearing thresholds are normal. However, when the test stimuli are delivered through the ear canal, a 40-dB hearing loss is present. This leads the audiologist to suspect the presence of some conductive disorder affecting the outer or middle ear transmission system that may be causing the hearing loss. Panel B displays findings for an individual with similar bone- and air-conduction deficits, indicating mild to moderate sensorineural hearing loss. Panel C in Figure 11.2 illustrates normal hearing threshold levels. It can be seen that both triangles (bone conduction) and Os (air conduction) cluster around the 0- to 10-dB range at each test frequency, suggesting no hearing loss.

Other Types of Hearing Assessment

Often, a hearing screening is the initial point at which hearing loss is suspected, and more sophisticated audiological procedures may be required. The American Speech-Language-Hearing Association (ASHA) (1993) has developed guidelines for hearing screening. ASHA suggests that the process involve (1) a case history; (2) visual inspection of the outer ear, ear canal, and eardrum; (3) pure-tone audiologic hearing screening; and (4) tympanometry screening. It is important to note that hearing screening aims to determine only whether a hearing loss may be present, not the degree or type of hearing impairment.

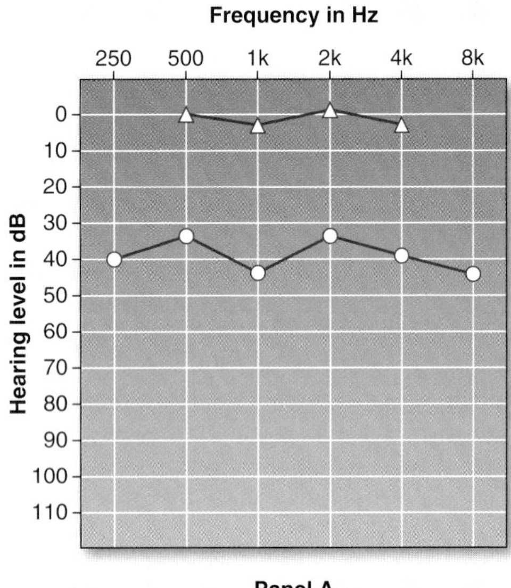

Panel A

An audiogram demonstrating that when the outer or middle ear is not functioning normally, resulting in a conductive hearing loss, the intensity of the air-conducted signals must be raised before threshold is reached while the bone-conduction thresholds remain normal.

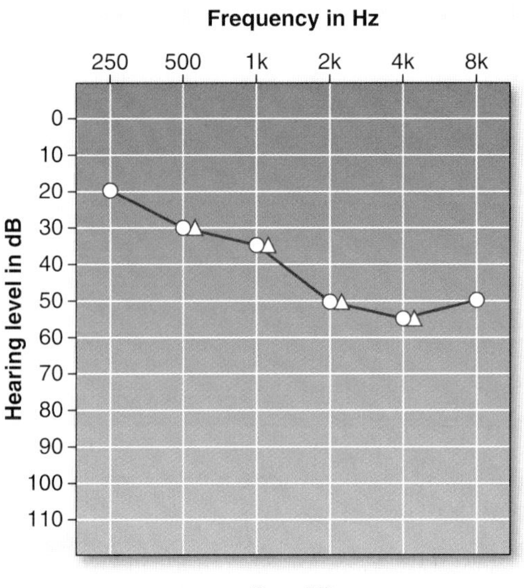

Panel B

An audiogram demonstrating that when a hearing loss is of cochlear origin, resulting in a sensorineural hearing loss, both air- and bone-conduction thresholds are affected similarly.

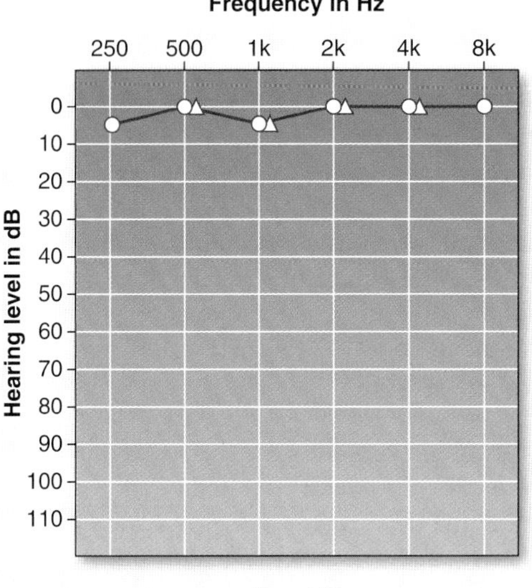

Panel C

An audiogram showing that when the outer and middle ear are functioning normally, air-conduction and bone-conduction thresholds are the same.

○ Air conduction △ Bone conduction

FIGURE 11.2 Audiograms Demonstrating Types of Hearing Loss

SOURCE: Adapted from B. Stach, *Clinical Audiology: An Introduction,* 2nd ed. (Clifton Park, NY: Delmar/Cengage Learning, 2010), pp. 89–91.

Audiologists are trained to conduct hearing screening programs in hospital newborn nurseries, in schools, and for adults. Some school systems employ audiologists, and hearing screening programs may fall within their purview. However, in most school settings, it is the speech–language pathologist who is best equipped to conduct hearing screening, refer students who are suspected of having a hearing loss for further audiologic evaluation, and make recommendations for school placement. Audiologic assessment is an essential component in the determination of a hearing loss and its impact on communication. However, a thorough assessment battery, including assessment of cognitive functioning, speech and language skills, social–emotional adjustment, and academic achievement, is required for appropriate school placement (Simeonsson & Rosenthal, 2001).

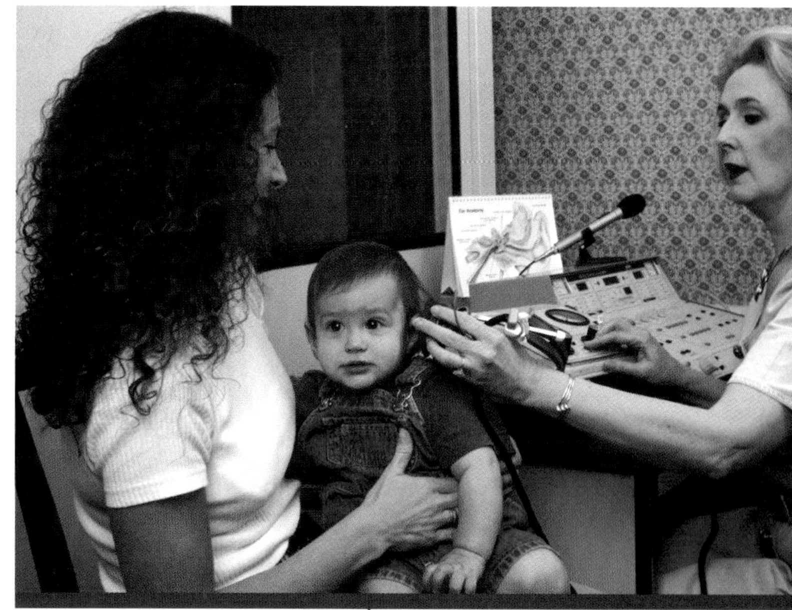

Special assessments are often used when evaluating the hearing of young children or students with special needs.

Hearing is a complex hierarchy of functions, the assessment of which requires highly sophisticated instrumentation and procedures in a clinical setting. Furthermore, test procedures appropriate for cooperative adults are not useful with young and many special-needs children. For example, **play audiometry** is often used with children who are difficult to test or unable to follow simple commands. In this procedure, the child is conditioned to respond to sounds in specific ways in order to determine the hearing threshold levels. **Speech audiometry** measures an individual's **speech recognition threshold (SRT)**, as well as that person's speech recognition ability in various listening conditions. Other types of auditory system assessment include electrophysiological measures of auditory function from the inner ear through the auditory brain stem to the cortex of the brain (**auditory evoked potentials**). **Evoked otoacoustic emissions** from the inner ear can be measured with sensitive microphones to examine functions in the inner ear far beyond the understanding of scientists in the past. To detect possible problems in the middle ear, **acoustic immittance** measures are used, placing a small probe in the ear to measure the transmission of sound through the eardrum and ossicular chain (American Speech-Language-Hearing Association, 2010a). Using all of these procedures, audiologists have opened new windows into mechanisms to evaluate human hearing, leading to better assessment and remediation for those with hearing impairments.

Age of Onset

The effects of hearing impairment depend significantly on the age at which the impairment occurs. **Prelingual** hearing impairment refers to disordered hearing present at birth or occurring before the development of speech and language. **Postlingual** impairment describes an auditory deficit acquired after the acquisition of speech and language (Berk, 2008). The age at which the hearing loss occurs is critical because normal language development is very much dependent on an intact auditory system.

Video Link 11.5
Watch a parent's perspective.

Not surprisingly, postlingually deaf children generally develop better speech, language, reading, and writing skills than prelingually deafened youngsters. Currently, great importance is placed on the early identification of hearing impairment in neonates and infants so that early intervention can reduce the effects of the hearing impairment on these skills, as well as on other areas such as social/cognitive development and academic achievement (Gallagher, Easterbrooks, & Malone, 2006).

The American Speech-Language-Hearing Association (2004, 2010d) estimates that one in every twenty-two infants born in the United States has some type of hearing loss, with about one in every thousand infants exhibiting a severe or profound hearing loss. Hearing loss is the most common congenital disorder in newborns. Forty states, the District of Columbia, and Puerto Rico currently have legislation that requires universal hearing screening for newborns. It is estimated that with this legislation, currently 95 percent of all newborns born in hospitals receive screening ("Early Hearing Campaign Honored," 2007).

A Brief History of the Field

The history of education of the hearing impaired is complex and controversial. Hearing impairments have probably existed in the North American region since the early settlement of this area by diverse Native American populations. Despite occasional references to provision of educational services for individuals with hearing impairments, however, there is no evidence of any organized program development until the nineteenth century (Moores, 2001).

In 1817, the first school in the United States for students with significant hearing impairments, the American Asylum for the Education of the Deaf and Dumb, was established in Hartford, Connecticut. This institution was begun through the efforts of a young divinity student named Thomas Hopkins Gallaudet. The name of the school was eventually changed to the American School for the Deaf, and the student population broadened to include individuals with hearing impairment from other states (Moores, 2001).

During this time period in France, a number of schools for the hearing impaired were experimenting with l'Epée's methods of communication, which were primarily manual. Gallaudet visited these schools and was greatly influenced by the work of l'Epée. In an effort to establish effective systems of **manual communication** in the United States, Gallaudet brought Laurent Clerc, a deaf Frenchman and well-known educator of the hearing impaired, to the United States. However, other American deaf educators went to Europe and were impressed by the **oral approaches** and philosophies. Of special interest were those methods that discouraged the use of any form of manual communication or sign language (Van Hasselt, Strain, & Hersen, 1988).

Many parents of children with significant hearing impairments assumed that living and learning with other individuals with similar problems was best for their children, and early formal education efforts were centered primarily in residential schools. Residential schools at this time were selective and would not serve all students with significant hearing impairments, especially those from minority groups or those with other significant disabilities. Day schools gained popularity partly because of these restrictive policies.

In 1864, Abraham Lincoln signed legislation establishing the nation's first college for the hearing impaired, known today as Gallaudet University. However, the debate over which method (oral or manual) was more appropriate for the instruction and communication of individuals with significant hearing impairments was now in full force. The two central figures in this debate were Thomas Gallaudet's son Edward, a renowned legal scholar, and Alexander Graham Bell, known to most as the inventor of the telephone and audiometer, who was an internationally recognized educator of the deaf. Bell's position centered on the issue of segregation in policy and practice. He believed that the manual philosophy, particularly in residential schools, as well as the use of sign language, fostered segregation of individuals with significant hearing impairments from the mainstream of society. Bell proposed a number of radical pieces of legislation that would (1) eliminate residential schools, (2) ban the use of manual communication in any form, (3) legislate that no adult with a significant hearing impairment could become a teacher of the deaf, and (4) forbid two adults with significant hearing impairments to marry. Interestingly, for many years the oral approach was more widely accepted than the manual position.

The issue of what constitutes the least restrictive environment for students with hearing impairments is controversial.

Edward Gallaudet strongly opposed these positions from both a moral and a methodological point of view. He believed that those who used the manual method (1) could learn when expectations were appropriately high, (2) would not feel isolated from society, (3) could and would participate in general life activities, and (4) would benefit socially by having friends with common interests (Moores, 2001). Eventually, Gallaudet's position gained support in Congress through appropriations to establish teacher preparation programs emphasizing the manual approach.

In the 1970s, **total communication (TC)**—combining a number of sensory modalities with manual and oral communication—was adopted by many professionals as the best approach to working with individuals with significant hearing impairments. Those who argued for TC criticized the practice of keeping many children with hearing impairments in oral programs until 9 or 10 years of age, especially those who had limited early success, because critical periods for attaining the basic linguistic principles were potentially missed. Those who argued against TC expressed concern that it would be difficult to emphasize all methods of communication and do justice to all. They further argued that the manual method would be the primary avenue of communication because it was significantly quicker and easier to learn. The debate continues today, indicated by the fact that Gallaudet University publishes a journal with a total communication orientation

(*American Annals of the Deaf*), and the AG Bell Association publishes one with an oral orientation (*Volta Review*). Both journals are world renowned for their quality of content and research articles.

The educational placement options available for hearing-impaired children today are a result of historical, political, and cultural forces. Since the 1980s, there has been a significant increase in the visibility of cultural advocacy groups for individuals who are hearing impaired. The "deaf rights" movement, embraced by many residential schools and deaf communities, increasingly polarized proponents of various methodologies. Advanced medical interventions such as gene therapy and cochlear implantation were not initially embraced by many culturally deaf adults, further complicating the cultural controversy. Educators today struggle to determine what constitutes the least restrictive environment (LRE) within the public school arena for children with significant hearing impairment. Although a number of educational placement options are available to facilitate LRE, parents as well as professionals frequently find themselves drawing legal and educational battle lines simply trying to *define* what constitutes such an environment.

The 1997 amendments to IDEA (PL 105–17) introduced a requirement to consider the communication needs of children with hearing impairments when making educational placement decisions. IDEA 2004 continues this stipulation. Communication-rich environments are an essential element in the education of children who are deaf and hard of hearing (Katz & Schery, 2006). What might be the LRE for many other children with disabilities may not be the LRE for a student with a hearing impairment because of the child's unique communication needs. Are there peers at the recommended placement site who can communicate with the child? Does the teacher have adequate skills in the communication mode typically used by the child? Does the teacher possess the skills necessary to meet the unique instructional needs of a student with hearing impairments? There are many questions regarding the implementation of the LRE requirement to consider—especially the communication needs of the pupil. Unfortunately, personnel responsible for making placement recommendations frequently do not have an adequate understanding of the educational needs of children who are deaf or hard of hearing (Easterbrooks & Baker, 2001; Katz & Schery).

Prevalence of Hearing Impairment

The number of Americans with a hearing loss has nearly doubled in the past three decades (American Speech-Language-Hearing Association, 2010d). Investigators estimate that hearing loss affects nearly 28 million people (American Speech-Language-Hearing Association, 2010c). Further, one in every twenty-two infants born in the United States has some degree of hearing impairment, and approximately one in every thousand infants has a severe or profound hearing impairment (American Speech-Language-Hearing Association, 2004; Herer et al., 2007).

Figure 11.3 shows the prevalence of hearing loss by age group in the United States. It is easily seen that prevalence of hearing loss increases as people age; persons above 65 years of age are about eight times more likely to have a hearing impairment than young adults in the 18–34 age category.

According to the U.S. Department of Education (2010), 70,781 students between the ages of 6 and 21 were defined as having a hearing impairment and receiving special education services during the 2008–2009 school year. These students represent 1.2 percent of all pupils with disabilities. At the same time, almost 8,400 preschoolers were receiving a special education because of a hearing impairment. This figure represents 1.1 percent of all preschoolers with a disability (U.S. Department of Education).

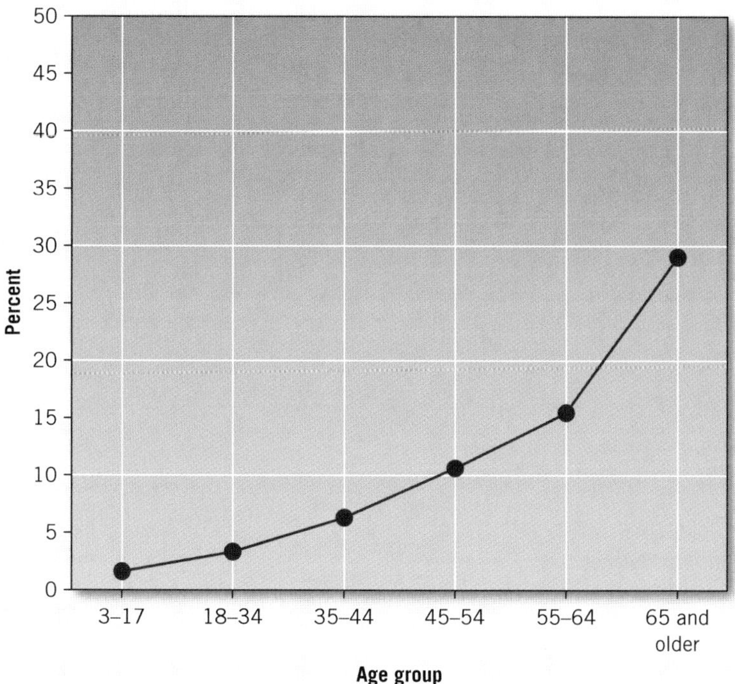

FIGURE 11.3 Estimate of the Prevalence of Hearing Impairment by Age Group

SOURCE: National Center for Health Statistics. (1994). *National Health Survey Interview,* Series 10, No. 188. Available at http://www.cdc.gov/nchs/data/series/sr_10/sr10_188.pdf

Etiology of Hearing Impairment

Causes of hearing loss can be classified in several ways. For example, hearing losses may be congenital (occurring before birth) or acquired (occurring after birth). Hearing losses occurring around the time of birth are generally considered to be congenital, whether or not the loss was actually documented at that time. Further, hearing losses may be classified as genetic or nongenetic. Genetic or hereditary factors are one of the leading causes of hearing impairments in children (Schirmer, 2001). It has been estimated that in approximately one third of all persons with hearing loss greater than about 55 dB, the origin of the loss is hereditary (Toriello, Reardon, & Gorlin, 2004). **Adventitious (acquired) hearing losses** of this magnitude constitute roughly another third of all cases, and unknown factors are responsible for the remaining third. The etiology of hearing loss is an important variable in determining immediate and long-range educational strategies.

Genetic/Hereditary Factors

Genetic causes are thought to account for more than a hundred and fifty different types of deafness (Bess & Humes, 2008). Researchers estimate that about one half of all congenital deafness is the result of genetic factors (Petersen & Willems, 2006). Of the several known modes of genetic inheritance, three mechanisms are most important. **Autosomal dominant** inheritance is characterized by expression of a trait (hearing loss) even if the gene for it is carried on only one chromosome of a matched pair. Conditions such as

Waardenburg syndrome (multicolored iris, white forelock, sensorineural hearing loss) and dominant progressive hearing loss (a sensorineural hearing loss that progresses over a period of years) are examples of autosomal dominantly inherited hearing losses.

In **autosomal recessive** inheritance, both genes of a pair must carry the characteristic in order for it to be expressed. Usher syndrome (bilateral sensorineural hearing loss and visual defects due to retinitis pigmentosa) is an example of autosomal recessive inheritance.

The third major mechanism of genetic transmission is **X-linked** inheritance. In the X-linked recessive form of this transmission mode, the parents are apparently normal, and the altered gene is associated with the X chromosomes of the male offspring. Most X-linked recessive hearing losses are sensorineural in type (Toriello et al., 2004).

Table 11.2 summarizes some of the disorders, both genetic and acquired, associated with hearing loss in children.

TABLE 11.2 Disorders Associated With Hearing Loss in Children

Cytomegalovirus (CMV)	• Most common congenital viral infection causing hearing loss today, occurring in one in one thousand live births • Contracted in utero or postnatally from the mother • Can result in sensorineural hearing loss as well as CNS, cardiac, optic, and growth abnormalities • Symptoms may not be apparent at birth, with onset about 18 months of age • Progresses rapidly during the first year
Down Syndrome	• Congenital chromosomal abnormality (trisomy 21) • Frequently have low set small ears, external canal stenosis, middle ear deformities, and facial nerve abnormalities • 30 percent of these children have sensorineural hearing loss • Most have poor Eustachian tube function, resulting in chronic middle ear disease with associated conductive fluctuant hearing loss
Meningitis	• Neonatal infection, can be viral or bacterial • Most common cause of acquired sensorineural hearing loss • Hearing loss can range from mild to profound, and may be progressive • Symptoms may include headache, neck stiffness, photophobia, and suppurative otitis media
Ototoxicity	• Can be caused by a wide variety of strong antibiotics such as aminoglycosides (gentamicin, kanamycin, etc.), chemotherapeutic agents such as cisplatin, or loop diuretics • Can also result from exposure to various chemical agents in the environment • Characterized by a progressive high-frequency sensorineural hearing loss following such exposure
Usher Syndrome	• Autosomal recessive • Occurs in 6 percent–12 percent of congenitally deaf children, and three in one hundred thousand of the general population • Involves retinitis pigmentosa and progressive moderate to severe sensorineural hearing loss • Can vary greatly in age of onset, severity, and progression
Waardenburg Syndrome	• Autosomal hereditary dominant • 20 percent have white forelock, 99 percent have increased distance between the eyes, 45 percent have two differently colored eyes (typically one brown and one blue) • Depigmentation of the skin and eyebrows that meet over the bridge of the nose • 50 percent have mild to severe sensorineural hearing loss, which can be unilateral or bilateral and is progressive

Infections

Many infectious agents that cause hearing loss are well documented; they can occur prenatally (before birth), at or around the time of birth (perinatally), or later in life (postnatally). During the mid-1960s, a rubella (German measles) outbreak caused an inordinate number of infants to be born with a hearing impairment. During that time span, approximately 10 percent of all congenital deafness was attributed to this disease, with half of these cases involving a severe sensorineural hearing loss. Fortunately, with the development of rubella vaccines, the incidence of this disease has dramatically decreased.

Common perinatal infections that may result in hearing impairment include cytomegalovirus (CMV), hepatitis B virus, and syphilis. Today, CMV infection is the leading viral cause of sensorineural hearing loss in children (Picard, 2004; Stach, 2010). Most children do not show clinical signs of the infection at birth but begin to demonstrate progressive evidence of it in the early years of life.

Measles and mumps viruses are examples of viral infections that can cause sensorineural hearing loss later in life, but for which there are now preventive vaccines. Hearing losses due to these viruses were all but completely eliminated, but failure to inoculate all children against these diseases has put them on the rise again and raised the risk of increased incidence of associated hearing loss.

Many nonviral infections can cause significant hearing loss. Bacterial meningitis can cause severe bilateral sensorineural hearing loss. Although viral meningitis can also cause hearing loss, most instances of hearing loss due to meningitis result from the bacterial form.

Otitis media is one of the leading causes of mild to moderate conductive hearing loss in children (Roizen, 2008). It is the most common reason for visits to physicians for children under age 6 (Schirmer, 2001). Fluid accumulation in the middle ear resulting from this disease typically causes a 15- to 40-dB conductive hearing loss and, if not treated, can lead to sensorineural impairment. Otitis media is most often treated by administering antibiotics or, in some instances, through placement of tubes in the ears.

Developmental Abnormalities

Some congenital causes of hearing loss involve abnormal development of outer or inner ear structure. **Atresia** (a narrowing or closure of the external ear canal and/or malformation of the middle ear) is a developmental disorder that affects the fetus early in pregnancy and results in malformation of the outer and/or middle ears. This frequently results in a conductive hearing loss that may or may not be treated successfully with surgical intervention.

Environmental/Traumatic Factors

Low birth weight, and its associated conditions, and asphyxia (breathing difficulties) are causes of serious hearing loss that frequently occur at birth or shortly thereafter. Both factors can result in conditions that actually cause hearing loss by traumatizing the ear. Some prescription drugs (including antibiotic medications) are known to be toxic to the inner ear, and the resulting hearing loss can occur prenatally when drugs are administered to the mother or during medical treatment later in life. The resulting hearing loss is typically sensorineural in type and permanent once damage is done. Intense noise, head injuries involving fractures of the skull, and dramatic pressure changes in the middle ear are all examples of traumatic causes of damage to the ear and hearing loss.

Hearing impairment has a wide range of causes, many of which have important implications for treatment and educational intervention to minimize the effects of hearing loss on children and adults.

Characteristics of Individuals With Hearing Impairments

Variations in etiology, onset, degree, and type of hearing loss, as well as family and educational situations, result in a widely diverse hearing-impaired population. However, children and adults with hearing disabilities characteristically experience significant issues with regard to social and intellectual development, speech and language, and educational achievement.

Intelligence

Over the past several years, reviews of the research on the intellectual characteristics of children with a hearing impairment have suggested that the distribution of intelligence or IQ scores for these individuals is similar to that of their hearing counterparts (Simeonsson & Rosenthal, 2001). Findings suggest that intellectual development for people with a hearing impairment is more a function of language development than cognitive ability. Any difficulties in performance appear to be closely associated with speaking, reading, and writing the English language, but are not related to level of intelligence (Marschark, 2006).

Speech and Language

Speech and language skills are the areas of development most severely affected for those with a hearing impairment, particularly for children who are born deaf. The majority of deaf children have a very difficult time learning to use speech (McLean, Wolery, & Bailey, 2004). Numerous papers published within the past fifty years on speech skills of children with a hearing loss suggest that the effects of a hearing loss on English language development vary considerably (Berk, 2008). For individuals who experience mild to moderate hearing losses, the effect may be minimal. Even for those with a prelingual moderate loss, effective communication skills are possible because the voiced sounds of conversational speech remain audible. Although the person with this type of hearing loss cannot hear unvoiced sounds and distant speech, language delays can be reduced or prevented by early diagnosis, the use of advanced technologies, and treatment. Thus, a vast majority of these individuals are able to use speech as the primary mode for English language acquisition.

For the individual with profound congenital deafness, most loud speech is inaudible, even with the use of the most sophisticated hearing aids. These individuals are unable to receive information through speech unless they have learned to speechread (lipread). Sounds produced by the individual who is deaf are often difficult to understand. Children who are deaf exhibit significant articulation, voice quality, and tone discrimination problems. Researchers have found that, even as early as 8 months of age, babies who are deaf appear to babble less than their hearing peers (Allen & Cowdery, 2009). This has been attributed to the fact that deaf infants do not experience the same auditory feedback from babbling as their hearing counterparts and therefore are not as motivated to continue the activity.

In 1990, the U.S. Food and Drug Administration approved cochlear implants for children between the ages of 2 and 17. Implants are now used at an even earlier age. Research indicates that the optimal age to implant a youngster is 10–15 months. New debates surround the potential benefit of early bilateral implantation. Early research indicates that pediatric implant users are receiving substantial benefit that will be evident in their development of speech and language (Berg, Ip, Hurst, & Herb, 2007).

Social Development

Video Link 11.6
Watch more about social development.

Social–emotional development in young children with hearing impairments shows the same developmental patterns as in those without a hearing loss with regard to preschool friendships and ethnic, age, and gender peer preferences. Social–emotional development, however, also depends heavily on the ability to use communication skills. A hearing loss modifies one's capacity to receive and process auditory stimuli; thus, the individual who is deaf or hard of hearing receives reduced auditory information and/or information that is distorted. As a result, there appear to be some differences in the way young deaf children play as compared to their hearing counterparts.

Young deaf children typically have less language interaction during play and appear to prefer groups of two rather than larger group sizes. These patterns may be attributed to the difficulty of dividing their attention, which is so visual in its nature, and their poorer knowledge of language appropriate to play situations. They also engage in less pretend play, possibly because language deficits impede their ability to script elaborate imaginary situations. Deaf children spend less time in cooperative peer play when they are with other deaf children; even though they are interested in and initiate the interaction, they frequently get no response from their play partner because of language deficits. When deaf and hearing children attempt to play but do not share a common communication system—both relying on oral skills or both relying on sign skills—they demonstrate little interest in playing together or sustaining a friendship (Lederberg, 1993; Marschark, 2006). This suggests a need to develop communication skills within the hearing peer group and among all teachers if children placed in inclusive classroom settings are to avoid social isolation. The poem "Deaf Donald" by Shel Silverstein is a poignant example of what may happen without such support (see Figure 11.4).

DEAF DONALD

Deaf Donald met Talkie Sue

But  was all he could do.

And Sue said, "Donald, I sure do like you."

But  was all he could do.

And Sue asked Donald, "Do you like me too?"

But  was all he could do.

"Good-bye then, Donald, I'm leaving you."

But  was all he did do.

And she left forever so she never knew

That  means I love you.

FIGURE 11.4 "Deaf Donald" by Shel Silverstein

There is an increasing awareness and acceptance of children with disabilities by their peer group. This is recognized and promoted by toy manufacturers as more "awareness" products become available on the open market. Mattel has assisted in awareness of hearing impairments through the introduction of the "Sign Language Barbie," which is distributed through Toys "R" Us.

Social and emotional development depend, in part, on a person's ability to communicate.

As children with a hearing impairment grow and mature, their capacity for receiving and using language hinders their overall social–emotional growth (developing friendships). Reviews of the literature on social and psychological development in adolescents who are deaf have suggested distinct differences from their hearing peers in such areas as maturity, awareness of social mores and attitudes, and social interactions (Marschark, 2007). The need for social interaction may tend to further isolate these individuals from the mainstream, as they seek and form social and professional relationships with others with hearing impairments. The Internet is providing more opportunity for interaction within the hearing-impaired peer group through the use of chat rooms.

Educational Achievement

The educational achievement of students with hearing impairments may be significantly delayed in comparison to that of their hearing peers. Students who are deaf or have a partial hearing impairment have considerable difficulty succeeding in an educational system that depends primarily on the spoken word and written language to transmit knowledge. Low achievement is characteristic of students who are deaf (Geers, 2006); they average three to four years below their age-appropriate grade levels. Even students with mild to moderate losses achieve below expectations based on their performance on tests of cognitive ability (Williams & Finnegan, 2003).

Reading is the academic area most negatively affected for students with a hearing impairment. Any hearing loss, whether mild or profound, appears to have detrimental effects on reading performance. Research suggests that pupils who are hearing impaired read at approximately a third- to fourth-grade level (Gallaudet Research Institute, 2003; Kuntze, 1998; Traxler, 2000). Consequently, many of these individuals will encounter difficulty reading a typical newspaper.

Although researchers report slight variations in educational achievement scores, there is no question that high-stakes testing is of great concern for this group of children. The difficulty the majority of students with hearing impairments across the country experience taking high school exit exams and the fact that most of them do not pass these tests are issues of profound concern among educators (Johnson, 2003).

Assessment of Individuals With Hearing Impairments

The primary objective of an assessment of individuals with a hearing impairment is to put together an accurate picture of cognitive, communicative, and personal characteristics (Simeonsson & Rosenthal, 2001). This information is central to designing individualized instructional plans and other experiential activities to promote development.

Cognitive Assessment

It is crucial that the intellectual assessment of students with hearing impairments use measures that do *not* rely primarily on verbal abilities as indicators of cognitive functioning. There are several nonverbal assessment options considered appropriate for individuals with hearing impairments. These include the nonverbal portion of the Kaufman Assessment Battery for Children (Kaufman & Kaufman, 2004) and the performance section of the Wechsler Intelligence Scale for Children (4th ed.) (Wechsler, 2003). Because of the nonverbal nature of these instruments, however, they have limited predictive validity in relation to achievement that requires verbal skills (Schum, 2004). As a result, their usefulness has yet to be determined in functional educational practice.

The two most widely used measures of academic achievement with this population are the Stanford Achievement Test (SAT) (Psychological Corporation, 2002) and individual state annual assessments. The psychometric qualities of the SAT include excellent data representing diverse performance levels of individuals with hearing impairments (Luckner & Bowen, 2006).

Communication Assessment

The most serious negative aspect of a hearing impairment is its effect on language and speech development. Inadequate auditory stimulation during early development almost always leads to marked problems in language acquisition and speech production (Allen & Cowdery, 2009). Language assessment with this population should examine both receptive and expressive communication skills, including (1) form of language, (2) content of language, and (3) use of language. However, most language assessments do not assess all these areas. In most cases, several different assessment tools and techniques (such as language sampling) are needed to accurately determine the individual's language abilities (Simeonsson & Rosenthal, 2001).

Speech assessment with this population should include a battery of tools designed to ascertain the individual's articulation, pitch, loudness, quality, and rate. Analysis of these speech functions will provide a basis for designing speech therapy objectives as part of the individualized education program (IEP) for the student with a hearing impairment.

Personal/Social/Behavioral Assessment

A number of measures of personal, social, and behavioral functioning are being used with individuals with hearing impairments. The assessment of personal/social characteristics with this population is very challenging given the language content of most of the measures in this area, which are designed to be completed by a rater in response to items in the domains of social adjustment, self-image, and emotional adjustment. Sattler and Hoge (2006) urge caution when inferring development in these areas. Individuals with a hearing impairment may respond atypically to a personality measure, not because they exhibit aberrant social–emotional development, but as a result of their linguistic difficulties.

Educational Considerations

One method of classifying hearing impairment is by degree. Hearing loss can range from mild to profound based on the level of intensity required (measured in decibels, or dB) at various frequencies (described in hertz, or Hz) to establish hearing threshold. This classification system is directly related to the individual's ability to hear and comprehend speech. Factors such as these, as well as whether the hearing loss is pre- or postlingual and fluctuant or stable, clearly have significant educational implications (see Table 11.3, page 414).

TABLE 11.3 Impact of Hearing Loss on Students

Degree of Hearing Loss	Possible Psychosocial Impact of Hearing Loss	Effect of Hearing Loss on Speech and Language	Potential Educational Needs and Programs
Minimal (borderline) 16–25 dB HL	May be unaware of subtle conversational cues, causing child to be viewed as inappropriate or awkward. May miss portions of fast-paced peer interactions, which could begin to have an impact on socialization and self-concept. May exhibit immature behavior. Child may be more fatigued than classmates because of greater listening effort.	May have difficulty hearing faint or distant speech. At 15 dB student can miss up to 10 percent of speech when teacher is at a distance greater than 3 feet and when the classroom is noisy, especially in the elementary grades when verbal instruction predominates.	May benefit from a hearing aid or personal FM system, depending on loss configuration. Would benefit from soundfield amplification if classroom is noisy and/or reverberant. Favorable seating. May need attention to vocabulary or speech, especially with recurrent otitis media history. Appropriate medical management necessary for conductive losses. Teacher requires in-service on impact of hearing on language development and learning.
Mild 26–40 dB HL	Barriers beginning to build, with negative impact on self-esteem as child is accused of “hearing when he or she wants to,” “daydreaming,” or “not paying attention.” Child begins to lose ability for selective hearing and has increasing difficulty suppressing background noise, which makes the learning environment stressful. Child is more fatigued than classmates because of listening effort needed.	At 30 dB can miss 25 percent–40 percent of speech. The degree of difficulty experienced in school will depend upon the noise level in the classroom, distance from the teacher, and the configuration of the hearing loss. Without amplification, the child with a 35- to 40-dB loss may miss at least 50 percent of class discussions, especially when voices are faint or speaker is not in line of vision. Will miss consonants, especially when a high-frequency hearing loss is present.	Will benefit from a hearing aid and use of a personal FM or soundfield FM system in the classroom. Needs favorable seating and lighting. Refer to special education for language evaluation and educational follow-up. Needs auditory skill building. May need attention to vocabulary and language development, articulation or speech reading, and/or special support in reading. May need help with self-esteem. Teacher in-service required.
Moderate 41–55 dB HL	Communication is often significantly affected, and socialization with peers with normal hearing becomes increasingly difficult. With full-time use of hearing aids/FM systems, child may be judged as a less competent learner. There is an increasing impact on self-esteem.	Understands conversational speech at a distance of 3–5 feet (face-to-face) only if structure and vocabulary controlled. Without amplification, the amount of speech missed can be 50 percent to 75 percent with a 40-dB loss and 80 percent to 100 percent with a 50-dB loss. Is likely to have delayed or defective syntax, limited vocabulary, imperfect speech production, and an atonal voice quality.	Refer to special education for language evaluation and for educational follow-up. Amplification is essential (hearing aids and FM system). Special education support may be needed, especially for primary-age children. Attention to oral language development, reading, and written language. Auditory skill development and speech therapy usually needed. Teacher in-service required.
Moderate to severe 56–70 dB HL	Full-time use of hearing aids/FM systems may result in child's being judged by both peers and adults as a less competent learner, resulting in poorer self-concept and diminished social maturity,	Without amplification, conversation must be very loud to be understood. A 55-dB loss can cause child to miss up to 100 percent of speech information. Will have marked difficulty in school situations requiring	Full-time use of amplification is essential. Will need resource teacher or special class depending on magnitude of language delay. May require special help in all language skills, language-based academic subjects, vocabulary, grammar, and

Degree of Hearing Loss	Possible Psychosocial Impact of Hearing Loss	Effect of Hearing Loss on Speech and Language	Potential Educational Needs and Programs
	and contributing to sense of rejection. In-service to address these attitudes may be helpful.	verbal communication in both one-to-one and group situations. Delayed language, syntax, reduced speech intelligibility, and atonal voice quality likely.	pragmatics, as well as reading and writing. Probably needs assistance to expand experiential language base. In-service of general educators required.
Severe 71–90 dB HL	Child may prefer other children with hearing impairments as friends and playmates. This may further isolate the child from the mainstream; however, these peer relationships may foster improved self-concept and a sense of cultural identity.	Without amplification, may hear loud voices about 1 foot from ear. When amplified optimally, children with hearing ability of 90 dB or better should be able to identify environmental sounds and detect all the sounds of speech. If loss is of prelingual onset, oral language and speech may not develop spontaneously or will be severely delayed. If hearing loss is of recent onset, speech is likely to deteriorate with quality becoming atonal.	May need full-time special aural/oral program with emphasis on all auditory language skills, speech reading, concept development, and speech. As loss approaches 80–90 dB, may benefit from a total communication approach, especially in the early language learning years. Individual hearing aid/personal FM system essential. Need to monitor effectiveness of communication modality. Participation in regular classes as much as possible. In-service of general educators essential.
Profound 91 dB HL or more	Depending on auditory/oral competence, peer use of sign language, parental attitude, and other factors, child may or may not increasingly prefer association with the Deaf culture.	Aware of vibrations more than tonal pattern. Many rely on vision rather than hearing as primary avenue for communication and learning. Detection of speech sounds dependent upon loss configuration and use of amplification. Speech and language will not develop spontaneously and are likely to deteriorate rapidly if hearing loss is of recent onset.	May need special program for children who are deaf, with emphasis on all language skills and academic areas. Program needs specialized supervision and comprehensive support services. Early use of amplification likely to help if part of an intensive training program. May be cochlear implant or vibrotactile aid candidate. Requires continual appraisal of needs in regard to communication and learning mode. Part-time in general education classes as much as benefits student.

SOURCE: Adapted from K. Anderson, "Hearing Conservation in the Public Schools Revisited," *Seminars in Hearing, 12*(4), 1991, pp. 361–363.

Individuals with a mild hearing loss may encounter difficulty hearing in a noisy classroom setting or distinguishing distant sounds; however, their speech discrimination ability is often within normal limits. Appropriate accommodations for such a student may include preferential seating, possible use of a hearing aid or personal FM system, greater redundancy in the instructional model, and increased collaboration with parents to facilitate learning.

Video Link 11.8
Watch a student's story.

The individual with a moderate hearing loss—depending on type, degree, and age of onset—may experience significant delays in speech and language. Articulation deficits, reduced vocabulary, difficulty mastering various grammatical and syntactical concepts, and poor voice quality are common problems. Hearing aid use coupled with personal FM systems is necessary for such students, in addition to the rehabilitative strategies cited previously.

Making Inclusion Work

My name is Catherine Davis, and I have been a teacher of the deaf and hard of hearing in the Blue Valley School District in Overland Park, Kansas, for four years. The first year I worked as an itinerant deaf education teacher serving six schools. Then I was lucky enough to get to start a center-based resource room program in a brand-new elementary school. There I teach preschool through fifth-grade students whose IEP teams have decided that due to the educational impact of their hearing loss—often accompanied by additional disabilities such as ADHD and/or cognitive, motor, and/or vision impairments—they would be best served in this program rather than in their neighborhood school. My students spend the majority of their day in the general education classroom but come to me for academic support as well as auditory training, speechreading, and sign language instruction.

I grew up in a small Midwestern town where there was not a lot of diversity. One boy in my high school was deaf, and I watched the other kids tease him, thinking he couldn't understand what they were saying because he couldn't hear them. He could. I decided to become his friend, learned to sign, and eventually started tutoring him. Thus, my love of teaching, combined with an interest in deafness and signing, began. After graduating from high school in 1992, I attended an interpreter-training program at the University of Kansas. Seeking to utilize my skills and have an adventure at the same time, I set out for Homer, Alaska, where I accepted a job interpreting for two Native Alaskan students. Miles from home, I encountered beauty and adventure, but also a challenge for which I was definitely unprepared. The two students with whom I worked had multiple disabilities and needed significant support. Unfortunately, the itinerant teacher was not always there to provide this support. Even though I loved Alaska and my job, this experience solidified my desire to teach, and I knew I needed more training. So after a year I returned to Kansas. I completed a B.S. in elementary education and an M.S. in deaf education, and I am now in my final year of my Ph.D. in special education with a focus on deaf education.

Inclusive Education Experience

The group of kids that I currently work with is truly representative of the type of caseload that a future teacher of the deaf can expect to have. My students are as different as they could be. I have one first grader who has a cochlear implant and communicates solely through sign language and another first-grade student who is hard of hearing, wears hearing aids, and uses an FM system. She is oral but learning to sign. A second-grade student has multiple disabilities including ADHD, aphasia, and vision loss. She wears hearing aids and an FM system, and uses both verbal and sign language. The fifth grader I teach has a severe hearing loss, wears hearing aids, uses an FM system, and also has multiple disabilities including motor, cognitive, and vision impairments. Her predominant mode of communication is oral.

At the beginning of every year I do an in-service for the entire staff in order to provide suggestions for working with students with a hearing loss. I also go into the general education classrooms and do lessons with all of the students explaining hearing loss, sign language, and Deaf culture. Often these lessons occur only with the classroom teacher or the special education teachers. However, I believe the whole school needs to be educated to really ensure that my students are fully included. I find that the more people know, the less apprehensive they are to interact with these kids. I let them try on hearing aids, listen to an FM system, watch a video on cochlear implants, learn some sign language, and even try to take a spelling test by reading lips to simulate what it might be like for students with a hearing loss.

A severe or profound hearing loss, again depending on the type, degree, and age of onset, may severely impede speech and language development. Individuals with severe to profound losses frequently have poor auditory discrimination, which often limits the effectiveness of conventional amplification devices. A team approach to remediation should be used, which involves substantial interaction with the child's managing audiologist to ensure accuracy of diagnostic information as well as appropriateness of amplification. Students with this degree of hearing loss will need significant accommodation in the educational environment to be successful, including intense visual language reinforcement for the instruction of grammar and syntax. See the accompanying Suggestions for the Classroom (page 418) on teaching students with hearing impairments.

Strategies for Inclusive Classrooms

Because of the diverse student needs, I am required to be versatile in my communication style. My philosophy on communication modality is not to have one! Instead, I go forward based on where the student is when he or she enters my program. At any given time, I use an eclectic combination of anything that works—sign, voice, gestures, drawing pictures, writing, acting—whatever it takes. In addition to working with the student at his or her level, it is critical to develop a good working relationship with the family.

One of the first things that I tell classroom teachers who are going to have a student who is deaf or hard of hearing in their classroom is that most accommodations are pretty simple. They shouldn't be scared! First of all, students with a hearing loss should be given priority seating so they will have a better opportunity to hear as well as have visual access to the teacher's mouth for lipreading or see their interpreter if they use one. I also tell teachers that anytime they can make their teaching more visual they should do so. This can be accomplished by writing new vocabulary on the board or accompanying it with a picture, or by using visual schedules. The students will have a much easier time following along with these visual cues added. If the child uses sign language, one of the best ways for the teacher and student to learn is to make it a part of the lesson for all students. I worked with a kindergarten teacher last year who really embraced this concept. She often invited me into her classroom to do lessons with her class. Eventually she and the interpreter took over the teaching. Anytime her class learned a new sight word, they paired it with the sign. She said that using this extra modality really accelerated the child's learning. A preschool teacher I worked with two years ago used sign language so much, and also encouraged her kids to sign, that a visiting parent had to ask which one of the students was deaf!

Our school music teacher is another good example of someone with whom I collaborate often. The school put on a musical last year, and the whole student body learned to sign the songs. The parent of one of my students came to my room the next day to thank me; she was nearly in tears. She said that she never thought that she would see her child up on a stage singing and signing with everyone else, just like one of the other kids. Obviously, this kind of integration and collaboration benefits not only the student who is deaf, but everyone involved as well.

Another thing I do is to encourage teachers to be good advocates for their students. This often takes sustained determination to educate others about the child's needs. Although the many meetings and abundance of paperwork that this can require can seem overwhelming at times, the results are worth it. Teachers also need to teach the children with hearing loss to be good advocates for themselves. Fostering independence in students with disabilities is a component that is sometimes overlooked. In order for them to have a quality life within their educational setting, and also outside of school, students need to know how to request an interpreter, manage their audiological equipment, and educate people about their hearing loss.

The reality is that hearing loss is a low-incidence disability. In my experiences in rural settings, both in Kansas and Alaska, I have seen how isolating it can be for the student to be the only one who is deaf or hard of hearing, or one of few, in his or her school. Therefore, it is especially important to me that I do everything I can to make sure the students I work with are included as much as possible. By being flexible and adaptable both in my teaching and in my communication style; by collaborating with staff, students, and parents; and by being a good advocate for my students and encouraging them to be good advocates for themselves, I find that my students are very successful in an inclusive setting.

—*Catherine Davis*
Liberty View Elementary School, Overland Park, Kansas
Teacher of the Deaf and Hard of Hearing

Where Are Students With Hearing Impairments Served?

Video Link 11.9
Watch a parent's perspective.

Under the contemporary philosophy of providing individualized instruction in the least restrictive environment (LRE), individuals with a hearing impairment can receive their education in a number of settings, generally classified into two broad categories: (1) regular public school programs and (2) special school programs. Family preference for educational placement may be influenced by such factors as the degree of loss, age of onset, mode of communication, presence of other disabilities, and available resources. (See the accompanying First Person feature on page 420.)

Suggestions for the Classroom

Suggestions for Teaching Students With Hearing Impairments

Suggestion #1: Promote acceptance of your students. Your student will benefit from a classroom where he or she feels accepted and where modifications are made without undue attention.

How to Do It

☑ Welcome the student to your class. Your positive attitude will help other students accept him or her.

☑ Discuss your student's hearing loss with him or her; let him or her know you are willing to help.

☑ As appropriate, have your student, the audiologist, or another person explain the student's hearing loss to your entire class.

☑ Make modifications seem as natural as possible so the student is not singled out.

☑ Accept your student as an individual; be aware of his or her assets as well as his or her limitations.

☑ Encourage your student's special abilities or interests.

Suggestion #2: Be sure hearing aids and other amplification devices are used when recommended. This will enable your student to use his or her hearing maximally.

How to Do It

☑ Realize that hearing aids make sounds louder, but not necessarily clearer. Hearing aids don't make hearing normal.

☑ Be sure your student's hearing aids or other devices are checked daily to see that they are working properly.

☑ Encourage the student to care for his or her hearing aid(s) by putting it on, telling you when it is not functioning properly, and so forth.

☑ Be sure your student always has a spare battery at school.

☑ Know whom to contact if your student's device is not working properly.

Suggestion #3: Provide preferential seating. Appropriate seating will enhance your student's ability to hear and understand what is said in the classroom.

How to Do It

☑ Seat your student near where you typically teach. It will be helpful if your student is at one side of the classroom so he or she can easily turn and follow classroom dialogue.

☑ Seat your student where he or she can easily watch your face without straining to look straight up. Typically the second or third row is best.

☑ Seat your student away from noise sources, including hallways, radiators, pencil sharpeners, and so forth.

☑ Seat your student where light is on your face and not in your student's eyes.

☑ If there is a better ear, place it toward the classroom.

☑ Allow your student to move to other seats when necessary for demonstrations, classroom discussions, or other activities.

Suggestion #4: Increase visual information. Your student will use lipreading and other visual information to supplement what he or she hears.

How to Do It

☑ Remember that your student needs to see your face in order to lipread!
- Try to stay in one place while talking to the class so your student does not have to lipread a "moving target."
- Avoid talking with your face turned downward while reading.
- Keep the light on your face, not at your back. Avoid standing in front of windows where the glare will make it difficult to see your face.

- ☑ Use visual aids, such as pictures and diagrams, when possible.
- ☑ Demonstrate what you want the student to understand when possible. Use natural gestures, such as pointing to objects being discussed, to help clarify what you say.
- ☑ Use the chalkboard—write assignments, new vocabulary words, key words, and so forth on it.

Suggestion #5: Minimize classroom noise. Even a small amount of noise will make it very difficult for your student to hear and understand what is said.

How to Do It

- ☑ Seat your student away from noisy parts of your classroom.
- ☑ Wait until all your students are quiet before talking to them.

Suggestion #6: Modify teaching procedures. Modifications will allow your student to benefit from your instruction and will decrease the need for repetition.

How to Do It

- ☑ Be sure your student is watching and listening when you are talking to him or her.
- ☑ Be sure your student understands what is said by having him or her repeat information or answer questions.
- ☑ Rephrase, rather than repeat, questions and instructions if your student has not understood them.
- ☑ Write key words, new words, new topics, and so forth on the chalkboard.
- ☑ Repeat or rephrase things said by other students during classroom discussions.
- ☑ Introduce new vocabulary to the student in advance. The speech–language pathologist or parents may be able to help with this.
- ☑ Use a "buddy" to alert your student to listen and to be sure your student has understood all information correctly.

Suggestion #7: Have realistic expectations. This will help your student succeed in your classroom.

How to Do It

- ☑ Remember that your student cannot understand everything all of the time, no matter how hard he or she tries. Encourage him or her to ask for repetition.
- ☑ Be patient when your student asks for repetition.
- ☑ Give breaks from listening when necessary. Your student may fatigue easily because he or she is straining to listen and understand.
- ☑ Expect your student to follow classroom routine. Do not spoil or pamper your student.
- ☑ Expect your student to accept the same responsibilities for considerate behavior, homework, and dependability as you require of other students in your classroom.
- ☑ Ask your student to repeat if you can't understand him or her. Your student's speech may be distorted because he or she does not hear sounds clearly. Work with the speech–language pathologist to help your student improve his or her speech as much as possible.
- ☑ Be alert for fluctuations of hearing due to middle ear problems.
- ☑ Request support from the audiologist, the speech–language pathologist, or others when you feel uncertain about your student and what is best for him or her.

SOURCE: Adapted from C. Johnson, P. Benson, and J. Seaton, *Educational Audiology Handbook* (San Diego, CA: Singular, 1997), pp. 370–371.

Figure 11.5 (page 421) shows the various educational environments attended by children with hearing impairments during the 2007–2008 school year. More than 86 percent of children with hearing impairments attend public schools. This is a dramatic shift from the historical educational placement of these children in residential education. Before 1975, when PL 94–142 was enacted, about 80 percent of students with hearing impairments were served in special schools, typically state residential schools for the deaf.

First Person: Mindy Believing in Yourself

Video Link 11.10
See parents talk about their experiences.

My experience growing up as a person who is deaf has been enriching. I have a successful career thanks to supportive parents who always treated me like a typical child. During my difficult times, they supported me wholeheartedly. Some parents of children who are deaf tend to be overprotective, but not my parents. They encouraged me to make my own decisions. I do not think that I would be as successful as I am today without them.

After my parents found out that I was deaf, they enrolled me in a preschool where I learned cued speech. A new teacher arrived and told my parents that Signing Exact English (SEE) would be more useful and social than cued speech. My parents then enrolled in sign language classes so that they could communicate with me.

In elementary school I was in a self-contained room with other students who were deaf and a teacher who used SEE. I loved that environment. At the time that I was about to enter the sixth grade, I was faced with a decision. Did I want to attend the Alabama School for the Deaf or an integrated middle school? I do not remember how I decided, but I chose the local middle school. I was in culture shock. My classroom was full of thirty hearing students. I was the only student who was deaf in the entire grade. (There were a few other students who were deaf, but they were in different grades.) I had to rely on my interpreter for everything, so I became shyer and less outgoing than I was in elementary school. Many of my classmates learned to sign or fingerspell, but I still missed so much information vital to socialization. I remember walking through the hallways, and my interpreter would walk with me and tell me all kinds of gossip she heard. I was shocked; I had no idea what the students were talking about. As I entered high school, I became very unhappy. I noticed that high school students were more into cliques. I felt as though I did not belong.

At a summer camp for children who are deaf, a camp counselor told me about the Model Secondary School for the Deaf (MSSD) at Gallaudet University in Washington, DC. I was interested, so I mentioned it to my parents. Of course, they said I was too young to be so far away. Yet the thought of attending this school stayed with me. I wrote a letter to Gallaudet asking for information about the school. They sent me a colorful, fancy brochure, and I was impressed. I brought it up once again with my parents, but they shrugged it off. I filled out the application anyway and asked them to sign the papers just in case. I think my parents thought that I would change my mind if things got serious. When MSSD called my parents to come for an intake interview, they kept asking me if I really wanted to do this. I was determined as ever to go. We made the trip to MSSD, and I fell in love with the school immediately. Once again, however, I was in culture shock because I was not aware of the Deaf culture. The students made fun of my clothes, my makeup, and my use of SEE. I was bewildered by all of this. I eventually learned American Sign Language, which was the language of choice. A friend once charged me a penny every time I signed using SEE. I loved the social aspects of being at MSSD. Unlike my middle school, I was able to be involved in any activity that I wished. I was viewed as the "deaf" girl at my middle school, but at MSSD, I was looked at as "Usher syndrome" girl.

I am currently a counselor at a school for the deaf, where I have worked for the past eight years. I have had to face many obstacles as I moved to a town where I knew no one. I chose to face my challenges rather than staying home and believing that things would not work out for me. I still face challenges now as a person who is deaf–blind. I am not completely blind yet, but my vision is slowly deteriorating. I have learned how to use Grade 1 Braille, and I am currently learning Grade 2. I have also completed orientation and mobility training so that I can become somewhat independent in challenging areas such as heavy traffic. I have learned everything possible in order to be independent in case I lose my sight completely.

In the summer of 2006 I had a cochlear implant because of concerns about my safety in the future. I will need to depend upon environmental sounds if and when I lose my vision. I now enjoy hearing the birds sing and water running. When the audiologist turned on my cochlear implant, it was the strangest sensation. The first sounds I heard were my husband's voice and that of the audiologist. Then I entered the bathroom. I did not realize that bathrooms were so noisy! Funny, I always thought that bathrooms were silent. After I got home, I noticed that flushing toilets even had a sound, so I was incredulous of that. I had never heard those sounds until I received my implant. It was one of the best decisions I ever made for myself.

I know I will face additional challenges as my vision deteriorates, but I have a wonderful support system consisting of my husband, family, and friends. I am confident that I will be able to overcome whatever obstacles come my way.

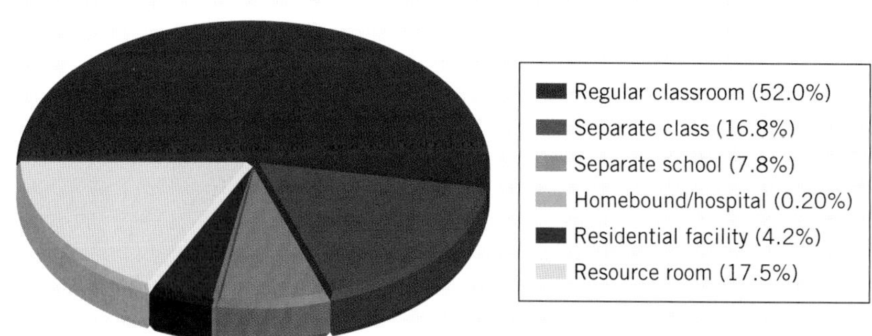

FIGURE 11.5 Educational Placement of Children With Hearing Impairments

NOTE: Figure represents percentages of enrollment of students with hearing impairments during the 2007–2008 school year.

SOURCE: U.S. Department of Education. (2009). *IDEA data.* Retrieved November 30, 2009, from https://www.ideadata.org/PartBReport.asp

Public School Programs

Public school programs include inclusive classroom settings, resource rooms, self-contained classrooms, and itinerant services. The overall goal of these settings is to include the student to the greatest extent possible in the educational/social processes in which all other children, with and without disabilities, participate. Since the implementation of IDEA, the vast majority of students who are deaf or hard of hearing are attending neighborhood schools with their hearing peers.

Video Link 11.11
Watch more about different educational settings.

Special School Programs

Special school programs include public and private residential and/or day schools with specifically prepared teachers and dormitory facilities for students when appropriate. The overall goal of these programs is to provide a positive learning environment, a sense of belonging, personal identification, and acceptance of hearing impairment (Scheetz, 2001). Residential schools also typically accept day and commuting students. As mentioned previously, these types of schools have experienced a dramatic decline in enrollment since the mid-1970s. This shift has caused great concern among deaf adults because residential schools have long been the support foundation in the establishment of Deaf culture.

Instructional Interventions

Methods of Communication

Communication implies a transfer (exchange) of knowledge, ideas, opinions, and feelings; it involves encoding and decoding messages. The basic foundation for communication is language, which is often defined as a system of rules governing sounds, words, meaning, and use. When a child is born with a hearing impairment, depending on the severity of the hearing problem, normal language acquisition is disrupted. Other means of communication are viable alternatives to spoken language. Sign language, in one of its multiple forms, and **fingerspelling** using the manual alphabet (see Figure 11.6, page 422) are examples of such alternatives. See Table 11.4 (see page 423) for a description of the three sign language systems that are most commonly used. Other methods

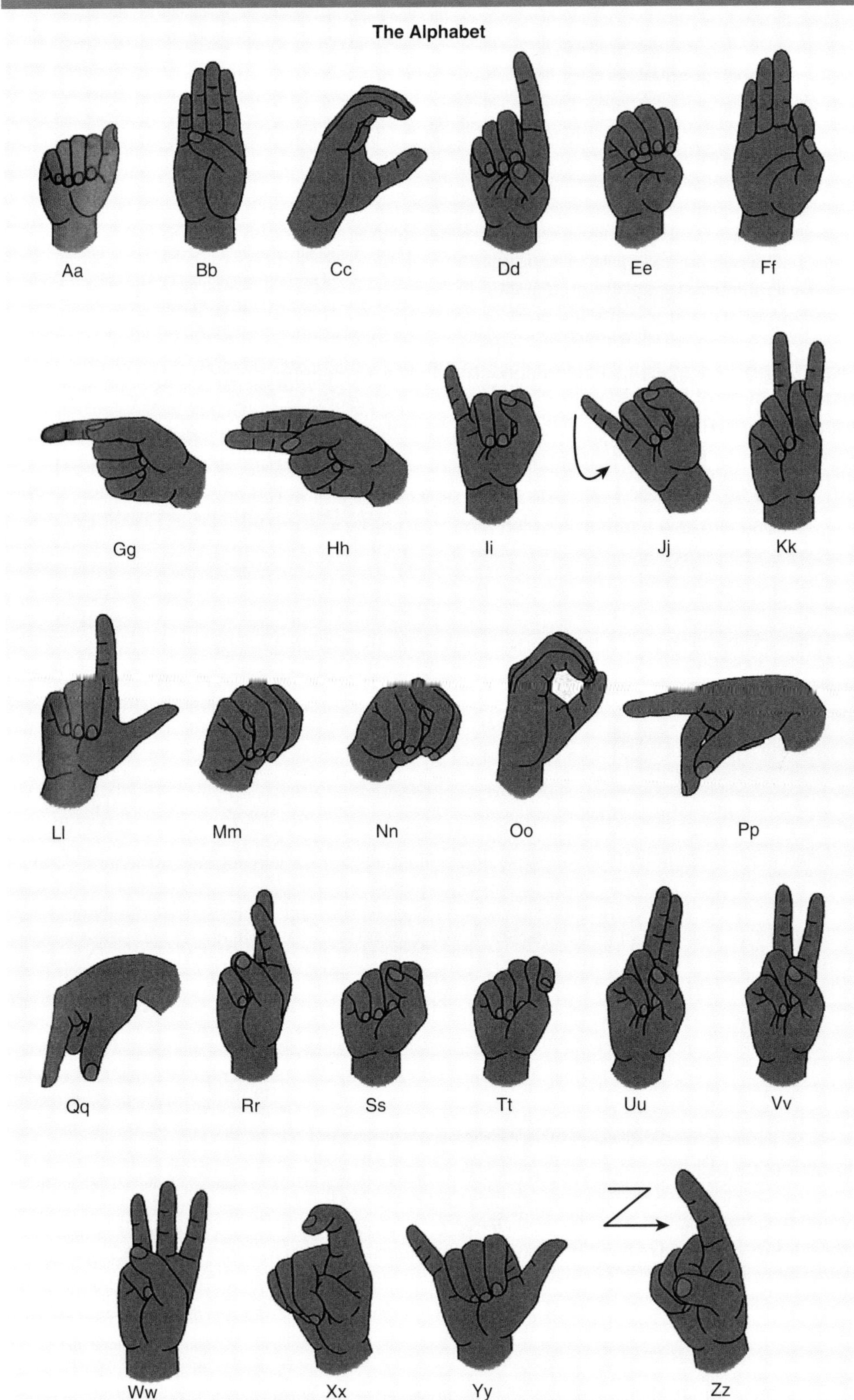

FIGURE 11.6 The Manual Alphabet

SOURCE: G. Gustason and E. Zawolkow, *Signing Exact English* (Los Alamitos, CA: Modern Signs Press, 1993), pp. xxvi, 1.

TABLE 11.4 Sign Language Systems

Sign System	Description	Advantages/Disadvantages
American Sign Language (ASL)	• Considered the natural language of the deaf • Has a unique syntax system, not a word-by-word interpretation • System most frequently used by interpreters in public settings (churches, concerts, ceremonies, etc.)	• Unique syntax could make transition to English more challenging
Signing Exact English	• Most like spoken English • Close match to ASL • Uses English word order • System most commonly used in public schools	• Can be understood by ASL users • English word order should make the transition to English less challenging
Signed English	• Uses ASL signs in English word order patterns	• Even closer match to ASL but with the advantage of English word order

SOURCE: Adapted from S. Kuder, *Teaching Students with Language and Communication Disabilities,* 3rd ed. (Boston: Allyn and Bacon, 2008), p. 235.

TABLE 11.5 Educational Approaches Used When Working With Students With Hearing Impairments

	Basic Position	Objective	Method of Communication
Bilingual–Bicultural	Considers American Sign Language (ASL) to be the natural language of the Deaf culture and urges recognition of ASL as the primary language choice with English considered a second language	To provide a foundation in the use of ASL with its unique vocabulary and syntax rules; ESL instruction provided for English vocabulary and syntax rules	ASL (American Sign Language)
Total Communication	Supports the belief that simultaneous use of multiple communication techniques enhances an individual's ability to communicate, comprehend, and learn	To provide a multifaceted approach to communication to facilitate whichever method(s) work(s) best for each individual	Combination of sign language (accepts the use of any of the sign language systems), fingerspelling, and speechreading
Auditory–Oral	Supports the belief that children with hearing impairments can develop listening/receptive language and oral language expression (English) skills; emphasizes use of residual hearing (the level of hearing an individual possesses), amplification (hearing aids, auditory training, etc.), and speech/language training	To facilitate the development of spoken (oral) English	Spoken (oral) English

of instruction include oral, auditory verbal, cued speech, total communication, and the Rochester Method (fingerspelling). For educators of the deaf and the Deaf culture, which method of communication to use is at the root of the current philosophical debate.

Within the placement options previously described, three different approaches to communication may be used: (1) an auditory–oral approach, (2) total communication (TC), or (3) a bilingual–bicultural (bi–bi) approach. See Table 11.5 for a description

Today, the majority of students with hearing impairments attend public schools.

of these approaches. A survey of deaf and hard of hearing educational programs in a thirty-nine-state sample found that more than two thirds of the programs used total communication (Meadows-Orlans, Mertens, Sass-Lehrer, & Scott-Olson, 1997). The majority of public school programs using TC employ a form of Signed English for the sign language component. Many residential programs and postsecondary programs for the deaf endorse the bi–bi approach, which uses American Sign Language (ASL). There are few data suggesting that one instructional approach is significantly better than another.

Audiologists

Audiologists have served hearing-impaired students within the context of educational settings for many years. The relatively high incidence of hearing impairment coupled with the explosive increase in rehabilitative technology for these students surely warrants an audiologist's inclusion as an educational team member. Using a collaborative approach to the education of hearing-impaired students, audiologists frequently provide support to classroom teachers and aides, speech–language pathologists, teachers of the hearing impaired, special educators, reading specialists, resource teachers, and interpreters. The American Speech-Language-Hearing Association (1993) recommends in its "Guidelines for Audiology Services in the Schools" that there be at least one audiologist for every twelve thousand students in a school system. Statistics indicate high

Interpreters play a very important role in the education of students with hearing impairments.

variability in the number of educational audiologists from state to state, with the overall number of such professionals significantly less than this recommendation (Johnson & Danhauer, 1999).

Interpreters

When an **interpreter** is used, three people are involved in the communication experience: the interpreter, the person who is deaf or hard of hearing, and the hearing person. The primary role of the educational interpreter is to relay to the student anything that is said in class by employing communication processes such as repetition, sign language, fingerspelling, body language, and verbal expressions. Many sign language systems (such as ASL, Signed English, or Signing Exact English) may be used, depending on the preferred communication mode or need of the individual with a hearing impairment. An **oral interpreter** may be used for cochlear implant users or individuals with a great deal of residual hearing. Oral interpreters use clear enunciation, slightly slower speech, and expressive mouth and facial movements to improve the visibility of the spoken message. In conjunction with the communication process, an interpreter may also use **transliteration.** For example, the interpreter may change the exact wording of the hearing person's communication in order to help the individual with a hearing impairment to better understand the context of the message. However, the interpreter is never a contributing member in the communication exchange.

Educational interpreters play diverse roles at all grade levels. They may assist students in the classroom, tutor individual students, assist regular and special educators in classroom activities, or interpret lectures. As increasing numbers of individuals with a hearing impairment choose to attend regular schools, the demand for interpreters is growing. A critical shortage of qualified interpreters exists in many educational settings, especially in rural areas. There is also a nationwide shortage of qualified interpreter preparation programs.

Services for Young Children With Hearing Impairments

Early intervention for the child with a hearing impairment is grounded in the same basic concepts as early intervention and early childhood special education programs for those with other disabilities (birth through age 5). Screening programs designed to detect hearing loss in school-age populations have existed for years. However, for those children born with a hearing impairment, identification and intervention as early as possible is critical. There is an obvious relationship between expressive and receptive communication skills and the hearing mechanism that facilitates such skills, which begin long before a child's first words are ever spoken. Because more children are being identified

EFFECTIVE INSTRUCTIONAL PRACTICES — Promoting Language Development in Young Children With Hearing Impairments

- ***Speak using an ordinary tone/volume.*** Make sure the student's attention is focused on the speaker. Talk naturally and clearly and use simple phrases or simple but complete sentences, depending on the pupil's language level. Do not shout or exaggerate words or slow down your speech unnaturally. Highlighting lips with lipstick can assist a young child in following speech. A mustache or long hair obscuring the face can cause loss of visual information.
- ***Clarify idioms.*** Explain idioms in context (e.g., explain "It's raining cats and dogs" when you have used the expression after dashing inside during a cloudburst). This prevents misunderstandings and enriches the child's language.
- ***Check with the student to ensure comprehension.*** Sometimes saying, "Tell me what I just said" provides information about how much a child understands. However, many children with a hearing loss have difficulty articulating their responses. Therefore, you may need to observe the child's actions for a short period to check for understanding. A perplexed look or doing nothing may indicate lack of understanding, and you will need to find additional, preferably visual, methods for getting the message across.
- ***Institute a buddy system to facilitate a child's understanding of directions and curriculum content.*** Many times children understand another child better than they do an adult, so have a child's buddy explain the information again after you have finished. Furthermore, attentive peer modeling of both speech and behavior is an excellent resource for the child with hearing deficits.
- ***Show real-life pictures when reading or talking about a topic, and use simple signs, point, or have an example of the object you're explaining.*** Pupils with a hearing loss need visual information to learn. Acting out experience-based language lessons or stories is helpful. Using environmental labels around the classroom can start such children on the road to learning language through print.
- ***Provide language boards or books for children who have difficulty producing intelligible speech or manual signs.*** Try providing a flannel board with pictures, words, or other graphic symbols to help communicate information such as available interest centers or answers to routine questions. The child can point to the board to indicate a response or choice. Preteach key vocabulary words from a story that will be read to the class, or send the book home with the child beforehand so that the words can be introduced by the family (and reinforced afterward).

SOURCE: Adapted from L. Katz and T. Schery, "Including Children with Hearing Loss in Early Childhood Programs," *Young Children, 61*(1), 2006, p. 94.

as hearing impaired at an earlier age, the emphasis of many early intervention programs has changed in order to meet the needs of younger children with hearing impairments, many of whom will receive cochlear implants.

Failure to identify and provide appropriate services for children who are hearing impaired has a profoundly negative impact on the development of language and speech, as well as educational achievement. Only about 50 percent of infants with hearing loss are identified using a **high-risk register** (Johnson, Benson, & Seaton, 2001). With the use of sophisticated diagnostic technology, universal newborn screening programs designed to identify hearing loss in infants have increased in number and scope. States that have legislated universal newborn screening programs, however, have encountered substantial difficulty with family compliance for follow-up testing. Because of this limitation, providing timely services to families of hearing-impaired infants has been difficult. Early intervention programs provide families with information on language development, communication skills, the use of residual hearing, amplification, self-help, and social–emotional development for children with hearing loss. These programs are usually not child centered in design, but place strong emphasis on parent and family instruction and involvement. Meeting the needs of each individual family requires unique design of interventional strategies.

As previously mentioned, the vast majority of hearing-impaired infants have normally hearing parents. Whether a deaf child is born to deaf or hearing parents may influence social, educational, and cultural issues that the family unit faces. For example, many hearing parents of children who are severely impaired probably do not know or use sign language. They may be unaware of cultural issues related to the deaf community, and how such issues might relate to their own child's education options. Some research indicates that deaf parents are more likely to view hearing-impaired children in a positive way, which may result in greater normalization of the parent–child relationship (Katz & Schery, 2006; Maxon, Brackett, & van den Berg, 1991). Allen and Cowdery (2009) suggest that early intervention programs focus on helping the child with a hearing impairment develop within the structure of his or her family, just as a child with normal hearing develops within this context.

Transition and Individuals With Hearing Impairments

The process of transition, enabling the person with a hearing impairment to make a comfortable and positive change from one environment to another, requires systematic planning and evaluation. IDEA mandates individualized transition plans (ITPs) for children with disabilities age 16 and older in public schools. It also requires ongoing modification to remain current and sensitive to the needs of these individuals and their families. As previously discussed, many students with severe to profound hearing impairments lag behind their peers in personal/social/behavioral maturity, which affects the structure of transition planning.

Video Link 11.12
See a student talk about her future.

Stress is often associated with changes, and transition can be especially difficult for the family as well as the pupil. Families learning to adjust to the new challenges of having an adolescent or a young adult who is deaf or hard of hearing are often assisted by teachers, counselors, or other specialists. Family life plays a key role in the transition process for deaf adolescents. Many times, the audiologist, social worker, speech–language pathologist, and special education teacher assist the family in gathering the information needed to make the initial educational placement and communication training decisions.

The Laurent Clerc National Deaf Education Center, located at Gallaudet University, provides excellent information families and teachers can use to promote transition and independence.

Legislation facilitating transition as a national priority for the hearing impaired began with the passage of PL 89–36 in 1968, which established the National Technical Institute for the Deaf (NTID) at the Rochester Institute of Technology, and Section 504 of the

Rehabilitation Act of 1973 (PL 93–112), which mandated that institutions of higher education provide accessible facilities and support services for individuals with disabilities. In addition, Congress currently funds six postsecondary programs for the deaf and hard of hearing: Gallaudet University, NTID, and regional postsecondary education programs for the deaf located at California State University at Northridge, St. Paul Technical College, Seattle Central Community College, and the University of Tennessee Center on Deafness.

Transition into a new educational or vocational environment involves a variety of community professionals and services. Itinerant teachers of the hearing impaired, in concert with the cooperation and coordination of the special education and general education teacher, the interpreter, and other support personnel, may assist in meeting the challenges of transitioning between special and general education programs or postsecondary educational and/or vocational programs.

The transition for many individuals with a hearing impairment also involves personal, social, and community adjustments. The new experiences are enlarged not only by communication difficulties but also by the diverse literacy skills needed in the new environment. Transition to postsecondary education, vocational training, and/or employment can be eased by career counseling and coursework centered on vocational skills and independent living, as outlined in the student's ITP. For students desiring a college degree, in addition to stressing academic achievement, a successful college preparatory training program involves instruction regarding dorm life, responsible social behavior, and problem-solving strategies for coping with the multitude of problems that college students who have hearing impairments are likely to encounter (King, De Caro, Karchmer, & Cole, 2001).

Services for Adults With Hearing Impairments

Adult support services often provide a vital link between the hearing impaired and the hearing world (Scheetz, 2001). These diverse services may be used to enhance public knowledge regarding deafness, facilitate communication, or aid in the transfer of information.

Two basic types of mandated services are offered statewide for adults who are deaf or hard of hearing. The first is a state commission or office on deafness, whose services include advocacy, information gathering and dissemination, referral to appropriate agencies, interpreting services, and job placement and development.

The second type of service is offered through each state's vocational rehabilitation service. A coordinator of rehabilitation services for the deaf and hard of hearing provides vocational evaluation, job placement, and counseling, often in conjunction with the transition plan while the student is still in high school. State rehabilitation offices can also help students preparing to enter postsecondary academic environments. Under the Americans with Disabilities Act, colleges and universities are required to provide qualified sign language interpreters and other auxiliary aids needed to ensure effective communication opportunities for the deaf and hard of hearing student population, even if these services are not provided by the state vocational rehabilitation system.

For more than a hundred and twenty years, the National Association of the Deaf (NAD) has been actively involved in obtaining the basic rights under the U.S. Constitution for individuals with hearing impairments. Additionally, NAD provides political advocacy at the state and federal levels and promotes issues important to the deaf population. NAD also publishes books on a wide range of topics and issues related to hearing impairment (Moores, 2001).

Another significant organization promoting the integration of the hearing impaired population into mainstream society is the Alexander Graham Bell Association. The philosophy of the AG Bell Association is based on the improvement of oral speech communication. This association serves as a clearinghouse of materials and information concerning oral teaching methods, technology, and related topics. See the end of this chapter for a detailed listing of organizations and agencies that have been established to provide services for the hearing impaired.

Another popular adult resource is Self-Help for Hard of Hearing People (SHHH). SHHH provides advocacy, information, and assistance to hard of hearing individuals. Extremely active, this organization has more than two hundred and fifty local chapters nationwide.

Family Issues

Family dynamics can be severely disrupted when a child is born with a significant hearing impairment. Parental, sibling, and grandparenting roles are often dramatically altered by such an event. Because the effects of hearing impairment are so pervasive, particularly with regard to communication, accepting and "normalizing" the child's disability can be quite difficult. The expected or fantasized child does not arrive, and the family experiences an initial state of emotional shock and disbelief. The level of impact on the family may vary, but for most families such an event can create a crisis atmosphere of considerable magnitude.

Family Reaction

Approximately 90 percent of all children with hearing impairments have hearing parents (Picard, 2004). After the initial emotional states of shock and disbelief, stresses on the family can increase as individual members come to understand that communicating with the child who is hearing impaired is different and likely always will be. From these initial reactions, parents go through different stages of grieving such as uncertainty, frustration, denial, depression, and anxiety (Ulrich & Bauer, 2003). They may initially blame their spouse, fate, or the professional community, or even misdirect anger and frustration toward themselves. Parents may have difficulty accepting assistance or recommendations from professionals, extended family, and friends. Some may become overprotective of the child and turn their attention away from other family members. Others may withdraw, finding isolation easier than coping with the child care demands placed upon them (Meadows-Orlans, 1995).

Perhaps the greatest factor in positive resolution of such emotionally charged issues is acceptance of the hearing impairment. Achieving genuine acceptance of any disability is, for most families, an ongoing process. Stages of this process are not necessarily completed independently and in successive order, just as achieving a measure of acceptance does not prevent certain situations from reopening old emotional wounds. Grieving and uncertainty may emerge time and again during the child's development, but will be less severe as the family's coping mechanisms improve. The stages of grieving that follow the birth of a baby with a hearing loss are healthy expressions of normal emotional reactions. The process of working through such feelings should not be hurried; it allows the family members opportunities to recognize and acknowledge change in their lives, as well as time to formulate positive strategies for accommodating the child with the hearing impairment. In this process, the development of positive relationships is individually and collectively encouraged (Meadows-Orlans, 1995). Parental support groups provide a very effective arena for expressing concerns, offering support and encouragement, and formulating effective parenting strategies.

Siblings and Grandparents

Siblings and grandparents are not immune to the emotional issues that accompany the birth of a hearing-impaired child. There is little formal research that examines the

Siblings can play an important role in families that have a child with a hearing impairment.

emotional impact of hearing impairment on either group. Siblings may feel unspoken pressure to compensate for perceived parental uncertainty and disappointment. Such perceptions may result in attempts to excel academically or socially. Some siblings describe very close relationships with their hearing-impaired brother or sister, assuming a great deal of responsibility for the child, and describe the relationship as almost a parental one. Others resent the time and attention parents devote to the sibling with hearing impairment. This resentment may take the form of jealousy or anger. Because of these and other factors, siblings of children with hearing impairments or other disabilities are at risk for behavior problems (Meadows-Orlans, 1995). Perhaps the best way to help siblings is for parents to communicate with them: ask about concerns, talk openly about family issues, have uniform behavioral expectations, and ensure that responsibilities are shared equally.

Luterman (2008) describes grandparents of hearing-impaired children as "the forgotten people." Grandparents experience a "double hurt," stemming from both the emotional pain of having a hearing-impaired grandchild and the pain associated with that experienced by their own child, the grieving parent. However, the role of grandparents can often provide much-needed emotional, logistical, and financial support for the family unit (Clark & Martin, 1994). Parent support groups often incorporate siblings, caregivers, and extended family members, affording them the opportunity to address the various dynamics of families dealing with hearing loss in a group setting.

Issues of Diversity

According to data from the Gallaudet Research Institute (2008), approximately 48 percent of all students in programs for the deaf and hearing impaired are persons from culturally diverse groups. Likewise, statistics from the U.S. Department of Education (2009) indicate that approximately 47 percent of students with hearing impairments, ages 6–21, are from culturally diverse populations.

From an educational standpoint, there has been significant recognition in the conceptual and research literature of the special academic, social, cultural, and linguistic needs of students from non-English-speaking (NES) families. Little attention has been paid, however, to the needs of children and youth with hearing impairments from NES families. As a result, teachers and related service providers may be insensitive to the specific needs of those students. For example, many of their families may not be knowledgeable regarding their educational options or the related service benefits available for their child with a hearing impairment.

Journal Link 11.1
Read more about issues of diversity.

Another issue of diversity involves the Deaf culture. Many individuals who are deaf or hard of hearing tend to identify with the deaf community. They contend that they should be viewed not as deficient or pathological, but as members of a different culture with its own language, traditions, values, and literature. This Deaf culture does not use the term *hearing impaired*. Its adherents view spoken English as an optional second language but ASL as the language of choice. This bilingual–bicultural approach stands in opposition to oralist philosophies and forms of sign language other than ASL. The Deaf culture was delayed in accepting cochlear implants, which seek to restore or enhance auditory information through surgery.

Technology and Individuals With Hearing Impairments

Modern technology is a very important component in the lives of all individuals with disabilities. Nowhere are the effects of today's technological advances more evident in working with special-needs students than in the area of hearing impairment. Sophisticated hearing aids, computers, alerting devices, cochlear implants, captioned media, and adaptive equipment are only a few of the items whose use has revolutionized education of the hearing-impaired child.

Hearing Aids and Auditory Training Devices

Video Link 11.14
Watch more about hearing aids.

There are several different types of hearing aids including in-the-ear and behind-the-ear aids (see Figure 11.7, page 432). Hearing aids are individually prescribed based on an audiologist's determination of the degree and nature of hearing impairment, along with age, additional disabilities or physical limitations, the individual's speech and language skills, cost considerations, and the environment in which the hearing aid will be used. The audiologist determines how much amplification—the difference between the level of acoustical input at the microphone and the level of acoustical output at the speaker—the hearing instrument will provide. All hearing aids contain miniaturized electronic components consisting of a microphone, an amplifier, a receiver, and a power source. The audiologist also determines the frequency response of the aid—that is, the range of frequencies amplified (usually between 250 Hz and 6,000 Hz). In the past, hearing aids simply amplified all incoming sounds equally. Recent technological advances have allowed for differential amplification so that hearing aid output depends somewhat on the nature of the incoming sound. In other words, the hearing aid does not respond to all incoming sounds in the same way. Programmable hearing aids can be linked to a computer and adjusted by the audiologist. Sound outputs at certain frequencies, or at various levels of loudness, can be varied during programming sessions. Today's increasingly sophisticated programmable hearing aids are individually tailored to closely match the configuration of an individual's hearing loss (Herer et al., 2007). The Insights feature (page 433) provides a basic hearing aid checklist for the classroom teacher.

Although current hearing aid technology offers substantial improvement over previously available personal amplification, such devices will not necessarily meet all of the listening needs of an individual with a significant degree of hearing loss. **Assistive listening devices (ALDs)** may be used to enhance the performance of people with hearing impairment in a variety of situations. Hearing-impaired children often use **auditory trainers,** particularly **FM systems**, in their educational settings. These amplification systems are easy to use and are often more effective than hearing aids in managing the acoustical problems inherent in most classrooms. Speech understanding in the presence of background noise presents a significant dilemma for students with hearing impairments, particularly those wearing some type of hearing aid. The **signal-to-noise ratio**, or loudness level of the desired sound source relative to unwanted noise, can be greatly enhanced by these systems. An FM system consists of a small transmitter with a tiny directional microphone worn by the teacher. A receiver can be worn separately by the student or in conjunction with his or her personal hearing aid. When using the FM system, the teacher's voice is heard directly and clearly regardless of his or her location in the classroom.

Sound field systems can also enhance signal-to-noise ratio in the classroom. With this type of system, the teacher wears a small microphone, and his or her voice is transmitted to various speakers strategically placed about the room, or on the desktop for a particular student. These systems have proven particularly successful for students with minimal hearing loss, recurrent otitis media (ear infections), cochlear implants, and a variety of

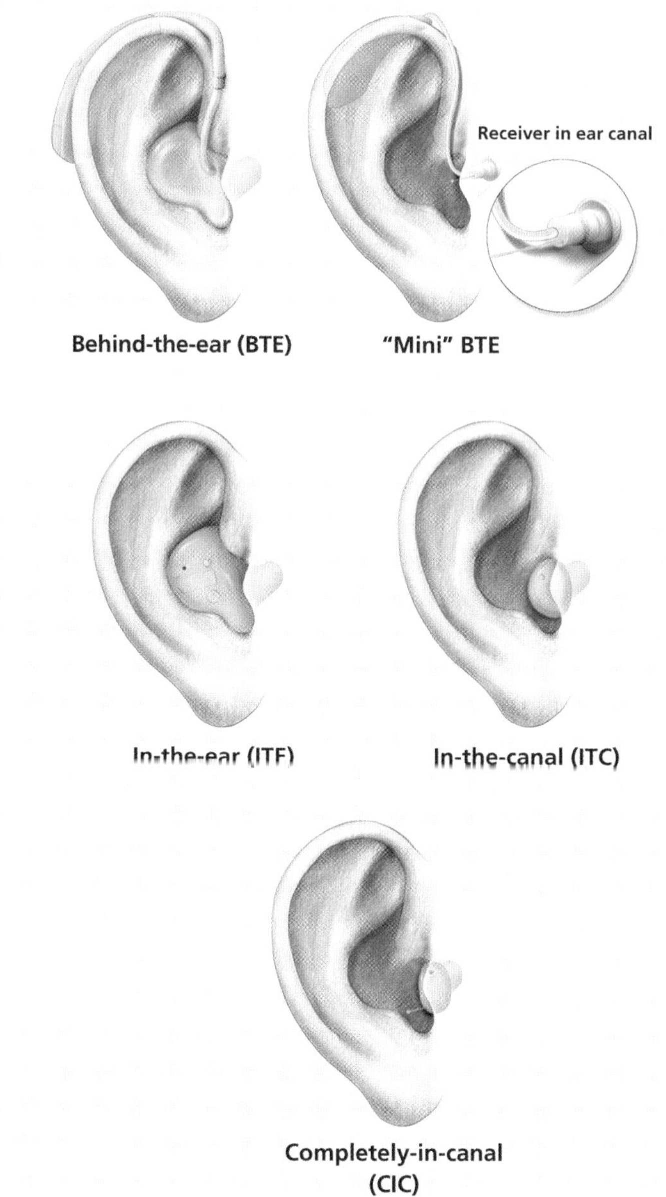

FIGURE 11.7 Styles of Hearing Aids

SOURCE: From the National Institute on Deafness and Other Communication Disorders (National Institute of Health).

communication problems, including those associated with attention deficit hyperactivity disorder, central auditory processing disorder (CAPD), and learning English as a second language (Iglehart, 2004).

Computers

Microcomputers have many applications for educating children with hearing impairments. Computer-assisted instructional programs offer students with hearing impairments

How to Check a Hearing Aid

For children who use hearing aids, it is helpful to check the aids on a regular basis to ensure functioning. With minimum effort and a few minutes a day, teachers can help students check their hearing aids. Depending on the age of the child, students should take appropriate responsibility for the checking process.

Know Background Information

Basic information on the child's hearing aid should be supplied by the audiologist or parents. Things to know about the aid include [the following]:

- Brand and model
- Recommended volume
- Internal settings
- Battery type

Check Hearing Aid Functions

Two inexpensive pieces of equipment—a hearing aid stethoscope and a battery tester—should be kept in the classroom and used to check hearing aids. Stethoscopes can usually be purchased through local hearing aid dealers for $10 to $15. The stethoscope is used to check the quality of sound provided by the hearing aid. Listen for the following problems:

- Sound cuts on/off when the volume control is changed.
- Sound cuts on/off when the cord of an FM system is jiggled.
- Voice quality sounds distorted.

Battery testers are also available through hearing aid dealers or local commercial outlets, such as Radio Shack. Depending on their quality and sophistication, testers are priced from $3 to $25. Use them according to directions to test hearing aid batteries. Only batteries working at full power will provide good hearing aid function.

Check Student Function With Hearing Aid

Described below is a quick, efficient check of how a child functions with a hearing aid. In addition to including if the hearing aid is working, this check can also detect other possible problems a child may be experiencing such as a change in hearing levels related to outer or middle ear problems or a change in sensorineural hearing levels.

- Have the student sit facing you at a distance of about three feet, wearing the aid.
- Cover your mouth with an index card or piece of paper.
- Individually present each of the following five sounds: ah, oo, ee, sh, s. (These sounds represent the variety of the frequencies present in speech.)
- Have the student raise one hand or place a block into a container when the sound becomes audible.
- Set a baseline for each student, consisting of the sounds the student can perceive from three feet away, using a functioning hearing aid with a good battery. Not all students will hear all five sounds.
- Check each student's awareness of the five sounds on a regular basis. If hearing deviates from the student's baseline, check the aid more carefully.
- If a thorough check of the aid confirms that it is working well, poor performance on the five-sound test may indicate that a problem such as fluid in the middle ear is impairing the student's ability to hear at baseline levels. Notify the student's family if you strongly suspect that middle ear fluid is causing problems.

(Continued)

(Continued)

Troubleshoot Hearing Aid Problems

When a student seems to be having difficulty with a hearing aid, some of the following signs may help you find or eliminate the problem. If you uncover any hearing aid problems that cannot be resolved in the classroom, let the student's family know so the aid can be repaired or replaced as necessary.

Problem: NO SOUND

- Try a new battery.
- Make sure the battery is properly placed. Match the positive (+) on the battery to the (+) in the battery compartment.
- The battery compartment may be corroded. Clean it gently with a pencil eraser, then try a new battery.
- Make sure the hearing aid is set at ON, not at T for telephone.
- Look for wax or dirt in the earmold. Clean the mold with a pipe cleaner, then with warm soapy water. Dry it completely before reattaching it to the aid. Do not use alcohol.
- Look for twists in the tubing.

Problem: SQUEALING/FEEDBACK

- Check to see if the earmold fits properly. If it looks too small, inform the student's parent or audiologist.
- Check the volume and turn it down to the appropriate setting. If it still squeals, the mold is too small or there is an internal problem in the aid.
- Check for loose tubing, or for cracks in the tubing attached to the aid or mold.

SOURCE: Laurent Clerc National Deaf Education Center, Gallaudet University, *How to Check a Hearing Aid, Series #5004*. Available at http://clerccenter.gallaudet.edu/SupportServices/series/5004.html

the opportunity to individualize the learning process at their own comfort level and pace, placing them in control of the interactive process with a variety of subjects. Special programs are also available on CD-ROM as well as on the Internet for speech drill, auditory training, sign language instruction, speechreading, and supplemental reading and language instruction. Computers can now synthesize speech from keyboard input and transcribe speech onto a printed display screen. This technology makes it easier for college and vocational students with hearing impairments and limited speechreading skills to understand verbal communications and to communicate verbally with others.

Alerting Devices

Many everyday devices have been adapted to meet the needs of persons with hearing impairments. Wristwatches can be equipped with vibratory devices rather than auditory alarms. Doorbells, fire alarms, and alarm clocks are available with vibratory mechanisms or flashing lights in addition to auditory signals. Flashing-light clocks are useful for those individuals who sleep lightly. For heavy sleepers or individuals who are deaf–blind, flashing lamps (eighty-five flashes per minute) or special pillow vibrators are available. For parents who are hearing impaired, alerting devices are available with lights that flash in response to a baby's cry. Certain high-frequency alarms, such as a smoke detector, can be converted to a lower frequency, ensuring that the signal falls within the frequency range where there is sufficient residual hearing for detection.

Real-Time Captioning/Interpreting Technology

Technological advancements and skills, some of which were originally intended for different applications, have made information more available to students with hearing impairments. Software that uses voice recognition and converts the spoken word to printed files in a computer is one such example. In this application, the teacher uses a microphone connected to a computer with voice recognition software, which picks up the instruction as spoken and translates it to a print file on a computer screen viewed by the student. Students with hearing impairments can follow the real-time instruction on the computer monitor and then save the print file to the computer when finished. The print file can then be reviewed, sorted into notes and study guides, and saved for the student to use whenever needed.

Children who are hearing impaired frequently use auditory trainers in the classroom.

For students who function better with sign language than with print, a software program is now available that works just as the voice recognition software does, with one significant difference. Instead of having a print file appear on the screen viewed by the student, the instruction from the teacher is presented by a computer-based character that signs the information in real time.

Another example of real-time interpreter/print technology is the CART (Communication Access Realtime Translation) program. CART uses the paid services of trained court reporters to record instruction in the classroom. The student is able to follow the instruction on a computer screen in real time and then save and use files of information later, just as with the voice recognition files described previously.

Captioning

Many current television programs and feature films are captioned to make entertainment more accessible to audiences with hearing impairments. Federal law now requires that all new televisions with screens thirteen inches and over have built-in caption functions. Video rental stores today provide a wide variety of movies and documentaries that are captioned.

Telecommunication Devices

Individuals with severe hearing impairments can communicate by telephone with a **telecommunication device for the deaf (TDD).** A TDD is a small keyboard with an electronic display screen and modem attached. The telephone receiver is placed in the modem, and messages typed onto a keyboard are carried as different sets of tones on the telephone line to the other party's telephone, which must be linked to a TDD in order to complete the call.

Audio Link 11.2
Listen to more about technology.

Amplified telephones are available with a wide range of styles, models, and capabilities. These devices are most often used by individuals with moderate to severe hearing impairments. The amplifier can be built into a special telephone, or designed for occasional use and strapped onto a conventional receiver when needed. Telecommunication devices available and used by the general population offer new and vibrant opportunities for communication between and among individuals with severe hearing impairments. Cell phones with text messaging are an increasingly popular and flexible option.

Cochlear Implants

Many persons have sensorineural hearing loss so severe that they may not derive significant benefit from conventional amplification devices. The cochlear implant

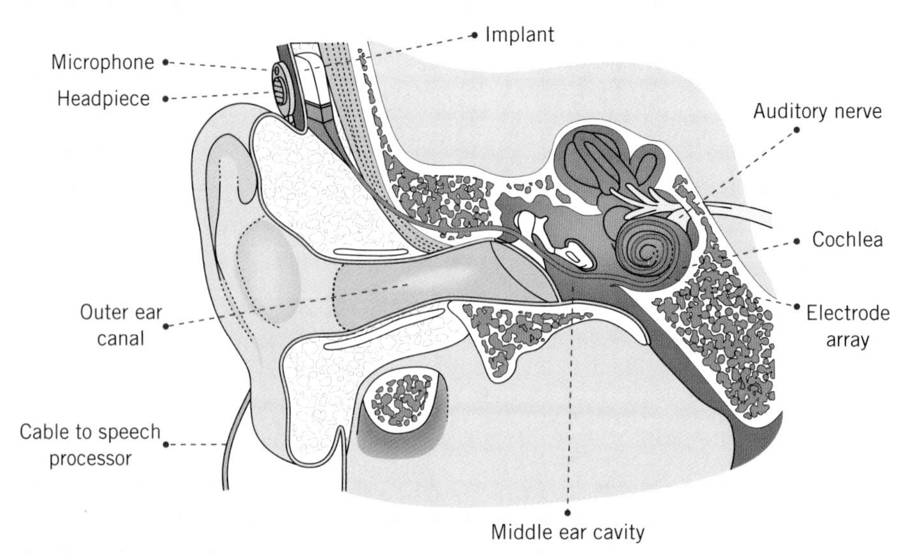

FIGURE 11.8 Cochlear Implant

SOURCE: Based on drawing from Advanced Bionics Corporation, Sylmar, CA.

Video Link 11.15
Watch more about cochlear implants.

(see Figure 11.8) is a surgically implanted device designed to make sounds audible for these individuals. Although somewhat controversial in the past, particularly with the Deaf culture community, large numbers of children and adults have been implanted, with favorable results. Worldwide, thousands of children and adults have received cochlear implants. Research indicates that cochlear implant users, particularly adventitiously deafened adults (those who lost their hearing after speech and language were developed) and children implanted at an early age, perform significantly better on a variety of tasks than most hearing aid users with a similar degree of hearing loss. When comparing the level of speech intelligibility between children with cochlear implants and children with normal hearing, distinct differences have been noted. By age 4, children with normal hearing develop adult or near adultlike speech intelligibility. Children with cochlear implants do not develop a similar ceiling of competence at such a rapid rate. Instead, they have a continuum of improvement that correlates to increased age and length of use of their implant. They continue to have a speech that is less intelligible than that of their same-age peer group with normal hearing. The question of how to bring them to the same level of intelligible speech as a normally hearing 4-year-old remains a challenge (Chin, Tsai, & Gao, 2003). Despite high variability in performance among users, cochlear implant technology is revolutionizing educational management of the profoundly deaf child.

A cochlear implant is not a hearing aid but rather a tiny array of electrodes that is implanted surgically in the inner ear (cochlea) and is attached to a receiver–stimulator implanted just behind the ear at the base of the skull. The individual wears a microphone and a small computer for speech processing, connected by electrical wiring. The transmitter is held in place over the implant site using a special magnet. Although many implant users wear larger processors similar in appearance to a body-type hearing aid, newer devices are a great deal smaller, fitting completely behind the ear, and are generally more cosmetically appealing. Continuous advancements in technology present ever-changing improvements in the options and results available to those opting for implantation (Chute, 2004).

Guidelines for implantation have become increasingly liberal (see Table 11.6). A number of factors affect the probability of success with implantation, including degree of hearing loss, age of onset, age at implantation, previous experiences with amplification, family support, and educational methodology. The earlier the child is implanted, the better the

TABLE 11.6 Guidelines for Cochlear Implants: Who Might Benefit?

Young Children: 12 months to 2 years	Does your child have: • Profound sensorineural hearing loss (nerve deafness) in both ears? • Lack of progress in development of auditory skill with hearing aid or other amplification? • High motivation and realistic expectations from family? • Other existing medical conditions that won't interfere with cochlear implant procedure?
Children: 2 to 17 years	Do you have: • Severe-to-profound sensorineural hearing loss (nerve deafness) in both ears? • Little or no benefit from hearing aids? • Lack of progress in the development of auditory skills? • High motivation and realistic expectations from family?
Adults: 18 years and older	Do you have: • Severe-to-profound sensorineural hearing loss in both ears? • Little or no useful benefit from hearing aids? • Scores of 50 percent or less on sentence recognition tests in the ear to be implanted and 60 percent or less in the nonimplanted ear or bilaterally?

SOURCE: From "Introduction to Cochlear Implants." Retrieved February 13, 2010, from http://www.cochlearamericas.com/378.asp

prognosis for success—especially for acquisition of intelligible speech. Implantation of older children (above 6 years) has shown some success, but improvement may be more limited.

The responsibility of public schools to children with cochlear implants was addressed in the final IDEA 2004 regulations. Because a cochlear implant is surgically implanted, it is not considered to be an assistive technology device. Therefore, schools are not required to pay for this appliance. The student, however, is entitled to receive related services as specified in the IEP. This can include speech pathology, audiological services, and the maintenance of the external components of the cochlear implant that are similar to those of a standard hearing aid (American Speech-Language-Hearing Association, 2010b).

Because cochlear implantation provides such an increase in residual hearing for the deaf child, educational management strategies are more likely to mirror those provided for children with a mild to moderate degree of loss. For example, profoundly deaf children often simply cannot hear many high-frequency consonants, even with technologically advanced amplification. Teaching such students to produce these sounds correctly in speech is extremely difficult. Children using cochlear implants generally have much better high-frequency hearing ability; as a consequence, encouraging correct production of high-frequency consonants becomes much easier. Although these children still have limitations with regard to complex grammatical structure, sophisticated vocabulary, and certain auditory skills, if implantation is done early and appropriate rehabilitative and educational supports are in place, linguistic and educational progress is generally more rapid for children using cochlear implants.

Trends, Issues, and Controversies

The debate regarding the most appropriate methodology for educating hearing-impaired children has raged for more than two hundred years and continues to be an emotionally charged issue. Overall, the research findings on efficacy of various communication styles and educational philosophies are inconclusive. It does appear that hearing-impaired infants born to deaf parents using American Sign Language (ASL) may exhibit significantly better language development (Hunt & Marshall, 2006). Determining the most appropriate methods for enhancing language acquisition, expressive and receptive communication skills, and resultant educational achievement for hearing-impaired children appears to be an issue of paramount importance. According to Paul and Quigley (1990), this issue has two major aspects: (1) kind of language and (2) form of communication. More specifically, there are two languages, American Sign Language (ASL) and Signed English systems, and two communication forms, oral and manual, to be considered. Any combination can produce a variety of approaches. The acquisition of one's native language is central to the development of functional literacy, which in turn provides the platform for future academic and societal success.

Research conducted by Moores (2001) suggests that parents who use a total communication approach, including manual signs, fingerspelling, and spoken language, with their child and with each other enhance their child's acquisition of language. Traditionally, the severity of hearing impairment has been viewed as a primary determinant of methodology. Before the availability of hearing aids, the greater the loss of hearing, the more difficulty the child had in developing speech and language skills. The merits of various methodologies are being reexamined in light of recent advances in amplification and cochlear implantation.

Audio Link 11.3
Listen to a debate about cochlear implants.

Transitioning from child-centered to family-centered interventional programs also appears to be an issue of great importance. Since the vast majority of hearing-impaired infants are born to hearing parents, simply attempting to provide families with comprehensive, unbiased information regarding educational options can be challenging. Current ideological and cultural controversies fueled by Deaf culture advocates and rigid proponents of various methodologies have polarized many educators. The bicultural–bilingual philosophy, often referred to as bi–bi, contends that deafness is a separate and viable culture within society, with ASL as its own unique and natural language. ASL has a unique grammar and syntax, and in the bicultural–bilingual approach English is learned as a secondary language.

Total communication (TC) is currently the communication approach of choice in many public school classrooms. Proponents of TC contend that by placing equal emphasis on signing, speaking, and speechreading skills, this method ensures a more normal rate of language acquisition and use of English as the primary language. Total communication has met with opposition for several reasons. Many educational programs that purport to be total communication in reality give little emphasis to oral skills. It has been argued that learning English as a primary language denies hearing-impaired children their cultural birthright by limiting their exposure to Deaf culture and ASL, its native language. Opponents of TC point to research by Strong and Prinz (1997) indicating that early exposure to ASL correlates positively with enhanced literacy and academic performance and may actually facilitate learning English as a second language.

Studies that examine human development confirm the importance of a child's early years in the development of functional, cognitive, communicative, social, and emotional abilities (Berk, 2008). Developing appropriate standards and procedures for early intervention programs, however, in concert with the debate surrounding communication methods and Deaf cultural issues, continues to be driven by philosophical perspectives (Paul & Quigley, 1990). As universal newborn screening programs for hearing loss are mandated and continue to expand, there is a pressing need for timely and effective intervention programs that allow families to make informed decisions regarding educational alternatives.

Within the context of inclusion, there is a growing concern regarding educational interpreters in general education classrooms at the elementary, secondary, and postsecondary levels. Minimum standards (preparation) and procedures (salary base) continue to affect preservice/in-service teacher development and have a residual effect on the education of students with hearing impairments (Moores, 2001). A number of educators, parents, and advocates have challenged inclusion as a viable placement option for individuals with hearing impairments (Innes, 1994). The main points of debate are that in inclusive settings (1) teachers are not familiar with the different dynamics of deafness, (2) teachers are not skilled in diverse communication techniques, and (3) students are stigmatized and often isolated socially (Moores, 2005).

Advocates for Deaf culture consider hearing impairment to be nonpathological and, therefore, not a condition requiring medical intervention. Individuals with significant hearing loss often work in the hearing world, but their family/social lives are usually sequestered within the deaf world. Proponents of Deaf culture claim that, when given a choice, individuals with significant hearing impairments would most often choose to spend the majority of their lives in the comfort of their own culture (Moores, 2001). Regrettably, the two societies, one deaf and the other hearing, often experience limited interaction and contact.

CHAPTER IN REVIEW

Definitions and Concepts in the Field of Hearing Impairment

- *Hearing impairment* is a generic term indicating a hearing disability that may range in severity from mild to profound.

- The term *deaf* refers to those in whom the sense of hearing is nonfunctional for the ordinary purposes of life. Deafness precludes successful processing of linguistic information through audition, with or without a hearing aid.
- An individual may be either congenitally deaf (born deaf) or adventitiously deaf—born with normal hearing that has become nonfunctional through illness or accident.
- Persons who are hard of hearing are those in whom the sense of hearing is defective but functional, either with or without a hearing aid, for the purpose of processing linguistic information.
- The ear is divided into three connected sections: the outer, the middle, and the inner ear. Hearing impairments are commonly classified according to their location in the hearing process and the severity of the loss.
- A conductive hearing loss is the interference of sound through the outer and middle ear.
- A sensorineural hearing loss is caused by defects of the inner ear (the cochlea), the auditory nerve that transmits impulses to the brain, or both.
- A mixed hearing loss involves both conductive and sensorineural loss.
- A central hearing loss is the result of damage to the central nervous system; an individual with this type of hearing loss may hear but not understand speech.
- Hearing loss is measured through testing procedures conducted by an audiologist and is graphed on an audiogram.
- The degree of hearing is usually reported in decibels (dB), a measure of sound intensity. It is also measured in hertz (Hz), or frequency of the sound.
- A hearing impairment is usually classified according to degree, ranging from mild to profound loss, based on different levels of intensity (dB) at different frequencies (Hz).
- One of the most common types of audiological tests is pure-tone audiometry, which is the practice of delivering sound tones to the individual via the air-conduction medium (headphones) and measuring them on an audiometer.
- Another common test is bone-conduction audiometry, which allows the signals to bypass the middle ear and be transmitted directly to the inner ear by vibrating the bones of the skull. It is used to ascertain whether there is a possible sensorineural or conductive hearing loss.
- More specialized types of hearing tests include play audiometry and speech audiometry.

Prevalence of Hearing Impairment

- Almost 71,000 students between the ages of 6 and 21 were receiving some type of specialized services because of a hearing impairment in the 2008–2009 school year. This accounts for approximately 1.2 percent of the students receiving services under IDEA.

Etiology of Hearing Impairment

- The cause of approximately one third of all hearing loss remains unknown; however, the known major causes are genetic or chromosomal anomalies, disease, and trauma.
- The etiology, location, and severity of the hearing loss are variables used in determining immediate and long-range treatment and programming.

Characteristics of Individuals With Hearing Impairment

- Children with hearing impairments have IQs similar to those of their nondisabled peers.
- Educational achievement in students with hearing impairments may be significantly delayed in comparison to that of their hearing peers, averaging three to four years below their age-appropriate grade levels.
- Play situations and the development of friendships are affected by difficulty with language development.

Educational Considerations

- The two principal educational settings for students with hearing impairment are public schools and special schools.
- There are three main instructional approaches to providing educational services to a child with a hearing impairment: (1) the auditory–oral method, (2) total communication, and (3) the bilingual–bicultural method.
- Currently a significant majority of educational and related service programs are using total communication.

Issues of Diversity

- Many persons who are deaf and hard of hearing contend that they should be viewed not as deficient or pathological, but rather as members of the Deaf culture with its own language, traditions, and values.

STUDY QUESTIONS

1. Define the terms *deaf* and *hard of hearing.*
2. Why is it important to know the age of onset, type, and degree of hearing loss?
3. What is the primary difference between prelingual and postlingual hearing impairments?
4. List the four major types of hearing loss.
5. Describe three different types of audiological evaluations.
6. What are some major areas of development that are usually affected by a hearing impairment?
7. List three major causes of hearing impairment.
8. What issues are central to the manualism-versus-oralism debate?
9. Define the concept of a Deaf culture.
10. What is total communication, and how can it be used in the classroom?
11. Describe the bilingual–bicultural approach to educating pupils with hearing impairments.
12. In what two academic areas do students with hearing impairments usually lag behind their classmates?
13. Why is early identification of a hearing impairment important?
14. Why do professionals assess the language and speech abilities of individuals with hearing impairments?
15. List five indicators of a possible hearing loss in the classroom.
16. What are three indicators in children that may predict success with a cochlear implant?
17. Identify five strategies a classroom teacher can use to promote communicative skills and enhance independence in the transition to adulthood.
18. Describe how to check a hearing aid.
19. How can technology benefit individuals with a hearing impairment?

KEY TERMS

hearing impairment 397
hearing sensitivity loss 397
deaf 397
residual hearing 397
hard of hearing 397
minimal hearing loss (MHL) 397
outer ear 397
middle ear 397
inner ear 397
central auditory nervous system 397
tympanic membrane 398
malleus 398
incus 398
stapes 398
ossicular chain 398
oval window 398
cochlea 398
organ of Corti 398
conductive hearing loss 398
otitis media 399
sensorineural hearing loss 399
mixed hearing loss 399
central hearing disorder 399
auditory neuropathy/auditory dys-synchrony 399
functional or nonorganic hearing loss 399
audiometric test 399
audiologist 400
audiogram 400
frequency 400
hertz (Hz) 400
decibels (dB) 400
pure-tone audiometry 400
air-conduction audiometry 400
bone-conduction audiometry 400
play audiometry 403
speech audiometry 403
speech recognition threshold (SRT) 403
auditory evoked potentials 403
evoked otoacoustic emissions 403
acoustic immittance 403
prelingual 403
postlingual 403
manual communication 404
oral approaches 404
total communication (TC) 405
adventitious (acquired) hearing loss 407
autosomal dominant 407
autosomal recessive 408
X-linked 408
atresia 409
fingerspelling 420
interpreter 421
oral interpreter 425
transliteration 425
high-risk register 427
assistive listening devices (ALDs) 431
auditory trainers 431
FM systems 431
signal-to-noise ratio 431
sound field systems 431
telecommunication device for the deaf (TDD) 435
amplified telephones 435

LEARNING ACTIVITIES

1. Observe an audiological examination of a student.
   a. Describe the individual being tested.
   b. What tests were administered?
   c. Were any hearing difficulties identified? If so, what kind of hearing loss was detected?
   d. What were your reactions to the assessment?
2. Observe an infant/toddler program as well as a school-age program for students with hearing impairments.
   a. Where did you observe the program?
   b. Describe the learning environment.
   c. Describe the activities you observed.
   d. What type(s) of communication modes were used?
   e. What were your reactions? What differences did you observe between the two programs?
3. Interview a general education teacher who has students who are deaf or hard of hearing in his or her class.
   a. How long has the teacher been educating students with hearing impairments?
   b. What type of professional training (preparation) does the teacher have?
   c. Ask the teacher about the primary purposes of the program and what kinds of problems he or she encounters.
   d. How would the teacher describe his or her classroom: mainstreamed or fully inclusive?
   e. What communication modes are used?
   f. How is technology used in the classroom?
   g. Describe your personal and professional reactions to this experience.

ORGANIZATIONS CONCERNED WITH HEARING IMPAIRMENTS

American Speech-Language-Hearing Association
2200 Research Boulevard
Rockville, MD 20850
(800) 638-8255
(301) 296-5650 (TTY)
(301) 296-8580 (Fax)
http://www.asha.org

Alexander Graham Bell Association for the Deaf and Hard of Hearing
3417 Volta Place N.W.
Washington, DC 20007–2778
(202) 337-5220
(202) 337-5221 (TTY)
(202) 337-8314 (Fax)
http://www.agbell.org

Council of American Instructors of the Deaf
P.O. Box 377
Bedford, TX 76095–0377
(817) 354-8414 (Voice/TTY)
http://www.caid.org

National Association of the Deaf
8630 Fenton Street
Suite 820
Silver Spring, MD 20910–3819
(301) 587-1788
(301) 587-1789 (TTY)
(301) 587-1791 (Fax)
http://www.nad.org

Self-Help for Hard of Hearing People
7910 Woodmont Avenue
Suite 1200
Bethesda, MD 20814
(301) 657-2248
(301) 657-2249 (TTY)
(301) 913-9413 (Fax)
http://www.icdri.org/dhhi/shhh.htm

REFLECTING ON STANDARDS

The following exercises are designed to help you learn to apply the Council for Exceptional Children (CEC) standards to your teaching practice. Each of the reflection exercises below correlates with a knowledge or skill within the CEC standards. For the full text of each of the related CEC standards, please refer to the standards integration grid located in Appendix B.

Focus on Learning Environments and Social Interactions ***(CEC Content Standard #5 CC5S8)***
Reflect on what you have learned about students with hearing impairments. If you were to have a student in your class with a hearing impairment, how might you help him or her learn skills for self-advocacy? What ways might you be able to help your student better understand his or her disability and communicate his or her learning needs?

Focus on Instructional Planning ***(CEC Content Standard #7 CC7S9)***
Reflect on what you have learned about the various assistive technologies available for students with hearing impairments. If you had a student in your class with a hearing impairment, how might you work with the student and his or her family to assess which assistive technologies might be best to use in your classroom? Who else might you need to involve from the school district to implement any new technologies?

STUDENT STUDY SITE

Visit the Student Study Site at www.sagepub.com/gargiulo4emedia for these additional learning tools:

- Video links
- Media links
- Self-quizzes
- E-flashcards
- Full-text SAGE journal articles
- Web exercises

CHAPTER 12

Learning Objectives

After reading Chapter 12 you should be able to:

- Define legally blind, functionally blind, and low vision.
- Explain the process of seeing and associated vision disorders.
- List the most common visual impairments affecting school-age children.
- Outline the historical evolution of educational services for children and youth with visual impairments.
- Provide examples of observable characteristics of vision difficulties.
- Describe how visual acuity is assessed.
- Define literacy medium and learning medium.
- Summarize educational services for persons with visual impairments across the life span.
- Explain how technology benefits individuals with visual impairments.

Individuals With Visual Impairments

CARRIE

The series of whistles sounds. She steps onto the starting block and bends into position as the official instructs. The beep of the starter propels the swimmers into the water. It is a good start. She and Jennifer surface at the same time, just short of Beth. Steadily Jennifer pulls ahead. "C'mon, Carrie, you can do it!" I think to myself. Jennifer's lead widens. I turn my head; I can't watch. She's worked so hard to not succeed now. At the turn, she flips just as Jennifer starts back for the last 50 meters. It's now or four more years. Suddenly she begins to narrow the margin. Is it too little too late? Maybe. I begin to yell (as do others around me). Please, dear God! She's doing it! Oh, no, the flags. It's so close. Yes, she does it! She out-touches Jennifer by hundredths of a second. But the clock does not register. Quickly the judges check the computers. Yes, she really did it! She doesn't know. Frantically I send word by a friend. When she hears the news, she stops in disbelief, and then her right arm shoots straight up with joy.

Video Link 12.1
Watch more about visual impairments.

She came through again. I don't know why I'm surprised. She has done it time and time again. That's just Carrie. All of her life she has amazed me as well as others she has encountered. While second place does not sound like much of an accomplishment, it is to a disabled child. Perhaps *disabled* is not the right word.

Carrie, now 22, was born with oculocutaneous albinism. As with all disabilities, this has a complex definition. For Carrie, it means she has no pigment in her eyes, skin, or hair; she is extremely sensitive to light; she has nystagmus; and she is legally blind. She has also had some other physical problems along the way, but has developed into an outstanding young lady earning her place on the U.S. Paralympic Team.

The road to victory has not been easy, and sometimes Carrie did not choose the easy route. Even as a small child many people saw the special qualities in Carrie and

---

Written by Carol Allison and Mary Jean Sanspree, University of Alabama at Birmingham encouraged and guided her. Others have been unable to see beyond her shortcomings. The key to her success has been her strength of character to focus on her abilities, not her disabilities. Her favorite saying is "I may not have eyesight, but I have vision."

Her academic life has definitely had its ups and downs. Her level of success and happiness seems to have been determined by her attitude, which is closely related to the attitude of her teachers and her classmates. The more creative and open the atmosphere, the more Carrie has achieved. Quite often the more creative teachers found ways to minimize her visual limitations and maximize her intellectual and creative abilities.

Swimming is not her only accomplishment. She is a college senior majoring in liberal arts with a concentration in visual arts. She is an award winner not only in the disabled world, but also in the "real world." Of all her talents, gifts, awards, recognitions, and other achievements, the one I am most proud of is the Right Stuff Award that she received at Space Camp in Huntsville, Alabama. This award is presented each camp session to one female and one male who have demonstrated outstanding leadership and personal effort. This shows me that she has developed into the kind of person who will contribute to society in a positive manner.

—*Jane Willoughby*

NOTE: For additional coverage of Carrie, check out the First Person box on page 465, written in her own words about her experience with her visual impairment.

Visual impairment is a term that describes people who cannot see well even with correction. Throughout history, *blindness* has been used as a term to mean that something is not understood, such as "I was blind to that idea" or the aged person is "old and blind." How many times do we use the stereotypes of the blind beggar on the street corner and the blind person groping for mobility in the environment? The stigma associated with loss of vision affects encounters with others, who may assume that the person is dependent on others for everything.

Famous success stories about persons who are blind include those of Helen Keller and Mary Ingalls. Helen Keller and her teacher, Annie Sullivan, pursued their lifelong journey from Tuscumbia, Alabama, to Perkins Institute for the Blind (now known as Perkins School for the Blind), to Radcliffe College, and then to employment with the American Foundation for the Blind. Keller helped develop schools for the blind all over the world (Lash, 1980).

Mary Ingalls was a student at Iowa College for the Blind (now Iowa Braille and Sight Saving School) in 1881. Her scholastic endeavors were made famous through Laura Ingalls Wilder's *Little House on the Prairie,* which later became a television series. Laura's portrayal of the determination of her sister Mary and their family to continue her education after she lost her vision at age 14 showed the world the success a person who is blind can achieve.

Movies about persons with visual impairments and publicity about musicians and athletes who are visually impaired have helped to change the image of persons with visual impairments. Braille in elevators, voice output on computers, and access to restaurant hosts who read the menu reflect a recognition that the person with vision loss is competent with only a visual acuity difference. Such changes allow for independence in the everyday world with only a few accommodations.

The goal of this chapter is to provide an understanding of the visual process, vision loss, the effects of vision loss on school performance and vocation, and the roles of the family and community. Historical foundations, classifications of vision loss, educational practices, and technological interventions are presented for you to examine how the general educational curriculum may be adapted for the student with a visual impairment.

Defining Visual Impairments

Visual impairment including blindness is defined in the Individuals with Disabilities Education Improvement Act (IDEA) (PL 108–446) as an impairment in vision that, even with correction, adversely affects an individual's educational performance. The term includes both partial sight and blindness. Educational services for students with visual impairments are determined by variations of the definition specified in IDEA. This definition encompasses students with a wide range of visual impairments, who may vary significantly in their visual abilities. One student may have no functional vision and must learn through tactual means; another may be able to read and write print with modifications such as enlarged print; still others may use a combination of both Braille and print. An appropriate learning medium for each student must be determined by the student's ability to use each of these means or a combination of both.

Visual impairments may include a reduction of **visual acuity** (the ability to visually perceive details) of near or distant vision or a restriction in the field of vision. In other words, acuity affects how well a child sees materials presented up close or how accurately the child can see work presented on chalkboards or maps across the room. An impairment involving the **visual field** refers to the amount of vision a student has in the quadrant regions to the right, to the left, above, and below while gazing straight ahead. Students may exhibit unusual head turning or positioning in order to view materials with the portion of the visual field that is functional. Students with a **field loss**, or a restriction to the visual field, must be taught to use auditory cues for safety purposes on the playground, in the classroom, and in other environments.

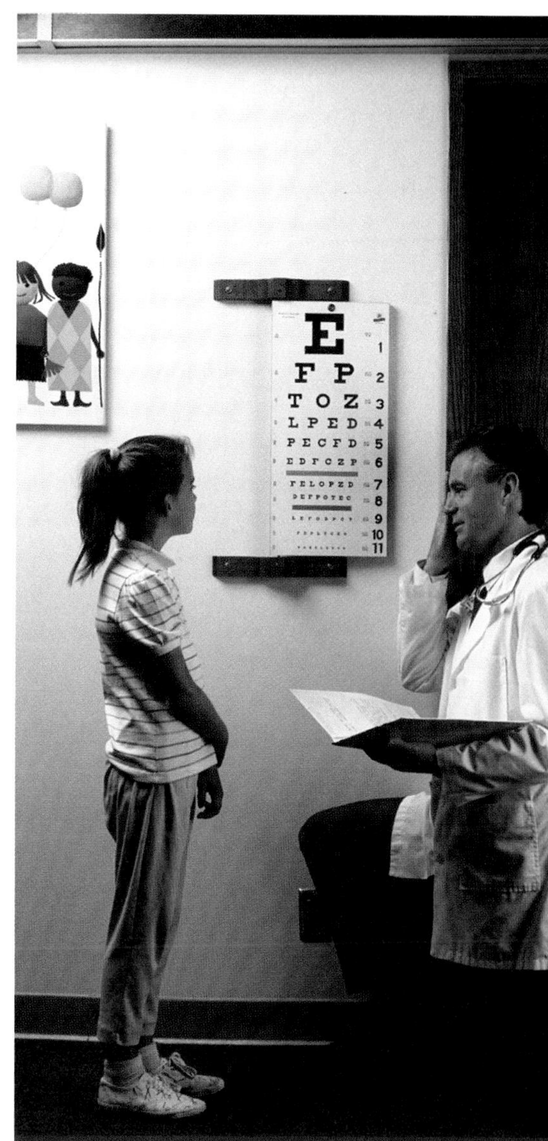

Legal blindness is visual acuity of 20/200 or less in the better eye after correction or a visual field that is no greater than 20 degrees.

Other areas of consideration in understanding a student's visual abilities include the age of the student at the time of the vision loss, the severity and stability of the eye condition, and whether the condition is the result of hereditary or congenital conditions. This information is usually obtained through a medical or clinically based assessment by an optometrist or ophthalmologist and does not necessarily include how the person functions in various settings throughout the school, home, or community.

Understanding the definitions of visual impairments is critical for the educational team in developing an appropriate educational program. Over the years, the term **legally blind** has been used as a federal definition of blindness. This definition involves using a **Snellen chart**, which is a clinical measurement of the true amount of distance vision an individual has under certain conditions. Legal blindness is a visual acuity of 20/200 or less in the better eye with correction or a visual field that is no greater than 20 degrees. In this definition, 20 feet is the distance at which visual acuity is measured. The *200* in this definition indicates the distance (200 feet) from which a person with normal vision would be able to identify the largest symbol on the eye chart. The second part of the definition refers to field restriction, which involves the amount of vision a person has to view objects peripherally. The legal definition is considered in education, but by itself has little value in planning a functional educational program for students with visual impairments.

Individuals identified as blind use tactile and auditory abilities as the primary channels of learning. They may have some minimal light or form perception or be totally without sight. Braille or other tactile media are commonly the preferred literacy channel. Orientation and mobility training is required for all students who are blind.

Individuals are considered **functionally blind** when the primary channel of learning is through tactile or auditory means. They may use limited vision to obtain additional information about the environment. These individuals usually use Braille as the **primary literacy medium** (most frequently used method of reading) and require orientation and mobility training.

A person is described as having **low vision** when the visual impairment interferes with the ability to perform daily activities. The primary channel of learning is through visual means with the use of prescription and nonprescription devices. The literacy medium varies with each individual according to the use of the remaining vision and the use of low vision devices. Orientation and mobility training is required for students to learn to use **residual vision** (usable vision).

Persons with deaf–blindness have limited vision and hearing that interfere with visual and auditory tasks. Individuals who are **deaf-blind** learn tactually. Braille and sign language are the preferred literacy and communication media. A sign language interpreter and orientation and mobility training are required for persons with deaf–blindness. The use of a variety of ways to communicate facilitates direct learning experiences for the person with deaf–blindness (Chen & Downing, 2006).

The Eye and How It Works

The human eye is the organ that gives us the sense of sight, which allows us to learn more about the surrounding world than any of the other four senses. We use our eyes in almost every activity we perform, whether reading, working, watching television, writing a letter, or driving a car. The eye allows us to see and interpret the shapes, colors, and dimensions of objects by processing the light. Light enters the eye first through the clear **cornea** and then through the circular opening in the **iris** called the **pupil**. Next the light is converged by the crystalline **lens**. The light progresses through the gelatinous **vitreous humor** to a clear focus on the **retina**, the central area of which is the **macula**. In the retina, light impulses are changed into electrical signals and sent along the **optic nerve** to the occipital (posterior) lobe of the brain, which interprets these electrical signals as visual images.

When an eyeball is longer than normal from front to back, the incoming rays of light focus in front of the retina instead of on the retina. This condition is known as **myopia** or nearsightedness. In this situation, a pupil can see near objects (for example, his or her textbook), but viewing objects at a distance—the chalkboard—may be problematic. If the eyeball is too short, the image will focus behind the retina. This condition is commonly referred to as **hyperopia** or farsightedness. A child with hyperopia typically has no problem seeing distant objects but encounters difficulty seeing near objects. Hyperopia is the most common refractive error in children (Miller & Menacker, 2007).

In the case of **astigmatism**, one or more surfaces of the cornea or lens (the eye structures that focus incoming light) are not spherical (shaped like the side of a basketball) but cylindrical (shaped like the side of a football). As a result, there is no distinct point of focus inside the eye but, rather, a smeared or spread-out focus.

The eyeball, which measures approximately one inch in diameter, is set in a protective cone-shaped cavity in the skull called the **orbit** or socket. The orbit is surrounded by layers of soft, fatty tissue that protect the eye and enable it to turn easily. Three pairs of muscles regulate the motion of each eye.

Figure 12.1 shows the anatomy of the human eye; Table 12.1 presents key terminology associated with the functioning of the eye.

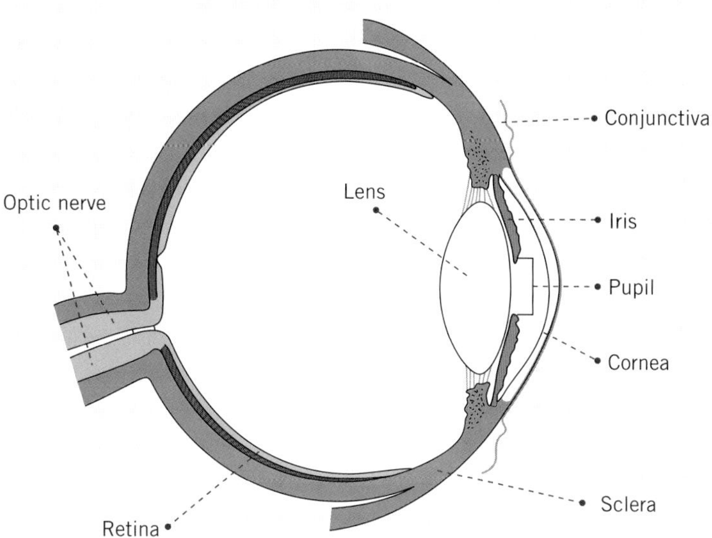

FIGURE 12.1 Schematic of the Eye

SOURCE: National Eye Institute. (2010). *Photograph and Image Catalog: Normal eye anatomy NEA05.* Available at http://www.nei.nih.gov/photo

TABLE 12.1 Terminology Describing Eye Functioning

Term	Description
Aqueous humor	A clear, watery fluid that fills the front part of the eye between the cornea, lens, and iris.
Choroid	The middle layer of the eyeball, which contains veins and arteries that furnish nourishment to the eye, especially the retina.
Conjunctiva	A mucous membrane that lines the eyelids and covers the front part of the eyeball.
Cornea	The transparent outer portion of the eyeball that transmits light to the retina.
Iris	The colored, circular part of the eye in front of the lens. It controls the size of the pupil.
Lens	The transparent disc in the middle of the eye behind the pupil that brings rays of light into focus on the retina.
Optic nerve	The important nerve that carries messages from the retina to the brain.
Pupil	The circular opening at the center of the iris that controls the amount of light allowed into the eye.
Retina	The inner layer of the eye containing light-sensitive cells that connect with the brain through the optic nerve.
Sclera	The white part of the eye; a tough coating that, along with the cornea, forms the external protective coat of the eye.
Vitreous body	A colorless mass of soft, gelatinlike material that fills the eyeball behind the lens.

Classification of Visual Impairments

Children are eligible for special education services according to the amount of vision loss and how that vision loss affects educational performance. The most common visual impairments affecting the school-age child include **cataracts, glaucoma, optic nerve atrophy**, myopia, **albinism**, eye injury, cortical visual impairment, and **retinopathy of prematurity (ROP)**. Examples of how children see with different eye diseases are shown in Figure 12.2.

Some visual impairments are secondary to systematic diseases such as diabetes, cancer, muscular dystrophy, and arthritis. A list of these visual impairments and their characteristics can be found in Table 12.2 (page 451).

(a)

(b)

(c)

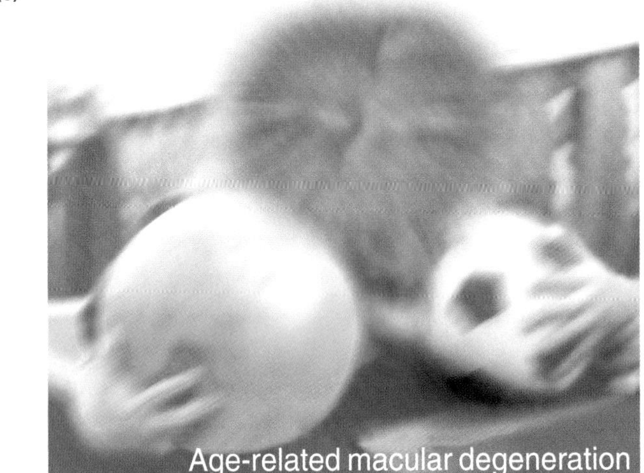

(d)

(e)

Diabetic retinopathy

FIGURE 12.2 Examples of Eye Diseases

SOURCE: National Eye Institute. (2010). *Photograph and Image Catalog: Eye disease simulation.* Available at http://www.nei.nih.gov/photo

TABLE 12.2 Common Visual Impairments of School-Age Children

Condition	Cause	Characteristics
Congenital cataracts	Congenital anomaly, infection, severe malnutrition, systemic disease, or trauma	Blurred vision, nystagmus
Congenital glaucoma	Increased pressure of the eye	Excessive tearing, cloudy lens, pain, restricted visual fields
Eye injury	Trauma	Poor visual acuity or blindness resulting from injury
Myopia	Elongation of the eye	Extreme nearsightedness, decreased visual acuity
Ocular albinism	Total or partial absence of pigment, hereditary condition	Nystagmus, light sensitivity, decreased visual acuity
Optic atrophy	Degeneration of the optic nerve, may be congenital or hereditary	Loss of central vision, color vision, and reduced visual acuity
Retinopathy of prematurity (ROP)	Prematurity and low birth weight	Loss of peripheral vision; total blindness may occur

A Brief History of Visual Impairments

Education for and changes of attitudes toward persons with visual impairments were of great interest to Diderot (1749), who wrote to King Louis of France a philosophical work called *Letter on the Blind for the Use of Those Who See.* Diderot had contact with two people who were blind: Nicholas Saunderson, a mathematics professor, and Maria Theresia von Paradis, a Viennese pianist and music teacher. Diderot was one of the early champions of the visually impaired and believed that persons who were blind could lead normal lives.

In 1784, Valentin Haüy established the Institut National des Jeunes Aveugles in Paris. This institution for blind youth was the first school for the education of children with vision loss. Haüy used Roman letters to teach students who were blind. His students, however, were using night writing codes within the school. In the 1800s, one of Haüy's students, Louis Braille, developed an embossed communication system so he could write to his friends in a simpler manner than using raised letters (Scholl, Mulholland, & Lonergan, 1986). His system of embossed dots was not accepted by educators until later, but his system of **Braille** dots remains today as the literacy code accepted throughout the world.

The first schools for the blind in the United States were financially supported through the school in Paris. These schools included the Perkins School for the Blind in Boston, established in 1829; the New York Institution for the Blind, incorporated in 1831; and the Overbrook School for the Blind in Philadelphia, opened in 1833. These residential schools, modeled after the Institut National des Jeunes Aveugles in Paris, were the brainchild of Samuel Gridley Howe, who had visited European schools to learn how to provide education for the blind in the United States (Scholl et al., 1986).

Residential programs were designed to prepare students with visual impairments for daily living skills and menial jobs. Students were expected to function within a sheltered environment and go into life as members of a separate society that was labeled as "helpless" or dependent. The schools were a type of experiment to see if students with disabilities could learn community skills and function as participating citizens instead of dependents of society.

In the early 1900s, children with visual impairments were served by various agencies such as hospitals, children's services for rehabilitation, and residential schools; there were

receive the light image and send it to the brain through the optic nerve. The optic nerve carries the light messages (electrical signals) to the brain, where they are interpreted as visual images known as sight.

Rods and cones are photoreceptive cells found in the retina. **Rod cells**, located mainly in the peripheral areas, are extremely light sensitive. Responsible for shape and motion, they function best in reduced illumination. Rod cells are not responsive to color. **Cone cells** are located mainly in the central area of the retina. Color is defined in the cone cells. Only special cones are found in the macula area, which is the area of best central vision, and the fovea area, which is the area of most acute vision. **Macular degeneration** is a common eye disease in adults, but it may also occur in young people. This disease involves damage to the central part of the retina cones, affecting central vision, photophobia, and color vision.

If a child has retinopathy of prematurity (ROP), vascular growth has been interrupted by premature birth. The veins and arteries begin to grow in an unorganized manner causing bundles, which pull together and detach the retina. The child first loses peripheral vision and then the whole field of vision unless surgical intervention is immediate. Spotty vision, retinal scarring, field loss, and glaucoma may also be present. Training in early intervention and sensory stimulation is an area of concern.

According to the Texas School for the Blind (2007), other retinal diseases include the following:

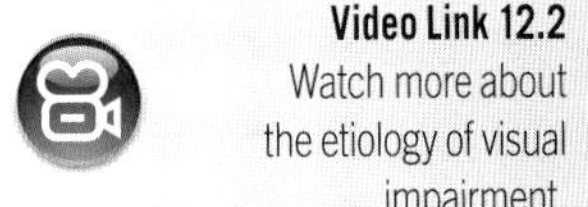

- **Retinitis pigmentosa** is a hereditary condition involving gradual degeneration of the retina, which can result in night blindness, photophobia, and eventually loss of macular vision.
- Toxoplasmosis is a severe infection transmitted through contact with domestic animals such as cats or chickens. Lesions on the retina can reduce visual acuity and field vision. Squinting is an observable characteristic of children with toxoplasmosis.
- Albinism is a congenital condition characterized by a lack of pigment (skin, hair, or eyes). If the eyes are the only area affected, it is called ocular albinism. These children may be extremely photophobic and sensitive to glare, both in the classroom and outdoors. They may have high refractive problems, but the visual fields are usually normal. Fatigue may become a factor in close work.
- **Coloboma** is a congenital condition that results in a teardrop shape of the pupil, iris, lens, retina, choroid, or optic nerve. Field of vision may be affected, problems with glare may also be present, and problems with depth perception may occur.
- Optic nerve atrophy is caused by a variety of diseases. Early treatment can prevent a loss of visual acuity. Without treatment, optic atrophy can result in conditions from low visual acuity to total blindness.

Prevention of Visual Impairments

Most visual impairments are genetic in source, but others can be prevented or controlled. Prenatal care can prevent eye problems secondary to sexually transmitted diseases, prematurity, or known hereditary problems. Screening of babies in the hospital nursery, youngsters in the preschool setting, and older students on a regular basis can help detect and prevent eye diseases that cause visual impairments.

Eye safety is a preventive measure against eye injuries that can hinder visual acuity and even cause blindness. Ocular trauma can affect the orbit, the eyelids, and other structures of the eye, and immediate intervention is necessary. Some trauma causes infections, changes in the appearance of the eye, and even blindness.

Early Detection

Vision screening is a necessary beginning to eye care, although such screening does not replace a professional eye examination. Vision problems affect one in twenty preschoolers and one in four school-age children (Prevent Blindness America, 2010a). Early screening and diagnosis can determine the prognosis for visual impairments. Screenings and eye examinations should take place shortly after birth, at 6 months of age, before entering school, and periodically throughout the school years.

Eye Safety

Eye injuries are common. They can range from a mild abrasion with bleeding in the front of the eye to retinal detachment, penetration of the eye, or actual rupture of the globe (eyeball). Some injuries heal without loss of vision; others result in the loss of the eye. At least 90 percent of all eye injuries to children can be prevented by understanding the dangers, identifying and correcting hazards, and using greater care when supervising children (Prevent Blindness America, 2010b). Some of the most frequent causes of eye injuries are listed as follows:

Many types of eye injuries can be prevented.

- Misuse of toys or altering toys
- Falls involving home furnishings and fixtures such as beds, stairs, tables, and toys
- Misuse of everyday objects, such as home repair and yard care products, personal use items, kitchen utensils, silverware, pens, and pencils
- Accidental exposure to harmful household and cleaning products, such as detergents, paints, pesticides, glues, and adhesives
- Automobile accidents (a leading cause of eye injuries to young children)
- Fireworks, which may cause injury to the user and bystanders alike (Kuhn et al., 2000)

Characteristics of Individuals With Visual Impairments

Visual impairment affects the type of experiences the child has, ability to travel within the environment, and actual involvement in the immediate and secondary communities. These factors will be affected differently depending on the amount of vision loss. The child with low vision has experiences that are different from those of the child who is legally blind or totally blind. The Optometric Extension Program Foundation (2010) has developed a checklist of observable characteristics of vision difficulties in children to assist teachers in making reliable observations of children's visual behavior (see Table 12.3).

Because the eye serves as the primary sensory input for most individuals, it becomes extremely important for those working with school-age children to be aware of the visual abilities necessary for maximum academic achievement:

- Clear visual acuity at both near and distance
- Ability to fixate at all distances and in all planes
- Binocular coordination
- Development of color preferences
- Central and peripheral visual abilities
- Visual perceptual imagery

Academic Performance

At one time it was believed that visual impairments were associated with lowered intellectual abilities, but we now know that this is not true. In fact, in many instances, the intellectual capabilities of students with visual impairments are similar to those of their

TABLE 12.3 Behavioral Characteristics in Vision Function Problems

Unusual turning of the head, body, or eye
Holding reading material extremely close to the face
Excessive rubbing of the eye
Watery eyes
Eye fatigue
Frequent eye pain
Frequent headaches
Squints or shades the eye to view objects
Constantly having difficulty in keeping up when reading and writing
Using markers such as pencils and fingers when reading
Difficulty copying from the board or transparencies
Confusion in writing letters and numbers appropriately
"Clumsy" movement from one environment to another
Poor posture in both standing and sitting
Reluctance to participate in social and physical activities
Poor grades
Difficulty with color identification or color coordination
Sensory perceptual coordination
Misaligns columns when writing math problems
Requires additional time to complete a task
Fails to make eye contact when talking to people
Behavior problems

SOURCE: Optometric Extension Program Foundation, *Educator's Guide to Classroom Vision Problems.* Available at http://oep.excerpo.com/index.php?action=show_details&product_id=3056

sighted peers (Gargiulo & Metcalf, 2010). Despite this, significant academic delays are not uncommon in learners with visual impairments. This is most likely due to their restricted opportunity to obtain information visually (Pogrund & Fazzi, 2007). For these children, unlike their sighted classmates, incidental learning derived from interacting with the environment is severely limited (Liefert, 2003). As a result, conceptual development and other learning in pupils with visual impairments primarily depend on tactile (touch) experiences and the use of sensory modalities other than vision (Bishop, 2004; Chen & Downing, 2006; Gargiulo & Metcalf).

Social and Emotional Development

The everyday experiences of children who have visual impairments are affected because these children do not respond visually to people in the environment. Maintaining eye contact during speech, smiling at someone in a friendly manner, and reaching out to touch someone nearby are not innate skills for the child who cannot see details in the immediate surroundings. For the child with visual impairment, knowledge about body parts, eating skills, age-appropriate behavior, clothing, and other social skills are not learned by viewing others in the family or community. Socially appropriate behaviors must be intentionally taught to the person with a visual impairment so that other people will be at ease during communication.

Social behaviors affect the emotional development of the child with a visual impairment. The child must feel accepted by peers and others in the community. If the eye contact or verbal communication is not appropriate for the age of the child, adults and children may tend to leave the child out of social events or talk for the child.

The child with a visual impairment should also talk about emotions and how to project those emotions in the sighted world. Often the child with a visual impairment is lonely and needs structure to integrate into community activities. The child may feel isolated and have low self-esteem because he or she appears to be on the fringe of events within the family or community. Physical communication within social interactions, such as touching people appropriately, affects the social and emotional facets of the child. It is necessary to address feelings and emotions so that the child with a visual impairment can know what emotions are and how others detect emotional changes in faces or body language.

Video Link 12.3
Watch more about social development.

A child who has low vision will display more visual and tactual skills in the social situation. The appropriate responses shown because of paired visual and tactile experiences will often make the child with low vision appear to have less of a vision loss than is really present. However, the child with low vision may have optical devices, enlarged materials, mobility devices, and technology for reading and writing with print. This may cause frustration for the child because of the complexity of the devices and materials needed to obtain information visually and auditorily.

The child who is legally blind will retrieve information tactually and auditorily, with minimal use of vision for tasks where large objects or light affects mobility decisions. Many parents notice that the young child does not turn his or her head toward the person talking and seems to grope for toys on the floor, hold onto the wall, or sit alone rather than explore the room. The child will also concentrate on items within the immediate environment, talk out when it is not appropriate, and ask questions to maintain voice contact with people in the room. The child who is legally blind will travel with a cane and will read and write with magnification, Braille, or both, according to reading speed, comprehension, and preference.

The child who is totally blind, with no light perception or possibly with prosthetic eyes, will depend on tactual and auditory skills for all information. The child will often not react to any visual cues, will usually sit in one place until someone guides him or her to another setting, and will be dependent on others for stimulation within the immediate environment. The child will use a cane to travel and will use the hands for locating and describing objects. The child will use Braille reading and writing for literacy and will have to use listening skills for learning new ideas.

Vocational Skills

Children with visual impairments begin vocational skills training at an early age if early intervention is provided or a preschool class is available. Children learn about dressing, eating, cooking, telling time, and using calendars for scheduling events in daily life. As the child progresses through school, a specialized curriculum may be introduced to teach about earning money, having a job, and traveling within the community.

Entering the world of work is an issue for vocational development. The student must know how to bathe, dress, prepare a meal, and plan the travel details to get to a job. After arriving at the workplace, the student must learn the building layout and the location of necessary sites such as the main office, restroom, lunchroom, and other important places

It is important that children with visual impairments feel accepted by their classmates.

within the company. Job duties and responsibilities must be explained so that job tasks can be completed successfully. Ethical behavior within the workplace must be learned before the first day of work. Ways to communicate with people within the work setting are also an educational issue.

The child with visual impairments faces quality-of-life issues that may differ from those faced by persons with other disabilities. The amount of vision loss, the intervention strategies, and the quality of life should all be taken into account. Independence begins in the early years and continues throughout life, affecting the quality of life at work, at home, and in the community. Vocational skills are a part of the preschool plan, the educational program, and the transition to adulthood so that age-appropriate skills are learned and used for independence.

Assessment of Students With Visual Impairments

Public Law 108–446 ensures that all students with disabilities will have available a free appropriate public education. A comprehensive assessment is required to determine eligibility for special education services and to develop an educational program that provides for the individual needs of each pupil. In developing an educational program for children with visual impairments, the assessment process must comply with the equivalent guidelines for other areas of exceptionality while also diagnosing and determining the unique needs and abilities of students with visual impairments.

Some children may be identified at birth as having a visual impairment through routine medical examinations, but many others are not identified as visually impaired until later. Parents or caregivers may notice unusual developmental behaviors caused by a vision loss. Some children may be diagnosed with a visual impairment following an accident or childhood illness. Other children may be identified through preschool or kindergarten vision screening programs.

A screening for visual acuity is often provided at school or in the physician's office. The acuity chart most often used for testing and reporting vision loss is the Snellen chart (see Figure 12.3). An example of a distance loss on the Snellen chart is 20/70, meaning that the person has to be 20 feet away from the chart to see what the normal eye can see from 70 feet. This chart is a 20-foot distance test; other tests are given for near vision and other vision problems.

Any student identified with a suspected vision problem should be referred to a licensed ophthalmologist or optometrist for further evaluation, including a medical examination and report. The information in this report should include etiology, medical history and diagnosis, ocular health, visual abilities, recommended low vision devices, orientation and mobility needs, and a reevaluation date. This information may be provided to the educational system through a written ocular report (see Figure 12.4).

Interpretation of these data for the educational team should be by a trained and certified teacher of the visually impaired. This information is crucial to the development of an appropriate educational experience. If conditions warrant, further assessment should be obtained and considered by the multidisciplinary team.

In addition to a medical examination, a clinical low vision evaluation is necessary to determine if a student could benefit from other optical or nonoptical low vision devices. The low vision examination involves acuity tests, visual field testing for peripheral or central vision loss, and an interview with the individual to see what he or she would like to do for work, school, or leisure activities. A personal prescription for low vision devices, technology, or referrals to community agencies is part of the low vision plan. If low vision devices cannot assist the student with reading, writing, or distant viewing, then auditory and tactual prescriptions are recommended as pre-Braille or listening skill practice. The student's vision teacher can attend this evaluation and bring materials relevant to the scheduled daily activities. Examples of educational materials pertinent to the student with visual impairments are reading texts, daily writing journals, workbooks, maps, and charts.

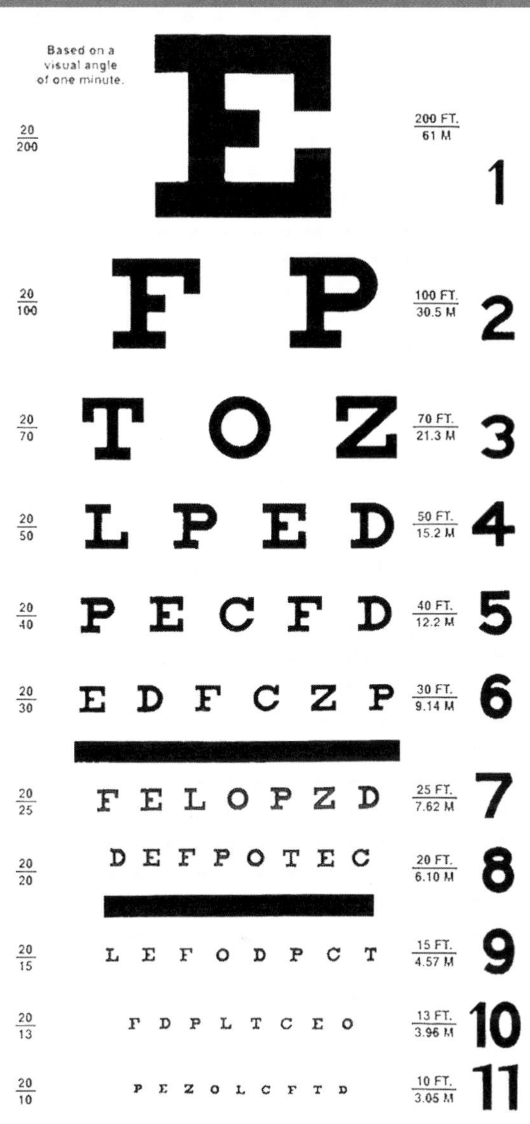

FIGURE 12.3 Snellen Chart

SOURCE: National Eye Institute. (2010). *Photograph and Image Catalog: Eye charts EC01*. Available at http://www.nei.nih.gov/photo

Functional Vision Evaluation

Each child's ability to use vision is unique, and the ability to use what vision the child has (visual efficiency) may be improved through specific programs of instruction. An important element in planning an educational program for children with visual impairments is assessment of a student's present **functional vision**. In other words, an assessment is needed to see how well each student uses vision to complete a specific task.

Because of the role that vision plays in the overall development of each child, a functional vision evaluation must be performed before all other educational evaluations. This is to ensure that each child will have access to the materials and equipment needed to participate and perform to the best of his or her abilities. Under the supervision of a teacher of students with visual impairments, each pupil must be observed in a variety of

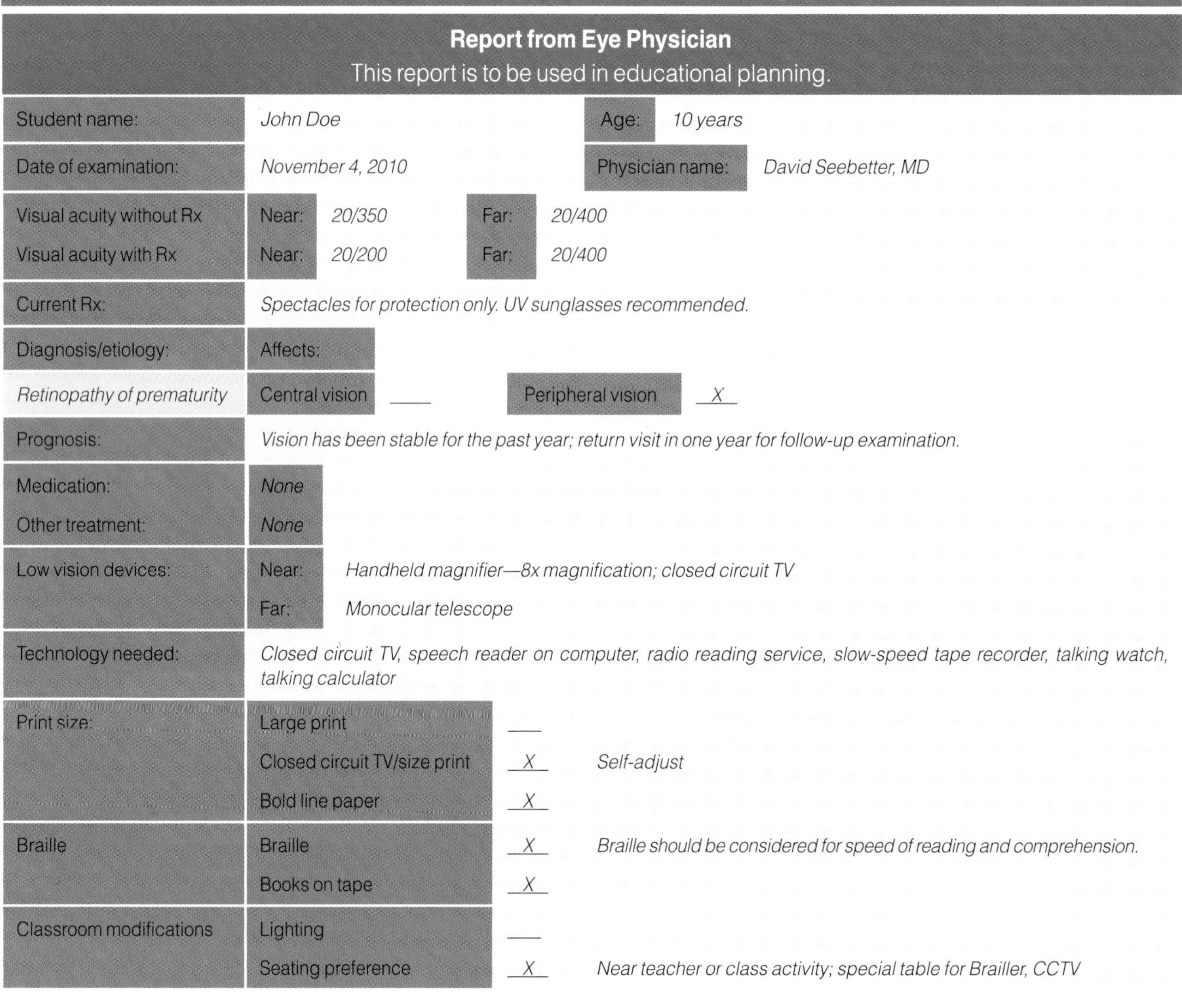

Report from Eye Physician
This report is to be used in educational planning.

Student name:	John Doe	Age:	10 years
Date of examination:	November 4, 2010	Physician name:	David Seebetter, MD
Visual acuity without Rx	Near: 20/350	Far: 20/400	
Visual acuity with Rx	Near: 20/200	Far: 20/400	
Current Rx:	Spectacles for protection only. UV sunglasses recommended.		
Diagnosis/etiology:	Affects:		
Retinopathy of prematurity	Central vision ___	Peripheral vision	X
Prognosis:	Vision has been stable for the past year; return visit in one year for follow-up examination.		
Medication:	None		
Other treatment:	None		
Low vision devices:	Near:	Handheld magnifier—8x magnification; closed circuit TV	
	Far:	Monocular telescope	
Technology needed:	Closed circuit TV, speech reader on computer, radio reading service, slow-speed tape recorder, talking watch, talking calculator		
Print size:	Large print	___	
	Closed circuit TV/size print	X	Self-adjust
	Bold line paper	X	
Braille	Braille	X	Braille should be considered for speed of reading and comprehension.
	Books on tape	X	
Classroom modifications	Lighting	___	
	Seating preference	X	Near teacher or class activity; special table for Brailler, CCTV

FIGURE 12.4 Ocular Report

environments that occur throughout the student's daily routine. This observation must include the student performing various tasks that require both near and distant visual abilities. Observations should encompass both individual and group activities, including oral and silent reading groups, desk work, and board work. The functional vision evaluation should also include travel within the school environment—playground, restroom, music room, lunchroom, and physical education sites—as well as accessing modes of transportation. The evaluation should also include samples of the student's work and reports of activities in the home and community.

The functional vision evaluation is a collaborative effort of the educational team for purposes of program planning. Specific recommendations, accommodations, modifications, and intervention strategies for the student in all environments can be based on a comprehensive evaluation. The team approach to the functional evaluation can provide a continuum of appropriate strategies in the educational and community settings.

Learning Media

Audio Link 12.1
Listen to more about learning media.

Another important component in the assessment process is to determine the most effective learning and literacy media. **Literacy medium** refers to sensory channels and is based on the student's preferred method of reading and writing—print, Braille, or both.

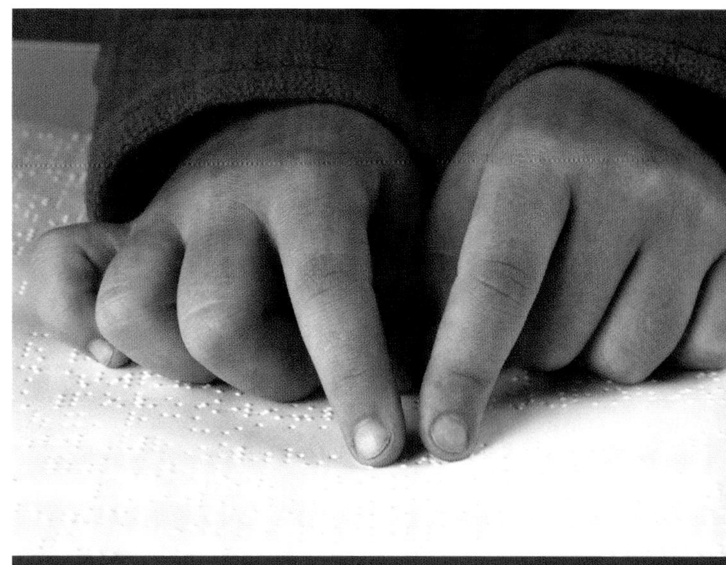

Braille is usually the reading medium of choice for pupils who are totally blind.

Regardless of the level of vision a student has or whether the pupil has an additional disability, a learning medium assessment must be conducted to determine the student's preferred mode of learning and literacy (American Foundation for the Blind, 2010c; Pugh & Erin, 1999).

Learning media include the materials and methods a student uses in conjunction with the sensory channels in the process of learning. Visual learning media include pictures, videos, imitation, and demonstration. Tactual learning media include models, real objects, and physical prompting. Auditory learning media include verbal communication, taped information, and environmental sounds (American Foundation for the Blind, 2010d; Levack, 1994). A hearing evaluation is required as a part of the auditory media determination. Determination of print size is important so that the child with a visual impairment can readily use low vision devices prescribed for reading, writing, and leisure activities. A vision specialist can inform the child and family about specific low vision devices, where to use them, and what size print is required for each device. The standard print sizes recommended range from 6 point, the size used in telephone directories, to 24 point, used in large print texts.

"This is 6 point type"

"This is 12 point type"

"This is 18 point type"

"This is 24 point type"

Braille as a literacy medium is used together with print and auditory input if the child has any residual vision. This enables the student to read print for survival skills, and to sign documents. An individual who is totally blind will use Braille and listening skills for input. Braille is addressed in the IEP so that the child with a visual impairment will have ongoing consideration of Braille as a reading medium.

Braille consists of patterns of six possible dots arranged in two columns of three (see Figure 12.5, page 462). The combination of dots indicates a certain letter of the alphabet. Each language has a Braille code that matches the letters in the alphabet of that language. American Braille has two "grades." In **Grade 1 Braille**, each letter of a word is spelled out using the Braille letter corresponding to the print letter. This is the first level taught so that the complete alphabet is learned. **Grade 2 Braille** is made up of contractions representing parts of words or whole words, similar to print shorthand. The primers begin with words contracted so that the child learns the spelling of the word with Grade 1 and the whole word in a sentence with Grade 2. Many elevators and signs use Grade 2, because that is the standard for Braille readers. Examples of Grade 1 and Grade 2 Braille are presented in Figure 12.6 (page 463).

Educational Assessment and Program Planning

Appropriate assessment strategies are a prerequisite to effective teaching. Assessments can provide critical information on the ways in which various visual impairments can affect learning and the need for instructional adaptations. Many students with visual impairments have the same educational goals as other pupils and can often be successfully included in the general education classroom. In planning an educational program for a student with visual impairments, other assessments must also be considered. However, educational assessments must be modified for accessibility, with either larger print, Braille, oral presentation, or omission of items that test visual skills. The evaluation must measure the skills of the student using the modifications with which the student is familiar so that the results will paint a picture of academic functioning level.

Students who have a visual impairment also have unique educational needs and should be evaluated in these areas to determine the appropriate educational placement and program. According to the American Foundation for the Blind (2010d), formal assessments used to determine strategies and needs in particular areas of instruction may include the following:

- Basic academic skills
- Learning and literacy media
- Verbal and nonverbal communication skills
- Social interaction skills
- Visual efficiency skills
- Orientation and mobility skills
- Independent living skills
- Career/vocational skills
- Use of assistive technology

Braille Alphabet and Numbers
Used by the Blind

Close your eyes and read this with your fingers.

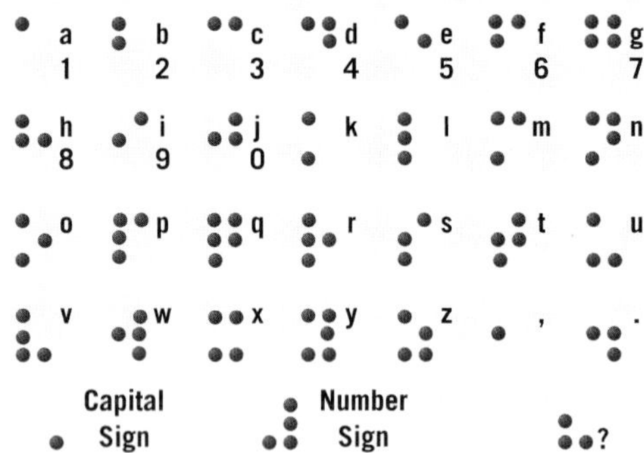

The Braille system is comprised of signs formed by the use of all the possible combinations of 6 dots numbered and arranged thus:

1 ●● 4
2 ●● 5
3 ●● 6

Letters are capitalized by prefixing dot 6. The first ten letters preceded by the number sign represent numbers. Punctuation marks are formed in the lower part of the cell.

In addition to ordinary print the Braille system provides for the writing of foreign languages, musical scores, mathematical and chemical notations, and other technical matter.

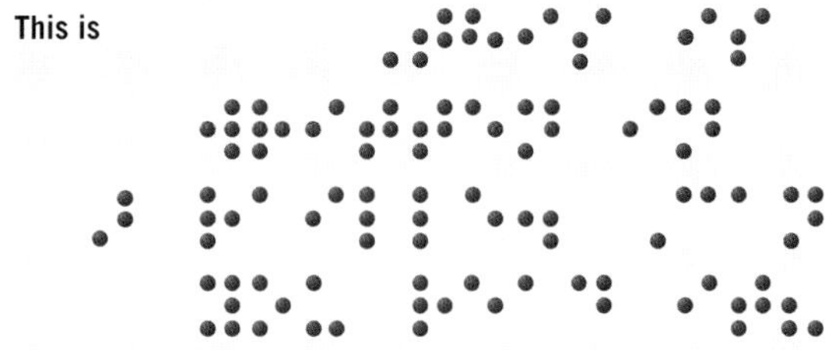

FIGURE 12.5 Braille Card

SOURCE: American Printing House for the Blind, Inc., Louisville, KY.

Eligibility Determination

Recall that to determine eligibility for special education because of a disability, the IEP team must base its decision on data from multiple sources. A functional vision evaluation and a learning media assessment should be part of the initial evaluation for individuals with visual impairments. However, a student with a visual disorder may not be eligible for or need specialized services if the disorder has no adverse effect on the student's educational progress.

Instructional planning requires a comprehensive assessment to establish current levels of performance. Using the information from multiple assessments, the IEP team determines the student's current levels of performance and develops an individualized education program. In keeping with the requirements of IDEA, parents and students are informed and involved in all areas of the planning process.

The success of the IEP depends on selecting and using appropriate instruments that address issues or concerns relevant to the needs of the student with a visual impairment. This process may be completed by having appropriately trained personnel use both formal and informal assessment instruments. Few formal instruments are available, however, because children with visual impairments are so diverse in age, background, and environmental influences, as well as in levels of visual abilities. Numerous factors, such as acuity, color blindness, age of onset, field vision restrictions, and other disabilities, affect a child's visual ability. Given the unique needs and diversity of these students, trained teachers of the visually impaired must be involved in the assessment process and the interpretation of test results.

Students with visual impairments are not usually included in standardized testing; however, they should participate with needed modifications or accommodations (see Table 12.4). Although the validity and reliability of the assessment may be compromised if too many modifications are made, instructional planning, including pupil and program

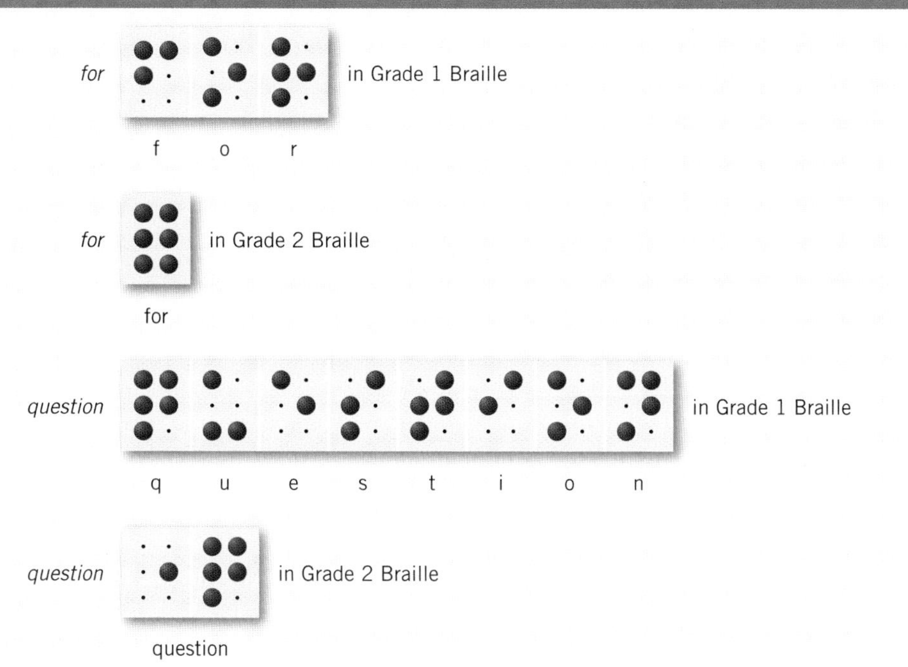

FIGURE 12.6 Examples of Braille

TABLE 12.4 Assessment Modifications for Students With Visual Impairments
Proctor for Braille transcription (recording or transfer scores)
Large print materials and tests
Oral presentation of materials (reader assistance for texts and other materials)
Assistive technology
Extended time limits (1.5 or twice the time is usually recognized for low vision and blind)
Small or individual group assessment
Preferred seating
Shorter periods of testing with rest breaks between sessions

evaluation, can be enhanced. In reporting test results, any modification or accommodations that were made should be recorded.

Many states require all students to participate in statewide testing programs, developed with specific guidelines and scores, to progress to the next grade or academic level. IDEA requires the IEP team to determine a student's participation in state- and district-wide assessment programs. The team must verify that the student is in need of modifications in order to participate, or if the student will not participate, the team must state why the assessment is not appropriate and what alternate assessments will be used.

Educational Considerations

Students with visual impairments require an educational plan to prepare for independent and productive lives. Educational goals delineate the needs of the child and the family. Appropriate accommodations allow for acquisition of information through incidental learning, observation and imitation, exploration, and social behavior.

Many students with visual impairments are able to participate in testing programs when appropriate modifications are made.

Where Are Students With Visual Impairments Educated?

Both the passage of IDEA and policy statements from professional organizations and agencies reinforce the principle that in order to meet the unique needs of children with sensory impairments and help them become responsible and independent members of a fully integrated society, we must offer a full continuum of services. According to the U.S. Department of Education (2009), well over half of all students with visual impairments received services in the general education classroom during the 2007–2008 school year. Approximately one out of ten pupils with visual impairments was assigned to a resource room, and only about 5 percent were placed in a residential facility (see Figure 12.7). The IEP team should determine the educational setting that is most appropriate for each student, keeping in mind current levels of academic, psychosocial, physical, and vocational functioning and the materials and instructional techniques that are successful with that child. (See the accompanying First Person feature.)

Instructional Considerations

Instructional goals for most students with visual impairment include communication skills, social competency, employability, and independence, in addition to academic progress (American Foundation for the Blind, 2010b). The IEP team must decide how these goals will be accomplished. Often an array of low vision devices will be required, depending on the needs of the student. The team will have to decide whether the child requires materials to be read, enlarged, or put into Braille and whether low vision devices or technology such as an abacus or a talking calculator will be used.

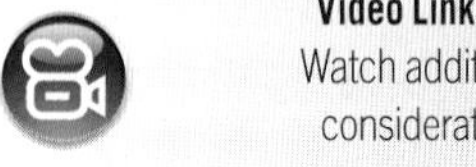

Video Link 12.4
Watch additional considerations.

The vision-related needs of the pupil should be supported within the general education curriculum wherever appropriate. The need for direct, specialized services also varies throughout the child's education, depending on the goals of the educational program and the way in which these goals are met in the classroom. Table 12.5 (page 468) describes some types of equipment that can be used to meet the needs of students with visual impairments in the general education classroom.

Individuals who are visually impaired should acquire compensatory skills and experiential learning by accessing the expanded core curriculum (Huebner, Merk-Adam,

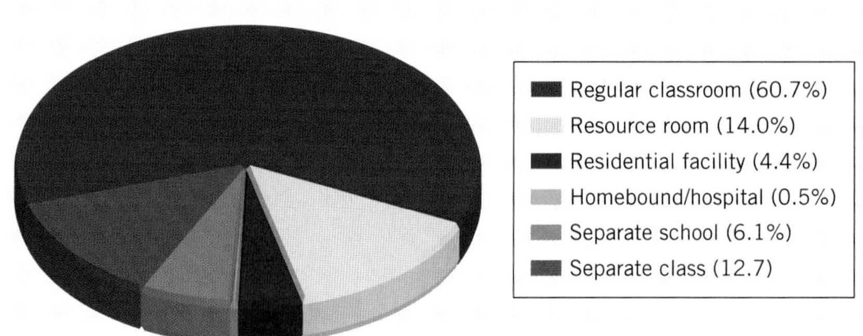

FIGURE 12.7 Educational Placements of Students With Visual Impairments

NOTE: Figure represents percentages of enrollment of students with visual impairments during the 2007–2008 school year.

SOURCE: U.S. Department of Education. (2009). *IDEA data.* Retrieved December 5, 2009, from https://www.ideadata.org/PartBReport.asp

First Person: Carrie
The Face of "Different"

It was a bright sunny day outside. The kids were going out to play, but a few of us were staying inside. I started to draw after staring at a friend's face. It was just a line with some curves. "That's different," remarked a classmate. "Wow, that's really good," said Mr. Tom. "Thank you," I replied.

At that point, I realized that I was good at something and at the same time realized that there was something "different" about me. I was drawing someone's face as if it were a silhouette. It was different from my classmates' drawings. These words of encouragement and approval would have seemed small to most, but to a 6-year-old they were awesome. I was just drawing what I saw. How could that have been different from anyone else, or even that good?

I was born with oculocutaneous albinism, which is the lack of pigment in the eyes, the skin, and the hair. A common side effect is a visual impairment, but this varies in severity from one person to another. The idea of being visually impaired and able to draw astounded Mr. Tom. He was surprised by my ability to depict how I saw the world. I enjoyed arts and crafts time during elementary school and still amazed many teachers by this talent. It was as if I was redefining their perception of my abilities.

In second grade there was a test to see how many addition problems we could solve correctly in two minutes. The teacher remarked that I would need extra time. Full of embarrassment, I wanted to prove her wrong. And I did. The same type of situation occurred in middle school. The challenge was reading maps for geography class. The maps were small with many black lines. "How is she going to do this with a visual impairment?" many remarked. I could see shapes and color. So I colored them in and then labeled them as I studied. It made things more difficult and was a different approach, but it worked. The test came back with a 97, and I was excited.

There were many times that I needed to take a different approach in my study tactics. I was more successful in class with teachers who were open-minded or who accentuated my strengths and minimized my weaknesses. My senior year in high school I read the book *Dr. Jekyll and Mr. Hyde* by Robert Louis Stevenson. Reading a novel was difficult because it took me longer to read than most students. I would feel discouraged and defeated, therefore losing motivation in the class. My teacher asked me to draw or paint how I envisioned the main characters, Dr. Jekyll and Mr. Hyde. The two characters are really one person but with a different look and contrasting personalities. She was pleased by the end result and distributed the grade on the ability to envision the description rather than the test alone.

There is not a map or a face that can guide and show a teacher how to educate a student with a visual impairment. I learned by doing and trying things by myself and with others. I was not the face of "different" as a child. Different is not a face to identify or a point to relate to; different is the line with curves between two points. Different is the process in which children as individuals learn, create, grow, and therefore succeed. It is the path and our attitude that depict our face. "We are all 'different,' and I thank you!"

—*Carrie Willoughby*

Stryker, & Wolffe, 2004). The expanded core curriculum is the body of knowledge and skills that are needed by pupils with visual impairments because of their unique disability-specific needs. Students who are visually impaired need the expanded core curriculum in addition to the core academic curriculum found in general education. The expanded core curriculum should be used as a framework for assessing pupils, planning individual goals, and providing instruction. According to Huebner et al., the expanded core curriculum typically includes the following:

- Compensatory skills
- Orientation and mobility
- Social skills
- Independent living skills
- Recreation and leisure skills
- Career education
- Assistive technology
- Visual efficiency skills
- Self-determination

EFFECTIVE INSTRUCTIONAL PRACTICES Accommodations for Students With Visual Impairments

Communication and accessibility are keys to providing an environment in which the student with visual impairments can realize his or her academic potential. Accommodations should provide the pupil with the ability to fully participate in the classroom as well as reduce the effects of the visual impairment.

Instructional Area	Accommodations
Reading	• Consult with the teacher of students with visual impairments on any optical devices the student may need to read printed materials. • Allow extra time for low vision readers, as they may experience eye fatigue. • Provide reading materials to the teacher of students with visual impairments in advance to be enlarged, scanned, Brailled, or recorded on tape. • Textbooks and books commonly used in educational settings are available on recorded tapes through Recording for the Blind & Dyslexic (www.rfbd.org). Students must be registered before ordering texts. • Recreational books in recorded or Braille format can be ordered through the National Library Service for the Blind and Physically Handicapped (http://www.loc.gov/nls/). This is a free service, but users must be registered before ordering. • Many local library systems have popular books available on audiotape.
Writing	• Some pupils with low vision need dark, bold, or raised lined paper for writing assignments. • Some individuals will need to use a typewriter or a computer for completing written assignments. • Braille readers may Braille their assignments and ask the teacher of students with visual impairments to transcribe them into print. • Some Braille readers use an electronic Braille note-taker such as Braille 'n Speak for written assignments. The assignment is inputted in Braille and then translated into a print copy for the classroom teacher.
Note-taking	• Students with visual impairments may take notes on their Brailler, electronic note-taker, or computer or may use a cassette recorder. • Any notes written on the board should be spoken aloud for the pupil who is visually impaired. • Students with visual impairments should be seated as close to an object or a display as possible. • Keep information in a visually simple and organized format for all students with visual perceptual difficulties. • Use high-contrast writing tools when using an overhead, a chalkboard, or a dry-erase board. • Use of a Smart Board attached to the student's or the classroom computer can provide the individual with an accessible version of the notes. • Use of a Smart Board with text conversion software allows the student to access the electronic version of the notes with a screen reading or voice output program.

SOURCE: Adapted from L. Schrenko, *Visual Impairment* (Georgia Department of Education, February 2002). Available at http://www.glc.k12.ga.us/passwd/trc/ttools/attach/accomm/visimp.doc

Making Inclusion Work

During the spring of my senior year as an undergraduate student in elementary education, I was required to complete a twenty-four-hour practicum for a special education course. The site I chose was the North Dakota School for the Blind. After my experiences at the school, I realized that I was very interested in working with children who were blind and visually impaired. This led me to search for graduate programs in the field of blindness. I was fortunate enough to locate the vision program at the University of Alabama at Birmingham. From my first day in the program, I had the opportunity to work with children of varying degrees of visual impairment, as well as additional disabilities. After completing my master's degree, I worked as an itinerant teacher for the visually impaired in southwestern Iowa for four years and went on to become the state consultant for children with deaf–blindness. I then returned to graduate school and earned my doctorate at Iowa State University.

Inclusive Education Experience

Working with children with visual impairments and multiple disabilities is definitely challenging, yet very rewarding. This is especially true when working with general education teachers in inclusive settings. You have to have a starting point that everyone can agree upon, including acceptance of the child with special needs as a full member of the general education class and an understanding that the general education teacher is that child's full-time teacher—not the five other service providers who also work with the child once a week. If the IEP team can come to such an agreement, then everything else seems to fall into place. For example, it may be that a teacher of the visually impaired works with the general education teacher to adapt lessons by creating tactile materials, creating story boxes, or even working with the entire class by teaching a class lesson.

One of my more memorable teaching experiences was collaborating with a first-year teacher who was working with a kindergartener, Andrew, who had multiple disabilities, including deaf–blindness. I taught a cooking lesson to the class once a month, in order to model interacting with Andrew for the other children and adults in the classroom. This worked well for the kindergarten teacher because it incorporated math, reading, and social skills. It was a wonderful opportunity, however, for the other children to see that Andrew could be an active and important member of the class, as they worked in small groups to get to know Andrew. By the end of the school year, the children were able to tell the adults what Andrew liked and disliked. The students also knew how to interact with Andrew so that he could respond to them with facial expressions and vocalizations.

Overall, as a teacher of the visually impaired, being able to work with the kindergarten class took extra time and preparation on my part. However, classrooms today are changing, as are the instructional expectations of both general education and special education teachers. It takes teamwork and collaboration to make programs work for children with special needs and to give them the best possible start to being active and contributing members of their community.

—*Susan A. Brennan*
Former teacher of students with visual impairments
Currently assistant professor, University of Northern Iowa

The expanded core curriculum essentially creates a parallel curriculum of disability-specific skills supplementary to the general education curriculum. The academic curriculum must be modified to meet the individual needs of each student so that progress is based on skill level and successful completion of expectations in each subject area. Specialized areas of the regular curriculum, such as art, music, and home economics, are also considered appropriate for pupils with visual impairments. Modifications and accommodations of lessons can often be achieved through the use of visual, auditory, or tactual experiences.

Adaptations of materials and the environment may be necessary to enable students who are visually impaired to participate in the educational program and derive maximum benefit from the experience (see Table 12.6, page 469). Adaptations may vary according to individual needs, which should be assessed before making special provisions available to the student.

TABLE 12.5 Examples of Core and Expanded Curriculum-Specific Equipment

Academics	• Magnifiers, glasses, Closed Circuit Television, Braille, bookstands, videotapes, scanners, optical character recognition system • Word processing programs, slate and stylus, electronic spell-checkers, bold line writing paper, embossed writing paper, signature writing guides • Abacus, scientific calculator, talking clock, Braille/print protractors and rulers, embossed and bold line grid pattern sheets, spreadsheet software • Tactile globes, relief maps, Braille and large print maps, tactile anatomy atlas, speech output devices such as thermometers and environmental controls
Leisure Time and Recreational Activities	• Adapted games, large print books, radio reading services, beeper balls, buzzers, wheelchair adapted for basketball and tennis play, lifts for swimming pools, adapted snow and water-skiing equipment, descriptive video
Daily Living and Self-Help	• Walkers, feeding adaptations, Braille labels, voice-activated switches, button switches, large print telephone buttons, automatic thermostats, Braille calendars, electronic address books and calendars, magnifiers for hand sewing and sewing machines, electronic mobility devices, lifts for automobiles and chairs

Table 12.7 (page 470) presents some general guidelines for working with students who have a visual impairment. These suggestions are offered using a "Do" and "Don't" format.

Video Link 12.5
Watch more about mobility.

Students with visual impairments require instruction in **orientation and mobility**, which is a related service according to IDEA. Orientation is being aware of where you are, where you are going, and the route to get there. Mobility is moving from place to place. A child must be able to put the orientation and mobility together to travel independently. Orientation and mobility training includes sensory training, concept development, and motor development. A certified orientation and mobility specialist can evaluate the child's functional level and prescribe specific training. See the accompanying Suggestions for the Classroom (page 470) for orientation and mobility tips for the general educator.

A child must be empowered to negotiate the environment skillfully and confidently. Opportunities for exploration must be provided for good posture, good health, and flexible muscles. With confident movement, the child can achieve good self-esteem and master independent travel within the community.

Young Children With Visual Impairments

The focus in early childhood education is not only on visual and auditory tasks, but also on the whole realm of developmental skills that must be taught, with modifications, to the child with visual impairments. These basic readiness skills should be integrated for age-appropriate cognitive development:

- Sensory development
- Gross motor development
- Fine motor development
- Social development
- Receptive language development
- Expressive language development
- Self-help development

The early intervention team can assist the family with activities that stimulate each of the developmental areas. Children are referred through state child-find activities, physicians,

TABLE 12.6 Environmental Adaptations for Students With Visual Impairments

	Lighting	Color and Contrast	Size and Distance	Time
What to observe	• Variety of lighting situations • Lighting at different times of day • Low vision devices used	• Contrast between object and background • Color contrast • Tactile tasks such as locker for books	• Placement and size of objects at near • Placement and size of objects at far	• Time for completion of visual discrimination during tasks
What to use	• Light sensitivity: shades, visors, tinted spectacles • Low light: lamp or illuminated low vision device • Room obstructions: preferential seating, furniture placement • Glare: Nonglare surface on areas such as chalkboards, computer screens, desktop, paper, maps, globes	• Bold line paper • Black print on white background • Dark markers • One-sided writing on paper • Dark placemat for contrast during eating • Floor contrast for mobility ease • Tactile markings for outline discrimination • Contrast to define borders on walls • Lock and key is preferred over combination locker	• Enlarged materials • Preferred seating • Electronic devices • Magnification • Optical character recognition • Adjustment of desks, tables, and chairs • Additional storage space for Braille, large print books, low vision devices near each workstation	• Verbal cues for actions in classroom • Increased time for task completion • Calling student by name • Announcements when entering or leaving room • Encourage participation in demonstrations • Opportunity to observe materials prior to lesson • Authentic manipulative objects • Schedule instructional time in early part of day • Convenient use and storage of materials
Desired results	• Better posture • Greater concentration • Less fatigue	• Better visual efficiency • Less fatigue • Safer travel	• Ease of viewing • Appropriate adaptations for specific vision loss	• Less fatigue • Inclusion in class activities • Time efficiency

and other agencies to early intervention services, which are available for children from birth to age 3. Services are provided according to the youngster's IFSP (individualized family service plan), with the child receiving services prescribed by the specialists involved on the team. The specialists who work with the child and family act as consultants, and some may provide direct services. Intervention may be offered in the youngster's home or an early childhood education program in the community.

Journal Link 12.1
Read more about young children with visual impairments.

At age 3, the child should transition to an early childhood class for youngsters with vision loss. A well-designed transition plan includes planning with the school administrators, general educators, parents or other caregivers, and related services personnel in support of the move to school. The service coordinator and vision specialist should also have input into the construction of the IEP. This will ensure that the receiving teacher knows about the child's progress and goals for the future. Age-related needs that should be addressed by the team when designing a transition plan include travel, low vision devices, educational activities, and leisure activities. Other services that family and school officials should consider include the following:

- Adaptive technology services
- Transcription services

TABLE 12.7 Suggestions for Working With Students Who Are Visually Impaired

DO	DON'T
• Feel comfortable using vision words such as *look*, *see*, and *watch*.	• Be fearful of touching a student who is visually impaired. Be sure to tell the student, however, that you are about to touch him or her. Be respectful of the individual's personal preference about being touched.
• Use the pupil's name when calling him or her.	• Overprotect. Allow the pupil to attempt as many things as he or she wishes to.
• Read aloud when writing on the board.	• Worry about personal feelings of awkwardness. Remember you are teaching a child who just happens to be visually impaired.
• Encourage independence. It is important that the student learn to do as much as possible for him- or herself	• Be afraid of having high expectations and demanding the pupil's best work.
• Include the pupil in as many class activities as feasible.	• Tolerate unacceptable behavior simply because the student is visually impaired. Discipline should be similar to that used with a pupil who has sight.
• Give explicit instructions.	
• Provide extra space for storage of equipment and specialized materials.	
• Encourage the use of supplementary aids and devices when necessary.	

SOURCE: Adapted from V. Bishop, *Teaching Visually Impaired Children,* 3rd ed. (Springfield, IL: Charles C Thomas, 2004), pp. 93–94.

Suggestions for the Classroom

Orientation and Mobility Tips

- ☑ Eliminate unnecessary obstacles; inform student of changes in room arrangement or of any temporary obstacles.
- ☑ Keep doors completely closed or completely open to eliminate the possibility of the student's running into a partially open door.
- ☑ Allow the student to travel with a companion to frequently used rooms such as the library, school office, restroom, and gym. Discuss routes with turns and landmarks.
- ☑ Allow the student to move about freely until the room and route are familiar.
- ☑ Encourage the use of a sighted guide for fire drills, field trips, assemblies, and seating in rooms that ordinarily have no assigned seats.
- ☑ Encourage independent travel in the familiar settings at school.

SOURCE: Adapted from R. Craig and C. Howard, "Visual Impairment," in M. Hardman, M. Egan, and D. Landau (Eds.), *What Will We Do in the Morning?* (Dubuque, IA: W. C. Brown, 1981), p. 191.

- Access to an equipment resource center
- Activities of daily living
- Community education
- Reader services
- Orientation and mobility
- Low vision examination

Transition Into Adulthood

IDEA mandates that the individualized education program include a transition plan for college preparation or vocational training. A full range of options and support services for appropriate placement in the least restrictive environment should be available (American Foundation for the Blind, 2010e). Student interests, family involvement in future education, and appropriate placement location and program are integral parts of the transition plan.

The goals for adolescents and young adults include vocation selection, continuing education, travel skills, low vision devices, reading material, community resources, family education, and independence on the job. The wide spectrum of individual needs quickly defines the goals with regard to job training, technical school education, or college entrance. A transition plan for each student must be designed no later than age 16.

Vocational training is an important component of transitional planning for adolescents who are visually impaired.

several different schools, time for travel and planning detracts from actual class time with the students. A reduction in class caseloads would enable teachers to fulfill IEP goals with more stable outcomes.

Prescriptions for reading and literacy media require a team approach based on the physician's and the teacher's educational recommendations. Reading media assessment is necessary to determine the appropriate low vision devices, enlargements, technology, or Braille use for each student. Some students need large print; others may require magnification or Braille; still others use books on tape. IDEA requires that the use of Braille be assessed in each student's IEP. Appropriate assessments of reading and writing media needs are limited. Teachers often use observations, work samples, and physician suggestions to validate media needs because functional levels are important for daily needs. With few certified teachers, it is difficult to provide this assessment for all students who are visually impaired.

Issues of transition center on evaluation and prognosis, vocational preparation, and how outcomes will be measured. Independence of students as they move into higher education or vocational training is a responsibility of the school and family and is often a problem with transition into the community. Because so many jobs require vision to complete the task, job training and higher education choices are sometimes difficult to select and implement. School representatives and families must construct a life plan with the student so that the benchmarks for success are attainable and reasonable and provide a meaningful and independent life of quality. Issues of community support also affect the successful outcomes of transition plans.

CHAPTER IN REVIEW

Defining Visual Impairments

Audio Link 12.3
Listen to a chapter summary.

- The educational definition of visual impairment is vision impairment that, even with correction, adversely affects an individual's educational performance.
- Visual impairment includes both partial sight and blindness.

The Eye and How It Works

- Light enters the eye first through the clear, transparent area in front of the eye known as the cornea and passes through the other structures to the retina.
- In the retina, light impulses are changed into electrical signals and travel along the optic nerve and back to the occipital lobe of the brain, which interprets the electrical signals as visual images.

Classification of Visual Impairments

- The most common visual impairments affecting school-age children are cataracts, glaucoma, optic nerve atrophy, myopia, albinism, eye injury, and retinopathy of prematurity (ROP).

Prevalence of Visual Impairments

- Visual impairment is one of the least prevalent disabilities, accounting for only 0.4 percent of pupils with a disability who are receiving a special education.

The Vision Process and Etiology of Visual Impairments

- If the cornea is damaged through trauma or disease, then the inner area may become infected, which could result in permanent visual impairment.
- Glaucoma is the major disease that occurs in the aqueous humor. This may result in a loss of visual acuity as well as a loss in the visual field.
- If the iris is malformed, the function of light control will be interrupted, and the child can become photophobic (sensitive to light).
- Cataracts are lenses that are opaque or cloudy due to trauma or age. Children with congenital cataracts often have the cataracts removed.
- Macular degeneration is a common eye disease in adults, but it may also occur in young people.
- Rods and cones are photoreceptive cells found in the retina.
- If a youngster has retinopathy of prematurity (ROP), vascular growth has been interrupted by premature birth.
- Retinitis pigmentosa is a hereditary condition involving gradual degeneration of the retina.

Prevention of Visual Impairments

- Most visual impairments are genetic in origin, but others such as injury can be prevented.

Assessment of Students With Visual Impairments

- The acuity chart that is most often used for testing and reporting vision loss is the Snellen chart.
- An important first step in planning an educational program for a child with visual impairments is to assess the pupil's present functional vision.
- Another important component in the assessment process is to determine the most effective learning and literacy media.
- Braille is used as a literacy medium along with print and auditory input if the child has any residual vision.

Educational Considerations

- Six out of ten pupils with visual impairments are served in the general education classroom.
- Many students with visual impairments have the same education goals as other pupils.
- Instructional goals for most students with visual impairment include communication skills, social competency, employability, and independence, in addition to academic progress.
- Students with visual impairments may also require instruction in orientation and mobility.

Technology and Individuals With Visual Impairments

- With appropriate assessment and training in technology, students who are blind or visually impaired can compete successfully in educational programs.
- Technology plays an integral role in learning and all aspects of daily living, from literacy to mobility to independent living.

STUDY QUESTIONS

1. What is the legal definition of blindness? How does it differ from the IDEA definition?
2. What does the Snellen chart assess? What does 20/200 mean?
3. Describe how the eye functions.
4. Define the terms *myopia, hyperopia,* and *astigmatism.*
5. List five eye problems common to school-age children.
6. Why is early detection of vision problems important?
7. Describe the social and emotional characteristics of persons with visual impairments.
8. What is functional vision, and how is it evaluated?
9. Define the term *learning media.* Give three examples of different forms of learning media.
10. In what two educational settings do the majority of students with a visual impairment receive a special education?
11. What are some common educational accommodations that a student with visual impairments may require?
12. List five signs of possible vision problems in children.
13. Identify three critical issues that must be addressed if an adolescent is to successfully transition to postsecondary education or enter the workforce.
14. Besides cultural differences, what diversity issue must be addressed for parents who are also visually impaired?
15. Identify five technology accommodations that can be provided in high school for a student who is legally blind.
16. Discuss the shortage of orientation and mobility specialists and how a child's educational plan is affected by a shortage of personnel.

KEY TERMS

visual impairment 446
visual acuity 447
visual field 447
field loss 447
legally blind 447
Snellen chart 447
functionally blind 448
primary literacy medium 448
low vision 448
residual vision 448
deaf–blind 448
cornea 448
iris 448
pupil 448
lens 448
vitreous humor 448
retina 448
macula 448
optic nerve 448
myopia 448
hyperopia 448
astigmatism 448
orbit 448
cataracts 449
glaucoma 449
optic nerve atrophy 449
albinism 449
retinopathy of prematurity (ROP) 449
Braille 451
visual efficiency 452
photophobic 453
aphakic 453
rod cells 454
cone cells 454
macular degeneration 454
retinitis pigmentosa 454
coloboma 454
vision screening 454
functional vision 459
literacy medium 460
learning media 461
Grade 1 Braille 461
Grade 2 Braille 461
orientation and mobility 468

LEARNING ACTIVITIES

1. Spend a day traveling with an itinerant teacher of the visually impaired. Describe the types of instruction this professional provided for one or two of the pupils. What IEP goals were addressed? How was technology used to adapt the general education curriculum? How did classmates relate to the child with a visual impairment? What type of assistance did the vision specialist offer to the general educator? What problems or difficulties, if any, did you observe? Write a summary of your experience and share it with your classmates.
2. Search the Internet for information about the following three educational tools: an electronic Brailler, screen readers, and optical character recognition systems. Develop IEP goals and accompanying benchmarks for a secondary

student who is legally blind and preparing to transition to a community college. How will this equipment be used to assist the adolescent in adapting to the general education curriculum? What individuals should be involved in planning the transition experience?

3. Interview an adult with a visual impairment. Find out about the type and age of onset of the vision loss. Ask about personal and family reactions to the loss of vision. What type of low vision devices or technology does this individual use on a daily basis? If possible, identify any adjustment concerns about independence, mobility, vocational and career issues, community involvement, and personal relationships. Share your impressions of this interview with your fellow students.

4. Travel with an orientation and mobility specialist and observe the training of a person with a visual impairment. What type of equipment was used? What travel techniques were addressed during the lesson? How did the orientation and mobility specialist evaluate the individual? Ask if you can use the various devices. How did it feel to navigate about the environment while simulating a visual impairment?

ORGANIZATIONS CONCERNED WITH VISUAL IMPAIRMENTS

American Council for the Blind
2200 Wilson Boulevard
Suite 650
Arlington, VA 22201
(800) 424-8666
(703) 465-5085 (Fax)
http://www.acb.org

American Foundation for the Blind
2 Penn Plaza
Suite 1102
New York, NY 10121
(800) 232-5463
(888) 545-8331 (Fax)
http://www.afb.org

American Printing House for the Blind
1839 Frankfort Avenue
P.O. Box 6085
Louisville, KY 40206–0085
(800) 223-1839
(502) 899-2274 (Fax)
http://www.aph.org

Helen Keller National Art Show, CEC Division on Visual Impairments, UAB School of Optometry Vision Science Research Center
924 S. 18th Street
Birmingham, AL 35294
(205) 934-6723

National Federation of the Blind
200 East Wells Street
Baltimore, MD 21230
(410) 659-9314
(410) 685-5653 (Fax)
http://www.nfb.org

National Dissemination Center for Children with Disabilities
1825 Connecticut Avenue N.W.
Suite 700
Washington, DC 20009
(800) 695-0285 (Voice/TTY)
(202) 884-8441 (Fax)
http://www.nichcy.org

The National Braille Press
88 Saint Stephen Street
Boston, MA 02115
(888) 965-8965
(617) 437-0456 (Fax)
http://www.nbp.org

Recording for the Blind & Dyslexic
20 Roszel Road
Princeton, NJ 08540
(800) 221-4792
http://www.rfbd.org

The Seeing Eye, Inc.
10 Washington Valley Road
Morristown, NJ 07960
(973) 539-4425
(973) 539-0922 (Fax)
http://www.seeingeye.org

The National Library Service for the Blind and Physically Handicapped
Publications and Media Section
Library of Congress
Washington, DC 20542
(888) 657-7323
(202) 707-0744 (TDD)
(202) 707-0712 (Fax)
http://www.loc.gov/nls

REFLECTING ON STANDARDS

The following exercises are designed to help you learn to apply the Council for Exceptional Children (CEC) standards to your teaching practice. Each of the reflection exercises below correlates with a knowledge or skill within the CEC standards. For the full text of each of the related CEC standards, please refer to the standards integration grid located in Appendix B.

Focus on Instructional Strategies ***(CEC Content Standard #4 CC4S3)***
Reflect on what you have learned about accommodations needed for students with visual impairments. If you were developing a reading program for your class and you had a student in your class with a visual impairment, in what ways might you modify your instruction to take into account all of your students' learning needs? How might you need to integrate assistive technology into your instruction?

Focus on Learning Environments and Social Interactions ***(CEC Content Standard #5 CC5S9)***
Reflect on what you have learned about students with visual impairments. If you were to have a student in your class with a visual impairment, how might you help him or her develop increased independence? How might you modify your classroom or your teaching strategies to create an environment where a student with visual impairments would feel comfortable? How might your other students assist you in creating this type of environment?

STUDENT STUDY SITE

Visit the Student Study Site at www.sagepub.com/gargiulo4emedia for these additional learning tools:

- Video links
- Media links
- Self-quizzes
- E-flashcards
- Full-text SAGE journal articles
- Web exercises

CHAPTER 13

Learning Objectives

After reading Chapter 13 you should be able to:

- List the disabilities associated with physical impairments.
- Identify disabilities associated with other health impairments.
- Define deaf–blindness.
- Summarize society's reaction to and treatment of persons with physical or health impairments.
- Provide examples of common causes of physical disabilities and health impairments.
- Outline representative conditions associated with orthopedic impairments, multiple disabilities, traumatic brain injury, other health impairments, and deaf–blindness.
- Describe the impact of a physical or health impairment on school performance.
- Explain the procedures that teachers and other professionals use to meet the educational needs of pupils with physical/health disabilities and deaf–blindness.
- Summarize educational services for individuals with physical or health impairments across the life span.
- Give examples of how technology benefits individuals with a physical or health disability.

Individuals With Physical Disabilities, Health Disabilities, and Related Low-Incidence Disabilities

NATALIE'S STORY

Natalie is an amazing young lady who has exceeded most of the expectations of those who made assumptions based on her "labels" and therefore had lowered expectations for her. Fortunately, she did not live down to their expectations! Natalie has cerebral palsy (severe spastic quadriplegic and athetoid) with poor head and trunk control and only some limited use of her left hand and arm. She has undetermined visual acuity, has a questionable degree of mental retardation, used to have seizures of varying types, and has a G-tube for most of her nutrition and caloric intake. She has had braces, splints, eye patching, and numerous surgeries (including spinal fusion).

Video Link 13.1
Watch more about disabilities.

Although Natalie is nonverbal, she can make approximately thirty words or sounds (that mean up to two hundred different things depending on the context or situation), and she uses an electronic augmentative communication device. Using a combination of two to four symbols, she can say approximately fifteen hundred sentences, three hundred words, and one hundred names!

Natalie is our third of three girls. She was born in 1975, five to six weeks premature. She was bluish-gray at birth, indicating a lack of oxygen, and had facial bruising, indicating a traumatic birth (face presentation). So she had the three leading causes of cerebral palsy going against her! She was diagnosed at 6 and a half months. She started therapy at 8 and a half months. At 6 and a half years, Natalie was given her first psychological test, which indicated an IQ of 65. Natalie was to be educated as if she had potential for normal intelligence, and she started school in an academically based class for students with orthopedic impairments.

Written by Kathryn Wolff Heller, Georgia State University, and Richard M. Gargiulo

Video Link 13.2
Watch a parent's perspective on traumatic brain injury.

Our family had to move, and it was then "determined" that Natalie would be placed in a self-contained, center-based class for students with severe mental retardation because all of the therapies were conveniently located there. I, of course, objected. We were told that she wouldn't really "fit" into the orthopedically impaired program as those kids were more "advanced." (Please note that the terms *convenient* and *fit into* seem in direct contradiction to what is stated for an IEP, or *individualized* education program.)

From 1985 to 1987, we were fortunate to have a teacher who, despite the label of severe mental retardation, knew Natalie had capabilities and academic potential. This teacher's philosophy was that if Natalie was having a problem with something, it was not that Natalie couldn't learn it, but more likely she just needed to change her approach. She worked with sight words and numbers and picture boards that increased in complexity as Natalie became proficient using them. As Natalie's skills developed, we started our search for the "right" augmentative communication device. After a yearlong assessment we found the ideal augmentative communication device for Natalie, a Touch Talker. Within six months, I had programmed two thirds of what is currently in her device. People began to see Natalie in a totally different way and to recognize her intelligence and humor and emotions, and lots of frustrations. They began to relate to her in a totally different way . . . all because she could finally communicate!

Natalie's label changed, and she was moved from the severe mental retardation class into a moderate mental retardation class in a public middle school. We tried again for placement in an orthopedic impairments class, and were again denied.

Finally, she was placed into an orthopedically impaired class her last year of middle school. It was probably her best year for academic learning, as she worked one-on-one on her individual goals, but also was part of group learning. She thrived in the group setting, and quite often had to be reprimanded for answering other students' questions!

Unfortunately, inclusion in high school, with the opportunity to go into general education classes, did not work for Natalie—it came too late. We tried, but it's a little hard to start with high school curriculum when you haven't had the basics! She was, for the most part, in a self-contained orthopedically impaired class for her last seven years. Her teacher involved peer tutors in much of Natalie's program, which was very motivating for Natalie and gave her the opportunity to make friends. It was kind of like bringing inclusion to Natalie. They definitely were a benefit to her, both socially and academically.

Transition planning for Natalie was a challenge because of the severity of Natalie's disabilities and the lack of experience with this type of student. We stressed the need to develop assertiveness, as Natalie—like so many folks with disabilities—was too often passive in situations that were not to her liking, but there was no such program. We encouraged goals based on our vision for Natalie's future, which was living and working in the community with supports.

Through school, she did participate in community-based vocational training, and worked in several locations. Although these were not jobs that she could actually do independently, they did offer an opportunity to work on her communication and mobility goals. And she brought an awareness to those stores—and the community that frequented them—of the possibility that a person with severe disabilities could work, wanted to work, and was excited about it!

One of our proudest moments was when Natalie received a standing ovation as she graduated from high school, and there have been many proud moments since. Natalie has had two paying jobs. She lives in her own home with a roommate and a live-in care provider. She is working on understanding and accepting more independence each day. She has given many presentations to community groups and is an active advocate for people who can't speak for themselves.

Through the years, Natalie has been blessed by many wonderful teachers, aides, therapists, and specialists who gave so much of themselves for her benefit. I hope that they will someday realize the impact that each one of them has had, individually and collectively, on Natalie and—through her—on the community as a whole. Natalie is an inspiration, and a wonderful example of what can be!

—*Beth Tumlin*

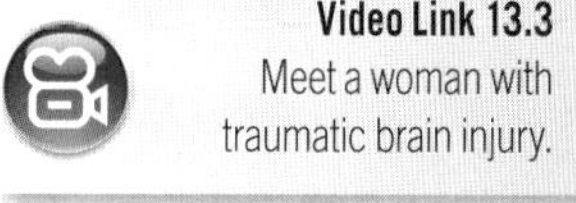

Video Link 13.3
Meet a woman with traumatic brain injury.

Students who have physical or health disabilities comprise one of the most diverse categories of learners in special education because of the wide range of diseases and disorders included in this category. Pupils with physical disabilities may range from those with severe physical conditions resulting in an inability to talk, walk, point, or make any purposeful movement to those students with only some difficulty walking or an unseen skeletal abnormality. Individuals with health disabilities may range from those with severe health problems forcing them to stay home to those with a hidden disability, such as a tumor. In addition, there are several **low-incidence**

Many individuals with physical or health disabilities are capable of living independent and productive lives.

disabilities that can also include physical or health disabilities, such as traumatic brain injury, deaf–blindness, and multiple disabilities. The term **low incidence** generally refers to a disability that occurs infrequently. In fact, children who exhibit the three impairments listed above account for only about 2.5 percent of all pupils receiving a special education (U.S. Department of Education, 2010). What places all of these students together in this chapter is that they frequently share some dimension or aspect of physical or health impairments.

At the beginning of this chapter, we read about Natalie, whose story is typical of many individuals who have a severe physical disability. Natalie has one of the most common physical disabilities (cerebral palsy) that occurs in schoolchildren. In her case, she also has a health disability (epilepsy). She has faced several challenges in her education, such as appropriate assessment, correct educational placement, selection of appropriate curriculum, and use of specialized strategies for teaching and adapting academics for a student who is essentially unable to speak. She uses several types of **assistive technology**, such as an **augmentative communication** device and a power wheelchair. Although she encountered problems regarding her placement and lack of inclusion, she has achieved successes in terms of acquired skills and transition to paid employment.

This chapter will examine what it means for a student to have a physical, health, or related low-incidence disability. Definitions will be given, along with a history of the field, data on the prevalence of these disabilities, and some of their causes. A sampling of some of the most common types of physical, health, and related low-incidence disabilities will be explored. A model will be presented explaining how school performance is affected by a physical, health, or related low-incidence disability, along with strategies to address these students' needs. Many other areas will also be reviewed, including services for young children, transition, adult issues, family issues, diversity, technology, and current issues in the field of physical and health disabilities. We begin by defining physical, health, and related low-incidence disabilities as they are addressed in education.

Defining Physical Disabilities, Health Disabilities, and Related Low-Incidence Disabilities

Many students have various physical or health conditions, but only those with physical or health disabilities that interfere with their educational performance require special education services. According to the Individuals with Disabilities Education Improvement Act of 2004 (IDEA; PL 108–446), students with physical impairments may qualify for special education services under three possible categories: **orthopedic impairments, multiple disabilities**, and **traumatic brain injury.** Students with health disabilities may qualify under the IDEA category of **other health impairments**. Children with the loss of both vision and hearing receive services under the label **deaf-blind.**

The federal definition of orthopedic impairments provides examples of impairments resulting from congenital anomalies (irregularities or defects present at birth), diseases, or other causes (see Table 13.1). In our chapter opener, Natalie was classified under this definition of orthopedic impairments and received special education services because of the impact of her cerebral palsy on her school functioning. Although Natalie had other impairments (seizures), she could be accommodated under the educational program in orthopedic impairments.

When students have two or more primary disabilities that cannot be accommodated by one special education program, they may be classified as having multiple disabilities. For example, a child who has a severe physical impairment and is deaf may be classified as having a multiple disability; this pupil may require services from a teacher certified to teach students with orthopedic impairments and another teacher certified to teach students who are deaf or hard of hearing. Many possible combinations of disabilities can fall under the category of multiple disabilities, but because a physical or health disability is often involved, this category is addressed in this chapter.

TABLE 13.1 Federal Definitions Pertaining to Physical or Health Disabilities and Deaf–Blindness

Deaf–blindness means concomitant hearing and visual impairment, the combination of which causes such severe communication and other developmental and educational needs that students cannot be accommodated in special education programs solely for children with deafness or children with blindness.

Multiple disabilities means concomitant impairments (such as mental retardation–blindness, mental retardation–orthopedic impairment, etc.), the combination of which causes such severe educational needs that students cannot be accommodated in special education programs solely for one of the impairments. The term does not include deaf-blindness.

Orthopedic impairment means a severe orthopedic impairment that adversely affects a child's educational performance. The term includes impairments caused by congenital anomaly (e.g., clubfoot, absence of some member, etc.), impairments caused by disease (e.g., poliomyelitis, bone tuberculosis, etc.), and impairments from other causes (e.g., cerebral palsy, amputations, and fractures or burns that cause contractures).

Other health impairment means having limited strength, vitality, or alertness, including a heightened alertness to environmental stimuli, that results in limited alertness with respect to the education environment that

i. Is due to chronic or acute health problems such as asthma, attention deficit disorder or attention deficit hyperactivity disorder, diabetes, epilepsy, a heart condition, hemophilia, lead poisoning, leukemia, nephritis, rheumatic fever, sickle cell anemia, and Tourette syndrome; and
ii. Adversely affects a child's educational performance.

Traumatic brain injury means an acquired injury to the brain caused by an external physical force, resulting in total or partial functional disability or psychosocial impairment, or both, that adversely affects educational performance. The term applies to open or closed head injuries resulting in impairments in one or more areas, such as cognition; language; memory; attention; reasoning; abstract thinking; judgment; problem-solving; sensory, perceptual, and motor abilities; psychosocial behavior; physical functions; information processing; and speech. The term does not apply to brain injuries that are congenital or degenerative, or to brain injuries induced by birth trauma.

SOURCE: 34 C.F.R. § 300.8 (c).

Children who have an acquired brain injury as a result of external force, such as from a car accident, may be served under the category of traumatic brain injury. Traumatic brain injury may result in impairments in several different areas, including physical disabilities, sensory impairments, cognitive abnormalities, language abnormalities, and behavioral disorders. This category does not include individuals who have brain injury that occurred before or during birth or that was acquired as a result of a degenerative disease.

Students with other health impairments have limited alertness to the educational environment because of health problems that limit strength, vitality, or alertness. This health impairment may be chronic (persisting over a long period of time) or acute (having a short and usually severe course). The federal definition in Table 13.1 gives several examples of health impairments, including asthma, heart conditions, diabetes, and attention deficit hyperactivity disorder. This is only a partial listing of all of the possible conditions that may be included in this disability area.

Pupils who have visual or hearing impairments of such magnitude that they cannot be appropriately accommodated in a special education program for children with deafness or blindness are identified as deaf–blind. Most of us could not imagine what it would be like to be without the use of both our hearing and our eyesight. We gather so much information about our surroundings through these two senses. The loss of both hearing and vision represents one of the most challenging of all disability categories. It would be wrong to assume, however, that students classified as deaf–blind are completely unable to see or hear—the term is not absolute. In reality, many children classified as deaf–blind experience a broad range of perceptions. Some pupils may be completely blind but only partially deaf, while in other instances a youngster might be partially sighted but have a be born with cerebral palsy, blindness, deafness, intellectual disabilities, and several other abnormalities, including heart defects, kidney defects, brain abnormalities, and deaf–blindness (Best & Heller, 2009b).

The fetus is also at risk of developing physical and health disabilities when exposed to certain drugs, chemicals, or environmental agents. Maternal abuse of alcohol, for example, has been linked to a range of physical, cognitive, and behavioral abnormalities that can result in lifelong damage (Merrick, Merrick, Morad, & Kandel, 2006; Tsai, Floyd, Green, & Boyle, 2007). Serious fetal abnormalities can also occur as a result of prescription medications taken for maternal illness or disease (for example, certain antibiotics and seizure medications). Environmental toxins such as radiation have been linked to birth defects, as have dietary deficiencies. Certain maternal diseases, such as diabetes, have also been associated with a higher risk of fetal disability. Maternal trauma from falls or car accidents can cause bleeding in the fetus's brain, resulting in neurological impairments (Akman, 2000).

Prematurity and Complications of Pregnancy

Infants are usually born at approximately 40 weeks of gestation, weighing approximately 7.5 pounds (Kliegman, Behrman, Jensen, & Stanton, 2007). An infant born before 37 weeks is considered premature.

Infants who are premature and born with very low birth weight (less than 1,500 grams) are at risk of having disabilities. These infants can develop neurological problems resulting in cerebral palsy, epilepsy, vision loss, hearing loss, deaf–blindness, and/or psychosis (Valcamonico et al., 2007). Cognitive functioning can be affected, resulting in intellectual or learning disabilities, which can lead to future educational difficulties (Hille et al., 2007).

In some instances, babies that are born on time and with average weight encounter complications during the perinatal period. The most common cause of brain injury during the perinatal period is asphyxia—a decrease of oxygen in the blood. Among infants who survive an episode of asphyxia, several disabilities may occur such as cerebral palsy, epilepsy, and cognitive deficits (Rennie, Hagmann, & Robertson, 2007).

Acquired Causes

Many physical and health disabilities in addition to related low-incidence disabilities are acquired after birth by infants, children, and adults. These acquired causes include trauma, child abuse, infections, environmental toxins, and disease. For example, deaf–blindness may be caused by meningitis. Traumatic brain injury is usually due to an acquired cause resulting from some type of trauma (for example, falls, accidents, child abuse). The extent of disability will depend on the cause and its severity.

Characteristics of Individuals With Physical Disabilities, Health Disabilities, and Related Low-Incidence Disabilities

The specific characteristics of an individual who has a physical or health disability will depend on the specific disease, its severity, and individual factors. Two individuals with identical diagnoses may be quite different in terms of their capabilities. Also, it is important to remember that students who have severe physical disabilities (even individuals who are unable to talk, walk, or feed themselves) may have normal or gifted intelligence. No one should judge a person's intellectual ability based on physical appearance.

TABLE 13.2 Examples of Physical and Health Disabilities

Physical Disabilities	Health Disabilities
Orthopedic Impairments	Other Health Impairments
Neuromotor impairments	Major health impairments
• Cerebral palsy	• Seizure disorders
• Spina bifida	• Asthma
Degenerative diseases	Infectious diseases
• Muscular dystrophy	• AIDS
Musculoskeletal disorders	
• Juvenile rheumatoid arthritis	
• Limb deficiency	
Multiple Disabilities*	
Physical disability plus another disability	
Traumatic Brain Injury*	
Physical disability resulting from traumatic brain injury	

NOTE: *Multiple disabilities and traumatic brain injury can occur without a physical disability being present. They only fall under the category of physical disabilities when a physical disability is present.

A multitude of physical and health disabilities may be encountered at school. Each of them has differing characteristics, treatments, and prognoses. To illustrate the range of conditions included under physical and health disabilities, this section describes a number of sample conditions across the four IDEA categories of orthopedic impairments, multiple disabilities, traumatic brain injury, and other health impairments. Table 13.2 gives an outline of the categories, subcategories, and sample conditions that will be discussed. Characteristics of individuals with deaf–blindness will also be reviewed.

Characteristics of Students With Orthopedic Impairments

The IDEA category of orthopedic impairments contains a wide variety of disorders. These can be divided into three main areas: neuromotor impairments, degenerative diseases, and musculoskeletal disorders. Each of these areas has unique characteristics and contains many different disabilities. Following is a sampling of some of the most commonly found orthopedic impairments in the school-age population.

Neuromotor Impairments

A **neuromotor impairment** is an abnormality of, or damage to, the brain, spinal cord, or nerves that send impulses to the muscles of the body. Neuromotor impairments often result in complex motor problems that can affect several body systems (for example, limited limb movement, loss of urinary control, loss of proper alignment of the spine). Individuals with neuromotor impairments have a higher incidence of additional impairments, especially when there has been brain involvement (for example, intellectual disabilities, seizures, visual impairments). Two types of neuromotor impairments that fall under the IDEA category of orthopedic impairments are cerebral palsy and spina bifida.

2. **Limb Deficiency**. A **limb deficiency** refers to any number of skeletal abnormalities in which an arm(s) and/or a leg(s) is partially or totally missing. A student may be born missing an arm or a leg or may lose a limb in an accident. Typically, individuals with limb deficiencies will be fitted with a prosthetic device (artificial limb). There are many different types of prosthetic devices with different levels of complexity. A student may have a leg prosthetic that allows for walking and running or an artificial hand that permits grasping and writing. If the limb has been missing from birth, the child may have learned to do things using other limbs. For example, some students who are missing both arms can write and feed themselves with their feet. Some students may type with their feet. Whether a prosthetic device is used or not, many students will still require some modifications and may need specialized instruction in such areas as one-handed keyboarding.

Characteristics of Students With Multiple Disabilities

Multiple disabilities is an umbrella term under which various educational, rehabilitation, government, and advocacy groups include different combinations of disabilities. In IDEA, this category refers to persons with concomitant impairments whose needs cannot be met in a special education program designed solely for one of the impairments. Although there is no single definition, the term does imply two or more disabilities whose combination usually creates an interactional, multiplicative effect rather than just an additive one. Some examples include learners with the following conditions:

- Intellectual disabilities and spina bifida
- Deafness and AIDS
- Behavior disorders and muscular dystrophy
- Cerebral palsy and seizures
- Learning disabilities and asthma

Some students may use their feet for such tasks as accessing a communication device.

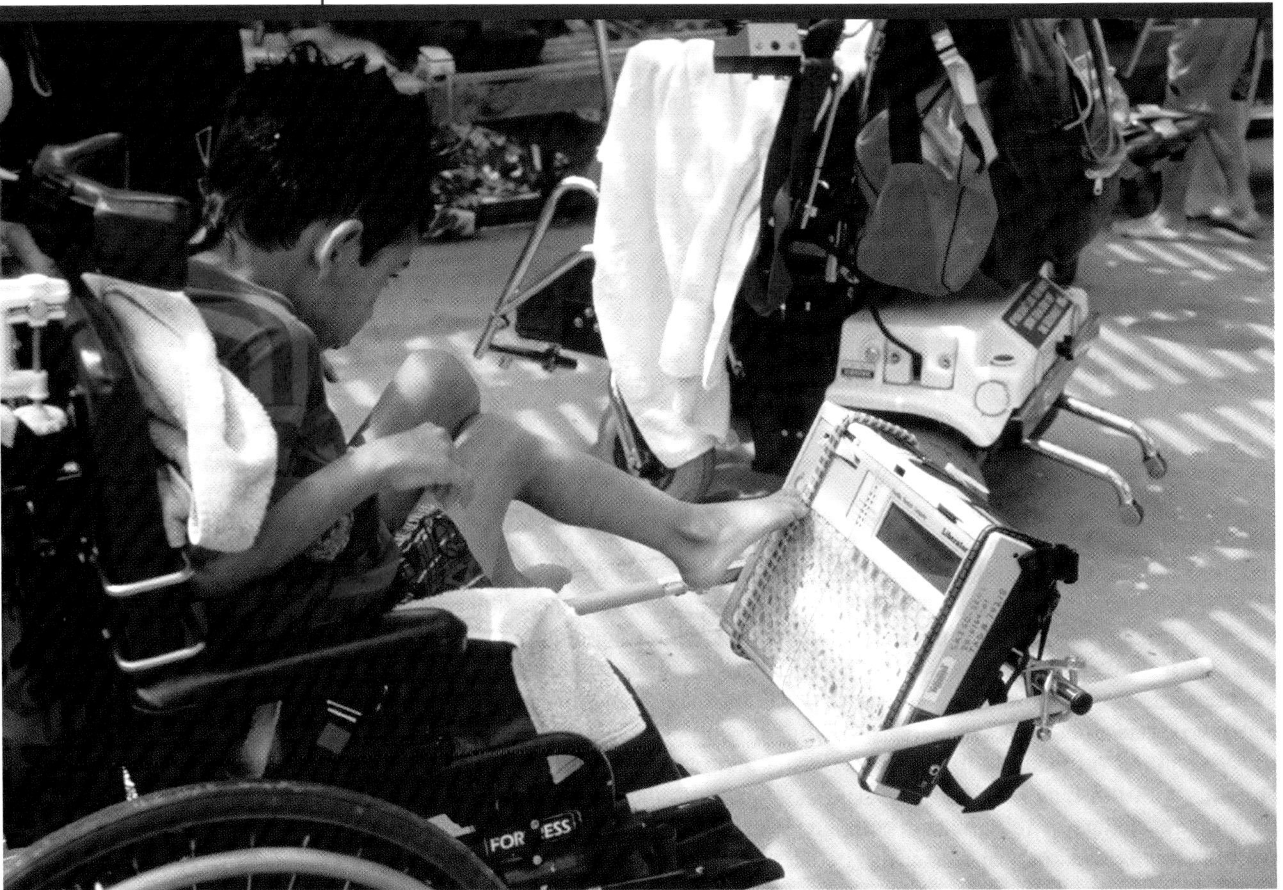

Depending on the type of multiple disabilities, cognitive functioning may vary from giftedness to profound intellectual disabilities. Usually there will be a need for modifications, assistive technology, and specialized teaching strategies.

Characteristics of Students With Traumatic Brain Injury

Traumatic brain injury refers to temporary or permanent injury to the brain from acquired causes such as car accidents, accidental falls, and gunshot wounds to the head; it does not include congenital or degenerative conditions or birth trauma. Approximately 5.3 million people in the United States have a disability as a result of a traumatic brain injury (Centers for Disease Control and Prevention, 2010). Although a person can acquire a traumatic brain injury at any age, one of the highest rates is among teenagers and young adults from 15 to 24 years of age.

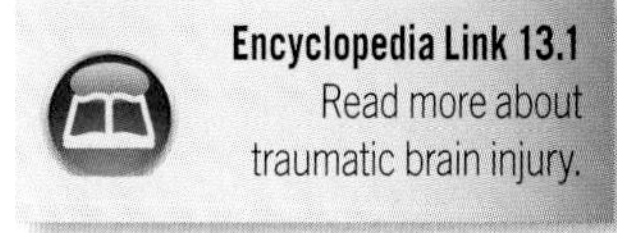

The effects of an injury will differ depending on the cause. A penetration injury, such as a bullet going through the brain, will result in certain specific effects. The effects of the injury are usually specific to the site of injury, with secondary effects occurring in other areas as a result of complications.

Traumatic brain injury can also be caused by car accidents and falls. This type of injury, known as an acceleration injury, results in diffuse damage throughout the brain. When the head hits the steering wheel of a car, for example, the brain (which is floating in cerebral spinal fluid) is thrown violently forward against the skull. This initial site of impact is referred to as "coup" (see Figure 13.3). The brain is then thrown backward and hits the back of the skull. This second site of impact is known as "contracoup." The brain continues to move back and forth, hitting against the skull, and suffering further damage against any sharp bony protrusions. Often the brain will be twisting as well,

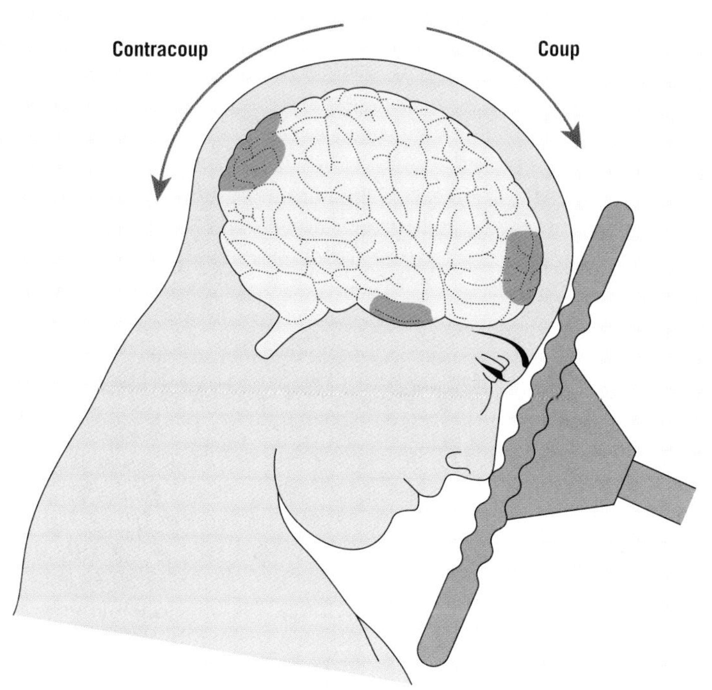

FIGURE 13.3 Traumatic Brain Injury

SOURCE: Adapted from S. Grandinette and S. Best, "Traumatic Brain Injury," in K. W. Heller, P. E. Forney, P. A. Alberto, S. Best, and M. N. Schwartzman (Eds.), *Understanding Physical, Health, and Multiple Disabilities,* 2nd ed. (Upper Saddle River, NJ: Pearson Education, 2009), p. 122.

breaking and damaging nerve cells throughout. The result is diffuse damage across the brain. Complications such as hemorrhage (bleeding) and edema (swelling) often cause further damage to the brain.

The effects of a traumatic brain injury range from no ill effects to severe disability. Most head injuries are mild, with no abnormalities found on neurological exams, and the person often does not require medical treatment. Even following a mild injury, however, problems such as headache, fatigue, distractibility, memory problems, and perceptual motor slowing can occur and persist for months, for years, or permanently. These problems often go undetected until difficulties arise during classroom activities. In one case, a girl fell out of a window and was taken to the emergency room. Although she had no apparent damage, she failed the school year. In retrospect, the teacher and parent were able to trace the student's academic difficulties as beginning after the accident and realized that some cognitive deficits must have occurred.

Students with moderate and severe cases of traumatic head injury typically require hospital stays and rehabilitation services before reentering school. The person with a severe traumatic brain injury often enters the hospital in a coma and slowly regains some or most abilities. Typically, motor skills return first, and higher-level cognitive skills return last. Improvement can be a long process, with the most dramatic gains occurring over the first year but skills continuing to improve over about a five-year period.

Some individuals may fully recover from a traumatic brain injury, while others may have permanent disabilities. A traumatic brain injury has the potential for causing lifelong disabilities across physical, cognitive, social, behavioral, health, and sensory domains. In the area of physical disabilities, some individuals are left without the ability to walk or use their hands. However, the permanent physical disability is often more subtle, with decreased balance and speed in walking and decreased hand speed and dexterity (Kuhtz-Buschbeck et al., 2003). Although these may seem mild, they can interfere with participation in sports and activities requiring good hand control.

Cognitive deficits can remain after a severe traumatic brain injury. These can range from severe intellectual disabilities to mild cognitive impairments. Individuals may have deficits in sustained attention, problem solving, shifting attention, planning, initiation, organization, and memory (Slomine et al., 2002). Impairments in these areas often result in learning problems and difficulty with setting goals, monitoring and evaluating performance, shifting strategies to address a problem, remaining focused over time, and remembering information. Teachers will need to use systematic instruction and specialized strategies to address these problems.

Impairments in social and behavioral functioning are common in individuals with traumatic brain injury. These may range from difficulty interacting with others to irritability and aggression (Alderman, 2003). Poor social interactions can occur when the injury has resulted in difficulty in reading social cues and monitoring social responses. Some individuals have personality changes with poorly controlled behavior in which they act on impulse, often with aggressive behavior (Slomine et al., 2002; Ylvisaker, Jacobs, & Feeney, 2003). These types of behaviors are often considered the most challenging to address in the classroom setting. A behavior management plan is usually constructed to provide guidelines on how to address the behavior problems.

During the reauthorization of IDEA in 1990, traumatic brain injury was added as a separate disability category, in part because of its unique and multiple characteristics that can interfere with learning and functioning. These students need to be constantly assessed, because skill levels do improve over time. For example, one student with a three-year-old severe traumatic brain injury was being taught to use pictures to communicate when suddenly she began to laugh at a misspelled word on a bulletin board. She had regained the ability to read most words without anyone realizing it. Unlike those with developmental disabilities, students with traumatic brain injury may be left with "splinter skills," meaning that they have some advanced skills but lack other simple ones. For example, one student with severe traumatic brain injury could identify any number, no matter how large, but had difficulty with the concept that 1 plus 1 equals 2. Teachers need to use various modifications and techniques to address the many problems that can occur in a student with a traumatic brain injury; some sample strategies are provided in the accompanying

Suggestions for the Classroom

Strategies That May Be Used With Students With Traumatic Brain Injury

Impairments	Strategies	Examples
Poor attention	Decrease distractions.	Move away extra pencils.
	Provide cues to attend.	Touch card that says "Listen."
	Limit amount of information.	Divide up information.
	Provide advance organizers.	Give list of important events.
Memory problems	Teach verbal rehearsal strategies.	Student repeats list of people.
	Teach use of visual imagery.	Student visualizes battle for history.
	Provide information in writing.	Give teacher's notes.
	Give a school schedule.	Put pictures by each subject.
	Repeat directions.	Repeat one direction at a time.
Decreased writing speed and accuracy	Give more time on tests.	Student takes test over two periods.
	Decrease assignment load.	Student writes two fewer papers.
	Have student type instead of writing by hand.	Student writes faster using keyboard.
Decreased stamina and endurance	Allow rest breaks.	Student rests for five minutes.
	Adjust school day.	Student comes for half day.
	Have peer carry books.	Friend helps with books.
Impulsive behavior	Encourage "thinking time."	Have student wait, then answer.
	Discuss rules each day.	Review rules.
	Redirect inappropriate behavior.	Tell student to sit, open book.
	Remove unnecessary material.	Book bags are placed at side of room.
	Role-play.	Practice different scenarios.

Suggestions for the Classroom. The special education teacher needs to work closely with the general education teacher in helping to use the most appropriate techniques.

Characteristics of Students With Other Health Impairments

Disabilities that fall under the IDEA category of other health impairments are often divided into two areas: major health impairments and infectious diseases. Students will not typically require special education services unless these conditions are severe. These impairments often result in more absences, fatigue, and decreased stamina.

Major Health Impairments

Many major health impairments fall under the category of other health impairments. Some of these can be treated effectively; others have no cure. Many of them can give rise to emergency situations that need to be handled immediately, and some can result in death. Two of the most commonly occurring health impairments are seizure disorders and asthma.

1. **Seizure Disorders.** A **seizure** is a sudden, temporary change in the normal functioning of the brain's electrical system as a result of excessive, uncontrolled electrical activity in the brain. A seizure may be due to a high fever, ingestion of certain drugs or poisons, certain metabolic disorders, or chemical imbalances. Seizures may also be the result of a prenatal or perinatal brain injury, head trauma, infections such as meningitis, congenital malformations, or unknown causes (Beers et al., 2009). A person has a seizure disorder, also known as **epilepsy**, when the seizures are recurrent. Often the reason for the seizure disorder is unknown.

Seizures are of many different types, depending on where in the brain the abnormal electrical activity occurs. Seizures may be characterized by altered consciousness, motor activity, sensory phenomena, inappropriate behaviors, or some combination of these. Three of the most commonly encountered seizure disorders are absence seizures, complex partial seizures, and tonic–clonic seizures.

An individual who has **absence seizures** (formerly known as *petit mal* seizures) will suddenly lose consciousness, stop moving, and stare straight ahead (or the eyes may roll upward). The person will not fall, but simply stop and appear trancelike. If the seizure occurs when the person is talking, the person will stop in midsentence and, when the seizure ends, continue the sentence as if nothing has happened. Typically, these seizures do not last more than thirty seconds, but they can occur several hundred times a day (Tovia, Goldberg-Stern, Shahar, & Kramer, 2005). Often the person is not aware of what has happened. When the seizure occurs during a teacher's lecture, the child often doesn't understand why the teacher is suddenly talking about something different. These seizures have been mistaken for daydreaming, but the student cannot be brought out of the seizure by touch or loud voices. Often it is the observant teacher who first detects that something is wrong with the student.

In a **complex partial seizure**, consciousness is impaired, and the person usually exhibits a series of motor movements that may appear voluntary but are beyond the person's control. For example, some individuals having a complex partial seizure will appear dazed and engage in purposeless activity such as walking aimlessly, picking up objects, or picking at their clothes. Some individuals may start laughing, gesturing, or repeating a phrase. Whatever the person's particular pattern, the same pattern will usually be repeated with each seizure. In other words, if a child walks in a circle when having a complex partial seizure, then that is what his or her seizures are expected to look like each time one occurs.

Tonic-clonic seizures (formerly known as *grand mal* seizures) are typically what people think of when they hear that a person has a seizure disorder. This is a convulsive seizure in which the person loses consciousness and becomes very stiff. A person who is standing when the seizure occurs will drop to the floor and may sustain injuries from the fall. This stiffness is followed by a jerking phase in which the body makes rhythmic jerking motions that gradually decrease. During this phase, saliva may pool in the mouth and bubble at the lips. Breathing may become shallow or irregular. Usually there is a loss of bladder control. These seizures usually last between two and five minutes. After the seizure, the student may be slightly disoriented at first and not realize what has happened. The person is usually exhausted and will often sleep. There are many misconceptions of what to do when this type of seizure occurs. See the accompanying Suggestions for the Classroom for information on the steps to take when a tonic–clonic seizure occurs.

Suggestions for the Classroom

Steps for Teachers to Take When a Tonic–Clonic Seizure Occurs

What to Do

- ☑ Stay calm; note time of onset.
- ☑ Move furniture out of the way to prevent injury.
- ☑ Loosen shirt collar and put something soft under head.
- ☑ Turn student on his or her side to allow saliva to drain out of mouth.
- ☑ If seizure continues more than five minutes, or if multiple seizures occur one right after another, or if this is the first seizure, call for an ambulance.
- ☑ If seizure stops but the student is not breathing, give mouth-to-mouth resuscitation (this rarely occurs).
- ☑ After the seizure is over, reassure student.
- ☑ Allow student to rest.

What *Not* to Do

- ☑ Do not put anything in the mouth.
- ☑ Do not restrain movements.
- ☑ Do not give liquids immediately after seizure.

The most common treatment for seizures is medication. Other treatments may be used when the seizures are severe and cannot be controlled by medication, such as surgery on part of the brain, special diets, and electrical stimulation of the vagus nerve (Wilfogn, 2002). However, these treatments are not always effective, and seizures may still occur.

It is important for teachers to know the steps to take when seizures happen. Often they will have a seizure information sheet to provide them with pertinent information. When a seizure occurs, teachers will often be asked to fill out a seizure report that describes what the seizure looked like, how long it lasted, and what treatment was given. The teacher will also need to be supportive of the child and try to minimize embarrassment (especially when there is a loss of bladder control). Often classmates will think seizures are contagious or their classmate is dead. It is important to help children understand that seizures are not contagious and to explain in simple terms what has happened.

2. **Asthma. Asthma** is the most common pulmonary disease of childhood and is on the increase (American Lung Association, 2010a). Children who have asthma breathe normally until they come in contact with a substance or situation that triggers an asthma attack, such as pollen, air pollution, a respiratory infection, or exercise. When an asthma attack is triggered, the person has difficulty breathing. Symptoms include shortness of breath, wheezing, coughing, and labored breathing.

Audio Link 13.1
Listen to more about asthma.

Asthma is treated by avoiding triggers and taking medication. In some instances, triggers can be removed or reduced. For example, if being close to the classroom hamster triggers an attack, then the hamster should be removed or placed in a different location.

If exercise is a trigger, the student may need some modifications in physical education class. Medication may be taken on a regular basis to decrease the possibility of an asthma attack. When an asthma attack occurs, the student often uses a prescribed inhaler (medication delivered in a spray form). It is important that the inhaler be used immediately if an attack occurs, so the inhaler needs to be readily accessible. If the student goes on a field trip, for example, the inhaler needs to go with him or her.

For most students, the asthma attack will stop once the inhaler is used. However, for some students, the inhaler will help but not stop the attack. It is very important that all school personnel know what steps to take should an asthma attack occur. Although it is rare for an asthma attack to be fatal, it is a possibility. If the student is experiencing severe respiratory problems, an ambulance should be called. When the asthma attack lasts for a long period of time (for example, several days), teachers will need to assist the student in completing missed work.

Infectious Diseases

Several infectious diseases fall under the heading of other health impairments. Some infectious diseases are readily transmittable (such as tuberculosis); others may pose no threat in the school environment (such as AIDS).

Acquired immune deficiency syndrome (AIDS) is one of the newest chronic illnesses of childhood. It is caused by the human immunodeficiency virus (HIV), which destroys the immune system, leaving the person open to serious, life-threatening diseases (such as pneumocystis carinii pneumonia). Transmission generally occurs in one of three ways: (1) having sex with an infected partner, (2) sharing contaminated needles during drug use, and (3) passing on the infection from mother to infant. It cannot be acquired through casual contact because it is only transmitted in blood, semen, vaginal secretions, and breast milk (Best & Heller, 2009a). Because it is not transmitted in saliva, even sharing toothbrushes or kissing will not transmit the infection.

Some students are born with the infection from an infected mother; adolescents may acquire the infection from sex with an infected partner or by sharing needles during drug use. Children born with HIV may have developmental delays, motor problems, nervous system damage, and additional infections. Adolescents acquiring the disease may also develop life-threatening infections, nervous system abnormalities, and other impairments (such as visual impairments). Treatment consists of a combination of medications that may slow the disease's effect on the immune system. However, the disease is considered terminal in most cases.

Often children with AIDS will not initially need any modifications in the school setting. However, as the disease progresses, they will require some modifications because of fatigue and frequent absences. A supportive attitude should be in place, especially given the social stigma surrounding the disease. Misconceptions that students or teachers have should be dispelled with accurate information.

Characteristics of Students With Deaf–Blindness

Describing the characteristics of pupils with deaf–blindness is a difficult task. This is an extremely heterogeneous population varying tremendously in members' needs, abilities, and educational requirements. Some consider deaf–blindness to be a spectrum disability (Brown & Bates, 2005) because of the enormous diversity exhibited by individuals who are deaf–blind.

As we stated at the beginning of this discussion, in addition to impaired hearing and vision, large numbers of students who are deaf and blind exhibit cognitive deficits (66 percent), physical impairments (57 percent), or complex health needs (38 percent) (Killoran, 2007). Speech and language impairments are also typical of individuals who are deaf–blind. Behavioral and social difficulties often accompany deaf–blindness. These deficits are frequently a result of the person's inability to understand language and effectively communicate with others (Miles, 2010). In addition to problems with communication, difficulties navigating the environment are common. The restrictions and challenges represented by these two areas usually lead to feelings of isolation among children and adults who are deaf–blind.

Assessment of Physical Disabilities, Health Disabilities, and Related Low-Incidence Disabilities

In order to qualify for special education services, students with a physical or health disability need to have a thorough assessment. The assessment will determine whether they qualify for special education services, and which ones are needed. The assessment for initial eligibility typically involves a medical evaluation and a series of educational evaluations. Depending on the student's medical condition and school functioning, other assessments involving related services and assistive technology will need to be performed.

First and foremost, a student will need a medical evaluation by a licensed physician that provides a diagnosis of the student's physical or health condition. The medical evaluation will typically include important information such as medications, surgeries, special health care procedures, and special diet or activity restrictions. Any sensory deficits should also be noted.

Once a medical diagnosis confirms a physical or health disability, a determination needs to be made as to whether the disability negatively affects the student's educational performance. A comprehensive educational assessment (or, for preschool children, a developmental assessment) will be performed to determine the effects of the physical or health disability. The precise educational assessment instruments will vary according to the student's age and abilities. Assessments will document deficits in areas such as preacademic functioning, academic functioning, adaptive behavior, motor development, language and communication skills, and social–emotional development.

A psychological evaluation may be given if there is a significant deficit in academic or cognitive functioning. However, it is often very difficult to evaluate cognitive functioning (possible intellectual disabilities) when the student has severe physical disabilities and is unable to speak. This is especially the case when the student has not yet learned to use a communication device, or cannot do so reliably because of severe motor constraints. Psychological and educational misdiagnosis and misplacement do occur, as they did in the case of Natalie.

If the educational evaluations demonstrate that the student's physical or health disability is affecting his or her educational performance, a decision will be made as to which educational category the student qualifies for: orthopedic impairments, multiple disabilities, traumatic brain injury, or other health impairments. Additional assessments will be performed based on the medical and educational evaluations. If the physician orders physical or occupational therapy, for example, the student will need to have assessments in these areas. If the student qualifies for speech–language pathology services, assessments will occur in that area as well. If the student has a physical disability, an assistive technology assessment may be performed by the special education teacher in conjunction with the educational team, or the school system may have a specialist or team of specialists in that area. If the student requires specialized health care procedures, such as tube feeding, an individual health (or health care) plan will be developed, and the student will be assessed to determine if he or she can be taught to self-perform the procedure. Depending on the student's needs, other assessments may be performed to provide appropriate educational services to the student.

Assessment of Students With Deaf–Blindness

The low-incidence nature of deaf–blindness coupled with the scarcity of appropriate assessment instruments presents a unique set of challenges to teachers and other professionals (Silberman et al., 2004). A team of individuals is typically needed to accurately assess the student with deaf–blindness. Valid assessment of individuals with deaf–blindness dictates collaboration among family members and professionals. The key is to conduct multiple assessments over both time and contexts.

Unfortunately, norm-referenced assessments are of little value when assessing pupils with deaf–blindness. Criterion-referenced tests, developmental scales (frequently normed on children without disabilities), and informal observations often yield useful information. Even these assessment strategies, however, are not without their limitations (Engleman, Griffin, Griffin, & Maddox, 1999). Experts recommend that assessments focus on what the child *has* learned as well as what he or she *needs* to learn (Silberman et al., 2004). For young children with deaf–blindness, developmental scales are often useful. The INSITE Developmental Checklist (Morgan, 1989) is one example of an assessment instrument appropriate for use with infants and young children with deaf–blindness. Older pupils are typically evaluated via tools that focus on desired outcomes of adulthood. For example, the Assessment Intervention Matrix (Wolf-Schein & Schein, 2009) focuses on basic daily living skills as well as housekeeping and food preparation.

Educational Considerations

Educational considerations for students with physical or health disabilities include the setting in which each student can receive an appropriate education, the impact of the physical or health disability on that student's school performance, and the best ways of meeting that student's needs in the educational setting. Each of these considerations will be discussed in turn.

Where Are Students With Physical or Health Disabilities Educated?

Video Link 13.7
Watch more about educational placement.

Students with physical and health disabilities are educated in a variety of settings. Settings can range from a regular classroom to a homebound or hospital setting, with several other settings in between (such as resource room, separate class, separate school, and residential facility). The appropriate setting is determined by the educational team, based on student assessments, educational goals, and planned interventions. For example, one student with cerebral palsy who is nonverbal may need special education services addressing reading and writing; this student may go to a resource room for the majority of the day to learn how to use an assistive technology device and receive specialized instruction. A second pupil with cerebral palsy may just need monitoring in regular education classes. A third student with cerebral palsy may be several grade levels behind across all areas; this individual may need to be in a separate class to meet his or her educational goals. Some children may have such severe health problems that homebound instruction is necessary; in this case, a teacher goes to the student's house to provide instruction.

Educational placement of students with physical and health disabilities varies greatly across the IDEA categories of orthopedic impairments, multiple disabilities, traumatic brain injury, other health impairments, and deaf–blindness (see Figure 13.4). The largest number of students with orthopedic impairments are educated in the regular classroom (50.1 percent), followed by a separate class (24.4 percent) and resource room (17.3 percent). This is not surprising, as most of this population does not have additional cognitive impairments. However, when the student's physical disability is severe, additional support is needed and may be provided in a resource room or separate class.

In contrast, the most common placement for students with multiple disabilities is a separate class (45.2 percent), followed by a separate school (20.4 percent), and then resource room (16.0 percent). Students with multiple disabilities often have severe physical disabilities with concomitant severe intellectual disabilities. Although many states are trying to phase out separate schools, they remain part of the range of options available to students.

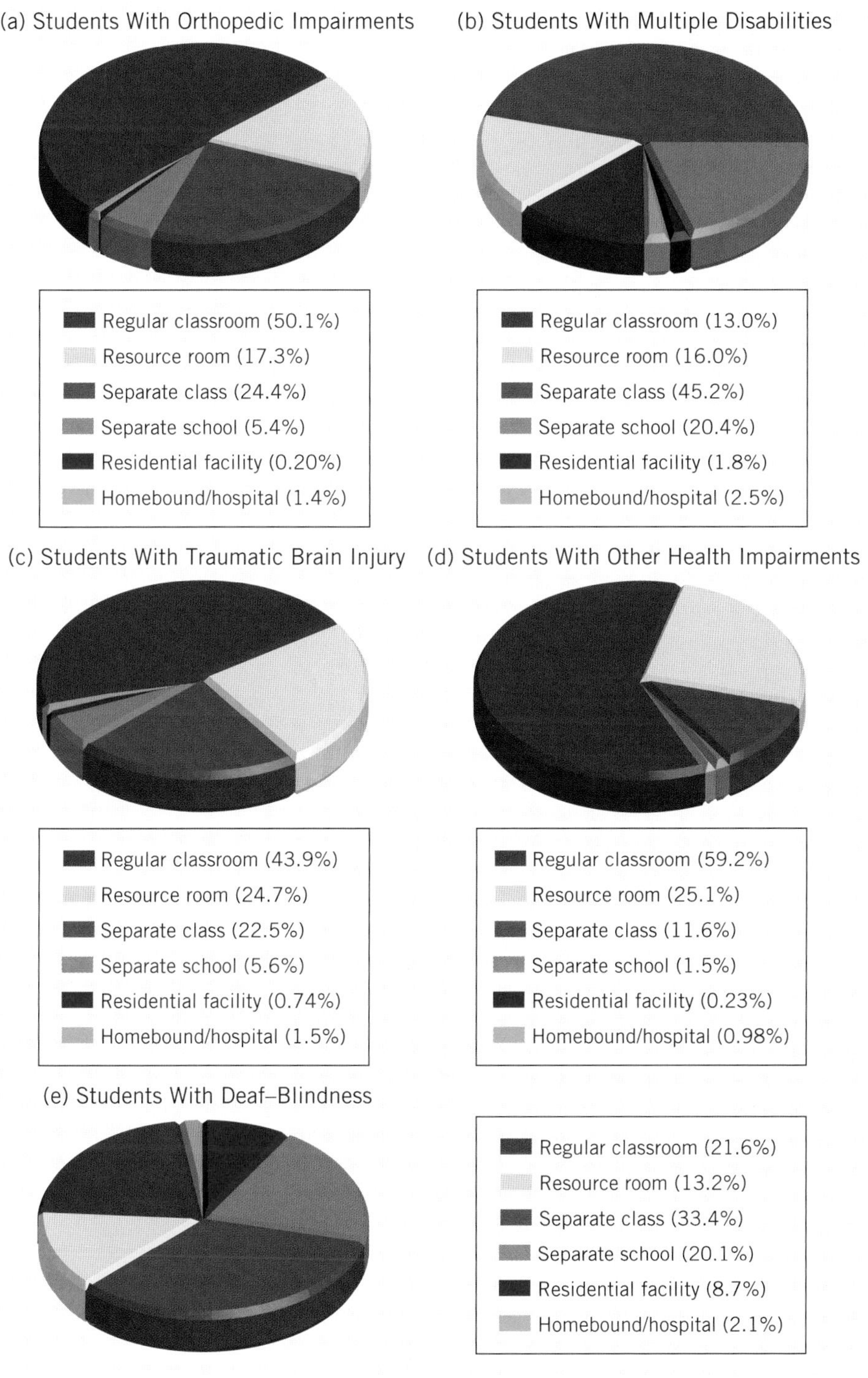

FIGURE 13.4 Educational Placement of Students With Physical Disabilities, Health Disabilities, or Deaf–Blindness (2007–2008 School Year)

SOURCE: U.S. Department of Education. (2009). *IDEA data.* Retrieved December 19, 2009, from https://www.ideadata.org/PartBReport.asp

Students with traumatic brain injury vary greatly in the severity of injury and its effects on the individual. Approximately four out of ten pupils with traumatic brain injury are served in the regular or general education classroom, with placement in a resource room (24.7 percent) or separate class (22.5 percent) about equally split. Functioning often improves during the first few years after injury, and the educational placement will typically change over a fairly short period of time.

Like pupils with orthopedic impairments, students with other health impairments are most likely to be educated in the regular classroom (59.2 percent). However, frequent absences, fatigue, inattention, pain, and other health-related factors often result in a need for placement in a resource room (25.1 percent) or separate class (11.6 percent).

At this time, individuals who are deaf–blind are often educated in more restrictive settings. Only about one out of five students (21.6 percent) is educated in the regular classroom, while over 50 percent of these pupils receive a special education in either a separate class (33.4 percent) or a separate school (20.1 percent).

Impact on School Performance

Several variables affect school performance for a student with a physical or health disability according to the Physical and Health Disabilities Performance Model (Heller, 2009a). These variables can be divided into three major areas: type of disability, functional effects, and psychosocial and environmental factors (see Figure 13.5). Students with physical or health disabilities will typically have one or more problems in each of these major areas, and their interaction can negatively affect the students' school performance. A better understanding of these areas and how they affect each child's school performance will help the teacher and the educational team make appropriate decisions regarding educational objectives and necessary modifications.

Type of Disability

The first major area to affect student performance is the type of disability. Pupils with orthopedic impairments, for example, will often have problems accessing materials while students with other health impairments are more likely to have problems of endurance and stamina. The severity of the specific disability will also be a factor. The teacher will need to be familiar with the student's specific disability, its severity, and its implications for academic performance.

Functional Effects of the Disability

The second area that affects student performance is the functional effects of the disability on each particular student. As shown in Figure 13.5, this area is divided into seven categories: (1) atypical movements and motor abilities, (2) sensory loss, (3) communication impairments, (4) fatigue and lack of endurance, (5) health factors, (6) experiential deficits, and (7) cognitive impairments and processing issues (Heller, 2009a). The student's disability, its severity, and how it affects the particular student will determine which of these seven categories is a factor in affecting academic performance.

1. **Atypical Movements and Motor Abilities.** The first category pertains to any atypical movements or limitations of movement of the limbs (arms and legs). A student whose disabilities limit the movement of arms, hands, and fingers may be unable to do school tasks involving writing or manipulating material without proper modifications. Even with modifications, performance may be affected. For example, a student who can only write using a computer with an adapted keyboard may only be able to write fifteen words a minute and cannot write for long periods of time because of fatigue.

2. **Sensory Loss.** Some physical disabilities will have a lack of sensation (for example, touch, temperature) affecting the arms or legs, which can subtly affect students' perception of items and certain concepts (for example, coldness of ice, smoothness of paper). In addition, there is an increased incidence of vision and hearing loss in many types of physical disabilities. Not being able to see an activity or hear what is being said will obviously impact student performance.

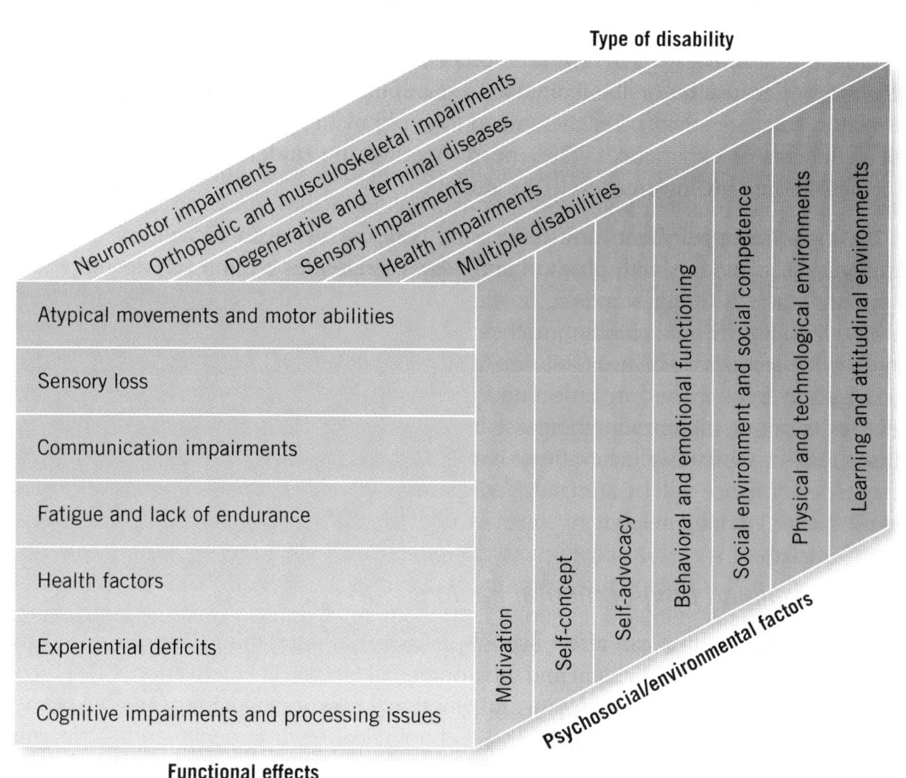

FIGURE 13.5 Physical and Health Disabilities Performance Model

3. **Communication Impairments.** When speaking is affected, students' performance can be severely affected. Questions may go unanswered, and teachers may have difficulty understanding students' responses. Students will typically use augmentative communication devices, but unless the students can spell, no augmentative communication device will have all the vocabulary needed to answer or ask questions. Also, it can take some time for students to learn to use their devices, during which time they will lose opportunities to communicate with others.

4. **Fatigue and Lack of Endurance.** The fourth category of functional effects is fatigue and endurance. Some students with physical and health disabilities may experience fatigue and limited stamina, which affects their ability to concentrate and hence their school performance. In some instances, fatigue may be so severe that the child needs short rest breaks throughout the day, a rest period within the school day, or a shortened school day.

5. **Health Factors.** The fifth category refers to various health issues associated with physical difficulties that can interfere with school performance. For example, some students may experience pain during the school day, such as a student with juvenile rheumatoid arthritis or a student with a poorly fitted artificial leg. A student who is experiencing pain or discomfort will be unable to attend fully to the lesson taught in class. Other health factors include the side effects of medications (for example, fatigue from seizure medications) or absences and missed information ranging from a few seconds because of an absence seizure to days as a result of illness.

6. **Experiential Deficits.** Some students with physical and health disabilities may lack experiences or concepts that are important to school performance. Students with severe

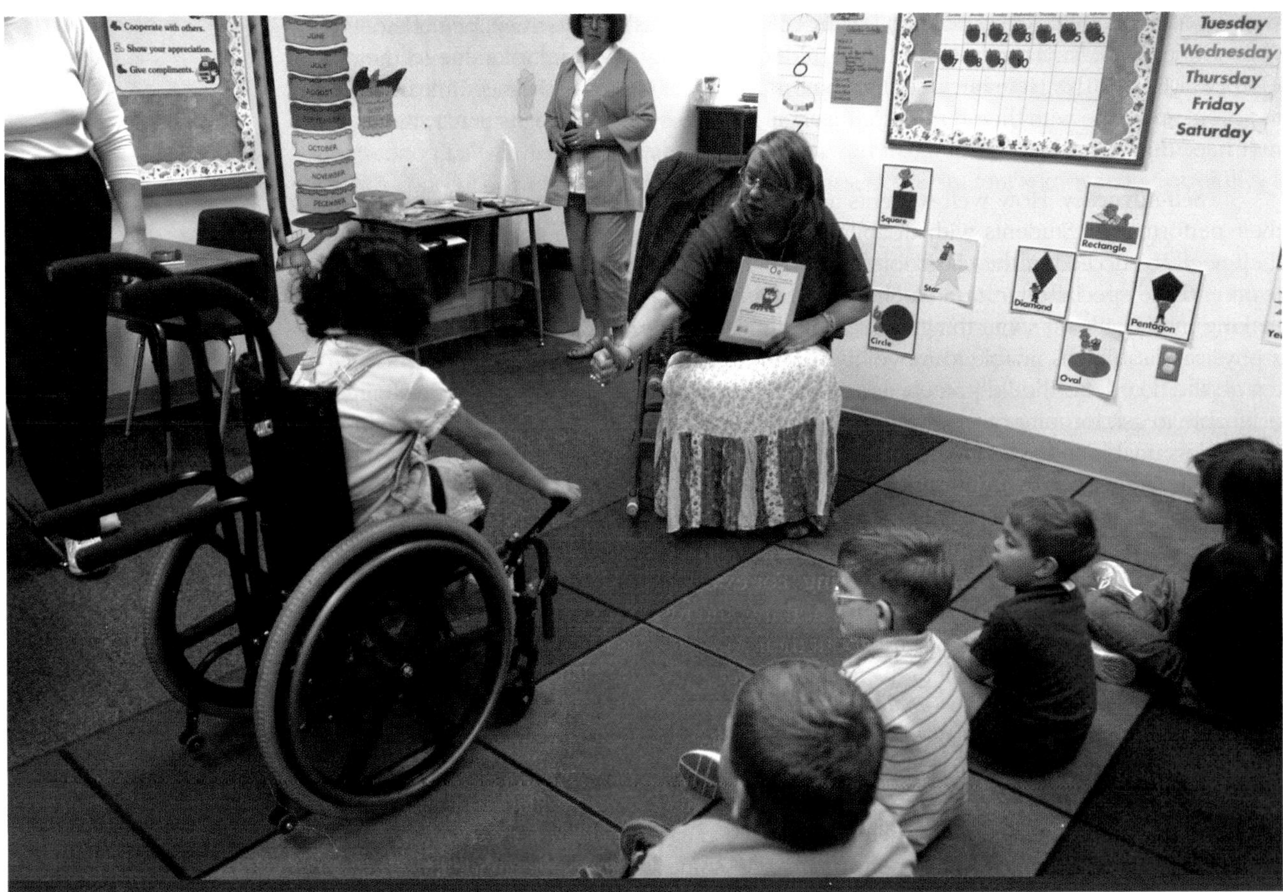

Classrooms, and other environments, must be arranged so as to allow ease of access for students with physical and health disabilities.

Meeting Educational Needs

Meeting the educational needs of students with physical or health disabilities requires several types of modifications. These will be discussed under four main headings: (1) physical/health monitoring, (2) modifications and adaptations, (3) specialized instructional strategies, and (4) specialized expanded curriculum areas.

Physical/Health Monitoring

It is the responsibility of teachers and school officials to maintain a safe, healthy environment for their students (DPHD Critical Issues and Leadership Committee, 1999; Heller, Fredrick, Best, Dykes, & Cohen, 2000). Maintaining a safe, healthy environment includes having efficient evacuation plans, school emergency procedures, proper infection control procedures, and teachers trained in CPR and first aid.

Teachers must know what type of medical condition each student has, how to monitor the student's physical or health impairment for problems, and what to do if a problem occurs. For example, if a student has a generalized tonic–clonic seizure, the teacher should have a plan in place and be able to immediately assist the student. In this example, immediate action is needed. Some monitoring may be more subtle, such as picking up signs that the student with muscular dystrophy is deteriorating and may need further modifications.

Modifications and Adaptations

Several modifications and adaptations may be needed to ensure that students with physical or health impairments are getting what they need to succeed in school. Major areas of concern include environmental arrangement, communication, instructional and curricular modifications, modifications and assistive technology for specific content areas, class participation, assignments and classroom tests, and sensory and perceptual modifications.

Often the special education teacher completes a checklist of needed modifications for each student with a physical or health disability and then discusses it with the general education teacher and other school personnel. Using a checklist helps ensure that a variety of modifications have been considered and that everyone is using the same modifications across environments.

1. **Environmental Arrangements.** Several types of environmental modifications may be needed to accommodate a student with a physical or health impairment. Fatigue or endurance issues may necessitate a modified day, rest breaks, or classrooms in close proximity. A student with very severe health issues may need a homeroom near an exit for easy access to an ambulance. In the classroom, a student may need widened aisles for wheelchair access or preferential seating in order to see the teacher or the board. In some cases, the student will need a special chair or desk to accommodate physical limitations. A student with restricted or impaired arm movement may need classroom materials to be positioned in a certain location or stabilized so they do not roll around.

2. **Communication.** Most students with physical and health disabilities will not need any adaptations in the area of communication. However, students with conditions such as severe cerebral palsy will often have speech that is not understandable. In our chapter opener, Natalie was able to communicate approximately thirty words or sounds that could mean up to two hundred different things depending on the context. Her use of an augmentative communication device opened up her world by allowing others to understand her.

It is very important that the teacher understand how the student communicates and how the teacher should present questions. Augmentative communication devices, for example, may range from a notebook with pictures to electronic devices with voice output, and may be used along with various sounds or words that the student can say. However, some students may not be able to use their communication device very reliably when they are still learning how to use it. The teacher may be instructed to ask questions giving answers in a multiple-choice format when calling on these students. For example, the teacher may ask the class, "On which mountain did the expedition take place?" Susan, a student with severe cerebral palsy, indicates she knows the answer. The teacher calls on her and asks, "Susan, is it (a) Mount Rainier, (b) Annapurna, (c) Mount Saint Helens, or (d) Mount Everest?" Upon hearing the correct one, Susan points to the *D* on her board to indicate her answer. The best way for communication to take place in the classroom setting will be discussed between the special and general education teachers and, once agreed upon, recorded on the modification checklist.

3. **Instructional and Curricular Modifications.** Often students with physical and health disabilities will require instructional and curricular modifications. Modifications in this area may include providing a study outline, extra repetition, or more frequent feedback. Students with physical disabilities who have speech impairments are often behind in their reading and may require material at a lower grade level. This may involve providing outlines at a reading level that the student can understand or using alternative textbooks that are easier to follow. Sometimes individual instruction from a special education teacher will be needed. Materials may need to be altered for accessibility (such as a larger calculator with bigger keys), and the curriculum may need to be altered to address the student's educational needs. Some students may need help with organizational skills, and others may need two sets of books because they are not physically capable of carrying their books back and forth between home and school.

Video Link 13.9
Watch more about modifications.

4. **Modifications and Assistive Technology for Specific Content Areas.** Often students will require modifications or assistive technology to access different school subjects. For example, to make a computer accessible for writing, some students with cerebral palsy

Making Inclusion Work

My inspiration and passion for teaching special education stems from a lifetime of experience: growing up with a sister with severe cerebral palsy who spent time in many different programs in the school system. I began my professional career teaching in a K–1 class for students with moderate, severe, and profound intellectual disabilities after graduating with a degree in mental retardation education. After four years in that setting, I completed my master's degree in orthopedic impairments (OI). I then taught students with orthopedic impairments at the high school level for eight years. Most of my students were fully included in the general education curriculum and were college or career bound. Other students were partially included in the general elective curriculum. Since that time, I completed my Ph.D. in physical disabilities and have worked with many educators who teach pupils with orthopedic impairments.

Inclusive Education Experience

In most cases, I favor inclusive education for students whose primary disability is physical. It is much easier to justify making physical modifications and accommodations for access to the general curriculum than it is to justify removing students due to modification and accessibility difficulties. Many different models exist for including students, ranging from intermittent checkups with the teacher to random student observations to having full-time assistance from either the OI teacher or a paraprofessional. Using an inclusion model allows teachers to collaborate, problem-solve, and inspire each other creatively. It also exposes teachers and students to a variety of teaching and learning styles. Because of multiple needs in the classroom, information is often explained in a variety of ways, and information is often presented through different modalities. Many students shine when they are given access to experiences they have not had before because of their physical limitations. Classmates are given the opportunity to look past the students' physical limitations and see their capabilities. The benefits for all students in the inclusive environment are reciprocal.

I have often run into lowered expectations and skepticism about the OI students' abilities. This is when it is necessary to get into the classroom and prove students' capabilities. The negativity usually doesn't last long. Another problem arises when OI students in inclusive environments use assistive technology (AT). Although AT often equalizes access, it can be tremendously frustrating as well. Some of the most common initial problems with inclusive OI are the general education teachers' fears of not being supported, not knowing how to interact or communicate with the student, or concerns over assistive technology use. Associated medical problems can be intimidating as well. One way to overcome these problems is through education, training, and modeling by the OI teacher.

may need to use a larger keyboard with bigger keys to correctly select the one they want. A student with a spinal cord injury may access the keyboard by using a voice recognition program in which the words appear on the screen as the student speaks into a microphone. In Natalie's case, she needed to use her augmentative communication device as a keyboard that connected to the computer in order to write.

5. **Class Participation**. Some modifications may be needed to allow a student with a physical or health disability to participate in class. It is important to determine how the student will gain the teacher's attention, especially if he is unable to raise his hand. Some students may need extra time to respond to a question in class because of motor difficulties using an augmentative communication system. Some teachers will patiently wait for the response. Others may elect to give the student some questions that will be asked the next day in class so the student can program his or her augmentative communication device with the answers. For some students, it is more appropriate to ask questions using a multiple-choice format, as described previously.

6. **Assignments and Tests**. Some students will need assignments and tests modified because of fatigue and endurance issues—either because of a health problem or because of the physical effort involved in slowly completing an assignment or a test. Assignments may need to be abbreviated or broken up into shorter segments, or students may need

Strategies for Inclusive Classrooms

A good schedule can make it or break it, so scheduling is first and foremost. Schedule your students to allow for the most support from you. This might mean manipulating everyone's schedule multiple times. It is imperative that the lines of communication between collaborating teachers be two-way. It is the responsibility of the special education teacher to communicate the specific needs of the students in the class to the general education teacher. It is not solely the general education teacher's responsibility to provide instruction. Here are some helpful hints:

Provide the general education teacher with IEP-driven modifications and strategies for success as well as emergency plans. Encourage the general education teacher to keep these strategies and plans in his or her grade book or another high-use area for quick reference.

Discuss expectations of the student and each teacher or paraprofessional supporting the student before beginning collaborative teaching.

Successful Collaboration

Successful collaboration means that the teachers have developed a good, professional working relationship and that all students have been enriched by the collaborative activities. This begins with open communication and effective planning. The structure of the class typically comes from the classroom teacher, with adaptations and individualization provided by the OI teacher. It is important, however, for both teachers to be able to switch roles and interact with all students in the class.

Working With Parents and Families

I have had the unique advantage of being on both sides: family and school system. As difficult as it might be, encourage the family to plan for the future early. Along with the parents, define realistic expectations for the students and strive to meet them. Parents know their children better than anyone. Listen to them and be sensitive to their needs. Establish how you will communicate with the parents regarding timelines, grades, progress, and parent–teacher conferences.

Advice for Making Inclusion and Collaboration Work

Transitioning into teaching in the OI classroom can be overwhelming. Teachers are always multitasking, supporting multiple students with multiple disabilities across multiple subjects in the same classroom at the same time. Trying to keep up with the pace of regular education while trying to work in extended time, technology, individualization, and physical access can be a vast undertaking. The best advice is to stay organized and stay focused on the needs of the students and on providing the best education in the most productive and appropriate learning environment possible.

—*Jennifer Tumlin Garrett, Ph.D.*
Former teacher of students with orthopedic impairments
Currently assistant professor, Georgia State University

extra time to complete assignments and tests. A student may be offered alternative ways to complete an assignment or a test, such as using a computer or telling the answers instead of writing them. Students may be unable to complete several essay questions because of the time and effort it takes to complete one question; a student with severe spastic quadriplegia cerebral palsy, for example, may take twenty minutes to type two sentences when using an alternative access mode for a computer. In these cases, the student may be given an alternative format such as multiple choice or short answer.

7. **Other Modifications.** Some students may need modifications or assistance in the areas of mobility, using the bathroom, and eating. If a party is given in class, the teacher needs to know if a student needs a special spoon or a special feeding technique. If a student needs to use the restroom, the teacher needs to know if the student cannot get onto the toilet without help. Advanced planning is necessary to determine what type of help a student needs and who will provide that help.

Specialized Instructional Strategies

Teachers need to know how to implement **specialized instructional strategies** for students with physical and health disabilities. Such strategies include using special techniques for teaching nonverbal students phonics, adapting assessment procedures, utilizing the student's reliable means of response, using alternative approaches for learning the writing process when alternative-access keyboarding is slow, and supporting chronically ill and terminally ill students. For example, when teaching students with severe speech and physical impairments to sound out a word, the special education teacher may use the Nonverbal Reading Approach (Heller & Alberto, 2010; Heller, Fredrick, Tumlin, & Brineman, 2002), which teaches the student who cannot talk to sound out the word using internal speech. Certain math algorithms that do not involve carrying a number may be advantageous for students using computers to write out their work (Heller, 2010). The special education teacher often uses these specialized approaches when teaching students with physical or health disabilities and will instruct other teachers regarding their use.

Teachers also need to know how to implement specialized strategies to prevent **communication breakdowns.** Often teachers and students who are using augmentative communication devices will have a communication breakdown—a misunderstanding or misinterpretation of what is being communicated. Heller and Bigge (2010) provide an example of a student (S) who was telling about a party at school, including the refreshments, activities, and people invited. The Boy Scout master (BSM) listened to the details and said, "You must have enjoyed that."

S: No.
BSM: You didn't?
S: No.
BSM: But you told me all about it. Did something bad happen?
S: No.
BSM: But you didn't enjoy it?
S: No.
BSM: Well, you did go, didn't you?
S: No.
BSM: You didn't! Why not? Were you somewhere else?
S: No.
BSM: Were you ill?
S: No.
BSM: I don't get it, then. (p. 272)

In this example, the student was trying to tell the Boy Scout master about a party that his class had planned, but that had not yet taken place. The Boy Scout master assumed that the party had already occurred.

Several strategies can be used to avoid a communication breakdown. The first is to be aware that you may be making an erroneous assumption that is leading to the breakdown. It is important to clarify or check each part of the information as it is being presented ("We are talking about a party?" "Yes." "At school?" "Yes." "That your class had?" "No."). Another strategy is to ask, "Am I missing something?" and then ask by categories, "Is it a person?" "A place?" "A feeling?" "A time?" and so on. It is also important to verify by asking, "Is that exactly right?" This will help ensure that you are understanding the message correctly. It is equally important that the student have a way of saying, "You are not understanding my message" (Heller & Bigge, 2010).

Specialized Expanded Curriculum Areas

The IEP team will determine the appropriate goals for a student with a physical or health disability. In some cases, a student will be on a regular academic curriculum; in others, a student with intellectual disabilities may be in a functional curriculum. In either case, students may also be taught additional curricular areas, referred to as *specialized expanded curriculum areas*. These areas often pertain to the technology they use, the adaptations they will need for independent living, and the health care they need because of their particular physical or health disability. For example, students may be taught to use their

EFFECTIVE INSTRUCTIONAL PRACTICES **Teaching Students With Physical or Health Disabilities**

Recommended Classroom Adaptations

Students with physical and health disabilities often require adaptations to accommodate their specific disabilities. This can include adaptations to the environment, instructional materials, and teaching strategies. Some effective practices are as follows:

- Make classroom adaptations to accommodate students' mobility and seating needs (e.g., widened aisles for wheelchairs, sit near side of room to see board and access computer, special desk).
- Use and properly arrange adaptations and assistive technology as determined by the special education teacher and educational team to provide access to the learning environment (e.g., slant board and stabilization of material on desk, alternative keyboard, augmentative communication device, books and worksheets scanned into the computer).
- Assist students with physical disabilities to participate as much as possible in classroom activities requiring a motor response (e.g., bring needed items to student, help student manipulate materials, partner student with peer to assist each other with task).
- Use a variety of systematic instructional strategies that effectively address the student's individual learning needs (e.g., learning strategies, content enhancement strategies, antecedent prompts, response prompts).
- Use specialized instructional strategies specifically developed for students with physical disabilities as appropriate (e.g., teach students who are nonverbal to use internal speech to decode words as in the Nonverbal Reading Approach).
- Assist students who use augmentative forms of communication to learn to use their communication devices successfully across learning and social environments during the school day. Also, allow students to answer questions using their most reliable form of communication.
- Allow more time for student to respond, take tests, or hand in assignments when oral or written communication is affected by the disability.
- Modify assignments or tests to accommodate student's disability (e.g., reduce paper tasks, break up assignments into shorter segments, alternate test or assignment format).
- Maintain a safe, healthy environment by observing for health-related problems and knowing the steps to take should a problem occur (e.g., seizure, fatigue, medication side effects).

SOURCE: Adapted from K. Heller and M. Coleman-Martin, "Classroom Adaptations for Students with Physical, Health, and Multiple Disabilities," in K. W. Heller, P. E. Forney, P. A. Alberto, S. Best, and M. N. Schwartzman (Eds.), *Understanding Physical, Health, and Multiple Disabilities,* 2nd ed. (Upper Saddle River, NJ: Pearson Education, 2009).

assistive technology and augmentative communication devices. Students who require health care procedures (such as tube feeding for nutrition) may be taught how to do the procedure themselves, along with other management issues related to the procedure (Heller & Tumlin, 2004). Independent living skills (such as cooking, cleaning, shopping, and dressing) often require adaptations, and students may be taught how to perform these tasks with the necessary modifications. Other possible specialized expanded curriculum areas include social skills, vocational skills, community skills, mobility skills, and leisure skills.

Meeting the Educational Needs of Students Who Are Deaf–Blind

Pupils who are deaf–blind frequently present a variety of instructional challenges for educators. The impact of the loss (or diminished capacity) of both vision and hearing results in significant educational needs. The consequences of this disability are much greater than simply adding up the effects of the individual sensory losses (Silberman et al., 2004). As a result, communication needs and navigation of the environment are typically the focus of attention for these students.

Individuals with deaf–blindness require highly individualized and specialized instruction, often on a one-to-one basis (Bowe, 2005). Direct teaching is also frequently required because, unlike other pupils (with and without disabilities), incidental learning is severely limited because of the loss of the distance senses of vision and hearing. Most students who are deaf–blind use their residual vision or hearing to learn. Those who totally lose vision and hearing (a minority of pupils) learn through other senses, such as the sense of touch, in which "their hands become their eyes" (Silberman et al., 2004, p. 506).

Like that for other students, the education of pupils with deaf–blindness addresses all domains of learning. Communication/language, however, is typically the priority subject for these children. "Without the ability to communicate other curriculum areas become meaningless" (Engleman et al., 1999, p. 65). Information gleaned from both formal and informal assessments is often used to establish areas of instructional emphasis as well as suggest teaching strategies (Silberman et al., 2004).

Communication

Encyclopedia Link 13.2
Read more about individuals with deaf-blindness.

Learning to communicate without the ability to hear is probably the most significant challenge that students with deaf–blindness will encounter. Yet it is also their greatest opportunity—for language opens the world to them (Alabama Institute for Deaf and Blind, 2010). Pupils who are deaf–blind vary tremendously in their communication abilities and consequently their educational needs. Recall that many of these children have some residual hearing and vision, and a few are capable of speech. In many instances, however, touch, gestures, and body movements are the primary form of communication, although some individuals will learn more complex forms of communication such as sign language. Conventional literacy skills often fail to develop in individuals with deaf–blindness, and language acquisition typically lags behind that of their peers (Engleman et al., 1999).

Because communication is critical to all activities at school, at home, and in the community, it is imperative that the pupil develop an effective and efficient system of communication. This may entail acquiring tactile means of receptive and expressive communication or developing the student's residual vision and hearing for purposes of communication. Multiple forms of communication are available to both teachers and parents. For instance, if vision is sufficient, some students who are deaf–blind will use the standard manual alphabet (see Figure 11.6, page 422). However, if the pupil's vision is inadequate, the alphabet can be traced in the palm of the individual's hand.

Some of the principal communication systems used with individuals who are deaf–blind include the following:

- Touch cues
- Object symbols
- Multiple versions of sign language
- Braille
- Fingerspelling
- Picture symbols
- Large print
- Tadoma method of speechreading
- Speechreading (Miles, 2010)

It is crucial that teachers, paraprofessionals, interpreters, **interveners**, and parents/family members incorporate as many of the communication systems as possible so that the child will have maximum access to the largest possible array of expressive and receptive modes of communication (Engleman et al., 1999). Table 13.3 presents additional information on some of these nonlinguistic communication forms.

TABLE 13.3 Representative Nonlinguistic Communication Systems

Intentional Behavior	Student is taught very deliberate actions to indicate a particular preference—an effort by the teacher to avoid confusing choice-making behavior from random movements.
Touch Cues	Minimal prompt used to convey information to a learner who is deaf–blind. Two taps on the shoulder, for example, tells the pupil to stand up.
Communication Shelves	This tactic helps bring a sense of order into the world of children with deaf–blindness. Placing items in a specific order on a shelf teaches the student that activities have a definite beginning and an end in addition to the concepts of time and sequence. Organizational skills are also aided.
Signals and Gestures	Body signs and other tactual cues indicating desired behaviors, such as reaching for or pushing away a particular object or pulling a person toward a desired location.
Sign Language	An alternative to spoken language. Multiple forms of this system are available, with American Sign Language (ASL) considered the natural language of persons who are deaf. (For additional information, revisit Chapter 11 on hearing impairments.)
Tadoma	In this mode of communication the individual places his or her thumb on the speaker's lips and his or her fingers along the jaw line, touching the speaker's cheek and throat while monitoring the particular movements and actions associated with speech.

SOURCE: Adapted from M. Engleman, H. Griffin, L. Griffin, and J. Maddox, "A Teacher's Guide to Communicating with Students with Deaf-Blindness," *Teaching Exceptional Children, 31*(5), 1999, p. 69.

As the student gains competency with nonverbal interactions, symbolic communication becomes a frequent adjunct to the student's system of communication. It is often beneficial to incorporate simple gestures or objects that serve as representations or symbols for various activities. For example, a spoon may indicate mealtime, a small rubber ball could represent recess, and a sweater might mean dismissal time. These representations help the pupil understand that one thing may represent another while also enabling the child to anticipate specific events. Reliable routines are particularly important to individuals who are deaf–blind. Consistency aids in reducing anxiety, helping the child feel secure, and increasing predictability. Unexpected or unanticipated events, such as the absence of a paraprofessional or a fire drill prior to lunch, need to be communicated as quickly as possible to minimize confusion and fearfulness (Engleman et al., 1999; Miles, 2010).

Orientation and Mobility

Being able to safely and independently navigate the environment (at school, at home, and in the community) is another major area of emphasis for individuals who are deaf–blind. Mobility training becomes a significant instructional challenge for the orientation and mobility (O&M) specialist when the student exhibits a dual sensory impairment. In some instances, a lack of motivation to explore the world coupled with difficulty in establishing an effective means of communication is but one obstacle confronting this professional. Generally speaking, the earlier the instruction begins, the greater the likelihood that the pupil will be able to successfully move about with confidence and independence.

Collaborative Efforts

It should be obvious from our discussion of these two key areas that multiple professionals are involved in the education of persons with deaf–blindness. It is not unusual to find vision teachers, O&M specialists, interpreters, physical and occupational therapists, and other professionals all working together to ensure that the individual needs of the pupil are fully met in an integrated and coordinated fashion. The needs of students with deaf–blindness far exceed the skills and knowledge of any one professional (Silberman et al., 2004). Collaboration, therefore, is imperative.

Services for Young Children With Physical Disabilities, Health Disabilities, and Related Low-Incidence Disabilities

As with school-age children, young children with physical disabilities, health disabilities, and related low-incidence disabilities typically need a collaborative approach utilizing expertise from a variety of disciplines. Professional staff such as physical therapists, occupational therapists, speech–language pathologists, special education teachers, preschool teachers, adapted physical education teachers, nurses, and physicians, as well as families, may be involved in the education of the young child with physical or health disabilities. This team of individuals will determine the major goals and objectives for the young child, including a safe and healthy environment, motor development and positioning, communication development, concept development, and early academic and functional skills.

Maintaining a safe, healthy environment involves special considerations for the young child. Young children may not understand why they have certain restrictions (such as no sweets if they have diabetes) or the exact nature of their disability (what is happening when they have a seizure, and why). The teacher needs to understand what restrictions are necessary and help the young child comply with them. Also, some young children may have the misconception that they have a particular condition because they did something bad. The teacher should be alert for such misconceptions and notify the parents.

Children with physical disabilities, multiple disabilities, and deaf–blindness often show delays or little progress in motor development—rolling over, sitting, crawling, walking, reaching for items, grasping items—and may receive the services of a physical therapist and an occupational therapist. These professionals can provide positioning suggestions and equipment, mobility devices, adaptive toys, devices for daily living (such as adapted feeding utensils and toothbrushes), and orthotics (such as leg braces). They may suggest changes in the environment to eliminate architectural barriers as they seek to integrate therapy intervention strategies into the child's daily routines (Effgen, 2005). Teachers will often integrate some of the therapy goals and objectives into the preschool classroom.

When young children with physical disabilities have communication problems, one of the major emphases of early intervention is to promote communication. It is often difficult to determine if a child will be understandable using speech or if the child will require an augmentative communication system. To encourage communication and decrease frustration, augmentative communication may be combined with speech therapy, giving the child a means of communicating while also working on speech production.

Some parents may not want their child to use augmentative communication for fear that it will hinder speech production and reduce their child's motivation to speak. Augmentative communication is never meant to replace speech, but meant to supplement it. There are no data to support the idea that augmentative or alternative communication interferes with speech production; in fact, research studies suggest just the opposite (Kaiser & Grim, 2006; Sevcik & Romski, 2010).

Because many young children with physical disabilities, health disabilities, and related low-incidence disabilities lack common experiences or the ability to manipulate common items, teachers will often need to work on concept development. Although concept development (for example, *round versus square, colors*) is typically addressed with the preschool child, even more basic concepts may need to be addressed with the child with a severe physical disability. Concepts such as "an orange is soft, not hard like a rock," or "a sponge can be squeezed" may need to be introduced. Failure to address these basic concepts can interfere with comprehension of material that will be addressed later in the school curriculum.

Children with physical disabilities, health disabilities, and related low-incidence disabilities will be participating in all or part of the preschool curriculum, and it is important that appropriate adaptations and modifications be in place. For coloring and drawing, for example, the child may need an adapted crayon or may begin using a simple drawing program on a computer. The special education teacher, with input from other members of the educational team, will assist in determining the appropriate modifications and assistive technology.

Transition Into Adulthood

As students with physical disabilities, health disabilities, and related low-incidence disabilities transition into adulthood, they often face major decisions regarding college, employment, and independent living. Hopefully, these issues have been discussed for many years with preparations made well in advance to make a smooth transition from high school to the next environment. Through the help of transition planning, legislation, technological advances, and options for support, more opportunities now exist for individuals with physical and health disabilities than ever before.

Video Link 13.10
Watch more about transitions.

With the passage of PL 101–476, each adolescent's IEP is required to include a **transition plan**. A transition plan identifies goals specific to that student aimed at meeting the student's needs after high school. Identification of transition needs and services is part of the planning process. Successful transition plans often base their programs on major life areas that will be important for adulthood. These may include daily living skills, personal–social skills, and occupational guidance and preparation (Clark, Bigge, & Best, 2010).

Career preparation should occur throughout students' school years. Some students will be preparing to go on to vocational school, community college, or university before seeking employment. Others will seek employment after finishing high school. Individuals with disabilities may use one of several vocational education service delivery programs, including secondary vocational education, secondary special needs vocational education, postsecondary vocational and technical education, apprenticeship programs, and vocational rehabilitation programs (Sitlington & Clark, 2006).

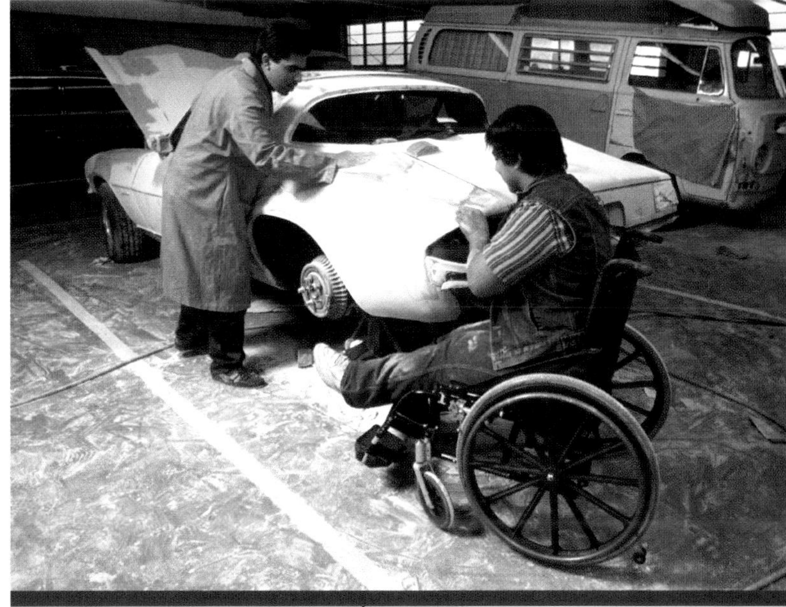

Vocational education is important for some adolescents with physical or health disabilities.

Students who are able to go to college, and who decide to do so, may find it very stressful to leave familiar surroundings and supports. However, colleges and universities typically offer services for individuals with physical and health disabilities to assist them with accommodations and accessibility issues. Other modifications, such as modified test taking or assignment adjustments, will also be addressed through these college and university services for individuals with disabilities. It is important in the high school years that students learn to be self-advocates and learn how to find and use available resources to make the appropriate accommodations.

Technology has made more jobs than ever before accessible for individuals with physical and health disabilities. Many jobs today are computer based, and individuals with severe physical and health disabilities can often work in these fields by adapting the computer to meet their specific needs. Modifications may be quite simple, such as having the keyboard placed in a different position for easy access or using a software program that provides a keyboard on the screen to be accessed with a joystick. Many other job opportunities are possible with often minor modifications. A willingness to figure out what is necessary to make a job possible and following through with appropriate modifications are critical for success.

Some individuals with physical disabilities, health disabilities, and related low-incidence disabilities who are unable to work in competitive employment may benefit from **supported (competitive) employment** or other employment models. In supported employment, the person with a disability works in the regular work setting and becomes a regular employee; however, training and continued support are necessary. A **job coach** (or job specialist) provides on-the-job assistance to the person with a disability. Often individuals who will benefit from this model have also received community-based vocational instruction during high school with a job coach. This previous training can help a student learn important job skills and also acquaints the student with a supported employment model.

Video Link 13.11
Watch more about transitions.

It is difficult to predict the employment outlook for individuals with physical disabilities, health disabilities, or related low-incidence disabilities. When the physical or health disability is mild, it may not interfere with employment opportunities. However, students with mild physical or health disabilities may have inappropriate social behaviors or poor work habits that make finding and keeping a job difficult without further training. Students who have severe physical disabilities will be unable to do many physically demanding jobs, but if they have normal cognitive functioning, they may be able to perform intellectually based jobs with the use of assistive technology. However, students with severe physical disabilities still face major barriers to employment when assistance is needed in personal skills (e.g., bathroom assistance) or there are mobility or communication difficulties. These problems, among others, contribute to a significant underemployment rate for individuals with cerebral palsy and other severe physical disabilities (Clark et al., 2010; Wehman, 2006) as well as those with deaf–blindness and multiple disabilities.

Adults With Physical Disabilities, Health Disabilities, and Related Low-Incidence Disabilities

Many adults with physical disabilities, health disabilities, and related low-incidence disabilities will make a positive transition into adulthood and be integrated into work and community environments. Their success will depend partly on community acceptance, as well as on the provision of necessary accommodations and support. With these kinds of disabilities, having appropriate medical and technological support will also be critical in ensuring a high quality of life.

Audio Link 13.2
Listen to more about long-term planning.

The impact of a physical or health disability in the adult years will vary greatly, depending on the specific impairment, its prognosis, and possible complications. Many individuals who have mild physical or health disabilities may experience only minor problems resulting from their disability. At the other extreme, individuals who have a terminal illness (Duchenne muscular dystrophy, AIDS, cystic fibrosis) may die in their early adult years, or not even survive to adulthood. Many other adults, such as those with cerebral palsy, may experience complications and multiple health issues, such as scoliosis (curvatures of the spine) and contractures, further limiting movement and mobility and resulting in pain. Multiple surgeries may be needed to address these types of musculoskeletal problems.

Some problems that occur in adults with physical disabilities can be prevented. A shocking lack of preventive medical care (general medical checkups, dental care) has been found among adults with cerebral palsy. As a result, adults with cerebral palsy are more susceptible to medical problems that could have been prevented or treated in their early stages. Providing preventive and appropriate medical care is key to adult health.

Family Issues

Families with children who have physical disabilities, health disabilities, or related low-incidence disabilities can be put under tremendous stress. Sources of stress include juggling the demands of the disability and ongoing medical treatment, dealing with uncertainties about the child's future health and independence, financial strains, lack of respite care, routine changes and disruptions, and overall exhaustion (Murphy, Christian, Caplin, & Young, 2007). For example, the young woman in our chapter opener has been to more than seventy-three doctors, therapists, and rehabilitation engineers, involving countless appointments, medications, and treatments, as well as thirteen surgeries. This is not unusual for a family that has a child with a severe physical disability.

Stress can also result from the additional care and daily activities that may need to be performed for the child. Absences from school because of illness, surgeries, and medical treatments may add stress when one of the parents needs to stay home (or in the hospital) with the child. Day to day, the child may need help with such basic tasks as eating, toileting, and obtaining desired items. Some children will require regular medical treatments at home (such as respiratory physical therapy to decrease respiratory secretions) or at a clinic (such as dialysis).

Stress may be associated with the type of physical or health impairment as well as its prognosis. Higher stress has been found in parents of children with degenerative diseases such as Duchenne muscular dystrophy than in parents of children with chronic illness such as cystic fibrosis (Barakat & Kazak, 1999). Both of these conditions are terminal, so issues of death and dying also arise. Some debilitating disabilities require extensive family support. Some families will provide lifetime care for a child with a severe physical or health disability.

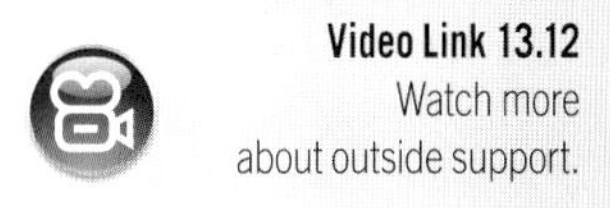

Video Link 13.12
Watch more about outside support.

Despite the added stress, most families are able to manage the demands of having a child with a physical or health disability with the child being a valued, loved, and contributing member of the family. Many factors contribute to the family's coping ability, including support from concerned others, positive family appraisal, spiritual support, advocacy, positive social interactions, education and information, parental involvement that enhances a sense of control, and consistency in the medical care of the child (Lin, 2000; Turnbull, Turnbull, Erwin, Soodak, & Shogren, 2011). Teachers can help families by being supportive, helping parents be an active part of the IEP team, and not being judgmental toward the parents.

Issues of Diversity

Physical disabilities, health disabilities, and related low-incidence disabilities occur in students from all backgrounds, cultures, and economic levels. Unlike other disabilities, such as intellectual and learning disabilities, there are no questions regarding misclassification and culture bias in identification of a physical or health disability. However, misunderstanding can result from cultural differences in how the disability is viewed and miscommunication between parents and school.

Different families cope with illness and disability in diverse ways, and some are influenced by their particular culture. For example, some Hmong view epilepsy as a sign of distinction that could qualify them for the divine office of shaman (Fadiman, 1997). More often the cultural influences are subtler.

Misunderstandings can occur between the school and family as a result of cultural differences. In one study (Geenen, Powers, & Lopez-Vasquez, 2001), for example, culturally and linguistically diverse parents described themselves as being very involved in the transition process while school officials reported far less involvement. This discrepancy can be explained by these parents' heavy involvement in talking with their children about life after high school and caring for their disability, but lack of participation in the school-based transition process. Many of these families viewed transitioning a student into adulthood as a family and community responsibility rather than an educational one. Understanding and respecting cultural differences is important to providing positive educational experiences for the student.

Technology and Individuals With Physical Disabilities, Health Disabilities, and Related Low-Incidence Disabilities

Technology encountered in the school setting can be grouped into five major categories: (1) technology productivity tools, (2) information technology, (3) instructional technology, (4) medical technology, (5) and assistive technology (Lindsey, 2008). Most students, whether they have disabilities or not, will use **technology productivity tools** (such as computers), **information technology** (such as the World Wide Web), and **instructional technology** (such as software programs teaching multiplication or map skills). In addition to these forms of technology, students with physical or health impairments will often require medical and assistive technology.

Many students with physical or health impairments require medical technology to sustain life and functionality. Medical technology devices can range from battery-powered artificial limbs that restore movement to individuals who have lost an arm or a leg to pumps that deliver medication. Other examples of medical technology are inhalers and nebulizers for individuals with asthma, glucose monitoring devices and injection systems for individuals requiring insulin, ventilators for individuals who need additional support to breathe, and gastrostomy tubes and supporting equipment for delivery of nutrition. Teachers should be knowledgeable about their students' medical technology and know what to do should a problem arise.

Assistive technology has opened doors for students with physical or health disabilities. The Technology-Related Assistance for Individuals with Disabilities Act of 1988 defines *assistive technology* as "any item, piece of equipment, or product system, whether acquired commercially off the shelf, modified or customized, that is used to increase, maintain, or improve functional capabilities of individuals with disabilities." Thus, assistive technology can range from something as simple as a bent spoon used when eating to a sophisticated computer-based augmentative communication system. Assistive technology can be divided into low-tech and high-tech categories, according to the complexity of the device. Table 13.4 gives some examples of both categories across several different activities.

Types of assistive technology commonly used by students with physical disabilities include computer assistive technology, augmentative communication, positioning and seating devices, mobility devices, assistive technology for daily living and environmental control, and assistive technology for recreation and leisure. These various types of assistive technology can greatly improve the students' functioning and be critical in providing access to school, home, community, and work environments.

Computer Assistive Technology

Students with physical or health disabilities use computers for communication, academic tasks, leisure, and socialization. Depending on the extent of the physical or health disability, a wide range of modifications can be made to the computer. These modifications typically fall into three categories: input modifications, processing aids, and output modifications (Alliance for Technology Access, 2004).

Input Modifications

Input devices provide information to the computer; standard input devices are the keyboard and mouse. For students with physical or health disabilities who have difficulty

TABLE 13.4 Examples of Low-Tech and High-Tech Assistive Technology Solutions

Activity	Low-Technology	High-Technology
Reading	• Book stand, nonslip mat • Turn pages with mouthstick or eraser tip of pencil • Ruler to help keep place on page	• Electric page turner • Software to scan book into computer to easily move through book, highlight material, or read text aloud
Writing	• Pencil with built-up grip • Wider-spaced paper • Mouthstick with pencil attached	• Computer with alternative input (switch or voice recognition)
Math	• Counter • Abacus • Money cards	• Graphing calculators • Electronic worksheet program that can correctly position the cursor for regrouping
Eating	• Spoon with built-up handle • Hand splint to hold spoon • Adaptive cup • Scoop dish	• Electric feeder • Robotic arm
Leisure	• Card holder • Bigger baseball	• Sport wheelchair • Adapted bicycle • Computer games

using these, a number of alternatives are available. Some students may need to activate the accessibility options available on most computers, such as the option to make keys not repeat when held down. Simple appliances may be placed over the standard keyboard to make it accessible. For example, some students drag their hand across the keyboard and need a keyguard (a plastic cover with holes for each key) to prevent accidentally pushing an unwanted key.

Students may use alternative keyboards that are larger, smaller, or differently configured than the standard keyboard in order to accommodate their physical impairment. Some students may use an on-screen keyboard; that is, the keyboard is displayed on the computer screen. A student may control the on-screen keyboard using any number of alternative input devices, such as a trackball, joystick, touchpad, touch monitor (directly touching the keyboard on the screen), or switch.

Some input devices do not use a keyboard at all. For example, voice recognition software enables a student to talk to the computer, which writes what is said.

Some students may use an alternative keyboard to access a computer.

Processing Aids

Once a student has a way of inputting information into the computer, there may be a problem with the speed at which the student can type. Whether the student is using a standard keyboard, using an alternative keyboard, using voice recognition software, or typing by raising an eyebrow, input may be slow. Several processing aids can increase the speed at which information is typed. One of the most common processing aids is a **word prediction program**. As a student types the first letter, the computer displays a list of words commonly used by this user that start with the letter typed. If the word is displayed, the student can type the corresponding number instead of the entire word. If the word is not displayed, the on-screen list continues to change as more letters are typed.

Output Modifications

Computers commonly have two types of output: the screen monitor and the printer. However, students with physical or health disabilities may require additional modifications. Some students may need to use speech synthesizers that allow the computer to "read aloud" what is on the screen. Others may need a larger monitor or a software program that can magnify what is on the screen. Printers can also be modified to allow for large fonts.

Augmentative Communication

Another form of assistive technology is augmentative communication, also known as augmentative or alternative communication. Augmentative communication refers to the various forms of communication that are used as a supplement or an alternative to oral language, including communication behaviors, gestures, sign language, picture symbols, the alphabet, communication devices, and computers with synthetic speech (Mirenda, 2005). Often students will use a combination of ways to communicate. The educational team will be involved in determining the most appropriate forms of augmentative communication for each individual student. (Refer to page 500 for a photo of an augmentative communication device.)

Learning to use augmentative communication is an essential part of a student's education when the student is unable to use speech effectively. Becoming proficient is critical in order to be able to make wants and needs known, communicate thoughts, participate in class activities, and socialize with others. Teachers play a vital role in teaching students to use their augmentative communication devices and supporting their use in all classroom activities. It is important that the teacher understand the forms of communication the student is using, and how they are used.

Positioning and Seating Devices

To provide access to activities, curriculum, and assistive devices, it is imperative that the student with a physical or health disability have proper positioning and seating. Position will always affect the quality and precision of a person's movement and ability to accomplish a task (Best, Reed, & Bigge, 2010). Proper positioning and seating are achieved through a wide range of special chairs and inserts that can go into a chair or wheelchair to achieve optimal positioning. Proper positioning not only helps the student move as efficiently as possible, but it can also reduce deformity and promote feelings of physical security. If students are unable to move themselves, their position may need to be changed frequently throughout the day to avoid any stiffness or pressure sores (skin breakdown from staying in one position for too long).

A student may use several different positioning devices throughout the day. Some devices may allow the student to sit a certain way, while other devices help the student lie on his or her side, stomach, or back. A prone stander may be used to support the student in a standing position. Such positioning devices may enable students to participate in activities they would not be able to do from a wheelchair, such as wash dishes at a sink while positioned in a prone stander. They can also increase muscle strength and movement, stimulate bone growth, improve circulation, and increase the movement of food through the gastrointestinal system. The physical therapist will determine the most therapeutic positions for the student and the types of devices to use to help the student achieve these positions.

Mobility Devices

Students with physical or health disabilities may use a wide range of mobility devices to move from one location to another. One of the most common devices is the wheelchair, either manual or power. Manual wheelchairs are pushed by the student (or someone else). Power wheelchairs have a motor that allows the wheelchair user to operate the chair by means of a joystick or other device. Self-operated wheelchairs can give their users tremendous independence.

Depending on the disability, a student may use the wheelchair all the time when moving about, or only when fatigued. Many people are surprised to see a student using a wheelchair one moment, then walking around the next. The type of chair and its frequency of use will depend on the student's disability.

Some students with cerebral palsy require the use of positioning equipment during the school day.

Individuals with physical disabilities use many other types of mobility devices. Some may use a power-operated scooter instead of a traditional wheelchair. A student who can stand and walk with support may use a **walker**. Others who need even less support may use canes or crutches. Older individuals may drive cars that have been modified for their use. Whichever mobility device is used, the teacher should be familiar with it and know what type of support the student needs in order to use it.

Environmental Control and Assistive Technology for Daily Living

An **environmental control unit (ECU)** is a device that allows the user to control electric appliances, telephones, and other items that use electric outlets. The device may be a stand-alone unit (that can be mounted onto a wheelchair) or be purchased as a software package that can be used with a computer or some electronic augmentative communication devices. The electrical appliances are equipped with receivers. The user then chooses an appliance (such as the TV or a room light) and what the user wants it to do (such as turn on or off) from a list on the ECU, which sends a signal to the appliance. ECUs can help students with physical or health disabilities to manipulate their surroundings independently.

Many other types of assistive technologies are available to help with daily living. Personal care items such as modified toothbrushes and hairbrushes can help the individual with a physical disability who has restricted arm and hand motion or who cannot grasp well. These items may have elongated handles, built-up handles, or Velcro straps. Modified washcloths that fit over the hand like a mitt and Velcro around the wrist may also be used.

Modifications for eating and preparing food include special cutting boards with edges and safety knives, modified dishes with one side higher than the other to help with scooping, and modified cups to help with drinking. Students who are unable to move their arms may use a mechanical feeder that scoops food onto a spoon and brings the spoon up to the mouth with the touch of a switch.

Dressing aids include special sticks with hooks on the end that can be used to pull pants and zippers up or down and devices to help put on socks when the individual cannot reach to the floor. Modified clothing, such as garments with Velcro along the seams to go over braces, can also make dressing easier.

Students with physical or health disabilities enjoy playing a variety of sports.

Assistive Technology for Play and Recreation

Numerous assistive technology devices are available for play and recreation. Children who cannot manipulate toys may have battery-operated toys they can activate by a switch. Switches may also be used to turn on and off radios or televisions. Computer games can often be accessed using joysticks or other input devices. Other types of recreational games, such as card games and board games, may require the use of a simple device to hold the cards, or a dice holder that can be knocked over to roll the dice.

Individuals with physical or health disabilities can also enjoy playing sports and engaging in physical activities. Some school systems have adapted sports teams, such as wheelchair basketball or wheelchair soccer, for students with physical disabilities. Many students with disabilities can participate in a wide variety of sports with minor modifications and assistive technology devices—for example, hitting a ball off a tee, allowing an extra swing at bat, or using a small adapted ramp that holds a bowling ball and allows the wheelchair user to push the ball down the ramp into the bowling lane. Individuals who like to exercise may be able to use adapted tricycles, bicycles, and mobility devices.

Trends, Issues, and Controversies

Three major issues in the field of physical disabilities, health disabilities, and related low-incidence disabilities are (1) assessing capabilities and needs of students with very severe physical disabilities; (2) provision of specialized technology, adaptations, and instructional strategies; and (3) selection of appropriate curriculum.

The first issue is appropriate assessment of students with severe physical disabilities in terms of cognitive functioning and evaluation of what the student has learned. When a young child cannot reliably move or speak, and is not yet using augmentative communication effectively, psychological testing can be of limited value or accuracy. We have come across twelve instances over the past decade in which young children with severe speech and physical impairments had been labeled as having severe intellectual disabilities, but whose intelligence was later determined to range from mild intellectual disabilities to giftedness. In our chapter opener, Natalie's category changed multiple times, although her intellectual capabilities remained the same. Assessment difficulties are also present for students with multiple disabilities and deaf–blindness.

Because of this difficulty, two major areas need to be addressed: finding a reliable response and providing an appropriate curriculum. While these students are learning augmentative communication, it is essential to find some **reliable means of response**—that is, a consistent, reliable way for the student to answer questions. This could be looking at the answer (eye gazing), touching the answer, hitting a switch to indicate the answer, or having the teacher move a finger across answers until the student makes a noise indicating a selection. Typically, this means that questions must be presented in a multiple choice format, at least until students have literacy skills and can type out their own responses. Having a reliable means of response makes it possible to assess what the student knows. Given the lack of experiences and inability to communicate thoughts and questions, intelligence testing may still not be accurate, even when the student has a reliable way to respond to the questions. However, it does give the teacher an accurate way of determining if the student has learned the material.

A second issue involves the provision of specialized technology, adaptations, and instructional strategies. Barriers to obtaining and using the necessary technology include funding issues, appropriate assessment, selection of devices, training to use the devices, and ongoing technical support.

The third area to consider is curriculum. Some students with physical or health disabilities will be on an academic curriculum; others will be on a more functional curriculum because of intellectual disabilities. However, when the student has severe speech and physical impairments, it may not be obvious where the student is functioning. If the student is on a functional curriculum, more advanced skills should also be taught periodically to determine if the student can learn them. For example, if the student is only introduced to pictures for communication, how do we know that the student is not capable of learning words? This concern is best summed up by Natalie's mom (B. Tumlin, personal communication, July 2001):

> A nonverbal child cannot provide her own opportunities to prove more than what is expected. When placement is based strictly on test scores and/or assumptions, quite often our kids end up living *down* to expectations, are isolated from normal interactions and experiences, and learn inappropriate behaviors to be what is "normal."

Placing students in inappropriate curriculums or teaching them less than they are capable of learning may be due to **spread** (Kirshbaum, 2000)—the overgeneralization of a disability into unrelated areas, often resulting in stereotyping. For example, people may assume that someone who uses a wheelchair has a cognitive impairment, or may react to a person who is blind by talking more loudly. It is important to interact with individuals with disabilities based on what they demonstrate, rather than on unfounded assumptions.

CHAPTER IN REVIEW

Defining Physical Disabilities, Health Disabilities, and Related Low-Incidence Disabilities

Audio Link 13.3
Listen to a chapter summary.

- Students who have physical and health disabilities comprise one of the most diverse categories of students receiving special education services.
- Depending on their disability, they may come under one of four IDEA categories: orthopedic impairments, multiple disabilities, traumatic brain injury, and other health impairments.
- Individuals with the concomitant loss of both vision and hearing are referred to as deaf–blind.

Prevalence of Physical Disabilities, Health Disabilities, and Related Low-Incidence Disabilities

- Physical and health disabilities vary widely in reported prevalence figures.
- Pupils with deaf–blindness are representative of a low-incidence disability accounting for only .02 percent of all individuals receiving a special education.
- Children with physical or health disabilities and low-incidence disabilities comprise about 15 percent of the special education population.

Etiology of Physical Disabilities, Health Disabilities, and Related Low-Incidence Disabilities

- Physical disabilities, health disabilities, and related low-incidence disabilities have many causes.
- Some of the more common etiologies can be grouped under chromosomal and genetic causes, teratogens, prematurity and complications of pregnancy, and acquired causes.

Characteristics of Individuals With Physical Disabilities, Health Disabilities, and Related Low-Incidence Disabilities

- The characteristics of individuals with physical disabilities, health disabilities, and related low-incidence disabilities depend on the specific condition and its severity.
- Individuals with such neuromotor impairments as cerebral palsy and spina bifida have impaired motor movements and often have additional disabilities associated with their condition.
- Children with degenerative diseases, such as Duchenne muscular dystrophy, have progressive loss of control to move their bodies and die early in life.
- Students with orthopedic and musculoskeletal disorders, such as juvenile rheumatoid arthritis and limb deficiencies, can have severe physical limitations.
- Individuals with multiple disabilities have a combination of disabilities, often including a physical or health impairment.
- Pupils with traumatic brain injury may have deficits across cognitive, motor, physical, health, sensory, language, social, and behavioral domains.
- Major health impairments (such as seizure disorders) and infectious diseases (such as AIDS) can affect an individual's endurance and attention.
- Students with deaf–blindness are an especially heterogeneous group of learners varying tremendously in their needs, abilities, and educational requirements.

Educational Considerations

- Educational placement of students with physical disabilities, health disabilities, and related low-incidence disabilities varies greatly.
- Physical and health disabilities vary in their impact on school performance according to the type of disability involved, the functional effects of the disability, and the psychosocial and environmental factors surrounding the disability.
- Meeting the educational needs of students with physical disabilities, health disabilities, and related low-incidence disabilities involves monitoring, modifications and adaptations, and specialized instructional strategies.

Technology and Individuals With Physical Disabilities, Health Disabilities, and Related Low-Incidence Disabilities

- Prominent is the role of medical and assistive technology. Advances in medical technology have helped individuals lead healthier lives.
- Types of assistive technology used by individuals with physical disabilities, health disabilities, and related low-incidence disabilities include computer assistive technology, augmentative communication, positioning and seating devices, mobility devices, environmental control and daily living devices, and play and recreation devices.

STUDY QUESTIONS

1. Which IDEA categories include students with a physical or health disability, and how are they defined?
2. What are the major causes of physical disabilities, health disabilities, and deaf–blindness?
3. Explain the following conditions: cerebral palsy, spina bifida, traumatic brain injury, Duchenne muscular dystrophy, limb deficiency, seizure disorders, AIDS, and deaf–blindness.
4. Explain the steps you would take if a tonic–clonic seizure occurred in your classroom.
5. How does a physical disability, health impairment, or low-incidence disability affect school performance?
6. What does it mean to maintain a safe, healthy environment?
7. What types of modifications and adaptations may need to be used in the classroom? Include seven major areas in your discussion.

8. Identify five of the principal communication systems used with pupils who are deaf–blind.
9. Describe how communication breakdowns can occur when talking with an individual using an augmentative communication device. Describe some techniques to prevent such breakdowns from occurring.
10. What are specialized instructional strategies and specialized expanded curriculum areas? Provide examples.
11. What are some stresses that occur in families that have a child with a physical or health impairment? How are these stresses different from those experienced by families with other types of disabilities?
12. What are the major types of assistive technology available to students with physical disabilities, health disabilities, or low-incidence disabilities?
13. What is augmentative communication? Does its use interfere with speech production?
14. What is "spread," and how may it affect a person with a physical or health disability?

KEY TERMS

low-incidence disabilities 487
assistive technology 488
augmentative communication 488
orthopedic impairments 488
multiple disabilities 488
traumatic brain injury 488
other health impairments 488
deaf–blind 488
CHARGE association 492
Usher syndrome 492
teratogen 493
neuromotor impairment 495
cerebral palsy 496
spastic cerebral palsy 496
athetoid cerebral palsy 496
ataxic cerebral palsy (ataxia) 496
mixed cerebral palsy 496
hemiplegia 496
diplegia 496
paraplegia 496
quadriplegia 496
orthotics 497
contractures 497
spina bifida 497
Duchenne muscular dystrophy 498
juvenile rheumatoid arthritis (JRA) 499
limb deficiency 500
seizure 504
epilepsy 504
absence seizure 504
complex partial seizure 504
tonic–clonic seizure 504
asthma 505
acquired immune deficiency syndrome (AIDS) 506
learned helplessness 512
specialized instructional strategies 517
communication breakdowns 518
interveners 520
transition plan 523
supported (competitive) employment 524
job coach 524
technology productivity tools 526
information technology 526
instructional technology 526
word prediction program 528
walker 529
environmental control unit (ECU) 529
reliable means of response 530
spread 531

LEARNING ACTIVITIES

1. Visit a website specializing in assistive technology (e.g., www.abledata.com or www.closingthegap.com). What types of assistive technology are provided on the site? Select five different assistive technology devices and describe their use, whom they are for, their price, and your overall impression of the devices.
2. Learn about your own state's disability definitions and special education certification categories. Does your state use the *orthopedic impairments, traumatic brain injury, multiple disabilities, other health impairments,* and *deaf–blind* categories? How are they defined? What types of special education certification does your state provide, and is there specialized training in physical and health disabilities?
3. Visit a school and observe students with low-incidence disabilities. What types of modifications, adaptations, and assistive technologies are being used? What are the roles of the occupational therapist, physical therapist, speech–language pathologist, nurse, special education teacher, general education teacher, student, and parents in determining modifications, adaptations, and selection of assistive technology?

4. Interview a high school student (or parent of a child) with a physical or health disability. Ask the student about his or her disability and its treatment. Ask the student what it is like to have the particular disability. Does he or she feel that it has interfered with school, activities, or making friends? What does the student think that teachers need to know about the disability?
5. Contact local chapters of organizations involved with physical and health disabilities, such as the Epilepsy Foundation of America or United Cerebral Palsy. Find out what services they provide. Obtain samples of literature they have for the public. Attend a support meeting to gain insight into some of the issues in their area of focus.

ORGANIZATIONS CONCERNED WITH PHYSICAL DISABILITIES, HEALTH DISABILITIES, OR RELATED LOW-INCIDENCE DISABILITIES

Most physical disabilities, health impairments, and low-incidence disabilities are represented by their own separate organization or support group; only a small sample of organizations is listed here. The reader is encouraged to locate organizations dealing with a specific disability by searching the World Wide Web.

Brain Injury Association of America
1608 Spring Hill Road
Suite 110
Vienna, VA 22182
(703) 761-0750
(703) 761-0755 (Fax)
http://www.biausa.org

Centers for Disease Control and Prevention
1600 Clifton Road N.E.
Atlanta, GA 30333
(800) 232-4636
(888) 232-6348 (TTY)
http://www.cdc.gov

Division for Physical and Health Disabilities, Council for Exceptional Children
1110 North Glebe Road
Suite 300
Arlington, VA 22201–5704
(888) 232-7733
(866) 915-5000 (TTY)
(703) 264-9494 (Fax)
http://www.cec.sped.org

Muscular Dystrophy Association
3300 E. Sunrise Drive
Tucson, AZ 85718
(800) 572-1717
http://www.mda.org

National Organization for Rare Disorders (NORD)
P.O. Box 1968
Danbury, CT 06813
(800) 999-6673
(203) 797-9590 (TDD)
(203) 798-2291 (Fax)
http://www.rarediseases.org

United Cerebral Palsy
1660 L Street N.W.
Suite 700
Washington, DC 20036–5602
(800) 872-5827
(202) 776-0414 (Fax)
http://www.ucp.org

REFLECTING ON STANDARDS

The following exercises are designed to help you learn to apply the Council for Exceptional Children (CEC) standards to your teaching practice. Each of the reflection exercises below correlates with a knowledge or skill within the CEC standards. For the full text of each of the related CEC standards, please refer to the standards integration grid located in Appendix B.

Focus on Learning Environments and Social Interactions ***(CEC Content Standard #5 CC5S1)***
Reflect on someone you know who has a physical disability or a related low-incidence disability. How is this person often misunderstood or treated by the general population? If you were to have a student in your class with a physical or related low-incidence disability, how might you need to educate your general education students so that your classroom is a safe, equitable, positive, and supportive learning environment?

Focus on Communication ***(CEC Content Standard #6 CC6S1)***
Reflect on what you have learned in this chapter about the educational needs of students with physical disabilities and related low-incidence disabilities. If you were to have a student with cerebral palsy in your class, what strategies might you need to implement to make sure communication with your student is clear? What assistive technologies might you need to implement?

STUDENT STUDY SITE

Visit the Student Study Site at www.sagepub.com/gargiulo4emedia for these additional learning tools:

- Video links
- Media links
- Self-quizzes
- E-flashcards
- Full-text SAGE journal articles
- Web exercises

CHAPTER 14

Learning Objectives

After reading Chapter 14 you should be able to:

- Describe various interpretations of giftedness.
- Explain the techniques typically used to assess a pupil's gifts and talents.
- Outline the history of educational services for students who are gifted and talented.
- List the characteristics of persons who are gifted and talented according to the five dimensions of giftedness.
- Summarize the various instructional strategies used by educators to teach individuals who are gifted and talented.
- Identify the service delivery options available to students with gifts and talents.
- Describe educational opportunities for young children and adolescents who are gifted and talented.
- Define twice exceptional.
- Discuss the challenges confronting girls who are gifted and talented as well as children with gifts and talents from culturally diverse backgrounds.

Individuals Who Are Gifted and Talented

IT'S ALL UP TO THE PARENT

My mom still laughs about it—knowingly laughs at my naïveté, joyfully laughs with his possibilities. At 18 months, Jake (my firstborn and only born at the time) was splashing in the tub playing "name that alphabet letter." Randomly I held up sponge letters as he giggled and shouted their names at me. But he misidentified the *I* as an *L*. When I told Mom about it, she was thrilled! I, on the other hand, explained, "But he missed one." There was silence, then laughter on the phone.

Video Link 14.1
Watch more about giftedness.

I've learned so much in the six years since then. For example, I've learned that most 18-month-olds can't speak in full sentences, much less know all the letters by name. And I've learned that most 4-year-olds can't read. In spite of all the child development books on the market and in my personal library, I've learned that gifted children are virtually ignored. Their educational, social, and emotional needs are very different from other children's, so unless the book solely deals with the gifted, it's not very beneficial. And I guess the most important thing I've learned is that, right or wrong, it's usually all up to the parent.

Academically, I have found that very few teachers understand or even recognize the gifted child. This became painfully clear to me as day after day I had to drag my first grader, my Jake, out from behind the couch forcing him to go to school. I have found that I am the one responsible to make sure he is challenged in the classroom and at home. I vividly remember the meeting I had with his teachers, then his principal. I had researched, read numerous books, prepared sample lessons, and organized the cognitive test results from an independent psychologist. I walked a fine line between concerned parent who wants the best for her child and so offers resources and suggestions—and the pushy, domineering mother who knows best. Luckily for Jake, it worked beautifully. I met with open-minded, open-hearted professionals. He

---

Written by Julia Link Roberts, Western Kentucky University

now has two very caring, understanding teachers from different grades individualizing instruction and challenging him. The couch is no longer an issue—this year.

The academic struggles Jake has battled in no way compare to the emotional issues we deal with almost daily. I see his confusion as people constantly expect more from him than other 7-year-olds because he is so bright. I see his frustration as he tries to explain some complicated make-believe game to his age peers. I see his boredom as he brings home worksheets that force him to "practice" a math skill twenty times that he knew after three. I see his hurt as he worries about the sick and misfortunate. And I see his anger over things that aren't fair.

Video Link 14.2
Meet the parent of a gifted child.

Oh, how I wish people understood! If administrators only knew that the best way to remove the learning ceiling is to cluster group by ability. If teachers only realized that gifted kids have very different academic and social needs. If they only knew how a little differentiation literally changes the life of a gifted child. (I well remember Jake's response to just the possibility of doing an independent project. He paced the floor rushing out his words about king cobras and books and where's the poster board! And I well remember the void of all expression when the teacher "didn't get around to it.") And if gifted kids only knew that there would be challenge, there would be intellectual peers who could share ideas, and there would be teachers and principals who just plain understood.

But until that happens, it seems to be up to the parent. I am the one who discovers the opportunities—The Center for Gifted Studies, the Super Saturdays enrichment classes, the summer reading programs, the independent learning. I am the advocate passing on information to the school, gifting the teacher with the latest curriculum book, serving on the School Council. And I see changes. I see how much information opens eyes. And I've seen how opened eyes facilitate change. And I am beginning to get the feeling I'm not alone.

—*Tracy Inman*

Stereotypes of children who are gifted and talented are numerous, and many people believe that they represent the truth about gifted children. Some people think that a person is not gifted unless he or she is radically accelerated or that being gifted means having few or diminished social skills. Others gather their impressions about giftedness from one or a few individuals they have known or heard about, and then they generalize about people who are gifted based on this limited information. Many of the resulting stereotypes are just that—stereotypes; they are often inaccurate or misleading when applied to students who are gifted or talented and gifted individuals in general.

Some people say that every child is gifted; if they mean all children are special, then, of course, they are right. However, they are using a different meaning of *gifted* from the one used in this chapter to describe a category of exceptional children. Other people use the term *gifted* only in connection with the arts or athletics; we often read about the gifted tennis player or the gifted violinist. As the term is used in education, however, children who are **gifted and talented** have abilities and talents that can be demonstrated or have the potential for being developed at exceptional levels. They are significantly different from age-mates in their area(s) of giftedness or talent. These children have needs that differ in some degree from those of other children.

In this chapter, we examine the concept of giftedness, the characteristics of children and young people who are gifted and talented, and the special needs created by these characteristics. We will trace the historical development of the concept of giftedness; describe trends in support, and lack of support, for addressing the needs of gifted individuals; and elaborate on strategies that can be used in schools and in other settings to develop students' maximum potential. Finally, we will explore some current issues and challenges in identifying and providing services for children who are gifted and talented.

See the accompanying Insights feature for a preview of frequently asked questions about students who are gifted and their education.

FAQs (Frequently Asked Questions) About Children and Youth Who Are Gifted and Talented

Q. Can all children become gifted?

A. From the data neurobiology is providing, it is evident that nearly all children are born with very complex and unique brain structures. Although each child is different, they all seem to have extraordinary potential. I believe that, if given the opportunity to develop optimally, most children could perform at the level we now call *gifted,* and it probably would be more natural for them to do so.

Q. Which is more important for the development of intelligence, heredity or environment?

A. Both are important, and current research recognizes that the interaction between them is complex and interdependent. At this time, few knowledgeable scientists even try to speak of one as being more important than the other.

Q. What is the biggest problem with labeling a child gifted? Would it be better to call children who are gifted by another word?

A. The word *gifted* does give an unfortunate connotation to the group of children who bear this label. People often think these children were given a gift; that is, they did nothing to earn their ability or talent. Americans tend to be suspicious of anyone who gets something for nothing. We think that people who didn't earn what they have probably do not deserve to have it, and certainly they should not have more. This line of thinking has been responsible for a lot of misunderstanding about gifted children. However, giving them a different label would still not solve the problems labeling causes. We have this label now, so perhaps the best we can do is to be sure everyone, including the child who is gifted, understands what we mean by it.

Q. Will grouping students who are gifted together result in "elitism"?

A. When this question is asked, "elitism" usually implies that the students who are gifted will become arrogant and snobbish and think they are better than other children. Research indicates that grouping gifted students together appropriately and flexibly in the areas in which they need advanced or accelerated work will not only result in their growth academically, but will give them a more realistic view of their abilities. Students who are always ahead of their classmates and do not have to study or are never challenged are in danger not only of becoming bored and dull, but of falsely assuming that they are superior to other students. Because they are never challenged, they do not learn good study skills and will have problems later as they try to pursue higher education. Arrogance can come either from unrealistic appraisal of their talent or from trying to cover up for the feeling of being different and not understanding why others continually reject them. In either case, flexible and appropriate grouping with intellectual peers will decrease that type of elitism, not increase it.

(Continued)

(Continued)

Q. Considering the focus on inclusion in the regular classroom, when is it appropriate to have special programs for students who are gifted?

A. When the material and the pacing used in the classroom are not allowing students to grow and learn, special provisions must be made. When there is no provision for students who are gifted to interact with intellectual peers, ways in which such groupings can occur must be planned. Research indicates that these are the minimum provisions that pupils who are gifted must have if they are to continue to develop and not regress, losing ability and motivation. For many students who are gifted, an appropriately individualized classroom can provide the differentiated materials and instruction needed. However, for children with gifts and talents whose pace and level of learning are significantly beyond those of their classmates, the least restrictive environment will *not* be the regular classroom. These students will need special classes and mentoring to grow and learn.

Q. Which is better for a gifted learner, acceleration or enrichment?

A. Pupils who are gifted need both acceleration and enrichment, and any gifted program should be designed to provide both. When to use each will depend on the student's needs.

Q. What is the difference between differentiation and individualization?

A. *Differentiation* for learners who are gifted is the preparation that is made for the curriculum to respond to their characteristic needs, such as allowing for a faster pace of learning and choosing themes and content that allow for more complex investigation. Individualization for children who are gifted is the process of adapting that curriculum to the needs and interests of a particular student. A program for gifted learners requires both to be really successful.

Q. Are most gifted children hyperactive?

A. Most children with gifts and talents have high levels of energy; they require less sleep, and they are very, very curious. These traits can look like hyperactivity, but there is a difference. The energy of a child who is gifted is focused, directed, and intense. The energy of a hyperactive child is diffuse, random, and sporadic. Gifted children can attend to an activity of their interest for long periods of time; hyperactive children cannot. The brighter the child, the more the energy may look excessive.

Q. Why do some teachers, principals, and other school personnel seem to have negative attitudes toward gifted students?

A. Unfortunately, studies show that this is too often true. Children who are gifted do not fit easily into the structure of most schools and classrooms. Because they can be two to four years ahead of the curriculum offered at any grade level, they make it very hard for a teacher of twenty to thirty other children to find appropriate curricular experiences for them. They often question and seek more information about ideas than the teacher is prepared to give. This can be seen as a challenge to the teacher's authority. They may refuse to do work that they consider boring or to repeat or practice lessons if they already understand the material. In a classroom where everyone is expected to do much the same work and cover the same material, this can be seen as a real problem. Pupils who are gifted can be demanding, challenging, intense, critical, oversensitive, highly verbal, and physically active, and they can devour material rapidly. None of these traits are problems in themselves, but they can present real problems for teachers who are not prepared to meet these needs. Some teachers do not know what to do with these youngsters and feel incompetent and threatened by them. For administrators, children who are gifted present needs for special services. This may be perceived as pressure on an already tight budget or cause special arrangements to be made that seem unnecessary. Fortunately, these attitudes often can be changed with in-service in gifted education.

Q. Do culturally diverse students require a separate curriculum?

A. If the instruction is individualized and the curriculum is differentiated, a separate curriculum is not necessary. What is important, however, is that the teacher and others involved in gifted programs in which cultural diversity exists hold positive attitudes toward cultural differences, that they be aware of cultural and ethnic history and traditions, that lots of resources related to diverse populations be made available, and that the program be flexible and responsive to each child's needs.

SOURCE: Adapted from B. Clark, *Growing Up Gifted,* 7th ed., © 2008. Adapted by permission of Pearson Education, Inc., Upper Saddle River, NJ.

Defining Giftedness: Refining the Meaning

During the early twentieth century, the public equated giftedness with high intelligence. Terman (1925), for instance, considered individuals gifted if they had an IQ greater than 140—the top 1 percent of the population. The connection between high intelligence and giftedness remains with us today. However, this restrictive view of giftedness has been expanded to include other dimensions and categories.

The first national report on gifted education, known as the Marland Report, offered the following definition, specifying six categories of giftedness (Marland, 1972, p. 10):

> Gifted and talented children are those identified by professionally qualified persons who by virtue of outstanding abilities are capable of high performance. These are children who require differentiated educational programs and/or services beyond those normally provided by the regular school program in order to realize their contribution to self and society.
>
> Children capable of high performance include those with demonstrated achievement and/or potential ability in any of the following areas: (1) general intellectual ability, (2) specific academic aptitude, (3) creative or productive thinking, (4) leadership ability, (5) visual and performing arts, and (6) psychomotor ability.

Many states have essentially adopted this definition, with the exception of psychomotor ability. Although individuals do demonstrate giftedness in psychomotor ability, the category has been removed because the development of athletic ability is generously funded in other ways.

The second national report on gifted education, *National Excellence: A Case for Developing America's Talent* (Ross, 1993), uses the term *talent* rather than *gifted:* "Children and youth with outstanding talent perform or show the potential for performing at remarkably high levels of accomplishment when compared with others of their age, experience, or environment" (p. 3). Like the Marland Report, it notes that "outstanding talent" can be evidenced in general intellectual ability, specific academic ability, creative thinking, leadership ability, and/or the visual and performing arts. At the same time, it stresses that "outstanding talents are present in children and youth from all cultural groups, across all economic strata, and in all areas of human endeavor" (p. 3). The recommendations contained in *National Excellence* provide a blueprint for states to use in expanding their definitions of children who are gifted and talented.

Renzulli (1978, 1998) has proposed a "Three-Ring" model of giftedness, represented visually as three intersecting circles (see Figure 14.1, page 542). Giftedness comprises three traits: creativity, above-average intellectual abilities, and task commitment. The focus of this model is on endeavors and activities that demonstrate giftedness; some examples of these behavioral manifestations are listed in Table 14.1 (page 543).

Piirto (2007) provides a definition of giftedness that applies to school settings. In this context, the gifted population includes

> those individuals who, by way of learning characteristics such as superior memory, observational powers, curiosity, creativity, and the ability to learn school-related subject matters rapidly and accurately with a minimum of drill and repetition, have a right to an education that is differentiated according to these characteristics because all children have a right to be educated according to their needs. (p. 37)

Giftedness manifests itself in many different ways.

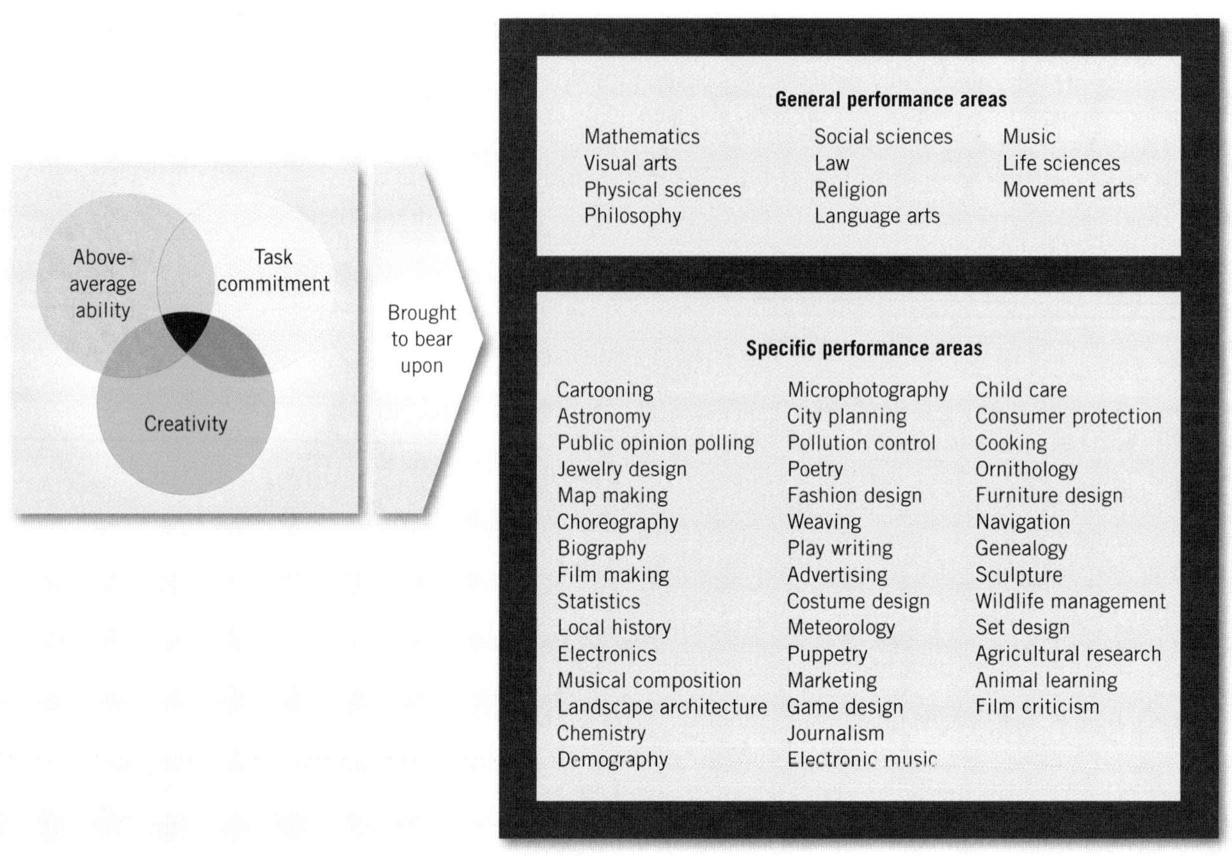

FIGURE 14.1 Renzulli's "Three-Ring" Definition of Giftedness

SOURCE: Adapted from J. Renzulli, "What Makes Giftedness? Reexamining a Definition," *Phi Delta Kappan,* 60, 1978, p. 184.

These children can be observed early, and their education should be planned to address their needs from preschool through college. Piirto also presents a model of talent development (see Figure 14.2, page 544) "in circular (not linear) form to indicate that the giftedness construct is not lines and angles, but a sphere, a circle, which enfolds all kinds of talent" (p. 37).

As you can see, definitions of gifted have evolved from an exclusive focus on high intelligence to a range of categories and indicators of talent. Identifying giftedness and talent in specific categories highlights the need for services to be customized to the individual's area(s) of identified strength(s). Identifying areas of giftedness is essential in order to match services and learning opportunities to need. Fairness is not offering the same educational opportunities to all children of the same age; rather, it is providing learning opportunities matched with needs, interests, and abilities.

Some examples may help. Jimmy was outstanding in many areas. He was so good at science that teachers encouraged him to become a physician or a research scientist; he was such an outstanding writer that his English teachers thought he was bound to be a journalist; he was also a talented musician and could have pursued a career in music. Jimmy was intellectually gifted, gifted in specific academic areas, and talented in the performing arts. Chin Lan was very talented in math and science and should have been identified as gifted in those specific academic areas; in other academic areas, she was ready for the academic challenges provided for others her age. Luis, who performed at grade level in academic subjects, was charismatic and had the ability to get others to do what

TABLE 14.1 Illustrations of Gifted Behavior as Portrayed by Renzulli's "Three-Ring" Model

Above Average Ability (general)	• High levels of abstract thought • Adaptation to novel situations • Rapid and accurate retrieval of information
Above Average Ability (specific)	• Applications of general abilities to specific area of knowledge • Capacity to sort out relevant from irrelevant information • Capacity to acquire and use advanced knowledge and strategies while pursuing a problem
Task Commitment	• Capacity for high levels of interest, enthusiasm • Hard work and determination in a particular area • Self-confidence and drive to achieve • Ability to identify significant problems within an area of study • Setting high standards for one's work
Creativity	• Fluency, flexibility, and originality of thought • Open to new experiences and ideas • Curious • Willing to take risks • Sensitive to aesthetic characteristics

SOURCE: J. Renzulli and S. Reis, *The Schoolwide Enrichment Model*, 2nd ed. (Mansfield Center, CT: Creative Learning Press, 1997), p. 9.

he wanted; he was gifted in leadership and needed opportunities to develop his skills as a leader. Albert was very creative; his teachers saw his ideas as pushing the limits. Gifted in creative thinking, he was also academically talented in English and social studies. Sara was an outstanding musician and took advantage of opportunities to develop her musical talents. All of these students were recognized as gifted and/or talented, but each one was unique. Each pupil needed services to allow him or her to make continuous progress in his or her area of strength.

Following are some important features of giftedness and talent, as used in this chapter and applied in school settings:

- Each state establishes its own definition of children and young people who are gifted and talented. Although there are similarities, it is important to know the definition in the state where you live and/or work.
- In states in which gifted children constitute a category of exceptionality, laws governing exceptional children also apply to children and young people who are gifted and talented.
- Being specific about the area of giftedness will make it possible to offer appropriate services and educational opportunities to allow continuous progress to be made in each category of talent or giftedness. Being specific also facilitates communication as you describe a young person as being gifted in mathematics, gifted in leadership, or intellectually gifted.
- Using giftedness and talent interchangeably will allow for concentration on the performance or potential for performance at levels that are exceptional in comparison with those of others of the same age, environment, or experience.
- Giftedness and talent will be found in children from all ethnic and racial groups and from all socioeconomic levels. Giftedness is also found among children with disabilities and English language learners.

gifted individuals often are considered valuable resources to be cultivated. During less tumultuous times, however, their value among the public diminishes, producing a roller-coaster effect.

In 1961, Virgil Ward coined the term *differential education* to describe a curriculum that would enable gifted students to learn at appropriate levels. In *Educating the Gifted: An Axiomatic Approach,* Ward set forth guidelines for writing such a curriculum. Although the curriculum does not need to be entirely different for academically talented students, it must be tied to their characteristics in order to enhance learning. It should be different in ways that encourage learning by young people who are ready to learn at more complex levels that would not be appealing to all students. By highlighting the need to design curriculum to address the needs of academically talented youth—a concept introduced decades earlier by Hollingworth—Ward's work provides a foundation for differentiating the curriculum in defensible ways.

The 1972 Marland Report, mentioned earlier, documented the lack of recognition of the needs of children who are gifted and talented. More than half the personnel in the schools surveyed responded that they had no gifted children in their districts, and twenty-one states reported no services for gifted students. This report, and materials appended to it, noted that the societal and personal costs of not providing services to this population of exceptional children are high. The Marland definition of giftedness (page 541) broadened the view of giftedness from one based strictly on IQ to one encompassing six areas of outstanding or potentially outstanding performance.

The passage of Public Law 94–142, the Education for All Handicapped Children Act, in 1975 led to an increased interest in and awareness of individual differences and exceptionalities. PL 94–142, however, was a missed opportunity for gifted children, as there is no national mandate to serve them. Mandates to provide services for children and youth who are gifted or talented are the result of state rather than federal legislation.

The 1980s and 1990s: The Field Matures and Provides Focus for School Reform

Building on Guilford's multifaceted view of intelligence, Howard Gardner and Robert Sternberg advanced their own theories of multiple intelligences in the 1980s. Gardner (1983) originally identified seven intelligences—linguistic, logical–mathematical, spatial, bodily–kinesthetic, musical, interpersonal, and intrapersonal (see Table 14.2). Describing these intelligences as relatively independent of one another, he later added naturalistic as an eighth intelligence (Gardner, 1993). Sternberg (1985) presented a triarchic view of "successful intelligence," encompassing practical, creative, and executive intelligences. Using these models, the field of gifted education has expanded its understanding of intelligence while not abandoning IQ as a criterion for identifying intellectually gifted children.

A Nation at Risk (National Commission on Excellence in Education, 1983) described the state of education in U.S. schools as abysmal. The report made a connection between the education of children who are gifted and our country's future. This commission found that 50 percent of the school-age gifted population was not performing to full potential and that mathematics and science were in deplorable condition in the schools. The message in this report percolated across the country and was responsible for a renewed interest in gifted education as well as in massive education reform that occurred nationally and state by state.

The Jacob K. Javits Gifted and Talented Students Education Act (PL 100–297) was passed in 1988. The Javits Act states that "gifted and talented students are a national resource vital to the future of the Nation and its security and well-being" [Sec. 8032 (a) (2)]. This legislation provided for the Office of Gifted and Talented Education, a national research center focusing on gifted children, and demonstration projects in gifted education. In the early nineties, *National Excellence: A Case for Developing America's Talent* (Ross, 1993), the second national report on gifted children, was issued by the Office

TABLE 14.2 Gardner's Multiple Intelligences

Intelligence	Characteristics	Possible Career Choices	Examples
Linguistic	Ability to use language effectively in written and oral expression; highly developed verbal skills; often think in words	Novelist, lecturer, lawyer, playwright	Ernest Hemingway, Martin Luther King, Jr.
Logical–mathematical	Ability to use calculation to assist with deductive and inductive reasoning; good at seeing patterns and relationships; think abstractly and conceptually; tend to be logical and systematic	Mathematician, physicist	Albert Einstein, Stephen Hawking
Spatial	Ability to manipulate spatial configurations; good at pattern recognition, sensitive to shape, form, and space; think in pictures or images	Architect, sculptor, interior decorator, engineer	I. M. Pei, Michelangelo
Bodily–kinesthetic	Ability to control and skillfully use one's body to perform a task or express feelings and ideas; able to communicate through body language; keen athletic ability	Dancer, athlete, surgeon	Mikhail Baryshnikov, Michael Jordan
Musical	Ability to discriminate pitch; sensitivity to rhythm, texture, and timbre; ability to hear themes; production of music through performance or composition	Musician, composer	Leonard Bernstein, Ludwig van Beethoven
Interpersonal	Ability to understand other individuals—their actions, moods, and motivations—and to act accordingly; sensitive to ideas and feelings of others, empathetic	Counselor, teacher, politician, salesperson	Carl Rogers, Nelson Mandela
Intrapersonal	Ability to understand one's own feelings, values, and motivations; self-reflective, inwardly motivated; insightful and self-disciplined	Therapist, religious leader	Sigmund Freud, Mother Teresa
Naturalist	Ability to understand interrelationships; capacity to discriminate and classify, recognizes patterns and characteristics; evidences a concern for the environment, sensitive to natural phenomena	Conservationist, forester	John Audubon, Charles Darwin

SOURCE: Adapted from N. Colangelo and G. Davis (Eds.), *Handbook of Gifted Education,* 3rd ed. (Boston: Allyn and Bacon, 2003), p. 102. Adapted by permission.

of Educational Research and Improvement in the U.S. Department of Education. The National Research Center on the Gifted and Talented continues to generate research that is used by school, district, state, and national decision makers as they design and implement policy and enact legislation. The demonstration projects have focused on developing talents in areas with a large percentage of children who have been underrepresented in gifted services. The Javits legislation, reauthorized in 2001 as part of the No Child Left Behind Act (PL 107–110), was funded at $11.14 million in fiscal year 2004; it was expanded to include grants to individual states to build an infrastructure in gifted education. Congress approved an appropriation of approximately $7.6 million for the Javits program in fiscal year 2008.

Myths and Truths About Gifted Students

Common Myths About Gifted Students

- Gifted students are a homogeneous group, all high achievers.
- Gifted students do not need help. If they are really gifted, they can manage on their own.
- Gifted students have fewer problems than others because their intelligence and abilities somehow exempt them from the hassles of daily life.
- The future of a gifted student is assured; a world of opportunities lies before the student.
- Gifted students are self-directed; they know where they are heading.
- The social and emotional development of the gifted student is at the same level as his or her intellectual development.
- Gifted students are nerds and social isolates.
- The primary value of the gifted student lies in his or her brain power.
- The gifted student's family always prizes his or her abilities.
- Gifted students need to serve as examples to others, and they should always assume extra responsibility.
- Gifted students make everyone else smarter.
- Gifted students can accomplish anything they put their minds to; all they have to do is apply themselves.
- Gifted students are naturally creative and do not need encouragement.
- Gifted children are easy to raise and a welcome addition to any classroom.

Truths About Gifted Students

- Gifted students are often perfectionistic and idealistic. They may equate achievement and grades with self-esteem and self-worth, which sometimes leads to fear of failure and interferes with achievement.
- Gifted students may experience heightened sensitivity to their own expectations and those of others, resulting in guilt over achievements or grades perceived to be low.
- Gifted students are asynchronous. Their chronological age [and] social, physical, emotional, and intellectual development may all be at different levels. For example, a 5-year-old may be able to read and comprehend a third-grade book but may not be able to write legibly.
- Some gifted children are "mappers" (sequential learners), while others are "leapers" (spatial learners). Leapers may not know how they got a "right answer." Mappers may get lost in the steps leading to the right answer.
- Gifted students may be so far ahead of their chronological age mates that they know more than half the curriculum before the school year begins! Their boredom can result in low achievement and grades.
- Gifted children are problem solvers. They benefit from working on open-ended, interdisciplinary problems—for example, how to solve a shortage of community resources. Gifted students often refuse to work for grades alone.
- Gifted students often think abstractly and with such complexity that they may need help with concrete study and test-taking skills. They may not be able to select one answer in a multiple choice question because they see how all the answers might be correct.
- Gifted students who do well in school may define success as getting an "A" and failure as any grade less than an "A." By early adolescence they may be unwilling to try anything where they are not certain of guaranteed success.

SOURCE: ERIC Clearinghouse on Disabilities and Gifted Education. Retrieved February 22, 2010, from http://eric.hoagiesgifted.org/fact/myths.html

Original source material: S. Berger, *College Planning for Gifted Students,* 2nd ed. (Reston, VA: Council for Exceptional Children, 1998), p. 16.

Suggestions for the Classroom

Differentiated Programming: What It Is and What It Isn't

Differentiated programming and *differentiated instruction* are terms for what is really a simple educational concept—providing instruction that meets the differing needs of all students. Although the concept is simple, making it a reality in the classroom is complex. For the student who is gifted, it means the opportunity to advance as far as possible. For a slower learner, it means offering support for advancement at a pace that allows for mastery. Other students have varying abilities, learning styles, interests, and needs, which also must be met. This is what differentiated programming attempts to do.

Differentiated instruction is:

- ☑ Having high expectations for all students.
- ☑ Providing multiple assignments within units that are oriented toward students with different levels of achievement.
- ☑ Allowing students to choose, with teacher direction, ways to learn and how to demonstrate what they have learned.
- ☑ Permitting students to demonstrate mastery of material they already know and progress at their own pace through new material.
- ☑ Structuring class assignments so they require high levels of critical thinking but permit a range of responses.
- ☑ Assigning some activities geared to different learning styles, levels of thinking, levels of interest, and levels of achievement.
- ☑ Providing students with opportunities to have choices about what they learn.
- ☑ Flexible. Teachers may move students in and out of groups after assessing their instructional needs.

Differentiated instruction is not:

- ☑ Individualization. It isn't a different lesson plan for each student each day.
- ☑ Giving all students the same work most of the time.
- ☑ Students spending significant amounts of time teaching material they have mastered to others who have not mastered it.
- ☑ Assigning more work at the same level to high-achieving students.
- ☑ All the time. Often, it is preferable for students to work as a whole class.
- ☑ Grouping students into cooperative learning groups that do not provide for individual accountability or do not focus on work that is new to all students.
- ☑ Using only the differences in student responses to the same class assignment to provide differentiation.
- ☑ Limited to acceleration. Teachers are encouraged to use a variety of strategies.

SOURCE: Susan Allan, unpublished manuscript.

Instructional Strategies

Curriculum Compacting

Curriculum compacting is a differentiation strategy that is often used in the general education classroom (Reis & Renzulli, 2005). Simply stated, **curriculum compacting** is an

Educators often use a variety of instructional strategies to meet the unique needs of pupils who are gifted and talented.

instructional procedure whereby the time spent on academic subjects is telescoped or reduced so as to allow the student(s) to make continuous progress. The first phase is to determine the goals and objectives of the regular curriculum. The second step in the process is to assess what the student or students already know before teaching a unit of study. If the preassessment indicates that one or more pupils have already mastered the content or a major portion thereof, this student or cluster of students will have time to delve into the content at a more complex level and to develop different and perhaps more sophisticated products. Curriculum compacting is a strategy that responds well to the characteristics of children who are gifted and talented intellectually, in specific academic areas, or in the visual and performing arts. Language arts and mathematics are two content areas where curriculum compacting has been shown to be effective (Reis et al., 2003). See the accompanying First Person feature for teaching suggestions from an award-winning educator (page 560).

Higher-Level Thinking and Problem Solving

Leaders of business and industry have told educators for decades that it is very important for students to develop higher-level thinking and problem-solving skills. When all teachers combine higher-level thinking skills with significant content, all children will thrive. Children who are gifted and talented will be ready for higher-level thinking and problem solving before many of their age-mates. Services provided by a teacher of gifted pupils can complement the teaching of thinking by the general educator. A gifted resource teacher can provide opportunities for individual and team projects that require higher-level thinking.

Flexible Grouping

The one-room school is a well-known example of **flexible grouping**. A 9-year-old child could spell with 13-year-olds but do math with 7-year-olds, if those groupings matched his or her level of achievement. Preassessment provides a defensible rationale for grouping and regrouping children to allow for continuous progress. Grouping by interests, needs, and abilities can be used within a heterogeneous classroom, in a homogeneous classroom, or between classrooms or teams. Flexible grouping is necessary if all children, including those who are gifted and talented, are to thrive in a classroom and make continuous progress.

Cluster Grouping

Cluster grouping is the practice of placing five or more students who have similar needs and abilities with one teacher. For example, seven fourth-grade students who are gifted in mathematics are placed together in a classroom. The purpose of cluster grouping is twofold. First, from a practical standpoint, a teacher is far more likely to plan instruction to address needs for more advanced content and a faster pace of instruction with a cluster than with a single student. Second, others who have similar needs and interests provide an intellectual peer group as well as age-mates for the students in the cluster.

Cluster grouping has advantages for both students and teachers. For the students who are gifted and talented, the cluster arrangement promotes challenging cognitive and positive social–emotional development. For teachers, the cluster provides a group for which to plan rather than single students sprinkled among all of the teachers.

Grouping students into clusters must be done before the school year begins. Consequently, the decision to cluster group must involve the individual responsible for class scheduling.

Tiered Assignments

This instructional strategy allows the teacher to offer variations of the same lesson to children with differing levels of ability. As an example, if the class is reading *Charlotte's Web,* one group of students (Tier 1) might be working on key information about the plot while Tier 2 might be asked to write a story that makes a change in the plot or in the development of a character. Pupils who are gifted and in Tier 3 might be asked to write their own chapter from the point of view of one of the characters. **Tiered assignments** allow for matching instruction to level of readiness.

Problem-Based Learning

The application of critical thinking skills and the development of problem-solving abilities along with the acquisition of knowledge are some of the benefits associated with using **problem-based learning** in the classroom. In this model, students are confronted with authentic, real-world situations, such as global warming, that are "ill-structured problems." The pupils are asked to solve the problem, which typically has multiple solutions rather than a "right answer." Teachers function as tutors and facilitators as the children work through various solutions and scenarios and evaluate their responses. Sometimes teachers model effective problem-solving strategies by thinking out loud and questioning their own hypotheses and recommendations. Pupils are often highly motivated and very engaged in their own learning (Smith, Polloway, Patton, & Dowdy, 2008).

Pacing Instruction

Individuals who are gifted and talented learn at a faster pace in their area of talent or special interest than their age-mates. This faster pace provides the rationale for differentiation strategies. *Prisoners of Time* (National Education Commission on Time and Learning, 1994) reports, "Some students take three to six times longer than others to learn the same thing. . . . Under today's practices, high-ability students are forced to spend more time than they need on a curriculum developed for students of moderate ability. Many become bored, unmotivated, and frustrated. They become prisoners of time" (p. 15).

Because children who are gifted and talented often complete their work in a fraction of the time that it takes their age-mates, teachers often provide more work to keep them busy. This practice is contrary to the needs of those children who can complete the assignment rapidly. The need for accelerated pacing must be linked with increasingly complex content and challenging learning experiences rather than more work at the same level.

Creativity

Creativity is important for all children. According to Clark (2008), it is "a highly complex human ability that is beyond giftedness and can bring forth that which is new, diverse, advanced, complex, or previously unknown, so that humankind can experience growth in life as fuller, richer, and/or more meaningful" (p. 188). Developing creative thinking skills is an especially important element of services for children who are gifted and talented. E. Paul Torrance (1969) describes four skills that are essential for a creative thinker: originality, fluency, flexibility, and elaboration. Originality is the ability to produce novel ideas. Fluency involves the ability to generate many ideas, and flexibility is the ability to switch categories of ideas. Elaboration is the ability to provide detail to

First Person: Patrice
One Size Does Not Fit All

Video Link 14.6
Watch more about supporting gifted students.

How might a classroom involved in the inclusion of gifted students look? Please take a glimpse into my Primary 1 (kindergarten) classroom, Room 21, for a moment, for inclusion is what you will see.

All of the children are working in math centers. Brandy and Alison are using random number generators (dice) to create simple addition sentences. Once they have generated two numbers to write down, they add the numbers together for the sum, and as all good mathematicians do, they double-check their work. At the same time, Lane and Shelby are busy using the random number generators to do double-digit addition. They squeal when they realize that their sum actually took them above 100. Sam and Megan are well above the regular addition process. They have stepped into the world of multiplication. They are using the random number generators and teddy bear counters to create groups representing multiplication. The entire room is a buzz of mathematical vocabulary and a celebration of learning . . . music to any teacher's ears. My journey to inclusion of the gifted student within my classroom was a result of realizing that I was not meeting the needs of my students.

As a seventeen-year teaching veteran, I have taught Grades K–6. Throughout those years, I have worn many hats. For a two-year period I was the curriculum coordinator for our building. I had the pleasant task of formally assessing students as a part of a verification process of our primary talent pool process. Bright-eyed primary students sat eagerly across from me amazing me with their high-ability thought processes. Each time a tiny student answered a question that was well above the typical/average level of learning for a primary student, I always asked, "Where did you learn about multiplication . . . square root . . . such difficult words to read?" The response was *always* the same: "My mom" or "My dad." I was saddened to never hear, "My teacher." When I returned to the classroom, I became determined to be in on the fun of removing the ceiling of learning for my students. When one of my students amazes everyone by sharing something brilliant, I am hoping she or he will be able to share, "My teacher taught me that!"

As our children walk through the door of our classrooms we must ever be cognizant of the fact that "one size does not fit all." Every classroom, without exception, is a classroom of diverse learners. Through a variety of means, teachers have the ability to orchestrate a classroom so that all needs can and will be met. The most important information a teacher must know before teaching all children includes what *each* of the children know, what they need to know, how they are able to apply what they have learned, and what kind of connection each child has made to his or her own world.

Before every thematic unit in our kindergarten classroom, the children help prepare a KWL (sometimes a KWHL) chart. *K* stands for "What do we know, or think we know, about this subject?" The *W* represents "What would we like to learn about this subject?" And the *L* is a follow-up for "What have we learned about this subject?" We also have a category for *H*, "How will we find out what we want to know?" The KWL chart is a good way for me to get a pulse of the class's knowledge and interest concerning the content I plan to present. I am able to use the information from the children to divide them into interest groups or to determine if the content needs to be modified in any way for particular students. The KWL is simply one form of preassessment used in our classroom on a regular basis. As the teacher, I simply must know ***what*** my children know. If a student or group of students is already equipped with the information I want to teach and I "plow ahead" with that unit without adjustments, then I have committed a grave injustice to my students. I have asked them to be patient as I teach the other students. As adults we are outraged when we are asked to sit still and listen to something we already know forward and backward. Our children are the same. When we teach content that a child has mastered, we are asking her or him to run in one spot over and over, much like a cartoon character that never seems to get anywhere.

Children not only come to us at different levels; they learn at different paces. Once you know what the children know individually, you must monitor progress through formative assessments. If a child has mastered a concept, he or she should be able to move on. If a child knows how to do simple addition with 100 percent accuracy, he or she should not be put through the nightmarish experience of extra work in simple addition. That child is ready to move on, not run in place! Math is one area in which I enjoy using the compacting process. For that quick learner, once I find out where he or she is, we move forward. The result of the pretesting is a learning atmosphere such as I described earlier. The overall assessment process is simply described. The pretest is the map for instruction. The formative tests are the detours. The posttesting is the determination of how successful we are in finding the final destination.

Literacy in a classroom should be individualized as much as math. In my classroom each child has his or her own word ring and reading assignments made on a weekly basis. Monitoring the word ring and reading progress at school enables the children to make continuous progress no matter what the reading level of each child may be. I love encouraging the children to go home and "impress" their parents or some other grown-up at home. When discussion of what they are learning is encouraged, the children are more prone to make school–learning connections transfer to home–learning connections. Parents are certainly vital participants in their child's education. But as the teacher, you will be looked upon as the one who should set the pace. We should be ever mindful that the pace for a child means continuous learning.

Textbooks are wonderful resources for teachers, but they are certainly no substitute for allowing children to think for themselves. I love to have the children use questioning . . . questioning of everything. I especially enjoy setting the stage for learning with a variety of materials centered on certain content and then turning the children loose on creating their own questions. Creativity, problem solving, and real-world learning become the products of such an environment.

Imagine the absolute misery Einstein would feel today sitting in a typical primary classroom. Sitting through simple addition would be torture for him! Every classroom today has the potential of having an Einstein in it. We must make it our duty and responsibility to meet the needs of the Einsteins of the future.

—*Patrice McCrary*
Cumberland Trace Elementary School
Warren County, KY
2003 Kentucky Teacher of the Year
2006 All-USA Teacher Team
2008 Kentucky Teacher Hall of Fame

ideas. All teachers should incorporate the teaching of creative thinking skills as an integral part of their curriculum.

Students who are gifted in creativity need opportunities to develop this talent in a risk-free learning environment (Piirto, 2007). They need to interact with creative adults, speculating on possibilities and examining the creative process as well as creative products. Pupils who are gifted thrive when given opportunities to combine their creativity with an interest in a content or talent area.

As educators, our goal should be to develop each child's gifts and talents to their fullest degree.

There is no one "correct" way to teach students who are gifted and talented. Teachers must skillfully match the needs of the pupil with the demands of the curriculum. Effective teaching of learners who are gifted and talented, as with other students, requires planning. It is a matter of constructing a "goodness of fit" between the individual's learning style and the specific content of the curriculum. As educators, our goal should be to develop each pupil's gifts and talents to their fullest degree. The accompanying Effective Instructional Practices feature offers suggestions for teaching students who are gifted (page 564).

Service Delivery Options

Pupils with gifts and talents require exposure to a curriculum that is rigorous and intellectually challenging. These students need instruction that is more complex and abstract than that provided to their typical peers (Burns, Purcell, & Hertberg, 2006). In many instances, this necessitates programming options outside of the general education classroom. The general education classroom, as traditionally

Making Inclusion Work

I am still somewhat of a rookie in the field of education. I taught eighth-grade language arts for three years. Although I loved that position and learned so much from it, I recently decided to take on a new challenge—the position of countywide gifted and talented teacher/coordinator. Throughout my career I have attended a wide variety of workshops related to teaching writing, reading across the curriculum, differentiated educational strategies, gender-based instruction, and gifted education. I have served as a model teacher for beginning teachers, and with my new position as gifted teacher/coordinator, I give workshops across the county about the selection process for children who are gifted and talented and strategies for differentiation and acceleration that can be used with all students. I work with four elementary schools and one high school, collaborating with teachers on service plans for students who are gifted and talented. Soon I will be teaching four days a week during which children in Grades 3–8 who are gifted and talented from across the county will come to my classroom and work in a resource room setting.

Strategies for Inclusive Classrooms

Based on my teaching experience, I believe that the key to effective instruction centers on two key ingredients—relationships with students and the belief that *every* child has strengths. I set high expectations for all my students. When I plan units, I try to begin with some sort of preassessment to find out what my students already know about the content that I am about to present. Based on the results, I can then adjust my activities to fit the needs of each of my students. Various preassessments that I have used include the following:

- Brainstorming: Students list questions that they have pertaining to that topic.
- KW Charts: Students chart what they already know, what they want to know about a topic, and how they want to learn it.
- Anticipation Guides: Students are given a list of statements that relate to the concepts that will be covered during the unit. They read each statement, put a check mark next to the ones with which they agree, engage in discussions about their answers, use the text and other materials for the chapter to either prove or disprove their answers, and finally review the statements and change them as necessary to make them true. The entire class debates the evidence that proves the statements and must come to consensus about each one.
- Most Difficult First: Students are presented with the most difficult vocabulary words from our list, and those who score 80 percent or better on a definition pretest are assigned another activity.

The beauty of each of these strategies is that each one can be used with any content area. Once I have diagnosed the situation, I can then decide which activities my students should complete.

I have found that cluster grouping is a highly effective strategy with students of all ability levels. In my opinion, the most positive outcome of this strategy is that the students who are gifted can excel to their fullest potential when presented with problem-solving activities, yet they don't feel burdened by the lack of motivation sometimes evidenced by their classmates. Additionally, those students who may lack academic confidence gain confidence in their abilities because they find that without someone else to carry the load, they can do it . . . and they usually do! It's a win–win situation for everyone.

Obviously, based on the repeated success of the differentiated projects, I would highly recommend them to all teachers at any grade level and ability level. In planning for these types of projects, I first reflect on the particular learning styles that exist in my classroom, choose a project type to fit each one, and then develop scoring criteria for each project choice. For example, for visual learners I might choose to include a poster option; for bodily–kinesthetic learners, I might choose a role play; for those who are verbally gifted, I might choose a newspaper article; and for those who are more intrapersonal in nature, I might choose creation of a webpage that requires individual work. Of course, with each new unit, I adjust the project choices accordingly because I don't want my students to become bored or accustomed to the same types of choices. I have never had a student complain about doing the projects—honestly! They much prefer them to tests, and so do I. In my opinion, these types of projects are true assessments of what students have learned because they tend to gravitate toward the choices that favor their own particular learning style, and consequently, they do well because they can show me what they know in the way that they know best. I have found that the products my students present to me provide me with an effective tool for building relationships with them because they have the freedom to demonstrate their understanding in a way that is completely unique to them.

Finally, my experience with independent studies has proven to be successful. I have found that allowing students to choose their topic to demonstrate a particular skill is very beneficial because they have the freedom to study something that is meaningful to them. Also, the types of products that they create will be specific to their own particular ability levels.

Successful Collaboration

My teaching experience has taught me one very important lesson . . . collaboration is crucial! Due to scheduling problems with planning time, our school cannot plan units by cross-curricular teams (including math, science, language arts, and social studies). However, during my first three years of teaching, I was fortunate enough to work very closely with another language arts teacher who had the same philosophy about teaching and learning that I did. We both believed that all students can learn, and we both were passionate about offering them challenges that expanded their minds and were enjoyable and fostered creativity in the process. We collaborated daily and often fed off one another in our planning of units. Once we were comfortable with one another, we decided to approach the eighth-grade social studies teacher and plan some activities that extended the students' learning of social studies concepts while in language arts class. Perhaps our most successful language arts–social studies collaboration resulted when we planned to read the Revolutionary War novel *My Brother Sam Is Dead* as the students were studying the Revolutionary War. The students loved it, and so did we! As we read the novel, I actually called upon the students to clarify some questions I had periodically, based on what they had learned previously about the war. It's a very gratifying experience to see students begin to make connections from one subject to another. When they master this skill, they are truly demonstrating higher-level thinking skills. My heart smiled as I listened to both my students who are gifted or talented and those with lower ability rattle off war facts without even blinking. Again, setting high expectations for everyone in the room paid huge dividends because students of varying levels gained confidence in their academic abilities.

Working With Parents and Families

While collaboration with other teachers has been beneficial for me, close contact with parents and families is also important. In fact, in some cases, it has saved me. I have had several students who were obviously gifted, yet they were unmotivated and were underperforming academically. When I realized that these students were underachieving, my first inclination was to contact the parents to ask for suggestions concerning tapping into their child's interests. I realized that if I could tweak assignments to cater to the children's areas of interest, they would be much more likely to get involved and have an appropriate learning experience. The line of communication was beneficial both ways, however. Making parents aware of the situation also gave them the chance to ask me for suggestions about ways to inspire their children at home. Although I have had many students who rose to every occasion and performed to the absolute best of their ability, I have had just as many who were less than excited about school because of sheer boredom and complacency. Those individuals definitely require more work, but inspiring them is worth all of the effort—for the student, the parent, and the teacher.

Advice for Making Inclusion and Collaboration Work

When students who are gifted or talented are involved, open-mindedness and flexibility are critical in making inclusion and collaboration work. I believe that the key to success in these situations is to appreciate each student for what he or she can offer the class. It is the teacher's responsibility to know each student's strengths and needs and to continuously assess his or her progress in order to promote academic growth. Modifying activities to fit students' needs, regardless of their ability level, is critical in providing appropriate learning experiences. Although I have always respected my students with gifts and talents, I have tried very hard to let all of my other pupils know that I value them just as much and to convey the message that everyone can learn something from someone else. I believe this philosophy creates an atmosphere of community, and when everyone cares about and helps everyone else, it's a truly productive, magical learning environment.

—*Erin DeHaven*
Breckinridge County Middle School, Breckinridge, KY
Gifted and Talented Teacher/Gifted Coordinator

EFFECTIVE INSTRUCTIONAL PRACTICES **Differentiated Instruction**

The goal of schools must be to create, support, and encourage lifelong learning. The most likely way to achieve that goal is differentiation, an instructional strategy that is a popular topic for educators to discuss but is less frequently implemented. Because all fourth or eighth graders, however, are not at the same level of achievement in any content area and their interests differ greatly, differentiation is very important. It is the strategy that is most likely to ensure continuous progress of all children, including those who are gifted and talented.

Effective instruction for learners with gifts and talents involves five steps:

Step 1. Preassess.

Once you have planned the unit of study, the starting point in planning differentiation must be to preassess.

Guiding Question: "Who already knows the content and can demonstrate the skills even before the unit of study begins?"

Step 2. Group children for instructional purposes.

Preassessment results provide information to help you decide which students can be clustered for instructional purposes for a particular unit of study. Grouping facilitates learning, providing the vehicle for differentiating learning experiences.

Guiding Question: "Which students are ready to learn the content at the same level and would benefit from being grouped for instruction?"

Step 3. Match learner experiences to the preassessment data (level of achievement, interests).

Differentiation does not just mean providing different learning experiences or offering choice; rather, differentiation is the intentional match of content (basic to complex), process (level of cognitive skill), and product (visual, written, oral, kinesthetic, and technological).

Guiding Question: "How can the learning experiences be shaped to match the preassessment results and to ensure intellectual stimulation?"

Step 4. Provide products (ways to demonstrate what has been learned) that will motivate and teach.

A variety of products can be used that will allow students to show what they have learned but in ways that will motivate them to learn.

Guiding Question: "What products will interest students and prepare them to build expertise for current and future use?"

Step 5. Reflect, reflect, reflect.

Learning experiences that remain isolated do not promote lifelong learning. If learning is to be ongoing, reflecting on what has been learned and what one wants to learn next is essential.

Guiding Question: "What questions will promote reflection and ongoing learning?"

organized in terms of curriculum and instruction, is seen as inadequate for meeting the needs of pupils who are gifted and talented (Clark, 2008). Silverman (1995b) believes that too many children who are gifted are "languishing in the regular classroom" (p. 220) because they are exposed to a curriculum that is too simple and was mastered long ago. The general education classroom is, in many cases, an exceedingly restrictive placement for pupils with special talents and gifts, rather than a least restrictive setting (Gallagher, 2003). As a result, many schools provide a range or continuum of service delivery options designed to meet the unique needs of students who are gifted. Figure 14.6 portrays an array of programming alternatives appropriate for gifted learners from elementary to high school.

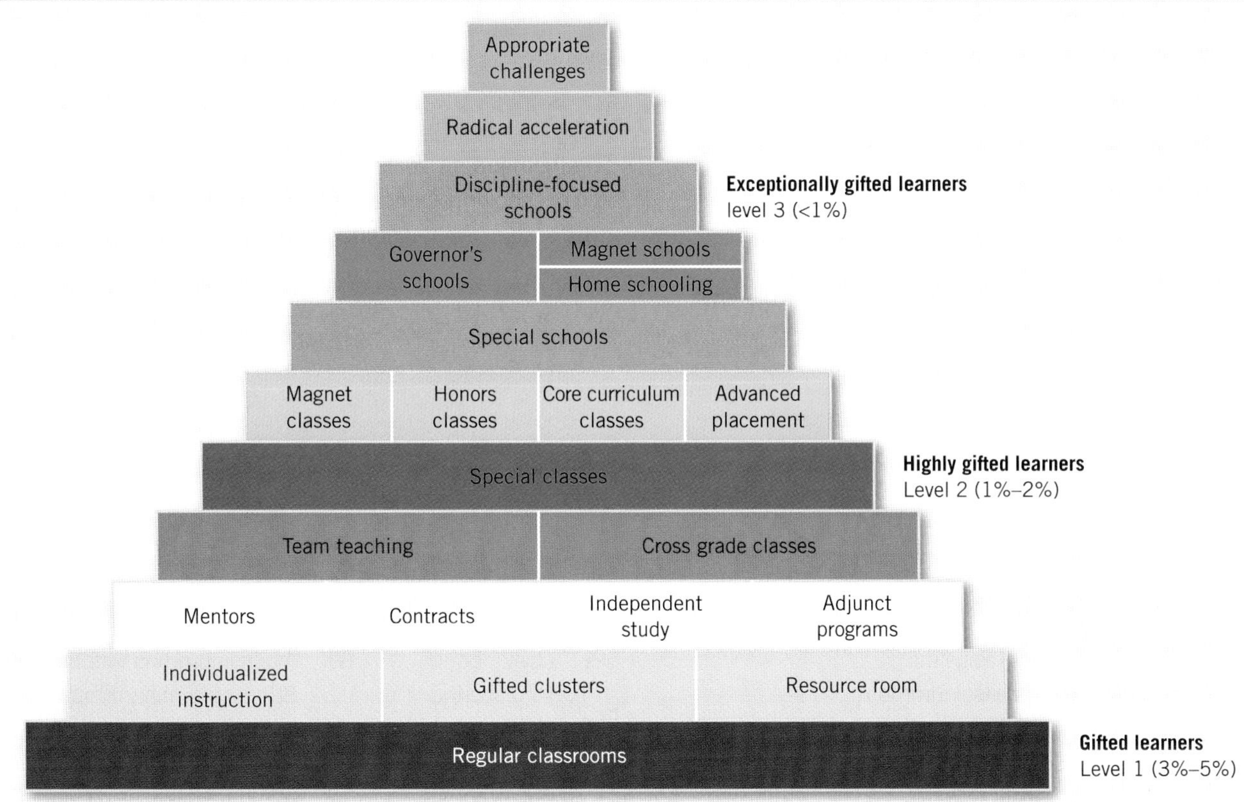

FIGURE 14.6 Levels of Programming Options for Gifted Learners

NOTE: All programs for gifted learners, regardless of how they are structured, must provide differentiation, flexible grouping, continuous progress, intellectual peer interaction, continuity, and teachers with specialized education.

SOURCE: Adapted from B. Clark, *Growing Up Gifted,* 7th ed. (Upper Saddle River, NJ: Pearson Education, 2008), p. 405. Reprinted by permission of Pearson Education.

Gifted Resource Services

Children identified in any area of giftedness or talent need some time with others who share their interests and abilities. Working with other children of similar abilities takes away the feeling that many children who are gifted have that they must hide their abilities in order to "fit in." This service is typically provided through a resource room or pull-out program. Such a program can be the highlight of the students' day or week. It is important that classroom teachers see the time with the gifted resource teacher as an important service but not the only one needed by these children. Children who are gifted and talented are gifted all day, all week; they need ongoing instruction that will remove the learning ceiling and allow for continuous progress. Table 14.4 (page 566) lists some of the advantages and disadvantages of a resource room model.

Acceleration

The child who is achieving above grade level and is ready to learn at increasingly advanced levels needs **acceleration**. Acceleration matches learning opportunities to the readiness of the student to learn at challenging levels. Researchers have found several beneficial outcomes for acceleration (Colangelo, Assouline, & Gross, 2004; Kulik, 2003). Among these positive outcomes are greater academic achievement, increased interest in school, and enhanced self-concept. Contrary to the worries of some parents

TABLE 14.4 Advantages and Disadvantages: The Resource Room and Pull-Out Models

Advantages	Disadvantages
1. Pull-out programs are relatively easy to set in motion.	1. Costs more as extra teachers have to be hired and special facilities provided.
2. The teacher in the regular classroom has more time to work with the other students.	2. The regular classroom teacher may get frustrated and feel that students leaving is a disruption to their educational plan.
3. Students who are left in classroom have a chance to shine.	3. Students in the regular classroom may feel resentful.
4. The teacher in the pull-out program can focus on critical and creative thinking because the teacher in the regular classroom focuses on the standard curriculum.	4. The academically talented students might have to make up work in the regular classroom while having more work in the pull-out classroom.
5. The differentiation of curriculum is separated from the classroom flow.	5. Curriculum may have no relationship to curriculum in the regular classroom.
6. Students receive special help in areas of strength.	6. Students are treated differently according to ability.
7. Teachers may feel as if they have "their" kids.	7. Teachers are isolated from the other teachers.
8. Students can have time with other students to discuss intellectual interests that may not be shared by students in the regular classroom.	8. Students may feel different from the rest of the students in their regular classroom.
9. Collaboration with other teachers is encouraged.	9. Students are academically talented all the time and not just during pull-out time.
10. Small groups of students can do special projects that would not be possible in the regular classroom.	10. Small groups of students may receive special privileges other students don't receive (e.g., access to computers, field trips).
11. Teachers of the talented can provide intensive instruction in areas of expertise (e.g., the arts, foreign language).	11. Turf issues with regular classroom teacher may arise (e.g., homework, lessons and assemblies missed).

SOURCE: J. Piirto, *Talented Children and Adults,* 3rd ed. (Waco, TX: Prufrock, 2007), p. 87.

and administrators, when properly implemented, acceleration does not contribute to social and emotional problems (Swiatek, 1993).

Acceleration may take several forms. Acceleration may focus on one content area, such as art or mathematics, or it may be a full-year acceleration known as grade skipping. It may also mean starting school at a younger age. Children who are reading when they come to school need to continue to improve their reading skills and to enhance their comprehension. Reading may be accelerated in the class with a cluster of children who are also early readers, or the child/children may join the first grade for the portion of the day devoted to reading. The skipping of a grade will usually be successful if the child wants to do it and if the receiving teacher wants the situation to work well. Acceleration includes taking high school classes while in middle school or taking College Board Advanced Placement classes throughout high school. It may involve taking advanced courses on the Internet or by correspondence. It may also include early entrance into college.

Besides acceleration, teachers have several other techniques at their disposal for modifying the curriculum in an effort to meet the needs of students with gifts and talents. Examples of these strategies can be found in Table 14.5. A variety of strategies and service options need to be in place in classrooms and schools to address the wide range of gifted learners' needs.

TABLE 14.5 Strategies for Addressing the Needs of Advanced Learners

Types	Focus of Opportunities	Examples
Enrichment	Opportunities to learn above and beyond what is usually provided at a particular grade level	• In-depth study • Junior Great Books • Competitions • Problem-solving programs • Interdisciplinary seminars • Project-based learning
Acceleration	Opportunities to learn at a pace that matches achievement and interest	• Subject acceleration • Early entrance (kindergarten or college) • Grade acceleration
Differentiation	Opportunities to have curriculum matched to levels of interest and achievement	• Tiered assignments based on content, process, and product
Grouping	Opportunities to learn with others at the same levels of interest and/or achievement	• Cluster grouping • Pull-out homogeneous classes • Magnet schools with a focus on math, science, or the arts

Independent Study

Independent study allows children of all ages to explore topics of interest and provides challenge if appropriate guidelines are established. These guidelines would include use of primary sources and resources that are matched to the child's level of reading and knowledge of the topic. This strategy enables the child to pose questions about topics of interest and to extend learning to related topics if he or she has demonstrated in a preassessment that he or she has mastered the core content. Independent study is a positive option for children, including those who are gifted and talented, only if they are taught to work independently. Because children are gifted does not mean that they have had the experiences that prepare them to take responsibility for their own learning. The skills needed to conduct primary research and to work independently must be taught. Once the young person refines these skills, independent study can provide alternative learning experiences that will allow the student to tap an area of interest and pursue it in depth.

Honors and Advanced Placement Courses

Honors and Advanced Placement classes are appropriate for young people who are ready to learn at advanced levels. Honors courses are offered to middle and high school students who are ready to work hard on advanced content. College Board Advanced Placement (AP) classes are available in approximately thirty different academic areas. Although the AP class is taken at the high school, a score of 3 or higher on the AP exam will earn three or more college credits at most institutions. AP classes may be taken by young people who demonstrate their readiness to learn at the college level no matter their year in school. Only local school policy restricts the grade at which a student is eligible to take AP classes.

Mentorships

"Most mentorships involving the gifted and talented are one-on-one, the relationship most supportive for providing specialized, individual attention to a protégé's development"

(Clasen & Clasen, 2003, p. 255). The **mentor** and young person share an interest, making the relationship important to both parties. A mentor may be an older student or an adult with similar interests, a professional, or an artist.

Mentorships are important for young people when pursuing passionate interests and for exploring careers. Working with a mentor can open doors to opportunities. Some mentors will communicate via technology. Some may be in a university, a laboratory, or an office. Mentorships may be formal or informal. They may be set up for a specific period of time, or they may be ongoing. Successful mentorships allow serious learners opportunities to pursue ideas in depth.

Self-Contained Classes and Special Schools

Learning with others who share their interests and have similar abilities is essential for children and youth who are gifted and talented. A self-contained class of students who are intellectually gifted provides a learning environment in which many of them will thrive. Special schools are found in many urban school districts. These magnet programs for middle and high school students typically focus on math and science or the visual and performing arts. Several states sponsor residential high schools that are academies for mathematics and science and/or the visual and performing arts.

Summer and Saturday Programs

Summer and Saturday programs should challenge young people to learn at high levels and provide opportunities to get to know others who share their interests and have similar abilities. Such programs are offered at colleges and universities as well as by some school districts. The academic content should take students beyond age-level expectations and content. National and state associations for gifted education can be a good source of information on summer and Saturday programs. The accompanying First Person feature offers one adolescent's perspective on a summer camp experience.

First Person: Graham Summer Programming

After much counting down, the long awaited end of the school year is finally here. The anxiously awaited three months of relaxation have arrived. For most gifted kids, this is a time for complete shutdown and withdrawal. They could spend hours sitting in the mind-numbing aura of a television or sleep for twelve hours a day. For some gifted kids, summer is recuperation from the harsh school year they just survived. But for others, myself included, summer is when the long anticipated summer camp takes place. Instead of shutting down and withdrawing, we are stimulated and placed in an environment where gifted kids have no problem "socializing." New information is absorbed, and the brain is kept awake and active. Things some gifted kids miss out on in the school year are presented in large quantities. Things like a caring mentor, an inspiring role model, or just a decent learning environment. Self-esteem skyrockets, and gifted kids begin to understand themselves more, by being around others like them. For me, summer programs were life changing. I gained assertiveness, self-confidence, and self-respect. I learned that I was not alone in the world. I learned that there were many other kids going through the same things I did each school day. I found out that I did, in fact, have the potential to do many things that I never knew I could, such as be popular among my peers, be accepted as who I am, and be known as something more than just "the smart kid."

—*Graham Oliver*
Paducah, KY
Ninth Grade

Competitions

Competitions do not constitute gifted education, but they do provide motivation and challenge for some young people who are gifted and talented. Just as athletes have both individual and team sports, some competitions are for individuals, others for pairs of children, and still others for teams. Information about a few competitions can be obtained from the websites listed at the end of the chapter, but there are many other competitions targeting a variety of interests and academic areas. *Competitions for Talented Kids* (Karnes & Riley, 2005) provides important information about competitions.

Services for Young Children Who Are Gifted and Talented

The educational needs of young children with special gifts and talents have largely been overlooked (Piirto, 2007). Among the reasons are a lack of federal legislation guaranteeing these children an education, difficulties in identifying this unique population of learners, problems in constructing developmentally appropriate educational experiences, and an inconsistent commitment to serving the nation's brightest and most advanced preschoolers.

Early identification is essential to meeting the needs of these youngsters. Parents and other adult caregivers are especially astute at recognizing talents and gifts. More often than not, when parents suspect that their son or daughter is gifted, follow-up assessments support the parents' beliefs (Robinson, Shore, & Enersen, 2007). Table 14.6 lists some of the characteristics typical of young children who are talented.

Despite the early evidence of gifts and talents, children are frequently not identified as gifted and talented until the third or fourth grade. In fact, professionals disagree about the appropriateness of early identification of young children with gifts and talents.

TABLE 14.6 Characteristics of Young Talented Children

1. They are precocious, regardless of the talent area. Some may demonstrate precocious behaviors in several talent areas.
    a. Verbally talented children acquire vocabulary and speak in sentences earlier than age-mates. They can break letter codes and make abstract verbal connections.
    b. Mathematically talented children acquire numeration and number concepts sooner than age-mates.
    c. Musically talented children may often sing on key, demonstrate an interest in the piano or other musical instruments, and stop what they are doing to listen to music.
    d. Children talented in visual arts demonstrate artwork that is similar to that of older children.
    e. Kinesthetically or psychomotor-talented children demonstrate advanced motor ability.
    f. Spatially talented children may want to take things apart to see how they work, and demonstrate an understanding of mechanics that is advanced for their age.
    g. Children talented in the inter- and intrapersonal areas will demonstrate advanced understanding of social relationships, and demonstrate emotion about such things that age-mates will not perceive.
2. They have excellent memories.
3. They concentrate intensely on what interests them, for longer periods of time than age-mates.
4. Dyssynchrony [uneven development] is obvious, especially in high-IQ children.
5. Affective precocity may lead to the assumption of leadership roles and to preferring older companions for play.

SOURCE: J. Piirto, *Talented Children and Adults,* 3rd ed. (Waco, TX: Prufrock Press, 2007), p. 225.

Early identification is crucial for meeting the needs of young children who are gifted and talented.

Critics of early programming argue that young children are rushed through their childhood. Supporters feel that there is a moral imperative to identify these youngsters and offer them challenging and stimulating opportunities to develop their unique abilities and gifts (Smutny, Walker, & Meckstroth, 2007). One common proposal is early admission to kindergarten or first grade. Howley, Howley, and Pendarvis (1995) consider this suggestion to be pedagogically sound and essential to the development of the child's gifts. When making such a decision, however, parents and educators need to carefully consider the individual's physical and emotional maturity so that an appropriate educational experience can be designed. Preschoolers who evidence gifts in one area, such as artistic talent, may be quite average in their verbal skills and social ability. Parents and professionals must be sensitive to this variability and be careful not to develop unrealistic expectations of advanced ability in all areas of development.

Early school experiences for academically talented pupils must be both enriching and accelerated. The primary concern, however, should always be the child, with his or her special abilities second (Piirto, 2007). Play, which is the "work" of a child, must be a critical component of any curriculum. The curriculum must be balanced and address all areas of development while reflecting the interests of the child. Finger painting and block building are just as important as counting and matching rhyming words.

Adolescents and Adults Who Are Gifted and Talented

Video Link 14.7
Watch more about future goals.

Adolescence is a time of awkwardness for most young people, and adolescents who are gifted and talented are no exception. At a time in life when differences can be a liability, adolescents with gifts and talents need opportunities to be with others who share their interests and have similar abilities in order to know that their needs, interests, passions, and characteristics are "normal" for them. Csikszentmihalyi, Rathunde, and Whalen (1997) conducted a longitudinal study of two hundred talented teenagers. They found some definite differences between talented teenagers and other adolescents. They describe the talented teens as having "personality attributes well suited to the difficult struggle of establishing their mastery over a domain: a desire to achieve, persistence, and a curiosity and openness to experience" (p. 82). Although we know that stereotyping adolescents who are gifted as misfits is not supported by research, "it must be understood that there are unique stresses and dynamic issues associated with a person's giftedness" (Robinson et al., 2007, p. 15).

Early adolescence is a challenging time for all young people, and middle school students who are gifted often feel pressure to "fit in." Middle schoolers who are gifted in any of the categories need challenging opportunities to make continuous progress in their talent areas and to share high-level learning experiences with others who are equally interested in this area. In reality, a lack of appropriately challenging instruction frequently leads to apathy and disengagement from the teaching and learning process (Tomlinson, 1994). Girls of middle school age frequently learn to compete "with boys" or "for boys"; these choices can profoundly affect their later choices. By the time young people enter high school, they set their course of study by the choices they make, selecting or avoiding the most rigorous courses. They also begin to consider and make career choices. Early adolescence is often a particularly complicated and difficult time for students with gifts and talents.

One of the key questions confronting professionals is how best to meet the educational needs of young people who are gifted and talented. Educators disagree as to which pedagogical strategy is best. Among the instructional options available to adolescents and young adults are enrolling in Advanced Placement (AP) classes, high school honors classes, or Saturday programs; seeking early admission to college; and attending a **magnet high school** (a secondary school with a particular focus such as science, mathematics, or the performing arts). Despite the general availability of these services, a fairly large portion of high school dropouts (estimated between 18 and 25 percent) are gifted (Davis, Rimm, & Siegle, 2011). We can only speculate that these students are unfulfilled and not academically challenged. Perhaps the lack of support services, the absence of a caring mentor, and the need to be accepted by peers interact to contribute to this phenomenon. For those individuals with gifts and talents who pursue postsecondary education, many colleges and universities offer a variety of honors classes and other opportunities for accelerated and in-depth study and investigation.

One well-known outlet for adults who are gifted is Mensa. Primarily a social organization, this international group consists of individuals who have an IQ in the top 2 percent of the general population. Mensa has approximately fifty thousand U.S. members who come from all walks of life but share one common trait—high intelligence (Mensa, 2010).

Family Issues

A synthesis of research evidence paints a picture of some of the characteristics of families who have children who are gifted (see Table 14.7). Families exert a powerful influence on any child, but especially on a child who is gifted (Subotnik, Kassan, Summers, & Wasser, 1993). If parents believe, Clark (2008) writes, that "their child has special ability, they will hold different expectancies [and] allow more opportunities to develop this ability" (pp. 65–66). Family support is vital if ability is to translate into achievement and accomplishment.

Video Link 14.8
Watch more about family.

TABLE 14.7 Characteristics of Families of Children Who Are Gifted
Few children in family
Gifted child oldest or only child
Early stimulation and enrichment given to children, including reading to them, encouraging language development, and exposure to a variety of experiences (e.g., museums, exhibits, and visual and performing arts)
Parents older and better educated than typical parents
Parents show high energy and love of learning
Strong work ethic and valuing of achievement modeled by parents
Parents set clear standards that are flexible and fairly administered
Parents respect the rights and dignity of children
All members of the family are encouraged to develop to the highest level of their ability as individuals
Family relationships and parent–child interactions are healthy
Parents and children share work, learning, and play
Parents involved in school-related activities

SOURCE: B. Clark, *Growing Up Gifted,* 6th ed. (Upper Saddle River, NJ: Prentice Hall, 2002), p. 152. Reprinted by permission.

Parents play a critical role in their son's or daughter's classroom performance. In a classic study of twelve thousand high school students over a four-year period, Steinberg (1996) found that parents and peers exerted the greatest influence on the young person's academic performance, greater than the teacher or the student's IQ score. Steinberg emphasizes the importance of parents' setting a priority on academic excellence.

Providing opportunities beyond school to develop talents or to further study in areas of interest can be expensive but critical to the student's future. Parents must understand how important it is for their children to find intellectual peers. It is well worth the time and resources that it takes to have the child who is interested in the violin play with a youth orchestra or the young person who is interested in any number of academic pursuits to drive to the nearest university to participate in a Saturday program. These experiences are often turning points that validate the need to work hard in order to achieve at high levels.

Parents may benefit from reading about children who are gifted and their needs. Parents can also benefit from joining state and national associations that advocate for gifted education. They need to know their legal rights and the regulations affecting gifted education in their state and local school system (Karnes, Stephens, & McHard, 2008). Parents need information about due process procedures if they believe that their child is not being provided with appropriate services and is not being challenged to learn at appropriately high levels.

Issues of Diversity

Children who are gifted and talented come from all socioeconomic, racial, and ethnic groups. A concern among educators is to be certain that children from all backgrounds are afforded quality educational opportunities that allow for gifts and talents to emerge and to ensure that students from diverse backgrounds receive appropriate services to develop their talents to optimal levels. A challenge to teachers is to become talent developers so that all pupils are able to demonstrate their special talents and gifts. Despite the best efforts of professionals, three particular dimensions of diversity remain issues today: (1) gifted and talented students with disabilities, (2) girls who are gifted and talented, and (3) the assessment and identification of gifts and talents in pupils from culturally and linguistically diverse populations.

Students With Gifts and Talents and Disabilities

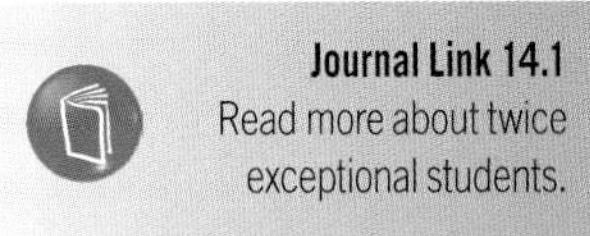

Journal Link 14.1
Read more about twice exceptional students.

Only recently have educators devoted attention to individuals with gifts and talents who also have a disability. All too often, the gifts and talents of these students are overlooked, and services are focused on the disability. It is tragic that people with disabilities are seldom thought of as possessing gifts and talents (Davis et al., 2011)—most likely because of biases, prejudices, and stereotypic expectations that prevent us from seeing their strengths. Yet think, for example, of the following eminent individuals who, although disabled, are truly gifted and talented in their respective fields of endeavor: Stephen Hawking, theoretical physicist (amyotrophic lateral sclerosis [ALS], also known as Lou Gehrig's disease); Franklin D. Roosevelt, U.S. President (polio); Helen Keller, author and social activist (dual sensory impaired); and Ray Charles, musician (visually impaired). In each of these instances, the individual's accomplishments overshadow his or her disability. Children who are gifted and disabled require programming aimed at remediating the deficit(s) caused by the disability and accommodations that minimize its impact, as well as opportunities that nurture and develop their gifts and talents to the fullest potential (Clark, 2008).

A student may have two (or more) disabilities. These **twice exceptional** learners often experience "double jeopardy." A child who is identified as gifted may also have a learning disability, a behavior disorder, a sensory impairment, a physical disability, or attention deficit hyperactivity disorder (ADHD). The challenge confronting professionals is to make a diagnosis that is appropriate. This can be a difficult task because one exceptionality may mask another or the characteristics of the two exceptionalities may be similar. For example, the pupil who has a learning disability but is intellectually gifted will likely perform at an average level, thereby camouflaging the need for gifted services as well as the need for services due to a learning disability. Another frequent problem is thinking that a child has ADHD when in actuality the child is gifted and exhibiting high energy and intense curiosity. "Gifted children with ADHD are usually labeled as underachieving or lazy long before they are ever labeled as ADHD" (Flint, 2001, p. 65). Knowing the characteristics of children who are gifted and talented in any category is the key to recognizing behaviors that reveal gifts and talents in children with and without other exceptionalities.

A great deal of attention is currently being directed to pupils who are gifted and talented and also learning disabled, a population that is frequently misunderstood. In many cases, these students are not receiving the services that would allow for the full expression of their potential. In too many instances, their disability masks their gifts and talents, or their giftedness allows them to compensate and achieve at or near grade level so their learning disability goes undetected; either way, these unique learners are not being appropriately served. Robinson et al. (2007) and King (2005) argue persuasively that these pupils require intervention specially tailored to their needs.

Children who are twice exceptional are sometimes referred to as *paradoxical learners*. Gifted students who are learning disabled exhibit characteristics such as distractibility, inattentiveness, and inefficient learning strategies while, at the same time, presenting patterns typical of students who are gifted. How can teachers best meet the needs of these children? Do we teach to their learning disability, their giftedness, or both? According to Weinfeld, Barnes-Robinson, Jeweler, and Shevitz (2005), students who have both gifts and learning disabilities require an intervention program that nurtures their gifts and talents while accommodating for learning weaknesses. Baum, Rizza, and Renzulli (2006) also recommend teaching to the gifts while providing strategies that compensate for the disability. Effective instructional programming for these pupils thus requires a blending of instructional practices, such as cognitive training coupled with differentiated programming or curriculum compacting.

Nielsen and Higgins (2005) identify four key elements that must be present for successful programming of students who are twice exceptional. According to these experts, these learners require

- a continuum of service delivery options ranging from the general education classroom to a self-contained classroom supported by related service professionals;
- a complex, integrated, and interdisciplinary curriculum because of their unique learning profiles;
- services and programs that address their social, emotional, and behavioral needs; and
- instruction that targets their gifts and talents while simultaneously providing individualized special education supports.

Girls Who Are Gifted

Although it may seem a bit unusual to include females who are gifted in a section devoted to diversity, there is ample evidence that girls who are gifted are an underrepresented population and an untapped national resource. This inequity appears to be embedded in a complex and interwoven web of educational, social, and personal barriers including sex-role stereotyping, unequal educational opportunities, and personal as well as parental expectations (Reis, 2006; Rimm, 2002). Collectively, these barriers frequently become obstacles to achievement and advancement. Some of the characteristics of gifted females are presented in Table 14.8 (page 574).

TABLE 14.8 A Profile of Gifted Females

Younger Gifted Girls	• Many gifted girls are superior physically, have more social knowledge, and are better adjusted than are average girls, although more highly gifted girls are not as likely to seem well adjusted. • Highly gifted girls are often second-born females. • Highly gifted girls have high academic achievement. • In their interests, gifted girls are more like gifted boys than they are like average girls. • Gifted girls are confident in their opinions and willing to argue for their point of view. • Gifted girls by age 10 express wishes and needs for self-esteem and are interested in fulfilling needs for self-esteem through school and club achievements, although highly gifted girls are often loners without much need for recognition. • Gifted girls are more strongly influenced by their mothers than are gifted boys. • Actual occupations of parents do not affect gifted girls' eventual career choices. • Gifted girls have high career goals, although highly gifted girls aspire to careers having moderate rather than high status.
Adolescent Females	• Gifted girls' IQ scores drop in adolescence, perhaps as they begin to perceive their own giftedness as undesirable. • Gifted girls are likely to continue to have higher academic achievement as measured by grade point average. • Gifted girls take less rigorous courses than gifted boys in high school. • Gifted girls maintain a high involvement in extracurricular and social activities during adolescence. • Highly gifted girls do very well academically in high school; however, they often do not receive recognition for their achievements. • Highly gifted girls attend less prestigious colleges than highly gifted boys, a choice that leads to lower-status careers.

SOURCE: Adapted from B. Kerr, *Smart Girls Two,* Rev. ed. (Scottsdale, AZ: Gifted Psychology Press, Inc., 1997).

The education of girls with gifts and talents cannot be neglected. Giftedness in females must be nurtured. Reis (2006) offers the following recommendations for developing this talent pool in both girls and boys:

- Provide equal treatment in a non-stereotyped environment and, in particular, provide encouragement for advanced coursework.
- Reduce sexism and stereotyping in classrooms and establish equity in classroom interactions.
- Help gifted adolescents understand healthy competition.
- Group gifted students homogeneously in separate classes or in clusters within heterogeneous classrooms.
- Expose gifted adolescents to other gifted adults who can act as role models through direct and curricular experiences—field trips, guest speakers, seminars, books, videotapes, articles, and movies.
- Provide educational interventions compatible with cognitive development and styles of learning (independent study projects, small group learning opportunities, etc.).
- Use a variety of authentic assessment tools such as projects and learning centers in addition to tests. (pp. 104–105)

Silverman (1995a) suggests that to preserve giftedness in girls, schools should offer them intellectually challenging courses and assistance in selecting career paths commensurate with their abilities. Additionally, girls who are gifted may require supplementary educational experiences in order to reach their potential (Noble, Subotnik, & Arnold, 1999). Instruction may be necessary to develop assertiveness, instill confidence, and enhance self-esteem. Exposure to female mentors who can offer girls personal and professional advice along with work experience is another common recommendation for fostering the talents and gifts of girls (Robinson et al., 2007). Table 14.9 offers additional suggestions and strategies for developing the gifts and talents of female students.

Identifying and Serving Children From Diverse Backgrounds

One contemporary challenge in the field of gifted education, as in other areas of exceptionality, is that of identifying and serving children from culturally diverse backgrounds

TABLE 14.9 Recommendations for Developing the Gifts and Talents of Female Students

Gifted and Talented Girls Should	Teachers Should	Parents, Teachers, and Counselors Should
• Have exposure to or personal contact with female role models and mentors who have successfully balanced career and family. • Participate in discussion groups and attend panel discussions in which gifted and talented girls and women discuss the external barriers they have encountered. • Pursue involvement in leadership roles and extracurricular activities. • Participate in sports, athletics, and multiple extracurricular activities in areas in which they have an interest. • Discuss issues related to gender and success such as family issues in supportive settings with other talented girls. • Participate in career counseling at an early age and be exposed to a wide variety of career options and talented women who pursue challenging careers in all areas.	• Provide equitable treatment in a nonstereotyped environment and, in particular, provide encouragement. • Reduce sexism in classrooms and create an avenue for girls to report and discuss examples of stereotyping in schools. • Help creative, talented females appreciate and understand healthy competition. • Group gifted females homogeneously in math/science or within cluster groups of high-ability students in heterogeneous groups. • Encourage creativity in girls. • Use problem solving in assignments and reduce the use of timed tests and timed assignments within class periods; rather, provide options for untimed work within a reasonable time frame. • Expose girls to other creative, gifted females through direct and curricular experiences—field trips, guest speakers, seminars, role models, books, videotapes, articles, movies. • Provide educational interventions compatible with cognitive development and styles of learning (i.e., independent study projects, small group learning opportunities, and so forth) and use a variety of authentic assessment tools such as projects and learning centers instead of just using tests. • Establish equity in classroom interactions. • Provide multiple opportunities for creative expression in multiple modalities.	• Form forces to advocate for programming and equal opportunities and to investigate opportunities for talented, creative girls. • Spotlight achievements of talented females in a variety of different areas; encourage girls and young women to become involved in as many different types of activities, travel opportunities, and clubs as possible. • Encourage girls to take advanced courses in all areas as well as courses in the arts and reinforce successes in these and all areas of endeavor; ensure equal representation of girls in advanced classes. • Encourage relationships with other creative girls who want to achieve. • Maintain options for talented, creative girls in specific groups such as self-contained classes, groups of girls within heterogeneous classes and in separate classes for gifted girls, science and math clubs, or support groups. • Consistently point out options for careers and encourage future choices but help girls focus on specific interests and planning for future academic choices, interests, and careers.

SOURCE: Adapted from S. Reis, "External Barriers Experienced by Gifted and Talented Girls and Women," *Gifted Child Today, 24*(4), 2001, pp. 33–34.

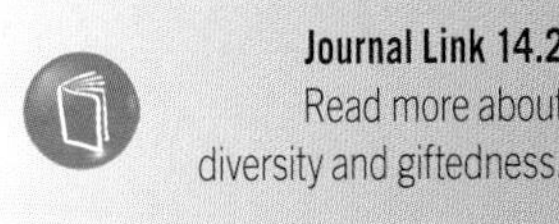

Journal Link 14.2
Read more about diversity and giftedness.

and from all socioeconomic groups. There is ample evidence that culturally diverse students are underrepresented in the pool of individuals identified as gifted (Clark, 2008; Davis et al., 2011; Ford, Harris, Tyson, & Trotman, 2002). African American pupils, for example, constitute approximately 16 percent of public school enrollment, but only about 8 percent of those in programs for the gifted and talented (Ford, 1998). The Javits legislation mentioned earlier in this chapter emphasizes that children with special gifts and talents can be found throughout society; our job as teachers is to find and provide services for these children. "Culturally diverse children," Plummer (1995) writes, "have much talent, creativity, and intelligence. Manifestations of these characteristics may be different and thus require not only different tools for measuring these strengths, but also different eyes from which to see them" (p. 290).

In a classic investigation, Frasier and her colleagues (1995) identified ten core attributes of giftedness in African American, Native American, and Hispanic children:

- Communication skills
- Imagination/creativity
- Humor
- Inquiry
- Insight
- Interests
- Memory
- Motivation
- Problem solving
- Reasoning

Students from culturally diverse backgrounds are significantly underrepresented in programs for children who are gifted and talented.

The process of identifying gifted children from culturally diverse backgrounds is sometimes described as finding "the light under the bushel basket" (Gallagher & Gallagher, 1994, p. 410). According to Gallagher and Gallagher, intellectual giftedness often resides within the individual; however, adverse environmental factors, such as poverty or language differences, can mask that gift—like placing a basket over a light. The task of educators is to find strategies that remove the basket and let the light shine forth.

Several factors are thought to contribute to the underrepresentation of culturally diverse learners in programs for gifted and talented pupils. Commonly mentioned variables include the deleterious consequences of poverty, test bias, faulty identification policies, conflicting cultural values, teacher attitudes and expectations, and rigid definitions of giftedness (Davis et al., 2011; Ford, 1998; Robinson et al., 2007). To combat these forces, recommendations have included the following:

- Culturally sensitive identification practices
- Establishing support services (career counseling, mentors, role models)
- Greater community and family involvement
- Multimodal assessment practices, including alternative (nontraditional) strategies (such as peer ratings, portfolios, teacher nominations, and checklists)
- Early identification

Portfolio assessment was thought to be one way of tapping into diverse talent areas. Its alignment with Gardner's concept of multiple intelligences makes it an especially attractive option for assessing giftedness. Unfortunately, this strategy as well as other proposed solutions have not solved the problem of underrepresentation.

Appropriate educational opportunities must be in place to develop the talents of children from low-income backgrounds; otherwise, millions of

TABLE 14.10 Suggestions for Teaching Culturally Diverse Students Who Are Gifted

African American Gifted Children	• Use small groups for instruction, building trust and belonging. • Provide structure by use of contracting, clear goals, and individualization. • Provide mentors and role models. • Emphasize use of oral language, providing many opportunities for debate, discussion, and oral presentations. • Provide for visual learning experiences, manipulative materials, and active real-life experiences in learning.
Native American Gifted Children	• Use storytelling, metaphor, and myths as media for delivering information. • Develop personal and group goals relevant to those of the tribal community as well as the student. • Provide visual and spatial experience. • Teach from whole to details. • Explore and honor belief in collective tribal self as an alternative worldview. • Use intuitive ability in learning experiences.
Hispanic Gifted Children	• Use cooperative intellectual peer groups for learning and encouraging independent production. • Provide visual and kinesthetic learning experiences. • Provide extensive experience with both English and Spanish. • Use successful Hispanic Americans as mentors. • Include the family as part of the educational team.

SOURCE: Adapted from B. Clark, *Growing Up Gifted,* 7th ed. (Upper Saddle River, NJ: Pearson Education, 2008), pp. 333–336.

high-ability children from challenging socioeconomic backgrounds will fail to stay in the upper quartile of achievement (Wyner, Bridgeland, & Diiulio, 2007). Special care must be taken to nurture their talents, encourage them to achieve at high levels, and pursue higher education opportunities. Wyner et al. are optimistic because a large number of children who fall in the upper quartile are from low-income backgrounds; however, it is discouraging that

> there are far fewer lower-income students achieving at the highest levels than there should be, they disproportionately fall out of the high-achieving group during elementary and high school, they rarely rise into the ranks of high achievers during these periods, and perhaps most disturbingly, far too few ever graduate from college or go on to graduate school. (p. i)

The challenge for educators in today's schools is to create learning environments that are intellectually stimulating and nurture the gifts and talents of all students so that it is just as attractive to be an outstanding student as it is to play on a championship team. See Table 14.10 for instructional suggestions designed to meet the unique needs of traditionally underrepresented groups of learners who are gifted and talented.

Technology and Individuals Who Are Gifted and Talented

Children and young adults with a passion for knowledge in areas of interest thrive when given access to technology. Access to mentors and colleagues who have similar interests

CHAPTER IN REVIEW

Defining Giftedness: Refining the Meaning

Audio Link 14.3
Listen to a chapter summary.

- Two national reports provide definitions of children who are gifted and talented; however, each state is responsible for establishing its own definition of giftedness. Generally speaking, definitions include high intellectual ability along with giftedness in specific academic areas, creativity, leadership, and/or the visual and performing arts.

Assessing Giftedness and Talent

- The assessment of gifts and talents necessitates multifactorial assessment of the student's strengths, using both formal and informal measures.

Prevalence of Giftedness and Talent

- Educators believe that approximately 3–5 percent of the school-age population is gifted. Some professionals estimate that 10–15 percent of school-age youth are gifted and talented.

Etiology of Giftedness and Talent

- The etiology or causes of giftedness are both genetic and environmental. The complex interaction of genetic patterns and environmental stimulation produces an individual with the capacity to learn or perform at exceptionally high levels in one or more areas of accomplishment.

Characteristics of Individuals Who Are Gifted and Talented

- The characteristics of children who are gifted and talented vary tremendously across the many dimensions of giftedness.
- The degree and intensity of characteristics are often the keys to understanding gifted behavior. Seldom, if ever, do children who are gifted and talented exhibit all of the cognitive and social–emotional characteristics associated with this exceptionality.

Educational Considerations

- The educational needs of pupils with gifts and talents are often best fulfilled via a variety of instructional strategies. Interventions must be planned to allow pupils to make continuous progress, even in areas in which they are advanced.
- Strategies to remove the learning ceiling include differentiating the curriculum and curriculum compacting.
- The curriculum must include learning experiences that combine complex content, high-level thinking and problem solving, and opportunities to think creatively. Other important accommodations addressing the needs of children who are gifted are cluster grouping, cooperative learning activities, and problem-based learning.
- A continuum of services is vital to ensure the development of talent to high levels.
- Acceleration is an appropriate option for many gifted children. Independent study, mentors, honors and Advanced Placement courses provide challenging learning experiences.
- Self-contained classrooms and special schools provide other venues for delivering services to gifted young people.
- Summer and Saturday programs are important options but should not be in lieu of services within the school setting.

Adolescents and Adults Who Are Gifted and Talented

- Adolescence can be an especially difficult time for students who are gifted and talented. Choosing between making continuous progress in their talent areas and remaining popular with their peers is one area of potential conflict.

Issues of Diversity

- Children who are gifted and talented come from all socioeconomic, racial, and ethnic groups.
- Professionals encounter three unique challenges when confronting issues of diversity: serving students with gifts and talents and a disability, meeting the needs of girls who are gifted and talented, and appropriately identifying and serving children with gifts and talents who happen to be culturally diverse.

STUDY QUESTIONS

1. How are children with gifts and talents identified in your area? Elsewhere?
2. In what ways is the assessment of giftedness an important and difficult process?
3. How have society's view and understanding of children with gifts and talents changed over time?
4. The etiology of giftedness is seen as the commingling or interaction of what variables?
5. Identify five characteristics typically associated with individuals considered gifted and talented. What implications do these characteristics have for the individuals' teachers?
6. Describe the various delivery models that are frequently used to meet the cognitive and social–emotional needs of children who are gifted and talented.
7. Define the following terms: *curriculum differentiation, preassessment, curriculum compacting, flexible grouping, cluster grouping,* and *pacing.*
8. Distinguish between the concepts of acceleration and enrichment. How can they be used together?
9. List five early indicators of gifts and talents.
10. What challenges do families of children who are gifted and talented frequently encounter?
11. Why are some groups of children underrepresented in programs for students who are gifted and talented? What can be done to remedy this situation?
12. How can technology be used to enhance learning opportunities for students with gifts and talents?
13. Why do some educators believe that full inclusion is not the best option for students who are gifted and talented?

KEY TERMS

gifted and talented 538
off-level testing 546
creativity 546
differentiation 555
preassessment 555
curriculum compacting 557
flexible grouping 558
cluster grouping 558
tiered assignments 559
problem-based learning 559
acceleration 565
mentor 568
magnet high school 571
twice exceptional 572

LEARNING ACTIVITIES

1. Write a statement about your philosophy of learning that could guide your teaching of students with gifts and talents.
2. Volunteer to assist with an academic competition, a Saturday program, or a summer program for children and youth who are gifted and talented. Keep a journal of your experiences. How do the children compare with their typical age-mates? What strengths did you observe among the participants? How do the children relate to and interact with their coaches and teachers? What are the advantages and benefits of these activities?
3. Interview two individuals of similar chronological age who are considered gifted and talented. Ask these persons to define what it means to be gifted. Have them describe their educational experiences, career goals, likes and dislikes, social relationships (including family members), and other topics of interest to you. What similarities and differences

did you observe between the two individuals? How do these persons differ from their typical age-mates?

4. Visit schools in your area that serve students with gifts and talents. What services are available for pupils who are gifted and talented? What differences did you observe between elementary and secondary programs? What instructional techniques did teachers use that were effective with students who are gifted and talented? How did the other pupils interact with their classmates who are gifted? What was your overall impression of the services—what specific features stood out? How are the individual needs of the students being addressed or ignored? Would you like to be a teacher of children who are gifted and talented? Why or why not?
5. What is the definition of children who are gifted and talented in your state? How does it compare with the definitions presented in this chapter?
6. Locate information about the advocacy organization in your state. What professional development opportunities does it offer? What information does it provide to teachers?

ORGANIZATIONS CONCERNED WITH GIFTEDNESS

The Council for Exceptional Children, The Association for the Gifted (CEC-TAG)
1110 N. Glebe Road
Suite 300
Arlington, VA 22201–5704
(888) 232-7733
(866) 915-5000 (TTY)
(703) 264-9494 (Fax)
http://www.cectag.org

National Association for Gifted Children (NAGC)
1707 L Street N.W.
Suite 550
Washington, DC 20036
(202) 785-4268
(202) 785-4248 (Fax)
http://www.nagc.org

National Research Center on the Gifted and Talented
NEAG Center for Gifted Education and Talent Development
2131 Hillside Road
Unit 3007
Storrs, CT 06269–3007
(860) 486-4626
(860) 486-2900 (Fax)
http://www.gifted.uconn.edu/nrcgt.html

Supporting Emotional Needs of the Gifted (SENG)
P.O. Box 488
Poughquag, NY 12570
(845) 797-5054
http://www.sengifted.org

World Council for Gifted and Talented Children, Inc.
c/o University of Winnipeg
515 Portage Avenue
Winnipeg, Manitoba
Canada R3B 2E9
(204) 789-1421
(204) 783-1188 (Fax)
http://www.world-gifted.org

REFLECTING ON STANDARDS

The following exercises are designed to help you learn to apply the Council for Exceptional Children (CEC) standards to your teaching practice. Each of the reflection exercises below correlates with a knowledge or skill within the CEC standards. For the full text of each of the related CEC standards, please refer to the standards integration grid located in Appendix B.

Focus on Instructional Strategies ***(CEC Content Standard #4 CC4S3)***
Reflect on what you have learned about students who are gifted and talented. If you had an individual who was gifted and talented in math, and well above the rest of your class, how might you use differentiated instruction to keep him or her challenged while still addressing the needs of the remainder of your pupils? What are some other instructional strategies you could incorporate in your class to meet his or her needs?

Focus on Learning Environments and Social Interactions ***(CEC Content Standard #5 CC5K5)***
Reflect on what you have learned about the social–emotional needs of students who are gifted and talented. If you were to have a pupil in your class who was gifted and talented and often received instruction outside your classroom at a higher grade level, what difficulties might this individual have in developing social skills with his or her peers? How might you help encourage or facilitate social interactions when the student is in your classroom during the day?

STUDENT STUDY SITE

Visit the Student Study Site at www.sagepub.com/gargiulo4emedia for these additional learning tools:

- Video links
- Media links
- Self-quizzes
- E-flashcards
- Full-text SAGE journal articles
- Web exercises

Postscript

You may recall that in Chapter 1 you were introduced to some of the students in Daniel Thompson's fifth-grade class. Mr. Thompson's classroom was like most classrooms in the United States: The majority of the students were typical learners, but five individuals were thought to have special learning needs.

- Victoria, age 11, is a very popular student with a great personality who has been blind since birth.
- Miguel is very shy and timid and interacts minimally with his classmates. Miguel only recently moved into the community from his home in Mexico.
- Jerome is particularly disliked by his peers. He is verbally abusive, often has temper tantrums, and frequently fights with other children. Mr. Thompson suspects that he might be a member of a local gang.
- Stephanie endures friendly teasing from her classmates, who secretly admire her intellectual gifts and talents.
- Robert is an outstanding athlete. In the classroom, however, he asks silly questions, has difficulty following class rules, and occasionally makes animal noises, much to the displeasure of his classmates. Robert has cognitive delays as a result of an automobile accident.

Mr. Thompson wondered why these students were in his class and how he could help them. Hopefully, after studying the preceding chapters, listening to your instructor's presentations, and completing course assignments, along with critically reflecting on the content, you are now in a position to respond to the six questions originally posed in Chapter 1:

1. Why are these pupils in a general education classroom?
2. Will I have students like this in my class?
3. Are these children called disabled, exceptional, or handicapped?
4. What does *special education* mean?
5. How will I know if some of my students have special learning needs?
6. How can I help these pupils?

Teaching children and young adults with exceptionalities is a very challenging yet richly rewarding career. When you stand before your class as a dedicated, committed, and caring professional, you possess the power to make a difference in the lives of all your students. I congratulate you on choosing to become a member of a dynamic profession—teaching.

Good luck!

Appendix A

Federal Definitions of Disabilities

Autism means a developmental disability significantly affecting verbal and nonverbal communication and social interaction, generally evident before age 3, that adversely affects a child's educational performance. Other characteristics often associated with autism are engagement in repetitive activities and stereotyped movements, resistance to environmental change or change in daily routines, and unusual responses to sensory experiences. The term does not apply if a child's educational performance is adversely affected primarily because the child has an emotional disturbance as defined below.

A child who manifests the characteristics of autism after age 3 could be diagnosed as having autism if the criteria in the preceding paragraph are satisfied.

Deaf-blindness means concomitant hearing and visual impairments, the combination of which causes such severe communication and other developmental and educational needs that they cannot be accommodated in special education programs solely for children with deafness or children with blindness.

Deafness means a hearing impairment that is so severe that the child is impaired in processing linguistic information through hearing, with or without amplification, that adversely affects a child's educational performance.

Emotional disturbance is defined as follows:

i. The term means a condition exhibiting one or more of the following characteristics over a long period of time and to a marked degree that adversely affects a child's educational performance:
   A. An inability to learn that cannot be explained by intellectual, sensory, or health factors.
   B. An inability to build or maintain satisfactory interpersonal relationships with peers and teachers.
   C. Inappropriate types of behavior or feelings under normal circumstances.
   D. A general pervasive mood of unhappiness or depression.
   E. A tendency to develop physical symptoms or fears associated with personal or school problems.

ii. The term includes schizophrenia. The term does not apply to children who are socially maladjusted, unless it is determined that they have an emotional disturbance.

Hearing impairment means an impairment in hearing, whether permanent or fluctuating, that adversely affects a child's educational performance but that is not included under the definition of deafness in this section.

Mental retardation means significantly subaverage general intellectual functioning, existing concurrently with deficits in adaptive behavior and manifested during the developmental period, that adversely affects a child's educational performance.

Multiple disabilities means concomitant impairments (such as mental retardation–blindness, mental retardation–orthopedic impairment, etc.), the combination of which causes such severe educational needs that they cannot be accommodated in special education programs solely for one of the impairments. The term does not include deaf-blindness.

Orthopedic impairment means a severe orthopedic impairment that adversely affects a child's educational performance. The term includes impairments caused by congenital anomaly (e.g., clubfoot, absence of some member, etc.), impairments caused by disease (e.g., poliomyelitis, bone tuberculosis, etc.), and impairments from other causes (e.g., cerebral palsy, amputations, and fractures or burns that cause contractures).

Other health impairment means having limited strength, vitality or alertness, including a heightened alertness to environmental stimuli, that results in limited alertness with respect to the educational environment, that

i. is due to chronic or acute health problems such as asthma, attention deficit disorder or attention deficit hyperactivity disorder, diabetes, epilepsy, a heart condition, hemophilia, lead poisoning, leukemia, nephritis, rheumatic fever, sickle cell anemia, and Tourette syndrome; and
ii. adversely affects a child's educational performance.

Specific learning disability is defined as follows:

i. ***General.*** The term means a disorder in one or more of the basic psychological processes involved in understanding or in using language, spoken or written, that may manifest itself in an imperfect ability to listen, think, speak, read, write, spell, or to do mathematical calculations, including conditions such as perceptual disabilities, brain injury, minimal brain dysfunction, dyslexia, and developmental aphasia.
ii. ***Disorders not included.*** The term does not include learning problems that are primarily the result of visual, hearing, or motor disabilities, of mental retardation, of emotional disturbance, or of environmental, cultural, or economic disadvantage.

Speech or language impairment means a communication disorder, such as stuttering, impaired articulation, a language impairment, or a voice impairment, that adversely affects a child's educational performance.

Traumatic brain injury means an acquired injury to the brain caused by an external physical force, resulting in total or partial functional disability or psychosocial impairment or both, that adversely affects a child's educational performance. The term applies to open or closed head injuries resulting in impairments in one or more areas, such as cognition; language; memory; attention; reasoning; abstract thinking; judgment; problem-solving; sensory, perceptual, and motor abilities; psychosocial behavior; physical functions; information processing; and speech. The term does not apply to brain injuries that are congenital or degenerative, or to brain injuries induced by birth trauma.

Visual impairment including blindness means an impairment in vision that, even with correction, adversely affects a child's educational performance. The term includes both partial sight and blindness.

SOURCE: Individuals with Disabilities Education Improvement Act, 34 C.F.R. Part 300 § 300.8 (C). August 14, 2006.

Appendix B

Professional Standards

Council for Exceptional Children (CEC) Standards Correlated by Chapter

Knowledge and Skill Base for All Beginning Special Education Teachers: Common Core

Standard #1: Foundations. Special educators understand the field as an evolving and changing discipline based on philosophies, evidence-based principles and theories, relevant laws and policies, diverse and historical points of view, and human issues that have historically influenced and continue to influence the field of special education and the education and treatment of individuals with exceptional needs both in school and in society. Special educators understand how these influence professional practice, including assessment, instructional planning, implementation, and program evaluation. Special educators understand how issues of human diversity can impact families, cultures, and schools, and how these complex human issues can interact with issues in the delivery of special education services. They understand the relationships of organizations of special education to the organizations and functions of schools, school systems, and other agencies. Special educators use this knowledge as a ground upon which to construct their own personal understandings and philosophies of special education.

Knowledge		Chapter													
		1	2	3	4	5	6	7	8	9	10	11	12	13	14
CC1K1	Models, theories, and philosophies that form the basis for special education practice.	•	•			•	•		•	•	•	•	•	•	•
CC1K2	Laws, policies, and ethical principles regarding behavior management planning and implementation.							•	•					•	
CC1K3	Relationship of special education to the organization and function of educational agencies.						•								
CC1K4	Rights and responsibilities of students, parents, teachers and other professionals, and schools related to exceptional learning needs.		•							•	•	•		•	•
CC1K5	Issues in definition and identification of individuals with exceptional learning needs, including those from culturally and linguistically diverse backgrounds.	•		•		•	•	•	•	•	•	•	•	•	•

Knowledge		Chapter 1	2	3	4	5	6	7	8	9	10	11	12	13	14
CC1K6	Issues, assurances, and due process rights related to assessment, eligibility, and placement within a continuum of services.		•				•		•		•	•	•	•	•
CC1K7	Family systems and the role of families in the educational process.		•		•					•		•		•	•
CC1K8	Historical points of view and contribution of culturally diverse groups.	•		•		•	•	•	•	•	•	•	•	•	•
CC1K9	Impact of the dominant culture on shaping schools and the individuals who study and work in them.			•						•					
CC1K10	Potential impact of differences in values, languages, and customs that can exist between the home and school.			•								•			
Skills		**1**	**2**	**3**	**4**	**5**	**6**	**7**	**8**	**9**	**10**	**11**	**12**	**13**	**14**
CC1S1	Articulate personal philosophy of special education.														

Standard #2: Development and Characteristics of Learners. Special educators know and demonstrate respect for their students first as unique human beings. Special educators understand the similarities and differences in human development and the characteristics between and among individuals with and without exceptional learning needs (ELN).[1] Moreover, special educators understand how exceptional conditions can interact with the domains of human development and they use this knowledge to respond to the varying abilities and behaviors of individuals with ELN. Special educators understand how the experiences of individuals with ELN can impact families, as well as the individual's ability to learn, interact socially, and live as fulfilled contributing members of the community.

Knowledge		Chapter 1	2	3	4	5	6	7	8	9	10	11	12	13	14
CC2K1	Typical and atypical human growth and development.					•	•				•	•	•	•	•
CC2K2	Educational implications of characteristics of various exceptionalities.	•				•	•	•	•	•	•	•	•	•	•
CC2K3	Characteristics and effects of the cultural and environmental milieu of the individual with exceptional learning needs and the family.					•	•	•	•	•	•	•	•	•	

1. "Individual with exceptional learning needs" is used throughout to include individuals with disabilities and individuals with exceptional gifts and talents.

(Continued)

(Continued)

Knowledge		Chapter 1	2	3	4	5	6	7	8	9	10	11	12	13	14
CC2K4	Family systems and the role of families in supporting development.				•	•			•		•	•	•	•	•
CC2K5	Similarities and differences of individuals with and without exceptional learning needs.	•	•			•		•	•	•	•	•	•	•	•
CC2K6	Similarities and differences among individuals with exceptional learning needs.		•					•		•		•		•	•
CC2K7	Effects of various medications on individuals with exceptional learning needs.							•						•	•

Standard #3: Individual Learning Differences. Special educators understand the effects that an exceptional condition[2] can have on an individual's learning in school and throughout life. Special educators understand that the beliefs, traditions, and values across and within cultures can affect relationships among and between students, their families, and the school community. Moreover, special educators are active and resourceful in seeking to understand how primary language, culture, and familial backgrounds interact with the individual's exceptional condition to impact the individual's academic and social abilities, attitudes, values, interests, and career options. The understanding of these learning differences and their possible interactions provides the foundation upon which special educators individualize instruction to provide meaningful and challenging learning for individuals with ELN.

Knowledge		Chapter 1	2	3	4	5	6	7	8	9	10	11	12	13	14
CC3K1	Effects an exceptional condition(s) can have on an individual's life.	•				•	•	•	•	•	•	•	•	•	•
CC3K2	Impact of learners' academic and social abilities, attitudes, interests, and values on instruction and career development.					•	•	•	•	•		•	•	•	•
CC3K3	Variations in beliefs, traditions, and values across and within cultures and their			•	•					•					

2. "Exceptional condition" is used throughout to include both single and coexisting conditions. These may be two or more disabling conditions or exceptional gifts or talents coexisting with one or more disabling conditions.

Knowledge		Chapter 1	2	3	4	5	6	7	8	9	10	11	12	13	14
	effects on relationships among individuals with exceptional learning needs, family, and schooling.														
CC3K4	Cultural perspectives influencing the relationships among families, schools, and communities as related to instruction.			•						•		•			
CC3K5	Differing ways of learning of individuals with exceptional learning needs including those from culturally diverse backgrounds and strategies for addressing these differences.			•		•				•					

Standard #4: Individual Learning Differences. Special educators possess a repertoire of evidence-based instructional strategies to individualize instruction for individuals with ELN. Special educators select, adapt, and use these instructional strategies to promote positive learning results in general and special curricula[3] and to modify learning environments appropriately for individuals with ELN. They enhance the learning of critical thinking, problem solving, and performance skills of individuals with ELN, and increase their self-awareness, self-management, self-control, self-reliance, and self-esteem. Moreover, special educators emphasize the development, maintenance, and generalization of knowledge and skills across environments, settings, and the life span.

Skills		Chapter 1	2	3	4	5	6	7	8	9	10	11	12	13	14
CC4K1	Evidence-based practices validated for specific characteristics of learners and settings.					•	•	•		•					
CC4S1	Use strategies to facilitate integration into various settings.	•				•			•	•		•		•	•
CC4S2	Teach individuals to use self-assessment, problem solving, and other cognitive strategies to meet their needs.					•	•	•	•			•			

3. "Special curricula" is used throughout to denote curricular areas not routinely emphasized or addressed in general curricula (e.g., social, communication, motor, independence, self-advocacy).

(Continued)

(Continued)

Skills		Chapter													
		1	2	3	4	5	6	7	8	9	10	11	12	13	14
CC4S3	Select, adapt, and use instructional strategies and materials according to characteristics of the individual with exceptional learning needs.					•	•	•	•	•			•	•	•
CC4S4	Use strategies to facilitate maintenance and generalization of skills across learning and environments.								•			•		•	•
CC4S5	Use procedures to increase the individual's self-awareness, self-management, self-control, self-reliance, and self-esteem.					•	•	•	•				•	•	•
CC4S6	Use strategies that promote successful transitions for individuals with exceptional learning needs.					•			•					•	•

Standard #5: Learning Environments and Social Interactions. Special educators actively create learning environments for individuals with ELN that foster cultural understanding, safety and emotional well-being, positive social interactions, and active engagement of individuals with ELN. In addition, special educators foster environments in which diversity is valued and individuals are taught to live harmoniously and productively in a culturally diverse world. Special educators shape environments to encourage the independence, self-motivation, self-direction, personal empowerment, and self-advocacy of individuals with ELN. Special educators help their general education colleagues integrate individuals with ELN in regular environments and engage them in meaningful learning activities and interactions. Special educators use direct motivational and instructional interventions with individuals with ELN to teach them to respond effectively to current expectations. When necessary, special educators can safely intervene with individuals with ELN in crisis. Special educators coordinate all these efforts and provide guidance and direction to paraeducators and others, such as classroom volunteers and tutors.

Knowledge		Chapter													
		1	2	3	4	5	6	7	8	9	10	11	12	13	14
CC5K1	Demands of the learning environment.						•		•	•		•	•	•	•
CC5K2	Basic classroom management theories and strategies for individuals with exceptional learning needs.						•	•	•	•				•	
CC5K3	Effective management of teaching and learning.						•		•	•		•	•	•	•

Knowledge		Chapter													
		1	2	3	4	5	6	7	8	9	10	11	12	13	14
CC5K4	Teacher attitudes and behaviors that influence behavior of individuals with exceptional learning needs.	•							•	•	•				•
CC5K5	Social skills needed for educational and other environments.								•	•	•	•	•	•	•
CC5K6	Strategies for crisis prevention and interventions.								•					•	
CC5K7	Strategies for preparing individuals to live harmoniously and productively in a culturally diverse world.			•						•		•			
CC5K8	Ways to create learning environments that allow individuals to retain and appreciate their own and each other's respective language and cultural heritage.			•								•			
CC5K9	Ways specific cultures are negatively stereotyped.														
CC5K10	Strategies used by diverse populations to cope with a legacy of former and continuing racism.														
CC5S1	Create a safe, equitable, positive, and supportive learning environment in which diversities are valued.			•						•		•		•	•
CC5S2	Identify realistic expectations for personal and social behavior in various settings.														•
CC5S3	Identify supports needed for integration into various program placements.								•						•
CC5S4	Design learning environments that encourage active participation in individual and group activities.									•		•	•	•	•
CC5S5	Modify the learning environment to manage behavior.						•	•	•					•	•

(Continued)

(Continued)

		Chapter													
Knowledge		1	2	3	4	5	6	7	8	9	10	11	12	13	14
CC5S6	Use performance data and information from all stakeholders to make or suggest modifications in learning environments.														
CC5S7	Establish and maintain rapport with individuals with and without exceptional learning needs.														
CC5S8	Teach self-advocacy.											•			
CC5S9	Create an environment that encourages self-advocacy and increased independence.											•	•		
CC5S10	Use effective and varied behavior management strategies.							•	•					•	
CC5S11	Use the least intensive behavior management strategy consistent with the needs of the individual with exceptional learning needs.								•						
CC5S12	Design and manage daily routines.								•						
CC5S13	Organize, develop, and sustain learning environments that support intracultural and intercultural experiences.			•											
CC5S14	Mediate controversial intercultural issues among students within the learning environment in ways that enhance any culture, group, or person.														
CC5S15	Structure, direct, and support the activities of paraeducators, volunteers, and tutors.														
CC5S16	Use universal precautions.														

Standard #6: Communication. Special educators understand typical and atypical language development and the ways in which exceptional conditions can interact with an individual's experience with and use of language. Special educators use individualized strategies to enhance language development and teach communication skills to individuals with ELN. Special educators are familiar with augmentative, alternative, and assistive technologies to support and enhance communication of individuals with exceptional needs. Special educators match their communication methods to an individual's language proficiency and cultural and linguistic differences. Special educators provide effective language models, and they use communication strategies and resources to facilitate understanding of subject matter for individuals with ELN whose primary language is not English.

		Chapter													
Knowledge		1	2	3	4	5	6	7	8	9	10	11	12	13	14
CC6K1	Effects of cultural and linguistic differences on growth and development.			•							•	•			
CC6K2	Characteristics of one's own culture and use of language and the ways in which these can differ from those of other cultures and uses of language.										•	•			
CC6K3	Ways of behaving and communicating among cultures that can lead to misinterpretation and misunderstanding.														
CC6K4	Augmentative and assistive communication strategies.					•					•	•		•	•
Skills		1	2	3	4	5	6	7	8	9	10	11	12	13	14
CC6S1	Use strategies to support and enhance communication skills of individuals with exceptional learning needs.										•	•		•	•
CC6S2	Use communication strategies and resources to facilitate understanding of subject matter for students whose primary language is not the dominant language.											•			

Standard #7: Instructional Planning. Individualized decision making and instruction is at the center of special education practice. Special educators develop long-range individualized instructional plans anchored in both general and special curricula. In addition, special educators systematically translate these individualized plans into carefully selected shorter-range goals and objectives, taking into consideration an individual's abilities and needs, the learning environment, and a myriad of cultural and linguistic factors. Individualized instructional plans emphasize explicit modeling and efficient guided practice to ensure acquisition and fluency through maintenance and generalization. Understanding of these factors as well as the implications of an individual's exceptional condition guides the special educator's selection, adaptation, and creation of materials and the use of powerful instructional variables. Instructional plans are modified based on ongoing analysis of the individual's learning progress. Moreover, special educators facilitate this instructional planning in a collaborative context including the individuals with exceptionalities, families, professional colleagues, and personnel from other agencies as appropriate. Special educators also develop a variety of individualized transition plans, such as transitions from preschool to elementary school and from secondary settings to a variety of postsecondary work and learning contexts. Special educators are comfortable using appropriate technologies to support instructional planning and individualized instruction.

		Chapter													
Knowledge		**1**	**2**	**3**	**4**	**5**	**6**	**7**	**8**	**9**	**10**	**11**	**12**	**13**	**14**
CC7K1	Theories and research that form the basis of curriculum development and instructional practice.					•	•			•			•	•	•
CC7K2	Scope and sequences of general and special curricula.									•					
CC7K3	National, state or provincial, and local curricula standards.														
CC7K4	Technology for planning and managing the teaching and learning environment.					•	•		•			•	•	•	•
CC7K5	Roles and responsibilities of the paraeducator related to instruction, intervention, and direct service.														
Skills		**1**	**2**	**3**	**4**	**5**	**6**	**7**	**8**	**9**	**10**	**11**	**12**	**13**	**14**
CC7S1	Identify and prioritize areas of the general curriculum and accommodations for individuals with exceptional learning needs.									•				•	•
CC7S2	Develop and implement comprehensive, longitudinal individualized programs in collaboration with team members.		•												
CC7S3	Involve the individual and family in setting instructional goals and monitoring progress.											•			
CC7S4	Use functional assessments to develop intervention plans.								•					•	
CC7S5	Use task analysis.					•									
CC7S6	Sequence, implement, and evaluate individualized learning objectives.														

Skills		Chapter													
		1	2	3	4	5	6	7	8	9	10	11	12	13	14
CC7S7	Integrate affective, social, and life skills with academic curricula.					•			•					•	•
CC7S8	Develop and select instructional content, resources, and strategies that respond to cultural, linguistic, and gender differences.			•						•					
CC7S9	Incorporate and implement instructional and assistive technology into the educational program.											•			•
CC7S10	Prepare lesson plans.														
CC7S11	Prepare and organize materials to implement daily lesson plans.														
CC7S12	Use instructional time effectively.								•						
CC7S13	Make responsive adjustments to instruction based on continual observations.														
CC7S14	Prepare individuals to exhibit self-enhancing behavior in response to societal attitudes and actions.					•									
CC7S15	Evaluate and modify instructional practices in response to ongoing assessment data.		•	•		•	•		•						•

Standard #8: Assessment. Assessment is integral to the decision-making and teaching of special educators, and special educators use multiple types of assessment information for a variety of educational decisions. Special educators use the results of assessments to help identify exceptional learning needs and to develop and implement individualized instructional programs, as well as to adjust instruction in response to ongoing learning progress. Special educators understand the legal policies and ethical principles of measurement and assessment related to referral, eligibility, program planning, instruction, and placement for individuals with ELN, including those from culturally and linguistically diverse backgrounds. Special educators understand measurement theory and practices for addressing issues of validity, reliability, norms, bias, and interpretation of assessment results. In addition, special educators understand the appropriate use and limitations of various types of assessments. Special educators collaborate with families and other colleagues to ensure nonbiased, meaningful assessments and decision making. Special educators conduct formal and informal assessments of behavior, learning, achievement, and environments to design learning experiences that support the growth and development of individuals with ELN. Special educators use assessment information to identify supports and adaptations required for individuals with ELN to access the general curriculum and to participate in school, system, and statewide assessment programs. Special educators regularly monitor the progress of individuals with ELN in general and special curricula. Special educators use appropriate technologies to support their assessments.

		Chapter													
Knowledge		1	2	3	4	5	6	7	8	9	10	11	12	13	14
CC8K1	Basic terminology used in assessment.		•			•	•		•	•			•		
CC8K2	Legal provisions and ethical principles regarding assessment of individuals.		•									•	•	•	•
CC8K3	Screening, prereferral, referral, and classification procedures.		•	•				•			•	•	•	•	•
CC8K4	Use and limitations of assessment.					•	•	•	•	•		•		•	•
CC8K5	National, state or provincial, and local accommodations or modifications.														
Skills		1	2	3	4	5	6	7	8	9	10	11	12	13	14
CC8S1	Gather relevant background information.														
CC8S2	Administer nonbiased formal and informal assessment strategies.			•											
CC8S3	Use technology to conduct assessments.														
CC8S4	Develop or modify individualized assessment strategies.								•						
CC8S5	Interpret information from formal and informal assessments.														
CC8S6	Use assessment information in making eligibility program and placement decisions for individuals with exceptional learning needs, including those from culturally and/or linguistically diverse backgrounds.			•											
CC8S7	Report assessment results to all stakeholders using effective communication skills.														
CC8S8	Evaluate instruction and monitor progress of individuals with exceptional learning needs.														
CC8S9	Create and maintain records.														

Standard #9: Professional and Ethical Practice. Special educators are guided by the profession's ethical and professional practice standards. Special educators practice in multiple roles and complex situations across wide age and developmental ranges. Their practice requires ongoing attention to legal matters along with serious professional and ethical considerations. Special educators engage in professional activities and participate in learning communities that benefit individuals with ELN, their families, and the special educators' colleagues and own professional growth. Special educators view themselves as lifelong learners and regularly reflect on and adjust their practice. Special educators are aware of how their own and others' attitudes, behaviors, and ways of communicating can influence their practice. Special educators understand that culture and language can interact with exceptionalities, and are sensitive to the many aspects of diversity of individuals with ELN and their families. Special educators actively plan and engage in activities that foster their professional growth and keep them current with evidence-based best practices. Special educators know their own limits of practice and practice within them.

		Chapter													
Knowledge		1	2	3	4	5	6	7	8	9	10	11	12	13	14
CC9K1	Personal cultural biases and differences that affect one's teaching.														
CC9K2	Importance of the teacher serving as a model for individuals with exceptional learning needs.														
CC9K3	Continuum of lifelong professional development.			•											
CC9K4	Methods to remain current regarding research-validated practice.														
Skills		1	2	3	4	5	6	7	8	9	10	11	12	13	14
CC9S1	Practice within the CEC Code of Ethics and other standards of the profession.														
CC9S2	Uphold high standards of competence and integrity and exercise sound judgment in the practice of the professional.														
CC9S3	Act ethically in advocating for appropriate services.														
CC9S4	Conduct professional activities in compliance with applicable laws and policies.														

(Continued)

(Continued)

Skills		Chapter													
		1	2	3	4	5	6	7	8	9	10	11	12	13	14
CC9S5	Demonstrate commitment to developing the highest education and quality-of-life potential of individuals with exceptional learning needs.														
CC9S6	Demonstrate sensitivity for the culture, language, religion, gender, disability, socioeconomic status, and sexual orientation of individuals.				•										
CC9S7	Practice within one's skill limit and obtain assistance as needed.														
CC9S8	Use verbal, nonverbal, and written language effectively.														
CC9S9	Conduct self-evaluation of instruction.														
CC9S10	Access information on exceptionalities.														
CC9S11	Reflect on one's practice to improve instruction and guide professional growth.														
CC9S12	Engage in professional activities that benefit individuals with exceptional learning needs, their families, and one's colleagues.			•											
CC9S13	Demonstrate commitment to engage in evidence-based practices.														

Standard #10: Collaboration. Special educators routinely and effectively collaborate with families, other educators, related service providers, and personnel from community agencies in culturally responsive ways. This collaboration ensures that the needs of individuals with ELN are addressed throughout schooling. Moreover, special educators embrace their special role as advocates for individuals with ELN. Special educators promote and advocate the learning and well-being of individuals with ELN across a wide range of settings and a range of different learning experiences. Special educators are viewed as specialists by a myriad of people who actively seek their collaboration to effectively include and teach individuals with ELN. Special educators are a resource to their colleagues in understanding the laws and policies relevant to individuals with ELN. Special educators use collaboration to facilitate the successful transitions of individuals with ELN across settings and services.

		Chapter													
Knowledge		1	2	3	4	5	6	7	8	9	10	11	12	13	14
CC10K1	Models and strategies of consultation and collaboration.	•			•			•			•				
CC10K2	Roles of individuals with exceptional learning needs, families, and school and community personnel in planning of an individualized program.	•								•	•	•	•	•	•
CC10K3	Concerns of families and individuals with exceptional learning needs and strategies to help address these concerns.				•									•	•
CC10K4	Culturally responsive factors that promote effective communication and collaboration with individuals and exceptional learning needs, families, school personnel, and community members.				•				•						
Skills		1	2	3	4	5	6	7	8	9	10	11	12	13	14
CC10S1	Maintain confidential communication about individuals with exceptional learning needs.														
CC10S2	Collaborate with families and others in assessment of individuals with exceptional learning needs.							•							
CC10S3	Foster respectful and beneficial relationships between families and professionals.				•										

(Continued)

(Continued)

		Chapter													
Skills		**1**	**2**	**3**	**4**	**5**	**6**	**7**	**8**	**9**	**10**	**11**	**12**	**13**	**14**
CC10S4	Assist individuals with exceptional learning needs and their families in becoming active participants in the educational team.				•										
CC10S5	Plan and conduct collaborative conferences with individuals with exceptional learning needs and their families.				•										
CC10S6	Collaborate with school personnel and community members in integrating individuals with exceptional learning needs into various settings.														
CC10S7	Use group problem-solving skills to develop, implement, and evaluate collaborative activities.														
CC10S8	Model techniques and coach others in the use of instructional methods and accommodations.														
CC10S9	Communicate with school personnel about the characteristics and needs of individuals with exceptional learning needs.														
CC10S10	Communicate effectively with families of individuals with exceptional learning needs from diverse backgrounds.				•										
CC10S11	Observe, evaluate, and provide feedback to paraeducators.														

SOURCE: Adapted from *What Every Special Educator Must Know,* 6th ed. (Arlington, VA: Council for Exceptional Children, 2009).

INTASC Standards Correlated by Chapter*

Interstate New Teacher Assessment and Support Consortium (INTASC) Standards for General and Special Education Teachers

Principle 1. The teacher understands the central concepts, tools of inquiry, and structures of the discipline(s) he or she teaches and can create learning experiences that make these aspects of subject matter meaningful for students.

		Chapter												
		1	2	3	4	5	6	7	8	9	10	11	12	13
1.03	All teachers understand that students with disabilities may need accommodations, modifications, and/or adaptations to the general curriculum depending on their learning strengths and needs.	•				•	•	•	•	•	•	•	•	•
1.04	All teachers have knowledge of the major principles and parameters of federal disabilities legislation.		•	•		•	•	•	•	•	•	•	•	•
1.05	All teachers know about and can access resources to gain information about state, district, and school policies and procedures regarding special education, including those regarding referral, assessment, eligibility, and services for students with disabilities.		•			•	•	•	•	•		•	•	•

Principle 2. The teacher understands how children learn and develop, and can provide learning opportunities that support the intellectual, social, and personal development of each learner. The teacher understands the central concepts, tools of inquiry, and structures of the discipline(s) he or she teaches and can create learning experiences that make these aspects of subject matter meaningful for students.

		Chapter												
		1	2	3	4	5	6	7	8	9	10	11	12	13
2.01	All general and special education teachers have a sound understanding of physical, social, emotional, and cognitive development from birth through adulthood.	•				•	•	•	•	•	•	•	•	•
2.02	All teachers continually examine their assumptions about the learning and development of individual students with disabilities.		•			•	•	•	•	•	•	•	•	•

*Chapter 14 is not included because INTASC standards do not directly address students who are gifted and talented.

(Continued)

(Continued)

		Chapter												
		1	2	3	4	5	6	7	8	9	10	11	12	13
2.03	All teachers recognize that students with disabilities vary in their approaches to learning depending on factors such as the nature of their disability, their level of knowledge and functioning, and life experiences.	•		•		•	•	•	•	•	•	•	•	•
2.04	All teachers are knowledgeable about multiple theories of learning and research-based teaching practices that support learning.					•	•	•	•	•	•	•	•	•

Principle 3. The teacher understands how students differ in their approaches to learning and creates instructional opportunities that are adapted to diverse learners.

		Chapter												
		1	2	3	4	5	6	7	8	9	10	11	12	13
3.01	All general and special education teachers build students' awareness, sensitivity, acceptance, and appreciation for students with disabilities who are members of their classrooms, schools, and communities.	•		•	•									
3.02	All teachers recognize that a specific disability does not dictate how an individual student will learn.	•	•			•	•	•	•	•	•	•	•	•
3.03	All teachers understand that a disability can be perceived differently across families, communities, and cultures based on differing values and belief systems.			•	•	•	•	•	•	•	•	•	•	•
3.04	All teachers understand and are sensitive to cultural, ethnic, gender, and linguistic differences that may be confused with or misinterpreted as manifestations of a disability.			•	•	•	•	•	•	•	•	•	•	•

Principle 4. The teacher understands and uses a variety of instructional strategies to encourage students' development of critical thinking, problem-solving, and performance skills.

		Chapter												
		1	2	3	4	5	6	7	8	9	10	11	12	13
4.01	All general and special education teachers have shared responsibility for the education of students with disabilities including the implementation of instructional strategies to support the student's learning in the general and/or expanded curriculums.	•	•			•	•	•	•	•	•	•	•	•
4.02	All teachers understand how different learning theories and research contribute to effective instruction for students with disabilities.					•	•	•	•	•	•	•	•	•
4.03	All teachers use research-based practices including explicit instruction and planned maintenance and generalization to support initial learning and generalization of concepts and skills for students with disabilities.					•	•	•	•	•	•	•	•	•
4.04	All teachers understand that it is particularly important to provide multiple ways for students with disabilities to participate in learning activities.			•		•	•	•	•	•	•	•	•	•
4.05	All teachers provide a variety of ways for students with disabilities to demonstrate their learning.	•				•	•	•	•	•	•	•	•	•
4.06	All teachers adjust their instruction in response to information gathered from ongoing monitoring of performance and progress of students with disabilities.		•					•	•	•			•	•
4.07	All teachers use strategies that promote the independence, self-control, and self-advocacy of students with disabilities.					•	•	•	•	•	•	•	•	•
4.08	All teachers expect and support the use of assistive and instructional technologies to promote learning and independence of students with disabilities.					•	•	•	•	•	•	•	•	•

Principle 5. The teacher uses an understanding of individual and group motivation and behavior to create a learning environment that encourages positive social interaction, active engagement in learning, and self-motivation.

		Chapter												
		1	2	3	4	5	6	7	8	9	10	11	12	13
5.01	All general and special education teachers identify the interests and preferences of students with disabilities and use this information to design activities that encourage students with disabilities to make positive contributions to the learning community.		•							•				•
5.02	All teachers help students with disabilities develop positive strategies for coping with frustrations in the learning situation that may be associated with their disability.					•	•	•	•	•	•	•	•	•
5.03	All teachers take deliberate action to promote positive social relationships among students with disabilities and their age-appropriate peers in the learning community.					•	•	•	•	•	•	•	•	•
5.04	All teachers recognize factors and situations that are likely to promote (or diminish) intrinsic motivation, and create learning environments that encourage engagement and self-motivation of students with disabilities.							•	•	•		•	•	•
5.05	All teachers participate in the design and implementation of individual behavioral support plans and are proactive in responding to the needs of individual students with disabilities within the learning community.		•						•	•				•

Principle 6. The teacher uses knowledge of effective verbal, nonverbal, and media communication technologies to foster active inquiry, collaboration, and supportive interaction in the classroom.

		Chapter												
		1	2	3	4	5	6	7	8	9	10	11	12	13
6.01	All general and special education teachers have knowledge of the general types of communication strategies and assistive technologies that can be incorporated as a regular part of their instruction.		•			•	•	•		•	•	•	•	•

		Chapter												
		1	2	3	4	5	6	7	8	9	10	11	12	13
6.02	All teachers collaborate with speech–language pathologists and other language specialists to identify the language and communication skills that need to be developed in students with disabilities, and to work cooperatively to teach those skills across settings.									•	•	•		•
6.03	All teachers understand that linguistic background has an impact on language acquisition as well as communication content and style.			•		•	•	•	•	•	•	•	•	•
6.04	All teachers provide multiple opportunities to foster effective communication among students with disabilities and other members of the classroom as a means of building communication and language skills.									•	•	•	•	•
6.05	All teachers are sensitive to the verbal and nonverbal messages they may convey to students with disabilities through their interactions during instruction.								•	•	•	•		•

Principle 7. The teacher plans instruction based on knowledge of subject matter, students, the community, and curriculum goals.

		Chapter												
		1	2	3	4	5	6	7	8	9	10	11	12	13
7.01	All general and special education teachers contribute their expertise as members of a collaborative team to develop, monitor, and periodically revise individualized educational plans for students with disabilities.		•	•					•	•				•
7.02	All teachers plan ways to modify instruction, as needed, to facilitate positive learning results within the general curriculum for students with disabilities.	•	•			•	•	•	•	•		•	•	•
7.03	All teachers collaborate to plan instruction related to expanded curriculum in general education classrooms for students with disabilities who require such curriculum.		•			•	•	•	•	•		•	•	•

(Continued)

(Continued)

		Chapter												
		1	2	3	4	5	6	7	8	9	10	11	12	13
7.04	All teachers design the learning environment so that the individual needs of students with disabilities are accommodated.	•	•			•	•	•	•	•	•	•	•	•
7.05	All teachers monitor student progress and incorporate knowledge of student performance across settings into the instructional planning process, using information provided by parents and others in those settings.		•			•	•	•	•	•	•	•	•	•

Principle 8. The teacher understands and uses formal and informal assessment strategies to evaluate and ensure the continuous intellectual, social, and physical development of the learner.

		Chapter												
		1	2	3	4	5	6	7	8	9	10	11	12	13
8.01	All general and special education teachers understand the purposes, strengths, and limitations of formal and informal assessment approaches for making eligibility, placement, and instructional decisions for students with disabilities.		•	•					•	•	•	•	•	•
8.02	All teachers use a variety of assessment procedures to document students' learning, behavior, and growth within multiple environments appropriate to the student's age, interests, and learning.			•		•	•	•	•	•	•	•	•	•
8.03	All teachers collaborate with others to incorporate accommodations and alternative assessments into the ongoing assessment process of students with disabilities when appropriate.					•	•	•	•	•	•	•	•	•
8.04	All teachers engage all students, including students with disabilities, in assessing and understanding their own learning and behavior.						•	•	•	•	•	•	•	•
8.05	All teachers understand that students with disabilities are expected to participate in district- and statewide assessments and that accommodations or alternative assessments may be required when appropriate.									•			•	•

Principle 9. The teacher is a reflective practitioner who continually evaluates the effects of his or her choices and actions on others and who actively seeks out opportunities to grow professionally.

		Chapter												
		1	2	3	4	5	6	7	8	9	10	11	12	13
9.02	All general and special education teachers continually challenge their beliefs about how students with disabilities learn and how to teach them effectively.	•				•	•	•	•	•	•	•	•	•
9.03	All teachers actively seek out current information and research about how to educate the students with disabilities for whom they are responsible, including information that will help them understand the strengths and needs of students with disabilities as well as ways to more effectively promote their learning.					•	•	•	•	•	•	•	•	•
9.04	All teachers reflect on the potential interaction between a student's cultural experiences and his or her disability.			•	•	•	•	•	•	•		•	•	•

Principle 10. The teacher fosters relationships with school colleagues, families, and agencies in the larger community to support students' learning and well-being.

		Chapter												
		1	2	3	4	5	6	7	8	9	10	11	12	13
10.01	All general and special education teachers share instructional responsibility for students with disabilities and work to develop well-functioning collaborative teaching relationships.	•								•		•	•	•
10.02	All teachers understand the purposes of, and are effective members of, the different types of teams within the special education process (e.g., child study and teacher assistance teams, multidisciplinary teams that focus on identification and placement, IEP/IFSP teams).	•										•		•
10.04	All teachers accept families as full partners in planning appropriate instruction and services for students with disabilities, and provide meaningful opportunities for them to participate as partners in their children's instructional programs and in the life of the school.			•	•	•	•	•	•	•	•	•	•	•

SOURCE: The Interstate New Teacher Assessment and Support Consortium (INTASC) standards were developed by the Council of Chief State School Officers and member states. Copies may be downloaded from the council's website at http://www.ccsso.org

Council of Chief State School Officers. (1992). *Model standards for beginning teacher licensing, assessment, and development: A resource for state dialogue.* Washington, DC: Author. Retrieved April 5, 2010, from http://www.ccsso.org/content/pdfs/corestrd.pdf

- Structuring and managing the learning environment, including
  - structuring the learning environment; for example: the physical-social environment for learning (expectations, rules, consequences, consistency, attitudes, lighting, acoustic characteristics, seating, access, safety provisions, and strategies for positive interactions); transitions between lessons and activities; grouping of students; integration of related services (occupational therapy, physical therapy, speech and language therapy)
  - classroom management techniques; for example: behavioral analysis (identification and definition of antecedents, target behavior, and consequent events); behavioral interventions; functional analysis; data gathering procedures (such as anecdotal data, frequency methods, and interval methods); self-management strategies and reinforcement; cognitive-behavioral interventions; social skills training; behavior management strategies
- Professional roles, including
  - specific roles and responsibilities of teachers; for example: teacher as a collaborator with other teachers, teacher educators, parents, community groups, and outside agencies; teacher as a multidisciplinary team member; maintaining effective and efficient documentation; selecting appropriate environments and services for students; critical evaluation and use of professional literature and organizations; reflecting on one's own teaching; teacher's role in a variety of teaching settings (self-contained classroom, resource room, itinerant, co-teacher in inclusion setting, etc.); and maintaining student confidentiality
  - influence of teacher attitudes, values, and behaviors on the learning of exceptional students
  - communicating with parents, guardians, and appropriate community collaborators; for example: directing parents and guardians to parent-educators or to other groups and resources; writing reports directly to parents; meeting with parents to discuss student concerns, progress, and IEPs; encouraging parent participation; reciprocal communication and training with other service providers

---

Glossary

absence seizure A type of epileptic seizure lasting for a brief period of time whereby the individual loses consciousness and stops moving, formerly known as a petit mal seizure.

acceleration An instructional strategy typically used with pupils who are gifted and talented; one approach is placing students in a grade level beyond their chronological age.

acoustic immittance A technical term for measurements of middle ear function.

acquired immune deficiency syndrome (AIDS) An infectious disease caused by HIV (human immunodeficiency virus) that destroys the immune system, leaving the person open to serious, life-threatening diseases.

active listening A type of listening in which a person is attentive to the feelings, as well as the verbal message, that are being communicated.

adaptability The ability of an individual or a family to change in response to a crisis or stressful event.

adaptive behavior The ability of an individual to meet the standards of personal independence as well as social responsibility appropriate for his or her chronological age and cultural group.

additions An articulation disorder wherein the speaker inserts extra sounds in spoken words.

adventitious (acquired) hearing loss Hearing loss that is acquired after birth, not inherited.

air-conduction audiometry A procedure for measuring hearing sensitivity at certain frequencies using pure tones presented to the listener through earphones or speakers.

albinism A hereditary condition with partial or total absence of pigment in the eye.

amniocentesis A diagnostic medical procedure performed to detect chromosomal and genetic abnormalities in a fetus.

amplified telephones Telephones containing a variable output control designed to increase volume for the listener.

anencephaly Cranial malformation; large part of the brain fails to develop.

anoxia Loss of or inadequate supply of oxygen associated with the birth process and frequently resulting in brain damage.

aphakic Absence of the lens, causing light sensitivity and loss of visual acuity.

aphasia Loss or impairment of language functions.

applied behavior analysis (ABA) Application of learning principles derived from operant conditioning; used to increase or decrease specific behaviors.

apraxia of speech Speech and language disorder comprising both a speech disorder, caused by oral–motor difficulty, and a language disorder, characterized by the resultant limitations of expression.

articulation disorders Errors in the formation of individual sounds of speech.

Asperger syndrome A pervasive developmental disorder with severe and sustained impairments in social interaction and the development of restricted, repetitive patterns of behavior, interests, and activities. Disorder causes clinically significant impairments in other important areas of functioning.

assessment The process of gathering information and identifying a student's strengths and needs through a variety of instruments and products; data used in making decisions.

assistive listening devices (ALDs) Devices such as FM or sound field systems that improve the clarity of what is heard by an individual with hearing impairments by reducing background noise levels.

assistive technology Any item, piece of equipment, or product system that increases, maintains, or improves functional capabilities of individuals with disabilities.

asthma A lung disease with acute attacks of shortness of breath and wheezing.

astigmatism One or more surfaces of the cornea or lens are cylindrical, not spherical, resulting in distorted vision.

ataxic cerebral palsy A type of cerebral palsy that is characterized by poor balance and equilibrium in addition to uncoordinated voluntary movement.

athetoid cerebral palsy A type of cerebral palsy in which movements are contorted, abnormal, and purposeless.

atresia The absence or closure of the ear canal; can be congenital or acquired from injury or disease.

at-risk An infant or a child who has a high probability of exhibiting delays in development or developing a disability.

attention deficit hyperactivity disorder (ADHD) A disorder characterized by symptoms of inattention, hyperactivity, and/or impulsivity. Frequently observed in individuals with learning disabilities.

auditory neuropathy/auditory dys-synchrony A hearing loss in which the cochlea is functioning normally but there is loss of neural function.

audiogram A graphic representation of audiometric findings showing hearing thresholds as a function of frequency.

audiologist A professional who studies the science of hearing, including anatomy, function, and disorders, and provides education and treatment for those with hearing loss.

audiometric test A test designed to measure auditory sensitivity and determine the nature and severity of any loss of hearing.

auditory evoked potentials Neural impulses produced from within the auditory system in response to stimulation of the auditory pathway and recorded as bioelectric events using a special computer.

auditory trainers Amplification systems used by children with hearing impairments in place of their hearing aids in educational settings.

augmentative or alternative communication (AAC) Symbols, aids, strategies, and techniques used as a supplement or alternative to oral language.

authentic assessment An evaluation of a student's ability by means of various work products, typically classroom assignments and other activities.

autism spectrum disorders Developmental disorders characterized by abnormal or impaired development in social interaction and communication and a markedly restricted repertoire of activity and interests.

autistic savant An individual with autism who possesses special skills in areas such as mathematical calculations, memory feats, artistic and musical abilities, or reading.

autosomal dominant A genetic form of inheritance involving the non-sex-linked chromosomes in which the individual has one normal and one abnormal gene in a gene pair.

autosomal recessive A genetic form of inheritance involving the non-sex-linked chromosomes in which both genes of a gene pair must be affected for the trait to be expressed.

behavioral curriculum model A curriculum approach based on learning principles derived from behavioral psychology.

behavioral inhibition A characteristic common in persons with ADHD; impacts executive functions. Typically affects the ability to (1) withhold a planned response, (2) interrupt an ongoing response, and (3) protect an ongoing response from distractions.

behavioral intervention plan A plan required by Public Law 105–17 for students with disabilities who exhibit problematic behavior; a proactive intervention approach that includes a functional behavioral assessment and the use of positive behavioral supports.

bilingual education An educational approach whereby students whose first language is not English are instructed primarily through their native language while developing competency and proficiency in English.

bilingual special education Strategy whereby a pupil's home language and culture are used along with English in an individually designed program of special instruction.

biologically at-risk Young children with a history of pre-, peri-, or postnatal conditions and developmental events that heighten the potential for later atypical development.

birth trauma Difficulties associated with the delivery of the fetus.

bone-conduction audiometry A procedure for measuring hearing sensitivity at certain frequencies using pure tones presented through an oscillator placed on the forehead or mastoid bone of the listener. Sound is conducted to the inner ear through the bones of the skull.

Braille A communication system utilizing raised representation of written materials for tactual interpretation.

brain injury Actual or assumed trauma to the brain.

breech presentation Fetus exits the birth canal buttocks first rather than typical headfirst presentation.

cataracts Lenses that are opaque or cloudy due to trauma or age.

category Label assigned to individuals who share common characteristics and features.

central auditory nervous system Part of the hearing mechanism connecting the ear to the brain.

central auditory processing disorder (CAPD) A problem in the processing of sound not attributed to hearing loss or intellectual capacity, involving cognitive and linguistic functions that directly affect receptive communication skills.

central hearing disorder Difficulty in the reception and interpretation of auditory information in the absence of a hearing loss.

cerebral palsy Several nonprogressive disorders of voluntary movement or posture that are caused by damage to the developing brain.

CHARGE association A rare genetic disorder resulting in deaf–blindness, a syndrome representing a cluster of physical anomalies present at birth.

child-find A function of each state, mandated by federal law, to locate and refer individuals who might require special education.

child maltreatment The neglect and/or physical, emotional, or sexual abuse of a child.

childhood disintegrative disorder A marked regression in multiple areas of functioning following a period of at least two years of apparent normal development; after the first two years of life (but before ten years), the child has a clinically significant loss of previously acquired skills in at least two of the following areas: expressive or receptive language, social skills or adaptive behavior, bowel or bladder control, play, and motor skills.

chorionic villus sampling (CVS) A diagnostic medical procedure used to detect a variety of chromosomal abnormalities, usually conducted in the first trimester of pregnancy.

classroom ambience The feeling or sense a person experiences upon entering a classroom; the appeal of the room.

classroom arrangement The physical layout of the classroom and its décor; a proactive intervention technique designed to minimize disruptions while increasing pupil engagement.

cleft lip/cleft palate A congenital defect in which the upper lip is split or there is an opening in the roof of the mouth. Can often be surgically corrected. Hypernasality is common.

clinically derived classification systems Systems frequently used by mental health professionals to describe childhood, adolescent, and adult mental disorders.

cluster grouping The practice of placing five or more students who have similar needs and abilities with one teacher; promotes challenging cognitive development and positive social–emotional development.

cluttering Type of fluency disorder involving cognitive, linguistic, pragmatic, speech, and motor abilities.

cochlea Shell- or spiral-shaped structure in the inner ear that is responsible for hearing.

cohesion Within a family, the degree of freedom and independence experienced by each member.

collaboration How individuals work together; a style of interaction among professionals.

coloboma A congenital condition that results in a teardrop shape of the pupil, iris, lens, retina, choroids, or optic nerve; may involve loss of field vision as well as problems with glare and depth perception.

communication The sharing or exchange of ideas, information, thoughts, and feelings. Does not necessarily require speech or language.

communication breakdowns Misunderstandings as to what is being communicated, especially as it relates to individuals who are using some form of augmentative communication.

community-based instruction A strategy for teaching functional skills in the environment in which they would naturally occur rather than in simulated settings.

comorbidity The simultaneous existence of two or more conditions within the same person.

complex partial seizure A type of epileptic seizure whereby the person exhibits purposeless motor activity for a brief period of time; consciousness is impaired.

conduct disorders Common psychiatric disorders among children and youth characterized by disruptive and aggressive behavior as well as other actions that violate societal rules.

conductive hearing loss The loss of sound sensitivity produced by abnormalities of the outer ear and/or middle ear.

cone cells Light-sensitive cells located mainly in the central area of the retina that define color.

conflict resolution Program designed to teach problem-solving skills along with strategies for negotiation and mediation.

consultation A focused problem-solving process in which one individual offers support and expertise to another person.

content enhancements Instructional aids designed to assist pupils in understanding major concepts, ideas, and vocabulary in a way that aids the acquisition, organization, and recall of material.

contractures Shortened muscles that result in the inability to fully extend a joint.

cooperative learning Instructional process whereby heterogeneous groups of students work together on an assignment.

cooperative teaching An instructional approach in which a special education teacher and a general educator teach together in a general education classroom to a heterogeneous group of students.

cornea The transparent outer portion of the eyeball that transmits light to the retina.

creativity A term with multiple meanings, generally referring to the production of novel or original ideas or products.

crisis prevention and management programs Techniques taught to teachers on how to effectively and proactively deal with students' violent, aggressive, and/or self-injurious behaviors; a proactive preventative approach.

criterion-referenced assessment An assessment procedure in which a student's performance is compared to a particular level of mastery.

cultural pluralism The practice of appreciating and respecting ethnic and cultural differences.

cultural sensitivity A perspective adopted by professionals when working with families in which there is an awareness of and respect for the values, customs, and traditions of individuals and families.

culture The attitudes, values, belief systems, norms, and traditions shared by a particular group of people that collectively form their heritage.

curriculum-based assessment (CBA) Assessment procedure in which test items are constructed based on local school curriculum.

curriculum-based measurement (CBM) Evaluation technique for monitoring student progress in core academic areas such as reading, writing, and arithmetic.

curriculum compacting An instructional technique whereby the time spent on academic subjects is reduced so as to allow for enrichment activities; typically used with students who are gifted or talented.

cytomegalovirus Known as CMV, a common virus that is part of the herpes group; if initial exposure occurs during pregnancy, severe damage to the fetus often results.

deaf Limited or absent hearing for ordinary purposes of daily living.

deaf–blind A dual disability resulting in impaired hearing and vision.

decibels (dB) Units of measure expressing the magnitude of a sound relative to the softest sound to which the normal human ear can respond.

deinstitutionalization A movement whereby persons with intellectual disabilities are relocated from large institutions into smaller, community-based, group living settings.

developmental delay A term defined by individual states referring to children ages 3 to 9 who perform significantly below developmental norms.

developmental language delay Slowness in the development of adequate vocabulary and grammar, or when a child's language age does not correspond to the child's chronological age.

developmental/cognitive model A curriculum approach based on the work of Piaget; cognitive development seen as resulting from maturation coupled with active interaction and involvement with children's environment.

differentiation A modification of the curriculum that enables students who are gifted to learn at a level appropriate to their ability.

diplegia Paralysis (or spasticity) of the legs and partly the arms.

Direct Instruction (DI) A teacher-directed instructional technique used to produce gains in specific academic skills; emphasizes drill and practice along with immediate feedback and reward.

disability An inability or incapacity to perform a task or an activity in a normative fashion.

discrepancy In regard to learning disabilities, the difference between the student's actual academic performance and his or her estimated ability.

distortions Articulation disorder in which a sound is said inaccurately but resembles the intended sound (e.g., *shlip* for *sip*).

doctor's office effect The absence of symptoms of ADHD when the individual is evaluated in a structured environment such as a physician's office.

Down syndrome A chromosomal abnormality frequently resulting in intellectual disabilities with accompanying distinctive physical features.

Duchenne muscular dystrophy An inherited disease that is characterized by progressive muscle weakness from the degeneration of the muscle fiber.

dyslexia A severe reading disability; difficulty in understanding the relationship between sounds and letters.

early childhood special education Provision of customized services uniquely crafted to meet the individual needs of youngsters with disabilities ages 3 to 5.

early intervention The delivery of a coordinated and comprehensive package of specialized services to infants and toddlers with developmental delays or at-risk conditions and their families.

educable mentally retarded (EMR) Classification of a person with mild intellectual disabilities who typically develops functional academic skills at a third- or fourth-grade level; IQ range generally between 50–55 and 70–75.

effective instructional cycle A teaching technique designed to enhance learning and student engagement.

emotional disturbance A term often used when referring to individuals with emotional or behavioral disorders.

emotional or behavioral disorders A chronic condition characterized by behaviors that significantly differ from age norms and community standards to such a degree that educational performance is adversely affected.

encephalitis An inflammation of the brain; may cause damage to the central nervous system.

environmental control unit (ECU) A device that allows the user to control electric appliances, telephones, and other items that use electric outlets from a distance.

environmentally at-risk Youngsters who are biologically typical yet encounter life experiences or environmental circumstances that are so limiting that there is the possibility of future delayed development.

epilepsy A chronic condition in which the person has reoccurring seizures.

established risk Youngsters with a diagnosed medical disorder of known etiology and predictable prognosis or outcome.

ethnocentrism A perspective whereby a person views his or her cultural practices as correct and those of other groups as inferior, peculiar, or deviant.

etiology A term frequently used when describing the cause of a disability.

eugenics movement A campaign that sought to improve the quality of humankind through carefully controlled selective breeding.

evoked otoacoustic emissions Sounds produced by the inner ear in response to auditory stimulation and measured in the ear canal.

exceptional children Children who deviate from the norm to such an extent that special educational services are required.

exclusionary clause In regard to learning disabilities, the elimination of possible etiological factors to explain a pupil's difficulty in learning.

executive functions Internal regulation of one's behavior through control of emotions, inner speech, working memory, arousal levels, and motivation. Considered impaired in individuals with attention deficit hyperactivity disorder.

expressive language The formation and production of language, verbal and nonverbal, that is understood by and meaningful to others.

external locus of control The belief that the consequences or outcomes of a person's actions are the result of circumstances and situations beyond one's control rather than a result of one's own efforts.

externalizing disorders Behavior disorders characterized by aggressive, disruptive, acting-out behavior.

familiality studies A method for assessing the degree to which a particular characteristic is inherited; the tendency for certain conditions to occur in a single family.

family characteristics One dimension of a family systems model; aspects include family size and form, cultural background, and socioeconomic status, as well as the type and severity of the disability.

family functions Interrelated activities found within a family systems model; functions range from affection to economics to socialization, among other variables.

family interactions One aspect of a family systems model; refers to the relationships and interactions occurring among and between various family subsystems.

family life cycle Developmental changes occurring within a family over time.

family systems model A model that considers a family as an interrelated social system with unique characteristics and needs.

family-centered early intervention (approach) A philosophy of working with families that stresses family strengths and capabilities, the enhancement of skills, and the development of mutual partnerships between service providers and families.

family-directed assessment A form of assessment, useful for infants, toddlers, and preschool-age youngsters, that focuses on information that families choose to provide regarding needs, concerns, resources, and priorities.

fetal alcohol effect (FAE) A less severe and subtler form of fetal alcohol syndrome; caused by drinking alcohol while pregnant.

fetal alcohol syndrome (FAS) Results from mother's consumption of alcohol while pregnant; mild to moderate intellectual disabilities are common, along with physical deformities. A leading cause of intellectual disabilities, although completely preventable.

field dependent/sensitive Students who approach learning intuitively rather than analytically and logically. These students tend to find success in cooperative learning situations and group work.

field independent Learners who are detail oriented and analytically inclined. These students tend to thrive in competitive settings.

field loss A restriction to the visual field within the quadrant regions to the right, to the left, above, and below while gazing straight ahead.

fingerspelling A form of manual communication; different positions or movements of the fingers indicate letters of the alphabet.

flexible grouping The combining or grouping of students according to needs and abilities matched to their level of achievement.

fluency disorders Disorders that involve the flow of speech, influencing the rate and smoothness of an individual's speech.

FM systems Wireless systems that allow for the transmission of a signal from the teacher wearing a microphone to the student wearing a receiver, increasing the volume of the teacher's voice over the volume level of classroom noise.

formal supports Assistance provided by government social programs, habilitation services, or advocacy groups.

fragile X syndrome A chromosomal abnormality leading to intellectual disabilities along with physical anomalies; believed to be the most common form of inherited intellectual disabilities.

frequency The number of vibrations per second of a given sound wave; typically measured as cycles per second (cps) or hertz (Hz).

full inclusion An interpretation of the principle of least restrictive environment advocating that all pupils with disabilities are to be educated in the general education classroom.

functional Etiologies of speech and language disorders that have no obvious physical basis (such as environmental stress).

functional academics The application of life skills as a means of teaching academic tasks; core of many instructional programs for students with mild or moderate intellectual disabilities.

functional behavioral assessment A behavioral strategy that seeks to determine the purpose or function that a particular behavior serves—what is occasioning and maintaining the behavior.

functional curriculum A curriculum that emphasizes practical life skills rather than academic skills.

functional or nonorganic hearing loss A hearing loss that has no organic or biological basis.

functional vision How well students use the vision they have to complete a specific task.

functionally blind An educational description when the primary channel of learning is through tactile and auditory means.

galactosemia An inborn error of metabolism that makes infants unable to process galactose, resulting in a variety of physical problems in addition to intellectual disabilities; dietary intervention reduces potential for problems.

generalizing The ability to transfer previously learned knowledge or skills acquired in one setting to another set of circumstances or situation.

gifted and talented Persons who possess abilities and talents that can be demonstrated, or have the potential for being developed, at exceptionally high levels.

glaucoma A disease caused by increased pressure inside the aqueous portion of the eye with loss in the visual field.

Grade 1 Braille A beginning level of Braille in which a word is spelled out with a Braille letter corresponding to each printed letter.

Grade 2 Braille A more complex level of Braille in which contractions are used to represent parts of words or whole words.

handicapism The unequal and differential treatment accorded individuals with a disability.

handicap Difficulties imposed by the environment on a person with a disability.

hard of hearing Refers to a person who has a hearing loss but uses the auditory channel as the primary avenue for oral communication, with or without a hearing aid.

hearing impairment Less than normal hearing (either sensitivity or speech understanding) resulting from auditory disorder(s).

hearing sensitivity loss Poorer than normal auditory sensitivity for sounds; usually measured in decibels using pure tones.

hemiplegia Paralysis (or spasticity) on the left or right side of the body.

heritability studies A method for assessing the degree to which a specific condition is inherited; a comparison of the prevalence of a characteristic in fraternal versus identical twins.

hertz (Hz) A unit of measurement for sound frequency, expressed as cycles per second (cps).

high-risk register A list of factors placing infants at increased risk for hearing impairment, including, but not limited to, low birth weight, congenital perinatal infections, a family history of childhood hearing impairment, severe asphyxia, and bacterial meningitis.

hydrocephalus A condition in which the head is unusually large due to accumulation of excessive cerebrospinal fluid; brain damage often minimized by surgically implanting a shunt to remove excess fluid.

hyperactive child syndrome A historical term commonly used to describe youngsters who exhibit impulsivity, inattention, and/or hyperactivity.

hypernasality Disorder of voice resonance, frequently observed as a result of cleft palate, in which too much air passes through the nasal cavities during the production of sounds, giving the speaker a distinctive nasal quality or "twang."

hyperopia Change in the shape of the eye, which shortens the light ray path and causes farsightedness.

hyponasality Disorder of voice resonance in which there is a restricted flow of air through the nostrils, often resulting in the speaker's sounding as if his or her nose is being held.

hypoxia Insufficient amount of oxygen to the brain; can result in brain damage.

incidence A rate of inception; number of new cases appearing in the population within a specific time period.

incus The second of the three middle ear bones for conducting sound to the inner ear, located between the malleus and the stapes; also called the anvil.

individualized transition plan (ITP) An individualized plan with identified goals and objectives used to prepare the student in making the transition from high school to work (or college).

individualized education program (IEP) A written detailed plan developed by a team for each pupil aged 3–21 who receives a special education; a management tool.

individualized family service plan (IFSP) A written plan developed by a team that coordinates services for infants and toddlers and their families.

infant stimulation Programs for infants with disabilities or those experiencing delays; emphasis usually on achieving developmental or cognitive milestones.

information technology Databases and computer-based information sources.

inner ear The snail-shaped part of the ear (cochlea) containing the organs of hearing and balance.

instructional technology Any apparatus or device that supports the teaching–learning process, such as computers or televisions; a tool for the delivery of instruction.

interdisciplinary team A group of professionals from different disciplines who function as a team but work independently; recommendations, however, are the result of sharing information and joint planning.

interindividual differences Differences between two or more persons in a particular area.

internalizing disorders Behavior disorders characterized by anxiety, withdrawal, fearfulness, and other conditions reflecting an individual's internal state.

interpersonal problem solving Teaching pupils the cognitive skills needed to avoid and resolve interpersonal conflicts, peer pressure, and ways of coping with stress and their own feelings.

interpreter A professional who signs, gestures, and/or fingerspells a speaker's message as it is spoken to enable individuals with hearing impairments to understand spoken language.

interveners People with specialized training and skills in deaf–blindness who provide individualized assistance to students.

intraindividual differences Differences within the individual; unique patterns of strengths and weaknesses.

iris The colored, circular part of the eye in front of the lens that controls the size of the pupil.

job coach An individual who supervises a person with a disability for all or part of the day to provide training, assistance, or support to maintain a job.

juvenile rheumatoid arthritis (JRA) A chronic arthritic condition affecting the joints that occurs before 16 years of age.

language A code used to communicate ideas via a conventional system of arbitrary signals.

language sample An observational evaluation that includes observing the speech and language characteristics of a child actively communicating.

lead poisoning Lead is an environmental toxin used at one time in the manufacture of gasoline and paint; ingestion of lead can cause seizures, brain damage, and impaired central nervous system functioning.

learned helplessness A lack of persistence at tasks that can be mastered; a tendency to expect failure.

learning disabilities A disability in which there is a discrepancy between a person's ability and academic achievement; individual possesses average intelligence.

learning media The materials and methods a student uses in conjunction with the sensory channels in the process of learning.

learning strategies Instructional methodologies focusing on teaching students how to learn; designed to assist pupils in becoming more actively engaged and involved in their own learning.

least restrictive environment (LRE) A relative concept individually determined for each student; principle that each pupil should be educated, to the maximum extent appropriate, with classmates who are typical.

legally blind A visual acuity of 20/200 or less in the better eye with correction or a visual field that is no greater than 20 degrees.

lens The transparent disc in the middle of the eye behind the pupil that brings rays of light into focus on the retina.

level of support A classification scheme for individuals with intellectual disabilities that is based on the type and extent of assistance required to function in various areas.

limb deficiency Any number of skeletal abnormalities in which an arm(s) and/or a leg(s) is partially or totally missing.

limited English proficient (LEP) A person with a reduced or diminished fluency in reading, writing, or speaking English.

literacy medium The student's preferred method of reading and writing.

low birth weight A term frequently used to describe babies who are born weighing less than 2,500 grams (5 pounds, 8 ounces).

low incidence disabilities A special education category representative of students with disabilities that occur relatively infrequently.

low vision A visual impairment that interferes with the ability to perform daily activities and in which the primary channel of learning is through the use of prescription and nonprescription devices.

macroculture The shared or national culture of a society.

macula The area of best central vision.

macular degeneration A common eye disease in adults, which may also occur in young people, involving damage to the central part of the retina cones, affecting central vision, light sensitivity, and color.

magnet high school A school with a strong instructional emphasis on a particular theme, such as performing arts or math and science; an option for secondary pupils who are gifted and talented.

mainstreaming An early term for the practice of integrating students with special needs into a general education classroom for all or part of the school day.

malleus The first and largest of the three middle ear bones for conducting sound to the inner ear. Also called the hammer, it is attached to the tympanic membrane.

manual communication Communication methods that utilize fingerspelling, signs, and gestures.

melting pot A metaphor describing the United States in the early decades of the twentieth century.

meningitis A viral or bacterial infection of the membranes covering the brain and spinal cord; associated with hearing loss and intellectual disabilities.

mentally ill A generic term often used by professionals outside of the field of special education to refer to individuals with emotional or behavioral disorders.

mentor The role fulfilled by an older individual who is an expert in a particular field and who works with and guides a student in an area of mutual interest.

metacognition The ability to evaluate and monitor one's own performance.

microcephaly A condition in which the head is unusually small, leading to inadequate development of the brain and resulting in intellectual disabilities.

microcultures Distinct subcultures within a larger culture; these groups maintain their own distinct values, norms, folkways, and identification.

middle ear The air-filled space behind the eardrum that contains three tiny bones (ossicles) that carry sound to the inner ear.

minimal brain injury A once popular term referring to individuals who exhibit behavioral signs of brain injury (such as distractibility or impulsivity) but with no neurological evidence.

minimal hearing loss (MHL) Technically not a hearing loss; however, individual experiences difficulty hearing spoken language at a distance or when background noise is present.

mixed cerebral palsy Cerebral palsy that consists of combinations of different types. A person who has both spastic and athetoid cerebral palsy would be considered to have mixed cerebral palsy.

mixed hearing loss Hearing losses resulting from both conductive and sensorineural hearing impairments.

mnemonic strategies A cognitive approach used to assist pupils in remembering material; the use of rhymes, pictures, acronyms, and similar aids to help in recall.

morphological disorder Difficulty learning and using morphological rules of language.

morphology Dictates how the smallest meaningful units of our language (morphemes) are combined to form words.

multiaxial system An assessment involving several axes, each of which refers to different domains of information, that may help a clinician plan treatment and predict outcome. Typically used by mental health professionals.

multicultural education An ambiguous concept that deals with issues of race, language, social class, and culture as well as disability and gender. Also viewed as an educational strategy wherein the cultural heritage of each pupil is valued.

multiculturalism Referring to more than one culture; acknowledges basic commonalities among groups of people while appreciating their differences.

multidisciplinary team A group of professionals from different disciplines who function as a team but perform their roles independent of one another.

multimodal interventions The use of concurrent treatment approaches with students who exhibit attention deficit hyperactivity disorder.

multiple disabilities Concomitant impairments that result in such severe educational needs that a student cannot be accommodated in a special education program solely on the basis of one of the impairments.

multiple intelligences An alternative perspective on intelligence suggesting that there are many different kinds of intelligence.

myopia Elongation of the eye that causes extreme nearsightedness and decreased visual acuity.

natural supports Assistance rendered by family members, friends, teachers, and coworkers.

neuromotor impairment An impairment involving abnormality of, or damage to, the brain, spinal cord, or nerves that send impulses to the muscles of the body.

noncategorical Programs developed based on student needs and common instructional requirements rather than on disability.

nondiscriminatory testing Federal mandate that assessments be conducted in a culturally responsive fashion.

normalization A principle advocating that individuals with disabilities be integrated, to the maximum extent possible, into all aspects of everyday living.

norm-referenced assessments Refers to standardized tests on which a pupil's performance is compared to that of his or her peers.

off-level testing The use of assessment instruments designed for older students when evaluating the academic ability of a child thought to be gifted.

omissions Articulation disorder that occurs when a sound is not pronounced in a word (e.g., *ban* for *band*).

optic nerve The nerve at the posterior of the eye that carries messages from the retina to the brain.

optic nerve atrophy Degeneration of the optic nerve, which may be congenital or hereditary, causing loss of central vision, color vision, and reduced visual acuity.

oral approaches Methods of instruction for children with hearing impairments that emphasize spoken language skills. Methodology attempts to use the child's residual hearing and employs auditory training and speechreading.

oral interpreter A professional who silently repeats a speaker's message as it is spoken so that a hearing-impaired person can lipread the message.

orbit A protective cone-shaped cavity in the skull, sometimes called the socket.

organ of Corti Organ of hearing found within the cochlea.

organic Etiologies of speech and language disorders that can be linked to a physiological deficit (such as cleft palate).

orientation and mobility Systematic techniques to plan routes and move from place to place for persons with visual impairments.

orthopedic impairments Physical disabilities that occur from congenital anomalies, diseases, or other causes that adversely affect a child's educational performance.

orthotics Various braces or splints that are used to help maintain alignment and decrease the development of contractures.

ossicular chain Three bones in the middle ear (malleus, incus, and stapes) that connect the eardrum to the inner ear and help to amplify sounds.

other health impairments A chronic or acute health problem that results in limited strength, vitality, or alertness and adversely affects educational performance.

otitis media Infection of the middle ear space, causing conductive hearing loss.

outer-directedness A condition characterized by a loss of confidence in one's own capabilities and a reliance on others for cues and guidance.

outer ear The most visible (external) part of the ear, useful in funneling sound to the ear canal and in localizing the source of sound.

oval window The link between the inner ear and the middle ear.

overrepresentation A situation in which a greater number of students from minority groups are placed in special education programs than would be expected based on the proportion of pupils in the general school population.

paraplegia Paralysis (or spasticity) of the legs.

perinatal Events occurring at or immediately after birth.

person-centered planning Useful when developing a student's individualized education program; creates a vision for pupil's future based on an analysis of his or her strengths, needs, and preferences.

pervasive developmental disorder, not otherwise specified (PDD, NOS) Label applied when there is a severe and pervasive impairment in the development of reciprocal social interaction associated with impairment in either verbal or nonverbal communication skills or with the presence of stereotyped behavior, interests, and activities.

pervasive developmental disorders Disorders characterized by severe and pervasive impairment in several areas of development: reciprocal social interaction skills, communication skills, or the presence of stereotyped behavior, interests, and activities.

phenylketonuria (PKU) An inherited metabolic disorder resulting from the inability of the body to convert phenylalanine to tyrosine; can be detected at birth and controlled by diet; left untreated, consequences are often severe.

phonation Includes speech factors of pitch, loudness, and quality.

phonemes Smallest unit of sound found in spoken language.

phonemic awareness The ability to recognize that words consist of different sounds or phonemes.

phonological awareness Possible explanation for the reading problems of some students with learning disabilities; difficulty in recognizing the correspondence between specific sounds and certain letters that make up words.

phonological disorder Abnormal organization of phonological system resulting in a significant deficit in speech production or perception.

phonology The sound system of a language, including the use of sounds to create meaningful syllables and words.

photophobic Sensitive to light.

play audiometry A method for measuring hearing sensitivity in young children by rewarding correct responses; turning the evaluation situation into a game in order to maintain interest and cooperation.

portfolio assessment A type of authentic assessment; samples of different work products gathered over time and across curriculum areas are evaluated.

positive behavioral support An alternative approach to punishment; a schoolwide, proactive way of addressing problematic behaviors.

postlingual Referring to the period of time after a child has developed language.

postnatal Events occurring after birth.

pragmatic difficulties Problems in understanding and using language in different social contexts.

pragmatics A sociolinguistic system involving the use of communication skills in social contexts.

preassessment An assessment of a pupil's previously acquired knowledge; allows teacher to provide differentiated learning experiences.

precipitous birth Birth that occurs in less than two hours.

prelingual Referring to the period of time prior to a child's development of language.

prelinguistic Communicative behaviors used by children before the formation of formal speech and language characteristics.

premature birth Babies born prior to 37 weeks of gestational age.

prenatal Events occurring before birth.

prereferral intervention Instructional or behavioral strategies introduced by a general educator to assist students experiencing difficulty; designed to minimize inappropriate referrals for special education.

prevalence The total number of individuals in a given category during a particular period of time.

primary literacy medium An individual's most frequently used method of reading and writing.

primary prevention Activities aimed at eliminating a problem or condition prior to its onset; may also refer to reducing the number of new instances of problematic behavior.

problem-based learning Instructional approach in which authentic problems having multiple solutions are addressed through the application of critical thinking skills.

progress monitoring The frequent and systematic assessment of a pupil's academic progress.

proximity and movement management A classroom management strategy focusing on the effective use of classroom space and the arrangement of the physical environment as a means of minimizing disruptive behavior.

psychogenic theories Freudian perspective that if basic psychological bonds are not established between the parent and the child, the child will not be able to establish relationships with others and will fail to progress. Individual psychotherapy recommended as the treatment of choice.

psychostimulants Medications typically prescribed for persons with ADHD. These drugs activate or enhance specific aspects of neurological functioning that in turn affect executive functions.

pupil The circular opening at the center of the iris that controls the amount of light allowed into the eye.

pure-tone audiometry A procedure for measuring hearing sensitivity at certain frequencies using tones that are presented at various intensities.

quadriplegia Paralysis (or spasticity) of both legs and both arms.

rebound effect The behavioral deterioration sometimes observed in persons with ADHD as the effect of psychostimulant medication gradually wears off.

receptive language The ability to understand what is meant by spoken communication.

referral A formal request by a teacher or parent that a student be evaluated for special education services.

regular education initiative (REI) An approach that advocates that general educators assume greater responsibility for the education of students with disabilities.

related services Services defined by federal law whose purpose is to assist a student with exceptionalities derive benefit from a special education.

reliable means of response A consistent, reliable way of answering questions.

residual hearing Remaining usable hearing in a person with hearing loss.

residual vision An individual's usable vision.

resonance Sound quality of speech.

respite care Temporary or occasional care of an individual with disabilities by nonfamily members.

response to intervention (RTI) A strategy used for determining whether a pupil has a learning disability. Student is exposed to increasing levels of validated instructional intervention; responsiveness to the instruction is assessed; a lack of adequate progress typically leads to a referral for possible special education services.

retina The inner layer of the eye containing light-sensitive cells that connect with the brain through the optic nerve.

retinitis pigmentosa Pigmentation of the retina that can result in night blindness, photophobia, and eventual loss of vision in various parts of the periphery.

retinopathy of prematurity (ROP) An interruption in the vascular system of the eye, due to premature birth, in which veins and arteries begin to grow in an unorganized manner and cause bundles that pull together and detach the retina, resulting in loss of peripheral vision or total blindness.

Rett's disorder A pervasive developmental disorder occurring in females following a period of normal functioning after birth. Signs include characteristic hand-wringing or hand washing, severe or profound retardation, and delayed social development.

Rh incompatibility A condition that results when a woman who is Rh negative carries an Rh positive fetus. Mother's body will produce antibodies that can affect babies resulting from future pregnancies; often leads to intellectual disabilities and other impairments if mother does not receive an injection of Rh immune globulin.

rod cells Light-sensitive cells located mainly in the peripheral areas of the retina that are responsible for shape and motion, function best in reduced illumination, and are not responsive to color.

rubella A viral disease also known as German measles; contact in first trimester of pregnancy often results in a variety of significant impairments.

scaffolding A cognitive teaching strategy in which teacher provides temporary support to student who is learning a new task; supports are gradually removed as pupil becomes increasingly competent with the activity.

schizophrenia A severe disorder characterized by psychotic symptoms, including hallucinations, delusions, disorganized thinking, and catatonic motor behaviors. These signs and symptoms are associated with marked social or occupational dysfunction.

secondary prevention Efforts focusing on minimizing or eliminating potential risk factors in regard to persons with emotional or behavioral disorders; refers to minimizing the possibility that maladaptive or inappropriate behaviors will occur.

seizure A sudden, temporary change in the normal functioning of the brain's electrical system due to excessive, uncontrolled electrical activity in the brain.

self-advocacy Speaking out for one's personal preferences; protecting one's own interests.

self-contained A separate classroom for children with disabilities, usually found in a public school.

self-determination Self-advocacy efforts by an individual with a disability; expression of desire to live one's life according to one's own wishes; assuming personal control over one's life.

self-instruction A cognitive strategy for changing behavior; pupils initially talk to themselves out loud while performing a task and verbally reward themselves for success.

self-monitoring strategies A behavioral self-control strategy; pupils compare their performance to a criterion, record their efforts, and obtain reinforcement if appropriate.

self-regulation The ability of an individual to manage or govern his or her own behavior.

semantic disorders Language difficulties associated with poor vocabulary development, inappropriate use of word meanings, and/or inability to comprehend word meanings.

semantics A psycholinguistic system that involves word meanings and word relationships and their use in communication.

sensorineural hearing loss The loss of sound sensitivity produced by abnormalities of the inner ear or nerve pathways beyond the inner ear to the brain.

sheltered workshop A structured work environment for persons with disabilities in which vocational and social skills are often the focus of attention; may be a temporary or permanent placement.

short-term memory The recall of information after a brief period of time.

signal-to-noise ratio The ratio of the signal level (in decibels) to the corresponding background noise level.

Snellen chart An eye chart of clinical measurement of the true amount of distance vision an individual has under certain conditions.

social skills training Using direct instruction to teach students appropriate social behaviors; goal is to increase individual's social competency and acceptance.

socially maladjusted Individuals whose social behaviors are atypical; often regarded as chronic social offenders.

sound field systems A system to assist students with hearing impairments in which the teacher wears a microphone that transmits a signal to a speaker strategically placed in the classroom rather than to a body-worn receiver.

spastic cerebral palsy A type of cerebral palsy in which the person has very tight muscles occurring in one or more muscle groups, resulting in stiff, uncoordinated movements.

special education Specially designed instruction to meet the unique needs of an individual recognized as exceptional.

specialized instructional strategies Teaching techniques specifically designed for a particular special education population to assist with learning specific material.

speech The expression of language via sounds; the oral modality for language.

speech audiometry A set of procedures for measuring auditory perception of speech, including syllables, words, and sentences.

speech recognition threshold (SRT) A measure of threshold sensitivity for speech. The SRT represents the softest sound level at which a listener can identify the stimuli 50 percent of the time.

spina bifida Failure of the neural tube to completely close during fetal development. In its most severe form, the baby is born with a sac on his or her back containing part of the spinal cord.

spread The practice of spreading inferences to other unrelated aspects of a disability, often resulting in stereotyping.

stage theory A hypothesized pattern of parents' reaction to the news that their child has a disability.

standard deviation (SD) A descriptive statistic that expresses the variability and distribution of a set of scores relative to the mean.

stapes The third of the middle ear bones for conducting sound to the inner ear. It resembles a stirrup in shape and is sometimes called the stirrup. It is the smallest bone in the body.

statistically derived classification systems System developed to analyze patterns of behaviors based on statistical procedures that characterize children and youth with emotional or behavioral disorders.

strength-based assessment An assessment model that looks at an individual's strengths, abilities, and accomplishments rather than focusing on his or her deficits.

Strauss syndrome A historical term applied to individuals with intellectual disabilities who exhibit high levels of distractibility and hyperactivity.

stuttering Type of fluency disorder in which word sounds are repeated.

substitutions Articulation disorder that occurs when one sound is substituted for another in the pronunciation of a word (e.g., *wabbit* for *rabbit*).

supported (competitive) employment At a work site for typical workers, individuals with disabilities are employed and work alongside their typical peers but receive ongoing assistance from a job coach.

syntactical deficits Difficulty in acquiring the rules that control word order and other aspects of grammar.

syntax A series of linguistic rules that determine word order and combinations to form sentences and how such word order is used in the communication process.

syphilis A sexually transmitted disease; infection of the mother in the last trimester of pregnancy can cause intellectual disabilities in the child.

systems of care model Providing an individually tailored and coordinated system of services and care to students with emotional or behavioral disorders; developed by family members and service providers.

task analysis An instructional methodology whereby complex tasks are analyzed and broken down into sequential component parts; each part is taught separately and then as a whole.

technology productivity tools Computer software, hardware, and related systems designed to help people work effectively.

telecommunication device for the deaf (TDD) An instrument for sending typewritten messages over telephone lines to be received by a person who is deaf or severely hearing impaired as a printed message. Sometimes called TT, TTY, or TTD.

teratogen Infections, drugs, chemicals, or environmental agents that can produce fetal abnormalities.

tertiary prevention Efforts that attempt to limit the adverse consequences of an existing problem while maximizing a person's potential; in regard to persons with emotional or behavioral disorders, refers to an intense level of intervention using strategies and supports designed for individuals with chronic and intense behavior problems.

theory of mind A hypothesis that attempts to explain the inability of the individual with autism to realize that other people have their own unique point of view about the world—different thoughts, plans, and perspectives from their own.

therapeutic abortion Elective termination of a pregnancy due to the presence of a birth defect.

tiered assignments An instructional strategy that allows the teacher to offer variations of the same lesson to students with differing levels of ability.

time management A proactive intervention strategy that attempts to maximize student engagement time and appropriately schedule class activities in addition to instruction in time management skills.

tonic–clonic seizure A convulsive seizure whereby the individual loses consciousness, falls, and begins making rhythmic jerking motions, formerly known as a grand mal seizure.

total communication (TC) A method of communication for students with hearing impairments, designed to provide equal emphasis on oral and signing skills to facilitate communication ability.

Tourette's syndrome A neurological disorder characterized by motor tics and uncontrollable verbal outbursts.

toxoplasmosis A maternal infection resulting from contact with parasites; especially devastating if exposure occurs during third trimester of pregnancy.

trainable mentally retarded (TMR) Classification of a person with moderate intellectual disabilities who is capable of learning self-care and social skills; IQ range generally between 35–40 and 50–55.

transdisciplinary team A group of professionals from different disciplines who function as a team but work independently; however, they share roles, and a peer is identified as the primary interventionist.

transition A broad term used to describe the movement of an individual from one educational environment to another, from one class to another, or from one phase of life (high school) to another (independent adulthood).

transition management The regulating of students as they move from one assignment to another or from one activity to another; a proactive behavioral intervention strategy.

transition plan *See* individualized transition plan.

transition services Individualized and coordinated services that assist the adolescent with a disability to successfully move from school to postschool activities.

transliteration Altering an interpreted message to facilitate understanding by a person who is hearing impaired.

traumatic brain injury An acquired injury to the brain caused by an external force that results in a disability or psychosocial impairment that adversely affects educational performance.

twice exceptional Students who are gifted and talented but also have a disability.

tympanic membrane A thin, membranous tissue between the ear canal and the middle ear that vibrates when struck by sound waves; also called the eardrum.

ultrasound The mapping or imaging of a fetus; useful in depicting a variety of defects.

underrepresentation A situation in which fewer children from minority groups are placed in special education programs than would be expected based on the proportion of pupils in the general school population.

universal design for learning The design of curriculum materials, instructional activities, and evaluation procedures that can meet the needs of learners with widely varying abilities and backgrounds.

Usher syndrome An inherited disorder resulting in deaf–blindness, deafness present at birth accompanied by progressive vision loss, sometimes associated with intellectual disabilities.

vision screening A simple measure to determine possible vision loss.

visual acuity The ability to visually perceive details of near or distant objects.

visual efficiency How well an individual uses remaining visual acuity at a distance or close up.

visual field The amount of vision in the quadrant regions to the right, to the left, above, and below while gazing straight ahead.

visual impairment An impairment in vision that, even with correction, adversely affects an individual's educational performance. The term includes both partial sight and blindness.

vitreous humor A colorless mass of soft, gelatinlike material that fills the eyeball behind the lens.

voice disorders May result from disorders of the larynx or disorders in phonation.

voice output communication aid (VOCA) Device that can be programmed to produce speech.

walker A mobility aid for individuals requiring support when walking.

word prediction program A software program that provides a list of potential words that correspond to the letters the user is typing so that the user does not have to type out the entire word.

working memory The ability to retain information while also engaging in another cognitive activity.

wraparound plan A coordinated interagency effort at providing supports and services to a student and his or her family in the natural environment—school, home, or community.

X-linked A pattern of inheritance involving the X chromosome, one of an individual's two sex chromosomes.

References

Chapter 1

Ballard, J., Ramirez, B., & Weintraub, F. (1982). *Special education in America: Its legal and governmental foundations.* Reston, VA: Council for Exceptional Children.

Bicard, S., & Heward, W. (2010). Educational equality for students with disabilities. In J. Banks & C. Banks (Eds.), *Multicultural education* (7th ed., pp. 315–341). Hoboken, NJ: Wiley.

Bogdan, R., & Biklen, D. (1977). Handicapism. *Social Policy, 7*(5), 14–19.

Brown, L., Albright, K., Rogan, P., York, J., Solnar, A., Johnson, F., et al. (1988). An integrated curriculum model for transition. In B. Ludlow, A. Turnbull, & R. Luckasson (Eds.), *Transitions to adult life for people with mental retardation: Principles and practices* (pp. 67–84). Baltimore: Paul H. Brookes.

Bruder, M. (1994). Working with members of other disciplines: Collaboration for success. In M. Wolery & J. Wilbers (Eds.), *Including children with special needs in early childhood programs* (pp. 45–70). Washington, DC: National Association for the Education of Young Children.

Bruder, M. (2010). Early childhood intervention: A promise to children and families for their future. *Exceptional Children, 76*(3), 339–355.

Clark, G., & Knowlton, H. (1988). A closer look at transition issues for the 1990s: A response to Rusch and Menchetti. *Exceptional Children, 54*(4), 365–367.

Cook, B. (2001). A comparison of teachers' attitudes toward their included students with mild and severe disabilities. *Journal of Special Education, 34*(4), 203–213.

Crutchfield, M. (1997, August). Who's teaching our children with disabilities? *National Information Center for Children and Youth with Disabilities News Digest, 27,* 1–23.

Dunn, L. (1973). *Exceptional children in the schools* (2nd ed.). New York: Holt, Rinehart & Winston.

Friend, M., & Cook, L. (2010). *Interactions: Collaboration skills for school professionals* (6th ed.). Needham Heights, MA: Allyn and Bacon.

Gargiulo, R., & Kilgo, J. (2011). *An introduction to young children with special needs* (3rd ed.). Belmont, CA: Wadsworth/Cengage Learning.

Gargiulo, R., & Metcalf, D. (2010). *Teaching in today's inclusive classrooms.* Belmont, CA: Wadsworth/Cengage Learning.

Giangreco, M., York, J., & Rainforth, B. (1989). Providing related services to learners with severe handicaps in educational settings: Pursuing the least restrictive option. *Pediatric Physical Therapy, 1*(2), 55–63.

Goodlad, J. (1984). *A place called school.* New York: McGraw-Hill.

Halpern, A. (1985). Transition: A look at the foundations. *Exceptional Children, 51*(6), 479–486.

Halpern, A. (1992). Transition: Old wine in new bottles. *Exceptional Children, 58*(3), 202–211.

Harris, L., & Associates. (2004). *National Organization on Disabilities/Harris Survey of Americans with Disabilities.* New York: Author.

Harry, B., & Klingner, J. (2007). Discarding the deficit model. *Educational Leadership, 64*(5), 16–21.

Hartman, M. (2009). Step by step: Creating a community-based transition program for students with intellectual disabilities. *Teaching Exceptional Children, 41*(6), 6–11.

Hitchcock, C., Meyer, A., Rose, D., & Jackson, R. (2002). Providing new access to the general curriculum: Universal design for learning. *Teaching Exceptional Children, 35*(2), 8–17.

Hobbs, N. (1975). *The futures of children.* San Francisco: Jossey-Bass.

Hobbs, T., & Westling, D. (1998). Promoting successful inclusion. *Teaching Exceptional Children, 31*(1), 10–14.

Hourcade, J., & Bauwens, J. (2003). *Cooperative teaching: Rebuilding and sharing the schoolhouse* (2nd ed.). Austin, TX: Pro-Ed.

Keefe, E., Moore, V., & Duff, F. (2004). The four "knows" of collaborative teaching. *Teaching Exceptional Children, 36*(5), 36–41.

Kitchin, R. (1998). "Out of place," "knowing one's place": Space, power and the exclusion of disabled people. *Disability and Society, 13,* 343–356.

Kliewer, C., & Biklen, D. (1996). Labeling: Who wants to be called retarded? In W. Stainback & S. Stainback (Eds.), *Controversial issues confronting special education: Divergent perspectives* (pp. 83–95). Boston: Allyn and Bacon.

Koppelman, J. (1986). Reagan signs bills expanding services to handicapped preschoolers. *Report to Preschool Programs, 18,* 3–4.

Lane, H. (1979). *The wild boy of Aveyron*. Cambridge, MA: Harvard University Press.

Lerner, J., & Johns, B. (2009). *Learning disabilities and related mild disabilities* (11th ed.). Belmont, CA: Wadsworth/Cengage Learning.

McCormick, L. (2003). Policies and practices. In L. McCormick, D. F. Loeb, & R. Schiefelbusch (Eds.), *Supporting children with communication difficulties in inclusive settings* (2nd ed., pp. 155–187). Boston: Allyn and Bacon.

McDonnell, J., Hardman, M., & McDonnell, A. (2003). *Introduction to persons with moderate and severe disabilities* (2nd ed.). Needham Heights, MA: Allyn and Bacon.

McLean, M., Wolery, M., & Bailey, D. (2004). *Assessing infants and preschoolers with special needs* (3rd ed.). Upper Saddle River, NJ: Pearson Education.

Meisels, S., & Shonkoff, J. (2000). Early childhood intervention: A continuing evolution. In J. Shonkoff & S. Meisels (Eds.), *Handbook of early childhood intervention* (2nd ed., pp. 3–31). Cambridge, England: Cambridge University Press.

Murawski, W., & Dieker, L. (2004). Tips and strategies for co-teaching at the secondary level. *Teaching Exceptional Children, 36*(5), 52–58.

National Center for Education Statistics. (2009). *Digest of education statistics 2008*. Washington, DC: U.S. Government Printing Office.

National Commission on Excellence in Education. (1983). *A nation at risk: The imperative for educational reform*. Washington, DC: Author.

National Longitudinal Transition Study 2. (2009). *The post-high school outcomes of youth with disabilities up to 4 years after high school*. Retrieved January 11, 2010, from http://www.nlts2.org/reports/2009_04/nlts2_report_2009_04_complete.pdf

Ohio State University Partnership Grant. (2010). *Fast facts for faculty: Universal design for learning*. Retrieved January 11, 2010, from http://ada.osu.edu/resources/fastfacts/Universal_Design.htm

Orkwis, R., & McLane, K. (1998). *A curriculum every student can use: Design principles for student access* (ED 423 654). Reston, VA: ERIC Clearinghouse on Disabilities and Gifted Education.

Pugach, M., & Johnson, L. (2002). *Collaborative practitioners, collaborative schools* (2nd ed.). Denver, CO: Love.

Reinhiller, N. (1996). Co-teaching: New variations on a not-so-new practice. *Teacher Education and Special Education, 19*(1), 34–48.

Reynolds, M., Wang, M., & Walberg, J. (1987). The necessary restructuring of special and regular education. *Exceptional Children, 53*(5), 391–398.

Rice, N., Drame, E., Owens, L., & Frattura, E. (2007). Co-instructing at the secondary level. *Teaching Exceptional Children, 39*(6), 12–18.

Sandall, S., Hemmeter, L., McLean, M., & Smith, B. (2005). *DEC recommended practices: A comprehensive guide for practical application in early intervention/early childhood special education*. Longmont, CO: Sopris West.

Scott, S., McGuire, J., & Shaw, S. (2003). Universal design for instruction: A new paradigm for adult instruction in secondary education. *Remedial and Special Education, 24*, 369–379.

Scruggs, T., Mastropieri, M., & McDuffie, K. (2007). Co-teaching in inclusive classrooms: A metasynthesis of qualitative research. *Exceptional Children, 73*(4), 392–416.

Smith, T., Polloway, E., Patton, J., & Dowdy, C. (2008). *Teaching students with special needs in inclusive settings* (5th ed.). Needham Heights, MA: Allyn and Bacon.

U.S. Department of Education. (1992). *Fourteenth annual report to Congress on the implementation of the Individuals with Disabilities Education Act*. Washington, DC: U.S. Government Printing Office.

U.S. Department of Education. (2009). *Twenty-eighth annual report to Congress on the implementation of the Individuals with Disabilities Education Act, 2006* (Vol. 1). Washington, DC: U.S. Government Printing Office.

U.S. Department of Education. (2010). *IDEA data*. Retrieved April 14, 2010, from https://www.ideadata.org/PartBReport.asp

Walther-Thomas, C., Korinek, L., McLaughlin, V., & Williams, B. (2000). *Collaboration for inclusive education*. Needham Heights, MA: Allyn and Bacon.

Wehmeyer, M., Lance, D., & Bashinski, S. (2002). Promoting access to the general curriculum for students with mental retardation. *Education and Training in Mental Retardation and Developmental Disabilities, 37*(3), 223–234.

Will, M. (1984). *OSERS programming for the transition of youth with disabilities: Bridges from school to working life*. Washington, DC: Office of Special Education and Rehabilitative Services.

Ysseldyke, J., Algozzine, B., & Thurlow, M. (1992). *Critical issues in special and remedial education* (2nd ed.). Boston: Houghton Mifflin.

Zigler, E. (2000). Foreword. In J. Shonkoff & S. Meisels (Eds.), *Handbook of early childhood intervention* (2nd ed., pp. xi–xv). Cambridge, England: Cambridge University Press.

Chapter 2

Bateman, B., & Linden, M. (2006). *Better IEPs* (4th ed.). Verona, WI: Attainment Co.

Bennett, T., DeLuca, D., & Bruns, D. (1997). Putting inclusion into practice: Perspectives of teachers and parents. *Exceptional Children, 64*(1), 115–131.

Buck, G., Polloway, E., Smith-Thomas, A., & Cook, K. (2003). Prereferral intervention process: A survey of state practices. *Exceptional Children, 69*(3), 349–360.

Center for Special Education Finance. (2004). *What are we spending on special education services in the United States, 1999–2000?* Retrieved January 14, 2010, from http://www.csef-air.org/index.php

Council for Exceptional Children. (1994). *CEC policies for delivering services to exceptional children*. Reston, VA: Author.

Council for Exceptional Children. (1997). What every teacher needs to know: A comparison of Section 504, ADA, and IDEA. *CEC Today, 4*(4), 1, 5, 15.

Council for Exceptional Children. (2003). *No Child Left Behind Act of 2001: Reauthorization of the Elementary and Secondary Education Act* (Technical assistance resource). Arlington, VA: Author.

Deno, E. (1970). Special education as developmental capital. *Exceptional Children, 37*(3), 229–237.

Dunn, L. (1968). Special education for the mildly retarded—Is much of it justifiable? *Exceptional Children, 35*(1), 5–22.

Fox, N., & Ysseldyke, J. (1997). Implementing inclusion at the middle school level: Lessons from a negative example. *Exceptional Children, 64*(1), 81–98.

Gargiulo, R., & Kilgo, J. (2011). *An introduction to young children with special needs* (3rd ed.). Belmont, CA: Wadsworth/Cengage Learning.

Gargiulo, R., & Metcalf, D. (2010). *Teaching in today's inclusive classrooms*. Belmont, CA: Wadsworth/Cengage Learning.

Henry, N., & Flynt, E. (1990). Rethinking special education referral: A procedural model. *Intervention in School and Clinic, 26*(1), 22–24.

Kauffman, J. (1995). Why we must celebrate a diversity of restrictive environments. *Learning Disabilities Research & Practice, 10*(4), 225–232.

Kennedy, C., & Horn, E. (Eds.). (2004). *Including students with severe disabilities*. Boston: Allyn and Bacon.

Lipkin, P., & Schertz, M. (2008). Early intervention and its efficacy. In P. Accardo (Ed.), *Capute & Accardo's neurodevelopmental disabilities in infancy and childhood* (3rd ed., Vol. 1, pp. 519–551). Baltimore: Paul H. Brookes.

Meyen, E. (1995). Legislative and programmatic foundations of special education. In E. Meyen & T. Skrtic (Eds.), *Special education and student disability* (4th ed., pp. 35–95). Denver, CO: Love.

Nolet, V., & McLaughlin, M. (2005). *Accessing the general curriculum* (2nd ed.). Thousand Oaks, CA: Corwin Press.

Noonan, M., & McCormick, L. (2006). *Young children with disabilities in natural environments*. Baltimore: Paul H. Brookes.

Osborne, A. (1996). *Legal issues in special education*. Needham Heights, MA: Allyn and Bacon.

Peterson, J., & Hittie, M. (2003). *Inclusive teaching: Creating effective schools for all learners*. Boston: Allyn and Bacon.

Polloway, E., Patton, J., & Serna, L. (2008). *Strategies for teaching learners with special needs* (9th ed.). Upper Saddle River, NJ: Pearson Education.

Pretti-Frontczak, K., & Bricker, D. (2004). *An activity-based approach to early intervention*. Baltimore: Paul H. Brookes.

Reynolds, M. (1962). A framework for considering some issues in special education. *Exceptional Children, 28*(7), 367–370.

Sailor, W. (Ed.). (2002). *Building partnerships for learning, achievement, and accountability*. New York: Teachers College Press.

Salend, S. (2011). *Creating inclusive classrooms* (7th ed.). Upper Saddle River, NJ: Pearson Education.

Skrtic, T. (1995). The special education knowledge tradition: Crisis and opportunity. In E. Meyen & T. Skrtic (Eds.), *Special education and student disability* (4th ed., pp. 609–672). Denver, CO: Love.

Smith, T. (2002). Section 504: What teachers need to know. *Intervention in School and Clinic, 37*(5), 259–266.

Smith, T., & Patton, J. (2007). *Section 504 and public schools: A practical guide* (2nd ed.). Austin, TX: Pro-Ed.

Trohanis, P. (1989). An introduction to PL 99–457 and the national policy agenda for serving young children with special needs and their families. In J. Gallagher, P. Trohanis, & R. Clifford (Eds.), *Policy implementation and PL 99–457: Planning for young children with special needs* (pp. 1–17). Baltimore: Paul H. Brookes.

Turnbull, A., Turnbull, H., Erwin, E., & Soodak, L. (2006). *Families, professionals, and exceptionality* (5th ed.). Upper Saddle River, NJ: Pearson Education.

Turnbull, A., Turnbull, H., Erwin, E., Soodak, L., & Shogren, K. (2011). *Families, professionals, and exceptionality* (6th ed.). Upper Saddle River, NJ: Pearson Education.

Turnbull, H. (1993). *Free appropriate public education: The law and children with disabilities* (4th ed.). Denver, CO: Love.

U.S. Department of Education. (1995). *Seventeenth annual report to Congress on the implementation of the Individuals with Disabilities Education Act*. Washington, DC: U.S. Government Printing Office.

U.S. Equal Employment Opportunity Commission. (2010). *Notice concerning the Americans with Disabilities Act (ADA) Amendments Act of 2008*. Retrieved January 14, 2010, from http://www.eeoc.gov/ada/amendments_notice.html

Weintraub, F., Abeson, A., Ballard, J., & LaVor, M. (Eds.). (1976). *Public policy and the education of exceptional children*. Reston, VA: Council for Exceptional Children.

Will, M. (1986a). Educating children with learning problems: A shared responsibility. *Exceptional Children, 52*(5), 411–415.

Will, M. (1986b). *Educating students with learning problems: A shared responsibility*. Washington, DC: U.S. Department of Education, Office of Special Education and Rehabilitative Services.

Yell, M. (2006). *The law and special education* (2nd ed.). Upper Saddle River, NJ: Pearson Education.

Ysseldyke, J. (2001). Reflections on a research career: Generalization from 25 years of research on assessment and instructional decision making. *Exceptional Children, 67*(3), 295–309.

Zirkel, P. (2009). What does the law say? New Section 504 student eligibility standards. *Teaching Exceptional Children, 41*(4), 68–71.

Chapter 3

Amos, J. (2008). *Dropouts, diplomas, and dollars*. Washington, DC: Alliance for Excellent Education.

Artiles, A., & Bal, A. (2008). The next generation of disproportionality research: Toward a comparative model in the study of equity in ability differences. *Journal of Special Education, 42*(1), 4–14.

Artiles, A., Kozleski, E., Trent, S., Osher, D., & Ortiz, A. (2010). Justifying and explaining disproportionality, 1968–2008: A critique of underlying views of culture. *Exceptional Children, 76*(3), 279–299.

Artiles, A., & Zamora-Durán, G. (1997). Disproportionate representation: A contentious and unresolved predicament. In A. Artiles & G. Zamora-Durán (Eds.), *Reducing disproportionate representation of culturally diverse students in special and gifted education* (pp. 1–6). Reston, VA: Council for Exceptional Children.

Baca, L., & Baca, E. (2004a). Bilingual special education: A judicial perspective. In L. Baca & H. Cervantes (Eds.), *The bilingual special education interface* (4th ed., pp. 76–99). Upper Saddle River, NJ: Pearson Education.

Baca, L., & Baca, E. (2004b). Bilingualism and bilingual education. In L. Baca & H. Cervantes (Eds.), *The bilingual special education interface* (4th ed., pp. 24–45). Upper Saddle River, NJ: Pearson Education.

Baca, L., Baca, E., & de Valenzuela, J. (2004). Background and rationale for bilingual special education. In L. Baca & H. Cervantes (Eds.), *The bilingual special education interface* (4th ed., pp. 1–23). Upper Saddle River, NJ: Pearson Education.

Banks, J. (2010). Multicultural education: Characteristics and goals. In J. Banks & C. Banks (Eds.), *Multicultural education issues and perspectives* (7th ed., pp. 3–30). Hoboken, NJ: Wiley.

Benner, S. (1998). *Special education issues within the context of American society*. Belmont, CA: Wadsworth.

Bicard, S., & Heward, W. (2010). Educational equity for students with disabilities. In J. Banks & C. Banks (Eds.), *Multicultural education: Issues and perspectives* (7th ed., pp. 315–341). Hoboken, NJ: Wiley.

Blanchett, W., Munford, V., & Beachum, F. (2005). Urban school failure and disproportionality in a post-Brown era. *Remedial and Special Education, 26*(2), 70–81.

Borland, J. (2004). *Issues and practices in the identification and education of gifted students from under-represented groups*. Storrs, CT: National Research Center on the Gifted and Talented.

Boyer, L., & Mainzer, R. (2003). Who's teaching students with disabilities? *Teaching Exceptional Children, 35*(6), 8–11.

Camarota, S. (2007). *100 million more: Projecting the impact of immigration on the U.S. population, 2007 to 2060*. Center for Immigration Studies. Retrieved January 14, 2010, from www.cis.org/impact_on_population.html

Children's Defense Fund. (2008). *Children in the United States*. Retrieved January 14, 2010, from http://www.childrensdefense.org/

Chinn, P., & Hughes, S. (1987). Representation of minority students in special education classes. *Remedial and Special Education, 8*(4), 41–46.

Clark, B. (2008). *Growing up gifted: Developing the potential of children at home and at school* (7th ed.). Upper Saddle River, NJ: Pearson Education.

Council for Exceptional Children. (1997). Making assessments of diverse students meaningful. *CEC Today*, October, 9.

Council for Exceptional Children. (2010). *New strategies to help diverse students succeed*. Retrieved January 14, 2010, from www.cec.sped.org/AM/Template.cfm?Section=Search&template=/CM/HTMLdisplay.cfm&contentID=11474

Coutinho, M., & Oswald, D. (2000). Disproportionate representation in special education: A synthesis and recommendations. *Journal of Child and Family Studies, 9*(2), 135–156.

Crawford, J. (2004). Language legislation in the USA. Cited in L. Baca & H. Cervantes (Eds.), *The bilingual special education interface* (4th ed.). Upper Saddle River, NJ: Pearson Education.

de Valenzuela, J., & Baca, L. (2004). Issues and theoretical considerations in the assessment of bilingual children. In L. Baca & H. Cervantes (Eds.), *The bilingual special education interface* (4th ed., pp. 162–183). Upper Saddle River, NJ: Pearson Education.

Donovan, S., & Cross, C. (Eds.). (2002). *Minority students in special and gifted education*. Washington, DC: National Research Council.

Figueroa, R. (1989). Psychological testing of linguistic-minority students: Knowledge gaps and regulations. *Exceptional Children, 56*(2), 145–152.

Ford, D. (1998). The underrepresentation of minority students in gifted education. *Journal of Special Education, 32*(1), 4–14.

Ford, D., Grantham, T., & Whiting, G. (2008). Culturally and linguistically diverse students in gifted education: Recruitment and retention issues. *Exceptional Children, 74*(3), 289–306.

Friend, M., & Bursuck, W. (2009). *Including students with special needs* (5th ed.). Boston: Pearson Education.

Garcia, S., & Malkin, D. (1993). Toward defining programs and services for culturally and linguistically diverse learners in special education. *Teaching Exceptional Children, 26*(1), 52–58.

Garcia, S., & Ortiz, A. (2006). Preventing disproportionate representation: Culturally and linguistically responsive prereferral interventions. *Teaching Exceptional Children, 38*(4), 64–68.

Gardner, H. (1983). *Frames of mind: The theory of multiple intelligence*. New York: Basic Books.

Gardner, H. (1993). *Multiple intelligences: The theory in practice*. New York: Wiley.

Gardner, H. (2006). *Multiple intelligences: New horizons*. New York: Basic Books.

Gargiulo, R., & Kilgo, J. (2011). *An introduction to young children with special needs* (3rd ed.). Belmont, CA: Wadsworth/Cengage Learning.

Gargiulo, R., & Metcalf, D. (2010). *Teaching in today's inclusive classrooms*. Belmont, CA: Wadsworth/Cengage Learning.

Gollnick, D., & Chinn, P. (2006). *Multicultural education in a pluralistic society* (7th ed.). Upper Saddle River, NJ: Pearson Education.

Gollnick, D., & Chinn, P. (2009). *Multicultural education in a pluralistic society* (8th ed.). Upper Saddle River, NJ: Pearson Education.

Harry, B. (1992). *Cultural diversity, families, and the special education system: Communication and empowerment*. New York: Teachers College Press.

Harry, B. (2008). The disproportionate placement of ethnic minorities in special education. In L. Florian (Ed.), *Sage handbook of special education* (pp. 69–84). London: Sage.

Harry, B., & Klinger, J. (2006). *Why are so many minority students in special education?* New York: Teachers College Press.

Harry, B., & Klinger, J. (2007). Discarding the deficit model. *Educational Leadership, 64*(5), 16–21.

Hoover, J., & Collier, C. (2004). Methods and materials for bilingual special education. In L. Baca & H. Cervantes (Eds.), *The bilingual special education interface* (4th ed., pp. 274–297). Upper Saddle River, NJ: Pearson Education.

Hoover, J., Klinger, J., Baca, L., & Patton, J. (2008). *Methods for teaching culturally and linguistically diverse exceptional learners*. Upper Saddle River, NJ: Pearson Education.

Hoover, J., & Patton, J. (2005). *Curriculum adaptation for students with learning and behavior problems: Principles and procedures* (3rd ed.). Austin, TX: Pro-Ed.

Janzen, R. (1994). Melting pot or mosaic? *Educational Leadership, 51*(8), 9–11.

Kaufman, A., & Kaufman, N. (2004). *Kaufman Assessment Battery for Children—Second Edition*. Circle Pines, MN: American Guidance Service.

Ladson-Billings, G. (1994). What we can learn from multicultural education research. *Educational Leadership, 51*(8), 22–26.

Linn, R., Miller, M., & Gronlund, N. (2010). *Measurement and assessment in teaching* (10th ed.). Upper Saddle River, NJ: Pearson Education.

Lustig, M., & Koester, J. (2010). *Intercultural competence: Interpersonal communication across cultures* (6th ed.). Boston: Allyn and Bacon.

MacMillan, D., & Reschly, D. (1998). Overrepresentation of minority students: The case for greater specificity or reconsideration of the variables examined. *Journal of Special Education, 32*(1), 15–24.

McLoughlin, J., & Lewis, R. (2008). *Assessing students with special needs* (7th ed.). Upper Saddle River, NJ: Pearson Education.

Meyer, L., Bevan-Brown, J., Park, H., & Savage, C. (2010). School inclusion and multicultural issues in special education. In J. Banks & C. Banks (Eds.), *Multicultural education: Issues and perspectives* (7th ed., pp. 343–368). Hoboken, NJ: Wiley.

National Center for Education Statistics. (2007a). *Condition of education 2007.* Washington, DC: U.S. Government Printing Office.

National Center for Education Statistics. (2007b). *Status and trends in the education of racial and ethnic minorities.* Washington, DC: U.S. Department of Education.

National Center for Education Statistics. (2009a). *Characteristics of public, private, and Bureau of Indian Education elementary and secondary school teachers in the United States: Results from the 2007–08 schools and staffing survey.* Retrieved January 14, 2010, from http://nces.ed.gov/pubs2009/2009324.pdf

National Center for Education Statistics. (2009b). *Condition of education 2009.* Washington, DC: U.S. Department of Education.

National Collaborative on Diversity in the Teaching Force. (2004). *Assessment of diversity in America's teaching force.* Washington, DC: Author.

National Education Association. (2010). *NEA and teacher recruitment: An overview.* Retrieved January 15, 2010, from http://www.nea.org/home/29031.htm

Ortiz, A., & Yates, J. (1988). Characteristics of learning disabled, mentally retarded and speech-language handicapped Hispanic students at initial evaluation and reevaluation. In A. Ortiz & B. Ramirez (Eds.), *Schools and the culturally diverse exceptional student* (pp. 51–62). Reston, VA: Council for Exceptional Children.

Quality Education for Minorities Project. (1990). *Education that works: An action plan for the education of minorities.* Cambridge, MA: Massachusetts Institute of Technology.

Ryan, F. (1993). The perils of multiculturalism: Schooling for the group. *Educational Horizons, 71,* 134–138.

Salend, S., & Salinas, A. (2003). Language differences or learning difficulties. *Teaching Exceptional Children, 35*(4), 36–43.

Shealey, M., & Callins, T. (2007). Creating culturally responsive literacy programs in inclusive classrooms. *Intervention in School and Clinic, 42*(4), 195–197.

Siccone, F. (1995). *Celebrating diversity: Building self-esteem in today's multicultural classrooms.* Boston: Allyn and Bacon.

Skiba, R., Simmons, A., Ritter, S., Rausch, M., Cuadrado, J., & Chung, C. (2008). Achieving equity in special education: History, status, and current challenges. *Exceptional Children, 74*(3), 244–288.

Sleeter, C., & Grant, C. (2009). *Making choices for multicultural education* (6th ed.). Hoboken, NJ: Wiley.

Smith, D., Smith-Davis, J., Clarke, C., & Mims, V. (2000). Technical assistance makes a difference: The Alliance 2000 story. *Teacher Education and Special Education, 23*(4), 302–310.

Tiedt, P., & Tiedt, I. (2010). *Multicultural teaching: A handbook of activities and resources* (8th ed.). Needham Heights, MA: Allyn and Bacon.

Tyler, N., Yzquierdo, Z., Lopez-Reyna, N., & Flippin, S. (2004). The relationship between cultural diversity and the special education workforce. *Journal of Special Education, 38*(1), 22–38.

U.S. Census Bureau. (2009a). *Annual estimate of resident population by sex, race, and Hispanic origin for the United States.* Retrieved January 15, 2010, from http://www.census.gov/popest/national/asrh/NC-EST2009-srh.html

U.S. Census Bureau. (2009b). *Statistical abstract of the United States: 2010* (129th ed.). Washington, DC: Author.

U.S. Census Bureau. (2009c). *U S. population projections, Table 6: Percent of U.S. population by race and Hispanic origin. 2010–2050.* Retrieved January 15, 2010, from www.census.gov/population/www/projections/2009hnmsSumTabs.html

U.S. Department of Education. (1997). *Nineteenth annual report to Congress on the implementation of the Individuals with Disabilities Education Act.* Washington, DC: U.S. Government Printing Office.

U.S. Department of Education. (2009). *Twenty-eighth annual report to Congress on the implementation of the Individuals with Disabilities Education Act, 2006* (Vol. 1). Washington, DC: U.S. Government Printing Office.

U.S. Department of Education. (2010). *IDEA data.* Retrieved April 14, 2010, from https://www.ideadata.org/PartBReport.asp

U.S. Department of Education, Office for Civil Rights. (1987). *Elementary and secondary school civil rights survey: National summaries* (ERIC Document Reproduction Service No. ED 304 485). Arlington, VA: DBS Corp.

U.S. English. (2010). *Official English: States with official English laws.* Retrieved January 15, 2010, from http://www.us-english.org/view/13

Utley, C., & Obiakor, F. (2001). Learning problems or learning disabilities of multicultural learners: Contemporary perspectives. In C. Utley & F. Obiakor (Eds.), *Special education, multicultural education, and school reform: Components of quality education for learners with mild disabilities* (pp. 90–117). Springfield, IL: Charles C Thomas.

Voltz, D. (1998). Cultural diversity and special education teacher preparation: Critical issues confronting the field. *Teacher Education and Special Education, 21*(1), 63–70.

Voltz, D., Sims, M., Nelson, B., & Bivens, C. (2005). M² ECCA: A framework for inclusion in the context of standards-based reform. *Teaching Exceptional Children, 37*(5), 14–19.

Winzer, M., & Mazurek, K. (1998). *Special education in multicultural contexts.* Upper Saddle River, NJ: Prentice Hall.

Chapter 4

Banks, M. (2003). Disability in the family: A life span perspective. *Ethnic Minority Psychology, 9*(4), 367–384.

Bauer, A., & Shea, T. (2003). *Parents and schools: Creating a successful partnership for students with special needs.* Upper Saddle River, NJ: Pearson Education.

Berry, J., & Hardman, M. (1998). *Lifespan perspectives on the family and disability.* Needham Heights, MA: Allyn and Bacon.

Bettelheim, B. (1950). *Love is not enough.* Glencoe, NY: Free Press.

Bettelheim, B. (1967). *The empty fortress: Infantile autism and the birth of the self.* London: Collier-Macmillan.

Blacher, J. (1984). Sequential stages of parental adjustment to the birth of a child with handicaps: Fact or artifact? *Mental Retardation, 22*(2), 55–68.

Blasco, P., Johnson, C., & Palomo-Gonzalez, S. (2008). Support for families of children with disabilities. In P. Accardo (Ed.), *Capute & Accardo's neurodevelopmental disabilities in infancy and childhood* (Vol. 1, 3rd ed., pp. 775–801). Baltimore: Paul H. Brookes.

Blue-Banning, M., Summers, J., Frankland, H., Nelson, L., & Beegle, G. (2004). Dimensions of family and professional partnerships: Constructive guidelines for collaboration. *Exceptional Children, 70*(2), 167–184.

Bronfenbrenner, U. (1977). Toward an experimental ecology of human development. *American Psychologist, 32*(7), 513–531.

Bronfenbrenner, U. (1979). *The ecology of human development: Experiments by nature and design.* Cambridge, MA: Harvard University Press.

Cook, R., Klein, M., & Tessier, A. (2008). *Adapting early childhood curricula for children in inclusive settings* (7th ed.). Upper Saddle River, NJ: Pearson Education.

D'Asaro, A. (1998). Caring for yourself is caring for your family: Methods of coping with the everyday stresses of care giving. *Exceptional Parent, 28*(6), 38–40.

Family Support Bulletin. (1991, Spring). Washington, DC: United Cerebral Palsy Association.

Flynn, L., & Wilson, P. (1998). Partnerships with family members: What about fathers? *Young Exceptional Children, 2*(1), 21–28.

Freidson, E. (1970). *Professional dominance.* Chicago: Aldine.

Gallagher, J., Beckman, P., & Cross, A. (1983). Families of handicapped children: Sources of stress and its amelioration. *Exceptional Children, 50*(1), 10–19.

Gallagher, P., Powell, T., & Rhodes, C. (2006). *Brothers and sisters: A special part of exceptional families* (3rd ed.). Baltimore: Paul H. Brookes.

Gannotti, M., Handwerker, W., Groce, N., & Cruz, C. (2001). Sociocultural influences on disability status in Puerto Rican children. *Physical Therapy, 81*(9), 1512–1523.

Gargiulo, R. (1985). *Working with parents of exceptional children.* Boston: Houghton Mifflin.

Gargiulo, R., & Graves, S. (1991). Parental feelings: The forgotten component when working with parents of handicapped preschool children. *Childhood Education, 67,* 176–178.

Gargiulo, R., & Kilgo, J. (2011). *An introduction to young children with special needs* (3rd ed.). Belmont, CA: Wadsworth/Cengage Learning.

Gargiulo, R., & Metcalf, D. (2010). *Teaching in today's inclusive classrooms.* Belmont, CA: Wadsworth/Cengage Learning.

Gearheart, B., Mullen, R., & Gearheart, C. (1993). *Exceptional individuals.* Pacific Grove, CA: Brooks/Cole.

Glidden, L., & Floyd, F. (1997). Disaggregating parental depression and family stress in assessing families of children with developmental delays: A multisample analysis. *American Journal on Mental Retardation, 102*(3), 250–266.

Gollnick, D., & Chinn, P. (2009). *Multicultural education in a pluralistic society* (8th ed.). Upper Saddle River, NJ: Pearson Education.

Graves, S., Gargiulo, R., & Sluder, L. (1996). *Young children: An introduction to early childhood education.* St. Paul, MN: West.

Grossman, F. (1972). *Brothers and sisters of retarded children.* Syracuse, NY: Syracuse University Press.

Hanson, M. (2004a). Ethnic, cultural, and language diversity in service settings. In E. Lynch & M. Hanson (Eds.), *Developing cross cultural competence* (3rd ed., pp. 3–18). Baltimore: Paul H. Brookes.

Hanson, M. (2004b). Families with Anglo-European roots. In E. Lynch & M. Hanson (Eds.), *Developing cross cultural competence* (3rd ed., pp. 81–104). Baltimore: Paul H. Brookes.

Harry, B. (1992). *Cultural diversity, families, and the special education system: Communication and empowerment.* New York: Teachers College Press.

Harry, B. (1995). African American families. In B. Ford, F. Obiakor, & J. Patton (Eds.), *Effective education of African American exceptional learners* (pp. 211–233). Austin, TX: Pro-Ed.

Harry, B. (2002). Trends and issues in serving culturally diverse families of children with disabilities. *Journal of Special Education, 36*(3), 131–138.

Harry, B., & Klinger, J. (2007). Discarding the deficit model. *Educational Leadership, 64*(5), 16–21.

Hayden, V. (1974). The other children. *Exceptional Parent, 4*(2), 26–29.

Hodapp, R., & Krasner, D. (1995). Families of children with disabilities: Findings from a national sample of eighth-grade students. *Exceptionality, 5*(2), 71–81.

Hutton, A., & Caron, S. (2005). Experience of families with children with autism in rural New England. *Focus on Autism and Other Developmental Disabilities, 20*(3), 180–189.

Kubler-Ross, E. (1969). *On death and dying.* New York: Macmillan.

Lamb, M., & Meyer, D. (1991). Fathers of children with special needs. In M. Seligman (Ed.), *The family with a handicapped child* (2nd ed., pp. 151–179). Boston: Allyn and Bacon.

Lambie, R. (2008). *Family systems within educational and community contexts* (3rd ed.). Denver, CO: Love.

Linan-Thompson, S., & Jean, R. (1997). Completing the parent participation puzzle: Accepting diversity. *Teaching Exceptional Children, 30*(2), 46–50.

Lovern, L. (2008). Native American worldviews and the discourse of disability. *Essays in Philosophy, 9*(1). Retrieved November 16, 2009, from http://sorrel.humboldt.edu/~essays/lovern.html

Lustig, M., & Koester, J. (2010). *Intercultural competence: Interpersonal communication across cultures* (6th ed.). Boston: Allyn and Bacon.

Lynch, E., & Hanson, M. (Eds.). (2004). *Developing cross cultural competence* (3rd ed.). Baltimore: Paul H. Brookes.

Mason, E., Kruse, L., Farabaugh, A., Gershberg, R., & Kohler, M. (2000). Children with exceptionalities and their siblings: Opportunities for collaboration between family and school. In M. Fine & R. Simpson (Eds.), *Collaboration with parents and families of children and youth with exceptionalities* (2nd ed., pp. 69–88). Austin, TX: Pro-Ed.

Matuszny, R., Banda, D., & Coleman, T. (2007). A progressive plan for building collaborative relationships with parents from diverse backgrounds. *Teaching Exceptional Children, 39*(4), 24–33.

McHugh, M. (2003). *Special siblings: Growing up with someone with a disability.* Baltimore: Paul H. Brookes.

Meyer, D. (2009). *Thicker than water.* Bethesda, MD: Woodbine House.

Meyer, D., & Vadasy, P. (1994). *Sibshops: Workshops for siblings of children with special needs.* Baltimore: Paul H. Brookes.

Meyer, L., Bevan-Brown, J., Park, H., & Savage, C. (2010). School inclusion and multicultural issues in special education. In J. Banks & C. Banks (Eds.), *Multicultural education: Issues and perspectives* (7th ed., pp. 343–368). Hoboken, NJ: Wiley.

Misra, A. (1994). Partnerships with families. In S. Alper, P. Schloss, & C. Schloss (Eds.), *Families of students with disabilities* (pp. 143–179). Boston: Allyn and Bacon.

Olson, D. (1988). Family types, family stress, and family satisfaction: A family developmental perspective. In C. Folicov (Ed.), *Family transitions: Continuity and change over the life cycle* (pp. 55–79). New York: Guilford Press.

Olsson, M., & Hwang, C. (2001). Depression in mothers and fathers of children with intellectual disability. *Journal of Intellectual Disability Research, 45*(6), 535–543.

Parette, H., & Petch-Hogan, B. (2000). Approaching families: Facilitating culturally/linguistically diverse family involvement. *Teaching Exceptional Children, 33*(2), 4–10.

Perl, J. (1995). Improving relationship skills for parent conferences. *Teaching Exceptional Children, 28*(1), 29–31.

Power, P., & Dell Orto, A. (2004). *Families living with chronic illness and disability.* New York: Springer.

Roos, P. (1978). Parents of mentally retarded children—Misunderstood and mistreated. In A. Turnbull & H. Turnbull (Eds.), *Parents speak out* (pp. 12–27). Columbus, OH: Charles Merrill.

Rump, M. (2002). Involving fathers of young children with special needs. *Young Children, 57*(6), 18–20.

Russell, C., Russell, C., & Russell, M. (2003). We're here too! *Exceptional Parent, 33*(6), 36–39.

Salend, S., & Taylor, L. (1993). Working with families: A cross cultural perspective. *Remedial and Special Education, 14*(5), 25–32, 39.

Santelli, B., Turnbull, A., Marquis, J., & Lerner, J. (1997). Parent-to-parent programs: A resource for parents and professionals. *Journal of Early Intervention, 21*(1), 73–83.

Scorgie, K., & Sobsey, D. (2000). Transformational outcomes associated with parenting children who have disabilities. *Mental Retardation, 38*(3), 195–206.

Scorgie, K., Wilgosh, L., & McDonald, L. (1998). Stress and coping in families of children with disabilities: An examination of recent literature. *Developmental Disabilities Bulletin, 26*(1), 22–42.

Seligman, M., & Darling, R. (2007). *Ordinary families, special children* (3rd ed.). New York: Guilford Press.

Seligman, M., Goodwin, G., Paschal, K., Applegate, A., & Lehman, A. (1997). Grandparents of children with disabilities: Perceived levels of support. *Education and Training in Mental Retardation and Developmental Disabilities, 32*(4), 293–303.

Trachtenberg, S., Batshaw, K., & Batshaw, M. (2007). Caring and coping. In M. Batshaw, L. Pellegrino, & N. Roizen (Eds.), *Children with disabilities* (6th ed., pp. 601–612). Baltimore: Paul H. Brookes.

Turnbull, A., Turnbull, R., Erwin, E., & Soodak, L. (2006). *Families, professionals, and exceptionality* (5th ed.). Upper Saddle River, NJ: Pearson Education.

Turnbull, A., Turnbull, R., Erwin, E., Soodak, L., & Shrogren, K. (2011). *Families, professionals, and exceptionality* (6th ed.). Upper Saddle River, NJ: Pearson Education.

Voltz, D. (1998). Cultural diversity and special education teacher preparation: Critical issues confronting the field. *Teacher Education and Special Education, 21*(1), 63–70.

Ziskin, L. (1978). The story of Jennie. In A. Turnbull & H. Turnbull (Eds.), *Parents speak out* (pp. 70–80). Columbus, OH: Charles Merrill.

Chapter 5

Alberto, P., & Troutman, A. (2009). *Applied behavior analysis for teachers* (8th ed.). Upper Saddle River, NJ: Pearson Education.

American Association on Intellectual and Developmental Disabilities. (2010a). *Diagnostic Adaptive Behavior Scale.* Retrieved January 20, 2010, from http://www.aamr.org/content_106.cfm?navID=23

American Association on Intellectual and Developmental Disabilities. (2010b). *FAQ on intellectual disability.* Retrieved January 17, 2010, from http://www.aamr.org/content_104.cfm

Beirne-Smith, M., Patton, J., & Kim, S. (2006). *Mental retardation* (7th ed.). Upper Saddle River, NJ: Pearson Education.

Belmont, J. (1966). Long-term memory in mental retardation. *International Review of Research in Mental Retardation, 1,* 219–255.

Blatt, B., & Kaplan, F. (1966). *Christmas in purgatory.* Boston: Allyn and Bacon.

Browder, D., & Snell, M. (2000). Teaching functional academics. In M. Snell & F. Brown (Eds.), *Instruction of students with severe disabilities* (5th ed., pp. 493–542). Upper Saddle River, NJ: Pearson Education.

Bybee, J., & Zigler, E. (1998). Outer-directedness in individuals with and without mental retardation: A review. In J. Burack, R. Hodapp, & E. Zigler (Eds.), *Handbook of mental retardation and development* (pp. 434–460). Cambridge, England: Cambridge University Press.

Channon, S., German, E., Cassina, C., & Lee, P. (2004). Executive functioning, memory, and learning in phenylketonuria. *Neuropsychology, 18,* 613–620.

Christenson, S., Ysseldyke, J., & Thurlow, M. (1989). Critical instructional factors for students with mild handicaps: An integrative review. *Remedial and Special Education, 10*(5), 21–31.

Conyers, C., Martin, T., Martin, G., & Yu, D. (2002). The 1983 AAMR manual, the 1992 AAMR manual, or the Developmental Disabilities Act: Which do researchers use? *Education and Training in Mental Retardation and Developmental Disabilities, 37*(3), 310–316.

Davidson, P., & Myers, G. (2007). Environmental toxins. In M. Batshaw, L. Pellegrino, & N. Roizen (Eds.), *Children with disabilities* (6th ed., pp. 61–70). Baltimore: Paul H. Brookes.

Denning, C., Chamberlain, J., & Polloway, E. (2000). An evaluation of state guidelines for mental retardation: Focus on definition and classification practices. *Education and Training in Mental Retardation and Developmental Disabilities, 35*(2), 135–144.

Detterman, D., & Gabriel, L. (2006). Look before you leap: Implications of the 1992 and 2002 definition of mental retardation. In H. Switsky & S. Greenspan (Eds.), *What is mental retardation? Ideas for an evolving disability in the 21st century* (Rev ed., pp. 135–146). Washington, DC: American Association on Mental Retardation.

Drew, C., & Hardman, M. (2007). *Intellectual disabilities across the lifespan* (9th ed.). Upper Saddle River, NJ: Pearson Education.

Edgar, E. (1988). Employment as an outcome for mildly handicapped students: Current status and future directions. *Focus on Exceptional Children, 2*(1), 1–8.

Ellis, N. (1963). The stimulus trace and behavioral inadequacy. In N. Ellis (Ed.), *Handbook of mental deficiency* (pp. 134–158). New York: McGraw-Hill.

Fiscus, R., Schuster, J., Morse, T., & Collins, B. (2002). Teaching elementary students with cognitive disabilities food preparation skills while embedding instructive feedback in prompt and consequent events. *Education and Training in Mental Retardation and Developmental Disabilities, 37*(1), 55–69.

Friend, M., & Bursuck, W. (2009). *Including students with special needs* (5th ed.). Upper Saddle River, NJ: Pearson Education.

Gargiulo, R. (1985). *Working with parents of exceptional children*. Boston: Houghton Mifflin.

Gargiulo, R., & Kilgo, J. (2011). *An introduction to young children with special needs* (3rd ed.). Belmont, CA: Wadsworth/Cengage Learning.

Gargiulo, R., & Metcalf, D. (2010). *Teaching in today's inclusive classrooms*. Belmont, CA: Wadsworth/Cengage Learning.

Gelof, M. (1963). Comparison of systems of classification relating degree of retardation to measured intelligence. *American Journal of Mental Deficiency, 68*, 297–317.

Graham, M., & Scott, K. (1988). The impact of definitions of high risks on services to infants and toddlers. *Topics in Early Childhood Special Education, 8*(3), 23–28.

Grossman, H. (1973). *Manual on terminology and classification in mental retardation*. Washington, DC: American Association on Mental Deficiency.

Grossman, H. (1983). *Classification in mental retardation*. Washington, DC: American Association on Mental Deficiency.

Harris, L., & Associates. (2004). *National Organization on Disabilities/Harris Survey of Americans with Disabilities*. New York: Author.

Hartman, M. (2009). Step by step: Creating a community-based transition program for students with intellectual disabilities. *Teaching Exceptional Children, 41*(6), 6–11.

Heber, R. (1961). A manual on terminology and classification in mental retardation (Rev. ed.). *Monograph Supplement to the American Journal of Mental Deficiency, 64*.

Hendricks, D., & Wehman, P. (2009). Transition from school to adulthood for youth with autism spectrum disorders. *Focus on Autism and Other Developmental Disabilities, 24*(2), 77–88.

Hickson, L., Blackman, L., & Reis, E. (1995). *Mental retardation: Foundations of educational programming*. Boston: Allyn and Bacon.

Hoover, J., & Patton, J. (2004). Differentiating standards-based education for students with diverse needs. *Remedial and Special Education, 25*(2), 74–78.

Hughes, C., Washington, B., & Brown, G. (2008). Supporting students in the transition from school to adult life. In F. Rusch (Ed.), *Beyond high school* (2nd ed., pp. 266–287). Upper Saddle River, NJ: Pearson Education.

Jared, J., Frantino, E., & Sturmey, P. (2007). The effects of errorless learning and backward chaining on the acquisition of Internet skills in adults with developmental disabilities. *Journal of Applied Behavior Analysis, 40*(1), 185–189.

Johnson, D., Johnson, R., & Holubec, E. (1998). *Cooperation in the classroom* (7th ed.). Edina, MN: Interaction Book Co.

Johnson, D., Johnson, R., & Holubec, E. (2002). *Circles of learning*. Edina, MN: Interaction Book Co.

Johnson, L. (2005). First, do no harm: An argument against mandatory high-stakes testing for students with intellectual disabilities. *Mental Retardation, 43*, 292–298.

Jones, K., Smith, D., Ulleland, C., & Streissguth, A. (1973). Pattern of malformation in offspring of chronic alcoholic mothers. *Lancet, 1*(7815), 1267–1271.

Katims, D. (2000). Literacy instruction for people with mental retardation: Historical highlights and contemporary analysis. *Education and Training in Mental Retardation and Developmental Disabilities, 35*(1), 3–15.

Kaufman, A., & Kaufman, N. (2004). *Kaufman Assessment Battery for Children—Second Edition*. Circle Pines, MN: American Guidance Service.

Lambert, N., Nihira, K., & Leland, H. (1993). *AAMR Adaptive Behavior Scale* (2nd ed.). Austin, TX: Pro-Ed.

Lejune, J., Gautier, M., & Turpin, R. (1959). Études des chromosomes somatiques de neuf enfants mongoliers. *Academie de Science, 248*, 1721–1722.

Lewis, R., & Doorlag, D. (2011). *Teaching students with special needs in general education classrooms* (8th ed.). Upper Saddle River, NJ: Pearson Education.

Lindman, F., & McIntyre, K. (1961). *The mentally disabled and the law*. Chicago: University of Chicago Press.

Luckasson, R., Borthwick-Duffy, S., Buntinx, W., Coulter, D., Craig, E., Reeve, A., et al. (2002). *Mental retardation: Definition, support, and systems of supports* (10th ed.). Washington, DC: American Association on Mental Retardation.

Luckasson, R., Coulter, D., Polloway, E., Reiss, S., Schalock, R., Snell, M., et al. (1992). *Mental retardation: Definition, classification, and systems of support* (9th ed.). Washington, DC: American Association on Mental Retardation.

Luckasson, R., & Reeve, A. (2001). Naming, defining, and classifying in mental retardation. *Mental Retardation, 39*(1), 47–52.

MacMillan, D. (1989). Mild mental retardation: Emerging issues. In G. Robinson, J. Patton, E. Polloway, & L. Sargent (Eds.), *Best practices in mild mental retardation* (pp. 1–20). Reston, VA: Division on Mental Retardation of the Council for Exceptional Children.

Mank, D., Cioffi, A., & Yovanoff, P. (2003). Supported employment outcomes across a decade: Is there evidence of improvement in the quality of implementation? *Mental Retardation, 41*, 188–197.

March of Dimes. (2007). *Public health education information sheet: Fragile X syndrome*. White Plains, NY: Author.

March of Dimes. (2008a). *Public health education information sheet: Drinking alcohol during pregnancy*. White Plains, NY: Author.

March of Dimes. (2008b). *Public health education information sheet: PKU*. White Plains, NY: Author.

March of Dimes. (2009a). *Public health education information sheet: Down syndrome*. White Plains, NY: Author.

March of Dimes. (2009b). *Public health education information sheet: Rh disease*. White Plains, NY: Author.

McDonnell, J., Hardman, M., & McDonnell, A. (2003). *An introduction to persons with moderate and severe disabilities* (2nd ed.). Boston: Allyn and Bacon.

McMaster, K., & Fuchs, D. (2002). Effects of cooperative learning on the academic achievement of students with learning disabilities. *Learning Disabilities Research and Practice, 17,* 107–117.

Meyer, G. (2007). X-linked syndromes causing intellectual disability. In M. Batshaw, L. Pellegrino, & N. Roizen (Eds.), *Children with disabilities* (6th ed., pp. 275–283). Baltimore: Paul H. Brookes.

Migliore, A., Mank, D., Grossi, T., & Rogan, P. (2007). Integrated employment or sheltered workshops: Preferences of adults with intellectual disabilities, their families and staff. *Journal of Vocational Rehabilitation, 26*(1), 5–19.

Morrison, G., & Polloway, E. (1995). Mental retardation. In E. Meyen & T. Skirtic (Eds.), *Special education and student disability* (4th ed., pp. 213–269). Denver, CO: Love.

Murphy, S., Rogan, P., Handley, M., Kincaid, C., & Royce-Davis, J. (2002). People's situations and perspectives eight years after workshop conversion. *Mental Retardation, 40,* 30–40.

National Down Syndrome Society. (2010). *Alzheimer's disease and Down syndrome.* Retrieved January 19, 2010, from http://www.ndss.org

National Longitudinal Transition Study 2. (2009). *The post-high school outcomes of youth with disabilities up to 4 years after high school.* Retrieved January 20, 2010, from http://www.nlts2.org/reports/2009_04/nlts2_report_2009_04_complete.pdf

Nihira, K., Leland, H., & Lambert, N. (1993). *AAMR Adaptive Behavior Scale—Residential and Community* (2nd ed.). Austin, TX: Pro-Ed.

Nirje, B. (1969). The normalization principle and its human management implications. In R. Kugel & W. Wolfensberger (Eds.), *Changing patterns in residential services for the mentally retarded* (pp. 179–195). Washington, DC: President's Committee on Mental Retardation.

Oswald, D., Coutinho, M., Best, A., & Nguyen, N. (2001). Impact of sociodemographic characteristics on the identification rates of minority students as having mental retardation. *Mental Retardation, 39*(5), 351–367.

Owens, R. (2009). Mental retardation/intellectual disabilities. In D. Bernstein & E. Tiegerman-Farber (Eds.), *Language and communication disorders in children* (6th ed., pp. 246–313). Boston: Pearson Education.

Owens, R. (2010). *Language disorders* (5th ed.). Boston: Pearson Education.

Polloway, E. (2004). Eulogy for "mild" mental retardation? *Division on Developmental Disability Express, 14*(3), 1, 8.

Polloway, E., Lubin, J., Smith, J., & Patton, J. (2010). Mild intellectual disabilities: Legacies and trends in concepts and educational practices. *Education and Training in Autism and Developmental Disabilities, 45*(1), 54–68.

Polloway, E., Patton, J., & Serna, L. (2008). *Strategies for teaching learners with special needs* (9th ed.). Upper Saddle River, NJ: Pearson Education.

Polloway, E., Patton, J., Smith, J., Antoine, K., & Lubin, J. (2009). State guidelines for mental retardation and intellectual disabilities: A revisitation of previous analyses in light of changes in the field. *Education and Training in Developmental Disabilities, 44*(1), 14–24.

President's Committee for People with Intellectual Disabilities. (2010). *Fact sheet.* Retrieved January 18, 2010, from http://www.acf.hhs.gov/programs/pcpid/pcpid_fact.html

Reiss, S. (1994). Issues in defining mental retardation. *American Journal on Mental Retardation, 99,* 1–7.

Roid, G. (2003). *Stanford-Binet Intelligence Scale—Fifth Edition.* Itasca, IL: Riverside.

Roizen, N. (2007). Down syndrome. In M. Batshaw, L. Pellegrino, & N. Roizen (Eds.), *Children with disabilities* (6th ed., pp. 263–273). Baltimore: Paul H. Brookes.

Schalock, R. (2010). *Bob Schalock interview.* Retrieved January 27, 2010, from http://www.aaidd.org/shalock-transcript.cfm

Schalock, R., Borthwick-Duffy, S., Bradley, V., Buntinx, W., Coulter, D., Craig, E., et al. (2010). *Intellectual disability: Definition, classification, and systems of supports* (11th ed.). Washington, DC: American Association on Intellectual and Developmental Disabilities.

Scheerenberger, R. (1983). *A history of mental retardation.* Baltimore: Paul H. Brookes.

Scheerenberger, R. (1987). *A history of mental retardation: A quarter century of concern.* Baltimore: Paul H. Brookes.

Schilit, J., & Caldwell, M. (1980). A word list of essential career/vocational words for mentally retarded students. *Education and Training of the Mentally Retarded, 15*(2), 113–117.

Simmons, J., & Flexer, R. (2008). Transition to employment. In R. Flexer, R. Baer, P. Luft, & T. Simmons (Eds.), *Transition planning for secondary students with disabilities* (3rd ed., pp. 230–257). Upper Saddle River, NJ: Pearson Education.

Sitlington, P., Neubert, D., & Clark, G. (2010). *Transition education and services for students with disabilities* (5th ed.). Needham Heights, MA: Allyn and Bacon.

Smith, T., Polloway, E., Patton, J., & Dowdy, C. (2008). *Teaching students with special needs in inclusive settings* (5th ed.). Needham Heights, MA: Allyn and Bacon.

Snell, M., & Brown, F. (2006). *Instruction of students with severe disabilities* (6th ed.). Upper Saddle River, NJ: Pearson Education.

Taylor, P., Collins, B., Schuster, J., & Kleinert, H. (2002). Teaching laundry skills to high school students with disabilities: Generalization of targeted skills and nontargeted information. *Education and Training in Mental Retardation and Developmental Disabilities, 37*(2), 172–183.

Taylor, R., Brady, M., & Richards, S. (2005). *Mental retardation.* Boston: Allyn and Bacon.

Test, D., Carver, T., Evers, L., Haddad, J., & Person, J. (2000). Longitudinal job satisfaction of persons in supported employment. *Education and Training in Mental Retardation and Developmental Disabilities, 35*(4), 365–373.

The Arc. (2005). *Q&A: Causes and prevention of mental retardation.* Retrieved January 18, 2010, from http://www.thearc.org/NetCommunity/Document.Doc?&id=147

Thoma, C. (1999). Supporting student voice in transition planning. *Teaching Exceptional Children, 31*(5), 4–9.

Thoma, C., Bartholomew, C., & Scott, L. (2009). *Universal design for transition.* Baltimore: Paul H. Brookes.

Thompson, J., Bryant, B., Campbell, E., Craig, E., Hughes, C., Rothholz, D., et al. (2004). *Supports Intensity Scale.* Washington, DC: American Association on Mental Retardation.

Tomporowski, P., & Tinsley, V. (1997). Attention in mentally retarded persons. In W. MacLean (Ed.), *Ellis' handbook of mental deficiency, psychological theory and research* (3rd ed., pp. 219–244). Mahwah, NJ: Erlbaum.

Turnbull, A., Turnbull, R., Erwin, E., Soodak, L., & Shogren, K. (2011). *Families, professionals, and exceptionality* (6th ed.). Upper Saddle River, NJ: Pearson Education.

U.S. Department of Education. (1991). *Thirteenth annual report to Congress on the implementation of the Individuals with Disabilities Education Act.* Washington, DC: U.S. Government Printing Office.

U.S. Department of Education. (1995). *Seventeenth annual report to Congress on the implementation of the Individuals with Disabilities Education Act.* Washington, DC: U.S. Government Printing Office.

U.S. Department of Education. (2006). *Twenty-sixth annual report to Congress on the implementation of the Individuals with Disabilities Education Act, 2004.* Washington, DC: U.S. Government Printing Office.

U.S. Department of Education. (2009). *IDEA data.* Retrieved September 5, 2009, from https://www.ideadata.org/PartBReport.asp

U.S. Department of Education. (2010). *IDEA data.* Retrieved April 14, 2010, from https://www.ideadata.org/PartBReport.asp

Vaughn, S., & Bos, C. (2009). *Strategies for teaching students with learning and behavior problems* (7th ed.). Upper Saddle River, NJ: Pearson Education.

Warren, S., & Yoder, P. (1997). Communication, language, and mental retardation. In W. MacLean (Ed.), *Ellis' handbook of mental deficiency, psychological theory and research* (3rd ed., pp. 379–403). Mahwah, NJ: Erlbaum.

Wechsler, D. (2003). *Wechsler Intelligence Scale for Children—Fourth Edition.* San Antonio, TX: Psychological Corporation.

Wehman, P. (2006). Applications for youth with intellectual disabilities. In P. Wehman (Ed.), *Life beyond the classroom* (4th ed., pp. 411–444). Baltimore: Paul H. Brookes.

Wehmeyer, M. (2003). Defining mental retardation and ensuring access to the general curriculum. *Education and Training in Developmental Disabilities, 38*(3), 271–282.

Wehmeyer, M., & Sailor, W. (2004). High school. In C. Kennedy & E. Horns (Eds.), *Including students with severe disabilities* (pp. 259–281). Boston: Allyn and Bacon.

Westling, D., & Fox, L. (2009). *Teaching students with severe disabilities* (4th ed.). Upper Saddle River, NJ: Pearson Education.

Wolfensberger, W. (1972). *Normalization: The principle of normalization in human services.* Toronto: National Institute on Mental Retardation.

Xin, J., & Holmdal, P. (2003). Snacks and skills: Teaching children functional counting skills. *Teaching Exceptional Children, 35*(5), 46–51.

Chapter 6

Aiken, L., & Groth-Marnat, G. (2006). *Psychological testing and assessment* (12th ed.). Boston: Allyn and Bacon.

Alley, G., & Deshler, D. (1979). *Teaching the learning disabled adolescent: Strategies and methods.* Denver, CO: Love.

American Psychiatric Association. (2000). *Diagnostic and statistical manual of mental disorders* (4th ed., text rev.). Washington, DC: Author.

Ariel, A. (1992). *Education of children and adolescents with learning disabilities.* New York: Macmillan.

Arnold, L., Christopher, J., Huestis, R., & Smeltzer, D. (1978). Megavitamins for minimal brain dysfunction: A placebo controlled study. *Journal of the American Medical Association, 240,* 2642–2643.

Association for Children with Learning Disabilities. (1986, September–October). ACLD definition: Specific learning disabilities. *ACLD Newsbrief,* pp. 15–16.

Bateman, B., & Linden, M. (2006). *Better IEPs* (4th ed.). Verona, WI: Attainment Co.

Belson, S. (2003). *Technology for exceptional learners.* Boston: Houghton Mifflin.

Bender, W. (2008). *Learning disabilities: Characteristics, identification, and teaching strategies* (6th ed.). Needham Heights, MA: Allyn and Bacon.

Bereiter, C., & Engelmann, S. (1966). *Teaching disadvantaged children in the preschool.* Englewood Cliffs, NJ: Prentice Hall.

Blair, C., & Scott, K. (2002). Proportion of LD placements associated with low socioeconomic status: Evidence for a gradient? *Journal of Special Education, 36*(1), 14–22.

Bradley, R., Danielson, L., & Doolittle, J. (2007). Responsiveness to intervention: 1997–2007. *Teaching Exceptional Children, 39*(5), 8–12.

Brooks, M. (2002). A look at current practice. In R. Bradley, L. Danielson, & D. Hallahan (Eds.), *Identification of learning disabilities: Research to practice* (pp. 335–340). Mahwah, NJ: Erlbaum.

Bryant, D., & Bryant, B. (2003). *Assistive technology for people with disabilities.* Boston: Allyn and Bacon.

Burns, M., Jacob, S., & Wagner, A. (2008). Ethical and legal issues associated with using response to intervention to assess learning disabilities. *Journal of School Psychology, 46*(3), 263–279.

Clements, S. (1966). *Minimal brain dysfunction in children: Terminology and identification* (Public Health Services Publication No. 1415). Washington, DC: U.S. Department of Health, Education, and Welfare.

Cortiella, C. (2006). *Response-to-intervention: An emerging method for LD identification.* Retrieved April 30, 2007, from http://www.schwablelearning.org/articles.asp?r=840

Cott, A. (1972). Megavitamins: The orthomolecular approach to behavioral disorders and learning disabilities. *Academic Therapy, 7*(3), 245–258.

Council for Exceptional Children. (2003). Strategies + technology = solutions for reading challenges. *CEC Today, 10*(1), 1, 5, 13, 15.

Council for Learning Disabilities. (1986). Use of discrepancy formulas in the identification of learning disabled individuals. *Learning Disabilities Quarterly, 9,* 245.

Crockett, J., & Kauffman, J. (2001). The concept of the least restrictive environment and learning disabilities: Least restrictive of what? Reflections on Cruickshank's 1997 guest editorial for the *Journal of Learning Disabilities.* In D. Hallahan & B. Keogh (Eds.), *Research and global perspectives in learning disabilities* (pp. 147–166). Mahwah, NJ: Erlbaum.

Cruickshank, W. (1972). Some issues facing the field of learning disabilities. *Journal of Learning Disabilities, 5*(5), 380–388.

Deiner, P. (1993). *Resources for teaching children with diverse abilities.* Fort Worth, TX: Harcourt Brace Jovanovich.

Deshler, D., Ellis, E., & Lenz, B. (1996). *Teaching adolescents with learning disabilities* (2nd ed.). Denver, CO: Love.

Dyson, L. (1996). The experiences of families of children with learning disabilities: Parental stress, family functioning and sibling self-concept. *Journal of Learning Disabilities, 29*(3), 280–286.

Engelmann, S. (1977). Sequencing cognitive and academic tasks. In R. Kneedler & S. Tarver (Eds.), *Changing perspectives in special education* (pp. 46–61). Columbus, OH: Merrill.

Ewen, J., & Shapiro, B. (2008). Specific learning disabilities. In P. Accardo (Ed.), *Capute & Accardo's neurodevelopmental disabilities in infancy and childhood* (3rd ed., Vol. II, pp. 553–577). Baltimore: Paul H. Brookes.

Feingold, B. (1975). Hyperkinesis and learning disabilities linked to artificial food flavors and colors. *American Journal of Nursing, 75,* 797–803.

Feingold, B. (1976). Hyperkinesis and learning disabilities linked to ingestion of artificial food colors and flavorings. *Journal of Learning Disabilities, 9*(9), 551–559.

Friend, M., & Bursuck, W. (2009). *Including students with special needs* (5th ed.). Upper Saddle River, NJ: Pearson Education.

Fuchs, D., & Fuchs, L. (2005). Responsiveness-to-intervention: A blueprint for practitioners, policymakers, and parents. *Teaching Exceptional Children, 38*(1), 57–59.

Fuchs, D., Fuchs, L., Compton, D., Bouton, B., Caffrey, E., & Hill, L. (2007). Dynamic assessment as responsiveness to intervention. *Teaching Exceptional Children, 39*(5), 58–63.

Fuchs, D., Fuchs, L., & Stecker, P. (2010). The "blurring" of special education in a new continuum of general education placements. *Exceptional Children, 76*(3), 301–323.

Fuchs, D., Mock, D., Morgan, P., & Young, C. (2003). Responsiveness-to-intervention: Definitions, evidence, and implication for the learning disabilities construct. *Learning Disabilities Research and Practice, 18*(3), 157–171.

Galaburda, A. (2005). Neurology of learning disabilities: What will the future bring? The answer comes from the successes of the recent past. *Learning Disabilities Quarterly, 28*(2), 107–110.

Gargiulo, R., & Kilgo, J. (2011). *An introduction to young children with special needs* (3rd ed.). Belmont, CA: Wadsworth/Cengage Learning.

Gersten, R., Carnine, D., & Woodward, J. (1987). Direct instruction research: The third decade. *Remedial and Special Education, 8*(6), 48–56.

Gollnick, D., & Chinn, P. (2009). *Multicultural education in a pluralistic society* (8th ed). Upper Saddle River, NJ: Pearson Education.

Graham, S., Harris, K., & Larsen, L. (2001). Prevention and intervention of writing difficulties for students with learning disabilities. *Learning Disabilities Research and Practice, 16*(2), 74–84.

Hallahan, D., Kauffman, J., & Lloyd, J. (1999). *Introduction to learning disabilities* (2nd ed.). Needham Heights, MA: Allyn and Bacon.

Hallahan, D., Lloyd, J., Kauffman, J., Weiss, M., & Martinez, E. (2005). *Learning disabilities: Foundations, characteristics, and effective teaching* (3rd ed.). Boston: Allyn and Bacon.

Hallahan, D., & Mercer, C. (2002). Learning disabilities: Historical perspectives. In R. Bradley, L. Danielson, & D. Hallahan (Eds.), *Identification of learning disabilities: Research to practice* (pp. 1–67). Mahwah, NJ: Erlbaum.

Hammill, D. (1990). On defining learning disabilities: An emerging consensus. *Journal of Learning Disabilities, 23*(2), 74–84.

Hammill, D., & Larsen, S. (1974). The effectiveness of psycholinguistic training. *Exceptional Children, 41*(1), 5–15.

Hoover, J., Baca, L., Wexler-Love, E., & Saenz, L. (2008). *National implementation of response to intervention (RTI): Research summary.* Alexandria, VA: National Association of State Directors of Special Education.

Hudson, B. (2006). Making and missing connections: Learning disabilities services and the transition from adolescence to adulthood. *Disability and Society, 21,* 47–60.

Isles, A., & Humby, T. (2006). Modes of imprinted gene action in learning disabilities. *Journal of Intellectual Disability Research, 50*(5), 318–325.

Jennings, J., Caldwell, J., & Lerner, J. (2010). *Reading problems: Assessment and teaching strategies* (6th ed.). Needham Heights, MA: Allyn and Bacon.

Kame'enui, E. (2007). A new paradigm: Responsiveness to intervention. *Teaching Exceptional Children, 39*(5), 6–7.

Kauffman, J. (1999). Commentary: Today's special education and its message for tomorrow. *Journal of Special Education, 32*(4), 244–254.

Kavale, K. (1990). Variances and verities in learning disability interventions. In T. Scruggs & B. Wong (Eds.), *Intervention research in learning disabilities* (pp. 3–33). New York: Springer-Verlag.

Kavale, K. (2002). Discrepancy models in the identification of learning disability. In R. Bradley, L. Danielson, & D. Hallahan (Eds.), *Identification of learning disabilities: Research to practice* (pp. 369–426). Mahwah, NJ: Erlbaum.

Kavale, K., & Forness, S. (1983). Hyperactivity and diet treatment: A meta-analysis of the Feingold hypothesis. *Journal of Learning Disabilities, 16*(6), 324–330.

Kavale, K., Holdnack, J., & Mostert, M. (2005). Responsiveness to intervention and the identification of specific learning disability: A critique and alternative proposal. *Learning Disability Quarterly, 28*(1), 2–16.

Kavale, K., & Mostert, M. (2004). Social skills interventions for individuals with learning disabilities. *Learning Disability Quarterly, 27*(1), 31–43.

Kirk, S. (1962). *Educating exceptional children.* Boston: Houghton Mifflin.

Klingner, J., & Edwards, P. (2006). Cultural considerations with response to intervention models. *Reading Research Quarterly, 41,* 108–117.

Klingner, J., Vaughn, S., Hughes, M., Schumm, J., & Elbaum, B. (1998). Outcomes for students with and without learning disabilities in inclusive classrooms. *Learning Disabilities Research and Practice, 13,* 153–161.

Lenz, B., & Deshler, D. (2004). *Teaching content to all.* Boston: Allyn and Bacon.

Lenz, B., Ellis, E., & Scanlon, D. (1996). *Teaching learning strategies to adolescents and adults with learning disabilities.* Austin, TX: Pro-Ed.

Lerner, J. (2003). *Learning disabilities* (9th ed.). Boston: Houghton Mifflin.

Lerner, J., & Johns, B. (2009). *Learning disabilities and related mild disabilities* (11th ed.). Belmont, CA: Wadsworth/Cengage Learning.

Lewis, B. (1992). Pedigree analysis of children with phonology disorders. *Journal of Learning Disabilities, 25*(9), 586–597.

Lyon, G., Fletcher, J., Shaywitz, S., Shaywitz, B., Torgesen, J., Wood, F., et al. (2001). Rethinking learning disabilities. In C. Finn, A. Rotherham, & C. Hokanson (Eds.), *Rethinking special education for a new century* (pp. 259–287). Washington, DC: Thomas B. Fordham Foundation and Progressive Policy Institute.

Lyon, G., Shaywitz, S., & Shaywitz, B. (2003). Defining dyslexia. *Annals of Dyslexia, 53,* 1–14.

MacArthur, C. (2000). New tools for writing: Assistive technology for students with writing difficulties. *Topics in Language Disorders, 20,* 85–100.

Manning, M., Bear, G., & Minke, K. (2006). Self-concept and self-esteem. In G. Bear & K. Minke (Eds.), *Children's needs III: Development, prevention, and intervention* (pp. 341–356). Bethesda, MD: National Association of School Psychologists.

Marchand-Martella, N., Slocum, T., & Martella, R. (Eds.). (2004). *Introduction to direct instruction.* Boston: Allyn and Bacon.

Marston, D., Muyskens, P., Lau, M., & Canter, A. (2003). Problem-solving model for decision making with high incidence disabilities: The Minneapolis experience. *Learning Disabilities Research and Practice, 18*(3), 187–200.

Martin, E. (2002). Response to "Learning disabilities: Historical perspectives." In R. Bradley, L. Danielson, & D. Hallahan (Eds.), *Identification of learning disabilities: Research to practice* (pp. 81–87). Mahwah, NJ: Erlbaum.

McLeskey, J., Hoppery, D., Williamson, P., & Rentz, T. (2004). Is inclusion an illusion? An examination of national and state trends toward the education of students with learning disabilities in the general education classroom. *Learning Disabilities Research and Practice, 19*(2), 109–115.

Meichenbaum, D. (1977). *Cognitive behavior modification.* New York: Plenum.

Meichenbaum, D., & Goodman, J. (1971). Training impulsive children to talk to themselves: A means of developing self-control. *Journal of Abnormal Psychology, 77,* 115–126.

Meltzer, L., & Krishnan, K. (2007). Executive function difficulties and learning disabilities: Understanding and misunderstandings. In L. Meltzer (Ed.), *Executive function in education* (pp. 77–105). New York: Guilford Press.

Mercer, C. (1997). *Students with learning disabilities* (5th ed.). Upper Saddle River, NJ: Prentice Hall.

Mercer, C., Forgnone, C., & Wolking, W. (1976). Definitions of learning disabilities used in the United States. *Journal of Learning Disabilities, 9*(6), 376–386.

Mercer, C., & Pullen, P. (2009). *Students with learning disabilities* (7th ed.). Upper Saddle River, NJ: Pearson Education.

Mull, C., Sitlington, P., & Alper, S. (2001). Postsecondary education for students with learning disabilities: A synthesis of the literature. *Exceptional Children, 68*(1), 97–118.

National Center for Education Statistics. (2009). *Digest of education statistics 2008.* Washington, DC: U.S. Department of Education.

National Joint Committee on Learning Disabilities. (2003). *A reaction to full inclusion: A reaffirmation of the right of students with learning disabilities to a continuum of services.* Retrieved March 21, 2010, from http://www.ldonline.org/?module=uploads&func=download&fileId=767

National Joint Committee on Learning Disabilities. (2006) *Learning disabilities and young children.* Retrieved March 22, 2010, from http://www.ldonline.org/about/partners/njcld/

Newman, L., Wagner, M., Cameto, R., & Knokey, A. (2009). *The post-high school outcomes of youth with disabilities up to 4 years after high school. A report of findings from the National Longitudinal Transition Study-2.* Menlo Park, CA: SRI International. Available at http://www.nlts2.org/reports/2009_04/index.html

Osborne, A. (1997). *Legal issues in special education.* Boston: Allyn and Bacon.

Paulson, F., Paulson, P., & Meyer, C. (1991). What makes a portfolio a portfolio? *Educational Leadership, 48*(5), 60–63.

Pearl, R., & Donahue, M. (2004). Peer relationships and learning disabilities. In B. Wong (Ed.), *Learning about learning disabilities* (3rd ed., pp. 133–165). San Diego, CA: Elsevier/Academic Press.

Peterson, J., & Hittie, M. (2010). *Inclusive teaching* (2nd ed.). Boston: Allyn and Bacon.

Polloway, E., Patton, J., & Serna, L. (2008). *Strategies for teaching learners with special needs* (9th ed.). Upper Saddle River, NJ: Pearson Education.

Raskind, M., Goldberg, R., Higgins, E., & Herman, K. (2002). Teaching life success to students with learning disabilities: Lessons learned from a 20-year study. *Intervention in School and Clinic, 37*(4), 201–208.

Raskind, W. (2001). Current understanding of the genetic basis of reading and spelling disability. *Learning Disability Quarterly, 24*(2), 141–157.

Reynolds, C. (1992). Two key concepts in the diagnosis of learning disabilities and the habilitation of learning. *Learning Disability Quarterly, 15,* 2–12.

Salend, S. (1998). Using portfolios to assess student performance. *Teaching Exceptional Children, 31*(2), 26–43.

Schumm, J., Moody, S., & Vaughn, S. (2000). Grouping for instruction: Does one size fit all? *Journal of Learning Disabilities, 33*(5), 477–488.

Sexton, M., Harris, K., & Graham, S. (1998). Self-regulated strategy development and the writing process: Effects on essay writing and attributions. *Exceptional Children, 64*(3), 295–311.

Shalev, R. (2004). Developmental dyscalculia. *Journal of Child Neurology, 19*(10), 765–771.

Shapiro, B., Church, R., & Lewis, M. (2007). Specific learning disabilities. In M. Batshaw, L. Pellegrino, & N. Roizen (Eds.), *Children with disabilities* (6th ed., pp. 367–385). Baltimore: Paul H. Brookes.

Simmons, D., Kame'enui, E., Coyne, M., & Chard, D. (2007). Effective strategies for teaching beginning reading. In M. Coyne, E. Kame'enui, & D. Carnine (Eds.), *Effective teaching strategies that accommodate diverse learners* (3rd ed., pp. 45–77). Upper Saddle River, NJ: Pearson Education.

Smith, T., Polloway, E., Patton, J., & Dowdy, C. (2008). *Teaching children with special needs in inclusive settings* (5th ed.). Needham Heights, MA: Allyn and Bacon.

Speece, D., Case, L., & Molloy, D. (2003). Responsiveness to general education instruction as the first gate to learning disabilities instruction. *Learning Disabilities Research and Practice, 18*(3), 147–156.

Spivak, M. (1986). Advocacy and legislative action for head-injured children and their families. *Journal of Head Trauma Rehabilitation, 1,* 41–47.

Stecker, P. (2007). Tertiary intervention: Using progress monitoring with intensive services. *Teaching Exceptional Children, 39*(5), 50–57.

Sturomski, N. (1997, July). Teaching students with learning disabilities to use learning strategies. *NICHY News Digest, 25*, 2–12.

Swanson, H. (2000). Issues facing the field of learning disabilities. *Learning Disability Quarterly*, 23(1), 37–50.

Swanson, H. (2005). Memory and learning disabilities: Historical perspective, current status, and future trends. *Thalamus, 23*, 30–44.

Swanson, H., Cooney, J., & McNamara, J. (2004). Learning disabilities and memory. In B. Wong (Ed.), *Learning about learning disabilities* (3rd ed., pp. 41–92). San Diego, CA: Elsevier/Academic Press.

Swanson, H., & Jerman, O. (2007). The influence of working memory on reading growth in subgroups of children with reading difficulties. *Journal of Experimental Child Psychology, 96*(4), 249–283.

Taylor, R. (2009). *Assessment of exceptional students: Educational and psychological procedures* (8th ed.). Boston: Allyn and Bacon.

Tymchuk, A., Lakin, K., & Luckasson, R. (2001). *The forgotten generation*. Baltimore: Paul H. Brookes.

U.S. Department of Education. (1994). *Sixteenth annual report to Congress on the implementation of the Individuals with Disabilities Education Act*. Washington, DC: U.S. Government Printing Office.

U.S. Department of Education. (2009). *IDEA data*. Retrieved October 22, 2009, from https://www.ideadata.org/PartBReport.asp

U.S. Department of Education. (2010). *IDEA data*. Retrieved April 14, 2010, from https://www.ideadata.org/PartBReport.asp

U.S. Office of Education. (1968). *First annual report of National Advisory Committee on Handicapped Children*. Washington, DC: U.S. Department of Health, Education, and Welfare.

U.S. Office of Education. (1977, December 29). Assistance to states for education of handicapped children: Procedures for evaluating specific learning disabilities. *Federal Register, 42*(250), 65082–65085.

Vaughn, R., & Hodges, L. (1973). A statistical survey into a definition of learning disabilities. *Journal of Learning Disabilities, 6*(10), 658–664.

Vaughn, S., & Bos, C. (2009). *Strategies for teaching students with learning and behavior problems* (7th ed.). Upper Saddle River, NJ: Pearson Education.

Vaughn, S., Elbaum, B., & Boardman, A. (2001). The social function of students with learning disabilities: Implications for inclusion. *Exceptionality, 9*, 47–65.

Vaughn, S., & Fuchs, L. (2003). Redefining learning disabilities as inadequate response to instruction: The promise and potential problems. *Learning Disabilities Research and Practice, 18*(3), 137–146.

Vaughn, S., & Linan-Thompson, S. (2003). What is special about special education for students with learning disabilities? *Journal of Special Education, 37*(3), 140–147.

Vaughn, S., Sinagub, J., & Kim, A. (2004). Social competence/social skills of students with learning disabilities. In B. Wong (Ed.), *Learning about learning disabilities* (3rd ed., pp. 341–373). San Diego, CA: Elsevier/Academic Press.

Wadsworth, S., & DeFries, J. (2005). Genetic etiology of reading difficulties in boys and girls. *Twin Research and Human Genetics, 8*(6), 594–601.

Walker, B., Shippen, M., Alberto, P., Houchins, D., & Cihak, D. (2005). Using the expressive writing program to improve the writing skills of high school students with learning disabilities. *Learning Disabilities Research and Practice, 20*(3), 175–183.

Wiener, J. (2004). Do peer relationships foster behavioral adjustment in children with learning disabilities? *Learning Disability Quarterly, 27*(1), 21–30.

Witte, R., Philips, L., & Kakela, M. (1998). Job satisfaction of college graduates with learning disabilities. *Journal of Learning Disabilities, 31*(3), 259–265.

Wood, F., & Grigorenko, E. (2001). Emerging issues in the genetics of dyslexia: A methodological preview. *Journal of Learning Disabilities, 34*(6), 503–511.

Yell, M. (2006). *The law and special education* (2nd ed.). Upper Saddle River, NJ: Pearson Education.

Zigmond, N. (2003). Where should students with disabilities receive special education services? *Journal of Special Education, 37*(3), 193–199.

Zigmond, N., & Baker, J. (1996). Full inclusion for students with learning disabilities: Too much of a good thing? *Theory into Practice, 35*(1), 26–34.

Zirkel, P., & Thomas, L. (2010). State laws for RTI: An updated snapshot. *Teaching Exceptional Children, 42*(3), 56–63.

Chapter 7

Alberto, P., & Troutman, A. (2006). *Applied behavior analysis for teachers* (7th ed.). Upper Saddle River, NJ: Pearson Education.

American Academy of Pediatrics. (2000). Clinical practice guideline: Diagnosis and evaluation of the child with attention-deficit/hyperactivity disorder. *Pediatrics, 105*(5), 1158–1170.

American Psychiatric Association. (2000). *Diagnostic and statistical manual of mental disorders* (4th ed., text rev.). Washington, DC: Author.

Atkins, M., & Mariñez-Lora, A. (2008). Attention-deficit/hyperactivity disorder and psychiatric comorbidity. In P. Accardo (Ed.), *Capute & Accardo's neurodevelopmental disabilities in infancy and childhood* (3rd ed., Vol. 2, pp. 693–703). Baltimore: Paul H. Brookes.

Barbaresi, W., Katusic, S., Colligan, R., Weaver, A., Leibson, C., & Jacobsen, S. (2006). Long term stimulant medication treatment of ADHD: Results from a population based study. *Journal of Developmental & Behavioral Pediatrics, 27*(1), 1–10.

Barkley, R. (1998). *Attention deficit hyperactivity disorder* (2nd ed.). New York: Guilford Press.

Barkley, R. (1999–2000). *ADHD in children and adolescents*. Fairhope, AL: Institute for Continuing Education.

Barkley, R. (2000). *Taking charge of ADHD: The complete authoritative guide for parents* (Rev. ed.). New York: Guilford Press.

Barkley, R. (2006). *Attention deficit hyperactivity disorder* (3rd ed.). New York: Guilford Press.

Barkley, R., Fischer, M., Smallish, L., & Fletcher, K. (2006). Young adult outcome of hyperactive children: Adaptive functioning in major life activities. *Journal of the American Academy of Child & Adolescent Psychiatry, 45*(2), 192–202.

Bender, W. (2008). *Learning disabilities: Characteristics, identification, and teaching strategies* (6th ed.). Needham Heights, MA: Allyn and Bacon.

Bos, C., Nahmias, M., & Urban, M. (1999). Targeting home–school collaboration for students with ADHD. *Teaching Exceptional Children, 31*(6), 4–11.

Bradley, W. (1937). The behavior of children receiving Benzedrine. *American Journal of Psychiatry, 94,* 577–585.

Brown, T. (2006). New understandings of AD/HD. In C. Dendy (Ed.), *CHADD educator's manual on attention-deficit/hyperactivity disorder* (pp. 3–12). Landover, MD: CHADD.

Brown, T. (2007). A new approach to attention deficit disorder. *Educational Leadership, 64*(5), 22–27.

Cantwell, D. (1979). The "hyperactive child." *Hospital Practice, 14,* 65–73.

Castellanos, F. (1997). Toward a pathophysiology of attention-deficit/hyperactivity disorder. *Clinical Pediatrics, 36,* 381–393.

Centers for Disease Control and Prevention. (2010). *State-based prevalence data of ADHD diagnosis.* Retrieved February 2, 2010, from http://www.cdc.gov/ncbddd/adhd/prevalence.html

Chronis, A., Jones, H., & Raggi, V. (2006). Evidence-based psychosocial treatments for children and adolescents with attention-deficit/hyperactivity disorder. *Clinical Psychology Review, 26,* 486–502.

Cohen, D. (2006). Critiques of the "ADHD" enterprise. In G. Lloyd, J. Snead, & D. Cohen (Eds.), *Critical new perspectives on ADHD* (pp. 12–33). London: Routledge.

Conners, C. (1997). *Conners' Teachers Rating Scale—Revised.* North Tonawanda, NY: Multi-Health Systems.

Cruickshank, W., Bentzen, F., Ratzeburg, F., & Tannhauser, M. (1961). *A teaching method for brain-injured and hyperactive children.* Syracuse, NY: Syracuse University Press.

Cruickshank, W., Bice, H., & Wallen, N. (1957). *Perception and cerebral palsy.* Syracuse, NY: Syracuse University Press.

Daley, D. (2006). Attention deficit hyperactivity disorder: A review of the essential facts. *Child: Care, Health and Development, 32,* 193–204.

Daly, P., & Ranalli, P. (2003). Using cartoons to teach self-monitoring skills. *Teaching Exceptional Children, 35*(5), 30–35.

Dodson, W. (2002). Attention deficit-hyperactivity disorder (AD/HD): The basics and the controversies. *Understanding Our Gifted, 14*(4), 17–21.

DuPaul, G. (2006). Academic achievement in children with ADHD. *Journal of the American Academy of Child & Adolescent Psychiatry, 45*(7), 766–767.

DuPaul, G., Power, T., Anastopoulos, A., & Reid, R. (1998). *ADHD Rating Scale–IV: Checklists, norms, and clinical interpretation.* New York: Guilford Press.

DuPaul, G., & White, G. (2004). An AD/HD primer. *Principal Leadership, 5*(2), 11–15.

Evans, S., Timmins, B., Sibley, M., White, L., Serpell, Z., & Schultz, B. (2006). Developing coordinated, multimodal school-based treatment for young adolescents with ADHD. *Education and Treatment of Children, 29,* 359–378.

Friend, M., & Bursuck, W. (2009). *Including students with special needs* (5th ed.). Upper Saddle River, NJ: Pearson Education.

Glanzman, M., & Blum, N. (2007). Attention deficit and hyperactivity. In M. Batshaw, L. Pellegrino, & N. Roizen (Eds.), *Children with disabilities* (6th ed., pp. 345–365). Baltimore: Paul H. Brookes.

Glanzman, M., & Blum, N. (2008). Genetics, imaging, and neurochemistry in attention-deficit/hyperactivity disorder. In P. Accardo (Ed.), *Capute & Accardo's neurodevelopmental disabilities in infancy and childhood* (3rd ed., Vol. 2, pp. 617–637). Baltimore: Paul H. Brookes.

Glynn, E., Thomas, J., & Shee, S. (1973). Behavioral self-control of on-task behavior in an elementary classroom. *Journal of Applied Behavior Analysis, 6*(1), 105–113.

Hallahan, D., Lloyd, J., Kauffman, J., Weiss, M., & Martinez, E. (2005). *Learning disabilities: Foundations, characteristics, and effective teaching* (3rd ed.). Boston: Pearson Education.

Harris, K., Friedlander, B., Saddler, B., Frizzelle, R., & Graham, S. (2005). Self-monitoring of attention versus self-monitoring of academic performance: Effects among students with ADHD in general education classroom. *Journal of Special Education, 39*(3), 145–156.

Honos-Webb, L. (2005). *The gift of ADHD.* Oakland, CA: New Harbinger.

Imperio, W. (2003). Community forums: Bridging the cultural gap. *Attention!, 9*(5), 12–13, 40–41.

Johnson, L., & Johnson, C. (1999). Teaching students to regulate their own behavior. *Teaching Exceptional Children, 31*(4), 6–10.

Jones, C., & Teach, J. (2006). Impact of AD/HD on elementary students. In C. Dendy (Ed.), *CHADD educator's manual on attention-deficit/hyperactivity disorder* (pp. 61–72). Landover, MD: CHADD.

Kessler, R., Adler, L., Barkley, R., Biederman, J., Conners, C., Demler, O., et al. (2006). The prevalence and correlates of adult ADHD in the United States: Results from the National Comorbidity Survey replication. *American Journal of Psychiatry, 163,* 716–723.

Larsson, J., Larsson, H., & Lichtenstein, P. (2004). Genetic and environmental contributions to stability and change of ADHD symptoms between 8 and 13 years of age. *Journal of the American Academy of Child & Adolescent Psychiatry, 43*(10), 1267–1275.

Lawrence, V., Houghton, S., Tannock, R., Douglas, G., Dunkin, K., & Whiting, K. (2002). ADHD outside the laboratory: Boys' executive function performance on tasks in videogame play and on a visit to the zoo. *Journal of Abnormal Child Psychology, 30,* 447–462.

Lerner, J., & Johns, B. (2009). *Learning disabilities and related mild disabilities* (11th ed.). Belmont, CA: Wadsworth/Cengage Learning.

Lerner, J., & Lowenthal, B. (1993). Attention deficit disorders: New responsibilities for the special educator. *Learning Disabilities: A Multidisciplinary Journal, 4*(1), 1–8.

Levy, F., Hay, D., & Bennett, K. (2006). Genetics of attention deficit hyperactivity disorder: A current review and future prospects. *International Journal of Disability, Development and Education, 53,* 5–20.

Martin, N., Levy, F., Pieka, J., & Hay, D. (2006). A genetic study of attention deficit hyperactivity disorder, conduct disorder, oppositional defiant disorder and reading disability: Aetiological overlaps and implications. *International Journal of Disability, Development and Education,* 53, 21–34.

McKinley, L., & Stormont, M. (2008). The school supports checklist: Identifying support needs and barriers for children with ADHD. *Teaching Exceptional Children, 41*(2), 14–19.

Mercer, C., & Pullen, P. (2009). *Students with learning disabilities* (7th ed.). Upper Saddle River, NJ: Pearson Education.

Mill, J., Caspi, A., Williams, B., Craig, I., Taylor, A., Polo-Tomas, M., et al. (2006). Prediction of heterogeneity in intelligence and adult prognosis by genetic polymorphisms in the dopamine system among children with attention-deficit/hyperactivity disorder. *Archives of General Psychiatry, 63,* 462–469.

Miranda, A., Jarque, S., & Tarraga, R. (2006). Intervention in school settings for students with ADHD. *Exceptionality, 14,* 35–52.

Moore, C., Biederman, J., Wozinak, J., Mick, E., Aleardi, M., Wardrop, M., et al. (2006). Differences in brain chemistry in children and adolescents with attention deficit hyperactivity disorder with and without comorbid bipolar disorder: A proton magnetic resonance spectroscopy study. *American Journal of Psychiatry, 163,* 316–318.

MTA Cooperative Group. (1999a). A 14-month randomized clinical trial of treatment strategies for attention-deficit/hyperactivity disorder. *Archives of General Psychiatry, 56,* 1073–1086.

MTA Cooperative Group. (1999b). Moderators and mediators of treatment response for children with attention-deficit/hyperactivity disorder. *Archives of General Psychiatry, 56,* 1088–1096.

Murphy, K., Barkley, R., & Bush, T. (2002). Young adults with attention deficit hyperactivity disorder: Subtype differences in educational and clinical history. *Journal of Nervous and Mental Disorders, 19,* 147–157.

National Dissemination Center for Children with Disabilities. (2004). *Fact Sheet No. 19: Attention deficit/hyperactivity disorder.* Washington, DC: Author.

National Institute of Mental Health. (2006). *Attention deficit hyperactivity disorder.* Retrieved April 3, 2007, from http://www.nimh.nih.gov/health/publications/adhd/summary.shtml

National Institute of Mental Health. (2008). *Attention deficit hyperactivity disorder.* Bethesda, MD: Author.

Pierce, K. (2003). Attention-deficit/hyperactivity disorder and comorbidity. *Primary Psychiatry, 10,* 69–70, 75–76.

Reid, R., Casat, C., Norton, H., Anastopoulos, A., & Temple, E. (2001). Using behavior rating scales for ADHD across ethnic groups: The IOWA Conners. *Journal of Emotional and Behavioral Disorders, 9*(4), 210–218.

Salend, S., & Rohena, E. (2003). Students with attention deficit disorders: An overview. *Intervention in School and Clinic, 38,* 259–266.

Silver, L. (1990). Attention deficit hyperactivity disorder: Is it a learning disability or a related disorder? *Journal of Learning Disabilities, 23,* 394–397.

Smith, T., Polloway, E., Patton, J., & Dowdy, C. (2008). *Teaching children with special needs in inclusive settings* (5th ed.). Needham Heights, MA: Allyn and Bacon.

Snider, V., Busch, T., & Arrowood, L. (2003). Teacher knowledge of stimulant medication. *Remedial and Special Education, 24*(1), 46–56.

Stein, M., & Shin, D. (2008). Disorders of attention: Diagnosis. In P. Accardo (Ed.), *Capute & Accardo's neurodevelopmental disabilities in infancy and childhood* (3rd ed., Vol. 2, pp. 639–656). Baltimore: Paul H. Brookes.

Still, G. (1902). Some abnormal psychical conditions in children. *Lancet, 1,* 1008–1012, 1077–1082, 1163–1168.

Strauss, A., & Werner, H. (1942). Disorders of conceptual thinking in the brain-injured child. *Journal of Nervous and Mental Disease, 98,* 153–172.

U.S. Department of Education. (2000). *Twenty-second annual report to Congress on the implementation of the Individuals with Disabilities Education Act.* Washington, DC: U.S. Government Printing Office.

U.S. Department of Education. (2008a). *Identifying and treating attention deficit hyperactivity disorders: A resource for school and home.* Washington, DC: Author.

U.S. Department of Education. (2008b). *Teaching children with attention deficit hyperactivity disorders: Instructional strategies and practices.* Washington, DC: Author.

U.S. Department of Education. (2010). *IDEA data.* Retrieved April 14, 2010, from https://www.ideadata.org/PartBReport.asp

Vaughn, S., Bos, C., & Schumm, J. (2011). *Teaching exceptional, diverse, and at-risk students in the general education classroom* (5th ed.). Upper Saddle River, NJ: Pearson Education.

Volkow, N., Wang, G., Newcorn, J., Telang, E., Solanto, M., Fowler, J., et al. (2007). Depressed dopamine activity in caudate and preliminary evidence of limbic involvement in adults with attention-deficit/hyperactivity disorder. *Archives of General Psychiatry, 64*(8), 932–940.

Weiss, S., & Illes, T. (2006). Advanced strategies for challenging behaviors. In C. Dendy (Ed.), *CHADD educator's manual on attention-deficit/hyperactivity disorder* (pp. 73–79). Landover, MD: CHADD.

Werner, H., & Strauss, A. (1941). Pathology of figure–background relation in the child. *Journal of Abnormal and Social Psychology, 36,* 236–248.

Weyandt, L. (2006). *The physiological bases of cognitive and behavioral disorders.* Mahwah, NJ: Erlbaum.

Weyandt, L. (2007). *An ADHD primer* (2nd ed.). Mahwah, NJ: Erlbaum.

Wilens, T., Faraone, S., Biederman, J., & Gunawardene, S. (2003). Does stimulant therapy of attention deficit/hyperactivity disorder beget later substance abuse? *Pediatrics, 111*(1), 179–185.

Chapter 8

Abelev, M. (2009). Advancing out of poverty: Social class worldview and its relation to resiliency. *Journal of Adolescent Research, 24*(1), 114–141.

Achenbach, T., & Edelbrock, C. (1978). The classification of child psychopathology: A review and analysis of empirical efforts. *Psychological Bulletin, 85,* 1275–1301.

Achenbach, T., & Edelbrock, C. (2001). *Manual for the Child Behavior Checklist* (2nd ed.). Burlington: University of Vermont, Department of Psychiatry.

Allen, R., & Petr, C. (1997). Family-centered professional behavior: Frequency and importance to parents. *Journal of Emotional and Behavioral Disorders, 5*(4), 196–204.

Allen-DeBoer, R., Malmgren, K., & Glass, M. (2006). Reading instruction for youth with emotional and behavioral disorders in a juvenile correctional facility. *Behavioral Disorders, 32*(1), 18–28.

American Psychiatric Association. (2000). *Diagnostic and statistical manual of mental disorders* (4th ed., text rev.). Washington, DC: Author.

Barton-Arwood, S., Wehby, J., & Falk, K. (2005). Reading instruction for elementary-age students with emotional and behavioral disorders: Academic and behavioral outcomes. *Exceptional Children, 72*(1), 7–27.

Beard, K., & Sugai, G. (2004). First step to success: An early intervention for elementary children at risk for antisocial behavior. *Behavioral Disorders, 29*(4), 396–398.

Blanchard, L., Gurka, M., & Blackman, J. (2006). Emotional, developmental, and behavioral health of American children and their families: A report from the 2003 National Survey of Children's Health. *Pediatrics, 117,* 1202–1212.

Boe, E., & Cook, L. (2006). The chronic and increasing shortage of fully certified teachers in special and general education. *Exceptional Children, 72*(4), 443–460.

Bower, E. (1960). *Early identification of emotionally disturbed children in school.* Springfield, IL: Charles C Thomas.

Bower, E. (1981). *Early identification of emotionally handicapped children in school* (3rd ed.). Springfield, IL: Charles C Thomas.

Bower, E. (1982). Defining emotional disturbance: Public policy and research. *Psychology in the Schools, 19,* 55–60.

Chandler, L., & Dahlquist, C. (2010). *Functional assessment: Strategies to prevent and remediate challenging behavior in school settings* (3rd ed.). Upper Saddle River, NJ: Pearson Education.

Children's Defense Fund. (2010). *Children & poverty 2008.* Retrieved March 11, 2010, from http://www.childrensdefense.org/helping-americas-children/ending-child-poverty/poverty-income-census-data-2008.html

Chitiyo, M., & Wheeler, J. (2009). Challenges faced by school teachers in implementing positive behavioral supports in their school systems. *Remedial and Special Education, 30*(1), 6–14.

Collins, S. (2003, July 17). Mentally ill children face life without necessary services. *USA Today,* p. 13A.

Connelly, V., & Graham, S. (2009). Student teaching and teacher attrition in special education. *Teacher Education and Special Education, 32*(3), 257–269.

Cooper, J., Heron, T., & Heward, W. (2007). *Applied behavior analysis* (2nd ed.). Upper Saddle River, NJ: Pearson Education.

Corbett, W., Clark, H., & Blank, W. (2002). Employment and social outcomes associated with vocational programming for youths with emotional or behavioral disorders. *Behavioral Disorders, 27*(4), 358–370.

Council for Children with Behavioral Disorders. (1990). Position paper on the provision of service to children with conduct disorders. *Behavioral Disorders, 15*(3), 180–189.

Council for Exceptional Children. (2001). New study of special education working conditions. *CEC Today, 8*(1), 9–12.

Coutinho, M., Oswald, D., Best, A., & Forness, S. (2002). Gender and sociodemographic factors and the disproportionate identification of culturally and linguistically diverse students with emotional disturbance. *Behavioral Disorders, 27*(2), 109–125.

Crundwell, R., & Killu, K. (2007). Understanding and accommodating students with depression in the classroom. *Teaching Exceptional Children, 40*(1), 48–54.

Cullinan, D. (2007). *Students with emotional and behavioral disorders* (2nd ed.). Upper Saddle River, NJ: Pearson Education.

Cullinan, D., Evans, C., Epstein, M., & Ryser, G. (2003). Characteristics of emotional disturbance of elementary school students. *Behavioral Disorders, 28*(2), 94–110.

Deno, S. (1998). Academic progress as incompatible behavior: Curriculum-based measurement (CBM) as intervention. *Beyond Behavior, 9*(3), 12–17.

Despert, J. (1965). *The emotionally disturbed child: Then and now.* New York: Brunner.

DeValenzuela, J., Copeland, S., Qi, C., & Park, M. (2006). Examining educational equity: Revising the disproportionate representation of minority students in special education. *Exceptional Children, 72*(4), 425–441.

Di Giulio, R. (2007). *Positive classroom management* (3rd ed.). Thousand Oaks, CA: Corwin Press.

Donovan, S., & Nickerson, A. (2007). Strength-based versus traditional social-emotional reports: Impact on multidisciplinary team members' perceptions. *Behavioral Disorders, 32*(4), 228–237.

Duckworth, S., Smith-Rex, S., Okey, S., Brookshire, M., Rawlinson, D., Rawlinson, R., et al. (2001). Wraparound services for young school children with emotional and behavioral disorders. *Exceptional Children, 33*(4), 54–60.

Dunlap, G., Strain, P., Fox, L., Carta, J., Conroy, M., Smith, B., et al. (2006). Prevention and intervention with young children's challenging behavior: Perspectives regarding current knowledge. *Behavioral Disorders, 32*(1), 29–45.

Eber, L., Breen, K., Rose, J., Unizycki, R., & London, T. (2008). Wraparound: A tertiary level intervention for students with emotional/behavioral needs. *Teaching Exceptional Children, 40*(6), 16–22.

Eber, L., & Keenan, S. (2004). Collaboration with other agencies: Wraparound and systems of care for children and youths with emotional and behavioral disorders. In R. Rutherford, M. Quinn, & S. Mathur (Eds.), *Handbook of research in emotional and behavioral disorders* (pp. 502–516). New York: Guilford Press.

Eber, L., Sugai, G., Smith, C., & Scott, T. (2002). Wraparound and positive behavioral interventions and supports in the schools. *Journal of Emotional and Behavioral Disorders, 10*(3), 171–180.

Epstein, M. (2002). *Behavioral and Emotional Rating Scale* (2nd ed.). Austin, TX: Pro-Ed.

Epstein, M., Rudolph, S., & Epstein, A. (2000). Strength-based assessment. *Teaching Exceptional Children, 32*(6), 50–54.

Erickson, M., Stage, S., & Nelson, J. (2006). Naturalistic study of the behavior of students with EBD referred for functional behavioral assessment. *Journal of Emotional and Behavioral Disorders, 14*(1), 31–40.

Etscheidt, S. (2002). Psychotherapy services for students with emotional or behavioral disorders. *Behavioral Disorders, 27*(4), 386–399.

Forgan, J., & Gonzalez-DeHass, A. (2004). How to infuse social skills training into literacy instruction. *Teaching Exceptional Children, 36*(6), 24–30.

Forness, S. (2003). Parting reflections on education of children with emotional or behavioral disorders. *Behavioral Disorders, 28*(3), 198–201.

Forness, S., & Kavale, K. (2000). Emotional or behavioral disorders: Background and current status of E/BD terminology and definition. *Behavioral Disorders, 25*(3), 264–269.

Forness, S., Kavale, K., & Davanzo, P. (2002). The new medical model: Interdisciplinary treatment and the limits of behaviorism. *Behavioral Disorders, 27*(2), 168–178.

Forness, S., Walker, H., & Kavale, K. (2003). Psychiatric disorders and treatments: A primer for teachers. *Teaching Exceptional Children, 36*(2), 42–49.

Frey, A. (2002). Predictors of placement recommendations for children with behavioral or emotional disorders. *Behavioral Disorders, 27*(2), 126–136.

Friend, M., & Bursuck, W. (2009). *Including students with special needs* (5th ed.). Upper Saddle River, NJ: Pearson Education.

Gresham, F., Sugai, G., & Horner, R. (2001). Interpreting outcomes of social skills training for students with high-incidence disabilities. *Exceptional Children, 67*(3), 331–344.

Gumpel, T., & David, S. (2000). Exploring the efficacy of self-regulatory training as a possible alternative to social skills training. *Behavioral Disorders, 25*(2), 131–146.

Gunter, P., Shores, R., Jack, S., Rasmussen, S., & Flowers, J. (1995). Teacher/student proximity: A strategy for classroom control through teacher movement. *Teaching Exceptional Children, 28*(1), 12–14.

Haslam, R., & Valletutti, P. (2004). *Medical problems in the classroom: The teacher's role in diagnosis and management* (4th ed.). Austin, TX: Pro-Ed.

Hayman, M. (1939). The interrelations between mental defect and mental disorder. *Journal of Mental Science, 85,* 1183–1193.

Hocutt, A., McKinney, J., & Montague, M. (2002). The impact of managed care on efforts to prevent development of serious emotional disturbance in young children. *Journal of Disability Policy Studies, 13*(1), 51–60.

Hooper, S., Roberts, J., Zeisel, S., & Poe, M. (2003). Core language predictors of behavioral functioning in early elementary school children: Concurrent and longitudinal findings. *Behavioral Disorders, 29*(1), 10–24.

House, A. (2002). *DSM-IV diagnosis in the schools.* New York: Guilford Press.

Janas, M. (2002). Twenty ways to build resiliency. *Intervention in School and Clinic, 38*(2), 117–121.

Janney, R., & Snell, M. (2008). *Teacher's guide to inclusive practices: Behavioral support* (2nd ed.). Baltimore: Paul H. Brookes.

Jensen, M. (2005). *Introduction to emotional and behavioral disorders.* Upper Saddle River, NJ: Pearson Education.

Johns, B., Mather, S., & McGrath, M. (2003). Leadership necessary to promote a call to action. *Beyond Behavior, 13*(1), 20–22.

Jones, V., Dohrn, E., & Dunn, C. (2004). *Creating effective programs for students with emotional and behavior disorders.* Boston: Allyn and Bacon.

Kauffman, J. (1981). *Characteristics of children's behavioral disorders* (2nd ed.). Columbus, OH: Merrill.

Kauffman, J., & Landrum, T. (2009). *Characteristics of emotional and behavioral disorders of children and youth* (9th ed.). Upper Saddle River, NJ: Pearson Education.

Kemp, S. (2006). Dropout policies and trends for students with and without disabilities. *Adolescence, 41*(162), 235–250.

Kendziora, K. (2004). Early intervention for emotional and behavioral disorders. In R. Rutherford, M. Quinn, & S. Mathur (Eds.), *Handbook of research in emotional and behavioral disorders* (pp. 327–351). New York: Guilford Press.

Kerr, M., & Nelson, C. (2010). *Strategies for managing behavior problems in the classroom* (6th ed.). Upper Saddle River, NJ: Pearson Education.

Kline, F., Silver, L., & Russell, S. (2001). *The educator's guide to medical issues in the classroom.* Baltimore: Paul H. Brookes.

Kutash, K., Duchnowski, A., Sumi, W., Rudo, Z., & Harris, K. (2002). A school, family, and community collaborative program for children who have emotional disturbances. *Journal of Emotional and Behavioral Disorders, 10*(2), 99–107.

Landrum, T., Katsiyannis, A., & Archwamety, T. (2004). An analysis of placement and exit patterns of students with emotional or behavioral disorders. *Behavioral Disorders, 29*(2), 140–153.

Lane, K. (2003). Identifying young students at risk for antisocial behavior: The utility of "teachers as tests." *Behavioral Disorders, 28*(4), 360–369.

Lane, K., Kalberg, J., & Edwards, C. (2008). An examination of school-wide interventions with primary level efforts conducted in elementary schools: Implications for school psychologists. In D. Molina (Ed.), *School psychology: 21st century issues and challenges* (pp. 253–278). New York: Nova Science.

Lane, K., Little, M., Redding-Rhodes, J., Phillips, A., & Welsh, M. (2007). Outcomes of a teacher-led reading intervention for elementary students at risk for behavioral disorders. *Exceptional Children, 74*(1), 47–70.

Lane, K., Robertson, E., & Graham-Bailey, M. (2006). An examination of school-wide interventions with primary level efforts conducted in secondary schools: Methodological considerations. In T. Scruggs & M. Mastropieri (Eds.), *Applications of research methodology* (Vol. 19, pp. 157–199). Oxford, England: Elsevier/JAI Press.

Lane, K., Wehby, J., Menzies, H., Doukas, G., Munton, S., & Gregg, R. (2003). Social skills instruction for students at risk for antisocial behavior: The effects of small-group instruction. *Behavioral Disorders, 28*(3), 229–248.

Lane, K., Weisenbach, J., Phillips, A., & Wehby, J. (2007). Designing, implementing, and evaluating function-based interventions using a systematic, feasible approach. *Behavioral Disorders, 32*(2), 122–139.

Leedy, A., Bates, P., & Safran, S. (2004). Bridging the research-to-practice gap: Improving hallway behavior using positive behavior supports. *Behavioral Disorders, 29*(2), 130–139.

Leffert, J., & Siperstein, G. (2003). A focus on social skills instruction for students with learning disabilities. *Current Practice Alerts, 9,* 1–4.

Lewis, C. (1974). Introduction: Landmarks. In J. Kauffman & C. Lewis (Eds.), *Teaching exceptional children with behavior disorders: Personal perspectives* (pp. 2–23). Columbus, OH: Merrill.

Logan, K., & Stein, S. (2001). The research lead teacher model: Helping general education teachers deal with classroom behavior problems. *Teaching Exceptional Children, 33*(3), 10–15.

Luiselli, J., Putnam, R., & Sunderland, M. (2002). Longitudinal evaluation of behavior support intervention in a public middle school. *Journal of Positive Behavior Interventions, 4*(3), 182–188.

Maag, J. (2006). Social skills training for students with emotional and behavioral disorders: A review of reviews. *Behavioral Disorders, 32*(1), 5–17.

Mastropieri, M., & Scruggs, T. (2002). *Effective instruction for special education* (3rd ed.). Austin, TX: Pro-Ed.

McIntyre, T., & Forness, S. (1996). Is there a new definition yet or are our kids still seriously emotionally disturbed? *Beyond Behavior, 7*(3), 4–9.

Milstein, M., & Henry, D. (2000). *Spreading resiliency: Making it happen for schools and communities*. Thousand Oaks, CA: Corwin Press.

Moffitt, T. (1994). Adolescence-limited and life-course persistent antisocial behavior: A developmental taxonomy. *Psychological Review, 100,* 674–701.

National Dissemination Center for Children and Youth with Disabilities. (2003). *Interventions for chronic behavior problems*. Washington, DC: Author.

National Institute of Mental Health. (2008). *The numbers count: Mental disorders in America*. Retrieved March 1, 2010, from http://www.nimh.nih.gov/publicat/numbers.cfm

National Institute of Mental Health. (2010). *Depression in children and adolescents*. Retrieved March 1, 2010, from http://www.nimh.nih.gov/health/topics/depression/depression-in-children-and-adolescents.shtml

Nelson, J., Babyak, A., Gonzalez, J., & Benner, G. (2003). An investigation of the problem behaviors exhibited by K-12 students with emotional or behavioral disorders in public school settings. *Behavioral Disorders, 28*(4), 348–359.

Nelson, J., Benner, G., & Cheney, D. (2005). An investigation of the language skills of students with emotional disturbance served in public schools. *Journal of Special Education, 39*(2), 97–105.

Nelson, J., Benner, G., Lane, K., & Smith, B. (2004). An investigation of the academic achievement of K-12 students with emotional and behavioral disorders in public school settings. *Exceptional Children, 71*(1), 59–73.

Nelson, J., Benner, G., & Rogers-Adkinson, D. (2003). An investigation of the characteristics of K–12 students with comorbid emotional disturbance and significant language deficits in public school settings. *Behavioral Disorders, 29*(1), 25–33.

New Freedom Commission on Mental Health. (2003). *Achieving the promise: Transforming mental health care in America*. Final report. DHHS Pub. No. SMA-03-3832. Rockville, MD: U.S. Department of Health and Human Services.

Newcomer, P. (2003). *Understanding and teaching emotionally disturbed children and adolescents* (3rd ed.). Austin, TX: Pro-Ed.

Nungesser, N., & Watkins, R. (2005). Preschool school teachers' perceptions and reactions to challenging classroom behavior: Implications for speech-language pathologists. *Language, Speech, and Hearing Services in Schools, 36*(2), 139–151.

Obiakor, F., Utley, C., Smith, R., & Harris-Obiakor, P. (2002). The Comprehensive Support Model for culturally diverse exceptional learners: Intervention in an age of change. *Intervention in School and Clinic, 38*(1), 14–27.

Oswald, D. (2003). Response to Forness: Parting reflections on education of children with emotional or behavioral disorders. *Behavioral Disorders, 28*(3), 202–204.

Polloway, E., Patton, J., & Serna, L. (2008). *Strategies for teaching learners with special needs* (9th ed.). Upper Saddle River, NJ: Pearson Education.

Quay, H., & Peterson, D. (1975). *Manual for the Behavior Problem Checklist*. Coral Gables, FL: Author.

Quay, H., & Peterson, D. (1996). *Manual for the Revised Behavior Problem Checklist*. Lutz, FL: Psychological Assessment Resources.

Quinn, M., Rutherford, R., Leone, P., Osher, D., & Poirer, J. (2005). Youth with disabilities in juvenile corrections: A national survey. *Exceptional Children, 71*(3), 339–345.

Raiser, L., & Van Nagel, C. (1980). The loophole in Public Law 94–142. *Exceptional Children, 46,* 516–520.

Rie, H. (1971). Historical perspectives of concepts of child psychopathology. In H. Rie (Ed.), *Perspectives in child psychopathology* (pp. 3–50). New York: Aldine-Atherton.

Rinaldi, C. (2003). Language competence and social behavior of students with emotional or behavioral disorders. *Behavioral Disorders, 29*(1), 34–42.

Robinson, D., Funk, D., Beth, A., & Bush, A. (2005). Changing beliefs about corporal punishment: Increasing knowledge about ineffectiveness to build more consistent moral and informational beliefs. *Journal of Behavioral Education, 14*(2), 117–139.

Rodgers-Adkinson, D. (2003). Language processing in children with emotional disorders. *Behavioral Disorders, 29*(1), 43–47.

Rogers-Adkinson, D., & Hooper, S. (2003). The relationship of language and behavior: Introduction to the special issue. *Behavioral Disorders, 29*(1), 5–9.

Rosenberg, M., Wilson, R., Maheady, L., & Sindelar, P. (2004). *Educating students with behavior disorders* (3rd ed.). Needham Heights, MA: Allyn and Bacon.

Rosenblum, K., Dayton, C., & Muzik, M. (2009). Infant social and emotional development. In C. Zeanah, Jr. (Ed.), *Handbook of infant mental health* (3rd ed., pp. 80–103). New York: Guilford Press.

Rosenshine, B., & Stevens, R. (1986). Teaching functions. In M. Wittrock (Ed.), *Handbook of research on teaching* (3rd ed., pp. 376–391). New York: Macmillan.

Rubin, R., & Balow, B. (1971). Learning and behavior disorders: A longitudinal study. *Exceptional Children, 38,* 293–299.

Ruef, M., Higgins, C., Glaeser, B., & Patnode, M. (1998). Positive behavioral support: Strategies for teachers. *Intervention in School and Clinic, 34*(1), 21–32.

Rutter, M. (2006). *Genes and behavior: Nature-nurture interplay explained*. Malden, MA: Blackwell Publishing.

Sabornie, E., & deBettencourt, L. (2009). *Teaching students with mild disabilities at the secondary level* (3rd ed.). Upper Saddle River, NJ: Pearson Education.

Safford, P., & Safford, E. (1996). *A history of childhood and disability*. New York: Teachers College Press.

Safran, S., & Oswald, K. (2003). Positive behavior supports: Can schools reshape disciplinary practices? *Exceptional Children, 69*(3), 361–373.

Salend, S. (2011). *Creating inclusive classrooms* (7th ed.). Upper Saddle River, NJ: Pearson Education.

Satcher, D. (1999). *Mental health: A report of the surgeon general*. Washington, DC: U.S. Department of Public Health Services.

Savage, T. (1999). *Teaching self-control through management and discipline* (2nd ed.). Needham Heights, MA: Allyn and Bacon.

Scheuermann, B., & Hall, J. (2008). *Positive behavioral supports for the classroom*. Upper Saddle River, NJ: Pearson Education.

Scott, T., Bucalos, A., Liaupsin, C., Nelson, C., Jolivette, K., & DeShea, L. (2004). Using functional behavior assessment in general education settings: Making a case for effectiveness and efficiency. *Behavioral Disorders, 29*(2), 189–201.

Scott, T., Payne, L., & Jolivette, K. (2003). Preventing predictable problem behaviors by using positive behavior support. *Beyond Behavior, 13*(1), 3–7.

Scruggs, T., & Mastropieri, M. (2000). Mnemonic strategies for students with behavior disorders: Memory for learning and behavior. *Beyond Behavior, 10*(1), 13–17.

Shaw, D., Gilliom, M., & Giovannelli, J. (2005). Aggressive behavior disorders. In C. Zeanah, Jr. (Ed.), *Handbook of infant mental health* (2nd ed., pp. 397–411). New York: Guilford Press.

Skiba, R., Poloni-Staudinger, L., Gallini, S., Simmons, A., & Feggins-Azziz, R. (2006). Disparate access: The disproportionality of African American students with disabilities across educational environments. *Exceptional Children, 72*(4), 411–424.

Sprague, J., & Walker, H. (2000). Early identification and intervention for youth with antisocial and violent behavior. *Exceptional Children, 66*(3), 367–379.

Stea, K., & Ristic, R. (2006). *Two peas in a pod: Integrating the Nonviolent Crisis Intervention training program and positive behavioral support strategies.* Brookfield, WI: Crisis Prevention Institute.

Stein, M., & Davis, C. (2000). Direct instruction as positive behavioral support. *Beyond Behavior, 10*(1), 7–12.

Sugai, G., Horner, R., Dunlap, G., Hieneman, M., Lewis, T., Nelson, C., et al. (1999). *Applying positive behavior support and functional assessment in schools.* Washington, DC: Office of Special Education Programs, Center on Positive Behavioral Interventions and Supports.

Sugai, G., Simonsen, B., & Horner, R. (2008). Schoolwide positive behavior supports. *Teaching Exceptional Children, 40*(6), 5–6.

Taylor, P., Gunter, P., & Slate, J. (2001). Teachers' perceptions of inappropriate student behavior as a function of teachers' and students' gender and ethnic background. *Behavioral Disorders, 26*(2), 146–151.

Taylor-Richardson, K., Heflinger, C., & Brown, T. (2006). Experience of strain among caregivers responsible for children with serious emotional and behavioral disorders. *Journal of Emotional and Behavioral Disorders, 14*(3), 157–168.

Umbreit, J., Ferro, J., Liaupsin, C., & Lane, K. (2007). *Functional behavioral assessment and function-based intervention.* Upper Saddle River, NJ: Pearson Education.

U.S. Department of Education. (1980). *Second annual report to Congress on the implementation of Public Law 94–142.* Washington, DC: Author.

U.S. Department of Education. (2000). *Safeguarding our children: An action guide.* Washington, DC: Author.

U.S. Department of Education. (2003). *Twenty-fifth annual report to Congress on the implementation of the Individuals with Disabilities Education Act.* Washington, DC: U.S. Government Printing Office.

U.S. Department of Education. (2009). *IDEA data.* Retrieved October 31, 2009, from https://www.ideadata.org/PartBReport.asp

U.S. Department of Education. (2010). *IDEA data.* Retrieved April 14, 2010, from https://www.ideadata.org/PartBReport.asp

Vaughn, S., Bos, C., & Schumm, J. (2011). *Teaching exceptional, diverse, and at-risk students in the general education classroom* (5th ed.). Needham Heights, MA: Allyn and Bacon.

Vaughn, S., & Lancelotta, G. (1990). Teaching interpersonal social skills to low accepted students: Peer-pairing versus no peer-pairing. *Journal of School Psychology, 28*(3), 181–188.

Vaughn, S., Levy, S., Coleman, M., & Bos, C. (2002). Reading instruction for students with LD and EBD: A synthesis of observation studies. *Journal of Special Education, 36*(1), 2–13.

Wacker, D., & Berg, W. (2002). PBS as a service delivery system. *Journal of Positive Behavior Interventions, 4*(1), 25–28.

Wagner, M., Cameto, R., & Newman, L. (2003). *Youth with disabilities: A changing population.* Retrieved March 2, 2010, from http://www.nlts2.org/reports/2003_04-1/nlts2_report_2003_04-1_complete.pdf

Wagner, M., & Davis, M. (2006). How are we preparing students with emotional disturbance in the transition to young adulthood? Findings from the National Longitudinal Transition Study-2. *Journal of Emotional and Behavioral Disorders, 14*(2), 86–98.

Wagner, M., Newman, L., Cameto, R., Garza, N., & Levine, P. (2005). *After high school: A first look at the post school experiences of youth with disabilities.* Retrieved March 2, 2010, from www.nlts2.org/reports/2005_04/nlts2_report_2005_04_complete.pdf

Wakschlag, L., & Danis, B. (2009). Characterizing early childhood disruptive behavior. In C. Zeanah, Jr. (Ed.), *Handbook of infant mental health* (3rd ed., pp. 392–408). New York: Guilford Press.

Walker, H., Kavanagh, K., Stiller, B., Golly, A., Severson, H., & Feil, E. (1997). *First Steps to Success: An early intervention program for antisocial kindergartners.* Longmont, CO: Sopris West.

Walker, H., Ramsey, E., & Gresham, F. (2004). *Antisocial behavior in schools: Evidence-based practices* (2nd ed.). Belmont, CA: Wadsworth.

Warger, C. (2002). *Full-service schools' potential for special education.* ERIC Clearinghouse on Disabilities and Gifted Education. Available at http://eric.hoagiesgifted.org/osep/topical/fullsvc.html

Webber, J., & Plotts, C. (2008). *Emotional and behavioral disorders: Theory and practice* (5th ed.). Boston: Allyn and Bacon.

Wehby, J., Falk, K., Barton-Arwood, S., Lane, K., & Cooley, C. (2003). The impact of comprehensive reading instruction on the academic and social behavior of students with emotional and behavioral disorders. *Journal of Emotional and Behavioral Disorders, 11*(4), 225–238.

Wehby, J., Symons, F., Canale, J., & Go, F. (1998). Teaching practices in classroom for students with emotional and behavioral disorders: Discrepancies between recommendations and observations. *Behavioral Disorders, 24,* 51–56.

White, C., Palmer, K., & Huffman, L. (2003). Technology instruction for students with emotional and behavioral disorders attending a therapeutic day school. *Beyond Behavior, 13*(1), 23–27.

Wicks-Nelson, R., & Israel, A. C. (2009). *Behavior disorders of childhood* (7th ed.). Upper Saddle River, NJ: Pearson Education.

Zigmond, N. (2006). Twenty-four months after high school: Paths taken by youth diagnosed with severe emotional and behavioral disorders. *Journal of Emotional and Behavioral Disorders, 14*(2), 91–107.

Chapter 9

Akshoomoff, N., Pierce, K., & Courchesne, E. (2002). The neurological basis of autism from a developmental perspective. *Development and Psychopathology, 14,* 613–634.

Alberto, P., & Troutman, A. (2009). *Applied behavior analysis for teachers* (8th ed.). Upper Saddle River, NJ: Pearson Education.

Altevogt, B., Hanson, S., & Leshner, A. (2008). Autism and the environment: Challenges and opportunities for research. *Pediatrics, 121*(6), 1225–1229.

American Psychiatric Association. (2000). *Diagnostic and statistical manual of mental disorders* (4th ed., text rev.). Washington, DC: Author.

Astington, J., & Barricult, T. (2001). Children's theory of mind: How young children come to understand that people have thoughts and feelings. *Infants and Young Children, 13*(1), 1–12.

Autism Society of America. (2010a). *About autism.* Retrieved February 4, 2010, from http://www.autism-society.org/site/PageServer?pagename=about_home

Autism Society of America. (2010b). *Life with autism.* Retrieved February 5, 2010, from http://www.autism-society.org/site/PageServer?pagename=life_home

Autism Society of America. (2010c). *Sibling perspectives: Guidelines for parents.* Retrieved February 5, 2010, from http://www.autism-society.org/site/DocServer/LWA-Siblings.pdf?docID=4183

Autism Society of America. (2010d). *Transition: Preparing for a lifetime.* Retrieved February 9, 2010, from http://www.autism-society.org/site/DocServer/Transition_Preparing_for_a_Lifetime.pdf?docID=10622

Bettelheim, B. (1967). *The empty fortress: Infantile autism and the birth of self.* New York: Free Press.

Blishak, D., & Schlosser, R. (2003). Use of technology to support spelling by students with autism. *Topics in Language Disorders, 23,* 293–304.

Bondy, A., & Frost, L. (1998). The picture exchange communication system. *Seminars in Speech & Language, 19*(4), 373–389.

Bowler, D. (2006). *Autism spectrum disorders.* Hoboken, NJ: Wiley.

Brobst, J., Clopton, J., & Hendrick, S. (2009). Parenting children with autism spectrum disorders. *Focus on Autism and Other Developmental Disabilities, 24*(1), 38–49.

Carter, A., Davis, N., Klin, A., & Volkmar, F. (2005). Social development in autism. In F. Volkmar, R. Paul, A. Klin, & D. Cohen (Eds.), *Handbook of autism and pervasive developmental disorders* (3rd ed., Vol. 1, pp. 312–334). Hoboken, NJ: Wiley.

Challman, T., Voigt, R., & Myers, S. (2008). Nonstandard therapies in developmental disabilities. In P. Accardo (Ed.), *Capute & Accardo's neurodevlopmental disabilities in infancy and childhood* (3rd ed., Vol. 2, pp. 721–741). Baltimore: Paul H. Brookes.

Charlop-Christy, M., Carpenter, M., Le, L., LeBlanc, L., & Kellet, K. (2002). Using the picture exchange communication system (PECS) with children with autism: Assessment of PECS acquisition, speech, social communicative behavior, and problem behavior. *Journal of Applied Behavior Analysis, 35,* 213–231.

Courchesne, E. (2004). Brain development in autism: Early overgrowth followed by premature arrest of growth. *Mental Retardation and Developmental Disabilities Research Reviews, 10*(2), 106–111.

Dahle, K. (2003a). Clinical and educational systems: Differences and similarities. *Focus on Autism and Other Developmental Disabilities, 18*(4), 238–246, 256.

Dahle, K. (2003b). Services to include young children with autism in the general classroom. *Early Childhood Education Journal, 31*(1), 65–70.

Dahle, K., & Gargiulo, R. (2003). Understanding Asperger disorder: A primer for early childhood educators. *Early Childhood Education Journal, 32*(3), 199–203.

Earles-Vollrath, T., Cook, K., Robbins, L., & Ben-Arieh, J. (2008). Instructional strategies to facilitate successful learning outcomes for students with autism spectrum disorders. In R. Simpson & B. Myles (Eds.), *Educating children and youth with autism* (2nd ed., pp. 93–178). Austin, TX: Pro-Ed.

Edelson, M. (2006). Are the majority of children with autism mentally retarded? *Focus on Autism and Other Developmental Disabilities, 21*(2), 66–83.

Edelson, S. (2000). *Autistic savant.* Salem, OR: Center for Study of Autism.

Ehlers, S., Gillberg, C., & Wing, L. (1999). A screening questionnaire for Asperger's syndrome and other high-functioning autism spectrum disorders in school-age children. *Journal of Autism and Developmental Disorders, 29*(2), 129–141.

Freeman, B. (1999). *Diagnosis of the syndrome of autism: Questions parents ask.* Bethesda, MD: Autism Society of America.

Freeman, B., & Van Dyke, M. (2006). Are the majority of children with autism mentally retarded? *Focus on Autism and Other Developmental Disorders, 21*(2), 86–88.

Gallagher, P., Powell, T., & Rhodes, C. (2006). *Brothers & sisters* (3rd ed.). Baltimore: Paul H. Brookes.

Gargiulo, R., & Kilgo, J. (2011). *An introduction to young children with special needs* (3rd ed.). Belmont, CA: Wadsworth/Cengage Learning.

Gerhardt, P., & Holmes, D. (2005). Employment: Options and issues for adolescents and adults with autism spectrum disorders. In F. Volkmar, R. Paul, A. Klin, & D. Cohen (Eds.), *Handbook of autism and pervasive developmental disorders* (3rd ed., Vol. 2, pp. 1087–1101). Hoboken, NJ: Wiley.

Haist, F., Adamo, M., Westerfield, M., Courchesne, E., & Townsend, J. (2005). The functional neuroanatomy of spatial attention in autism spectrum disorder. *Developmental Psychology, 27*(3), 425–458.

Handleman, J., & Harris, S. (Eds.). (2008). *Preschool programs for children with autism* (3rd ed.). Austin, TX: Pro-Ed.

Harris, S., Handleman, J., & Jennett, H. (2005). Models of educational intervention for students with autism: Home, center, and school-based programming. In F. Volkmar, R. Paul, A. Klin, & D. Cohen (Eds.), *Handbook of autism and pervasive developmental disorders* (3rd ed., Vol. 2, pp. 1043–1054). Hoboken, NJ: Wiley.

Heflin, L., & Alaimo, D. (2007). *Students with autism spectrum disorders.* Upper Saddle River, NJ: Pearson Education.

Hendricks, D., & Wehman, P. (2009). Transition from school to adulthood for youth with autism spectrum disorders. *Focus on Autism and Other Developmental Disabilities, 24*(2), 77–88.

Howlin, P., Goode, S., Hutton, J., & Rutter, M. (2004). Adult outcome for children with autism. *Journal of Child Psychology and Psychiatry, 45*(2), 212–229.

Hume, K., Bellini, L., & Pratt, R. (2005). The usage and perceived outcomes of early intervention and early childhood programs for young children with autism. *Topics in Early Childhood Education, 25*(4), 195–207.

Hyman, S., & Towbin, K. (2007). Autism spectrum disorders. In M. Batshaw, L. Pellegrino, & N. Roizen (Eds.), *Children with disabilities* (6th ed., pp. 325–343). Baltimore: Paul H. Brookes.

Italia, C. (2007, April/May). One in 150. *Spectrum Magazine,* pp. 26–30.

Johnson, C. (1994, November/December). Interview with Ivar Lovaas. *Advocate,* pp. 2–12.

Johnson, C., & Myers, S. (2007). Identification and evaluation of children with autism spectrum disorders. *Pediatrics, 120*(5), 1183–1215.

Kanner, L. (1985). Autistic disturbance of affective contact. In A. Donnellan (Ed.), *Classic readings in autism* (pp. 11–50). New York: Teachers College Press. (Original work published 1943)

Klin, A., McPartland, J., & Volkmar, F. (2005). Asperger syndrome. In F. Volkmar, R. Paul, A. Klin, & D. Cohen (Eds.), *Handbook of autism and pervasive developmental disorders* (3rd ed., Vol. 1, pp. 88–125). Hoboken, NJ: Wiley.

Kogan, M., Blumberg, S., Schieve, L., Boyle, C., Perrin, J., Ghandour, R., et al. (2009). Prevalence of parent-reported diagnosis of autism spectrum disorder among children in the US, 2007. *Pediatrics, 124*(5), 1395–1403.

Kravits, T., Kamps, D., Kemmerer, K., & Potucek, J. (2002). Brief report: Increasing communication skills for an elementary-aged student with autism using picture exchange communication system. *Focus on Autism and Other Developmental Disabilities, 30,* 225–230.

Laramie, R. (2001). Asperger syndrome: Advice for school personnel. *Preventing School Failure, 45,* 148–152.

LaVigna, G. (1985). Commentary on positive reinforcement and behavioral deficits of autistic children by C. B. Fester. In A. Donnellan (Ed.), *Classic readings in autism* (pp. 53–73). New York: Teachers College Press.

Levy, S., Hyman, S., & Pinto-Martin, J. (2008). Autism spectrum disorders: Overview and diagnosis. In P. Accardo (Ed.), *Capute & Accardo's neurodevelopmental disabilities in infancy and childhood* (3rd ed., Vol. 2, pp. 495–511). Baltimore: Paul H. Brookes.

Levy, S., Kim, A., & Olive, M. (2006). Interventions for young children with autism: A synthesis of the literature. *Focus on Autism and Other Developmental Disabilities, 21*(1), 55–62.

Levy, S., Kruger, H., & Hyman, S. (2008). Treatments for children with autism spectrum disorders. In P. Accardo (Ed.), *Capute & Accardo's neurodevlopmental disabilities in infancy and childhood* (3rd ed., Vol. 2, pp. 523–543). Baltimore: Paul H. Brookes.

Lipkin, P., & Schertz, M. (2008). Early intervention and its efficacy. In P. Accardo (Ed.), *Capute & Accardo's neurodevlopmental disabilities in infancy and childhood* (3rd ed., Vol. 1, pp. 519–551). Baltimore: Paul H. Brookes.

Lord, C., Risi, S., DiLavore, P., Schulman, C., Thurm, A., & Pickles, A. (2006). Autism from 2 to 9 years of age. *Archives in General Psychiatry, 63,* 694–701.

Lord, C., Rutter, M., DiLavore, P., & Risi, S. (1999). *Autism Diagnostic Observation Schedule.* Los Angeles: Western Psychological Services.

Lovaas, I. (1987). Behavioral treatment and normal educational and intellectual functioning in young autistic children. *Journal of Consulting and Clinical Psychology, 55,* 3–9.

Lovaas, I. (1993). The development of a treatment-research project for developmentally disabled and autistic children. *Journal of Applied Behavior Analysis, 26*(4), 617–630.

Marcus, L., Kunce, L., & Schopler, E. (2005). Working with families. In F. Volkmar, R. Paul, A. Klin, & D. Cohen (Eds.), *Handbook of autism and pervasive developmental disorders* (3rd ed., Vol. 2, pp. 1055–1086). Hoboken, NJ: Wiley.

Mesibov, G., Shea, V., & Schopler, E. (2005). *The TEACCH approach to autism spectrum disorders.* New York: Springer.

Millar, D., Light, J., & Schlosser, R. (2006). The impact of augmentative and alternative communication intervention on the speech production of individuals with developmental disabilities: A research review. *Journal of Speech, Language, & Hearing Research, 49*(2), 248–264.

Muller, R. (2007). The study of autism as a distributed disorder. *Mental Retardation and Developmental Disabilities Research Reviews, 13*(1), 85–95.

Myers, S., & Johnson, C. (2007). Management of children with autism spectrum disorders. *Pediatrics, 120*(5), 1162–1182.

Myles, B., & Simpson, R. (2002). Asperger syndrome: An overview of characteristics. *Focus on Autism and Other Developmental Disabilities, 17*(3), 132–137.

National Education Association. (2006). *The puzzle of autism.* Washington, DC: Author.

National Institute of Child Health and Human Development. (2005). *Autism overview: What we know.* Rockville, MD: National Institute of Child Health and Human Development Clearinghouse.

National Institute of Mental Health. (2010). *Autism spectrum disorders (pervasive developmental disorders).* Retrieved February 6, 2010, from http://www.nimh.nih.gov/health/publications/autism/complete-index.shtml

National Institute of Neurological Disorders and Stroke. (2010). *Autism fact sheet.* Retrieved February 8, 2010, from http://www.ninds.nih.gov/disorders/autism/detail_autism.htm

National Research Council. (2001). *Educating children with autism.* Washington, DC: National Academies Press.

Nordin, V., & Gillberg, C. (1998). The long-term course of autistic disorders: Update on follow-up studies. *Acta Psychiatrica Scandinavica, 97*(2), 99–108.

Owens, R. (2010). *Language disorders* (5th ed.). Boston: Pearson Education.

Paul, R., & Sutherland, D. (2005). Enhancing early language in children with autism spectrum disorders. In F. Volkmar, R. Paul, A. Klin, & D. Cohen (Eds.), *Handbook of autism and pervasive developmental disorders* (3rd ed., Vol. 2, pp. 946–976). Hoboken, NJ: Wiley.

Polleux, F., & Lauder, J. (2004). Toward a developmental neurobiology of autism. *Mental Retardation and Developmental Disabilities Research Reviews, 10*(4), 303–317.

Rank, B. (1949). Adaptation of the psychoanalytic technique for the treatment of young children with atypical development. *American Journal of Orthopsychiatry, 19,* 130–139.

Rapin, I. (2008). Etiologies of autism spectrum disorders. In P. Accardo (Ed.), *Capute & Accardo's neurodevlopmental disabilities in infancy and childhood* (3rd ed., Vol. 2, pp. 513–521). Baltimore: Paul H. Brookes.

Rimland, B. (1985). The etiology of infantile autism: The problem of biological versus psychological causation. In A. Donnellan (Ed.), *Classic readings in autism* (pp. 84–103). New York: Teachers College Press. (Original work published 1964)

Ronald, A., Happe, F., Bolton, P., Butcher, L., Price, T., Wheelwright, S., et al. (2006). Genetic heterogeneity between the three components of autism: A twin study. *Journal of the American Academy of Child & Adolescent Psychiatry, 45*(6), 691–699.

Rutter, M. (1978). Diagnosis and definition. In M. Rutter & E. Schopler (Eds.), *Autism: A reappraisal of concepts and treatment* (pp. 1–25). New York: Plenum.

Rutter, M. (1994). Psychiatric genetics: Research challenges and pathways forward. *American Journal of Medical Genetics (Neuropsychiatric Genetics), 54,* 185–198.

Rutter, M. (2005). Aetiology of autism: Findings and questions. *Journal of Intellectual Disability Research, 49*(4), 231–238.

Rutter, M., Le Couteur, A., & Lord, C. (2003). *Autism Diagnostic Interview–Revised.* Los Angeles: Western Psychological Services.

Santos, M., Coelho, P., Maciel, P. (2006). Chromatin remodeling and neuronal functioning: Exciting links. *Genes, Brain and Behavior, 5*(Suppl. 2), 80–91.

Schechter, R., & Grether, J. (2008). Continuing increases in autism reported to California's developmental services system: Mercury in retrograde. *Archives of General Psychiatry, 65*(1), 19–24.

Seligman, M., & Darling, R. (2007). *Ordinary families, special children* (3rd ed.). New York: Guilford Press.

Simpson, R., Myles, B., & Ganz, J. (2008). Efficaious interventions and treatments for learners with autism spectrum disorders. In R. Simpson & B. Myles (Eds.), *Educating children and youth with autism* (2nd ed., pp. 477–512). Austin, TX: Pro-Ed.

Simpson, R., Myles, B., & La Cava, P. (2008). Understanding and responding to the needs of children and youth with autism spectrum disorders. In R. Simpson & B. Myles (Eds.), *Educating children and youth with autism* (2nd ed., pp. 1–59). Austin, TX: Pro-Ed.

Smith, T., Polloway, E., Patton, J., & Dowdy, C. (2008). *Teaching students with special needs in inclusive settings* (5th ed.). Upper Saddle River, NJ: Pearson Education.

Sullivan, R. (2005). Community-integrated residential services for adults with autism: A working model. In F. Volkmar, R. Paul, A. Klin, & D. Cohen (Eds.), *Handbook of autism and pervasive developmental disorders* (3rd ed., Vol. 2, pp. 1255–1264). Hoboken, NJ: Wiley.

Trottier, G., Srivastava, L., & Walker, C. (1999). Etiology of infantile autism: A review of recent advances in genetic and neurobiological research. *Journal of Psychiatry and Neuroscience, 24*(2), 193–215.

Tsai, L. (2007). Asperger syndrome and medication treatment. *Focus on Autism and Other Developmental Disabilities, 22*(3), 138–148.

U.S. Department of Education. (1993). *Fifteenth annual report to Congress on the implementation of the Individuals with Disabilities Education Act.* Washington, DC: U.S. Government Printing Office.

U.S. Department of Education. (2009). *IDEA data.* Retrieved November 5, 2009, from https://www.ideadata.org/PartBReport.asp

U.S. Department of Education. (2010). *IDEA data.* Retrieved April 14, 2010, from https://www.ideadata.org/PartBReport.asp

Volkmar, F., & Nelson, D. (1990). Seizure disorders in autism. *Journal of the American Academy of Child Psychiatry, 29,* 127–129.

Volkmar, F., & Pauls, D. (2003). Autism. *Lancet, 362*(9390), 1133–1141.

Volkmar, F., & Wiesner, L. (2009). *A practical guide to autism.* Hoboken, NJ: Wiley.

Williams, J., Scott, F., Stott, C., Allison, C., Bolton, P., Baron-Cohen, S., et al. (2005). Childhood Asperger Syndrome Test. *Autism, 9*(1), 45–68.

Wolfe, P., Condo, B., & Hardway, E. (2009). Sociosexuality education for persons with autism spectrum disorders using principles of applied behavior analysis. *Teaching Exceptional Children, 42*(1), 50–61.

Chapter 10

American Speech-Language-Hearing Association. (1993). Definitions of communication disorders and variations. *ASHA, 35*(Suppl. 10), 40–41.

American Speech-Language-Hearing Association. (2008). *Advancing into the 21st century: Care for individuals with cleft palate or craniofacical differences.* Retrieved February 8, 2010, from http://www.asha.org/Publications/leader/2008/080506/f080506a.htm

Bell, M. (2007). Infections and the fetus. In M. Batshaw, L. Pellegrino, & N. Roizen (Eds.), *Children with disabilities* (6th ed., pp. 71–82). Baltimore: Paul H. Brookes.

Bernthal, J., Bankson, N., & Flipsen. P. (2009). *Articulation and phonological disorders* (6th ed.). Boston: Allyn and Bacon.

Brigance, A. (2004). *Inventory of Early Development—Brigance Diagnostic II.* North Billerica, MA: Curriculum Associates.

Bryant, D., Smith, D., & Bryant, B. (2008). *Teaching students with special needs.* Boston: Pearson Education.

Bunce, B. (2003). Children with culturally diverse backgrounds. In L. McCormick, D. Loeb, & R. Schiefelbusch (Eds.), *Supporting children with communication difficulties in inclusive settings* (2nd ed., pp. 367–407). Boston: Allyn and Bacon.

Cohen, L., & Spenciner, L. (2007). *Assessment of children and youth with special needs* (3rd ed.). Boston: Allyn and Bacon.

de Cohen, C., & Clewell, B. (2007). *Putting English language learners on the educational map.* Washington, DC: Urban Institute.

Desch, L. (2008). The spectrum of assistive and augmentative technology for individuals with developmental disabilities. In P. Accardo (Ed.), *Capute and Accardo's neurodevelopmental disabilities in infancy and childhood* (3rd ed., Vol. 1, pp. 691–719). Baltimore: Paul H. Brookes.

Friend, M., & Bursuck, W. (2009). *Including students with special needs: A practical guide for classroom teachers* (5th ed.). Upper Saddle River, NJ: Pearson Education.

Gargiulo, R., & Kilgo, J. (2011). *An introduction to young children with special needs* (3rd ed.). Belmont, CA: Wadsworth/Cengage Learning.

Goldman, R., & Fristoe, M. (2000). *Goldman-Fristoe Test of Articulation 2.* Circle Pines, MN: American Guidance Service.

Hoff, E. (2009). *Language development* (4th ed.). Belmont, CA: Wadsworth/Cengage Learning.

Johnson, J., & Wong, M. (2002). Cultural differences in beliefs and practices concerning talk to children. *Journal of Speech, Language, and Hearing Research, 45,* 916–927.

Kangas, K., & Lloyd, L. (2006). Augmentative and alternative communication. In G. Shames & N. Anderson (Eds.), *Human communication disorders: An introduction* (7th ed., pp. 436–470). Boston: Allyn and Bacon.

Lipkin, P., & Schertz, M. (2008). Early intervention and its efficacy. In P. Accardo (Ed.), *Capute and Accardo's neurodevelopmental disabilities in infancy and childhood* (3rd ed., Vol. 1, pp. 519–551). Baltimore: Paul H. Brookes.

Luterman, D. (2008). *Counseling persons with communication disorders and their families* (5th ed.). Austin, TX: Pro-Ed.

March of Dimes. (2007). *Cleft lip and cleft palate.* Retrieved February 8, 2010, from http://www.marchofdimes.com/pnhec/4439_1210.asp#

McCormick, L. (2003a). Introduction to language acquisition. In L. McCormick, D. Loeb, & R. Schiefelbusch (Eds.), *Supporting children with communication difficulties in inclusive settings* (2nd ed., pp. 1–42). Boston: Allyn and Bacon.

McCormick, L. (2003b). Language intervention in the inclusive preschool. In L. McCormick, D. Loeb, & R. Schiefelbusch (Eds.), *Supporting children with communication difficulties in inclusive settings* (2nd ed., pp. 333–366). Boston: Allyn and Bacon.

Millar, D., Light, J., & Schlosser, R. (2006). The impact of augmentative and alternative communication intervention on the speech production of individuals with developmental disabilities: A research review. *Journal of Speech, Language, and Hearing Research, 49,* 248–264.

National Dissemination Center for Children with Disabilities. (2004). *Fact sheet 11: Speech and language disorders.* Washington, DC: Author.

Owens, R. (2008). *Language development: An introduction* (7th ed.). Boston: Pearson Education.

Owens, R. (2010). *Language disorders* (5th ed.). Boston: Pearson Education.

Owens, R., Metz, D., & Farinella, K. (2011). *Introduction to communication disorders: A lifespan evidence-based perspective* (4th ed.). Boston: Allyn and Bacon.

Piaget, J. (1952). *The origins of intelligence in children* (Margaret Cook, Trans.). New York: International Universities Press.

Ramig, P., & Shames, G. (2006). Stuttering and other disorders of fluency. In G. Shames & N. Anderson (Eds.), *Human communication disorders: An introduction* (7th ed., pp. 183–221). Boston: Allyn and Bacon.

Ratner, N. (2009). Atypical language development. In J. Gleason & N. Ratner (Eds.), *The development of language* (7th ed., pp. 315–390). Boston: Pearson Education.

Turner, J. (2008). Assessment of speech and language disorders in children. In P. Accardo (Ed.), *Capute and Accardo's neurodevelopmental disabilities in infancy and childhood* (3rd ed., Vol. 2, pp. 425–455). Baltimore: Paul H. Brookes.

Urban Institute. (2010). *Immigrants.* Retrieved February 8, 2010, from http://www.urban.org/immigrants/index.cfm

U.S. Department of Education. (2009). *IDEA data.* Retrieved November 21, 2009, from https://www.ideadata.org/PartBReport.asp

U.S. Department of Education. (2010). *IDEA data.* Retrieved April 14, 2010, from https://www.ideadata.org/PartBReport.asp

Van Hattum, R. (1969). *Clinical speech in the schools.* Springfield, IL: Charles C Thomas.

Van Riper, C., & Emerick, L. (1996). *Speech correction: An introduction to speech pathology and audiology* (9th ed.). Boston: Allyn and Bacon.

Vaughn, S., & Bos, C. (2009). *Strategies for teaching students with learning and behavioral problems* (7th ed.). Upper Saddle River, NJ: Pearson Education.

Chapter 11

Allen, K., & Cowdery, G. (2009). *The exceptional child: Inclusion in early childhood special education* (5th ed.). Clifton Park, NY: Delmar/Cengage.

American Speech-Language-Hearing Association. (1993). Guidelines for audiology services in the schools. *ASHA, 35*(Suppl. 10), 24–32.

American Speech-Language-Hearing Association. (2004). *The prevalence and incidence of hearing loss in children.* Retrieved June 2, 2004, from http://www.asha.org/hearing/disorders/children

American Speech-Language-Hearing Association. (2010a). *Hearing assessment.* Retrieved January 26, 2010, from http://www.asha.org/public/hearing/testing/assess.htm

American Speech-Language-Hearing Association. (2010b). *IDEA issue brief: Cochlear implants.* Retrieved January 26, 2010, from http://www.asha.org/uploadedFiles/advocacy/federal/idea/CochlearImplantsBrief.pdf

American Speech-Language-Hearing Association. (2010c). *Noise and hearing loss.* Retrieved January 26, 2010, from http://www.asha.org/public/hearing/disorders/noise.htm

American Speech-Language-Hearing Association. (2010d). *The prevalence and incidence of hearing loss in children.* Retrieved January 26, 2010, from http://www.asha.org/public/hearing/disorders/children.htm

Berg, A., Ip, S., Hurst, M., & Herb, A. (2007). Cochlear implants in young children: Informed consent as a process and current practices. *American Journal of Audiology, 16*(1), 13–28.

Berk, L. (2008). *Child development* (8th ed.). Boston: Allyn and Bacon.

Bess, F., & Humes, L. (2008). *Audiology: The fundamentals* (4th ed.). Baltimore: Williams and Wilkins.

Chin, S., Tsai, P., & Gao, S. (2003). Connected speech intelligibility of children with cochlear implants and children with normal hearing. *American Journal of Speech-Language Pathology, 12,* 440–451.

Chute, P. (2004). Cochlear implants: An evolving journey. *ASHA Leader, 9,* 7.

Clark, J., & Martin, F. (1994). *Effective counseling in audiology: Perspectives and practice.* Englewood Cliffs, NJ: Prentice Hall.

Early hearing campaign honored. (2007, November 6). *The ASHA Leader, 12,* 3.

Easterbrooks, S., & Baker, S. (2001). Enter the matrix! Considering the communication needs of students who are deaf or hard of hearing. *Teaching Exceptional Children, 33*(3), 70–76.

Gallagher, P., Easterbrooks, S., Malone, D. (2006). Universal newborn hearing screening and intervention. *Infants & Young Children: An Interdisciplinary Journal of Special Care Practices, 19*(1), 59–71.

Gallaudet Research Institute. (2003). *Literacy & deaf students.* Retrieved January 26, 2010, from http://research.gallaudet.edu/Literacy/

Gallaudet Research Institute. (2008). *Regional and national summary report of data from the 2007–2008 annual survey of deaf and hard of hearing children and youth.* Washington, DC: Gallaudet University.

Geers, A. (2006). Spoken language in children with cochlear implants. In P. Spencer & M. Marschark (Eds.), *Advances in spoken language development of deaf and hard-of-hearing children* (pp. 244–270). New York: Oxford University Press.

Herer, G., Knightly, C., & Steinberg, A. (2007). Hearing: Sounds and silences. In M. Batshaw, L. Pellegrino, & N. Roizen (Eds.), *Children with disabilities* (6th ed., pp. 157–183). Baltimore: Paul H. Brookes.

Hunt, N., & Marshall, K. (2006). *Exceptional children and youth* (4th ed.). Boston: Houghton Mifflin.

Iglehart, F. (2004). Speech perception by students with cochlear implants using sound-field systems in classrooms. *American Journal of Audiology, 13*(1), 62–72.

Innes, J. (1994). Full inclusion and the deaf student: A deaf consumer's issue. *American Annals of the Deaf, 139,* 152–156.

Johnson, C., Benson, P., & Seaton, J. (2001). *Educational audiology handbook* (2nd ed.). Albany, NY: Delmar.

Johnson, C., & Danhauer, J. (1999). *Guidebook for support programs in aural rehabilitation.* San Diego, CA: Singular Publishing Group.

Johnson, R. (2003, Fall). High stakes testing conference held at Gallaudet. *Research at Gallaudet,* 1–12.

Kaderavek, J., & Pakulski, L. (2002). Minimal hearing loss is not minimal. *Teaching Exceptional Children, 34*(6), 14–18.

Katz, L., & Schery, T. (2006). Including children with hearing loss in early childhood programs. *Young Children, 61*(1), 86–95.

Kaufman, A., & Kaufman, N. (2004). *Kaufman Assessment Battery for Children—Second Edition.* Circles Pines, MN: American Guidance Service.

King, S., De Caro, J., Karchmer, M., & Cole, K. (2001). *College and career programs for deaf students* (11th ed.). Washington, DC: Gallaudet Research Institute.

Kuder, S. (2008). *Teaching students with language and communication disabilities* (3rd ed.). Boston: Allyn and Bacon.

Kuntze, M. (1998). Literacy and deaf children: The language question. *Topics in Language Disorders, 18*(4), 1–15.

Lederberg, A. (1993). The impact of deafness on mother–child and peer relationships. In M. Marschark & M. Clark (Eds.), *Psychological perspectives on deafness* (pp. 93–119). Hillsdale, NJ: Erlbaum.

Luckner, J., & Bowen, S. (2006). Assessment practices of professionals serving students who are deaf or hard of hearing: An initial investigation. *American Annals of the Deaf, 15*(4), 410–417.

Luterman, D. (2008). *Counseling persons with communication disorders and their families* (5th ed.). Austin, TX: Pro-Ed.

Marschark, M. (2006). Intellectual functioning of deaf adults and children: Answers and questions. *European Journal of Cognitive Psychology, 18*(1), 70–89.

Marschark, M. (Ed.). (2007). *Raising and educating a deaf child* (2nd ed.). New York: Oxford University Press.

Maxon, A., Brackett, D., & van den Berg, S. (1991). Self-perception of socialization: The effects of hearing status, age, and gender. *Volta Review, 93*(1), 15–17.

McLean, M., Wolery, M., & Bailey, D. (2004). *Assessing infants and preschoolers with special needs* (3rd ed.). Upper Saddle River, NJ: Pearson Education.

Meadows-Orlans, K. (1995). Source of stress for mothers and fathers of deaf and hard of hearing infants. *American Annals of the Deaf, 140,* 352–357.

Meadows-Orlans, K., Mertens, D., Sass-Lehrer, M., & Scott-Olson, K. (1997). Support services for parents and their children who are deaf or hard of hearing. *American Annals of the Deaf, 142,* 278–288.

Moores, D. (2001). *Educating the deaf: Psychology, principles, and practices* (5th ed.). Boston: Houghton Mifflin.

Moores, D. (2005). The No Child Left Behind Act and the Individuals with Disabilities Education Acts: The uneven impact of partially funded mandates on education of deaf and hard of hearing students. *American Annals of the Deaf, 150*(2), 75–80.

Paul, P., & Quigley, S. (1990). *Education and deafness.* White Plains, NY: Longman.

Petersen, M., & Willems, P. (2006). Non-syndromic, autosomal-recessive deafness. *Clinical Genetics, 69*(5), 371–392.

Picard, M. (2004). Children with permanent hearing loss and associated disabilities: Revisiting current epidemiological data and causes of deafness. *Volta Review, 104*(4), 221–236.

Psychological Corporation. (2002). *Stanford Achievement Test* (10th ed.). San Antonio, TX: Author.

Roeser, V., Valente, M., & Hosford-Dunn, H. (Eds.). (2008). *Audiology diagnosis* (2nd ed.). New York: Thieme.

Roizen, N. (2008). Hearing loss. In P. Accardo (Ed.), *Capute & Accardo's neurodevelopmental disabilities in infancy and childhood* (3rd ed., Vol. 2, pp. 457–470). Baltimore: Paul H. Brookes.

Salvia, J., Ysseldyke, J., & Bolt, S. (2010). *Assessment* (11th ed.). Belmont, CA: Wadsworth/Cengage Learning.

Sattler, J., & Hoge, R. (2006). *Assessment of children: Behavioral, social, and clinical foundations.* La Mesa, CA: Sattler.

Scheetz, N. (2001). *Orientation to deafness* (2nd ed.). Boston: Allyn and Bacon.

Schirmer, B. (2001). *Psychological, social, and educational dimensions of deafness.* Boston: Allyn and Bacon.

Schum, R. (2004). Psychological assessment of children with multiple handicaps who have hearing loss. *Volta Review, 104*(4), 237–255.

Scott, T. (2003). Auditory neuropathy in children. *AHSA Leader, 8,* 17–18.

Simeonsson, R., & Rosenthal, S. (Eds.). (2001). *Psychological and developmental assessment: Children with disabilities and chronic conditions.* New York: Guilford Press.

Stach, B. (2010). *Clinical audiology: An introduction* (2nd ed.). Clifton Park, NY: Delmar/Cengage Learning.

Strong, M., & Prinz, P. (1997). A study of the relationship between American Sign Language and English literacy. *Journal of Deaf Studies and Deaf Education, 2,* 37–46.

Toriello, H., Reardon, W., & Gorlin, R. (2004). *Hereditary hearing loss and its syndromes* (2nd ed.). New York: Oxford University Press.

Traxler, C. (2000). The Stanford Achievement Test, 9th Edition: National norming and performance standards for deaf and hard-of-hearing students. *Journal of Deaf Studies and Deaf Education, 5*(4), 337–348.

Ulrich, M., & Bauer, A. (2003). Levels of awareness: A closer look at communication between parents and professionals. *Teaching Exceptional Children, 35*(6), 20–23.

U.S. Department of Education. (2009). *IDEA data.* Retrieved November 30, 2009, from https://www.ideadata.org/PartB Report.asp

U.S. Department of Education. (2010). *IDEA data.* Retrieved April 14, 2010, from https://www.ideadata.org/PartBReport.asp

Van Hasselt, V., Strain, P., & Hersen, M. (1988). *Handbook of developmental and physical disabilities.* New York: Pergamon Press.

Wechsler, D. (2003). *Wechsler Intelligence Scale for Children—Fourth Edition.* San Antonio, TX: Psychological Corporation.

Williams, C., & Finnegan, M. (2003). From myth to reality: Sound information for teachers about students who are deaf. *Teaching Exceptional Children, 35*(3), 40–45.

Chapter 12

American Foundation for the Blind. (2010a). *Accommodations and modifications at a glance.* Retrieved February 9, 2010, from http://www.familyconnect.org/parentsite.asp?SectionID=72&TopicID=347&DocumentID=3820

American Foundation for the Blind. (2010b). *Expanded core curriculum.* Retrieved February 9, 2010, from http://www.familyconnect.org/parentsite.asp?SectionID=72&TopicID=382

American Foundation for the Blind. (2010c). *Learning media assessment.* Retrieved February 9, 2010, from http://www.familyconnect.org/parentsite.asp?SectionID=72&TopicID=369&DocumentID=4068

American Foundation for the Blind. (2010d). *Overview of assessment.* Retrieved February 9, 2010, from http://www.familyconnect.org/parentsite.asp?SectionID=72&TopicID=369

American Foundation for the Blind. (2010e). *Transition from high school to adult life.* Retrieved February 9, 2010, from http://www.familyconnect.org/parentsite.asp?SectionID=72&TopicID=343&DocumentID=3814

American Foundation for the Blind. (2010f). *Transition happens, ready or not!* Retrieved February 15, 2010, from http://www.afb.org/Section.asp?SectionID=7&TopicID=269&DocumentID=3535

Barraga, N. (1973). Utilization of sensory-perceptual abilities. In B. Lowenfeld (Ed.), *The visually handicapped children in school* (pp. 117–151). New York: John Day.

Best, H. (1919). *The blind.* New York: Macmillan.

Bishop, V. (2004). *Teaching visually impaired children* (3rd ed.). Springfield, IL: Charles C Thomas.

Chen, D., & Downing, J. (2006). *Tactile strategies for children who have visual impairments and multiple disabilities.* New York: American Foundation for the Blind.

Council for Exceptional Children. (1996). Advocacy in action: CEC proves it makes a difference! *CEC Today, 2*(8), 4–5.

Diderot, D. (1749). *Lettre sur les aveugles à l'usage de ceux qui voient.* London.

Erin, J. (2000). Students with visual impairments and additional disabilities. In A. Koenig & M. Holbrook (Eds.), *Foundations of education: Instructional strategies for teaching children and youths with visual impairments* (2nd ed., Vol. 2, pp. 730–752). New York: American Foundation for the Blind.

Ferrell, K. (2007). *Issues in the field of blindness and low vision.* National Center on Severe and Sensory Disabilities. Retrieved December 24, 2009, from http://www.unco.edu/ncssd/resources/issues_bvi.shtml

Gargiulo, R., & Metcalf, D. (2010). *Teaching in today's inclusive classrooms.* Belmont, CA: Wadsworth/Cengage Learning.

Griffin, H., Williams, S., Davis, M., & Engleman, M. (2002). Using technology to enhance cues for children with low vision. *Teaching Exceptional Children, 35*(2), 36–42.

Huebner, K., Merk-Adam, B., Stryker, D., & Wolffe, K. (2004). *The national agenda for the education of children and youths with visual impairments, including those with multiple disabilities—Revised.* New York: American Foundation for the Blind.

Johnson, J. (2003). Expanded core curriculum: Technology. In S. Goodman & S. Wittenstein (Eds.), *Collaborative assessment* (pp. 237–263). New York: American Foundation for the Blind.

Koenig, A. (1992). A framework for understanding the literacy of individuals with visual impairments. *Journal of Visual Impairments and Blindness, 86*(7), 277–284.

Kuhn, F., Morris, R., Witherspoon, D., Mann, L., Mester, V., Modis, L., et al. (2000). Serious fireworks-related eye injuries. *Ophthalmic Epidemiology, 7*(2), 139–148.

Lang, M. (1992). Creating inclusive, nonstereotyping environments: The child with a disability. In R. Swallow & M. Sanspree (Eds.), *Project Video.* Los Angeles: California State University at Los Angeles.

Lash, J. (1980). *Helen and teacher: The story of Helen Keller and Anne Sullivan Macy.* New York: Delacorte Press.

Levack, N. (1994). *Low vision: A resource guide with adaptations for students with visual impairments.* Austin: Texas School for the Blind and Visually Impaired.

Liefert, F. (2003). Introduction to visual impairment. In S. Goodman & S. Wittenstein (Eds.), *Collaborative assessment* (pp. 1–12). New York: American Foundation for the Blind.

Miller, M., & Menacker, S. (2007). Vision: Our window to the world. In M. Batshaw, L. Pellegrino, & N. Roizen (Eds.), *Children with disabilities* (6th ed., pp. 137–155). Baltimore: Paul H. Brookes.

National Eye Institute. (2010). Retrieved February 15, 2010, from http://www.nei.nih.gov/

Optometric Extension Program Foundation. (2010). *Educator's guide to classroom vision problems.* Available at http://oep.excerpo.com/index.php?action=show_details&product_id=3056

Pogrund, R., & Fazzi, D. (2007). *Early focus: Working with young blind and visually impaired children and their families* (3rd ed.). New York: American Foundation for the Blind.

Prevent Blindness America. (2010a). *Common eye problems in children.* Retrieved February 15, 2010, from http://www.preventblindness.org/children/ch_eye_problems.html

Prevent Blindness America. (2010b). *Eye safety.* Retrieved February 15, 2010, from http://www.preventblindness.org/safety

Pugh, G., & Erin, J. (Eds.). (1999). *Blind and visually impaired students: Educational service guidelines*. Watertown, MA: Perkins School for the Blind.

Scholl, G., Mulholland, M., & Lonergan, A. (1986). Education of the visually handicapped: A selective timeline. In G. Scholl (Ed.), *Foundations of education for blind and visually handicapped children and youth: Theory and practice* (Inside cover charts). New York: American Foundation for the Blind.

Southern California College of Optometry. (2010). *Visual efficiency evaluation*. Retrieved February 15, 2010, from http://www.sccoeyecare.com/visiontherapy/visualefficiency.html

Texas School for the Blind. (2007). *Selected anomalies and diseases of the eye*. Retrieved February 15, 2010, from http://www.tsbvi.edu/Education/anomalies/index.htm

U.S. Department of Education. (2009). *IDEA data*. Retrieved December 5, 2009, from https://www.ideadata.org/PartBReport.asp

U.S. Department of Education. (2010). *IDEA data*. Retrieved April 14, 2010, from https://www.ideadata.org/PartBReport.asp

Chapter 13

Akman, C. (2000). Intrauterine subdural hemorrhage. *Developmental Medicine and Child Neurology, 42*, 843–846.

Alabama Institute for Deaf and Blind. (2010). *Information about deaf-blindness*. Retrieved January 5, 2010, from http://www.aidb.org/Information+on+Deafblindness.aspx?Page=1f27f144-2069-4e68-bd4e-ab692ae724d3

Alderman, N. (2003). Contemporary approaches to the management of irritability and aggression following traumatic brain injury. *Neuropsychological Rehabilitation, 13*, 211–240.

Alliance for Technology Access. (2004). *Computer resources for people with disabilities* (4th ed.). Alameda, CA: Hunter House.

American Lung Association. (2010a). *Asthma & children fact sheet*. Retrieved January 7, 2010, from http://www.lungusa.org/asthmaandchildren

American Lung Association. (2010b). *Trends in asthma morbidity and mortality*. Retrieved January 4, 2010, from http://www.lungusa.org/finding-cures/our-research/trend-reports/asthma-trend-report.pdf

Barakat, L., & Kazak, A. (1999). Family issues. In R. Brown (Ed.), *Cognitive aspects of chronic illness in children* (pp. 333–364). New York: Guilford Press.

Beattie v. Board of Education, 169 Wis. 231, 233, 172 N.W. 153, 154 (1919).

Beers, M., Porter, R., Jones, T., Kaplan, J., & Berkwits, M. (2009). *The Merck manual of diagnosis and therapy* (18th ed.). Whitehouse Station, NJ: Merck & Co.

Best, S. (2010). Physical disabilities. In S. Best, K. Heller, & J. Bigge (Eds.), *Teaching individuals with physical or multiple disabilities* (6th ed., pp. 32–58). Boston: Pearson Education.

Best, S., & Heller, K. (2009a). Acquired infections and AIDS. In K. Heller, P. Forney, P. Alberto, S. Best, & M. Schwartzman (Eds.), *Understanding physical, health, and multiple disabilities* (2nd ed., pp. 368–386). Upper Saddle River, NJ: Pearson Education.

Best, S., & Heller, K. (2009b). Congenital infections. In K. Heller, P. Forney, P. Alberto, S. Best, & M. Schwartzman (Eds.), *Understanding physical, health, and multiple disabilities* (2nd ed., pp. 387–398). Upper Saddle River, NJ: Pearson Education.

Best, S., Reed, P., & Bigge, J. (2010). Assistive technology. In S. Best, K. Heller, & J. Bigge (Eds.), *Teaching individuals with physical or multiple disabilities* (6th ed., pp. 175–220). Upper Saddle River, NJ: Pearson Education.

Bowe, F. (2005). *Making inclusion work*. Upper Saddle River, NJ: Pearson Education.

Brown, D., & Bates, E. (2005). A personal view of changes in the deaf-blind population, philosophy, and needs. *Deaf-Blind Perspectives, 12*(3), 1–5.

Centers for Disease Control and Prevention. (2009). *AIDS surveillance—general epidemiology*. Retrieved January 5, 2010, from http://www.cdc.gov/hiv/topics/surveillance/resources/slides/epidemiology/

Centers for Disease Control and Prevention. (2010). *Overview: TBI*. Retrieved January 6, 2010, from http://www.cdc.gov/ncipc/tbi/overview.htm

CHARGE Syndrome Foundation. (2010). *About CHARGE*. Retrieved January 6, 2010, from http://www.chargesyndrome.org/about-charge.asp

Clark, G., Bigge, J., & Best, S. (2010). Self-determination and education for transition. In S. Best, K. Heller, & J. Bigge (Eds.), *Teaching individuals with physical or multiple disabilities* (6th ed., pp. 343–372). Upper Saddle River, NJ: Pearson Education.

DPHD Critical Issues and Leadership Committee. (1999). Position statement on specialized health care procedures. *Physical Disabilities: Education and Related Services, 18*(1), 3–5.

Dunn, N., McCartan, K., & Fuqua, R. (1988). Young children with orthopedic handicaps: Self-knowledge about their disabilities. *Exceptional Children, 55*, 249–252.

Eberle, L. (1922, August). The maimed, the halt and the race. *Hospital Social Service, 5*, 59–63. Reprinted in R. Bremner (Ed.), *Children and youth in America, a documentary history: Vol. II. 1866–1932* (pp. 1026–1028). Cambridge, MA: Harvard University Press.

Effgen, S. (2005). *Meeting the physical therapy needs of children*. Philadelphia: F. A. Davis.

Engleman, M., Griffin, H., Griffin, L., & Maddox, J. (1999). A teacher's guide to communicating with students with deaf-blindness. *Teaching Exceptional Children, 31*(5), 64–70.

Epilepsy Foundation of America. (2010). *About epilepsy & seizures*. Retrieved January 4, 2010, from www.epilepsyfoundation.org/about/statistics.cfm

Fadiman, A. (1997). *The spirit catches you and you fall down*. New York: Farrar, Straus & Giroux.

Gallaudet Research Institute. (2006). *Regional and national summary report of data from the 2005–2006 annual survey of deaf and hard of hearing children and youth*. Washington, DC: Gallaudet University.

Gargiulo, R. (1985). *Working with parents of exceptional children*. Boston: Houghton Mifflin.

Geenen, S., Powers, L., & Lopez-Vasquez, A. (2001). Multicultural aspects of involvement in transition planning. *Exceptional Children, 67*, 265–282.

Griffin, H., Fitch, C., & Griffin, L. (2002). Causes and interventions in the area of cerebral palsy. *Infants and Young Children, 14(3)*, 18–23.

Heller, K. (2009a). Learning and behavioral characteristics of students with physical, health, or multiple impairments. In K. Heller, P. Forney, P. Alberto, S. Best, & M. Schwartzman (Eds.), *Understanding physical, health, and multiple disabilities* (2nd ed., pp. 18–34). Upper Saddle River, NJ: Pearson Education.

Heller, K. (2009b). Monitoring health impairments and individualized healthcare plans. In K. Heller, P. Forney, P. Alberto, S. Best, & M. Schwartzman (Eds.), *Understanding physical, health, and multiple disabilities* (2nd ed., pp. 349–366). Upper Saddle River, NJ: Pearson Education.

Heller, K. (2009c). Traumatic spinal cord injury and spina bifida. In K. Heller, P. Forney, P. Alberto, S. Best, & M. Schwartzman (Eds.), *Understanding physical, health, and multiple disabilities* (2nd ed., pp. 94–117). Upper Saddle River, NJ: Pearson Education.

Heller, K. (2010). Mathematics instruction and adaptations. In S. Best, K. Heller, & J. Bigge (Eds.), *Teaching individuals with physical or multiple disabilities* (6th ed., pp. 457–493). Upper Saddle River, NJ: Pearson Education.

Heller, K., & Alberto, P. (2010). Reading instruction and adaptations. In S. Best, K. Heller, & J. Bigge (Eds.), *Teaching individuals with physical or multiple disabilities* (6th ed., pp. 375–406). Upper Saddle River, NJ: Pearson Education.

Heller, K., & Avant, J. (2009). Juvenile rheumatoid arthritis, arthrogryposis, and osteogenesis imperfecta. In K. Heller, P. Forney, P. Alberto, S. Best, & M. Schwartzman (Eds.), *Understanding physical, health, and multiple disabilities* (2nd ed., pp. 172–190). Upper Saddle River, NJ: Pearson Education.

Heller, K., & Bigge, J. (2010). Augmentative and alternative communication. In S. Best, K. Heller, & J. Bigge (Eds.), *Teaching individuals with physical or multiple disabilities* (6th ed., pp. 221–254). Upper Saddle River, NJ: Pearson Education.

Heller, K., Fredrick, L., Best, S., Dykes, M., & Cohen, E. (2000). Specialized health care procedures in the schools: Training and service delivery. *Exceptional Children, 66,* 173–186.

Heller, K., Fredrick, L., Tumlin, J., & Brineman, D. (2002). Teaching decoding for generalization using the nonverbal reading approach. *Journal of Physical and Developmental Disabilities, 14,* 19–35.

Heller, K., Mezei, P., & Schwartzman, M. (2009). Muscular dystrophies. In K. Heller, P. Forney, P. Alberto, S. Best, & M. Schwartzman (Eds.), *Understanding physical, health, and multiple disabilities* (2nd ed., pp. 232–248). Upper Saddle River, NJ: Pearson Education.

Heller, K., & Tumlin, J. (2004). Using expanded individualized healthcare plans to assist teachers of students with complex healthcare needs. *Journal of School Nursing, 20*(3), 150–160.

Heller, K., & Tumlin-Garrett, J. (2009). Cerebral palsy. In K. Heller, P. Forney, P. Alberto, S. Best, & M. Schwartzman (Eds.), *Understanding physical, health, and multiple disabilities* (2nd ed., pp. 72–93). Upper Saddle River, NJ: Pearson Education.

Herring, J. (2007). *Tachdjian's pediatric orthopaedics* (4th ed.). Philadelphia: W. B. Saunders.

Hille, E., Weisglas-Kuperus, N., van Goudoever, J., Jacobusse, G., Ens-Dokkum, M., de Groot, L., et al. (2007). Functional outcomes and participation in young adulthood for very preterm and very low birth weight infants: The Dutch Project on preterm and small for gestational age infants at 19 years of age. *Pediatrics, 120,* 587–595.

Holmbeck, G., Westhoven, V., Phillips, W., Bowers, R., Guse, C., Nikolopoulos, T., et al. (2003). A multi-method, multi-informant, and multidimensional perspective on psychosocial adjustment in preadolescents with spina bifida. *Journal of Counseling and Clinical Psychology, 71,* 782–797.

Hsu, C., Lin, Y., Yang, Y., & Chiang, B. (2004). Factors affecting clinical and therapeutic outcomes of patients with juvenile rheumatoid arthritis. *Scandinavian Journal of Rheumatology, 33,* 312–317.

Iddon, J., Morgan, D., Loveday, C., Sahakian, B., & Pickard, J. (2006). Neuropsychological profile of young adults with spina bifida with or without hydrocephalus. *Journal of Neurology, Neurosurgery & Psychiatry, 75,* 1112–1118.

Jacobs, R., Northam, E., & Anderson, V. (2001). Cognitive outcome in children with myelomeningocele and perinatal hydrocephalus: A longitudinal perspective. *Journal of Developmental and Physical Disabilities, 13,* 389–405.

Kaiser, A., & Grim, J. (2006). Teaching functional communication skills. In M. Snell & F. Brown (Eds.), *Instruction of students with severe disabilities* (6th ed., pp. 447–488). Upper Saddle River, NJ: Pearson Education.

Killoran, J. (2007). *The national deaf-blind child count: 1998–2005 in review.* Retrieved January 7, 2010, from http://www.nationaldb.org/documents/products/Childcountreview-0607Final.pdf

Kirshbaum, M. (2000). A disability culture perspective on early intervention with parents with physical or cognitive disabilities and their infants. *Infants and Young Children, 13,* 9–10.

Kliegman, R., Behrman, R., Jensen, H., & Stanton, B. (2007). *Nelson textbook of pediatrics* (18th ed.). Philadelphia: Elsevier.

Kuhtz-Buschbeck, J., Hoppe, B., Golge, M., Dreesmann, M., Damm-Stunitz, U., & Ritz, A. (2003). Sensorimotor recovery in children after traumatic brain injury: Analysis of gain, gross motor, and fine motor skills. *Developmental Medicine and Child Neurology, 45,* 821–828.

La Vor, M. (1976). Federal legislation for exceptional persons: A history. In F. Weintraub, A. Aberson, J. Balard, & M. La Vor (Eds.), *Public policy and the education of exceptional children* (pp. 96–111). Reston, VA: Council for Exceptional Children.

Lazzaretti, C., & Pearson, C. (2004). Myelodysplasia. In P. Allen & J. Vessey (Eds.), *Primary care of the child with a chronic condition* (4th ed., pp. 630–643). St. Louis, MO: Mosby.

Lin, S. (2000). Coping and adaptation in families of children with cerebral palsy. *Exceptional Children, 66,* 201–218.

Lindsey, L. (2008). *Technology and exceptional individuals* (4th ed.). Austin, TX: Pro-Ed.

Liptak, G. (2005). Complementary and alternative therapies for cerebral palsy. *Mental Retardation and Developmental Disabilities Research Reviews, 11,* 156–163.

Macmillan, D., & Hendrick, I. (1993). Evolution and legacy. In J. Goodlad & T. Lovitt (Eds.), *Integrating general and special education* (pp. 23–48). New York: Merrill.

Management of Myelomeningocele Study. (2010). *Overview of management of myelomeningocele.* Retrieved January 6, 2010, from http://www.spinabifidamoms.com/English/overview.html

Mavinkurve, G., Bagley, C., Pradilla, G., & Jallo, G. (2005). Advances in the management of hydrocephalus in pediatric patients with myelomeningocele. In M. Zesta (Ed.), *Trends in spina bifida research* (pp. 1–29). New York: Nova Biomedical Books.

Melancon, F. (2000). A group of students with Usher syndrome in south Louisiana. *Deaf-Blind Perspectives, 8*(1), 1–3.

Merrick, J., Merrick, E., Morad, M., & Kandel, I. (2006). Fetal alcohol syndrome and its long-term effects. *Minerva Pediatrica, 58,* 211–218.

Miles, B. (2010). *Overview on deaf-blindness.* Retrieved January 6, 2010, from http://www.nationaldb.org/NCDBProducts.php?prodID=38

Miller, F. (2005). *Cerebral palsy.* New York: Springer.

Mirenda, P. (2005). Augmentative and alternative communication techniques. In J. Downing (Ed.), *Teaching communication skills to students with severe disabilities* (2nd ed.). Baltimore: Paul H. Brookes.

Miyahara, M., & Piek, J. (2006). Self-esteem of children and adolescents with physical disabilities: Quantitative evidence from meta-analysis. *Journal of Developmental and Physical Disabilities, 18,* 219–234.

Morgan, E. (1989). *INSITE Developmental Checklist: 0–6 Years.* Logan: Utah State University.

Murphy, N., Christian, B., Caplin, D., & Young, P. (2007). The health of caregivers for children with disabilities: Caregiver perspectives, *Child: Care, Health and Development, 33,* 180–187.

National Consortium on Deaf-Blindness. (2007). *The national deaf-blind child count.* Retrieved January 10, 2007, from http://www.tr.wou.edu/ntac/index.cfm?path=publications/publications_census.html

National Consortium on Deaf-Blindness. (2009). *The 2008 national child count of children and youth who are deaf-blind.* Retrieved January 5, 2010, from http://www.nationaldb.org/documents/products/2008-Census-Tables.pdf

National Consortium on Deaf-Blindness. (2010). *Primary etiologies of deaf-blindness—alphabetically.* Retrieved January 4, 2010, from http://www.nationaldb.org/ISSelectedTopics.php?topicID=989&topicCatID=24

Nehring, W. (2004). Cerebral palsy. In P. Allen & J. Vessey (Eds.), *Primary care of the child with a chronic condition* (4th ed., pp. 327–346). St. Louis, MO: Mosby.

Rennie, J., Hagmann, C., & Robertson, N. (2007). Outcome after intrapartum hypoxic ischaemia at term. *Seminars in Fetal and Neonatal Medicine, 12,* 398–407.

Sacks, S., & Silberman, R. (2000). Social skills. In A. Koenig & M. Holbrook (Eds.), *Foundations of education: Instructional strategies for teaching children and youths with visual impairments* (2nd ed., Vol. 2, pp. 616–648). New York: American Foundation for the Blind Press.

Sevcik, R., & Romski, M. (2010). *AAC: More than three decades of growth and development.* Retrieved January 7, 2010, from http://www.asha.org/public/speech/disorders/AACThreeDecades.htm

Silberman, R., Bruce, S., & Nelson, C. (2004). Children with sensory impairments. In F. Orelove, D. Sobsey, & R. Silberman (Eds.), *Educating children with multiple disabilities* (4th ed., pp. 425–527). Baltimore: Paul H. Brookes.

Sitlington, P., & Clark, G. (2006). *Transition education and services for students with disabilities* (4th ed.). Needham Heights, MA: Allyn and Bacon.

Slomine, B., Gerring, J., Grados, M., Vasa, R., Brady, K., Christensen, J., et al. (2002). Performance on measures of executive function following pediatric traumatic brain injury. *Brain Injury, 16,* 759–772.

Spina Bifida Association of America. (2010). *Spina bifida.* Retrieved January 5, 2010, from http://www.spinabifidaassociation.org

Temkin, O. (1971). *The falling sickness: A history of epilepsy from the Greeks to the beginning of modern neurology* (2nd ed.). Baltimore: Johns Hopkins University Press.

Tovia, E., Goldberg-Stern, H., Shahar, E., & Kramer, U. (2005). Outcome of children with juvenile absence epilepsy. *Journal of Child Neurology, 21,* 766–768.

Tsai, J., Floyd, L., Green, P., & Boyle, C. (2007). Patterns and average volume of alcohol use among women of childbearing age. *Maternal and Child Health Journal, 11,* 437–445.

Turnbull, A., Turnbull, R., Erwin, E., Soodak, L., & Shogren, K. (2011). *Families, professionals, and exceptionality* (6th ed.). Upper Saddle River, NJ: Pearson Education.

U.S. Department of Education. (2009). *IDEA data.* Retrieved December 19, 2009, from https://www.ideadata.org/PartBReport.asp

U.S. Department of Education. (2010). *IDEA data.* Retrieved April 14, 2010, from https://www.ideadata.org/PartBReport.asp

United Cerebral Palsy. (2010). *Cerebral palsy: Facts and figures.* Retrieved January 5, 2010, from http://www.ucp.org/ucp_generaldoc.cfm/1/9/37/37-37/447

Vachha, B., & Adams, R. (2003). Language differences in young children with myelomeningocele and shunted hydrocephalus. *Pediatric Neurosurgery, 39*(4), 184–189.

Valcamonico, A., Accorsi, P., Sanzeni, C., Martelli, P., La Boria, P., & Frusca, T. (2007). Mid- and long-term outcome of extremely low birth weight (ELBW) infants: An analysis of prognostic factors. *Journal of Maternal-Fetal and Neonatal Medicine, 20,* 465–471.

Wehman, P. (2006). *Life beyond the classroom: Transition strategies for young people with disabilities* (4th ed.). Baltimore: Paul H. Brookes.

Wilfogn, A. (2002). Treatment considerations: Role of vagus nerve stimulator. *Epilepsy & Behavior, 3,* S41–S44.

Wolf-Schein, E., & Schein, J. (2009). *AIM: Assessment Intervention Matrix.* Coconut Creek, FL: Three Bridge Publishers.

Ylvisaker, M., Jacobs, H., & Feeney, T. (2003). Positive supports for people who experience behavioral and cognitive disability after brain injury. *Journal of Head Trauma Rehabilitation, 18,* 7–32.

Ysseldyke, J., & Algozzine, B. (1982). *Critical issues in special and remedial education.* Boston: Houghton Mifflin.

Chapter 14

Archambault, F., Jr., Westberg, K., Brown, S., Hallmark, B., Zhang, W., & Emmons, C. (1993). Classroom practices used with gifted third and fourth grade students. *Journal for the Education of the Gifted, 16*(2), 103–119.

Baum, S., Rizza, M., & Renzulli, S. (2006). Twice-exceptional adolescents: Who are they? What do they need? In F. Dixon & S. Moon (Eds.), *The handbook of secondary gifted education* (pp. 137–164). Waco, TX: Prufrock Press.

Blackbourn, J., Patton, J., & Trainor, A. (2004). *Exceptional individuals in focus* (7th ed.). Upper Saddle River, NJ: Pearson Education.

Burns, D., Purcell, J., & Hertberg, H. (2006). Curriculum for gifted education students. In J. Purcell & R. Eckert (Eds.), *Designing services and programs for high-ability learners* (pp. 87–111). Thousand Oaks, CA: Corwin Press.

Clark, B. (2008). *Growing up gifted: Developing the potential of children at home and at school* (7th ed.). Upper Saddle River, NJ: Pearson Education.

Clasen, D., & Clasen, R. (2003). Mentoring the gifted and talented. In N. Colangelo & G. Davis (Eds.), *Handbook of gifted education* (3rd ed., pp. 254–267). Needham Heights, MA: Allyn and Bacon.

Colangelo, N., Assouline, S., & Gross, M. (2004). *A nation deceived: How schools hold back America's brightest students*. Iowa City: University of Iowa.

Cote, D. (2005). *Wicked: The grimmerie*. New York: Hyperion.

Csikszentmihalyi, M., Rathunde, K., & Whalen, S. (1997). *Talented teenagers: The roots of success and failure*. Cambridge, England: Cambridge University Press.

Davis, G., Rimm, S., & Siegle, D. (2011). *Education of the gifted and talented* (6th ed.). Upper Saddle River, NJ: Pearson Education.

Evans, M. (2001). *Developing and testing an innovation component configuration map for gifted education in the elementary school*. Unpublished dissertation, University of Louisville and Western Kentucky University.

Flint, L. (2001). Challenges of identifying and serving gifted children with ADHD. *Teaching Exceptional Children, 33*(4), 62–69.

Ford, D. (1998). The underrepresentation of minority students in gifted education: Problems and promises in recruitment and retention. *Journal of Special Education, 32*(1), 4–14.

Ford, D., Harris, J., Tyson, C., & Trotman, M. (2002). Beyond deficit thinking: Providing access for gifted African American students. *Roeper Review, 24*, 52–58.

Frasier, M., Hunsaker, S., Lee, J., Mitchell, S., Cramond, B., Krisel, S., et al. (1995). *Core attributes of giftedness: A foundation for recognizing the gifted potential of minority and economically disadvantaged students*. National Research Center on the Gifted and Talented. Storrs: University of Connecticut.

Gallagher, J. (2003). Issues and challenges in the education of gifted students. In N. Colangelo & G. Davis (Eds.), *Handbook of gifted education* (3rd ed., pp. 11–23). Boston: Allyn and Bacon.

Gallagher, J., & Gallagher, S. (1994). *Teaching the gifted child* (4th ed.). Boston: Allyn and Bacon.

Gardner, H. (1983). *Frames of mind: The theory of multiple intelligences*. New York: Basic Books.

Gardner, H. (1993). *Multiple intelligences: The theory in practice*. New York: Basic Books.

Gibson, S., & Efinger, J. (2001). Revisiting the schoolwide enrichment model: An approach to gifted programming. *Teaching Exceptional Children, 33*(4), 48–53.

Gubbins, E. (2006). Constructing identification procedures. In J. Purcell & R. Eckert (Eds.), *Designing services and programs for high-ability learners* (pp. 49–61). Thousand Oaks, CA: Corwin Press.

Guilford, J. (1967). *The nature of human intelligence*. New York: McGraw-Hill.

Hollingworth, L. (1926). *Gifted children: Their nature and nurture*. New York: Macmillan.

Howley, C., Howley, A., & Pendarvis, E. (1995). *Out of our minds: Anti-intellectualism and talent development for American schooling*. New York: Teachers College Press.

Karnes, F., & Riley, T. (2005). *Competitions for talented kids*. Waco, TX: Prufrock Press.

Karnes, F., Stephens, K., & McHard, E. (2008). Legal issues in gifted education. In F. Karnes & K. Stephens (Eds.), *Achieving excellence: Educating the gifted and talented* (pp. 18–35). Upper Saddle River, NJ: Pearson Education.

King, E. (2005). Addressing the social and emotional needs of twice-exceptional students. *Teaching Exceptional Children, 38*(1), 16–20.

Kulik, J. (2003). Grouping and tracking. In N. Colangelo & G. Davis (Eds.), *Handbook of gifted education* (3rd ed., pp. 268–281). Boston: Allyn and Bacon.

Landrum, M., Callahan, C., & Shaklee, B. (Eds.). (2001). *Aiming for excellence*. Waco, TX: Prufrock Press.

Landrum, M., & Shaklee, B. (Eds.). (1998). *Pre-K–grade 12 gifted program standards*. Washington, DC: National Association for Gifted Children.

Marland, S. (1972). *Education of the gifted and the talented: Report to the Congress of the United States by the U.S. Commissioner of Education*. Washington, DC: U.S. Government Printing Office.

Mensa. (2010). Retrieved February 20, 2010, from http://www.us.mensa.org/

National Association for Gifted Children. (2010). *Frequently asked questions*. Retrieved February 20, 2010, from http://www.nagc.org/index.aspx?id=548

National Center for Education Statistics. (1998). *Pursuing excellence: A study of U.S. twelfth-grade mathematics and science achievement in international context*. Washington, DC: U.S. Department of Education.

National Center for Education Statistics. (2009). *Digest of education statistics 2008*. Washington, DC: U.S. Department of Education.

National Commission on Excellence in Education. (1983). *A nation at risk: The imperative for school reform*. Washington, DC: U.S. Government Printing Office.

National Council of Teachers of Mathematics. (1989). *Curriculum and evaluation standards for school mathematics*. Reston, VA: Author.

National Council of Teachers of Mathematics. (2000). *Principles and standards for school mathematics*. Reston, VA: Author.

National Education Commission on Time and Learning. (1994). *Prisoners of time*. Washington, DC: U.S. Government Printing Office.

National Governors Association Center for Best Practices. (2010). *Common core state standards initiative*. Retrieved February 20, 2010, from http://www.corestandards.org/

Neal, D., & Schanzenbach, D. (2007, August). *Left behind by design: Proficiency counts and test-based accountability* (NBER Working Paper No. W13293). Retrieved February 20, 2010, from http://ssrn.com/abstract=1005606

Nielsen, M., & Higgins, L. (2005). The eye of the storm: Services and programs for twice-exceptional learners. *Teaching Exceptional Children, 38*(1), 8–15.

Noble, K., Subotnik, R., & Arnold, K. (1999). To thine own self be true: A new model of female talent development. *Gifted Child Quarterly, 43*, 140–149.

Pfeiffer, S., & Jarosewich, T. (2003). *Pfeiffer-Jarosewich Gifted Rating Scales*. San Antonio, TX: Psychological Corporation.

Piirto, J. (2007). *Talented children and adults: Their development and education* (3rd ed.). Waco, TX: Prufrock Press.

Plummer, D. (1995). Serving the needs of gifted children from a multicultural perspective. In J. Genshaft, M. Birely, & C. Hollinger (Eds.), *Serving gifted and talented students* (pp. 285–300). Austin, TX: Pro-Ed.

Reis, S. (2006). Gender, adolescence, and giftedness. In F. Dixon & S. Moon (Eds.), *The handbook of secondary gifted education* (pp. 87–111). Waco, TX: Prufrock Press.

Reis, S., Gubbins, E., Briggs, C., Schreiber, F., Richards, S., Jacobs, J., et al. (2003). *Reading instruction for talented readers: Case studies documenting few opportunities for continuous progress* (Research Monograph No. 03184). Storrs: National Research Center on the Gifted and Talented, University of Connecticut.

Reis, S., & Renzulli, J. (2005). *Curriculum compacting: An easy start to differentiating for high-potential students*. Waco, TX: Prufrock Press.

Renzulli, J. (1978). What makes giftedness? Reexamining a definition. *Phi Delta Kappan, 60,* 180–184, 261.

Renzulli, J. (1998). A rising tide lifts all ships: Developing the gifts and talents of all students. *Phi Delta Kappan, 80,* 104–111.

Renzulli, J., & Reis, S. (2003). The schoolwide enrichment model: Developing creative and productive giftedness. In N. Colangelo & G. Davis (Eds.), *Handbook of gifted education* (3rd ed., pp. 184–203). Boston: Allyn and Bacon.

Rimm, S. (2002). *How Jane won*. New York: Crown.

Roberts, J. (2010, Winter). Preassessment: The linchpin for defensible differentiation. *The Challenge, 24,* 10, 12.

Roberts, J., & Inman, T. (2009). *Differentiated student products: A protocol for development and assessment*. Waco, TX: Prufrock Press.

Roberts, J., & Roberts, R. (2005). Writing units that remove the learning ceiling. In F. Karnes & S. Bean (Eds.), *Methods and materials for teaching the gifted and talented* (2nd ed., pp. 179–210). Waco, TX: Prufrock Press.

Robinson, A., Shore, B., & Enersen, D. (2007). *Best practices in gifted education*. Waco, TX: Prufrock Press.

Roid, G. (2003). *Stanford-Binet Intelligence Test—Fifth Edition*. Itasca, IL: Riverside.

Ross, P. (Ed.). (1993). *National excellence: A case for developing America's talent*. Washington, DC: U.S. Department of Education, Office of Educational Research and Improvement.

Sanders, W. (1998). Value-added assessment. *School Administrator, 55,* 24–27.

Silverman, L. (1995a). Gifted and talented students. In E. Meyen & T. Skrtic (Eds.), *Special education and student disability* (4th ed., pp. 379–413). Denver, CO: Love.

Silverman, L. (1995b). Highly gifted children. In J. Genshaft, M. Bireley, & C. Hollinger (Eds.), *Serving gifted and talented students: A resource for school personnel* (pp. 217–240). Austin, TX: Pro-Ed.

Smith, T., Polloway, E., Patton, J., & Dowdy, C. (2008). *Teaching students with special needs* (5th ed.). Upper Saddle River, NJ: Pearson Education.

Smutny, J., Walker, S., & Meckstroth, E. (2007). *Acceleration for gifted learners, K–5*. Thousand Oaks, CA: Corwin Press.

Steinberg, L. (1996). *Beyond the classroom: Why school reform has failed and what parents need to do*. New York: Simon & Schuster.

Sternberg, R. (1985). *Beyond IQ: A triarchic theory of intelligence*. New York: Cambridge University Press.

Subotnik, R., Kassan, L., Summers, E., & Wasser, A. (1993). *Genius revisited: High IQ children grow up*. Norwood, NJ: Ablex.

Swiatek, M. (1993). A decade of longitudinal research on academic acceleration through the study of mathematically precocious youth. *Roeper Review, 15*(3), 120–123.

Terman, L. (1925). *Mental and physical traits of a thousand gifted children: Vol. 1, Genetic studies of genius*. Stanford, CA: Stanford University Press.

Tomlinson, C. (1994). Gifted learners: The boomerang kids of middle school? *Roeper Review, 16*(3), 177–181.

Tomlinson, C. (1999). *The differentiated classroom: Responding to the needs of all learners*. Alexandria, VA: Association for Supervision and Curriculum Development.

Torrance, E. (1966, 1998). *Torrance Tests of Creative Thinking: Norms and technical manual*. Bensenville, IL: Scholastic Testing Service.

Torrance, E. (1969). Creative positives of disadvantaged children and youth. *Gifted Child Quarterly, 13,* 71–81.

Ward, V. (1961). *Educating the gifted: An axiomatic approach*. Columbus, OH: Charles Merrill.

Wechsler, D. (2003). *Wechsler Intelligence Scale for Children—Fourth Edition*. San Antonio, TX: Psychological Corporation.

Weinfeld, R., Barnes-Robinson, L., Jeweler, S., & Shevitz, B. (2005). What we learned: Experiences in providing adaptations and accommodations for gifted and talented students with learning disabilities. *Teaching Exceptional Children, 38*(1), 48–53.

Westberg, K., Archambault, F., Jr., Dobyns, S., & Salvin, T. (1993). The classroom practices observation study. *Journal for the Education of the Gifted, 16*(2), 120–146.

Westberg, K., & Daoust, M. (2003, Fall). The results of the replication of the classroom practices survey replication in two states. *The National Research Center on the Gifted and Talented Newsletter,* pp. 3–8.

Williams, F. (1993). *Creativity Assessment Packet*. Austin, TX: Pro-Ed.

Woodcock, R., McGrew, K., & Mather, N. (2001). *Woodcock-Johnson III Tests of Achievement*. Itasca, IL: Riverside.

Wyner, J., Bridgeland, J., & Diiulio, J., Jr. (2007). *Achievement trap: How America is failing millions of high-achieving students from lower-income families*. Retrieved February 19, 2010, from http://www.jkcf.org/news-knowledge/research-reports/

Photo Credits

Photo, Making Inclusion Work features.

Chapter 6: © Jack Hollingsworth/Thinkstock.

Chapter 9: © Hemera Technologies/Getty Images/Thinkstock.

Chapter 10: © Brand X Pictures, SW Productions.

Photo, Suggestions for the Classroom features. © iStockphoto.com/daaronj.

Part I

Part-opening photo, page 1. © iStockphoto.com/Aldo Murillo.

Chapter 1

Chapter-opening photo, page 2. © Getty Images/Thinkstock.

Photo 1.1, page 5. © iStockphoto.com/Cliff Parnell.

Photo 1.2, page 9. © Bill Aron/PhotoEdit.

Photo 1.3, page 11. © 1996 Joel Pett, Lexington Herald-Leader. All rights reserved.

Photo 1.4, page 19. © Frances Benjamin Johnston, Library of Congress Prints and Photographs Division.

Photo 1.5, page 22. © Robin Nelson/PhotoEdit.

Photo 1.6, page 28. © iStockphoto.com/Bonnie Jacobs.

Photo 1.7, page 33. © iStockphoto.com/Wendy Shiao.

Photo 1.8, page 36. © George Doyle/Thinkstock.

Chapter 2

Chapter-opening photo, page 42. © Michael Newman/PhotoEdit.

Photo 2.1, page 50. Public Domain; State of Wyoming.

Photo 2.2, page 51. © LWA-Dann Tardif/Corbis.

Photo 2.3, page 57. © Ed Kashi/Corbis.

Photo 2.4, page 61. © Robin Nelson / PhotoEdit.

Photo 2.5, page 66. Nottingham Toddler Lab, University of Nottingham, UK Preschool Language Scale–Third Edition (PLS–3). Copyright © 1992 by NCS Pearson, Inc. Reproduced with permission. All rights reserved. "Preschool Language Scale" and "PLS" are trademarks, in the US and/or other countries, of Pearson Education, Inc. or its affiliates(s).

Photo 2.6, page 70. © Spencer Grant / PhotoEdit.

Photo 2.7, page 77. © Nancy Sheehan/PhotoEdit.

Photo 2.8, page 79. © Richard Hutchings / PhotoEdit.

Chapter 3

Chapter-opening photo, page 84. ©Gabe Palmer/Corbis.

Photo 3.1, page 89. © Thinkstock.

Photo 3.2, page 90. © iStockphoto.com/Bonnie Jacobs.

Photo 3.3, page 97. © Catherine Karnow/Corbis.

Photo 3.4, page 101. © Corbis.

Chapter 4

Chapter-opening photo, page 112. © iStockphoto.com/Diloute.

Photo 4.1, page 117. © Michael Newman/PhotoEdit.

Photo 4.2, page 119. © Tony Freeman / PhotoEdit.

Photo 4.3, page 121. © Photodisc.

Photo 4.4, page 128. © iStockphoto.com/Wendy Shiao.

Photo 4.5, page 129. © Michael Newman/PhotoEdit.

Part II

Part-opening photo, page 136. © Getty Images.

Chapter 5

Chapter-opening photo, page 138. © Richard Hutchings/PhotoEdit.

Photo 5.1, page 148. © A. Ramey/PhotoEdit.

Photo 5.2, page 159. © Richard Hutchings/PhotoEdit.

Photo 5.3, page 162. © iStockphoto.

Photo 5.4, page 165. © Bob Daemmrich/PhotoEdit.

Photo 5.5, page 171. © Robin Nelson/PhotoEdit.

Photo 5.6, page 174. © iStockphoto.com/Bonnie Jacobs.

Photo 5.7, page 182. © James L. Shaffer/PhotoEdit.

Photo 5.8, page 183. © James L. Shaffer/PhotoEdit.

Chapter 6

Chapter-opening photo, page 192. © iStockphoto.com/Ekaterina Monakhova.

Photo 6.1, page 196. © iStockphoto.com/Chris Schmidt.

Photo 6.2, page 202. © iStockphoto.com/Lajos Repasi.

Photo 6.3, page 209. © iStockphoto.com/Cliff Parnell.

Photo 6.4, page 210. © Thinkstock.

Photo 6.5, page 210. © iStockphoto.com/Bonnie Jacobs.

Photo 6.6, page 227. © iStockphoto.com/Aldo Murillo.

Chapter 7

Chapter-opening photo, page 238. © O'Brien Productions/Corbis.

Photo 7.1, page 241. © Tatiana Mironenko.

Photo 7.2, page 244. © iStockphoto.com/Jani Bryson.

Photo 7.3, page 246. © David Young-Wolff/PhotoEdit.

Photo 7.4, page 255. © Thinkstock/David Sacks.

Photo 7.5, page 260. © Photoscom.

Chapter 8

Chapter-opening photo, page 270. © iStockphoto.com/lvdesign77.

Photo 8.1, page 277. © Spencer Grant/PhotoEdit.

Photo 8.2, page 287. © iStockphoto.com/Brandy Taylor.

Photo 8.3, page 291. © David Young-Wolff/PhotoEdit.

Photo 8.4, page 302. © Kristina Buskirk.

Photo 8.5, page 308. © iStockphoto.com/ Cliff Parnell.

Photo 8.6, page 309. © Dan Eckert.

Photo 8.7, page 311. © Forest Woodward.

Chapter 9

Chapter-opening photo, page 320. © Robin Nelson/PhotoEdit.

Photo 9.1, page 325. © iStockphoto.com/Morgan Lane Studios.

Photo 9.2, page 328. © iStockphoto.com/Sean Locke.

Photo 9.3, page 334. © Mary Kate Denny/PhotoEdit.

Photo 9.4, page 335. © David Young-Wolff/PhotoEdit.

Photo 9.5, page 347. © James Shaffer/PhotoEdit.

Chapter 10

Chapter-opening photo, page 356. © Christina Kennedy/PhotoEdit.

Photo 10.1, page 370. © Photodisc.

Photo 10.2, page 375. © iStockphoto.com/Bradley Mason.

Photo 10.3, page 380. © Mary Kate Denny/PhotoEdit.

Photo 10.4, page 388. © BrandXPictures.

Photo 10.5, page 389. © Bob Daemmrich/Stock, Boston, Inc.

Chapter 11

Chapter-opening photo, page 394. © Gabe Palmer/Corbis.

Photo 11.1, page 400. © Mark Richards/PhotoEdit.

Photo 11.2, page 403. © Robin L. Sachs/PhotoEdit.

Photo 11.3, page 405. © Richard Lord/PhotoEdit.

Photo 11.4, page 412. © Robin Sachs/PhotoEdit.

Photo 11.5, page 424. © Will Hart/PhotoEdit.

Photo 11.6, page 425. © Michael Newman/PhotoEdit.

Photo 11.7, page 430. © David Young-Wolff/PhotoEdit.

Photo 11.8, page 435. © David Young-Wolff/PhotoEdit.

Chapter 12

Chapter-opening photo, page 444. © Tony Freeman/PhotoEdit.

Photo 12.1, page 447. © Photodisc.

Photo 12.2, page 455. © Renee Lee.

Photo 12.3, page 458. © Robin Sachs/PhotoEdit.

Photo 12.4, page 461. © iStockphoto.com/Carmen MartAnez Bana.

Photo 12.5, page 464. © Robin Sachs/PhotoEdit.

Photo 12.6, page 471. © Michael Newman/PhotoEdit.

Photo 12.7, page 475. © Michael Newman/PhotoEdit.

Chapter 13

Chapter-opening photo, page 484. © Ariel Skelley/Corbis.

Photo 13.1, page 487. © Zigy Kaluzny/ Getty Images.

Photo 13.2, page 500. © Bob Daemmrich/Stock, Boston, Inc.

Photo 13.3, page 514. © Bob Daemmrich/PhotoEdit.

Photo 13.4, page 523. © Bob Daemmrich/PhotoEdit.

Photo 13.5, page 527. © Courtesy of Kathryn Wolff Heller.

Photo 13.6, page 529. © Courtesy of Kathryn Wolff Heller.

Photo 13.7, page 530. © iStockphoto.com/Alistair Scott.

Chapter 14

Chapter-opening photo, page 536. © iStockphoto.com/Lesley Lister.

Photo 14.1, page 541. © Julia L. Roberts.

Photo 14.2, page 547. © Julia L. Roberts.

Photo 14.3, page 549. © Julia L. Roberts.

Photo 14.4, page 558. © iStockphoto.com/Jamie Wilson.

Photo 14.5, page 561. © iStockphoto.com/Catherine Yeulet.

Photo 14.6, page 570. © iStockphoto.com/Chris Schmidt.

Photo 14.7, page 576. © iStockphoto.com/Laurence Gough.

Author Index

Subject Index

About the Contributors

Carol Allison is an instructor in the program for the visually impaired offered by the Department of Leadership, Special Education, and Foundations at the University of Alabama at Birmingham (UAB). She has a dual assignment as the project coordinator for the Alabama Deafblind Project and as a consultant to local and state education agencies and individual families in the field of visual impairments. She received her M.A. from UAB and completed her postgraduate certification in the area of deaf–blind multihandicapped. She served as an adjunct faculty member at UAB from 1979 until she became a full-time member in 1999. Ms. Allison is a native of Louisiana, where she earned her undergraduate degree and worked with children with hearing impairments and emotional disabilities. She has worked in both the public and private sectors of general and special education for the past forty years.

Ms. Allison's special interests have included the development of a statewide program with an international foundation that serves as a coordinating agency for creating and promoting arts programs for individuals with disabilities. Other areas of interest include the development and creation of distance education teacher training programs in the field of visual impairments. Additionally, she has been assisting in the development and implementation of a program providing vision services to individuals living in poverty in Alabama.

Ms. Allison has made numerous professional presentations to local, state, and international conferences and has served on advisory boards for many educational and civic organizations.

Karen Bowen Dahle has a doctorate in special education, administration, and supervision; a master's degree in clinical psychology; and a bachelor's degree in behavior disorders and autism. With over thirty years' experience in the field of autism, she is a nationally certified school psychologist and a nationally board-certified counselor with an endorsement in clinical mental health counseling, and she holds equivalent state and educational licenses and certifications.

Dr. Dahle is also trained in the administration of both the ADOS-R and the ADI-R. With this background, she has participated in autism clinics for more than thirty years and does independent evaluations and advocacy work on behalf of parents and schools.

Dr. Dahle is recognized for her teaching excellence at both the public school and university level and for her work as an administrator in a private facility for individuals with autism spectrum disorders where she managed more than ten programs for students ages 3 to 21. She has published extensively and is a field editor for *Focus on Autism and Other Developmental Disabilities*.

Kathryn Wolff Heller is a professor of special education at Georgia State University, where she coordinates a master's program in physical and health disabilities. She also advises and teaches students who are working toward their doctorate with a concentration in the area of physical and health disabilities. She also directs several projects, including a statewide grant that provides technical assistance to school personnel and families in the area of deaf–blindness.

Dr. Heller, a registered nurse with experience in pediatric medicine, worked for five years in intensive care units and then went on to obtain master's and doctoral degrees in special education. She has worked as a classroom teacher of students with orthopedic impairments, intellectual disabilities, traumatic brain injury, and visual impairments. She has coauthored three books, several book chapters, and numerous articles. She chairs and participates on several advisory boards and committees, and she makes frequent presentations. One of her primary interests is in providing effective educational instruction and health care for students with physical, sensory, and health impairments.

Betty Nelson, Ph.D., is the interim chair of the Department of Leadership, Special Education, and Foundations at the University of Alabama at Birmingham. At the university level, Dr. Nelson has taught preservice and graduate special education majors. She also has teaching experience in programs for children with disabilities ranging from early intervention to secondary and postsecondary education. Her experience includes working with children in all areas of disabilities and within public schools, private institutions, and home-based and hospital-based settings. Assistive and instructional technology is the main focus of her teaching, research, and service activities.

Dr. Nelson has authored several books, monographs, teacher training modules, and multimedia resources. She has given numerous presentations to local, state, national, and international conferences. She has also served as the president of the Technology and Media (TAM) Division of the Council for Exceptional Children. In addition, she has been the president of the Special Education Technology and Special Interest Group (SETSIG) of the International Society for Technology in Education.

Julia Link Roberts, Ed.D., is the Mahurin Professor of Gifted Studies at Western Kentucky University. She is also executive director of The Center for Gifted Studies and the Carol Martin Gatton Academy of Mathematics and Science in Kentucky. She was honored in 2001 as the first recipient of the National Association for Gifted Children David W. Belin Advocacy Award. Dr. Roberts serves on the boards of the Kentucky Association for Gifted Education and the Association for the Gifted, an affiliate of the Council for Exceptional Children, and she is a member of the Executive Committee of the World Council for Gifted and Talented Children. She has published books, chapters, and journal articles and is a frequent speaker at state, national, and international meetings. *Strategies for Differentiating Instruction: Best Practices for the Classroom,* co-authored with Tracy Inman, received the Legacy Book Award for the 2009 outstanding book for educators in gifted education, awarded by the Texas Association for the Gifted and Talented. As the founding director of The Center for Gifted Studies, Dr. Roberts has initiated and implemented many programs and services for children and adolescents who are gifted and talented as well as for educators and parents. She earned a B.A. at the University of Missouri and an Ed.D. at Oklahoma State University.

Mary Jean Sanspree, Ph.D., is on the faculty of the School of Optometry and has an appointment as a research professor in the School of Education at the University of Alabama at Birmingham (UAB), and is an associate scientist in the UAB Vision Science Research Center. She has served as president of the Council for Exceptional Children Division on Visual Impairments, is a member of the National Institutes of Health National Eye Institute Public Liaison Program Committee, and has served as chair of the Alabama Early Intervention Interagency Coordinating Personnel Preparation Committee, among other service responsibilities. She conducts vision research concerning rural eye care and access to eye care for persons with diabetes and glaucoma.

Dr. Sanspree has trained teachers in the field of visual impairments in underdeveloped countries and has published extensively on the topics of Braille literacy, distance education, multiple disabilities, and dual sensory impairment, as well as low vision habilitation. She serves on the Helen Keller Birthplace Foundation board of directors and has been associated with the Helen Keller Art Show of Alabama and the Helen Keller International Art Show since its inception in 1984.

Lou Anne Worthington received her Ph.D. from the University of Alabama. Her bachelor's and master's degrees are from Auburn University. She has been a special educator for thirty-four years. Her areas of expertise include assessment, special education law, behavioral interventions, functional assessment, cultural diversity, attention deficit hyperactivity disorder, and inclusion/collaboration. Dr. Worthington has taught children and youth with emotional and behavioral disorders in a variety of settings, including both public schools and private residential facilities. She has also served in a number of administrative special education positions in private residential schools.

Dr. Worthington is currently an associate professor and associate dean for programs at the University of Alabama at Birmingham. She is an educational consultant to a number of school systems. Dr. Worthington has been the recipient of several teaching and service awards. She has presented at numerous international, national, regional, state, and local conferences and workshops. Areas in which she has published include autism, attention deficit hyperactivity disorder, cultural diversity, emotional and behavioral disorders, academic and behavioral interventions, prenatal cocaine exposure, and health care plans.